KITCHEN

How to Plan, Install & Remc

Rick Harrison

Published by HPBooks
P.O. Box 5367
Tucson, AZ 85703
602/888-2150
ISBN: 0-89586-217-4
Library of Congress Catalog Card Number: 83-82405

Printed in U.S.A.

HPBooks®

Publishers
Bill and Helen Fisher

Executive Editor
Rick Bailey

Editorial Director
Randy Summerlin

Editor
Jim Barrett

Art Director
Don Burton

Book Design
Kathleen Koopman

ACKNOWLEDGMENTS

A book such as this is never the product of one person, or even a few people. Many have contributed time, effort, ideas, information and contacts with others who might help. Included are many homeowners who allowed us to photograph their kitchens.

Our thanks to these people extends to any we might have inadvertently omitted in the following list. Special thanks to those manufacturers listed here who have contributed photographic material for use in this book.

American Woodmark Corp., Woodmark Cabinets, Berryville, VA
Armstrong World Industries Inc., Lancaster, PA
The Atkins Company Community Builders, Tucson, AZ
Bainbridge Manufacturing, Inc., Bainbridge, WA
Belwood, Ackerman, MS
Jeff Case, CKD & Emma Weinel, Scan Design, Bellvue, WA
Ed Day, D & S Construction, Issaquah, WA
Ditz-Crane Associates, Tucson, AZ
Al and Patty Freitchen, Tucson, AZ
GE-Hotpoint, Fairfield, CT
Haas Cabinet Co., Sellersburg, IN
Herder Construction Co., Tucson, AZ
Chuck & Barbara Hertzler, Fine Wood Cabinets, Oak Harbor, WA
Kemper (division of Tappan), Richmond, IN
Kitchen Kompact, Inc., Jeffersonville, IN
Kitchens of Distinction, Tucson, AZ
The Maytag Co., Newton, IA
Marian Noble, Redmond, WA
Mary M. Powers Public Relations, Tustin, CA
Chris Schmidt, European Kitchens, Bellvue, WA
David Soleim, New Country Homes, Issaquah, WA
Sub-Zero Freezer Co., Madison, WI
Thermador/Waste King, Los Angeles, CA
Ralph Wilson Plastics Co., Wilsonart Division, Temple, TX

Special thanks to our technical consultants who contributed to the accuracy of information in this book:

Ed Mertz, Rued Construction, Tucson, AZ
Jerry Young, Architectural Visions, Tucson, AZ
Hugh Young, Tucson, AZ

Photography
All photography by Rick & Betty Harrison, except as noted in captions.

Illustrations
Rick Harrison

Cover Photograph:

Patterned tiles and oak are unifying design elements in this large Southwestern kitchen. With two sinks, four ovens (two not shown), gas cooktop and electric range, kitchen is equipped to entertain large groups. Beyond kitchen through entry is serving area to dining room. It has sink, hot-water dispenser, microwave oven, dishwasher and food warmer. Kitchen is featured on pages 14-16, 179. Design: Helen Fisher and Janean Kitchens, Tucson AZ. Tile design: Steve Dirks. Cabinets: Jorgensen Cabinets. Photo by Rick Harrison.

Contents

Your Kitchen

Kitchen counters don't always have to run straight. This kitchen has sink installed in diagonal section, so no storage space is wasted. Design: John Klassen & Co.

Center of almost every household, the kitchen is a gathering place for the family. It's a place of warmth, light and good aromas—the happy and busy place where food is prepared. The kitchen is one of humankind's oldest ideas, far older than the idea of the house. If you define a kitchen as a separate place to store and prepare food, examples have been found in caves and rock shelters dating back thousands of years. These earliest kitchens consisted only of a hearth or firepit and a few niches to hold clay pots or baskets. Kitchens have come a long way since then.

Kitchen fads and fashions have come and gone over the years. From a central hearth or fireplace within the dwelling, the kitchen first shifted to a separate shed or small building. The age of servants brought the kitchen back into the house, often on a separate floor or in the basement. These kitchens were usually split into two parts—a food preparation and storage room, and a serving pantry. Later developments brought the kitchen back near the eating area, but still in a separate, closed-off room in the house.

Early in this century, the kitchen came full circle. With architect Frank Lloyd Wright in the lead, designers started taking out doors and tearing down walls. The kitchen again became a part of the living area.

PLANNING FOR FAMILY USES

You have a number of choices on how open or closed your new kitchen will be. You can decide what family activities will be included in the kitchen and which will be kept separate. Organization of family activity can have a great effect on how well a kitchen works.

If there are small children in the family, the cook may want them in sight while preparing meals. This gives kids a sense of belonging and a chance to watch how it's done. But if children and toys are constantly underfoot, meal preparation can be much more difficult, and even hazardous. A harried parent may find that children in the work area make cooking too time-consuming. Think ahead and design spaces not only for kids but also for spectators and extra cooks.

In most families, members spend large amounts of time in and around the kitchen. The kitchen is the most-used room in the house during waking hours, so it deserves more planning than other rooms. It should not only function efficiently, but it should also be a pleasant place. Many kitchens are not.

Splendid example of great kitchens found in Victorian mansions during the 1890s. Home was a summer residence built by millionaire William K. Vanderbilt, called *Marble House*. It was completed in 1892 at a cost of 11 million dollars. Restoration was completed in 1983, by the Preservation Society of Newport County, Newport, Rhode Island.

Luckily, subsequent owners had stored much of the kitchen furniture and original monogrammed copper pots and pans, now polished and back on their racks. Normal staff for this kitchen was five people. Cast-iron coal stove is 25 feet long, and has six ovens. The Society keeps this great house and six others open for public viewing. *Photo courtesy of the Preservation Society of Newport County.*

GOOD KITCHEN DESIGN

Some kitchens are "unfriendly" for reasons related to their function. If the layout is poor or equipment is rundown, the kitchen becomes a miserable place to cook. But in other kitchens, the layout and equipment can be *too efficient*. Such kitchens are so clinical and well-organized that they leave no room for anything *but* cooking. There's no place to sit down for coffee, no corner for a child and toys, no sunny windowsill for a plant. Such kitchens say, *"Cook. Clean up. Then get out!"*

Noise—Many kitchens are unpleasant because of noise. Smooth, hard, sound-reflecting walls and surfaces amplify every small clink and clatter. Because of a kitchen's function, noises can be difficult to suppress.

A throw rug, curtains, wall hangings or upholstered furniture help absorb sound. So do acoustical ceilings and, to a certain extent, wood countertops.

Often overlooked is the shape of the room's surfaces. Changes and breaks in surfaces act as sound baffles. For instance, interrupting a large, flat ceiling with a dropped luminous panel or an opening for a skylight can help reduce sound.

Lighting—Poor lighting is responsible for more unpleasant kitchens and unhappy cooks than any other problem. To some extent, any kitchen can be helped by lighting revisions. In many older kitchens, lighting was never really planned. Also, most kitchens have so many angles and out-of-the-way corners that even well-thought-out lighting often falls short of the designer's intentions.

No two cooks use the same kitchen the same way. Lighting that's good for one cook's methods may not fit another's. If two people cook in the same kitchen, some adjustments may have to be made so both of them have adequate light. For more information on lighting, see page 53.

Counter and Cabinet Heights—If the cook is not of average height, changes may be needed. Kitchen cabinet dimensions are standardized to suit the majority of users. But there's no rule against using non-standard dimensions.

A 5-foot-2 cook might be much happier with some counter space that's only 32 or 33 inches high instead of the standard 34 to 36 inches. The same cook would consider wall cabinets over the standard 84-inch height to be wasted. But the 6-foot-2

Sliding drawers help organize cans, jars and bottles, making them easily accessible. Drawers also provide more usable storage than shelves in the same amount of space.

Oak trim gives these cabinets a unique personality. Custom accents like this help individualize a kitchen.

cook may appreciate wall cabinets extending to 8 or even 9 feet above the floor. The tall cook may also like some counter area at 38 or 39 inches, especially at the sink.

Some height adjustments might dictate custom-made cabinets, but many adjustments can be made to standard, factory-made cabinets. Many manufacturers offer 42-inch-tall wall cabinets. When mounted, they easily provide storage up to 8 feet. On most cabinets, you can make minor changes in countertop height by cutting or adding to the *toe board* at the bottom of the cabinets. See page 155.

To make a dropped-counter area for things like dough-kneading, first remove the top drawer assembly and surrounding frame from the top of a cabinet or two. Then fit a piece of countertop in the lowered section.

Planning Ahead—A good kitchen is flexible. It adapts to changing uses and family circumstances without sacrificing efficiency. A well-built kitchen can last a long time, so think ahead when you're planning. Ten years from now, favorite family recipes may be different. But basic food-preparation operations will be much the same. Each specialized area within the kitchen must be flexible if overall flexibility is to be achieved.

GETTING THE JOB DONE

This book is heavily oriented toward helping you do your own work, from initial planning stages to final cleanup. But you don't have to do more than you want to and are capable of. You can hire a subcontractor to do any procedures shown in this book. Or you can have a kitchen dealer or a general contractor handle

If you do much outdoor eating and entertaining, a pass-through window from kitchen to yard will save steps. Here, tile countertop extends outside to provide a serving counter

Shallow cooktop allows storage directly beneath. Spices and condiments are stored closest to where they're used.

the entire job. Review the nuts-and-bolts procedures anyway, even if you're planning to contract some or all of the work. It will help you understand what's being done as work progresses. You'll also appreciate the difficulties and limitations a contractor faces. This knowledge will help you plan a realistic and workable kitchen design.

If you deal with a contractor or subcontractors, they may not follow procedures exactly as described in this book. Don't be alarmed at this. There are several ways of tackling most situations involved in remodeling or new construction. Methods in this book have been selected to apply to many situations, to require a minimum number of special tools and to help the beginner. If you have prior remodeling experience, use your own judgment in modifying procedures to your liking.

Most subcontractors have years of experience and many expensive special tools and equipment. But that doesn't mean you can't do a job as well as a subcontractor. You probably just can't do it as quickly.

As you work, take all the time and trouble you feel are necessary. There's no hurry-up next job to get to, no reason why the remodel can't be worked at until you're satisfied. Beware of one pitfall: You will see every tiny flaw in your work. You will not be able to eliminate them all. This is true even if your work is excellent. Relax. Nobody else will see those tiny flaws. In a little while, you'll lose track of them too. Don't be afraid to tackle most kitchen remodeling jobs. It's a myth that "owner-built" means sloppy and badly done.

Styles

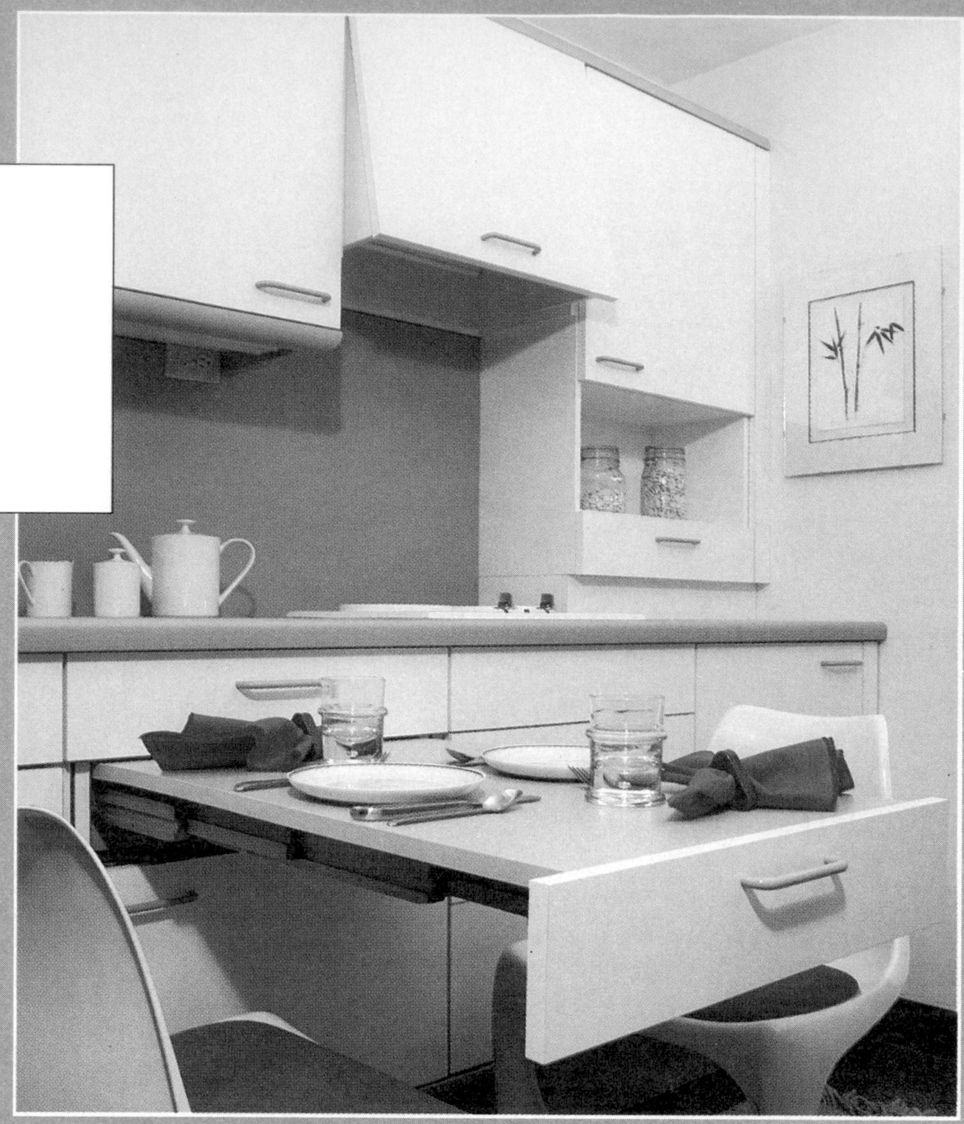

A kitchen can fit into a surprisingly small space. See facing page.

Kitchens come in many shapes and sizes, but each has a personality—a *style*. The mysterious quality we call *style* is made up of tangible elements and intangible ones.

Tangible elements are easy to see. For instance, sleek plastic-laminate cabinets are typically contemporary. Raised-panel cabinets in cherry or maple with antique-brass handles are characteristic of a Colonial kitchen. Intangible style elements are harder to define. They're also difficult to design and execute. They are the subtle touches that reflect your personality and lifestyle, making the kitchen unique.

You can affect tangible style elements by your choice of cabinets, surface materials, appliances and floor plan. Select a style or group of styles early, one that's comfortable for you and your family. Then modify or adapt it to fit your tastes and needs. As you plan your kitchen, the harmony of tangible and intangible elements will evolve by itself.

Fashions come and go, in kitchens as in other things. Don't pick a style only because it's fashionable. If the style doesn't fit you, your family and your home, you won't be comfortable with it. Even if the kitchen is fine in terms of appearance and function, it will feel like it belongs in someone else's home, not yours.

The *eclectic* style is tougher than any other to do effectively. It combines bits of many styles into a harmonious and unique whole. When the eclectic approach works, it's magnificent. When it doesn't, the result is an unworkable jumble.

Feel free to try an eclectic style, but approach it cautiously. Start by choosing a familiar object or small piece of furniture that seems to belong in the new kitchen. Then find other things that seem to belong with that object. Keep incorporating various elements such as appliances, furniture, cabinets and knick-knacks, until you're satisfied with the result. You can always change your mind or rethink things just before you buy expensive items like cabinets or appliances.

As you approach the process of designing and building or remodeling a kitchen, the number of available options may surprise you. You'll find many ideas and possibilities in the photographs and descriptions in this chapter. Others will occur to you as you put the kitchen together. Now's the time to let ideas flow, become creative and do some dreaming.

FLOOR-PLAN KEY

Use this key to identify symbols in floor plans in this chapter. You can also use the symbols when making drawings of your kitchen design, pages 59-61.

S	SINK
CT	COOKTOP
G	GRILL
DW	DISHWASHER
REF	REFRIGERATOR
F	FREEZER
R	RANGE
O	OVEN
M	MICROWAVE
TC	TRASH COMPACTOR
FP	FIREPLACE

Studio Kitchen

This example of a tiny corridor kitchen is perfect for a small city apartment, or even an office. It would also work well in a guest apartment, mother-in-law suite or family room.

All the necessities are here. Most are concealed when not in use. The range hood tips out for use, and drops back flat when you're done. Enameled covers disguise the two burners when not in use. The undercounter refrigerator at the right end is paneled to match the cabinets.

Then there's the "magic table" that pulls out farther than the depth of the cabinets by means of folding sections. The table seats two comfortably, three in a pinch.

At the right end of the counter is an enclosure for a microwave oven, not yet installed when these photos were taken.

The corridor kitchen is one of the most efficient layouts for a limited space. For more information on kitchen layouts, see page 54. *Design: Jeff Case, CKD.*

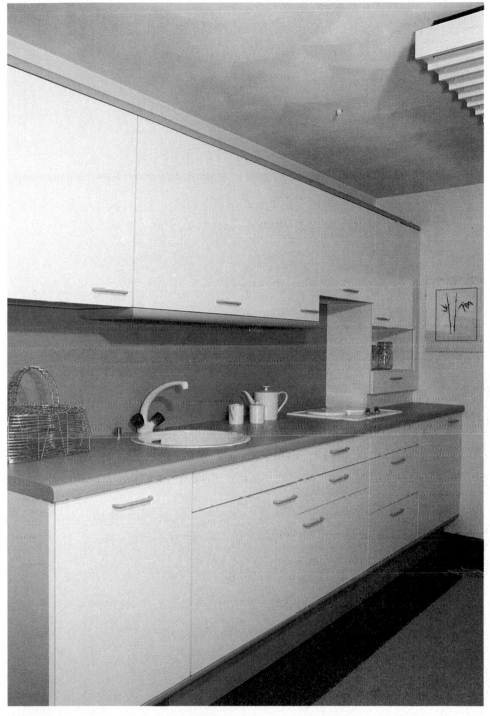

Drawer front conceals breakfast table that seats two comfortably. Range hood above cooktop tilts out for use, drops back when through. Microwave will be installed in niche holding decorative jars.

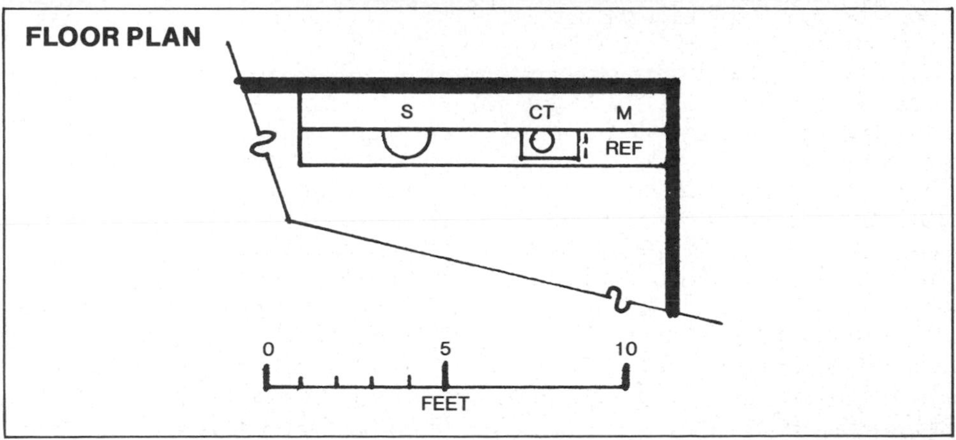

Blue, White & Oak

The soaring, skylighted ceiling sets the tone for this expansive kitchen. The fluid design is a blend of *island* and *zoned* kitchen layouts. See page 55 for more on these concepts. Because some work areas are separated, several people can work at once on different tasks. One example is the small sink at the end of the island near the refrigerator. See photo at top of page 11. Refrigerator and sink, along with cabinet and counter space in the corner to the right of the refrigerator, also make a perfect spot for a wet bar while entertaining.

The tile backsplash shown in the bottom left photo on page 11 represents an interesting solution to a technical problem. The design called for radiused corners for the full-height backsplashes. This would have been easy with plastic laminate or small tiles. But the owner selected large, patterned tile to accent streamlined plastic-laminate cabinets and DuPont Corian countertops. The builder declared that either large tile or radiused corners had to go. After all, 8x8" tiles don't bend.

Unwilling to give up either, the owner consulted the tilesetter and came up with the solution you see here. Tiles at the radiused corners were cut into three vertical strips each, and reassembled on the wall. Normal grout joints were used where the "whole" tiles met, and the smallest possible grout joints were used at the cut lines. The result produces a moment of mental upset for those who have worked with large tiles—"they just don't bend like that!"—but very effectively softens the corners.

The oak toprail is unobtrusive but serves several design purposes. As a midlevel unifying element, it picks up the color of the wood framing on the skylight, the color of the parquet floor and the color of the grout in the tile backsplashes.

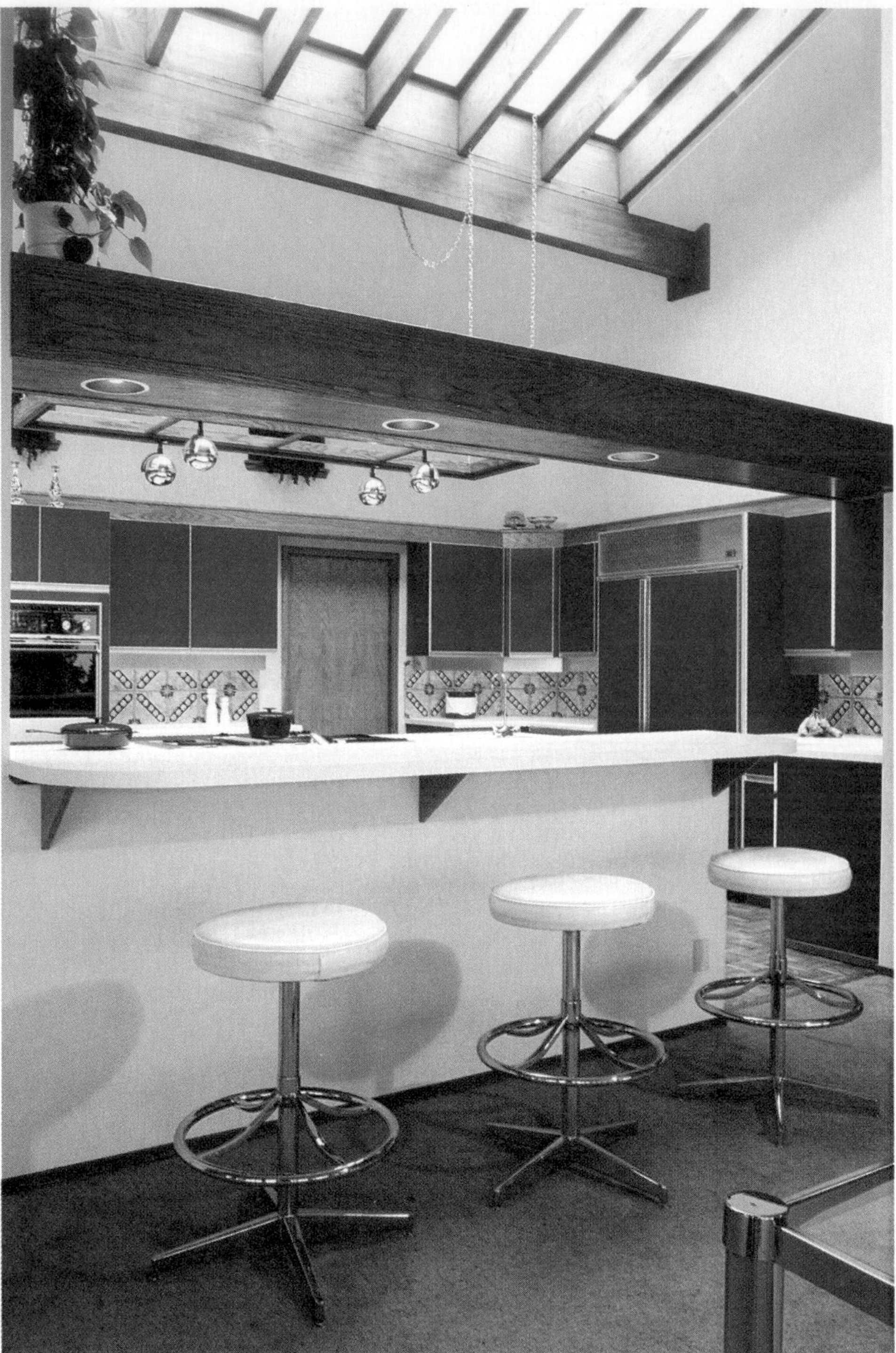

Skylight provides even, natural light during day. Suspended task lights illuminate work areas within kitchen.

The oak toprail also ties into the box structure above the snack bar. At that location it adds visual separation between kitchen and adjoining sitting area, and provides a place to install recessed lighting over the snack bar and sink. See photo above.

Task lighting is provided by recessed lights over the snack bar and by spotlights on the frame over the island. The aluminum strip below the wall cabinets conceals a series of fluorescent lights.

The slightly raised snack bar helps hide clutter at the sink area and beyond. Small brackets provide extra support for the snack bar. *Design: Marian Noble & Chris Schmidt.*

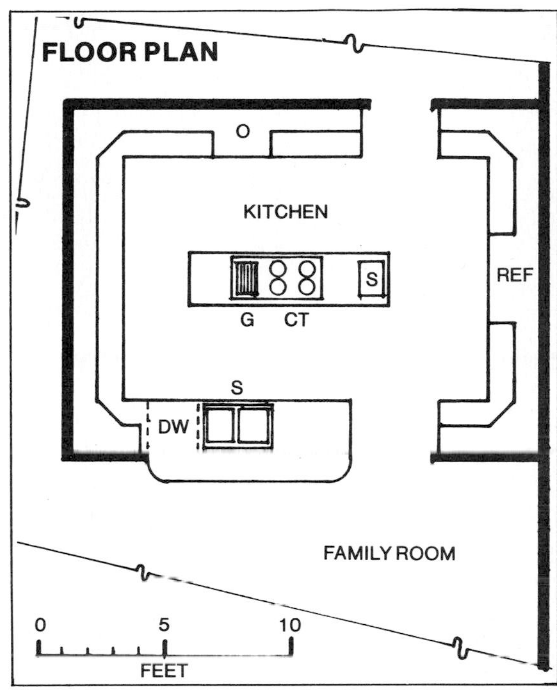

Right: Small, island sink near refrigerator is perfect for mixing drinks, rinsing off fruits and vegetables.
Below: Large ceramic tiles were cut in sections to make radiused corners on backsplash.
Below right: Raised snack bar hides sink-countertop clutter from dining area in foreground.

Great-Room Approach

When this lakefront home was gutted to the outside walls and renovated, the owners wanted to keep a view of the lake in as much of the living area as possible. Other homes close by on both sides made it difficult to open up lake views with side windows. The solution was to treat the living room, U-shape kitchen, entry and the dining room—all formerly walled off—as one open space. Designers often call this a *great room.*

An overhead skylight and bay window over the sink admit natural light to the kitchen. To maximize light from the bay window, mullions were omitted and the three pieces of glass connected with beads of silicone adhesive. The header for the bay window runs straight across the opening, in line with the wall. The roof overhang forms a top for the projecting bay.

Most appliances in the old kitchen were recent, so the owners decided to reuse them. They added a down-venting broiler grill.

The kitchen is designed for one-person cooking, with most of the appliances clustered at the head of the U. But the coffeemaker and refrigerator are located convenient to the open end of the U. This provides easy access by guests and family, in keeping with the informal entertaining that's so much a part of this lakeside community.

Cabinet doors with square-top panels have been used on the base cabinets, harmonized with crowned panels on wall-cabinet doors. Wood edge strips have been applied to the countertop only within the kitchen, where the top is directly adjacent to cabinet fronts. On the overhanging outer edge of the snack bar, edging matches the plastic-laminate top. This careful balancing of variations within a kitchen can be more pleasing than a forced, sterile consistency. *Design: Rick Harrison.*

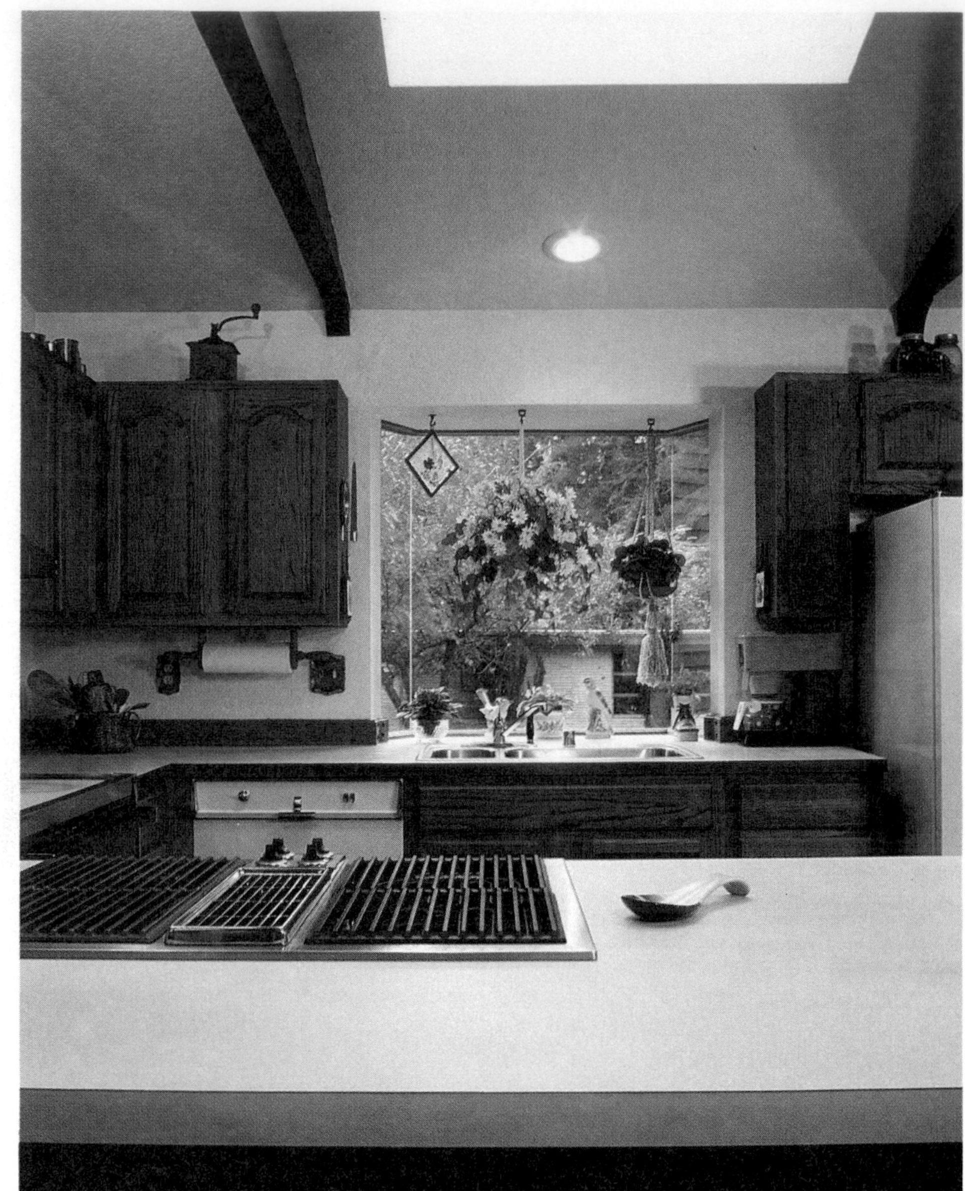

Bay window and skylight help open this kitchen to outdoors. Vertical strips between window panes, called *mullions,* were omitted. Panes are joined with beads of silicone adhesive.

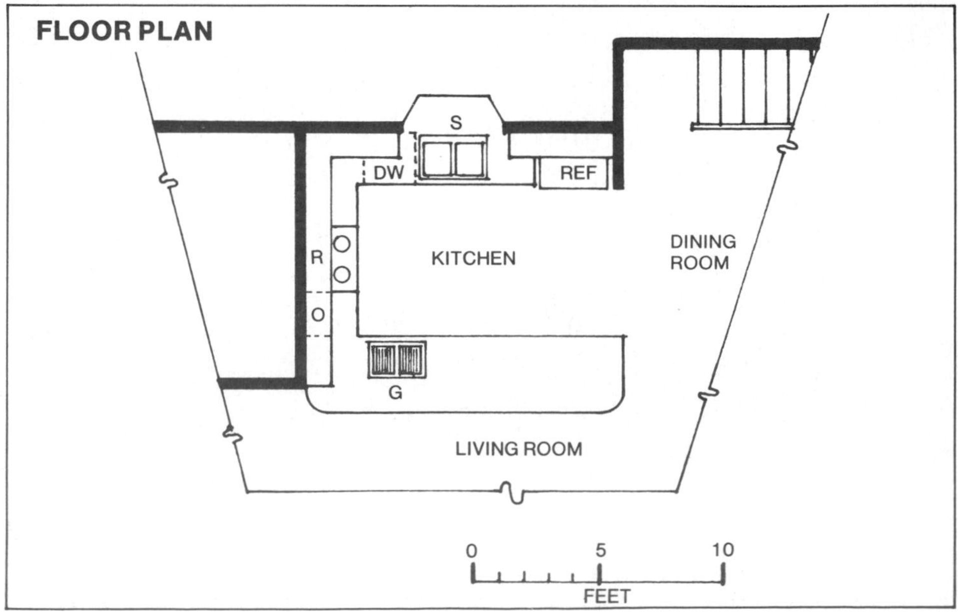

All appliances except refrigerator are grouped at head of this U-shape kitchen. Appliance layout is convenient for one-person cooking.

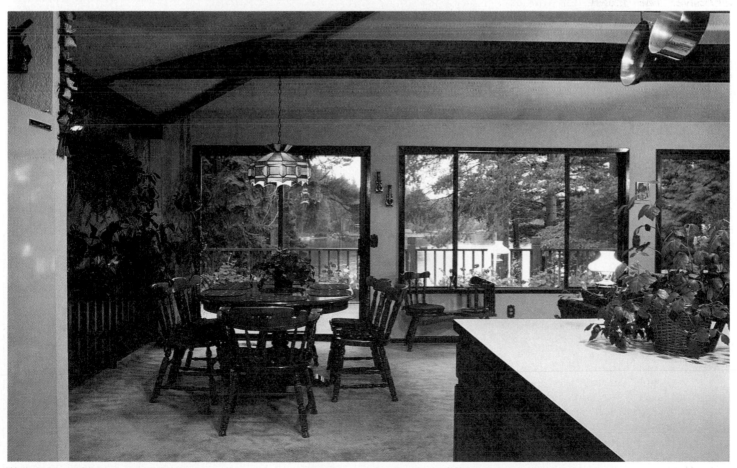

Walls between kitchen, entry and dining room were removed to open up lake view from all three areas.

Made to Match

This large Southwestern kitchen faces the south slope of a mountain range that extends to nearly 6,000 feet. The view changes constantly. Occasionally, mountain wildlife can be seen browsing in the garden. The kitchen was designed to bring in the mountains and garden through tall windows. The high, gently sloped ceiling helps to bounce north light through the kitchen all day long.

The kitchen's unifying design element is the patterned tiles. Tiles were handmade to match the owners' favorite china, visible on the island and on the breakfast table in the photo at right. The owners insist that if the tiles outlast the china, they'll have new china made to match the tiles.

Instead of a standard hood over the ranges, the recess is lined with ceramic tile on sides, back and top. A narrow slot at the top front edge of the recess vents heat, smoke and moisture through a roof-mounted fan. Access to the filters is through a trap door concealed by the tile. The heavy door must be opened carefully.

A two-burner gas cooktop was installed alongside the electric range with 30-inch oven, for recipes that benefit from gas cooking. Since these appliances were installed, combination gas-electric units have become available in the United States. Such units have been in use in Europe for years.

In the short hallway to the dining room is a small serving counter. It's equipped with a bar sink, an instant hot-water dispenser and another dishwasher. An infrared food-warming unit is installed under the wall cabinet to the right of the sink. See photo on facing page.

Ceramic tiles were handmade to match owner's favorite china. They're used creatively as borders throughout kitchen.

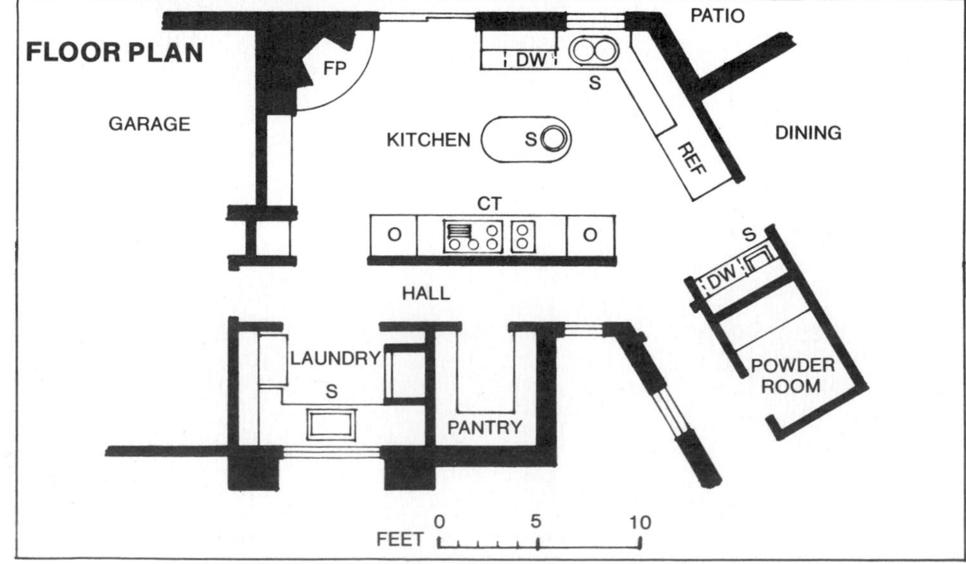

Cooking area is designed for entertaining large groups. Gas and electric burners offer versatility in surface-cooking methods.

Serving counter is in hall between kitchen and dining room. It includes sink, hot-water dispenser, dishwasher and infrared food-warmer. Vertical glass strip in swinging door helps prevent collisions.

Made to Match

A swinging door installed between a kitchen and dining room often results in collisions. This happens when two people use the door from opposite sides at the same time. A solid door causes many such collisions, and large glass panels defeat the reason for the door. In this home, the problem was ingeniously solved by installing a narrow, vertical strip of glass. People sitting in the dining room can see almost nothing through the glass. But people moving on either side of the door can see much larger areas on the other side, including approaching traffic. See photo on page 15.

The drawer and appliance-garage area to the left of the refrigerator is capable of hiding large amounts of kitchen clutter. For example, a complete spice collection occupies only two of the 15 drawers. Because extra space was available behind the cabinets, the drawers and appliance garage are extra deep.

Oak panels for refrigerator, right, and dishwasher, page 14, were custom-made to match cabinets. Marble top on island sink, page 14, is used for pastry-making; top is slightly lower for owner's comfort. Design: *Helen Fisher and Janean Kitchens. Tile design by Steve Dirks. Cabinets by Jorgensen Cabinets.*

Appliance garage keeps portable appliances handy but out of sight.

Tall window over sink opens up mountain view.

Extra-deep drawers provide added storage space.

Free-Standing Kitchen

This unusual kitchen is not on an outside wall. It's surrounded by three free-standing walls, not connected to the sloping beamed ceiling above. The fourth side is open over the breakfast bar to a wall of glass only a few feet away. To maximize this openness, built-in ovens and refrigerator are stepped back behind the line of the cabinet fronts. The formal dining room is around the corner, left of the refrigerator.

In a kitchen like this, under-cabinet lighting assumes extra importance in providing adequate task lighting. Another approach would have been to suspend several lights at appropriate points above the work areas. *Design: Rick Harrison.*

Open ceiling lends spacious feeling to free-standing kitchen. Sink counter is extended to serve as snack bar. Refrigerator and oven are recessed in alcove to provide additional floor space in kitchen.

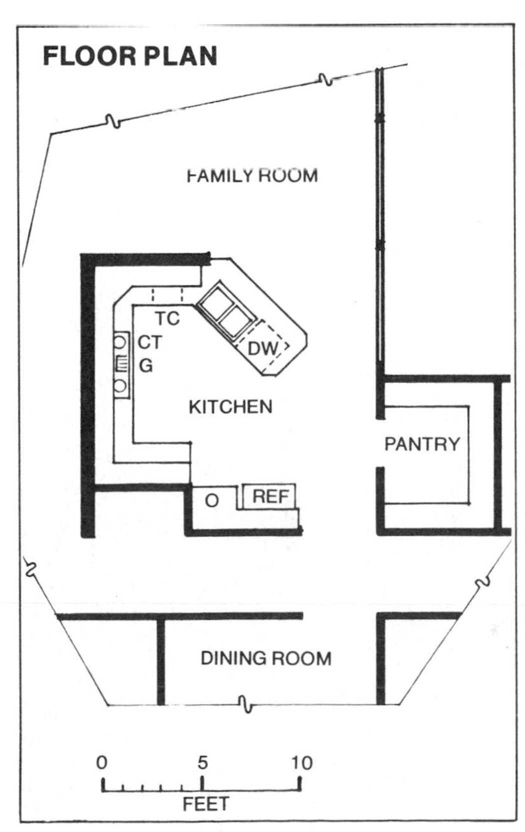

Cabinet tops make excellent plant display area. Plants can be viewed from both sides of wall.

Traditional Cherry

This large but workable kitchen is done in a traditional American style. Solid-cherry cabinets are factory-made. They were stained and finished on the job to match custom-milled cherry moldings and trim that extend throughout the house. The room doors are faced in cherry veneer and finished to match. Surface moldings were custom-milled to match cabinets and applied to all room doors. Unfortunately, it wasn't possible to carry this detail to the pocket doors, because the moldings wouldn't fit into existing wall pockets.

The basic design approach was an integration of kitchen, breakfast area and family room, in keeping with the home's informal country location. All three areas are linked together around a large brick fireplace. The size of the fireplace structure isn't a facade. It not only houses a closet, wood storage and the ovens, but another fireplace on the living-room side. The fireplaces are the heat-circulating type, ducted to a central heat-storage rock bin. A fire for a few hours every evening provides thermostatically controlled heat for the whole house most of the night.

The trash compactor and dishwasher are ideally located on either side of the sink for efficient after-meal cleanups. Front panels that match cabinets have been installed on both appliances. Due to careful planning by the builder, the window over the sink is located exactly the right height so window trim meets the countertop backsplash. Good detailing like this helps a kitchen look its best.

The pot rack over the bar is from a restaurant-supply store. These racks come in many shapes, sizes and finishes. Or, you can make your own without too much difficulty. Chain mounting makes it easy to suspend a rack under a sloping ceiling like this one.

The antique chairs in the breakfast area are carved oak, stained to match the cherry cabinets and trim. *Design: Rick Harrison.*

Massive fireplace structure houses 2 fireplaces, kitchen oven, wood storage area and closet.

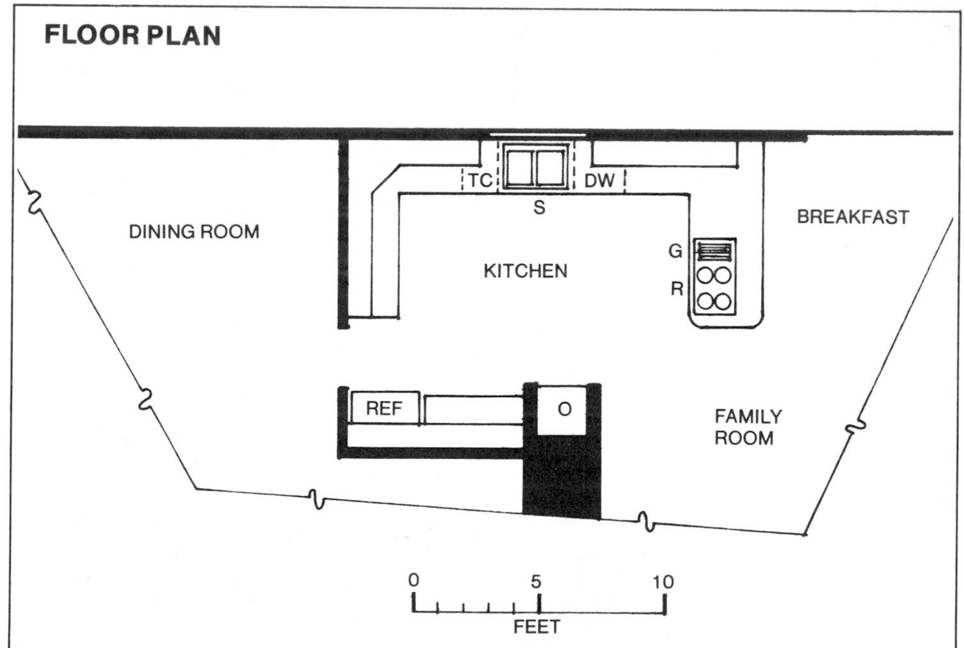

Peninsula with drop-in cooktop and suspended pot rack visually separates kitchen from breakfast area. Antique chairs were stained to match rest of woodwork.

Floor, doors and all trim work were stained to match dark cherry cabinets. Dishwasher and trash compactor are conveniently located on either side of sink.

Steel & Marble

Sharing its gray-and-white Taiwanese-marble floor with many other areas in the house, this cool-white kitchen is made for the owners' entertaining needs. A true zoned kitchen, it's suitable for cooking and serving by three or four. But it's organized so one person can cook without needing a bicycle to travel between work centers.

A wall of windows topped with large skylights provides natural lighting all day long. Supplemental light is provided by recessed fixtures in the ceiling and track lights mounted on mullions between skylights. Strategically placed undercabinet lights provide task lighting at counters.

The double-width center island is topped with heavy-gage stainless steel. This large, durable top will stand up to jobs like cutting up a beef hindquarter. It isn't damaged by hot pots and pans. This feature is especially useful on the end that serves the ovens. Both cooktop and broiler unit are down-venting, so no hood is needed over the island.

To the left of the ovens is the walk-in pantry door. Left of that, a short hall leads to a powder room, then to a service door opening onto a small courtyard off the parking area. This makes the kitchen ideal for catered entertaining of large groups. See top photo on facing page.

The serving counter can be shut off from the dining room side by folding doors. Drawers underneath open from both sides so serving utensils, tablecloths and napkins can be reached from dining room or kitchen.

It's the small details that make this kitchen special. Open space was left over some wall cabinets. Over others where a solid wall couldn't be avoided, smoked-glass mirrors cover the wall. This makes the spaces over all wall cabinets look much the same.

Another small detail is an electrical plug-in strip running across the back of the appliance garage. This allows the many small appliances to be left plugged in all the time. As a safety

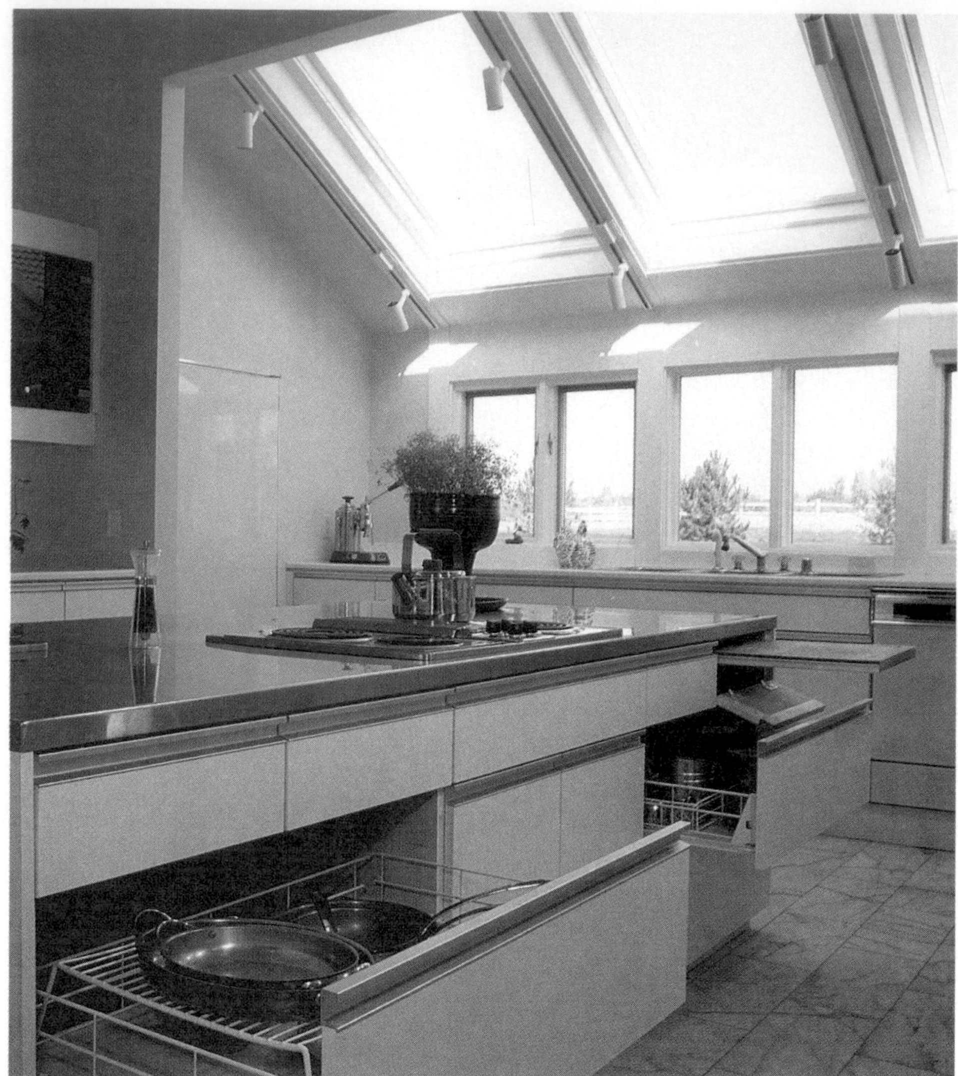

Wall of windows topped by skylights provides natural lighting all day long. Stainless-steel countertop is durable, easy to clean.

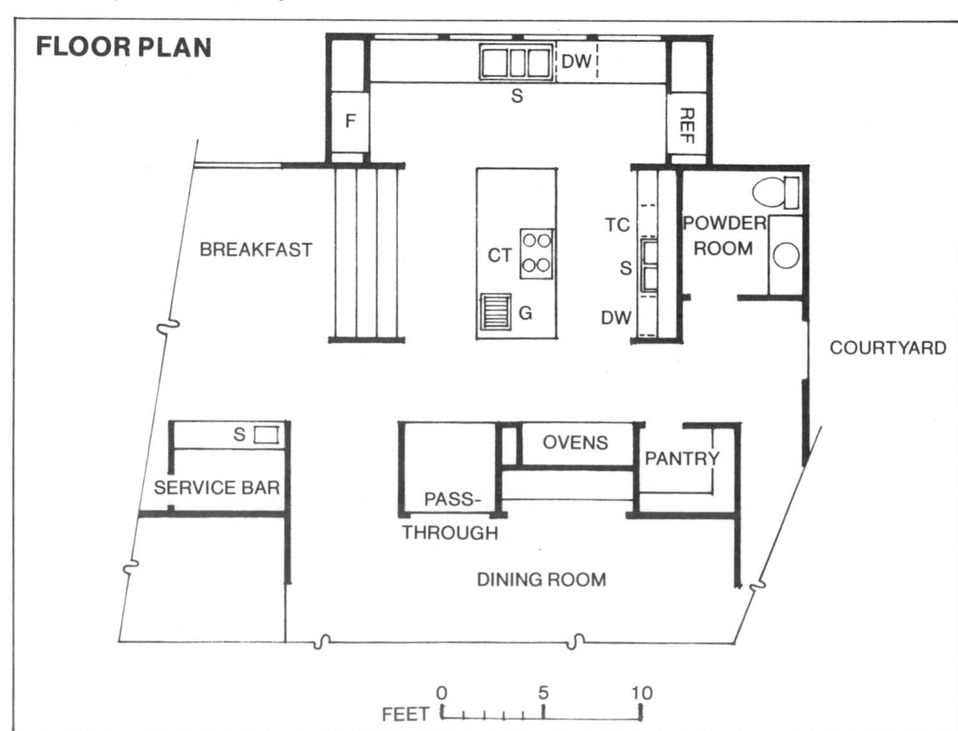

Drawers under pass-through serving counter can be opened from both sides. Folding doors close off pass-through from dining area.

precaution, the plug-in strip is controlled by a wall switch that disconnects power when none of the appliances are in use.

Adjustable wire storage racks in many of the cabinets offer efficient storage for utensils and containers of many different sizes and shapes. See photo at right. *Design: Marian Noble & Chris Schmidt.*

Adjustable wire racks hold many various-size items.

Appliance garage features electrical-outlet strip that allows all appliances to remain plugged in for immediate use.

Small But Elegant

This cozy little kitchen packs a lot of storage space, work space and a breakfast corner into a surprisingly small area—about 140 square feet.

One space-saving technique was to extend cabinets all the way to the ceiling. Additional small cabinets were installed near the ceiling in space not normally used—over the window and over the sliding-glass door. The owners are tall enough to reach these cabinets. To free up counter space, the toaster was recessed into the wall to the right of the refrigerator, as shown in the photo on the facing page.

Despite its appearance, the finish material on wall and ceiling is not tile. It's wallpaper with a glossy finish. The background color of the wallpaper was chosen to match the plastic laminate on the cabinets. The widely spaced pattern on walls and ceiling contrasts with the plain background color on the cabinets. This visual trick tends to make the cabinets recede, so they're less obtrusive. Light-color countertops and built-in refrigerator also make this kitchen seem larger.

When this kitchen was remodeled, the original window was removed and a greenhouse window installed in the opening. The greenhouse window captures outside space and adds it to the apparent volume of the kitchen. The greenhouse window is a prefabricated unit. Most prefab greenhouse windows are as easy to install as a standard window. *Design: Jeff Case, CKD.*

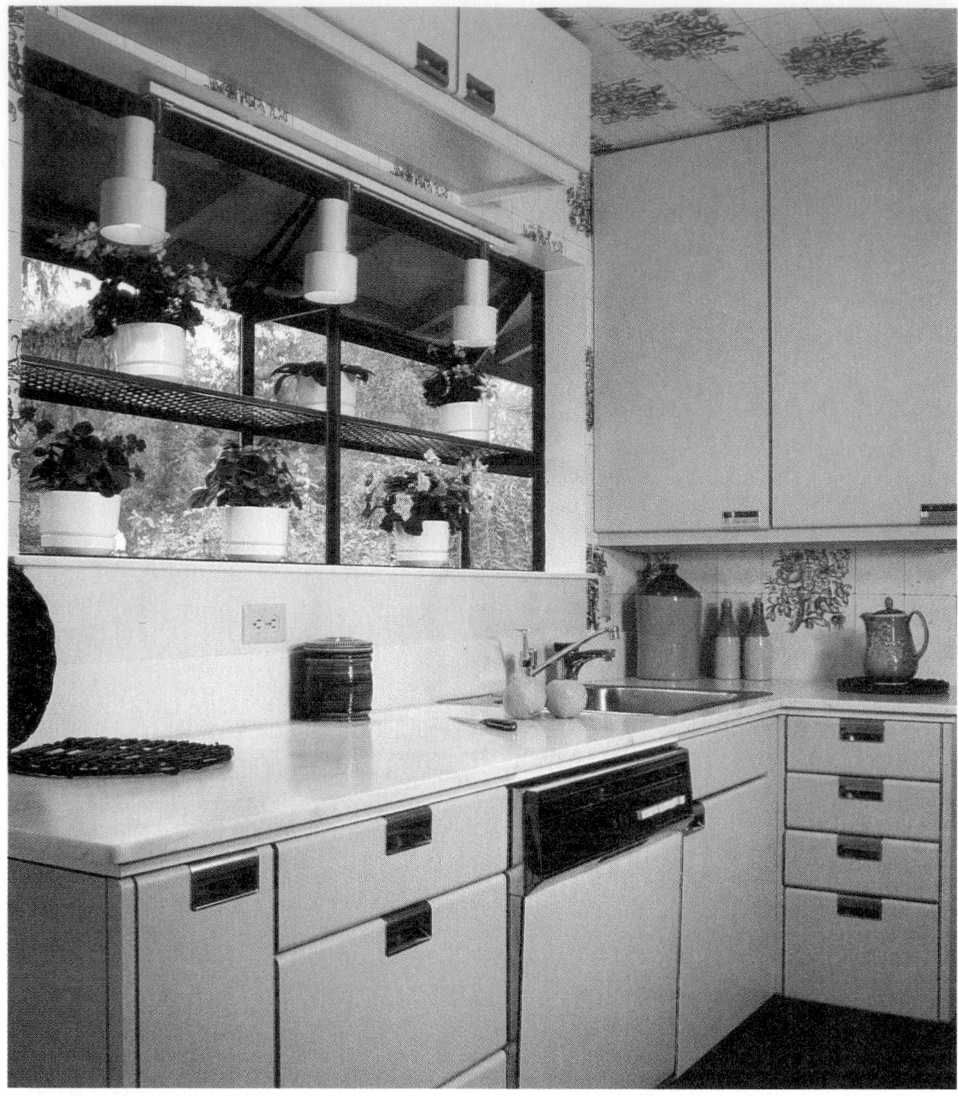

Greenhouse window lights sink area by day, directional task lighting illuminates by night. Overhead cabinets provide extra storage space for tall owners.

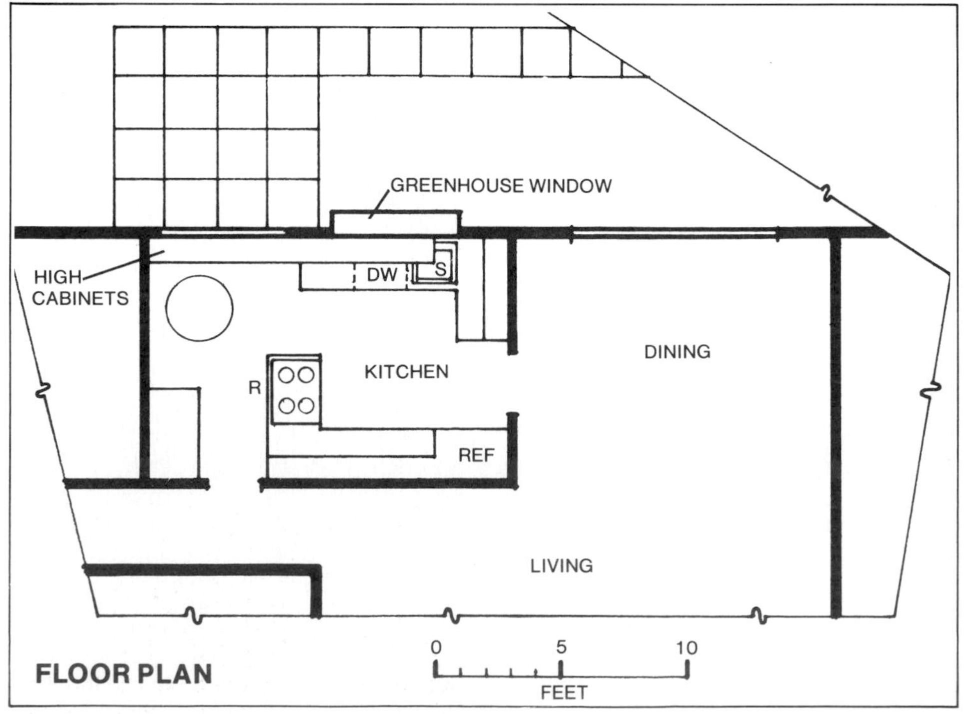

Recessed refrigerator provides additional floor space. Toaster to right is also recessed to free up counter space. Range with pyroceram surface is at right.

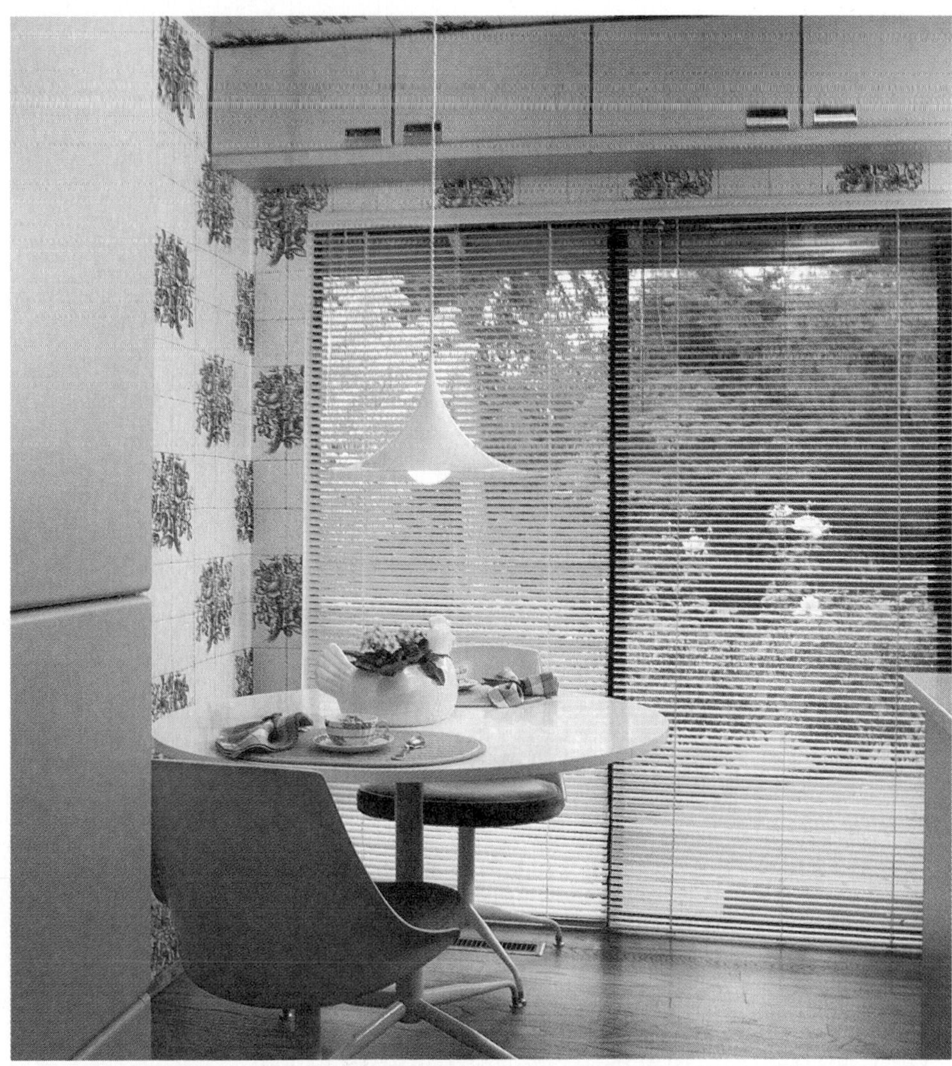

Cozy breakfast area seats two comfortably. Note storage cabinets above sliding-glass door. Full-height cabinets are in foreground at left.

Skylight Opens Treetop View

The lighting in this second-story kitchen is unusual in its thoroughness. A large skylight-window gives a wide-angle view of forest treetops from the sink area and brightens the entire kitchen during daylight hours.

There are recessed fixtures in the high ceiling and track lights inside the upper edge of the skylight. Fluorescent fixtures under wall cabinets illuminate counters.

Wood soffit above wall cabinets has recessed fixtures that illuminate cabinet interiors when doors are open. Front edge of the soffit is about even with front edge of countertop below. See photo on facing page, top right.

Two kinds of countertop materials have been combined in this kitchen—butcher block and soft-tan ceramic tile. The butcher-block top on the island has been cut into a complex-polygon shape to provide traffic clearance. See photo on facing page, top left. The island overhang on the family-room side provides seating for two people to enjoy snacks or converse with the cook.

There's no clear-cut dividing line between kitchen and the rest of the house. Roll-top desk and entertainment center were custom-made to match kitchen cabinets. They are separated from the kitchen itself by a door to the dining room. TV set at top of entertainment center is on a tray mounted on heavy-duty drawer hardware. The set can be rolled back into the cabinet or rolled out and swiveled toward the kitchen or family room. Another piece of matching cabinetwork is the bar, beyond the desk and entertainment center. *Design: Barbara Hertzler.*

T-shape skylight gives wide-angle view at sink location. Track lights in upper edge of skylight provide general lighting.

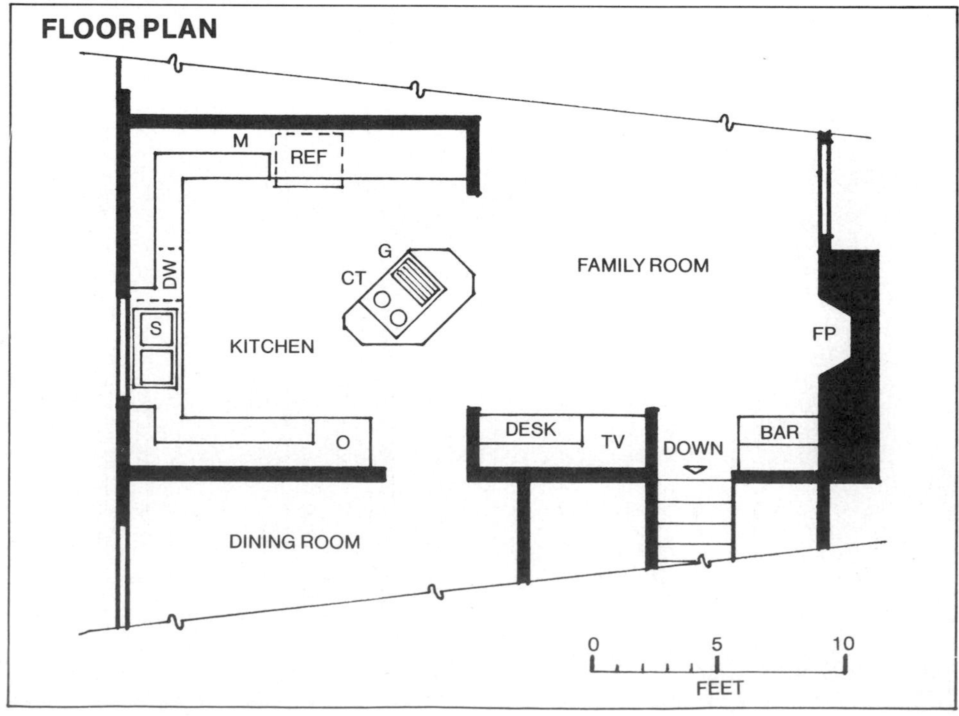

Above left: Butcher-block top on island counter is shaped to allow traffic clearance.
Above: Recessed lights in soffit illuminate cabinet interiors when doors are open. Roll-up door between base cabinets and wall cabinets conceals appliance garage and electrical outlet.
Left: Cabinetry and roll-top desk in adjoining entertainment center were designed to match kitchen cabinets. TV is mounted on roll-out base that swivels to face kitchen area.

Leaded-Glass Doors

Because this kitchen faces the street, it has no windows in the main wall. Instead, a long skylight was installed. The skylight panels are separated by structurally necessary rafters. These are kept above the skylight and capped with U-shape metal flashing. This is a technically difficult bit of carpentry. It's usually easier to run the rafters straight through, stained to match, and construct the skylight assembly on top.

The skylight also illuminates muted colors of leaded-glass panels in cabinets below. Leaded-glass panels can be installed in custom cabinets or can replace inset panels in some factory-made cabinets.

Massive range hood over the island is suspended on four heavy chains and turnbuckles, hooked to stout ringbolts solidly anchored into roof structure. Under certain circumstances, a hood this heavy may require reinforcing of the roof structure itself. Hood fan is roof-mounted.

At far left end of kitchen, a suspended rack has been installed to catch notes, receipts and other pieces of paper a household accumulates. There's also a swing-down cookbook rack. *Design: Roger Beckmann.*

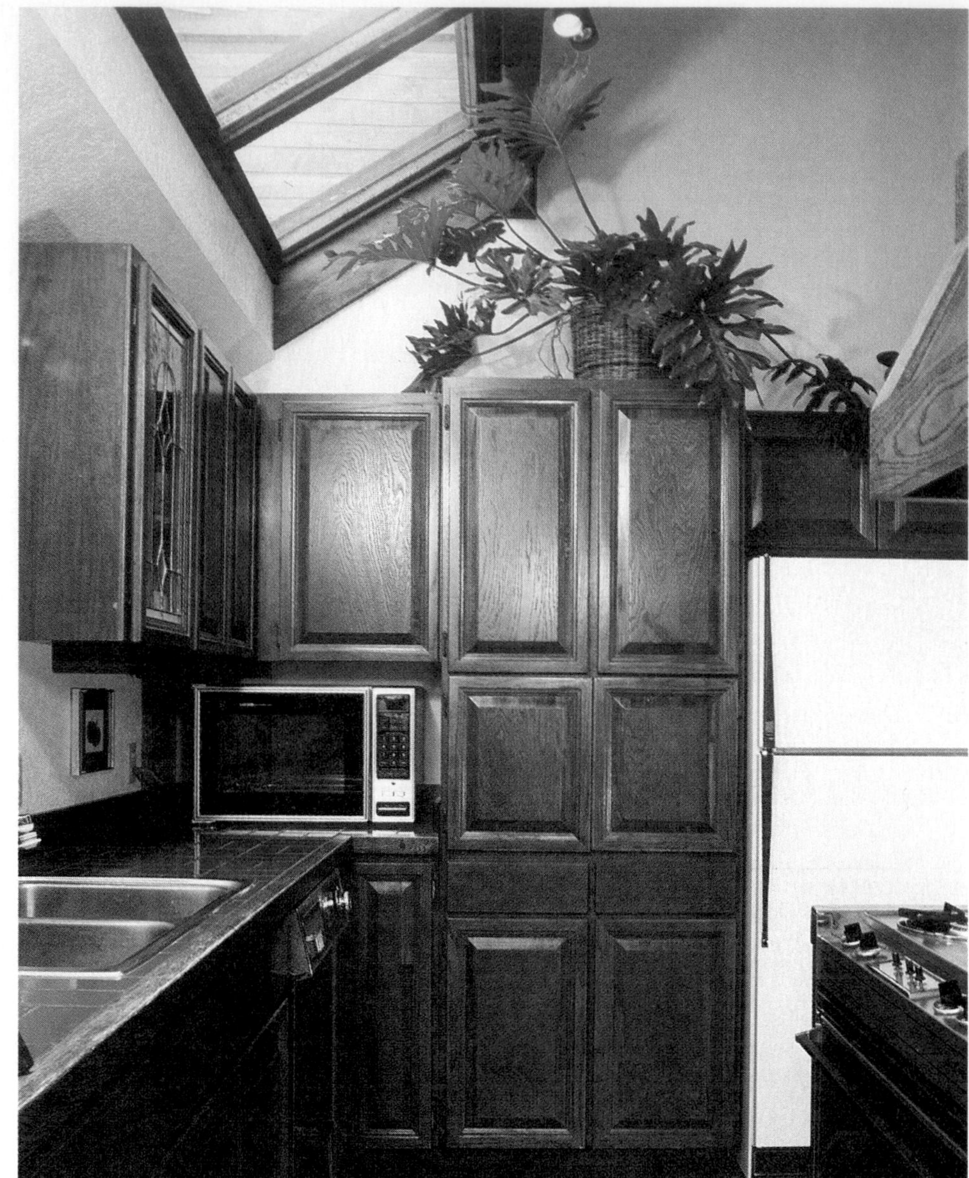

Wall behind kitchen sink at left faces street. High skylights offer privacy.

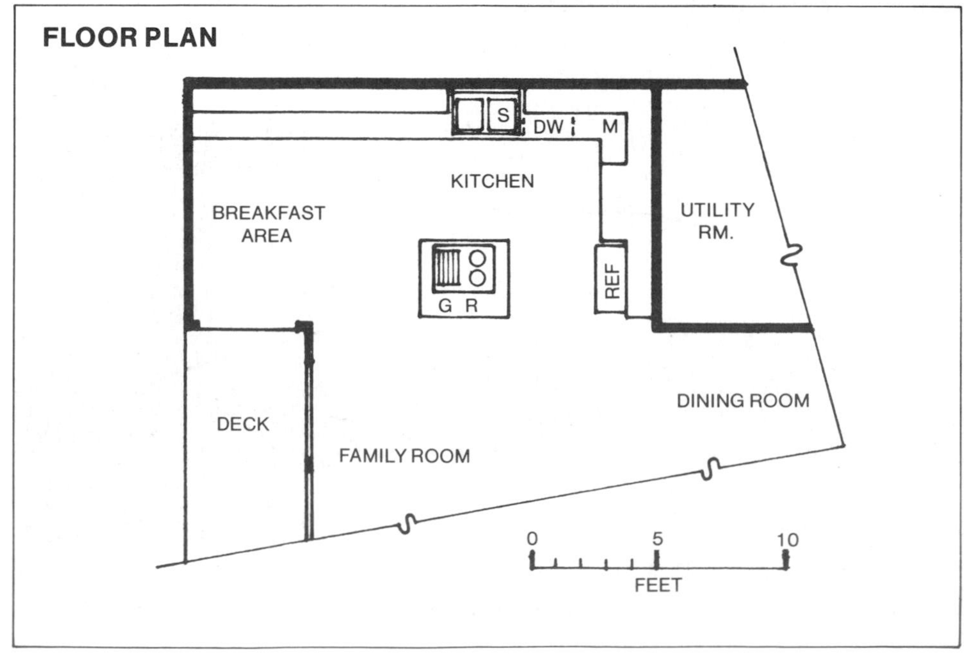

Massive range hood is supported by heavy chains and turnbuckles. Roof on this house is designed to carry the additional weight. Wood panels were replaced with leaded glass on cabinet doors either side of sink. This is an easy way to customize some factory-made cabinets.

Rack suspended below wall cabinets is efficient way to organize miscellaneous notes and mail. Swing-down cookbook rack frees cook's hands while reading.

Many unrelated features are pulled together to give this kitchen an eclectic look. Stained-glass panel conceals overhead lights.

Modern Country

The dominant material in this country kitchen is oak. Other materials are skillfully blended in to demonstrate pleasing diversity of the *eclectic style,* defined on page 8.

Material choices for this kitchen seem to come in pairs and are used in original ways. For instance, none of the cabinet-door panels are oak. Most are sheet copper. Those on the peninsula cabinets are etched glass. The sheet copper was chemically treated to produce a mottled effect. See photo on facing page, top right.

A modern-looking fluorescent fixture was installed under peninsula cabinets. It contrasts with lights concealed by a stained-glass panel in the ceiling's center. Solid-color tile on countertops contrasts with a totally unrelated patterned tile on the floor. Tile insets on floor simulate a scatter rug. The overall effect is a bit cluttered but homey and comfortable.

The main design point that makes this small kitchen efficient is the recessed refrigerator. In a conventional design, the refrigerator would have been located just left of the present range. See floor plan at right. That would have squeezed the other work locations clockwise around the kitchen. The bulk of the exposed refrigerator would have visually reduced the size of the kitchen. Using about 6 square feet of an adjacent closet produced a better result. For the same reasons, wall ovens couldn't be used in this kitchen unless more closet space was used to make room for them.

An interesting touch in this kitchen is the use of wood accessories. These include the towel rack and the spice rack/pot rack, both made to match the cabinets. *Design: Roger Beckmann.*

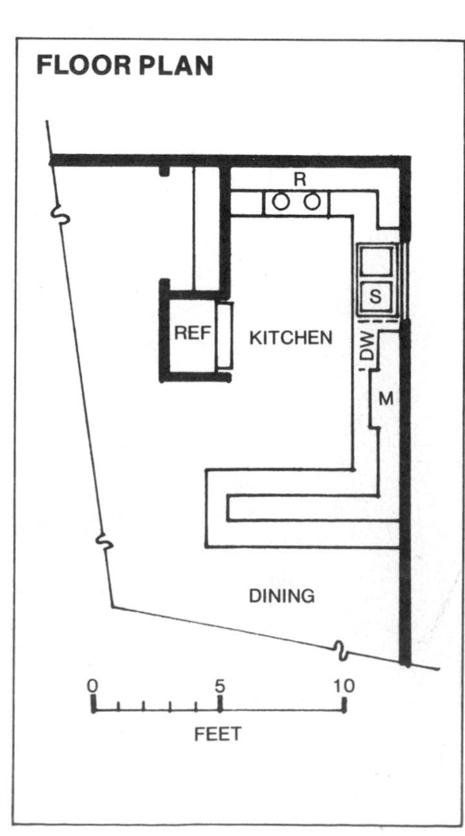

Above left: Cabinets suspended by chains provide overhead space to display basket collection. Modern fluorescent fixture under cabinet adds to eclectic style.
Above: Ceramic tile inset provides durable floor surface in high-traffic area. Pattern is totally unrelated to countertop tiles.
Left: Kitchen is designed to provide as much display space as possible. Custom-made spice rack/pot rack is a good example.

Black & White Tile

Remodeling a kitchen in an old house can be challenging. This solid, century-old house was worth the effort, but finding enough space for the kitchen was a problem.

Originally, the space that's now the kitchen was a small kitchen and pantry, divided by cellar stairs. The stairs were relocated to the end wall, leaving a larger, though somewhat irregular, open space. Other structural elements, such as a large masonry fireplace, couldn't be moved.

The end result was an unorthodox but functional new kitchen. Cabinets extending up to the ceiling provide extra storage space. Crown molding at cabinet tops is in keeping with the character of the rest of the house. Additional storage was provided by installing Lazy Susans and pullout drawers inside the cabinets.

Off-white cabinets in the dining room are identical to those in the kitchen except for color and the glass panels in the wall cabinets. All countertops are DuPont Corian. Backsplashes were omitted on the dining-room countertops. The small bar sink in the dining room is molded into the countertop. See photo on facing page. *Design: Cheryl Davis.*

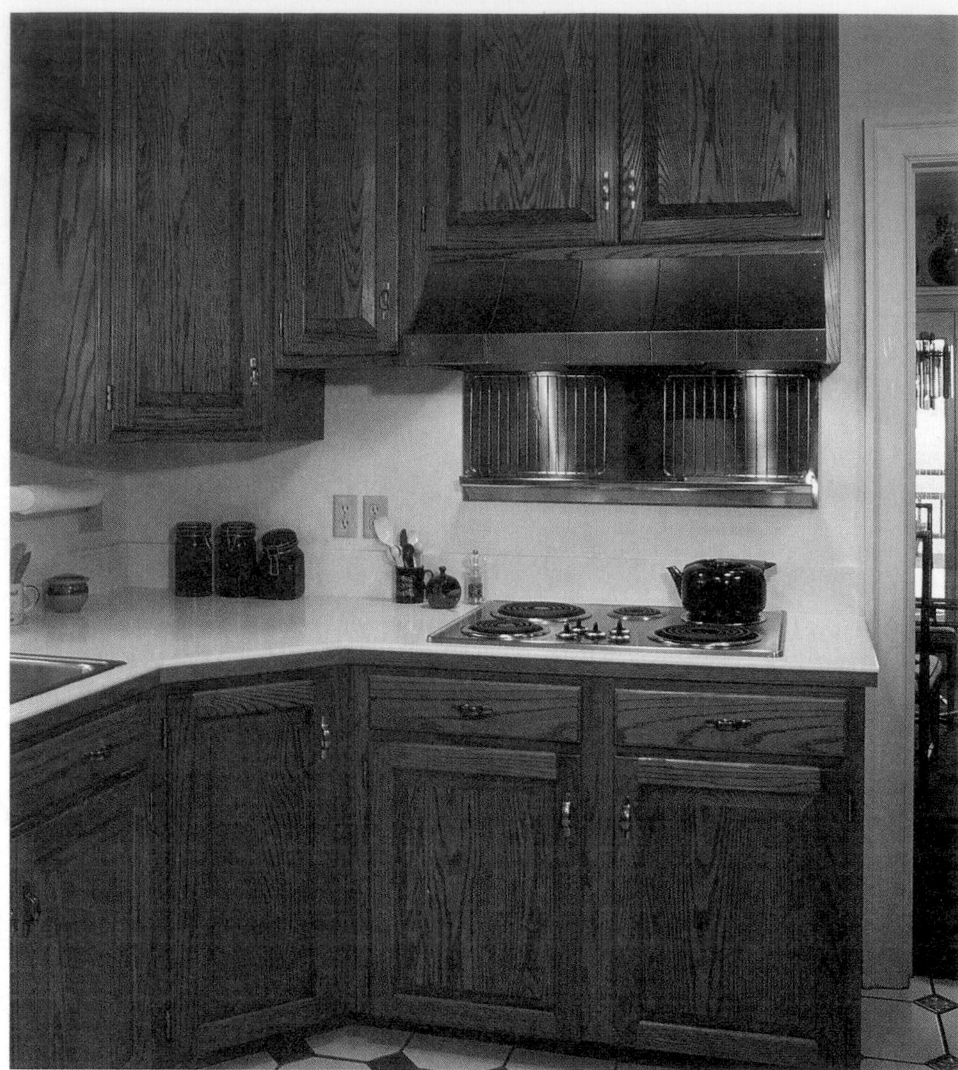

Floor-to-ceiling cabinets increase storage space in small kitchen. Drop-down warming racks are integral to range hood above cooktop.

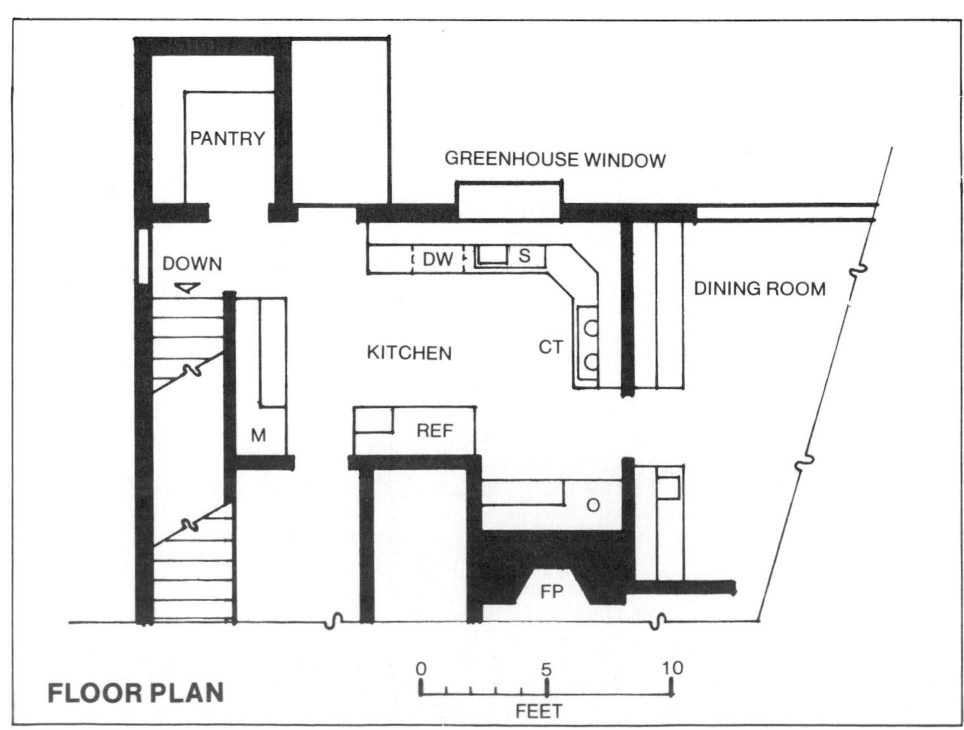

Lazy Susans make best use of corner-cabinet space. Countertops are DuPont Corian.

Panels in refrigerator were custom-made to match cabinets. Matching side panels and cabinet above complete disguise. Many newer refrigerators and freezers are designed to accept door inserts such as this. Black-and-white tile and crown molding at cabinet tops is in keeping with style of this century-old house.

Except for color, hardware and glass panels, dining-room cabinets are identical to those in kitchen. Small bar sink is molded into Corian countertop.

Wall of Glass

The angled projection in this kitchen counter has been used to break up the kitchen's rectangular shape. The projection permits large glass areas while preserving adequate space elsewhere for wall cabinets. Window trim was custom-made to match cabinets. Matching trim was used in adjoining dining area.

All interior walls in this home's living areas have been held down below the sloping ceiling, providing a spacious feeling throughout the house. This allows a skylight in the entry beyond the kitchen to light the kitchen also. *Design: Roger Beckmann.*

Angular countertop lends geometric interest to this kitchen. Suspended overhead lights and partial interior walls make kitchen seem more spacious than it really is. Oak cabinets and yellow ceramic tile are restful to eyes.

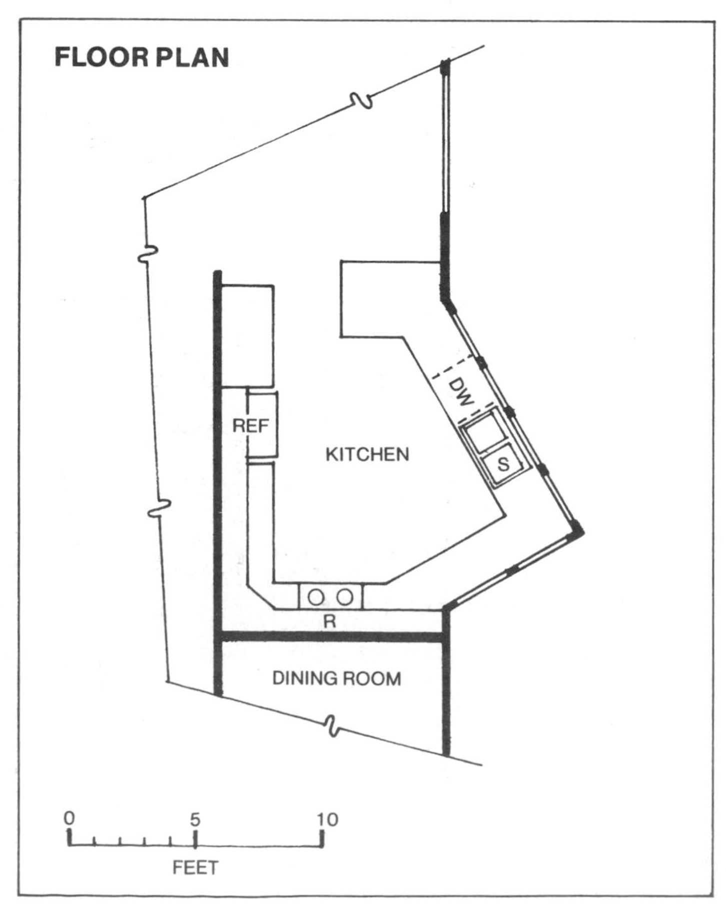

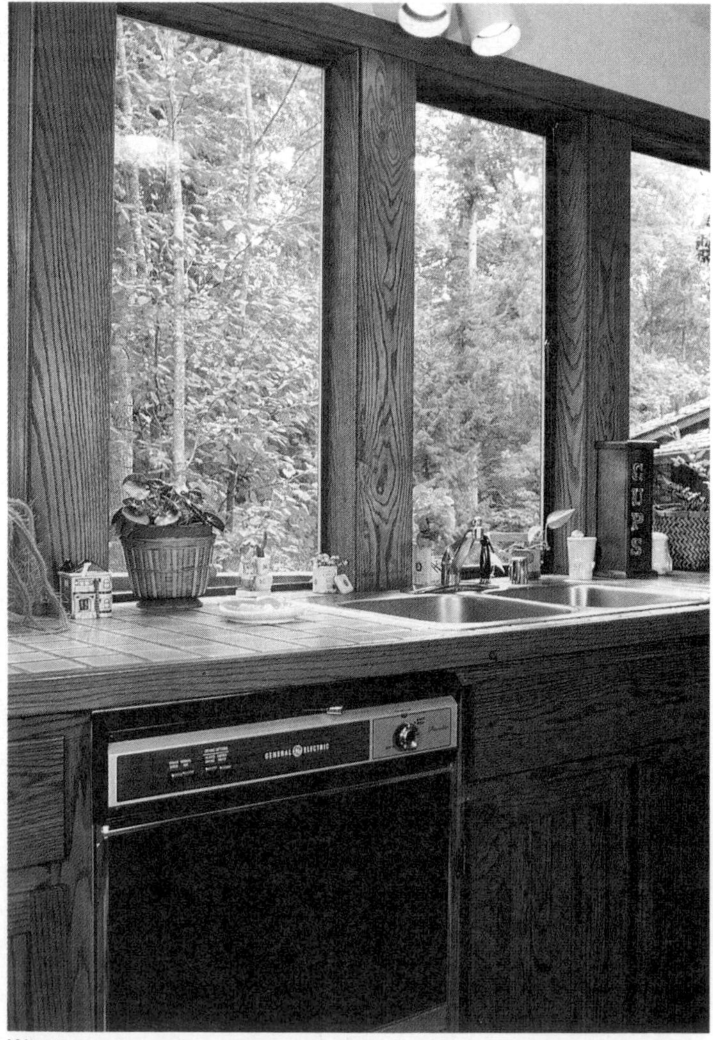

Window trimmed to match cabinets is unifying design element in this kitchen. Tall windows and absence of backsplash behind sink open sink area to outdoors.

Country Style

Variations of the American country kitchen are still with us. In this example, the eating area has been moved to one end, out of the middle of the room. Layout is a large *galley* type, with a small L at the end of one side to give some separation to the breakfast area. Kitchen layouts are discussed on pages 54-55. Cabinets carry through the country look, as does the wallpaper. Relatively dark wallpaper on the high ceiling visually lowers it and ties it to the rest of the kitchen. Techniques for visually altering space are discussed on page 48.

The niche in the soffit above the refrigerator is one way to make use of space above wall cabinets in a high-ceiling room. The niche and its contents are visible from adjacent formal dining room.

The two-sided bar is ideal for entertaining. Appetizers or snacks can be stocked on the counter from the kitchen side and sampled from the living-room side. The depth of the bar is made feasible by the walk-in pantry to its left. The pantry is behind door between the bar and refrigerator.

In this kitchen, the floor covering continues up cabinet toe boards. This application makes the floor easy to clean, and is easy to do with flexible resilient-flooring materials. Solid backing must be provided where the resilient-floor covering curves up the toe board. Otherwise the floor covering is easily damaged where it bends. A special wood cove molding is used for this purpose. *Design: Herder Construction Co.*

Cabinets and wallpaper are main design elements in country kitchen. Galley-kitchen design was modified with small L-shape counter to separate kitchen from breakfast area.

Niche above refrigerator is used for display. Wallpaper on ceiling visually lowers it, making room more cozy.

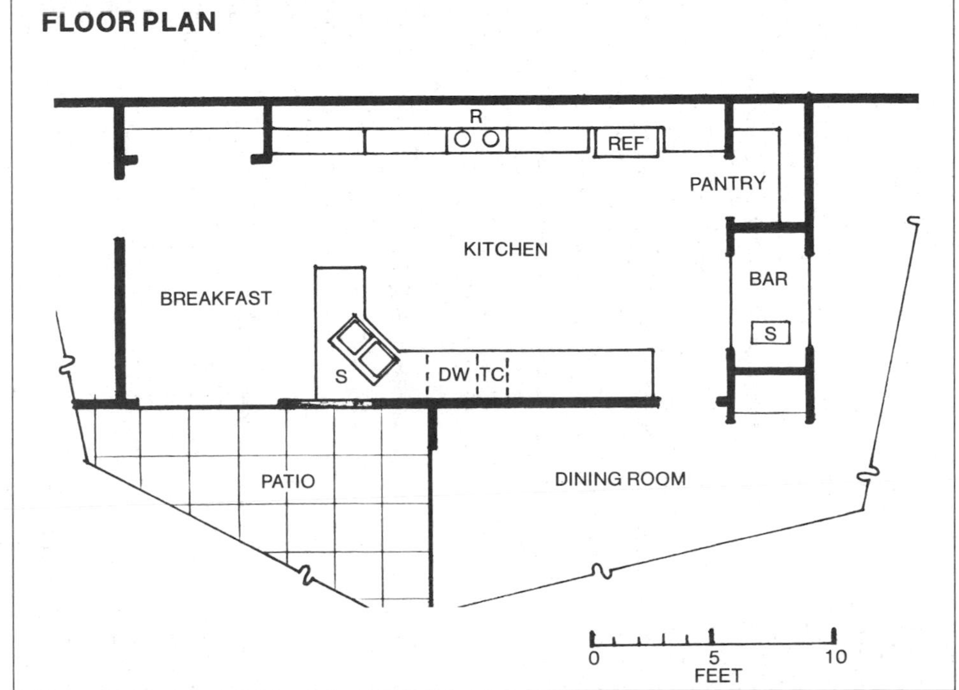

Surfaces & Equipment

Indoor version of familiar gas barbecue. Unit features electronic, solid-state ignition, variable heat control and adjustable grill. Glazed ceramic tile makes durable, heat-resistant countertop. Unit is self-venting.

A kitchen consists of hundreds of different parts and pieces selected to match a concept. Because of the full, rich marketplace of ideas and products available, you have hundreds of choices to make. Suppliers will tell you what features and advantages their products have, but not what's available from other suppliers. They may not even know alternative features or products exist. It is up to you to research what is available, compare products and features and make the best choices for your situation.

This chapter does not cover all of the available products and their variations. It will give you a good idea of what products and features are available and what to look for when making choices. For instance, if you've had problems with the kids chipping enamel off the interior surface of the dishwasher, you might want to consider one lined with stainless steel, as described on page 44. Another feature in your package may include a cooktop or range with controls located out of a toddler's reach. When you know what features you want and which are available, you can begin shopping and comparing products.

Some items discussed here change slowly, if at all. Others, such as cooking appliances and resilient floor coverings, change rapidly. Styles, colors, patterns and other features are modified or added yearly. Some products and features described in this chapter may soon be outdated. With some products it is best to get up-to-date information from the manufacturers. A list of names and addresses can be found on page 188.

SURFACES

Walls, floors and ceilings form most of the visible area of a kitchen. The materials available for finishing these surfaces are covered in this section. Countertops and cabinets are discussed on pages 38-40.

CHOICES IN FLOOR COVERINGS

In selecting a flooring material, first consider the floors of adjoining rooms. Although trim strips are available to bridge seams where two kinds of flooring meet, some floor combinations will be unsightly and even dangerous. Adjoining floor areas can sometimes be built up to compensate if the new kitchen floor is at a higher level.

Next, consider the existing floor structure. Materials such as thick ceramic tile or brick are heavy and brittle. They require a strong, rigid subfloor. If your present floor is not strong or rigid enough, it may sag under the load. You will have to reinforce the floor. Check local codes for subfloor requirements. If your floor is rough, lumpy concrete, it may require too much work to make it smooth and level for a flexible, resilient floor covering. Quarry tile in a thick mortar bed may be a better solution.

Certain types of floor coverings have inherent resistance to various kinds of wear. If mud and grit are regularly tracked into the kitchen, the finish on a high-gloss wood floor will quickly be destroyed. A cushioned vinyl floor with a strong pattern to hide dirt would be more suitable. It would also be more skid-resistant under wet feet.

Wear as it relates to traffic patterns should be considered. Many kitchen layouts have tight spots where all traffic is funneled over a small section of floor. If you use more than one floor covering in the kitchen, arrange them so high-traffic areas are surfaced with a wear-resistant material. Extend this material to a cutoff point where traffic is more diffused. This way the area where the two flooring materials meet won't become shabby from wear.

Carpet—This material is particularly prone to wear, crushing and matting in high-traffic areas. Under heavy use, carpet will develop a visible trench in a few years. If you must use carpet in a high-traffic area, buy extra carpet and pad so you can replace worn sections when necessary.

Kitchen and bath carpet is different from ordinary carpet, and from indoor-outdoor carpet. Kitchen carpet is all-synthetic, will withstand frequent cleaning and has a waterproof backing. Most ordinary carpets contain natural materials that can absorb water and harbor bacteria. The backing is usually porous. Indoor-outdoor carpet is usually all-synthetic, but the backing is designed to let water drain through and away, which is not suitable in a kitchen.

The comfort and resiliency of kitchen carpet are hard to match with any other material, but spills and routine cleaning are major drawbacks. If spills are rare in your home, and routine carpet cleaning is frequent, carpet may work out well.

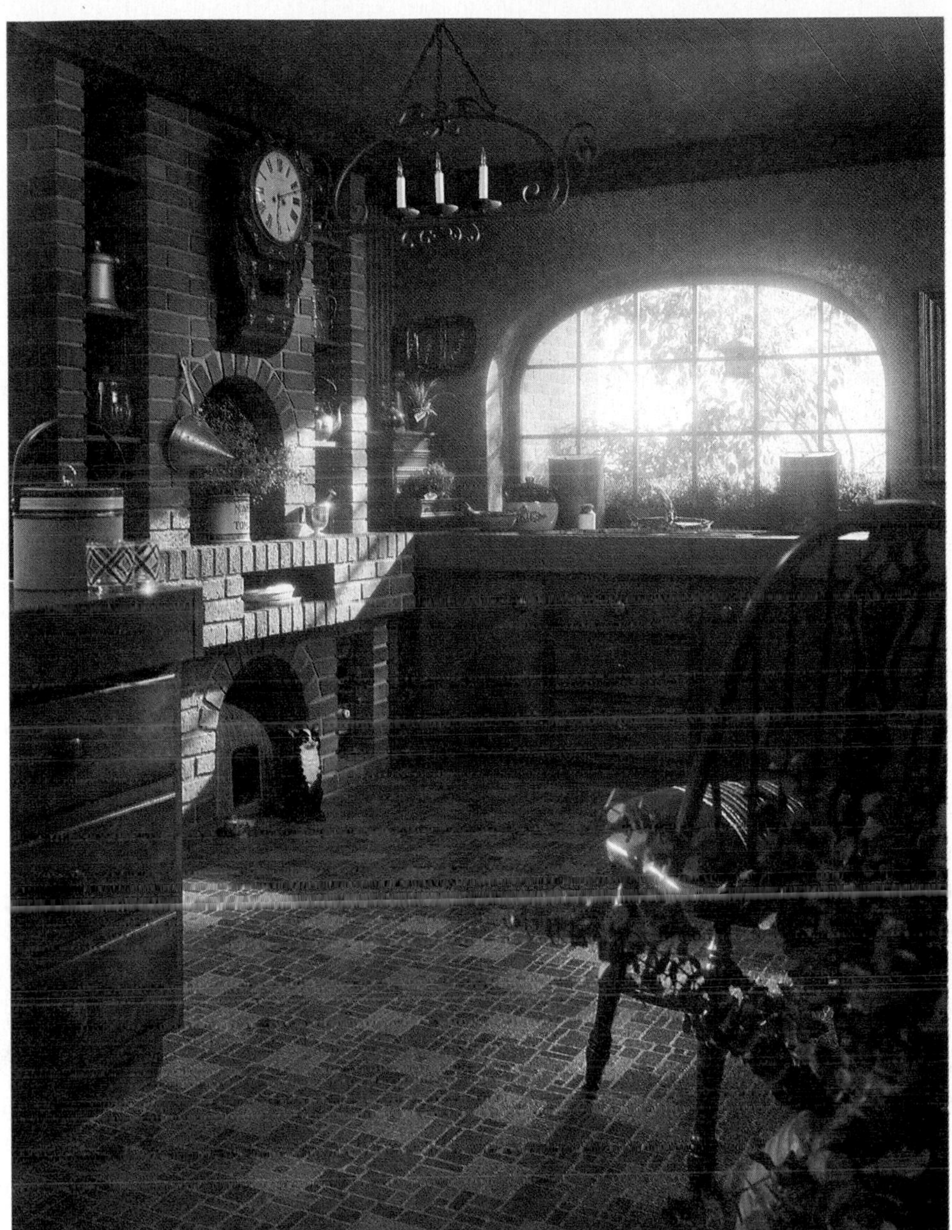

Resilient floor coverings are attractive, wear well and are easy to clean. They can be selected to suit any decor.

Resilient Floor Coverings—These have come a long way since the times when choices for kitchen floors consisted of burlap-backed linoleum or brittle asphalt tile. But the proliferation of resilient flooring materials led to confusion about installation techniques. With the early linoleum and asphalt tile, you first put down a layer of brown-black mastic and laid your choice of floor covering. Now there's a greater variety of resilient floorings, adhesives and installation techniques.

Resilient tiles usually require adhesive over the whole floor surface. Some sheet floorings only require adhesive around the perimeter. A few sheet floorings can be stapled around the perimeter and not glued at all. Some resilient tiles are self-adhesive. You peel release paper from the backs and place them into position.

Asphalt tile was the first resilient tile made, and isn't readily available today. Limited in color choice and made only in a marbleized pattern, asphalt tile is brittle and subject to staining from grease. Even if you're creating a 1930s or 1940s period kitchen, pass it by. There's a solid-vinyl look-alike available, discussed on page 36. Tile size is 9x9".

Vinyl-asbestos tile is made up of a patterned layer of vinyl over a fibrous backing, with or without a clear vinyl or urethane top layer. Vinyl-asbestos is economical because it is inexpensive to produce and is long-lasting. As a result, it's widely used in new construction. A wide variety of colors, patterns and grades are available. Tile size is 12x12".

Vinyl tile is somewhat more expensive than vinyl-asbestos but more luxurious. Some types are manufactured by printing a pattern on a layer of vinyl. Others, called *inlaid vinyl,* fuse tiny particles of several colors, arranged to form a pattern. Both types are made with or without a clear surface coating, called a *wear layer.* Solid-color vinyl tiles are also available. Tile size is 12x12".

One type of solid-vinyl tile is made by rolling out and fusing the factory-produced scraps and trimmings from other vinyl tile lines. The result is a mottled, marbleized pattern reminiscent of old asphalt tile. These tiles are usually inexpensive, and make an excellent substitute for asphalt tile in a period kitchen. They're as durable as the other solid vinyls. Tile size is 12x12".

Vinyl sheet flooring is made in many variations. Sheet floorings may or may not have a clear vinyl or urethane wear layer. Vinyl sheet flooring is made in long rolls 6, 9, 12 and sometimes 15 feet wide.

Printed vinyl is generally the least expensive. The top layer is printed with a pattern and laminated to a felt backing. Better grades are embossed, and have a clear wear layer.

Cushioned vinyl has a resilient-foam layer between the patterned vinyl layer and the backing. This produces a cushioned feeling underfoot. A textured, cushioned vinyl is ideal for floors subjected to grit and mud. Grit particles are kept from cutting into the floor by the cushioning. A top-line variation of the cushioned vinyl floor is all-vinyl. It consists of a clear wear layer, pattern layer, cushioning and backing.

The resilience of cushioned vinyl has its drawbacks. The top surface is subject to damage from sharp objects. Also, heavy appliances make permanent dents.

Inlaid-vinyl sheet flooring is similar to the tile version. It's made by creating the color pattern with small granules, then fusing the granules together into a solid sheet. This process makes for brilliant coloring and high durability.

The signs of quality are similar for all resilient flooring materials. Generally, the thicker the flooring the higher the quality. Also, the thickness of the clear wear layer and the pattern layer are indicators. If possible, check a sample for damage resistance. Check the clear wear layer for its reaction to heat, such as hot grease or a dropped cigarette. Damage caused by such mishaps can be repaired, but a clear wear layer that's resistant to damage is preferable.

Wood floors fit in well with country kitchens.

Wood Flooring—Wood is one of the oldest and most universal flooring materials. Some wood floorings are prefinished, others must be sanded and finished after installation. Some are presanded but still must be finished. Some wood floorings are glued down. Others are nailed over resin paper.

Wood-block flooring is available in a wide variety of types, sizes, thicknesses and wood species. Flooring that is a number of pieces of wood made into a block is commonly called *parquet.* Original parquet floors were painstakingly assembled from many small pieces of wood in an inlay. Many of the currently available parquet blocks duplicate the old patterns. Parquet flooring is sold prefinished or unfinished. Parquet comes in many block sizes—12x12" is the most common.

A common parquet flooring looks like several lengths of strip flooring splined together into a block, milled into tongues and grooves on the edges. It is usually thick and can be blind-nailed like strip flooring, page 152, or applied with adhesive.

Some parquet flooring is laminated flat, like plywood. Plies are offset to form tongues and grooves. The wear surface might be one piece of wood, or several pieces joined in a pattern.

A third type of parquet is strips of wood joined together by paper facing. The facing preserves the relationship of the strips in the pattern. This type has square edges, but is difficult for the owner-builder to work with. Square-edge parquet is installed much the same as resilient tile. But any curving of the wood segments tends to scoop adhesive off the floor, extruding it under the paper facing. The resulting blotch can be difficult to remove when it's discovered after removing the facing paper.

Wood strips come in a number of sizes, species, grades and finishes. Strips are usually 3/4 inch thick and vary in width from 1-1/2 to 3-1/4 inches. They are sold in bundles of random lengths, from 2 to 8 feet. Strips of other widths and thicknesses are available.

Oak is the most popular species for wood-strip flooring. It harmonizes well with today's oak cabinets. The durability of oak strip flooring ranks with tile. While tedious to install, a wood floor, with proper maintenance, will outlast the house itself. Like any of the thicker flooring materials, wood strip flooring is usually installed before you put in the cabinets and appliances.

Ceramic Tile—In a way, a ceramic tile floor is a primeval dirt floor reborn in a slightly different form. Ceramic tile floors have existed in almost every culture. Tile floors reflect the widest artistic spectrum you'll find anywhere, but the roots of any ceramic tile design stem from primitive cultures.

Unglazed tile is the color of the clay it's made of, modified by the heat of firing. This ranges from adobe-red of Mexican tile to pale greens and tans. Such tiles must be sealed after laying because they're absorbent. Shapes range from square to hexagonal, octagonal and serpentine, but sizes are usually large. Mexican tiles are larger, thicker and more irregular than quarry tiles. Because they haven't been fired as long, they are usually softer.

Glazed tile is hard-fired, coated with glaze and fired again. This produces a coating called *bisque*. It's gritty but skidproof. The bisque glaze mostly serves as an undercoat for a final glaze. Temperature of this last firing controls the degree of melting of the glaze and the finish on the tile. Finishes range from glossy and semi-glazed to matte.

Sizes of glazed tiles range from barely 1/2 inch square to 14 or 15 inches on a side. All sorts of shapes are available commercially. Tiles can also be custom-made.

Ceramic tile makes an excellent floor. It's long-lasting, and easy to keep good-looking with a minimum of care. The wide range of colors and patterns makes it possible to use ceramic tile with almost any kitchen design. But the hard surface of ceramic tile means it reflects sound, and it's more tiring underfoot than softer materials. If you drop a dish or glass on a ceramic tile floor, the object is likely to break. If you drop something heavy, it's possible to crack a tile or two. A repair job can be difficult unless you've kept spare tiles and some matching grout. A rigid subfloor is required to hold the weight of the tile and prevent cracking. Check local codes for subfloor requirements.

Masonry—Brick can be used for a kitchen floor, although it's heavy and tedious to install. Brick looks at home in country or Southwestern kitchens. Brick pavers specifically made for

Acoustical-tile ceilings can solve noise problems. Many new patterns and textures are available, including simulated cork. Installation is easy.

flooring should be used. Paving brick is also available in reduced thickness, called *split pavers*. Sizes vary with the manufacturer—brick is almost always made locally. Colors available are usually similar to quarry-tile colors, which are derived from local clay colors. Brick floors are even more porous than unglazed tiles and should be sealed or finished.

Stone makes an interesting and attractive kitchen floor—if you can find it in your area. Because of the extreme weight, the expense of shipping stone more than a couple of hundred miles becomes prohibitive. If there's a local source of a good flooring stone, a stone floor is entirely feasible. But the installation is so specialized and difficult that it should be left to an experienced stonemason.

An exception to this are *gaged stone* products. In certain parts of the United States and Canada, it's possible to buy these products. Slate is most often found in this form. Marble is occasionally available. Gaged slate, for instance, has been ground on the back to an approximately uniform thickness—1/4 to 1/2 inch. It is then sawed into regular squares and rectangles. The face is just as it was originally split. Gaged stone products come in a box, just like tile, and are installed and finished much the same as unglazed tile.

WALLS AND CEILINGS

Walls and ceilings are often the forgotten parts of a new kitchen. Most often, they're simply drywall covered with a coat of paint. But they can benefit from better treatment. Use a primer-sealer and a finish coat of high-quality semigloss or gloss enamel. For maximum resistance to washing and scrubbing, use exterior-acrylic house paint.

Gloss and semigloss enamel is made in water-base and solvent-base forms. Each has its adherents, but the differences have become small. The water-base products have the advantages of easy cleanup, less smell and somewhat more manageable consistency. Solvent-base products tend to self-level a bit better, reducing brush marks. Coverage and durability might also be better. Whichever type you decide to use, don't skimp on quality. A high-quality product of one type will outperform an average-quality product of the other type.

Paint that is true white produces way too much glare. *Gray-white,* typically labeled *off-white,* isn't much better, unless the shade harmonizes with the rest of the kitchen. For general use, especially with wood cabinets, look for some variation of *cottage-white,* or *antique-white.* Many shades are available. The general idea is an off-white tempered with golds, beiges or creams.

Textures, light or heavy, help to add interest to walls and ceilings. A too-heavy texture can present problems with cabinet installation. Texturing is best done before cabinets go in, but avoid placing lumps and bumps where cabinets will meet wall. If you don't, be prepared to do a good bit of scraping and sanding to get a tight fit.

Masonry walls of all kinds, like heavy texture, present some fitting problems. About the only realistic solution is to plan on scribing moldings to the contour. See page 171.

Wallpapers—These can be used in a kitchen, but must be selected carefully. Plain wallpaper is subject to water and humidity damage. It should not be used without a protective coating. Vinyl-impregnated wallpapers, vinyl-coated wallpapers and all-vinyl wallcoverings are more resistant to moisture damage, but still may be marred by grease spatters. Foil wallcoverings work well, as long as they can withstand scrubbing without shedding their decorative pattern.

Some wallcoverings require an application of paste before hanging. Others come with adhesive already applied, called *prepasted* wallcoverings. They're dipped in water to activate the adhesive before hanging. Although convenient, they don't allow use of high-strength adhesives or adhesive additives. Such adhesives and additives are better at withstanding exposure to steam and water, common to a kitchen environment.

Strippable wallcoverings have a lower-strength bond to the wall than nonstrippable kinds. They tend to come loose when exposed to moisture. *Peelable wallcoverings* are designed to strip off between the layers when you want to remove them. When they are removed, they leave adhesive and paper backing on the wall.

Hundreds of variations of wallcoverings are available. The best source of information is a knowledgable wallcovering dealer. Explain the project you're doing, and he or she will help you select the right wallcovering and adhesive for a successful job.

Wall preparation is as important with wallcoverings as it is with paint, and the steps are much the same. Seal porous surfaces and remove grease, wax and dirt. Thoroughly degloss shiny surfaces. After the wall surface is ready, you may need to *size* it. Sizing is a material applied to the wall surface to help ensure a better bond. Check with your dealer to obtain the correct sizing for your particular project.

Wood Paneling—Paneling and wood tongue-and-groove material can be attractive in a kitchen. Tongue-and-groove cedar on walls and ceiling combined with neutral, plastic-laminate cabinets is striking. But there are technical problems. Bare wood isn't very tolerant of moisture, and isn't washable at all. It's necessary to finish the wood.

Some types of prefinished paneling and varnished tongue-and-groove paneling won't survive steam, grease and repeated scrubbing. Several coats of flat or semigloss polyurethane are fairly durable under these conditions. Heat over long periods of time can discolor wood and wood finishes.

A good source of wood paneling for application to walls is cabinet manufacturers. Most produce fairly large *finish panels* that match their cabinets. Such panels are normally used for closing off exposed ends and backs of cabinet runs. Finish panels can be used to surface walls, and they're as durable as the cabinets.

Many kinds of prefinished paneling can be found on the market. Some have a surface of wood veneer. Others have a vinyl surface with printed or photographically reproduced wood grain. This paneling is often the only way to get the appearance of rare or expensive wood, or wood that doesn't cut well into veneer. Paneling should have resistance to moisture, heat and grease spatters if it is to be used in the kitchen. Check the manufacturer's literature to see if paneling is recommended for kitchen use.

Ceilings—Any material or treatment that's used on walls can be used on a ceiling. But ceilings have three finishes of their own: *acoustical tile, acoustical coatings* and *luminous ceiling panels.*

Acoustical tile is a natural solution for a kitchen that tends to be noisy, or has a high ceiling. Many colors and patterns are available. The tile can be applied directly to the present ceiling or suspended below it. Be aware that an acoustical tile ceiling won't solve the problem of an old, loose, broken plaster or drywall ceiling. Acoustical tile may disguise the mess for a year or two, but there is a danger of it all coming down. Avoid this by doing the job right. Take down the old ceiling and put up new drywall, plaster or an acoustical-tile ceiling that will stay in place.

Acoustical coatings are applied with a paint roller or by spraying. They have a light, fluffy texture and are more sound-absorbent than ordinary drywall texture. They do not absorb sound nearly as well as acoustical tile.

Custom cabinetry often includes appliance garage. Roll-down door hides coffeemaker.

Luminous ceilings are the answer if you want lots of nondirectional light in a kitchen, but don't want the clutter of several light fixtures. Most luminous ceilings consist of a recessed light fixture covered with a diffuser panel. Panels are usually set flush with the ceiling surface. The diffuser panels used for luminous ceilings can also serve to diffuse light from skylights.

Any translucent material can be used for diffuser panels. Sheets of rigid plastic are made for this purpose. They come in many patterns, colors and degrees of translucency. Installing custom-made stained-glass panels is a creative option.

Diffuser panels can be suspended on metal L- and T-channels made for acoustical ceilings, or suspended on wood frames. Wood frames can be finished to match cabinets or trim work. Be sure to provide clearance and ventilation for hot light bulbs.

CABINETS AND COUNTERTOPS

Selection of cabinets and countertops is probably the largest financial commitment involved in creating your kitchen. Be certain of your choices before you place the orders.

CUSTOM OR FACTORY CABINETS?

Cabinets are produced in three basic ways. They can be built to fit a kitchen, either on the job or in a local shop. They can be mass-produced in a factory to standard sizes and types. Or they can be built to order in a factory, with variations from standard sizes and shapes. The method you choose depends on time, money and demands of the kitchen you're creating.

You can solve just about any design problem—odd heights, widths, shapes and poor storage—with custom-made cabinets. If your new kitchen is unusual, a custom cabinetmaker can deal with it. If the kitchen you have in mind doesn't seem to mesh with the standard sizes and shapes of cabinets, visit some local cabinet shops.

Take inventory of utensils, portable appliances and supplies that will be stored in the cabinets. Note sizes and shapes of each. Custom cabinets may be needed to fit large appliances, wide dishes, or tall glasses and goblets.

Custom cabinets are not necessarily expensive. Most custom shops have specific cabinet styles they can make for a reasonable price. But if you want cabinets to match a piece of antique furniture, the bill will be high.

Delivery time for custom cabinets varies according to the backlog of work at the individual shop. It can range from 1 or 2 weeks, to 1 year or more for a nationally renowned cabinetmaker.

Built-to-order factory cabinets cost somewhere between factory and custom. They're built from standard materials in a factory with precision equipment, basically to standard types and sizes. But they can be modified from standard to some extent to better suit your needs. The details and extent of modifications vary from one factory to another. Check with local dealers.

Built-to-order factory cabinets cost somewhere between factory and custom. They're built from standard materials in a factory with precision equipment, basically to standard types and sizes. But they can be modified from standard to some extent to make them suit your needs. Details and extent of modifications vary from one factory to another. Check with local dealers.

Most built-to-order factory cabinets allow modifications to front frames and toe boards, but not to doors, drawers or the interior shape and size of the cabinet. Cabinet finish can often be modified. Some manufacturers provide unfinished cabinets.

Cabinets without face frames are convenient if you're planning on highly structured storage in the cabinets. Dividers and rollouts are easily slipped into place. More and more manufacturers are producing accessories to fit inside cabinets. These range from fixed dividers and racks to a host of removable drawers, bins and racks. These accessories can double or triple the storage capacity of your cabinets.

Although a few manufacturers still make steel cabinets, most cabinets are made of wood or plastic laminate. Wood cabinets have that age-old appeal. When properly cared for, they develop a pleasing patina with the passing of time. Plastic-laminate cabinets look sleek and modern, are easy to keep clean and wear well. But combinations are also possible. Plastic-laminate doors and drawer fronts are available with many kinds of wood trim. Perhaps the best combination is wood fronts and plastic laminate lining the interiors.

Whatever the exterior finish of your new cabinets, the structure will be built of plywood, particle board or wafer board. Face frames, doors and drawer fronts on wood cabinets are often made of solid wood.

Look for solid cabinet construction with rabbeted, glued and fastened joints. Edges should be as well finished as the rest of the cabinet, especially where they will show. Hardware, especially drawer hardware, should be sturdy and of high quality. Drawers should be built of solid wood or plywood, not lightweight particle board, especially the bottoms. High-quality molded-plastic drawer assemblies have recently appeared on the market. Those that are made well have the potential to outlast wood drawers.

It is important to check the nature of the wood when assessing the quality of wood cabinets. Wood constantly absorbs and releases moisture as humidity rises and falls. This causes the wood to swell and shrink. If two sides of a piece of wood have been finished differently, they will swell and shrink differently. In extreme cases, this can cause a cabinet door to be cupped one week and bowed the next!

Look for panels that are treated the same on both sides so they will swell and shrink in unison. If the face of a door is finished with plastic laminate, see if the back of the door has a similar finish. If the back is covered with only a coat of paint, you might have problems with warpage. The back laminate may look different from the face material but that will have no effect.

Selecting Hardware—Whether you have chosen custom cabinets or factory ones, an infinite variety of pulls, hinges and other hardware await your perusal. On factory cabinets, you might want to use door hardware from one manufacturer on cabinets from another. You are not limited to the hardware that comes with the cabinet.

Some cabinet designs do not lend themselves to visible hardware. If you have difficulty finding knobs or pulls that complement your cabinets, you can modify doors and drawers to provide an inconspicuous hand hold. Many factory cabinets come without knobs or pulls. Door and drawer edges are beveled or chamfered on one or more sides for a hand hold.

Customizing—In addition to hardware, many kinds of custom moldings can be attached to flat doors and finished to match or contrast. Doors with panels can be altered by replacing panels with metal mesh, etched glass, stained glass or fabric.

Plastic laminate covers more countertops than any other material. Wood trim strips are inset into beveled edges of top to match cabinets.

COUNTERTOPS

The quickest and easiest approach to countertops is the post-form top. These tops are plastic laminate, preformed over a particle-board core. They have a curved, molded backsplash and front edge. Post-form tops come ready to install and are widely available. They're sold by the running foot in stock lengths, usually in 2-foot increments. Simplicity, quick installation and moderate price are their main appeal.

Post-form tops can have their drawbacks for more elaborate kitchens. Corners and finished ends can be troublesome, and width is not adjustable for snack bars or other irregular shapes. Colors and pattern selection are often limited.

Plastic Laminate—This surface material is more widely used than you might think, often masquerading as another material. Consider substituting plastic laminate if you want the appearance of a fragile or hard-to-work with material such as slate or leather. Often, laminate is easier to get and apply than the material it simulates. Wear characteristics may be better than the real item.

Plastic laminates come in standard widths of 24, 30, 36 and 48 inches. Standard lengths are from 4 to 12 feet in 2-foot increments. Thicknesses are normally 1/16 inch for tops and 1/32 inch for wall areas and cabinets.

Wood—Most wood countertops come in the form of butcher block. The term *butcher block* comes from the large blocks of end-grain hardwood that used to occupy the middle of the floor in butcher shops. Most of today's butcher block is edge-grain rather than end-grain, and will never see a meat cleaver.

Butcher block is useful in the kitchen for the same reason it's useful to the butcher. It wears well and needs little maintenance beyond a soapy sponge and some mineral oil occasionally. Burns, gouges, worn areas and stains can be easily sanded or scraped out and refinished. Stock sections of butcher block are available, and many small woodworking shops can make it to order.

Butcher block can be inset into other top materials to provide a durable, repairable cutting surface. Unless you have access to jointing-planing equipment, a large section of butcher block isn't a make-it-yourself item.

Ceramic tile makes a durable countertop. It has versatility in color, texture and pattern.

Wood countertops are available in all of the wood-flooring materials such as maple and oak, in tongue-and-groove strips and parquet blocks. Strips or blocks should be edge-glued and given a thorough coat of mineral oil to help prevent water penetration. Polyurethane or a similar finish can be substituted for areas such as snack bars. Countertops can be matched to wood cabinets and blended right into the tops of the cabinets.

Ceramic Tile—This is nothing more than plates of fire-hardened clay. Along with wood, ceramic tile is among the oldest and most versatile materials. Ceramic tile is available in a myriad of sizes, shapes, colors and finishes. Tile is impervious to heat, cold, acids and cleaning products, although its grout joints might not be. Tile is easy to clean, but the porous grout joints absorb water and stain and soil easily. Grout sealers are available, but they have to be applied frequently to keep grout impervious to water and dirt. Unglazed tiles should also be sealed to resist staining.

Because ceramic tile has been a part of almost every culture, there are designs to complement any kitchen. Tiles 4x4" or larger are best used for large, flat surfaces. Small mosaic tiles are best on contoured or irregular surfaces. Although tile is traditionally set in a bed of mortar, modern adhesives make tile easy to install. See page 164 for information on installing ceramic-tile countertops.

Dishes and glassware can break if dropped on ceramic tile. Also, some tile glazes are prone to show pot marks, especially from aluminum or copper-bottom pots. The same kinds of tile used for floors, page 144, can be used for countertops.

Stainless Steel—This is a high-cost, custom-made countertop material. It harmonizes well with futuristic kitchens, but must be made and installed by a specialist. It is expensive, but stainless steel is close to being a permanent countertop material. It resists burns, scratches and stains, and is easy to keep clean. You can set hot pots and pans directly on stainless steel. Be aware that it dulls knives if you use it as a cutting surface.

Marble—Marble has a place in the kitchen, but the real thing is easily stained and scratched. Pastry cooks find small marble slabs handy. They can be chilled in the refrigerator and used as a surface for rolling out dough, without allowing the dough to heat up.

Synthetic marble materials come in two kinds. One is an acrylic resin, often having marble chips or dust as filler. The other is a DuPont product called *Corian.* The acrylics are suitable for light-duty areas, but the glossy finish is thin and subject to wear. Corian is the same all the way through, so marred areas can be sanded and polished out fairly easily. Both can be worked with hand tools and are easy to install. Corian can also be cut with a power saw and shaped with a router.

APPLIANCES

Not that long ago, it was simple to choose your kitchen appliances. This was mostly because there were only two appliances to select—a stove and a refrigerator. They came in white. You could have gas or electric, but there wasn't much else to consider. Today's marketplace provides many more alternatives. It pays to take your time and examine the options so you will make the right choices.

Color—White appliances are still available, and probably always will be. Some manufacturers still produce old favorites avocado and harvest gold. Others supply specialty colors such as red. But the current, widely available colors are white, almond—the color of the inside of an almond, not the outside—and wheat, a light gold. Gaining rapidly is the black-glass and bright-metal look, with some manufacturers producing dark-brown glass.

Some manufacturers provide a trim kit for their appliances that allows you to add and even periodically change custom panels. These panels can range in patterns from quilts to wallpaper to wood. Some appliances can be built into the cabinets and fitted with wood panels to match the cabinet doors.

ENERGY EFFICIENCY

Some appliances are more energy-efficient than others. Until the 1975 Energy Policy and Conservation Act, there was no good way to assess energy efficiency. Most new appliances are required to wear a sticker such as shown below. This sticker shows how that appliance performs in standardized tests. The numbers, like EPA mileage figures for automobiles, are guidelines. They aren't accurate in predicting operating costs in your own kitchen.

The stickers help you make comparisons of appliances of similar size and with similar features. For instance, a refrigerator-freezer with an energy-cost sticker showing $75 can be expected to use roughly 25% more energy than one with the sticker below. If both refrigerators have the same capacity and features, the one with the lower energy-cost estimate will be more energy-efficient.

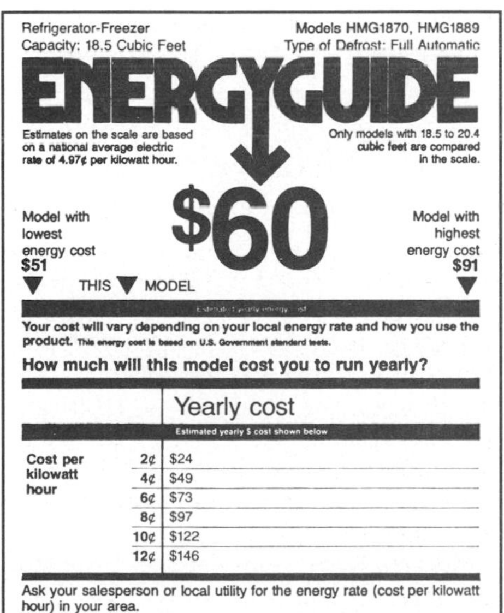

Refrigerator-Freezer
Capacity: 18.5 Cubic Feet

Models HMG1870, HMG1889
Type of Defrost: Full Automatic

ENERGYGUIDE

Estimates on the scale are based on a national average electric rate of 4.97¢ per kilowatt hour.

Only models with 18.5 to 20.4 cubic feet are compared in the scale.

$60

Model with lowest energy cost **$51**

THIS ▼ MODEL

Model with highest energy cost **$91**

Your cost will vary depending on your local energy rate and how you use the product. This energy cost is based on U.S. Government standard tests.

How much will this model cost you to run yearly?

		Yearly cost
		Estimated yearly $ cost shown below
Cost per kilowatt hour	2¢	$24
	4¢	$49
	6¢	$73
	8¢	$97
	10¢	$122
	12¢	$146

Ask your salesperson or local utility for the energy rate (cost per kilowatt hour) in your area.

REFRIGERATORS AND FREEZERS

One basic choice you must make when purchasing a refrigerator and freezer is whether you want the freezer and/or refrigerator to be free-standing or built-in. Another basic choice is whether you want a combination refrigerator-freezer or separate units. After you've made these decisions, you have a number of options and features to consider.

Sizes—Free-standing refrigerators and freezers generally do not exceed 36 inches in width. Larger-size, free-standing models are deeper and often project farther into the room than a standard-depth countertop. If possible, recess these big boxes into the wall. Or install the cabinets out from the wall and use a deeper countertop.

The makers of built-in units maintain standard countertop depth. Larger built-in units are often wider than 36 inches, up to 48 inches for a side-by-side unit. Separate refrigerator and freezer units can total 72 inches in width.

Although models with multiple-door layouts are available, most free-standing refrigerators and freezers follow a pattern. The basic door configurations and approximate size ranges for each are as follows:

Doors	Type	Total Capacity (cu. ft.)
1	undercounter refrigerator	5-6
1	refrigerator, no freezer	16-20
1	refrigerator, top freezer	10-13
2	refrigerator, top freezer	12-20
2	refrigerator, bottom freezer	16-24
2	side-by-side	19-24
1	undercounter freezer	5-6
1	chest freezer	5-25
1	upright freezer	15-21

Defrosting—Three defrosting systems are available. *Manual defrosting* is the old-fashioned way—remove contents, turn the freezer off, scrape and chip, mop up, put contents back. Refrigerators and freezers equipped this way use the least energy. Chest and upright freezers that aren't opened often generally work fine with manual defrost.

Automatic defrost refrigerators and freezers are at the high end of the energy-use scale. These defrost themselves periodically without requiring attention.

Between manual defrost and automatic defrost are the *manually cycled self-defrosting* refrigerators and freezers. These defrost themselves only when you activate a defrosting mechanism. If you live in a part of the country where humidity varies markedly from one season to another, a manually cycled system is worth considering.

Side-by-side refrigerator-freezer is 24 inches deep and 48 inches wide. It has a total capacity of 30.5 cubic feet. Features include automatic defrosting and icemaker. Two separate refrigeration systems allow independent temperature control to provide maximum efficiency. Wood insets on doors match surrounding walls and cabinets. *Sub-Zero model 3211.*

Controls—Most large refrigerator-freezers have separate controls for each compartment. Some also have complete, separate refrigeration systems. On top-line models, look for separate temperature or humidity controls for vegetable and meat bins.

Many refrigerators and freezers have a heater under the outside shell to eliminate condensation on the outside on hot, humid days. Some have a switch that reduces or shuts off this heater to save energy when heat is not needed.

Doors—A refrigerator or freezer door should be hinged on the side *away* from a service counter to allow for easy access. Doors on most refrigerators and some freezers are reversible, but some must be ordered in the correct *hand.* Many manufacturers offer trim kits for customizing doors. See photo above.

Doors on side-by-side refrigerator-freezers can be a problem. The freezer is generally on the left, and the refrigerator on the right, with the hinges on the outside edges. If you're considering purchasing a side-by-side, locate it carefully in relation to service counters so doors don't get in the way.

Interiors—Most refrigerators and freezers have shelves that can be removed for cleaning. Some have adjustable shelves. Extra shelves are optional on some models. Some manufacturers offer adjustable shelves in the door. Units with a one-piece, molded-plastic liner and tempered-glass shelves are the easiest to clean.

Most refrigerators have one or more bins for use as a vegetable crisper. Many have special bins for meats, cheeses and produce that need a temperature or humidity range different from general cooling.

Many refrigerator-freezers can be equipped with an automatic icemaker in the freezer compartment. Direct water hookup is required. Some top-line models dispense ice or cold water on the outside of the freezer door.

COOKING EQUIPMENT

The two main energy sources for today's cooking equipment are gas and electricity, although a few companies still make wood and coal ranges. Each cooking method has its advantages and drawbacks.

Gas provides instant-on and instant-off heat. An electric burner takes time to heat and cool. But a gas burner produces a lot of hot air and some byproducts from combustion, including water vapor. An electric burner doesn't. The choice is essentially a question of personal preference and which energy source is readily available. Usually, a natural gas or a 240-volt outlet will be provided in the kitchen area—seldom both. Consider cost and difficulty of supplying the energy source for the cooking equipment before you make your choice.

If you want gas equipment but natural gas isn't available, liquid petroleum (LP) gas can often be substituted, with some modifications. In standard gas appliances, the gas orifices must be changed to accept LP gas. See an appliance dealer or LP-gas supplier for details. Using LP gas is useful if you want only a gas grill. Check codes for hookup and gas-storage details.

OVEN FEATURES

Conventional kitchen ovens take two forms. Built-in ovens are individual units, installed separately from other cooking appliances. Ranges include both oven and cooktop. Ovens for ranges and built-in ovens share most of the same features discussed here. Microwave ovens can be either built-in or free-standing.

Ovens are becoming more and more versatile and automated. Features include timers and programmable controls that allow you to preset times and temperatures throughout the day. Temperature probes and rotisseries are available. A few ovens have a low-temperature thermostat for warming or slow cooking. More and more gas ovens are available with electronic ignition, so they don't require pilot lights. Look for thin-wall construction or a shielded lower element for larger shelf area and a greater range of shelf positions.

Cleaning—In addition to old-style, manual-clean ovens, *continuous-clean* ovens—provided you're not too messy a cook—burn up drips and spills as the oven is used. The relatively rough texture of the inside surface conceals remnants that haven't yet disintegrated. Other ovens are self-cleaning. You simply lock the door and push a button. Some self-cleaning ovens even lock their own door. This feature has been available for some years on electric ovens, but has only recently become available on gas ovens.

Multiple Functions—The cooking duties of ovens are expanding. Baking and broiling are still standard, but many combine conventional operation and microwave, and convection and microwave. Gas ovens generally bake and roast only in the upper oven, and broil only in the lower one. Electric ovens provide broiling in upper or lower oven or both.

Built-in Ovens—These come in single and double units, but it's possible to stack single units to get almost any combination of features you want. There are also warming ovens and drawers for even more versatility.

Convection Ovens—A convection oven cooks by circulating hot air at lower temperatures than a conventional oven. This speeds cooking by improving heat transfer, seals the surface of the food to retain moisture and produces an appetizing brown glaze. Convection ovens are generally more energy-efficient than conventional gas and electric ovens. Most do not require venting.

Microwave Ovens—These ovens cook by generating radio-frequency energy that excites water molecules in food into increased motion. The resulting friction generates heat, cooking the food. The main advantage of microwave ovens is that they cook foods two to three times as fast as conventional gas and electric ovens. This feature is not only convenient, it saves energy.

Microwaves can cause injury if

Microwave with 2-speed fan and cooktop light replaces standard range hood over conventional range. Microwave has 10 settings for time- or temperature-controlled cooking. Includes temperature probe and programmable controls. *General Electric model JVM62 "Spacemaker" microwave.*

you're exposed to them, all microwave ovens have a standard fail-safe device. The oven shuts off as soon as the door is opened.

Microwave cooking has a few disadvantages. Microwaves will not penetrate metal, so plastic, glass or ceramic cookware must be used in these ovens. Cookware is available specifically for use in microwave ovens. Microwave ovens cook foods evenly throughout. You can't use them for broiling meats. Some models have a *browning element* that can be used to brown meats and other foods.

SURFACE COOKING FEATURES

In addition to features we've become used to on cooktops and range surfaces, many new features are available. Electric surface burners are now made with high-speed elements that heat much faster than standard burners. Infinite-heat elements provide a continuous heating range, which gives you more control over the heat. Thermostatically controlled elements let you set the burner to a precise temperature that is maintained throughout cooking.

Some electric units have burners that unplug so they can be replaced with a plug-in grill, griddle or rotisserie. Some units don't have conventional burners at all.

The top surface of some electric units is a flat ceramic plate in white or black. Markings on the surface indicate areas that heat. One advantage is plates are easy to clean. But they take longer to heat and cool than standard burners. Try one before buying.

Other manufacturers have eliminated conventional electric burners. The surface unit doesn't even generate heat. These are called *magnetic-induction* units. The unit works by generating a magnetic field. When you place a ferrous-metal pot or pan in the magnetic field, the pot or pan heats. When you remove the pot or pan, the magnetic field shuts off automatically. Any utensil made of iron, steel, stainless steel or enameled steel will work. If a magnet sticks to the pot or pan, the utensil will work on a magnetic-induction unit.

New features for gas surface units include pilotless electronic ignition. European-style equipment eliminates individual black grates over each gas burner in favor of an overall rack made of stainless-steel rod.

Both gas and electric surface units are available with one or more thermostatically controlled burners. Many units have tops that lift up or off for easy cleaning. Built-in grills or griddles are available as an alternative to plug-in versions. Combination gas and electric surface units are also available.

Cooktops—A wide variety of cooktops are made, from two burners to six burners and a grill. Widths run from 14 inches to 42 inches. Front-to-back dimensions range from 18 inches to 22 inches. Some cooktops are only 3 inches deep, allowing for a drawer underneath for cooking utensils.

All of the features mentioned above are available in cooktops, including flat, ceramic cooking surfaces and magnetic-induction systems. A few manufacturers offer 2-burner electric cooktops that operate on 120 volts if you don't have 240 volts available.

Surface-burner elements on electric cooktop have infinite-heat controls. Grill is interchangable with non-stick griddle. Rotisserie is optional. *Thermador model TMH36.*

RANGES

Ranges combine oven and cooktop in a single appliance. These appliances are more suitable for smaller kitchens. Separate units offer more versatility in larger ones. All features discussed for ovens and cooktops are available in ranges.

Free-standing ranges are available with four to six burners in sizes from 21 to 40 inches wide, with one or two ovens. The backsplash-control panel is typical of the free-standing range. This control panel enables you to end the countertop at one side of the range and begin it again on the other side of the opening. This saves material and reduces detail work on the

Range features self-cleaning oven, two 8-inch and two 6-inch burner units. Digital clock, minute timer and automatic oven timer are standard features on this model. Range is 30 inches wide. *Hotpoint model RB747GA.*

countertop. But if you want to install a range in an island or peninsula, the control panel or backsplash presents a problem. It's possible to raise the far side of the island or peninsula above the top of the control panel to conceal it. Or use a drop-in range.

Drop-in ranges must be installed in a cutout in both countertop and cabinets. Most drop-in ranges are 30 inches wide, and don't have a control panel at the backsplash. The flat top makes the drop-in range useful for installation in islands and peninsulas. Some manufacturers supply an accessory backsplash kit for drop-ins.

Single-oven, free-standing ranges use a conventional oven. Some electric ranges are available with a combination conventional and microwave oven. Two-oven, free-standing ranges are generally of the high-low type, with the second oven above the surface burners. Lighting is built-in. Venting is either built-in or attachable. Many combinations of ovens are made. The lower oven is usually conventional, but the upper, secondary oven can be any of the combinations discussed on page 42. Some secondary ovens have removable inner panels that can be cleaned in the main self-cleaning oven.

DISHWASHERS

Unheard of in home kitchens before World War II, the dishwasher has become commonplace. At first all were portable. Now most are built-in, standardized at 24 inches wide. The few portables available are usually convertible to undercounter installation. If you have a recently manufactured portable and want to install it permanently, check with a dealer for an undercounter installation kit.

The external appearance of dishwashers follows the pattern of all the other appliances. See page 40. Inside finish varies from plastic liners to enameled steel, to stainless steel on top-line models.

A few manufacturers are producing a dishwasher designed to be installed undercounter below a special 6-inch-deep sink. This way a dishwasher and a single-bowl sink can be fitted into only 24 inches of cabinet front. A double-bowl sink with a garbage disposer and a dishwasher can be installed in only 36 inches.

Most dishwashers can be elevated to make them easier to load. This may be especially helpful for handicapped or elderly users, or people with back problems.

Generally, using a dishwasher consumes less water and less energy than washing the same batch of dishes by hand. By making the right choices of available features you can save more. The more versatile the controls, the better. For instance, rinse-and-hold and short-wash features handle small batches of dishes. A dishwasher that heats its own water allows you to set your water heater lower than with a dishwasher that requires high-temperature water. A machine with a heavy-duty cycle washes loads that are part dishes and part pots and pans. The more adjustable the racks and baskets, the easier it is to do mixed loads. Also, it isn't always necessary to dry a finished load with hot air. Some dishwashers have a cycle that dries dishes with unheated air.

Consider noise when shopping for a dishwasher. Look for good sound insulation. If possible, listen to the models while they are in operation before you make the purchase.

As with refrigerators, some dishwashers have optional trim kits to match doors to cabinets or other appliances.

DISPOSERS

Disposers are made with motors ranging from 1/3 to 3/4 HP. Generally, top-line models have the highest horsepower and best soundproofing. But insulation is only part of the noise problem. The type of sink a disposer is attached to plays a big part in the noise level. Stainless-steel and enameled-steel sinks usually transmit more noise than massive, cast-iron ones.

Disposers are made in two basic types—*batch-feed* and *continuous-feed.* Batch-feed models are first loaded, then a cover is locked over the inlet that switches on the disposer. Continuous-feed disposers are controlled by an external switch, and can be turned on and fed continuously. Some building departments have regulations about which you can use.

Batch-feed disposers are designed so they will not operate unless sealed. But on some models it's possible to actuate the switch by accident while groping around inside to clear a jam. Also, if you drop a piece of silverware or bottle cap into a continuous-feed disposer while it's running, it can eject the obstruction violently.

All disposers work by means of a spinning plate that forces food waste against a grinding ring, pulverizing it. Some use fixed teeth on the plate to propel the food waste, while others use hammers attached to the plate. The hammers are free to swivel, providing additional impact on the waste. Some disposers are wired to

This dishwasher features stainless-steel interior for long life. Multi-cycle features range from *heavy steam* to *energy saver* short cycle, as well as an electronic delay start. Soft-waste disposer is standard. *Thermador model TD122.*

reverse direction if they jam, providing self-clearing action.

All disposers in current production are built with permanently oiled and sealed bearings. All have thermal overload protection for the motor, with a reset button. If your disposer ever quits, let it cool for a while and try again after clearing the jam by pushing the reset button. You might save yourself a service call.

Disposers are normally furnished with some means of dealing with jams. This is usually a wrench of some sort that operates the plate manually to loosen the jam so it can be removed. Some wrenches insert from the top and lock into slots in the plate. Another type of wrench plugs into the bottom end of the motor shaft from underneath and is somewhat more convenient.

TRASH COMPACTORS

After the disposer has dispensed with the garbage, what's left is trash. A trash compactor reduces trash to about one-fourth its original volume with a motor-driven ram. This means one trip to the garbage can instead of four for the same amount of trash. You also need fewer garbage cans.

Trash compactors are installed undercounter and vary from 12 to 18 inches wide. Standard undercounter height is 34-1/2 inches. All models have a safety switch so the unit won't run when the door is ajar or the removable container isn't in place.

If you allow trash with food residues to build up in a trash compactor for any length of time—they'll swallow a surprising amount—odor can be a problem. Most compactors have an automatic spray-deodorant dispenser. Some are sealed with an activated charcoal vent/filter.

All trash compactors load from the front. They're available in popular appliance colors. Some have optional trim kits to match front panel to surrounding cabinets. Motor size varies from 1/2 to 3/4 HP and operate on 120 volts. Trash compactors are relatively inexpensive to operate.

SINKS AND FAUCETS

Sinks are made of stainless steel, enameled steel and cast-iron. Copper or brass sinks are available but not common. Rarer still are sinks made of vitreous china. Most sinks are *self-rimming.* They're dropped into the countertop cutout and attached with

Only 12 inches wide, this trash compactor handles average load of 22 28 pounds of trash. No special bags are required. Unit plugs into 120-volt outlet. Safety switch prevents operation if door is open or container is not in place.

clips. Other sinks have rims that are attached to the sink or countertop before installation.

Stainless Steel—These sinks are hard to damage and easy to repair. Most scrapes and stains can be removed with scouring powder, steel wool or a rotary wire brush.

The alloy and degree of hand-finishing separates the price ranges of stainless-steel sinks. A quality sink has a carefully finished surface.

Metal thickness is also a consideration. Standard gages are 18 and 20 gage, with 18 gage being thicker. If the sink will have a garbage disposer, use the thickest gage and sturdiest design you can afford. This cuts down on vibration and noise. Some stainless-steel sinks come with a sprayed-on material for sound insulation.

Stainless-steel sinks come in the widest variety of bowl sizes, shapes and configurations, from small bar sinks to large triple-bowl sinks. Some have integral drainboards. At least one manufacturer will make a sink of any size you want, with types and combinations of bowls you specify. You must stick to bowl sizes the manufacturer has tooling for, although there's a wide selection of these.

Enameled Steel—These sinks are made like stainless-steel sinks, but of plain steel that has an enamel coating. Enameled steel comes in several colors, but the selection of bowl configurations is limited. The enamel coating is subject to chipping and shows marks from metal pots. Scouring powder will remove some marks. Touch-up kits are available to cover chipped areas.

Cast Iron—These sinks are much more durable than enameled steel but won't tolerate the the same amount of impact as stainless steel. Available in a variety of colors and bowl configurations, cast-iron sinks are solid and quiet. Sheer mass reduces disposer and water-flow noises.

The coating on a cast-iron sink is a glaze put on as a powder and then fused to the iron at high temperature. You must take certain precautions with this type of finish. The thin, fused surface of the coating can be quickly worn away by abrasive cleaners such as scouring powder. Once the glass-smooth finish is abraded, stains and dirt penetrate the coating. Then, the harder you scrub it, the worse it will look. If you don't use abrasive cleaners on a cast-iron sink, it will look new for years.

Faucets—Almost all sink faucets currently produced avoid old problems of washer-and-seat construction. The operating parts are most often contained in a cartridge. It is relatively trouble-free and easily replaced if a malfunction occurs. The familiar two-handle type is available, but single-handle faucets are more widely used. Gooseneck, bar-sink faucets are usually two-handle.

The finish on a faucet can be matched with the rest of the metal trim in the kitchen. Look for brass and chrome in polished and brushed finishes. Unusual handle designs and materials are available from some specialty manufacturers.

Double-bowl sink of European design is a specialty item. An interior designer can often help you find unusual or hard-to-get fixtures such as this.

FACTORY CABINETS

STANDARD SIZES

Most cabinets are made in a factory, rather than custom built. Factory cabinets follow a standard dimension system which includes standardized cabinet units. With few exceptions, any cabinet manufacturer can supply basic cabinet types shown here.

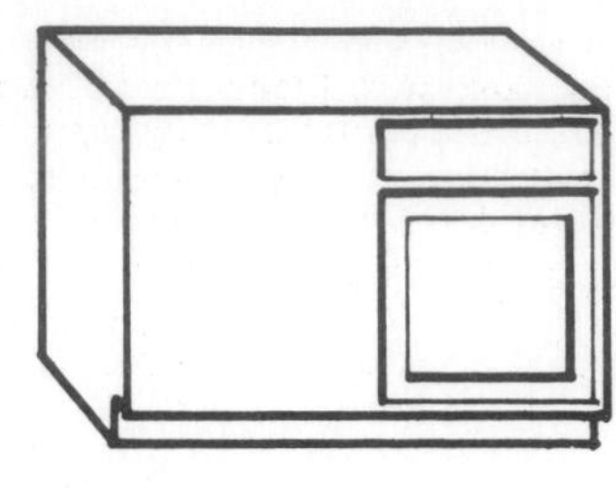

REACH-IN CORNER
Widths (inches): 36, 42, 48
Note: Reach-in cabinets can usually be pulled out of the corner a few inches if necessary.

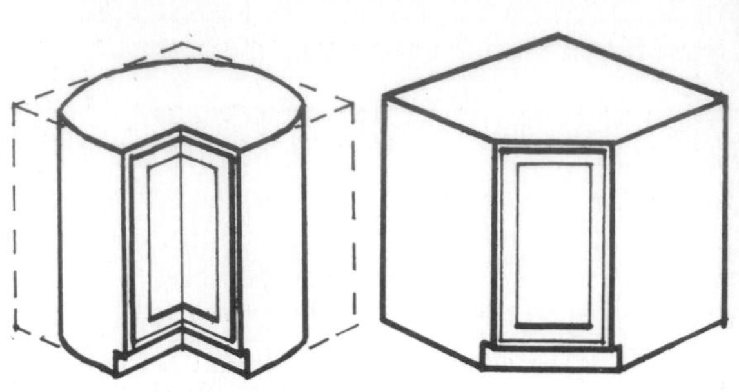

LAZY SUSAN
Widths: 33" each way, 36" each way
Note: Doors may hinge aside, or may rotate with the shelves.

DIAGONAL CORNER
Width: 36" each way
Note: Sometimes available just as a front panel.

BASE CABINETS

Note: Standard base-cabinet height is 34-1/2 inches.

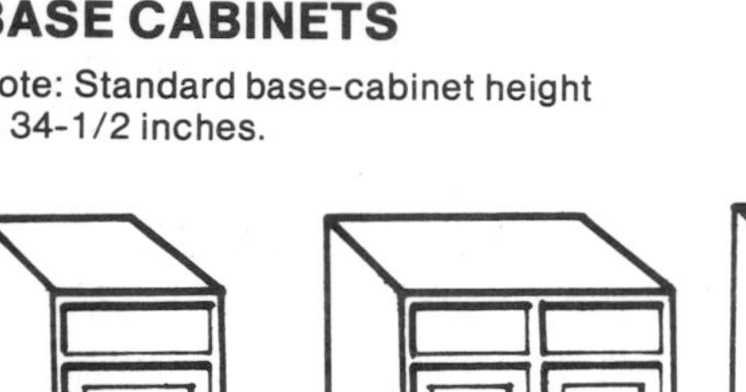

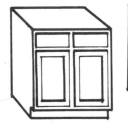

SINGLE DOOR
Widths (inches): 12, 15, 18, 21, 24

DOUBLE DOOR
Widths (inches): 27, 30, 33, 36, 39, 40, 42, 45, 48

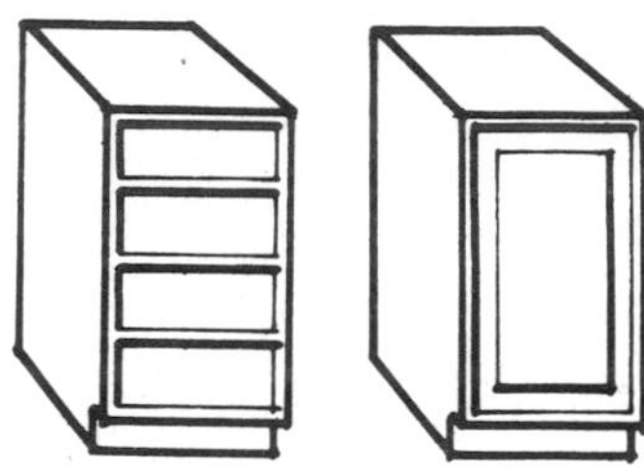

DRAWER BASE
Widths (inches): 12, 15, 18, 21, 24

TRAY BASE
Width (inches): 9, 12

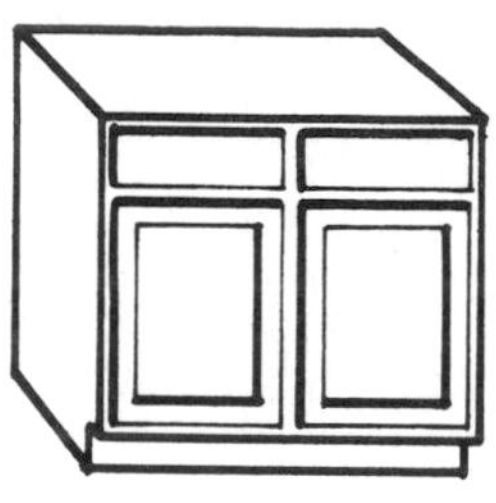

SINK/RANGE BASE
Widths(inches): 30, 33, 36, 39, 42, 45, 48

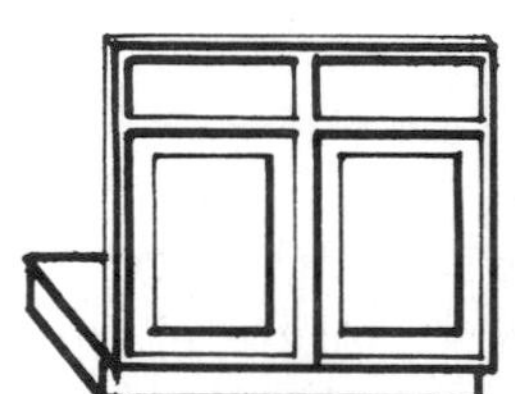

SINK/RANGE FRONT
Widths (inches): 30, 36, 42, 48
Note: Bottom is sometimes separated from front.

WALL CABINETS

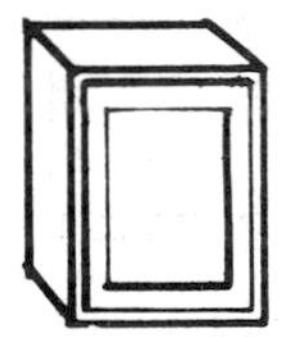

SINGLE DOOR
Widths (inches): 9, 12, 15, 18, 24
Heights (inches): 12, 15, 20, 30, 42

DOUBLE DOOR
Widths (inches): 24, 27, 30, 33, 36, 39, 42, 45, 48
Heights (inches): 12, 15, 20, 30 42

REACH-IN
Widths (inches): 24, 30, 36, 42, 48
Height: 30"
Note: Reach-in cabinets can be pulled several inches out from end wall to lengthen cabinet run.

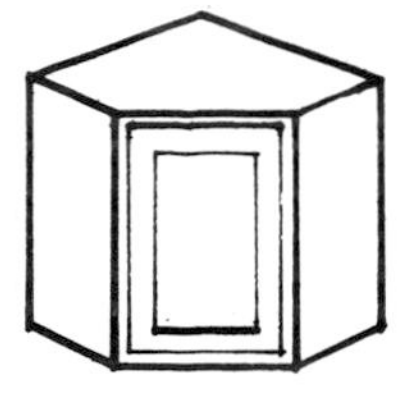

DIAGONAL CORNER
Width: 24" each way
Height: 30"
Note: Available with fixed shelves or Lazy Susan.

END CABINET
Width: 12" each way
Height: 30"
Note: Often available with door.

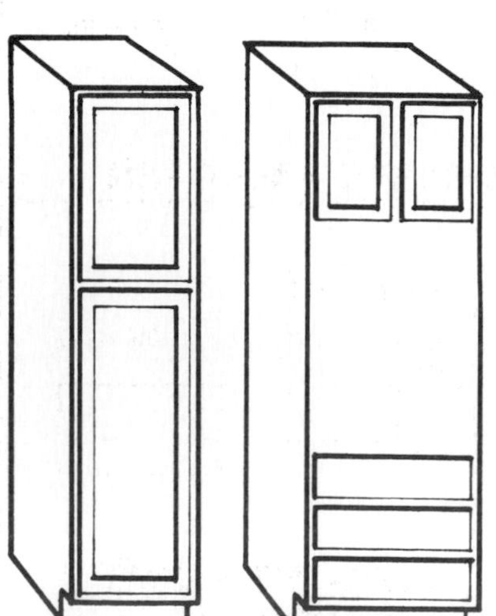

FULL HEIGHT CABINETS

Note: Standard full-cabinet height is 83-1/2 inches.

OVEN CABINET
Widths (inches): 27, 30, 33
Note: Oven opening cut to minimum dimensions; can be enlarged to fit larger ovens.

STORAGE
Widths (inches): 18, 21, 24
Note: Often available 12" deep or 24" deep.

MISCELLANEOUS

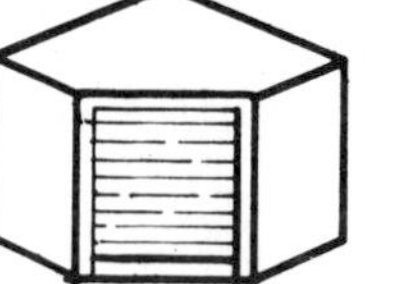

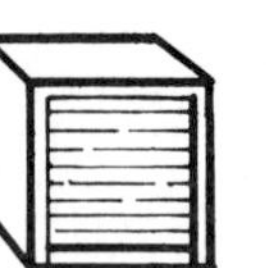

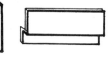

CORNER APPLIANCE GARAGE
Width: 23-1/2" each way
Height: 17-1/2"

STRAIGHT APPLIANCE GARAGE
Width: 24"
Height: 17-1/2"

RANGE/OVEN FRONT
Widths (inches) 30, 36
Heights: varies 12" to 15"
Note: Used to cover space below drop-in appliances.

FINISHED PANELS
Come in variety of heights, widths and thicknesses to cover exposed sides, ends and backs of cabinets.

APPLIANCE SIZES

Shown below are many types of appliances. These will be useful for planning purposes. Because these dimensions may vary from one manufacturer to the next, don't use these dimensions for construction, only for planning. Measure the actual appliance after it's selected, or check the manufacturer's literature on it.

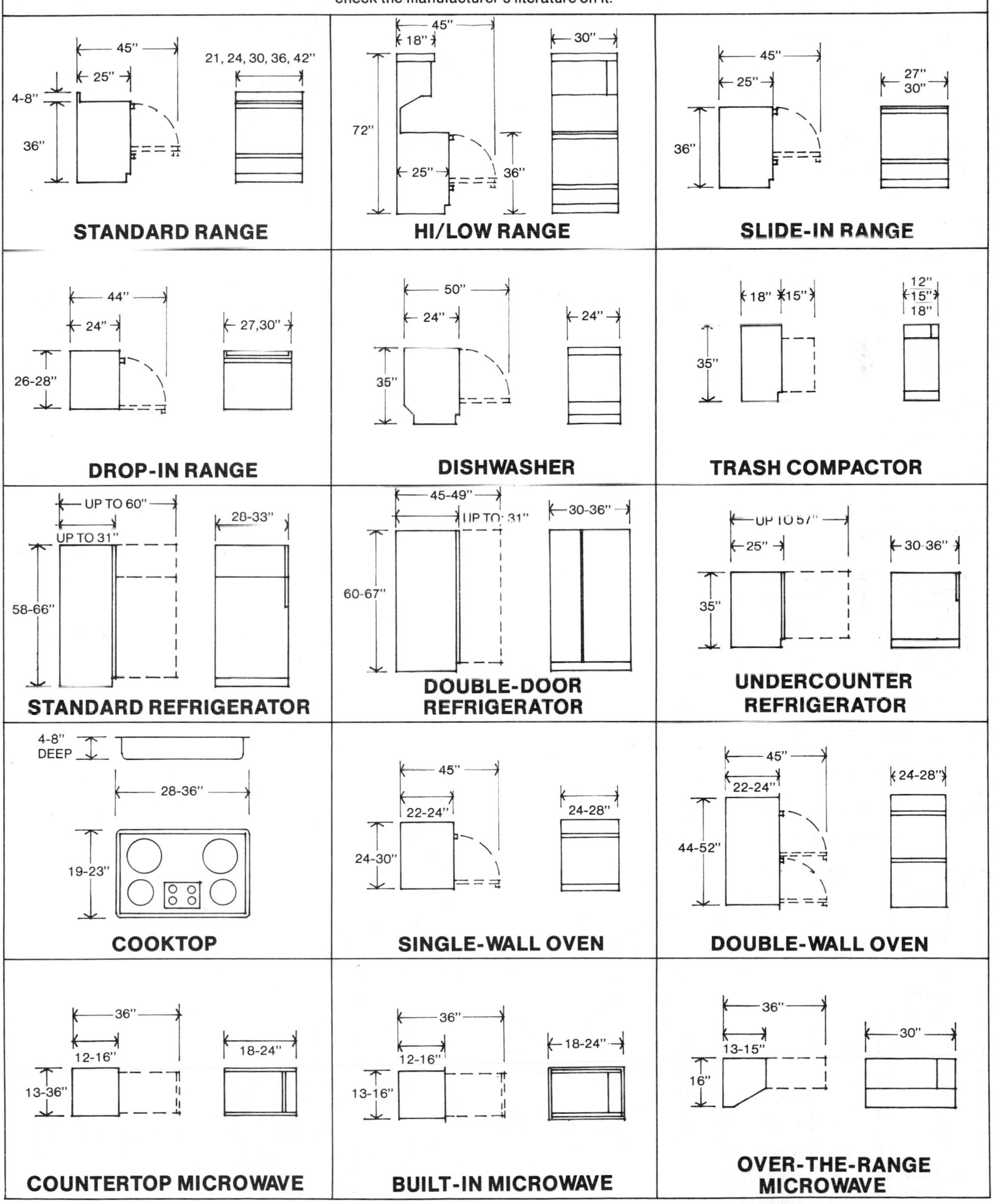

Planning Your Kitchen

Designing a functional, attractive kitchen takes careful planning. First research and consider what's available, then draw your plans.

Designing a new kitchen or redesigning an existing one is like assembling a giant jigsaw puzzle. If you've read the chapter, *Surfaces and Equipment*, starting on page 34, you know that you can pick the puzzle pieces. In the designing process, you'll determine the overall picture those puzzle pieces will fit into—the kitchen space.

Planning space for your new or remodeled kitchen requires a careful examination of your family's lifestyle. Consider habits and living patterns, and even the sizes and shapes of every member. The object is to achieve a custom fit to the space available and to the kitchen users. This chapter tells how to gather necessary design information and how to work with it to design your kitchen.

UNDERSTANDING SPACE

One of the first steps in designing your kitchen is to distinguish *real* space from *apparent* space. Real space is the actual square footage you have. Apparent space is the amount of space you perceive, or see.

The spaces you see are affected by optical illusions. One illusion is caused by color. You can alter the *apparent* size and shape of a kitchen by the way you handle color. For instance, in a long, narrow kitchen, light-color cabinets on the long walls and dark paneling on the short walls make the room seem much more square. Switching the light and dark colors creates a reverse effect. See drawings on facing page.

Patterns also create optical illusions. Patterns with horizontal lines—lines running across the line of sight—make a room seem lower and wider. Patterns with strong vertical lines—lines running in the same direction as the line of sight—make the room seem higher and narrower. Consider this effect when choosing wall and floor coverings.

You can learn more about these illusions by estimating dimensions of various rooms and then measuring them. You may find you've been seeing apparent space rather than real space all your life.

Another way to manipulate apparent space is by altering *available lines of sight*. This means shortening or extending a view from a particular spot in the room.

For instance, a large window that extends the line of sight to an outside deck railing 15 or 20 feet away can make a kitchen space seem larger. So would a pass-through that allows you to see the far wall of the family room from the kitchen. A large opening or window to these areas is more effective than a small one in achieving this effect. The drawings at right show how a boxed-in kitchen can be opened up to give the illusion of more space.

On the other hand, you may want to block lines of sight to give an area intimacy or to screen an undesirable view. For instance, you can block the sight of a messy kitchen work area from an adjoining dining area. This technique will make both areas seem smaller.

A good compromise is to install a sliding or accordion-style door that can be left open or closed as needed. The door can be used in conjunction with a permanent divider, such as a snack bar. Often, just raising a snack bar or serving counter about 6 inches above the kitchen counter will solve the problem.

A good kitchen design combines several illusions to create the desired effect. For example, a small kitchen will seem larger with a light color scheme, a recessed refrigerator, a large window overlooking a deck outside, or a pass-through opening. Conversely, a large kitchen with a light ceiling, medium-tone walls and cabinets, dark countertops and dark floor will feel smaller and cozier.

You can use optical illusions for visually separating areas within a room without actually separating them with a wall or partition. Start by using two different types and colors of floor covering. Then add a false beam in a contrasting color to the ceiling. Your mind begins to see two rooms. A dark floor next to a light one will appear to be higher, further separating the two areas. To complete the effect, you can use different wall coverings in each area.

These two kitchens are identical in size and shape, but they don't look it. All that's been changed is color scheme. You can use colors to change apparent size of kitchen.

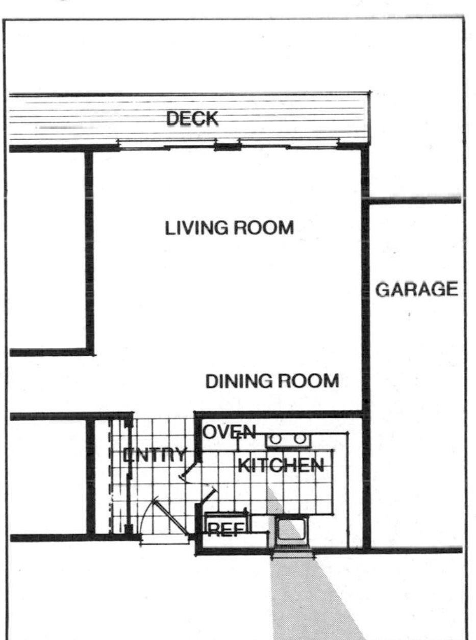

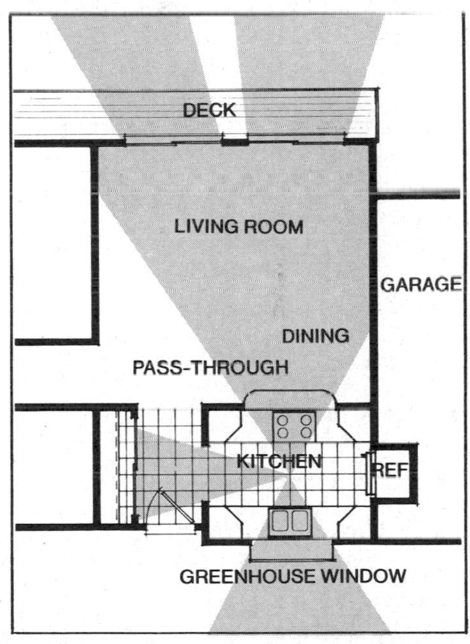

This kitchen is no larger than a large walk-in closet. It feels small because its openings are small. Providing openings to extend lines of sight, as shown at right, makes kitchen feel more spacious.

STYLE SELECTION

Select a style for your new kitchen as early as possible in the planning stage. In most cases, you'll want the kitchen style to match the rest of the house. If your house has low, beamed ceilings, pine paneling and antique furniture, you'll probably be more comfortable with a country or colonial look in the kitchen. If the house has soaring angular spaces and is full of chrome and glass, contemporary or Scandinavian kitchen styles will be best. But style is a matter of personal choice and preference. A few well-chosen accessories can tie a kitchen of one style into a house of another style, or can integrate a kitchen that combines many styles.

Style selection should not be dictated only by fashion. A well-built kitchen lasts a long time. You don't want the kitchen or its elements to become dated because of a short-lived fad. For more on styles, see pages 8-33.

YOUR LIFESTYLE

Your family's needs will affect your kitchen design more than any other factor except the amount of space available. By now you've probably begun to assess these needs and ask yourself many questions. Beyond the obvious questions are others you should ask. Some are listed below, along with some of the things your answers should tell you.

Consider these questions about your present kitchen even if you are designing a kitchen for another house. Use the questions to review

WORK AND STORAGE CENTERS

A good way of analyzing and understanding how a kitchen will function is to look at its design in terms of *work centers* and *storage centers.* You not only need space for a work activity; you also need storage space for utensils and supplies. To create a kitchen that saves time and steps, provide storage space as close as possible to the point of use.

MINIMUM STORAGE NEEDS—Total shelf area in a kitchen shouldn't be less than 50 square feet. Don't count any shelf area more than 74 inches above the floor, or above a refrigerator. Count 50% of shelf area at inside corners. You should have 12 square feet or more of drawer area. Drawers deeper than 6 inches can be counted as shelves.

To establish your minimum needs, take an inventory. List all items in your current kitchen—or your *ideal* kitchen—under their appropriate work centers. Make an estimate of storage space you'll need for each work center.

FOOD-STORAGE CENTER—This includes refrigerator and freezer. You'll need at least 18 inches of counter space on the handle side of the refrigerator for general food storage. A pantry can serve as part of the food-storage center, or if it's remote, as a backup. If you're planning on a pantry *cabinet,* it should be 24 inches deep and located at the hinge side of the refrigerator.

The food-storage center must be set up for handling incoming grocery bags. Plan countertop areas for this.

Primary movement from food-storage center will be to sink and food-preparation center. Consider the relationship to the serving area also—some foods are served directly from the refrigerator. Handling leftovers should also be considered.

FOOD-PREPARATION CENTER—This center is usually placed between refrigerator and sink. The practical minimum countertop length is 30 inches, provided it's adjacent to the countertop over the food-storage center. Otherwise, add 6 or more inches. The disposer should be convenient to the food-preparation center. Stored within reach should be knives, peelers, graters, salad bowls and other utensils used for food-preparation jobs.

CLEANUP CENTER—Located in the cleanup center are sink, dishwasher and provisions for trash and garbage. Allow at least 32 inches for sink and 30 inches or more of countertop for stacking dirty dishes for washing. Think about the cleanup center as it functions with the dishwasher door *open,* not closed. A dishwasher in a corner cuts off access to 4 feet of counter, 2 feet each way. Door should not cut off access to counter where dirty dishes are stacked.

Cabinet space for dishes and drawers for silverware should be nearby. If you do a lot of entertaining or special activities like canning, consider adding a second sink in a separate, secondary preparation and cleanup center.

MIXING AND BAKING CENTER—In a smaller kitchen, the food-preparation center can double as a mixing and baking center. But if you do much baking, the mixing and baking center should be separate. About 42 inches of countertop is needed. It's helpful if this section of countertop is dropped to a height of 30-32 inches. A lower work surface makes mixing and kneading more comfortable. Mixing and baking center should be convenient to oven or ovens.

A baking center is the most-specialized area in a kitchen, because baking traditions and equipment vary so much. If you'd like to try some of the more exotic baked goods, check several cookbooks for tools and techniques needed. Special equipment includes marble slabs for puff-pastry work, appliances such pasta and ravioli machines, dough mixers, flour mills, and a host of available bins and built-in canisters. An appliance garage can be useful for storing special appliances. A small two-burner cooktop can be handy for preparing sauces.

COOKING CENTER—This should be located closer to the serving or eating area than should the preparation center. The range or cooktop should not be located within 12 inches of a window. It should not be closer than 30 inches from an unprotected cabinet above, or 24 inches from a protected one. Avoid putting a range in a corner. There should be at least 30 inches of countertop on one side of the range or cooktop and at least 15 inches on the other side. A built-in oven should have at least 18 inches of countertop immediately to one side.

Herbs and seasonings should be handy to the cooking center, but in a *cool* location. Pots and pans occupy lots of space, so plan for them. Lids and cooking utensils can be kept in drawers or on wall racks for easy access.

SERVING AREA—The most convenient location is just outside the busy traffic pattern but not out of reach. If you plan on a pass-through to a dining area, it shouldn't have less than 24 inches of countertop. Such a pass-through is best combined with the cleanup center on the kitchen side, and with dish storage.

Plan places for linens and place mats, serving utensils, and extras like candles, candlesticks and vases. A warming oven or a heat lamp makes a handy addition to a serving area. A bar sink can reduce traffic in the kitchen.

PLANNING CENTER—Locate the planning center out of the main work pattern. The center can be as simple as a wall phone, a bulletin board and a cookbook rack. Or a planning center can include a desk with a telephone, intercom and file drawers. A fully equipped planning center is shown at right.

A standard chair can be used if the desk surface is no higher than 30 inches. The desk area can be as narrow as 24 inches if not hemmed in by walls. Average width is 30 to 36 inches.

past kitchens and friends' and relatives' kitchens.

What are the traffic patterns in and through the present kitchen?

If you have a well-worn older kitchen, traffic patterns can be easily determined from the wear pattern in the old flooring. In newer kitchens, you'll have to study the way traffic moves through the kitchen at various times of the day.

If you're comfortable with the traffic patterns in your kitchen, strive to maintain them when you begin redesigning. If you have a problem with present traffic patterns, a system for analyzing and correcting them appears on page 57. Perhaps you've seen kitchens with traffic patterns you prefer. Now's the time to study them.

Are people and pets always underfoot?

This problem can relate to traffic patterns, but it may also alert you to the need to allow room for spectators and assistants.

What kind of cooking or baking would you like to do more of?

It's possible to create special work areas for many activities, such as pastry making, meat cutting or flower arranging. Be prepared to adapt counter height to these specialized areas. Heavy work such as dough kneading is often much more comfortable on a lower counter.

This kitchen planning center has plenty of shelf and drawer space. Cabinets match those in kitchen.

Does the process of cooking, serving and cleaning up after a meal require a lot of walking?

This problem might be the result of a poor layout or obstacles in the traffic pattern. Or the kitchen may be too big. A large kitchen can work well if it is zoned for various functions. But if it's 50 feet from refrigerator to sink to stove and back, the kitchen needs reorganizing.

Is the present kitchen plagued with small disasters such as spills, cuts and bumped heads?

Accidents indicate the kitchen may be poorly designed or laid out. Traffic patterns or lighting could be at fault, but often it's a question of elbow room. For instance, locating a refrigerator directly adjacent to a range inevitably leads to a pot or pan handle being hit by the refrigerator door, tipping the pot. If the refrigerator is to the right of the stove and the cook is right-handed, handling pots and pans on the back burners becomes difficult. A common cause of bumped heads is a misplaced wall-cabinet door. The same door causes the same accident time after time. Always plan an appliance or work area for the people using it.

Would you like to entertain more in the kitchen, but can't?

Entertaining in informal areas rather than formal ones has become more acceptable in recent years. Naturally, a dingy old kitchen is a deterrent, but the way the space is organized is just as important. Plan room for spectators and assistants. Think about snack bars, wet bars and other places for people where they won't interfere with the cook's work.

How long are you planning to stay in the house or apartment?

Ordinarily, you might not think of remodeling a rented apartment, but in many big cities, some people live in the same apartment for decades. Under such circumstances, it can make sense to adapt the kitchen to your needs—with the owner's permission, of course. Even if you don't plan to stay for long, some small improvements could be worthwhile.

Will the present kitchen interfere with resale of the property?

While it usually doesn't pay to do major remodeling just for resale purposes, a thorough cleanup and reorganization can help. If the kitchen is the only problem room in an otherwise presentable home, a few cosmetic improvements may help. This might include painting or papering walls, replacing old floor covering or countertops, or refinishing cabinets.

This Colonial-style kitchen required attention to detail. All features were carefully selected, all spaces carefully planned. *Photo courtesy of Armstrong World Industries Inc.*

What do you like or dislike about the equipment in your present kitchen?

Your feelings about your present appliances will influence you to select different or similar new ones. You might decide to keep a faithful old appliance, even if everything else in the kitchen is to be changed. If you keep older appliances, harmonize the new ones with the old in color and style. If you change the color scheme, the old appliance can be painted to match new ones.

For an expert paint job, consult an appliance repair service. Some autobody shops paint appliances as a sideline business.

Are there any hot or cold areas?

Pinpoint any such areas. The cause might be an improperly sized heating duct that can be corrected. You might need to replace an old window that leaks cold air all winter. A window that lets in afternoon sun all summer might benefit from an awning or removable sun screen. You may need to weatherstrip existing windows and exterior doors or install a ceiling fan for air circulation.

Are there any bright or dim areas?

As with heat and cold, lighting problems should be corrected. If your kitchen is sunny, work surfaces away from direct sun need more light to reduce the contrast. Work surfaces in direct sun need measures to control glare. A dark-color surface reflects less light than a light-color one.

Many bright kitchens have a big light in the middle of the ceiling. But you're in your own shadow when you're working at a counter. Consider installing lighting under wall cabinets or soffits to illuminate countertops.

Recessed lights in the soffit or ceiling in front of the wall cabinets can provide shadow-free lighting on countertops and illuminate the insides of cabinets when their doors are open. For more on lighting, see page 53.

COLOR

When planning your kitchen, choose a color scheme early. This will help you select appliances, cabinets, floor and wall coverings, and other materials.

The Color Wheel—Shown below, the color wheel is the basic tool of color selection. Applying various patterns to the wheel generates color combinations we perceive as harmonious. Each segment represents a light-frequency range that we recognize as a separate color. About half of the wheel is sensed as *warm* and the other half as *cool.* Color segments marked "P" are *primary* colors, from which all others can be blended. Ones marked "S" are *secondary* colors, formed by blending equal parts of the primary colors on either side of them on the wheel. Segments marked "T" are *tertiary* colors, formed by a 1/4-3/4 blend of the primaries on either side.

Color Schemes—You can apply any of the patterns below to the color wheel to come up with harmonious color combinations. Start with colors that are a fixed part of the overall design, and work from there. Before you start selecting colors, get an idea of values and intensities you want for various areas.

A *monochromatic* color scheme (pattern A) uses several colors from one segment of the color wheel, in a range of values and intensities. A *related* color scheme (pattern B) uses colors from two or more segments that are side by side on the color wheel. Start by picking the central segment, and working out from there. A *complementary* color scheme (pattern C) uses colors from two segments directly opposite each other. A *related-complementary* color scheme (pattern D) uses colors from two pairs of segments, directly opposite each other. A *split-complementary* color scheme (pattern E) uses colors from one segment and the two segments on either side of the one opposite it. A *triad* color scheme (pattern F) uses colors from three segments equally spaced around the color wheel. A *tetrad* color scheme (pattern G) uses colors from four segments equally spaced around the color wheel. All of these patterns can be rotated to any position on the color wheel.

Color Accents—A kitchen affords many opportunities for strong color accenting. Keep accent-color options open so you can vary accents from time to time. Crockery, baskets, dish towels and flowering plants can be used to generate a fresh look every few months. High-intenstiy, low-value colors work well for accents. You can pick accent colors from the patterns shown above. Or accent colors can be picked from wall-coverings or other patterns in the kitchen. Just match a minor color in the pattern, and use it at full intensity for an accent.

Color Tips—Color and light are interrelated. While color shading in artificial "white" light is faint, it's still there. Incandescent light is slightly yellow or amber. Fluorescent light can have a faint green, blue or pink cast. The light source you use can slightly alter the color of room surfaces and objects. Try to view color samples under the actual mix of lighting you'll be using, day and night.

Basically, the closer a color is to the color of the light, the more it's intensified. The farther away a color is from the color of the light, the more it fades. For instance, the color of natural-oak cabinets is accentuated by incandescent lighting, and suppressed by fluorescent lighting that has a blue or green cast.

When selecting colors and textures for your kitchen, don't let the current season of the year affect your choices. Think in terms of how the choices will work through the whole year. On the other hand, if you have a favorite season of the year, the right color combinations can recall it for you every time you walk into the kitchen.

Don't view your kitchen as an isolated area. It should harmonize with color schemes of adjoining rooms. Or you can make changes in color schemes of adjoining rooms to match the kitchen, especially if the kitchen is open to these rooms.

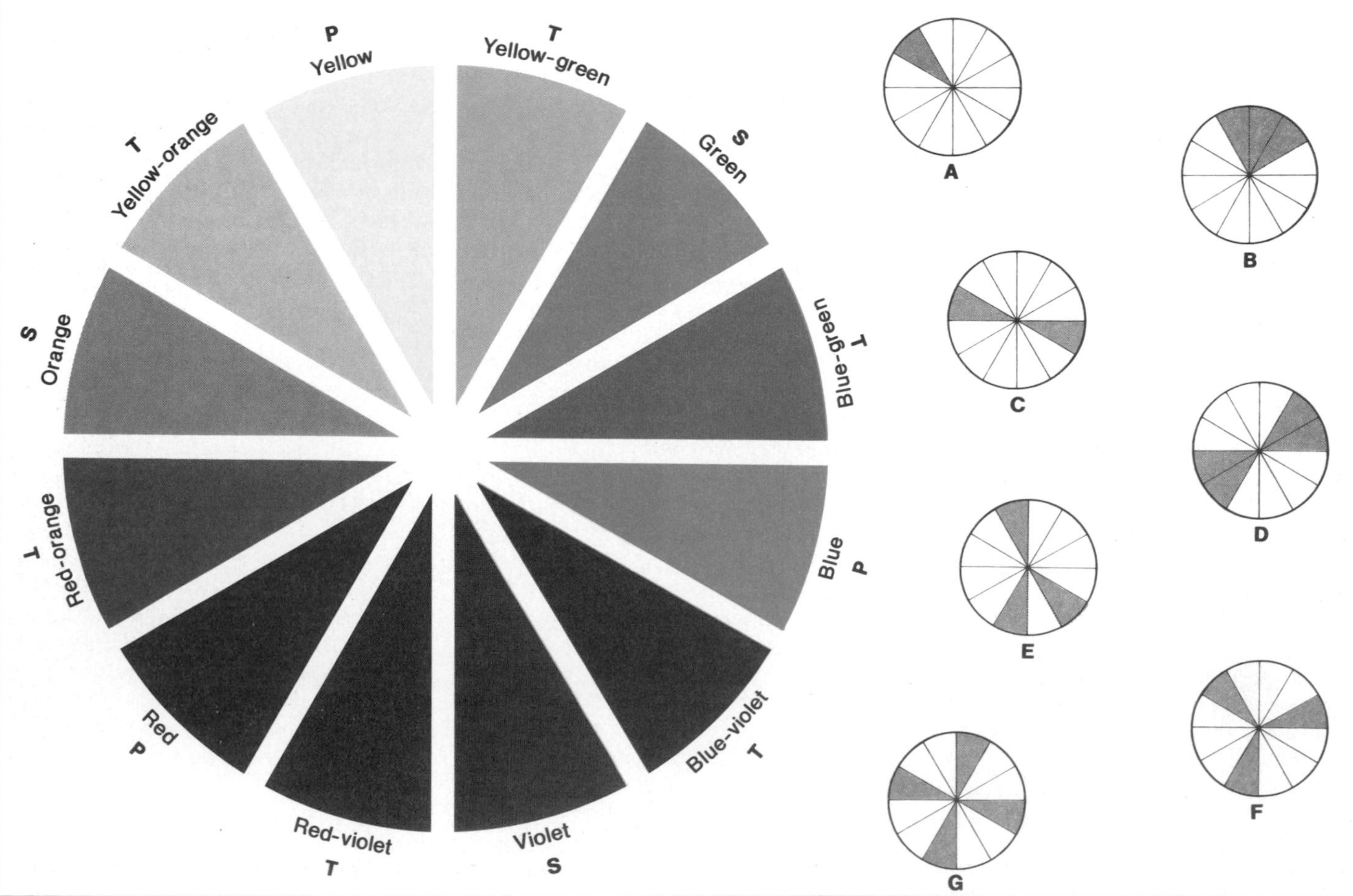

LIGHTING

Natural Light—Because a kitchen is used a lot in the daytime, natural sunlight is important. Sunlight can be admitted by windows, skylights or high clerestory windows. Direct sunlight is generally bluish-white unless it's tinted by diffuser panels. But once direct sunlight strikes a surface, it picks up some of its color. Reflected, indirect sunlight can be more useful than direct sunlight in creating desired lighting in a kitchen.

Glare from direct sunlight on glossy surfaces can be a problem. Textured surfaces can also create glare. Another difficulty is high contrast between sunlit areas and shaded ones. This contrast can be hard on your eyes.

You can reduce glare by several means. Diffuser panels, either fixed or moveable, reduce and scatter direct sunlight. Outside sunshades or awnings can cut off direct sun altogether, allowing only scattered skylight to enter the room. Landscaping outside a window can make a big difference. Trees, vines and tall shrubs can directly shade a window. Lawns, ground covers and low plantings reduce the amount of reflected sunlight through the window. Curtains or blinds help, especially if direct light enters the window a short time each day, or only during part of the year.

Orientation of windows, skylights and clerestories is important. North facing windows and clerestories rarely admit direct sun. East-facing ones admit morning sun. West-facing windows let in afternoon sun, and possibly excessive heat and glare. South-facing windows and clerestories admit direct sun most of the day, with attendant problems.

Skylights, especially clear ones, are less predictable. Depending on the slope and orientation of the roof, the amount of sunlight admitted can differ. For instance, a skylight in a flat roof will light the center of the west wall of the room on a summer morning, then the floor, then the east wall in the afternoon. In the winter the same skylight will admit light that moves from the north end of the west wall, across the north wall to the east wall. A skylight in the north slope of a pitched roof may admit direct sun only in the summer, being shaded by the roof the rest of the year. Before putting in a skylight, think about how the sun moves throughout the year. To reduce glare, use translucent skylights or diffuser panels.

Artificial Light—The job of artificial lighting is to substitute for sun when it isn't there, and to supplement sun when it is. There are two basic artificial light sources.

Incandescent Lights are small, bright light sources that generate heat as well as light. Power consumption is higher for the amount of light generated than with fluorescents. Incandescent light has a gold or amber cast, though the eyes automatically adjust for the color shift from natural sunlight.

Basic incandescent fixture types are recessed, surface-mounted and suspended. Recessed fixtures are installed in a ceiling or wall. Surface-mounted fixtures are made in both fixed types and directional spots and floods. In these groups are track assemblies that let you move lights anywhere you want along a track. Suspended fixtures hang down from the ceiling, and are useful for lighting a kitchen when the ceiling is high or sloping.

Incandescent bulbs vary widely in price and lifespan. Bulb cartons usually list the wattage and the *lumens*, the amount of light produced. Bulbs that produce the highest number of lumens per watt generally have the shortest life, especially in a fixture that doesn't vent accumulated heat very well. So if a bulb shape is expensive, or a fixture is hard to get to, pick a bulb with the lowest lumens-per-watt you can find.

Fluorescent Lights produce two or three times as much light per watt as incandescents. They emit relatively little heat. The light is produced over a fairly large surface. Light from early fluorescent tubes had an unpleasant greenish cast. Tubes are now available that emit a "warm" light and others that emit a "cool" light.

Fluorescent light fixtures are limited in size and shape by the fluorescent tubes themselves. Also, the box that forms the body of the fixture includes room for the *ballast*, or transformer, required to make the tube function. Most fluorescent fixtures tend to look utilitarian. Unless the utilitarian look fits with your design, plan on disguising fluorescents behind diffuser panels, or in an enclosed fixture.

General Lighting—Though general lighting and task lighting can come from the same source, they're more often provided separately. General lighting ideally provides relatively uniform and shadowless lighting all over the kitchen. Fluorescent fixtures work well for this, as do regular patterns of incandescent lights. For fluorescent lights, comfortable light levels run around 1-1/4 watts per square foot of surface to be lit; around 3-1/2 watts per square foot with incandescent. Considerable variation from these levels may be necessary to adapt to a very light-color or reflective kitchen, or to a very dark-color or light-absorbent one. For instance, a wall of dark-brown brick can absorb large quantities of general light, leaving the kitchen dim.

Task Lighting—Plan on providing additional light anywhere work is done. The primary areas to consider are the major work centers described on page 50. A good starting point for task lighting is 100 to 150 watts incandescent or 40 watts fluorescent for each work center. Be careful not to introduce harsh shadows. As in general lighting, surface color and reflectivity affect the amount of light needed. Also, the more evenly task lighting is provided, the lower the total levels can be. Light-color, reflective surfaces tend to even out lighting.

Special-Effect Lighting—Lighting can be installed for effect rather than purely functional reasons. Just as a spotlight might be used to highlight a painting on a wall, objects in a kitchen can be highlighted by spotlights or showcase lights. A row of miniature lights might be installed on tops of wall cabinets not for its contribution to general lighting, but to relieve a dark area there. The lights can illuminate a plate collection displayed there. Many such treatments are possible.

Controls—Lights can be controlled either by standard switches or by dimmer switches. Make sure dimmer switches have adequate capacity for the lights they're controlling. General lighting should be controlled by a switch at every entry to the room. This may require 3-way switching—see page 95. Task lighting, on the other hand, is best controlled where it's used. You can provide separate switches for each work center, or use switches to control groups of task lights.

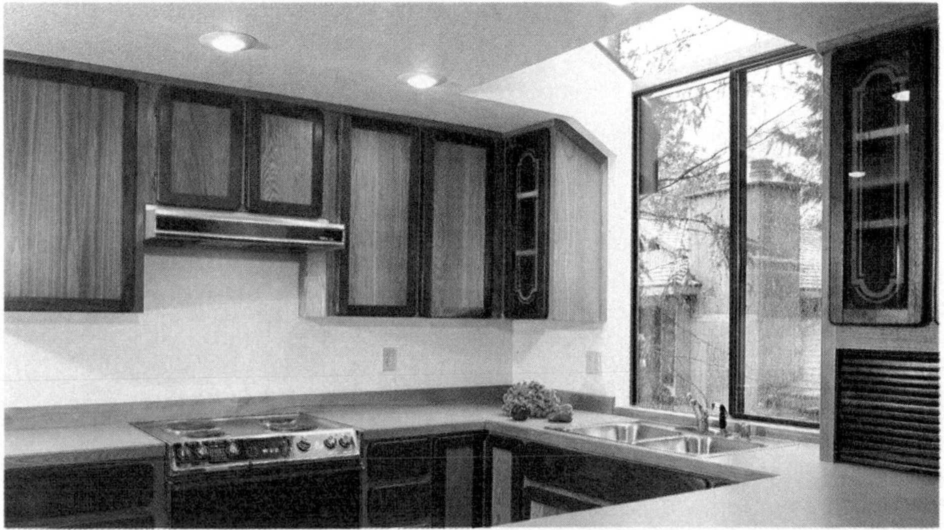

Skylight admits natural light during day, recessed floodlights in ceiling provide general lighting at night.

COMPROMISES

Designing a kitchen involves compromises. Most of the creative work lies in identifying and resolving conflicts. The largest is the conflict of square footage in the house for kitchen activities—cooking, cleanup, storage and dining—versus square footage for all other uses in a house. Close behind comes the battle of appliance space in the kitchen versus food and utensil storage space, seating space and moving-around space. A third major conflict is the need for counter area opposed to the need to shorten distance between work centers.

The first approach to resolving these problems is priority. List the conflicting items in order of their importance to you. Then include as many as you can of the top items on the list and pass up those farther down. You might include a trash compactor and give up the small amount of storage space it displaces, if enough storage space is available anyway. Or you might steal a small amount of space from a dining room to make room for a snack bar. In many cases, this trading-off technique isn't enough.

If you still have conflicts, try merging various functions. If you never use two adjacent work areas at the same time, you might consider using one work area to serve both functions. For example, a food preparation area may double as a mixing and baking center.

Consider borrowing space wherever it can be found. A pantry door looks like any other door, so a pantry can be anywhere it's convenient. A nearby hall closet could be converted to a pantry, as could space in a dining room or utility room.

If the conflict is mostly financial, your perfect kitchen can be staged over a period of months, or even years. Make changes a step at a time, starting with the most important ones. Make sure each modification follows your overall plan, so all elements in the finished kitchen fit together when the project is complete.

BASIC LAYOUTS

Over the centuries, millions of kitchens have been built and used. Every one of them belongs to one of eight basic layouts. These are the *L*, the *Broken-L*, the *U*, the *Broken-U*, the *Island*, the *Galley*, the *Corridor* and the *Zoned*. While some are superficially similar, they differ in the way work patterns and traffic patterns interact. These patterns are discussed on pages 56 and 57.

In the layouts shown on the following pages, the work patterns are shown as dotted lines and the traffic patterns are shown in color. Each basic layout has its advantages and its disadvantages.

The L Kitchen is commonly used because of its economical use of space. See drawing at right. It's also efficient, as seen from the relatively short sides of the work pattern and the lack of interference between traffic pattern and work pattern.

The main drawback of the L kitchen is that storage space in the corner can be difficult or impossible to get to. Any appliance near the corner can be difficult to use due to the proximity of cabinets on the adjacent wall. Lazy Susan corner units help provide better access and space the appliances and cabinets away from the corner. Lazy Susan units are discussed on page 31. The L kitchen is more easily adapted to square spaces than long, narrow ones.

The Broken-L Kitchen is fundamentally a poor one, due to the unavoidable conflict between work pattern and traffic pattern. This layout is often the result of a kitchen with too many doorways.

The U Kitchen is becoming more popular because of the trend toward open kitchens and snack bars. Interference between work pattern and traffic pattern is low. Spectators are easily accommodated at a snack bar.

The economies of the L kitchen are doubled in the U kitchen, because of the short distance between work centers. Difficulties of access to corner storage and corner crowding are also doubled. Unless a diagonal cabinet or Lazy Susan is installed, much of the space in the corner where cabinets meet will be inaccessible.

U kitchens get big in a hurry as you pencil in appliances. A refrigerator, built-in oven, range, sink, dishwasher and trash compactor add up to about 14-1/2 feet of cabinet frontage. Add two Lazy Susan units at the corners, and you use about 26-1/2 feet of room perimeter. Consider a U kitchen for a relatively square space, with no less than 9 feet across the short wall. Consider providing access to cabinets from dining-room side of the U.

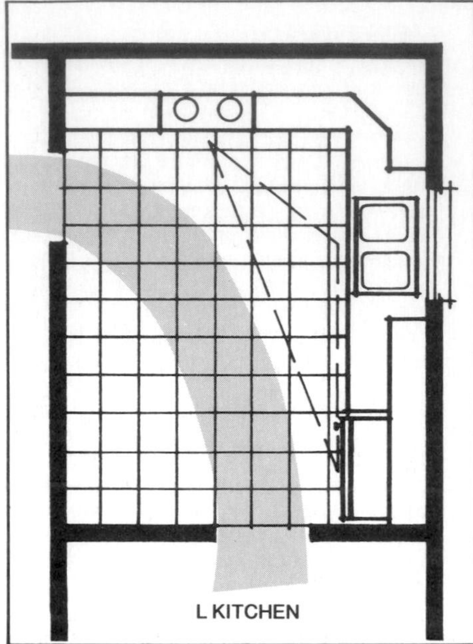
L KITCHEN

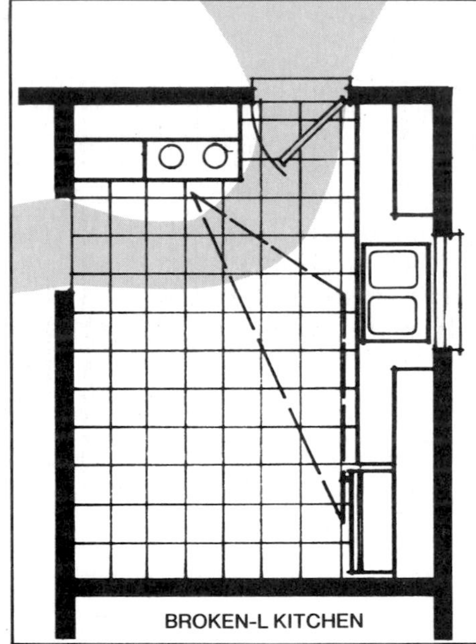
BROKEN-L KITCHEN

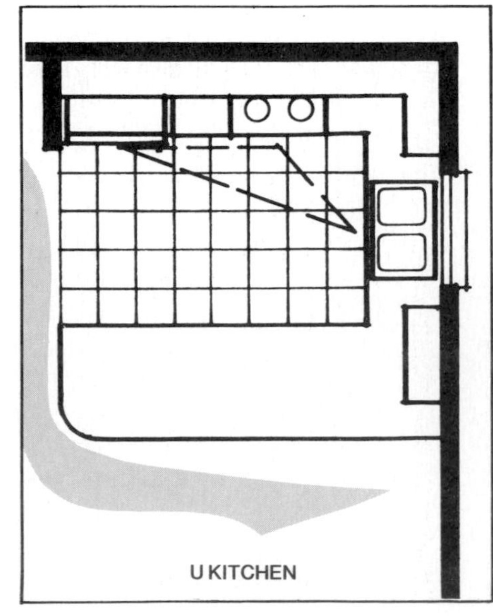
U KITCHEN

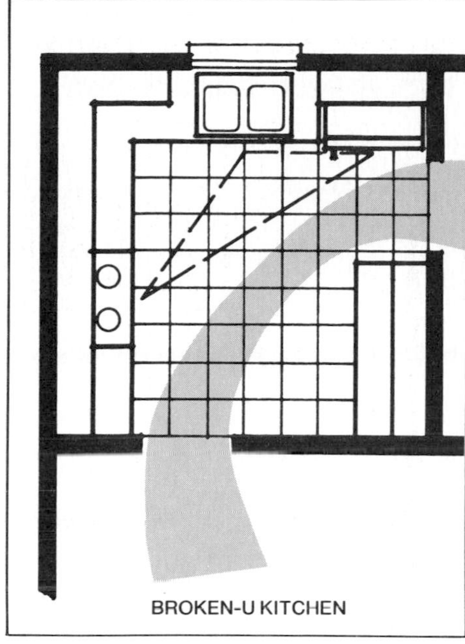

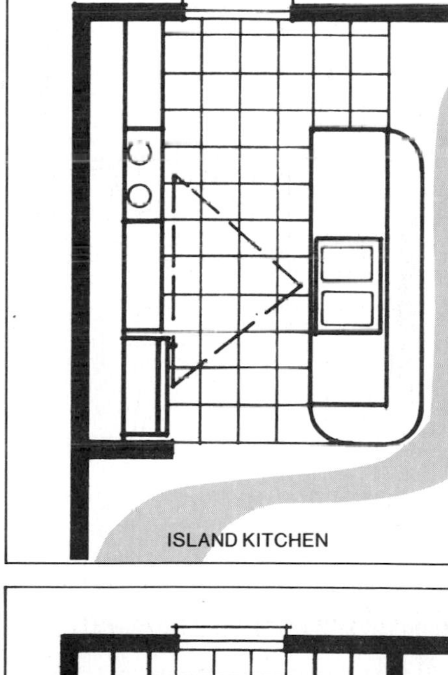

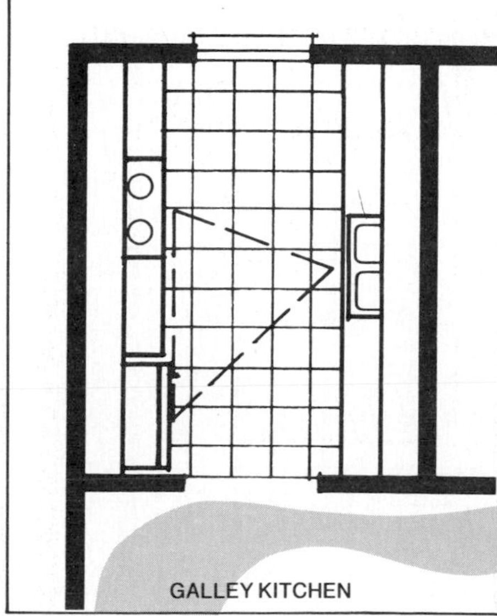

The Broken-U Kitchen works well when there are no major appliances in the detached segment. It's a poor choice when there are major appliances in the detached segment. Many L kitchens with an associated pantry are really broken-U kitchens. The broken-U layout provides little or no space for spectators.

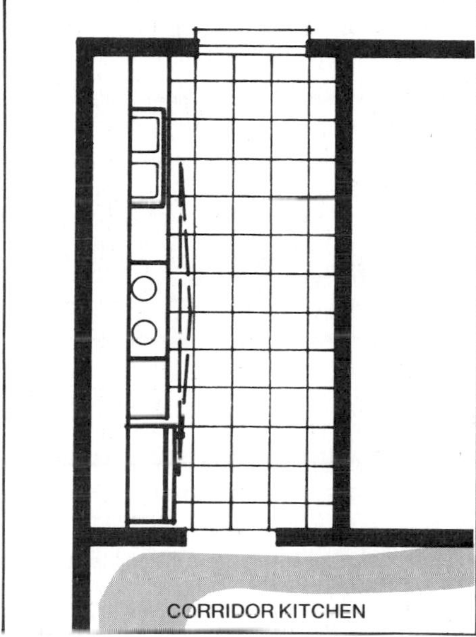

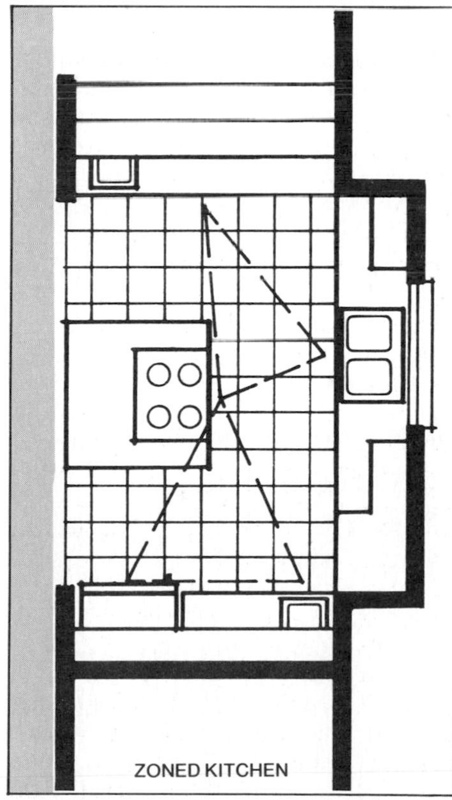

The Island Kitchen provides a great deal of fluidity in traffic pattern. When the kitchen is not in use, traffic can flow either way around the island. When cooking is under way, traffic will naturally divert to the outer path.

Island kitchens must always be carefully organized so there is a good outer path around the island. Open-island kitchens provide a sense of freeness and informality to a house. If an island kitchen is enclosed, the space across the back counter, the island and the two open spaces should not measure less than 12 feet.

The Galley Kitchen is one of the most efficient layouts, provided the traffic pattern passes by the door instead of through the kitchen. When augmented by a walk-in pantry at the dead end and a snack bar or pass-through in one side, it's excellent. When counters are too close together, natural lighting is poor and major traffic flows down the middle, a galley kitchen can be a disaster. Counters should be a minimum of 4 feet apart.

The Corridor Kitchen is a one-sided galley. It's useful when you need a small kitchen. The corridor kitchen fits nicely into odd spaces, but in longer ones, the work pattern becomes unworkable quickly. As with the galley kitchen, a traffic pattern through a corridor kitchen should be avoided.

The Zoned Kitchen separates the functions of a kitchen at the cost of some equipment duplication. It also requires a lot of space. While the zoned kitchen usually has an island, it is much more disciplined than the informal island kitchen. A design that is a confusion of the two forms will be disappointing and difficult to work in.

A true zoned kitchen is a series of interrelated but separate kitchens that are equipped only for their limited function. A typical zoned kitchen might have separate areas for food storage, preparation, baking, cooking, serving and cleanup. An extreme example might include all of the above areas, a self-contained family kitchen, and a service entrance and facilities for a caterer. The same kitchen could accommodate one person cooking for one or two, three people cooking for 12 or a catering company providing food for a party of 100.

WORK PATTERNS

A little time spent working in a kitchen soon reveals that a cook's movements are not random. Movements soon begin to fall into patterns that are repeated over and over. To get maximum function and efficiency in a kitchen, patterns should be analyzed and considered during the design process.

Elements of a kitchen work pattern are measured from the center front of the work areas. The line from sink to refrigerator should not measure less than 4 feet, nor more than 7 feet. The line from range to sink should not measure less than 4 feet, nor more than 6 feet. The line from refrigerator to range should not be less than 4 feet, nor more than 9 feet. In the simplest kitchens, these three lines form a triangle that should not be less than 12 feet, nor more than 22 feet.

These dimensions are not hard and fast, even in a simple kitchen. A kitchen designed for one small cook may measure a little less than the minimums. A kitchen for two or three large cooks who often work together might be several feet over the maximums, to provide extra elbow room and passage space.

As a kitchen design becomes more complex, the simple triangular work pattern is subject to modification. Additional, secondary work centers modify the work pattern. Sometimes additional, subsidiary triangles come into being. Adding a pantry to a kitchen, for instance, can cause the nearest side of the triangle to grow a bump showing trips to the pantry for supplies while preparing a meal. Remember, these work patterns are not abstract. They're an estimated representation of the cook's movements.

Often, the work pattern in a kitchen can be two or more triangles rather than one. This is characteristic of the zoned kitchen. Even adding something like a baking center can radically change the work pattern. A baking center, for example, generates a work pattern from the storage space for supplies and utensils, to the refrigerator, to the oven, to the sink. This secondary pattern needs to be assessed just like the primary one, or the baking center won't work.

There's an easy way to shorten secondary work patterns when it's not feasible to move elements like the refrigerator. Try adding a secondary work center, like a sink or an oven, to serve only the secondary function. This is the way zoned kitchens grow, but there's no reason the same technique can't be used in other layout types.

If you can't be sure how the work patterns will look in a proposed kitchen design, sit down with the principal cook of the household. Trace the movements for three or four typical meals on the design with a pencil. You'll see lines pile up to reveal the work pattern. Don't forget to include *all* operations, from putting away groceries to putting away clean dishes after the meal.

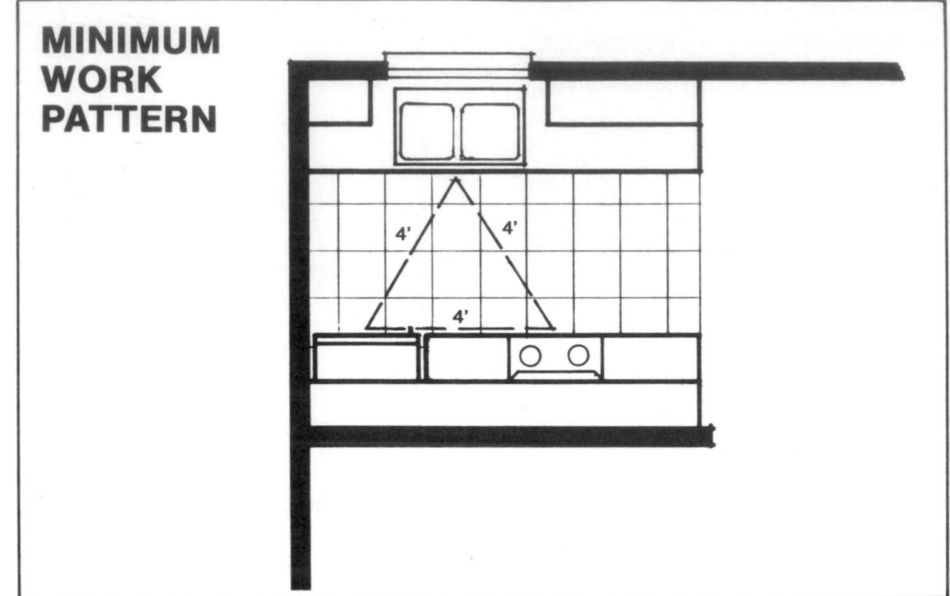

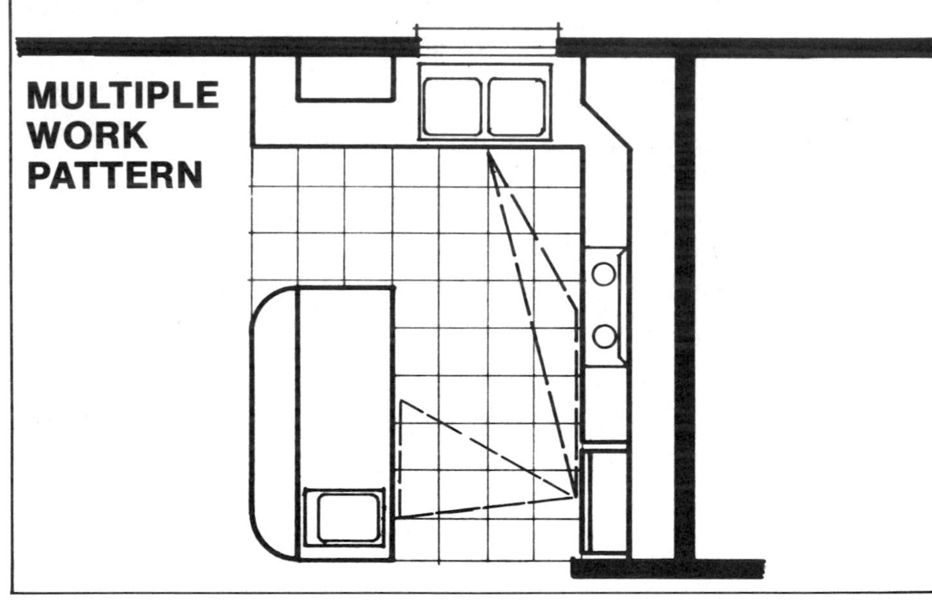

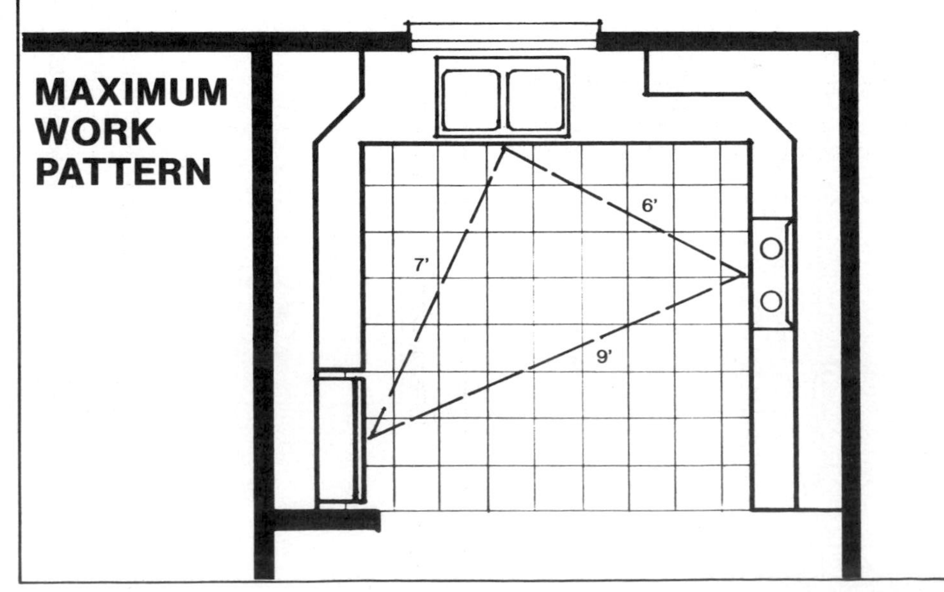

TRAFFIC PATTERNS

Unlike *work patterns,* which are determined by placement of appliances and cabinets, *traffic patterns* are mostly controlled by placement of doors and openings to other rooms. All traffic through and around a kitchen is restricted to paths related to these openings. By changing door and opening locations, and by moving any in-room obstacles, you can change the kitchen's traffic pattern

Certain floor areas will receive more wear than others. The top floor plan at right shows effect of traffic through a kitchen over a period of time. Traffic is lightest at edges of shaded area and gets heavier moving toward the center. Shaded area shows only traffic to, through, and from the kitchen, not actual cooking traffic between appliances.

For planning purposes, you have to predict only where the main paths will run, not lighter traffic toward edges of shaded area.

Try to visualize the floor plan as if you you're looking down into the kitchen and surrounding areas from above. You can easily spot main traffic lanes. Don't assume that people will walk where they're supposed to. People will usually take the shortest path between two points. Also, people usually don't make sharp right-angle turns when they change course. They follow a curved path much of the time. A normal traffic path is 30 to 36 inches wide. If the kitchen has frequent traffic in both directions at the same time, plan for a path 48 to 60 inches wide.

Plan the kitchen so traffic patterns and work patterns do not intersect. The higher the amount of traffic, the more important this is. A conflict is shown in the center drawing at right. The drawing shows the same kitchen as the first, but indicates interference between work pattern and traffic pattern. The bottom drawing shows the same kitchen with a few minor changes that make a big difference in traffic flow. Locations of window and sliding-glass door have been reversed. A doorway has been opened to divert some of the traffic from the dining room. This kind of improvement illustrates why you should spend some time working with traffic patterns in the design phase of your new kitchen.

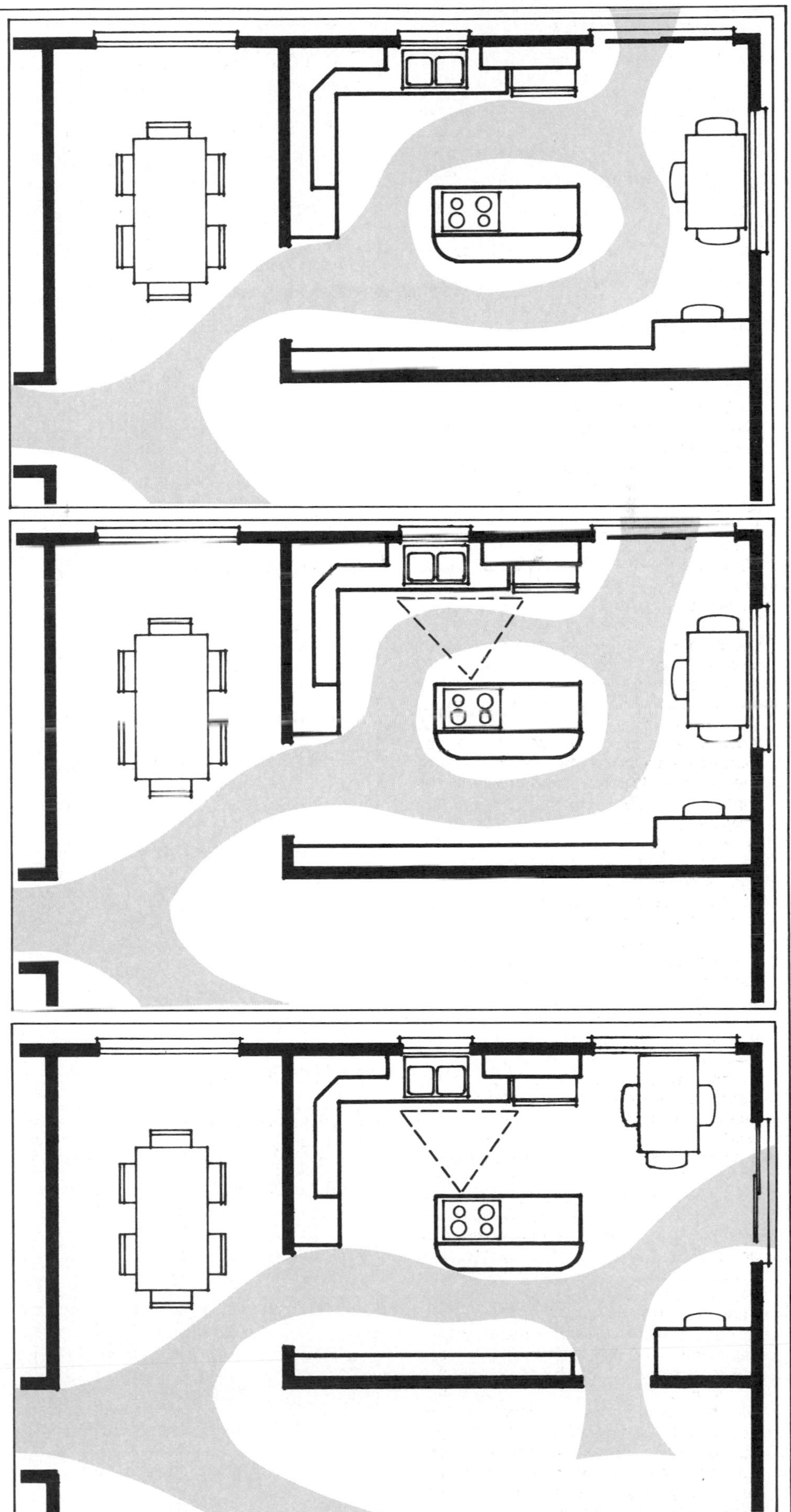

MEASURING

Accurate measurement is important to successful planning. Measure the kitchen area and all the rooms or spaces surrounding it. Once you get measurements for the whole area around the kitchen down on paper, many improvements will suggest themselves. They may not be apparent when you're looking at the actual space.

If you've lived with a house for several years, you've gotten used to it and have ceased to notice its problems. A good drawing gives you a fresh two-dimensional view.

If you measure and draw only the present kitchen, you'll probably end up with a design much like it, flaws and all. So include adjoining spaces also.

To clarify the space even more, don't measure existing cabinets. Measure the space as if the cabinets had not yet been installed.

ROUGH SKETCH FIRST

Start by drawing a rough sketch of the area you're going to measure. This doesn't need to be fancy or to scale. But the rough sketch must show that walls have thickness, and it must be big enough so you have room to work. Show all windows and doorways on the sketch, but ignore doors themselves. If you draw in a door as it is—right or left-handed—you might keep yourself from seeing that it's been swinging the wrong way for years. Or that there should be a pocket door there. Or no door at all. Especially when dealing with an older house, doors can be taken out, resulting in a major improvement to the traffic pattern. A sample rough sketch is shown above.

DIMENSIONS

On the rough sketch, mark two sets of *dimension lines.* One is an overall dimension line for each inside wall of each space, measured from corner to corner inside the room. The other is a dimension line that breaks at each interruption—door or window edge, jog or offset—in the wall. This second line also indicates wall thickness.

Measure the overall dimensions of the walls first, noting them on the sketch. Don't assume that walls at opposite ends of a room are the same length. Often they're not. Ignore baseboards and door and window casings.

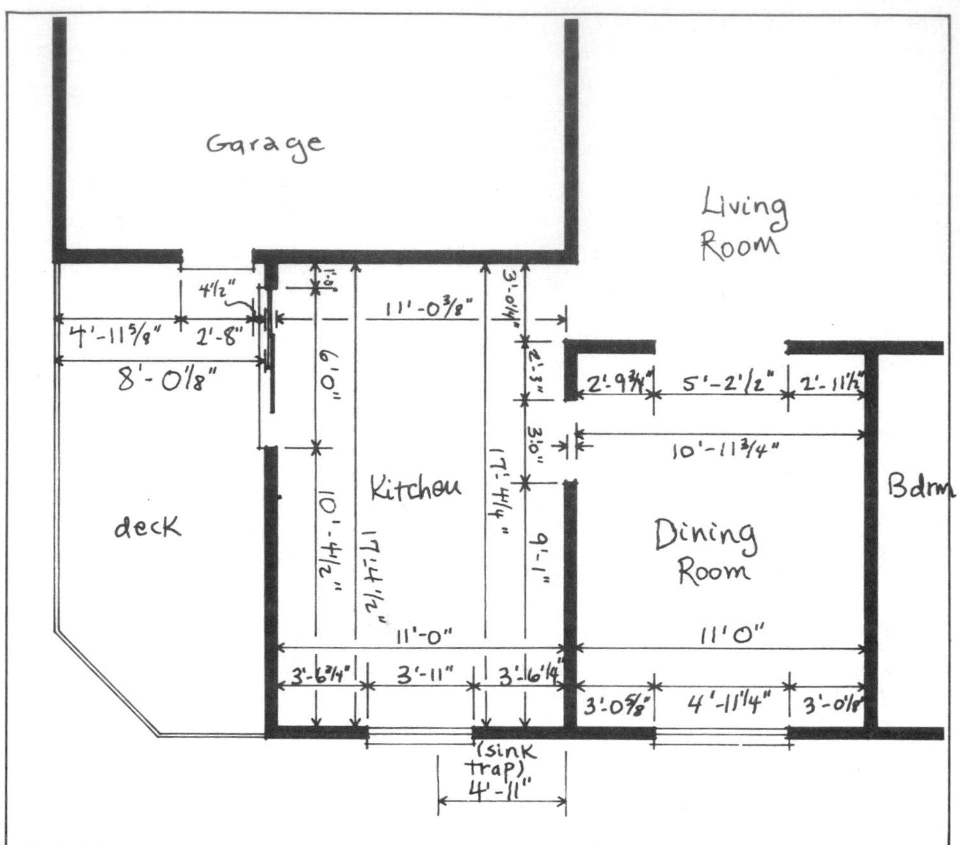

Make a rough sketch of kitchen and surrounding spaces and measure *everything.* Double-check by adding step-by-step measurements and comparing to overall ones. They should add up the same.

After the overall dimension lines are filled in, measure from each interruption to the next for each wall.

When you have all the measurements, add the shorter dimensions. Compare them to the overall dimensions to detect any errors in measurement.

Measure to the face of any door or window jamb. Also measure the thickness of each wall. Don't assume that all walls are the same thickness. If there isn't an opening in a wall so you can measure thickness, find a way to measure from fixed points, as shown in the drawing at right. Then subtract to get wall thickness. Indicate wall thicknesses on the sketch.

SQUARENESS, LEVEL AND SAG

Whether you're planning a new kitchen or a remodeled one, become aware of the peculiarities of the space you're working with. Walls and floors are rarely straight, level and square.

To determine problems you have, you need a 4-foot level, two perfectly straight 8-foot lengths of 1x2. Move one of the 1x2s on edge from place to place on all surfaces where you might want to install cabinets. Note any

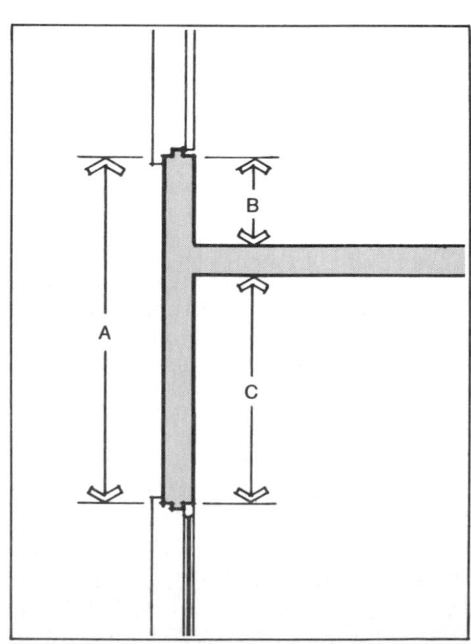

Here's how you find out how thick a wall is when there aren't any openings in it. Measure between openings in adjacent rooms (A). Then measure from wall to opening in each room (B and C). Subtract total of B and C from measurement A to get wall thickness.

humps or hollows over about 1/8 inch. Check for curving or bowing of walls. Where you measure on the curve can affect the accuracy of your measurements. *Cabinet runs* are the combined length of a series of cabinets. They should be sized for the shortest dimension between two walls. If both side walls bow out and you measured between them across the middle of the back wall, your cabinet run could end up an inch or more too big. See drawing below.

Use the 1x2 and the level to detect any bowing or sagging in floor and ceiling, and to find the approximate high spots. The ceiling height measurement should be based on the vertical distance between highest point on the floor to the lowest point on the ceiling.

Also use the level to find any leaning walls. If any walls lean, your dimensions should take this into account.

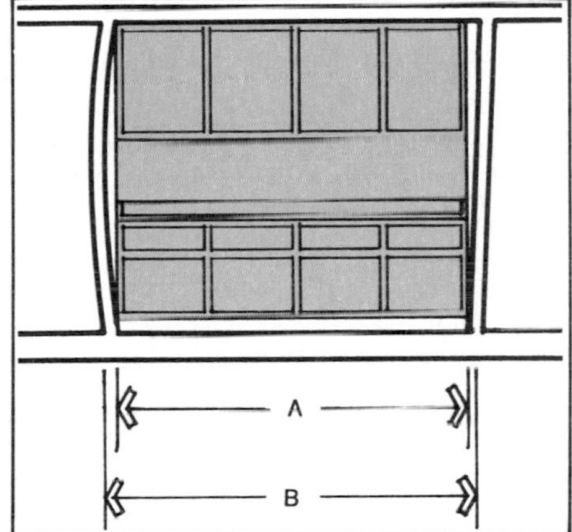

All cabinet runs have to fit between closest points on opposite surfaces—in all directions.

CORNERS

Corners are the last area of concern when you're sizing up your existing space. Corners are rarely square, for two reasons. First, when drywall or plaster corners are finished, plaster or joint compound builds up at corners. While the rest of the walls might be fairly flat, the last 4 or 5 inches at the corner may have a curve. If it's a minor deviation at the critical level—at the countertop height—it can be ignored. If the curve is severe, over 1/8 inch or so, correct it before installing cabinets. This can be done by shaving down the corner or building up one or both walls to the level of the corner. Decide now which to do so you can adjust your dimensions accordingly.

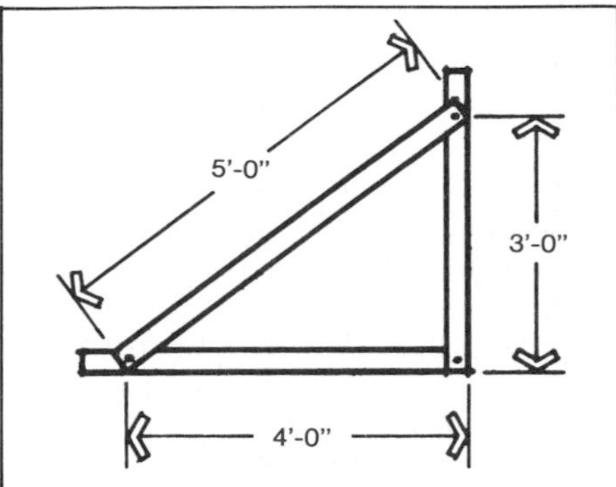

Construct a right-angle gage as shown here to detect out-of-square corners.

The second cause of out-of-square corners is more serious. Sometimes walls don't meet at a 90° angle. This corner problem is more difficult to detect. Sometimes, but not always, you'll be tipped off when walls at opposite ends of the room are not the same length.

You can use a framing square to check for out-of-square corners, as shown in the photo below. A more accurate method is to construct a *right-angle gage* from 1x2s. Cut the 1x2s into three pieces, one about 3-1/2 feet long, one about 4-1/2 feet long and a third exactly 5 feet long. Assemble as shown in the drawing above, by nailing through overlaps.

If you think you'll be using this device for future projects, make it easier to store by substituting carriage bolts and wing nuts for the nails. If you don't have room for a full-size gage, make a half-scale one or use a framing square.

Apply your right-angle gage to corners you'll be working with. If any aren't square, measure the amount of the offset at the front and back of any planned cabinet runs. Make sure you plan with the *shortest dimension* so the cabinets will fit in. For instance, if the corner is less than 90°, plan to the dimension at the front of cabinets. If the corner is more than 90°, plan to the dimension at the back of cabinets. Be sure to adjust dimensions both ways from the corner if cabinets will run across both walls.

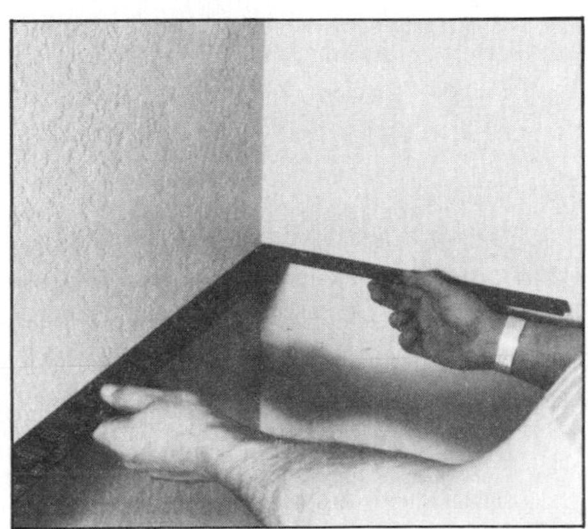
If you have a carpenter's framing square, you can use it to check your kitchen's corners.

Out-of-square corners also cause problems in countertop installation. Pre-mitered tops are ruled out, unless you're willing to recut the corner miters, which is not an easy job. Large ceramic tiles are also out, unless you don't mind tapered grout joints near the corner. Most other materials can be adapted fairly well.

DRAWING PLANS

When you've gathered the data on your new kitchen space, make accurate scale drawings. This isn't as difficult as you might think. The secret is in the kind of paper you use. Don't use common school-type graph paper with the 1/4-inch grid. Find a store that sells drafting supplies. Buy tracing papers with accurately printed *fadeout grids*. The grid is a network of faint blue or blue-green lines that do not reproduce on a blueprint machine. You want paper with an 8x8 grid. This grid has heavy lines at 1-inch spacing and light lines at 1/8-inch spacing.

Note: If you're working with metric cabinets, get 10x10 grid. After you've taken all measurements, convert them to metric dimensions in the spaces where the cabinets will be installed.

If you work on 8x8 fadeout grid paper in 1/2"=1'-0" scale, half an inch on the paper equals 1 foot in reality. Each big block equals 2x2', and each small block equals 3x3". Because standard factory cabinets come in increments of 3 inches, the grid works perfectly for cabinet planning. Tracing papers with fadeout grids come in rolls or precut sheets.

TOOLS

Aside from the right paper, you need only a few simple tools to do usefully accurate drawings. The simplest tool kit includes a *straightedge*, a roll of *masking tape*, a fairly hard *lead pencil* and a piece of *fine sandpaper*. The sandpaper is used to keep a sharp, even point on the pencil lead. Any smooth hard surface will do for a work area—a table with a plastic-laminate top is fine.

There are other tools available at a drafting-supply store that can make the process quicker and easier, though it's possible to get by without them. The first extra tool to consider is a *scale rule*. Shown below, a scale rule has several different scales on it, and makes it possible to read scaled measurements directly instead of having to count squares on the graph paper.

A scale rule reads differently than a ruler. There's a zero point near one end of each scale. Whole feet are marked from the zero point, going *away* from that near end. You'll find a finely divided section extending from the zero point *toward* the near end. These small divisions subdivide a single foot, usually into 2-inch increments on smallest scales, up to 1/8-inch increments on largest scales.

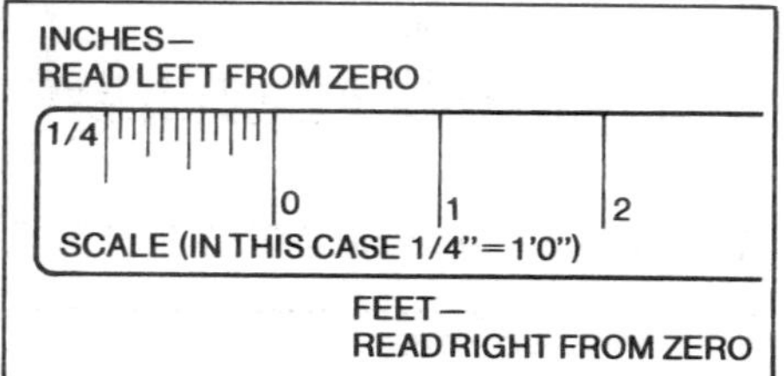

If you have a table with at least one straight side and a hard smooth edge such as plastic laminate, you could add a small *T-square* and one or two convenient-size *triangles* to your tool kit. The T-square hooks over the table edge and slides along to let you draw parallel horizontal lines. The triangles butt against the T-square so you can make parallel, vertical or diagonal lines.

For another few dollars, you can add a *mechanical drafting pencil* of the type pioneered by Pentel. It accepts leads that are a uniform 0.3, 0.5 or 0.9 mm in diameter. This makes it easy to get consistent line widths in your drawings. Leads for these pencils come in varying degrees of hardness. These range from 6B (softest) to 6H (hardest). The drafting pencils usually come with F or HB leads in them, so get a tube each of H and 2H leads. Experiment on the paper you're using to find the lead grade you like.

GETTING STARTED

Tape a sheet of tracing paper to your tabletop or drafting board with a piece of masking tape at each corner. Be sure to position your drawing so it's oriented the *same direction* as the spaces you're drawing, even if you're working in an another room. If the drawing is rotated from the real thing, you'll confuse yourself constantly.

Look at your rough sketch and find an outside wall. Add up the dimensions from the outside wall to the innermost area you want to draw. Roughly center that measurement on the sheet. That gives you a starting location for the outside wall.

Lightly draw in a pair of *guidelines* for the outside wall. The lines should show actual thickness of the wall. These guidelines form the framework for the actual drawing. Make them just dark enough to see, and as thin and as accurately placed as possible. Find the next wall parallel to the outside wall, mark your measurements and draw in another pair of guidelines. When parallel walls are marked by guidelines, do the same for all cross walls. If a wall isn't exactly parallel to the others, make sure to adjust guidelines to match the actual wall location.

When all guidelines are in place and checked, refer to your sketch and draw in openings, one wall at a time. When openings in a wall are marked with heavy end lines, fill in where walls are with heavy lines, right over the guidelines. When you complete this process, you'll have an exact duplicate in miniature of the real spaces.

TRIAL SOLUTIONS

When you've brought the drawing this far, don't do anything more to it. This applies even if you're just thinking about modifying an existing kitchen. Resist the impulse to go directly to a final drawing. This drawing will be your *base drawing* on which to sketch various ideas on tracing-paper *overlays*.

Tape a second piece of tracing paper over the base drawing, aligning grids on top and bottom sheets. Label this sheet with a number 1 in the corner so you can identify it. You'll be able to see the heavy lines of the first drawing right through the overlay sheet. As a starting point, draw in guidelines 1 foot (wall cabinets) and 2 feet (base cabinets) from any walls where you're thinking of putting cabinets.

Non-standard cabinet depths are often entirely possible, so don't feel locked in by these cabinet guidelines. When guidelines are drawn in, block in the design you've got in mind. See sample trial solution at right.

When you're done with sheet 1, take an important step. Pull sheet 1 off the base drawing and put on another sheet of tracing paper. Label this sheet 2. Now ask yourself: "If I never had the first idea I just took off the board, how would I make a kitchen out of this space?"

After you've done a second trial solution, do a third. Keep this up until you start repeating yourself. Trial solutions don't have to be carefully drawn. Freehand work with a felt-tip pen is good enough. But the scale of counters and appliances must be close to correct. The purpose of this exercise is to free your thinking. Ideas and details may occur to you that you hadn't thought of. Jot down these ideas or sketch them so you can compare them with each other.

Your first thoughts may have been the right ones. Or your first thoughts may have been blocking you from thinking further. Getting those first thoughts out on sheet 1 lets you have a look at what next occurs to you. If you run out of ideas, review the basic layouts on pages 54-55, and make sure you've considered them all.

Analyzing Trial Solutions—Don't try to weigh the relative merits of solutions as you draw them. Critical analysis comes after all trial solutions are on paper, with the work patterns sketched in. Go through each sheet and draw in the work pattern, usually a triangle shape. Work patterns are discussed on page 56.

Measure all sides of the triangle and note the total length on your drawing. The total length of a work pattern should not be much less than 12 feet,

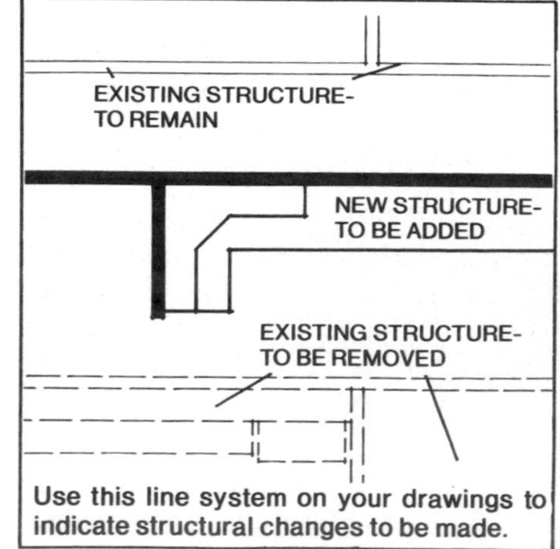

Use this line system on your drawings to indicate structural changes to be made.

nor much more than 22 feet. Study any of your trial solutions that exceed these limits and try to rearrange things to correct the work pattern. If the work pattern can't be corrected, discard that solution.

Then check traffic patterns. Use a colored pencil to shade in the traffic patterns the layout will generate. Ideally, traffic patterns should not intersect work patterns. Again, rework trial solutions that have problems. If rework isn't possible, discard that solution.

After the trial solutions have been reviewed for work patterns and traffic patterns, consider each of the following in turn. Has a place been provided for spectators, assistants and guests? Does the trial solution fit fairly closely with existing windows, doors, plumbing, gas piping and wiring? Does the trial solution present any obvious safety hazards, such as oven doors that open across doorways or window curtains hanging over a stove? Can you see ways to get proper lighting, ventilation, heating and cooling where it's needed?

Consider the practicality of each trial solution. How well will each work as a finished kitchen? Kitchen utensils and supplies should be stored so they're readily available where they'll be used. Simultaneous functions shouldn't conflict. Think through the preparation of several typical meals to see what problems there might be.

Then consider cost and degree of difficulty. Major window and door changes in a masonry house or major plumbing changes under a concrete slab are difficult and expensive. Relocating an interior doorway or running a few extra plumbing lines in a crawl space is relatively easy and inexpensive.

If the work or cost for a particular design is too much, the remodel can be split into several phases for completion over a period of time. If the work isn't a problem but the cost is, check with your mortgage lender to see if financing is feasible. If the cost is no obstacle but time and effort is, check with subcontractors about doing some of the specialized work. Sooner or later you'll arrive at the kitchen design that's right for you. Then make a drawing.

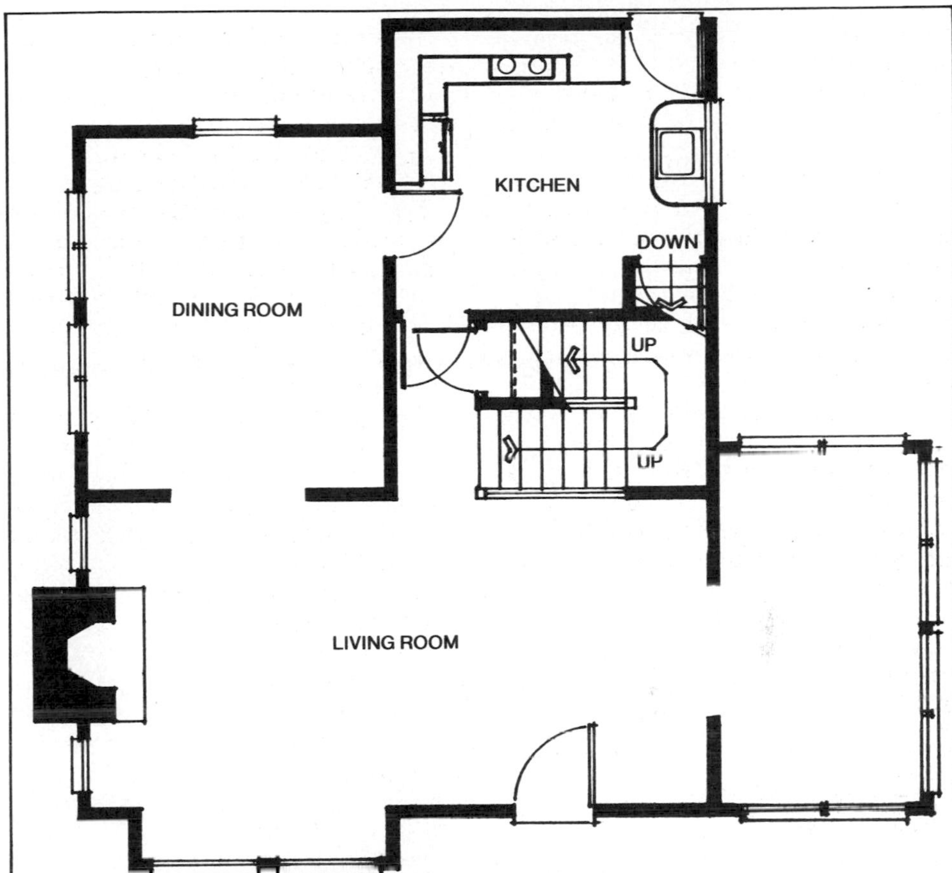

A finished base drawing shows kitchen area and surrounding rooms.

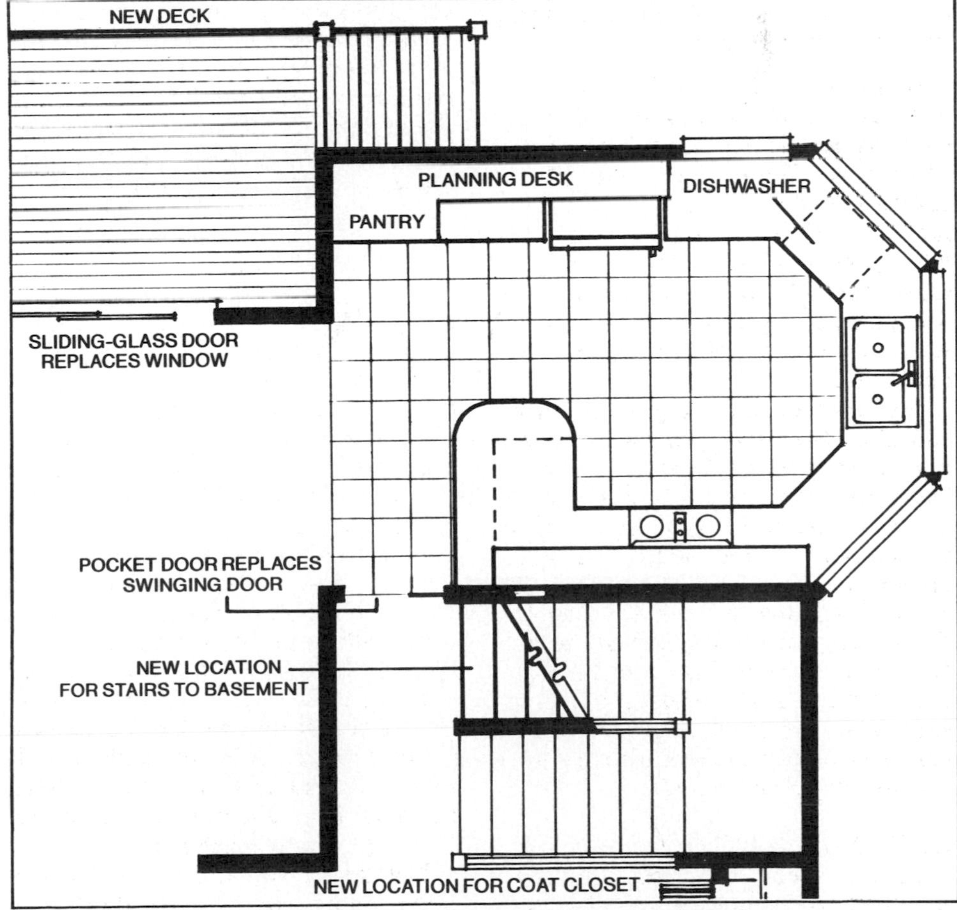

Trial solution for kitchen shown above is one of several workable alternatives.

Preparing to Build

Tearing out your old kitchen can be dirty and dangerous. Use correct safety equipment. Wear safety goggles, hard hat and gloves. Ear plugs prevent damage to hearing when using power tools.

Preparation is the key to a successful kitchen project. It's tempting to rush into the job, but preparing before you start is smarter. This chapter covers major preparations to be made, and why they're important.

PERMITS, CODES AND INSPECTIONS

Work beyond the minor and nonstructural requires a building permit. Electrical or plumbing work also requires a permit. If you're installing a kitchen in a new house or in a new addition, you should already have your permits. If you're remodeling, call your local building department before you do anything else.

Building department requirements and procedures vary widely from place to place, so find out what the details are in your area. Most building departments can supply information sheets detailing the entire permit and inspection process.

BUILDING CODES

Most local building codes are based on the master codes published by regional groups. In the western United States, master codes are the Uniform Building Code, the Uniform Plumbing Code and the Uniform Mechanical Code. These are issued every 3 years by the International Conference of Building Officials (ICBO) in Whittier, California.

In the East and Midwest, master codes are issued by Building Officials and Code Administrators International (BOCA). In the Southeast, they are issued by the Southern Conference of Building Officials. For electrical work, the master code is the National Electrical Code, issued by the National Fire Protection Association (NFPA), Boston, Massachusetts. *Even if a master code has been adopted in your area, local variations can apply.*

If you doubt whether or not something will comply with local codes, don't guess. Call up and ask. Or stop in at your local library and look it up in the codes. If you want a more permanent reference, the building department can sell you a copy of each of the codes or direct you to a place where you can buy them.

BUILDING OFFICIALS

In building-safety agencies, all employees above the secretarial level are known collectively as "building officials." These include plan checkers, administrators and others, as well as building inspectors. When applying for a permit in all but the smallest jurisdictions, you'll deal with someone other than the inspector who will actually inspect your work.

Deal carefully with building officials. They are public officials with great power. Most take their responsibilities seriously. If you approach them with a casual attitude about code compliance, this may prompt them to look at your plans and work even more critically than they ordinarily would. This, in turn, may hold up the job and make your life miserable.

Take codes seriously. Let building officials know you do. Dealing with building officials can sometimes be frustrating, but it is necessary. In short, work with officials, not against them.

The inspector may look at your work in great detail. This attention on his part is not malicious. The house you're working on will be standing for many years. It may have many owners and occupants after you. Most building officials feel a strong obligation to the health and safety of all present and future owners and occupants. Whether you're a contractor or an owner-builder, you're also responsible for their health and safety.

BUILDING INSPECTIONS

The building inspector will inspect your work as various stages are completed. It's up to you to notify the building department and arrange for inspections at proper times. Ask the department at what stages they require building, electrical and plumbing inspections. Most departments require an inspection when rough framing is complete, another when rough plumbing and wiring is installed, and a final inspection when the job is complete. Initial plumbing and electrical inspections are usually done while the framing is still exposed so the inspector can see the work.

PAPER WORK

In most jurisdictions, you'll need at least a detailed scale floor plan, and possibly other detailed drawings and information. Include all structural information, such as lumber sizes and material descriptions, for both new work and the existing structure. If you're making changes to outside walls, you'll probably need exterior-elevation drawings.

Interior elevations can be useful as a visualizing tool, even if they're not required by the building department. An example is shown below. If you've drawn them, make a copy for the building department anyway. It will help you get your plans approved. For information on drawing plans, see pages 59-61.

Get a building application form and fill it out at home, rather than at the building department. Print in ink, or type. Prepare a list of any technical questions and get them answered when you go to file the application. Get the name of the person answering your questions, in case you have to cite these answers to the inspector later on.

COSTS

Permit costs include the cost of inspections. Costs vary from place to place. Some jurisdictions may charge extra for reinspections. As a general rule, permit fees range from 0.5% to 3% of the cost of the work.

PURCHASING

Before you shop for materials, refer to your drawings and make material lists. If you're uncertain about material requirements, refer to Chapters 6 through 12 and read the appropriate section on the installation of that material. Separate the materials by supplier on separate sheets of paper.

Consult the Yellow Pages and make a list of suppliers you want to get quotations from. Then visit the suppliers you chose and get quotations for materials on your list. Don't settle for *estimates*, which do not commit the supplier to a firm price. Quotations should indicate exactly what the dealer proposes to supply, and should be priced item by item. You'll also need to know delivery terms and costs, payment terms and *lead times*. Lead time is the time from placement of order to delivery of goods.

Get at least three prices on each item. If the three prices are scattered over a range of 5% or so, that's normal. If prices vary much more than 5% on an item of significant value, get more quotations for that item until some of the prices group in about a 5% range.

Be wary of the sensationally low price. It may be legitimate—the result

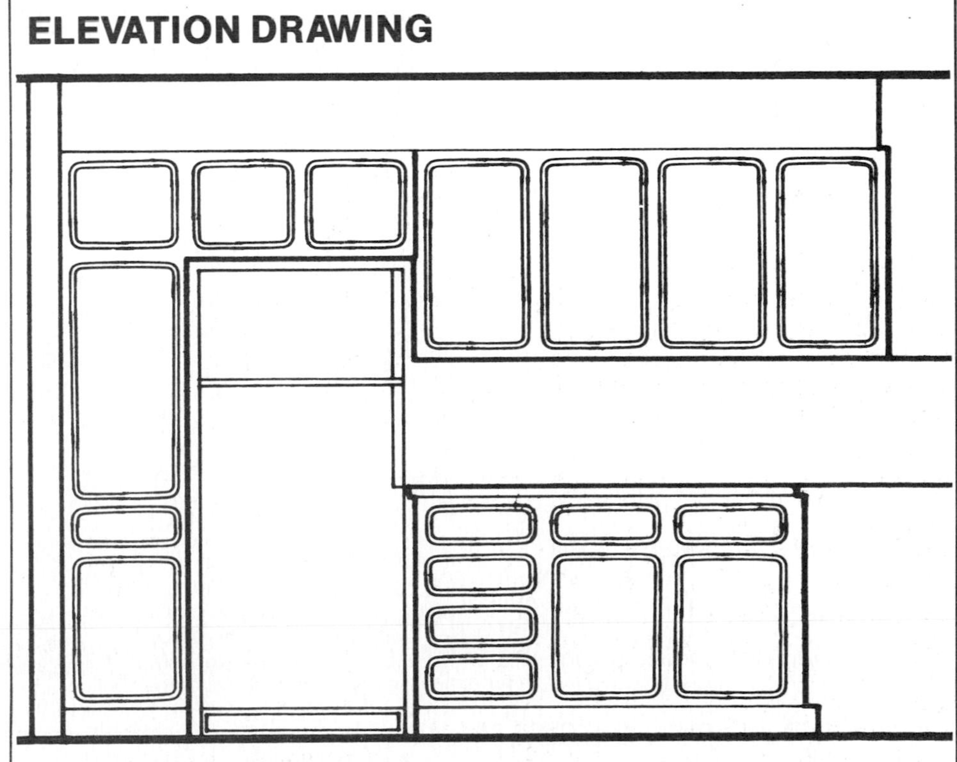

Your local building department may require elevation drawings of your kitchen. Even if they don't, the drawings are helpful in getting your plans approved.

of an oversupply or a closeout—or just efficient business operation. Or a mistake could have been made in the figures. Or the supplier may have misunderstood what you wanted. Double-check extremely low prices to avoid later corrections that may upset your job budget.

You may find one or more suppliers capable of supplying all the materials for the job. If so, ask if they will provide an additional discount if you give them the order for the whole job. Be sure their net price is at or below the sum of your separate quotations.

If payment is to be cash on delivery—COD is often required of owner-builders—ask about prompt-payment discounts. Many suppliers give these discounts to their open-account customers. You may get one if you ask.

COD is not a reflection on your credit status. Opening an account involves a lot of paper work for some suppliers. They don't often open accounts for one or two orders.

After you've got your quotations, take one more money-saving step. Visit every do-it-yourself store in your area. They often have loss-leaders or closeouts. Make sure you're getting first-quality, comparable goods, though. Comparative shopping is a lot of work, but it can cut the cost of the job by as much as 25%.

DISCONTINUED ITEMS

The problem of discontinued items occurs most often with appliances, floor coverings, plastic-laminate products and ceramic tile. Most manufacturers change their lines at least every year. Some add colors and patterns and discontinue others almost constantly. A critical element in your color scheme can suddenly become unobtainable. Have several alternative choices for all finish materials, including cabinets.

If you must have a particular vinyl flooring or plastic-laminate pattern, make your final selection early. Then buy the materials and store them. Or give the dealer a firm order, and a deposit if necessary, to hold the goods for you. Many dealers won't mind storing materials if they know they're already sold. But there is some risk in having the dealer store the materials. They could be sold in error. If possible, store critical items yourself.

PLANNING YOUR TIME

After you've done the space planning and money planning, do the time planning. Most people tend to *underestimate* the time a job will take. Remodeling work often takes longer than you think it will, especially if you're working in your spare time. Unforeseen problems come up—the cabinets you ordered are out of stock, your boss wants you to work some overtime. As a rule of thumb, double the amount of time you initially think an operation will take. You'll come out about on schedule. The following sequencing method will help you accurately plan the amount of time your kitchen project will take.

SEQUENCING

Use the chart below to help plan your job sequence. Rearrange items to suit your circumstances or inclinations. To sequence the job, start with the last procedure and review steps in reverse order. This makes it easier to see what needs to be done before you start the next operation, and you're less likely to miss a step.

Take your finished sequence sheet and pencil in approximate start and finish dates for each item. Note at what points in the sequence you'll need materials on hand to keep the work going. Working from the lead times your suppliers gave you—with any adjustments—note when you'll have to place orders to keep on schedule. Keep the finished sequence sheet with your plans and sketches, so you can refer to it.

SUPPLIER LEAD TIMES

Not all lead times can be trusted. With best intentions, suppliers sometimes make promises they or manufacturers can't keep.

If the materials are ordinary goods, such as 2x4 studs in a lumberyard, lead times will be short and missing items rare. If the lumberyard you pick does run out of studs, you can easily find another source. This is not the case with low-volume materials, such as custom-made cabinets and certain appliances.

If you need to special-order anything, do it well before you start the job. A week or so after the order is placed, the manufacturer should be able to provide your supplier with a

CONSTRUCTION SEQUENCE

Plan space.
Plan money.
Plan time.
Plan purchasing.
Obtain permit.
Set up temporary kitchen.
Remove all kitchen contents and decorations.
Seal off area.
Remove appliances.
Remove plumbing fixtures and cap off.
Remove electrical fixtures and cap off.
Remove countertops.
Remove cabinets.
Remove baseboards, trim and built-ins.
Remove finish-floor materials.
Remove wallcoverings.
Remove unwanted non-bearing walls.
Clean up and remove trash and debris.
Repair floors.
Shore up and remove unwanted bearing walls.
Revise and repair wall framing.
Revise and repair ceiling framing.
Install windows or exterior doors.
Revise and repair water supply.
Revise and repair drainage.
Revise and repair wiring.
Revise and repair insulation in exterior walls/floor/ceiling.
Clean up and remove trash and debris.
Get rough-in inspections.
Install drywall.
Tape and finish drywall.
Install other wall and ceiling finish materials.
Paint walls and ceiling.
Install interior doors.
Install floor coverings.
Install wall cabinets.
Install base cabinets.
Install cabinet trim.
Make countertops.
Install countertops.
Install countertop finish materials.
Install baseboards and trim.
Install and hook up finish plumbing.
Install and hook up finish electrical.
Install appliances.
Clean up and remove trash and debris.
Test all systems—repair and touch up as required.
Get final inspections.
Throw a kitchen-warming party.

Note: This sequence is a general one that will fit most kitchen remodeling jobs but by no means all. Feel free to add, subtract, or rearrange to suit your particular job conditions and preferences.

Use this list when sequencing your kitchen remodeling project. Start at bottom of list and review steps in reverse order. This way, you're less likely to miss a step.

projected shipping date. Shipping dates aren't infallible, but any information is a help.

You may have to place a deposit to secure the order. Have the supplier note on the receipt that the deposit is refundable if a reasonable, specific delivery date is not met.

Waiting for materials before you start the job can be frustrating. But cooking in the garage for two months while you wait for your new cabinets is even more frustrating.

TYPICAL SUPPLIER LEAD TIMES

Product	High volume, local stock	Low volume, factory or regional stock	Factory-made to order or custom made
Cabinets	2 to 10 days	1 to 6 weeks	3 to 13 weeks
Appliances	2 to 7 days	1 to 4 weeks	2 to 13 weeks
Plumbing fixtures & fittings	2 to 7 days	1 to 8 weeks	3 to 13 weeks
Lights & vents	2 to 10 days	1 to 8 weeks	3 to 13 weeks
Plastic laminates	2 to 10 days	2 to 8 weeks	
Ceramic tile	2 to 7 days	2 to 13 weeks	2 to 26 weeks
Butcher block	2 to 7 days	2 to 8 weeks	3 to 13 weeks
Floor covering	2 to 15 days	1 to 13 weeks	3 to 13 weeks
Brick & stone	2 to 14 days	2 to 8 weeks	1 to 26 weeks

Note: Lead times are approximate and can vary according to manufacturers and suppliers you're dealing with. Also, the state of the construction industry has a bearing on lead times. When building is brisk, both suppliers and manufacturers build up their inventories to meet demand. Many low-volume items can be obtained more quickly. But if building is booming, extreme demand can lead to spot shortages and backorders of even common materials. Conversely, during slow times, manufacturers and custom shops are usually more able and eager to get out a special or custom order without delay.

MATERIAL STORAGE

You'll need storage space for both inbound and outbound materials. Most incoming supplies will be transported on at least a medium-size truck, so plan for truck access to the storage area. Some items should be placed under cover, others secured against possible theft. The ideal storage area is an enclosed two-car garage. Clear out enough space to store all materials. This may involve parking a car outside for the duration of the project. The driveway should provide easy access for delivery and materials will be under cover. Keep the garage locked to discourage theft.

If you don't have a garage, shed or other enclosed storage area, the storage problem is more complicated. Materials such as lumber can be stacked outside and covered until used. Block any such stacks off the ground to prevent moisture damage. Unload materials at the storage location to avoid double handling.

More valuable or fragile materials should be stored inside the house. These include materials that might be stolen or damaged by weather. Look for a room that's convenient to the work area. If necessary, redistribute some of the furniture to other rooms. You'll need a space about the same size as the kitchen. Don't use the kitchen for storage unless it has an out-of-the-way corner of adequate size.

CLEARING THE FIELD

If you're remodeling an existing kitchen, you'll need to remove and store food, kitchen utensils, appliances, and old cabinets and hardware you wish to save. You'll also have to set up temporary cooking and eating facilities.

Load a large cardboard box with cooking and eating utensils you'll need for temporary use. Then load a small cardboard box with cleaning supplies and tools you'll need in your temporary eating facilities. Finally, pack up the rest of the movable kitchen contents and store them in an out-of-the-way place.

Provide storage space for salvaged old cabinets, appliances and other items you'll be reusing. You can store the movable appliances at this time. For information on removing and disposing of old cabinets, see page 68.

SECURING THE AREA

The early phases of remodeling are dirty and incredibly dusty. Take measures to keep dirt and dust from migrating through the house. Remove all heating/cooling registers and block the ducts with cardboard. Fasten cardboard in place with duct tape. Close off cold-air returns to the heater also.

Closets or pantries that are not going to be worked on should be taped shut, especially at the bottom. Install door sweeps, made of two pieces of duct tape, on the bottoms of any doors leading to the work area.

In large open areas, borrow a trick from the remodelers who work on large department stores. Use lengths of 1x2 and screws to attach large plastic dropcloths to the ceiling to screen off the work area. Fasten screws into the ceiling framing, not just the drywall. Use other lengths of 1x2 to weight down the bottom edges. On commercial remodels, 6-mil polyethylene or canvas dropcloths are used. But the thin plastic dropcloths sold in paint stores are much safer for home use. If someone steps on the plastic, it will more likely rip than bring the 1x2 crashing down.

All protective coverings should stay in place until all heavy sanding and cleanup is done. This is usually at the end of the drywall taping described on pages 121-122. If you're planning to spray paint or varnish, leave dropcloths up until finished.

REQUIRED TOOLS

You don't need many tools for tearout work, but the right tools make the job easier. One of the most useful tools is a hammer with *ripping claws.* Ripping claws are straighter than the hooked claws you find on most hammers. They're more versatile for tearing things apart. You'll also need a brick set, a 3-inch scraper, a 3/32-inch pin punch or a nailset, a utility knife, assorted screwdrivers, small and large adjustable wrenches and a small, flat pry bar.

Pry bars are made by several manufacturers. Two popular trade names are Wonderbar and Superbar. The forerunners of these pry bars were handmade from lengths of automobile leaf spring. These days, they're available in almost any hardware store. Get one that's fairly thin, sharp-edged, and spring-tempered.

Brick sets are all steel, including the handle. They're similar in appearance to a broad-blade cold chisel. But the blade has a bevel only on one side, like a wood chisel.

Tools for specific tearout procedures described in this book are listed where they are used. Look over your kitchen in detail to get a better idea of what specific tools you'll need, such as screwdrivers.

As an additional safety precaution, turn off breakers to the kitchen circuits before doing tearout work. Wall-removal procedures start on page 69, floor-covering removal page 68 and subfloor removal page 71.

APPLIANCE REMOVAL

Remove all free-standing appliances. A hand truck is helpful for this. If electric appliances are wired in rather than plugged in, turn off the power before unwiring them. To remove gas appliances, turn off the quarter-turn gas-shutoff valve before disconnecting the appliance gas line. Quarter-turn gas-shutoff valves have a flat blade-type handle. When the handle is parallel to the pipe, the valve is *on.* When the handle is perpendicular to the pipe, the valve is *off.* Check the appliance pilot lights, if any, to make sure the valve is shut off completely. Disconnect the gas line on the appliance side of the shutoff valve. See photo below.

In some areas, the gas company prohibits work on gas systems by anyone but licensed personnel. Other gas companies prohibit work by anyone other than their own employees. Luckily, companies with this policy usually provide this service free. Call your gas company for further information.

The best way to avoid hazards from dismantled electrical circuitry while you're working is to leave circuit off until done. If you have to turn circuit back on and work near wires, cut off exposed end of each wire. Then screw a small wire nut on each wire and fold wires back into box out of the way.

Exposed utility connections should be capped while work is in progress. Securing electrical connections is shown above. Capping water lines is described on page 80, sewer lines on page 84. Cap lines as you encounter them during the tearout phase.

TEAROUT PROCEDURES

Brute-force methods are *not* recommended in the removal of appliances, sinks, cabinets and so forth. Brute force has its place in some demolition work, such as the removal of masonry walls or old concrete. For most interior work, tearout is best accomplished by removing all fasteners, and the judicious use of wedging and leverage.

Whenever something won't move, check for hidden fasteners. Then ask yourself how you can apply some leverage or wedging action. Let the tools do the work. Cabinets and other fixtures must be removed carefully if you wish to reinstall them later, or salvage them for use elsewhere.

Never tear into a wall, floor or ceiling until you know the location of wires and pipes. If you carefully dismantle cabinets, walls and other structural members, you can usually leave existing plumbing and electrical lines undisturbed and intact. Then you can work with them easily, as described on pages 96-97.

Some quarter-turn gas-shutoff valves have a lever handle, some have a flat handle with a hole in it. They work the same. Both types are shown here, where several appliances hook up to one gas line.

SINK REMOVAL

Dismantle and remove the sink *trap.* The trap connects the sink to the drain line inside the wall. The trap pieces are usually connected by a series of *slip nuts.* See drawing at right. If the trap won't come apart, you can avoid mangling the surrounding pipes by cutting the trap loose with a hacksaw. You can then work with the remaining pipe after the sink and cabinets are removed.

Turn off the water at the *water supply-pipe valves* and disconnect or cut the *risers.* See drawing at right. If supply-pipe valves won't shut off all the way, or there aren't any, turn off the main valve that supplies water to the house. Then remove the supply-pipe valves. You can clean them and put them back, or just cap the pipe stubs that project from the wall.

Wall-hung sinks are connected to a wall bracket by one or more clamps. Remove the clamps and *carefully* lift the sink off the wall bracket. Most old wall-hung sinks are heavy cast iron, and are usually stuck fast to the bracket. A few heavy upward blows with a length of 2x4 will usually jar the sink loose without lifting it off the bracket. Have a helper steady the sink while you do this, just in case the sink unexpectedly jumps off the bracket.

Most modern sinks are top-mounted in the countertop. Lightweight enameled-steel or stainless-steel sinks can be left in the countertop and removed with it. Heavier cast iron top-mounted sinks should be removed from the countertop. Support the sink from underneath with several wood props and unscrew the *anchor clips* underneath. Then lift out the sink carefully.

COUNTERTOP REMOVAL

In most cases, professionally installed countertops are attached from underneath with screws. Remove all screws and ease the top loose with your flat pry bar. The trick is to find all the screws. Once you get an end loose, you can wedge the top up with the pry bar and use a flashlight to look for remaining screws.

On owner-built tops, you may find almost any sort of attaching method. If you can't find and remove all fasteners, tap the pry bar between top and cabinets and lever the top up and off.

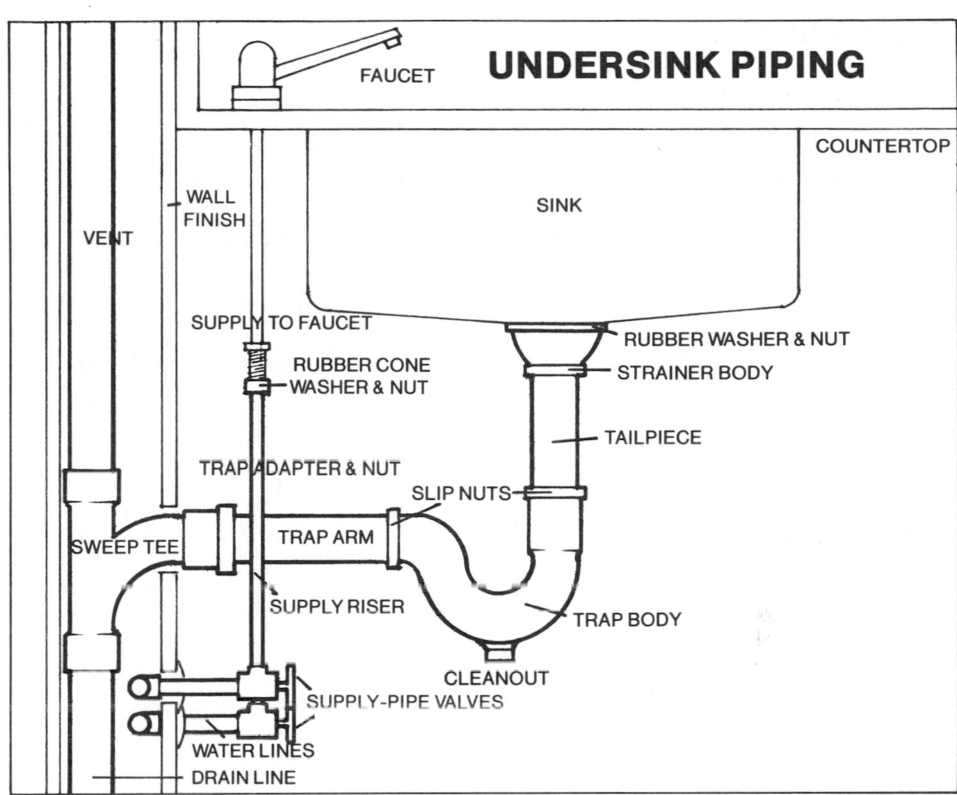

This drawing shows parts of typical sink and faucet. Your sink may include additional or different parts.

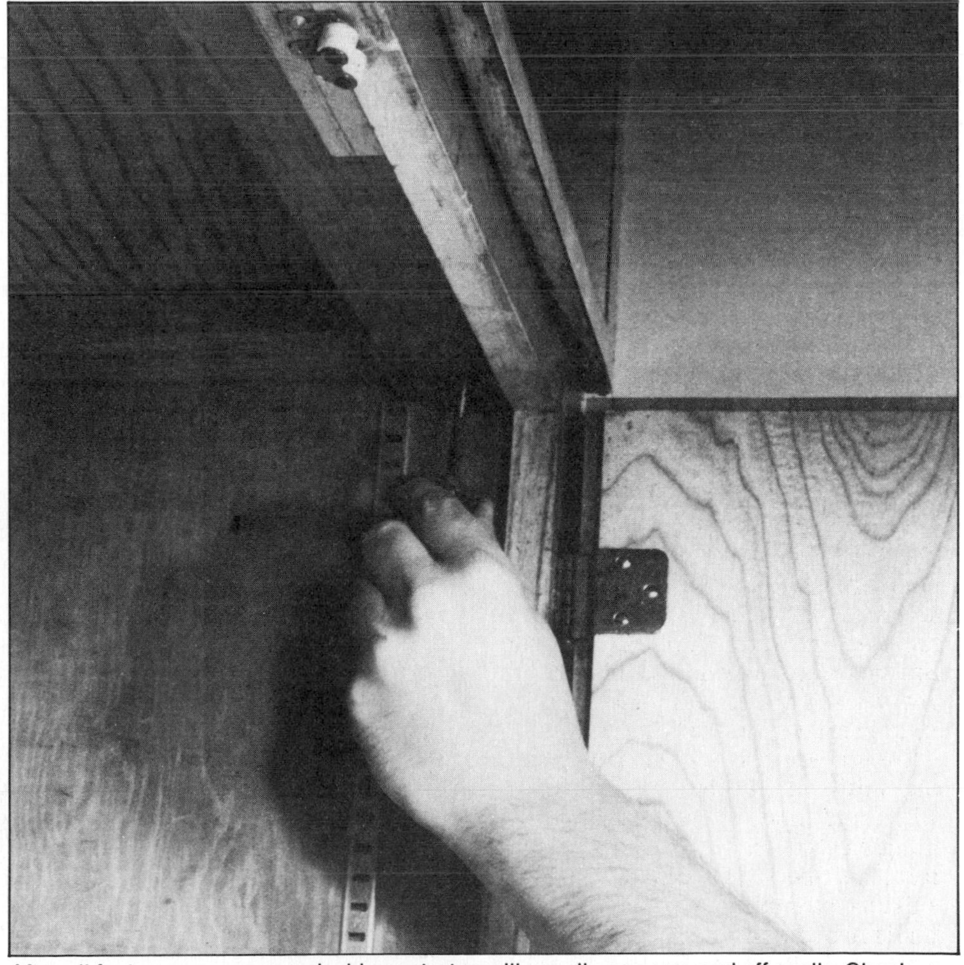

After all fasteners are removed, old countertop will usually come up and off easily. Check underneath for hidden screws and fasteners.

CABINET REMOVAL

Starting with the upper cabinets, look inside for mounting screws or nails that attach them to the wall or ceiling. If there are screws or nails holding individual cabinets together, remove these first. Then remove cabinets one at a time. Support the cabinet while removing all mounting screws. Lower the cabinet to the top of the base cabinets. If you don't want to save the cabinets, nail wood props to them for support. If you want to save the cabinets, have a helper hold up the cabinet while you remove the last of the screws.

If the cabinets are nailed on, drive the short end of the pry bar up behind the cabinet and ease it loose at the bottom. Then pull out at the bottom of the cabinet to lever the upper nails out of the wall.

If the base cabinets are fastened together, remove screws or nails before you remove mounting screws that attach the cabinets to the wall or floor. The base cabinets should then lift out easily. If they're attached with nails, drive the short end of the pry bar between the wall and the top rear of the cabinet. To avoid damaging the wall, use a nail and hammer to locate studs and center the prybar over them. Then lever the cabinet away from the wall.

Cabinet Removal Problems—Some cabinets are nailed at the back and on one or more sides. Remove the side nails first. To get them out, position your pin punch or nailset in the center of each nailhead. Then drive the nail, head and all, right through the cabinet. This technique also works on badly corroded or stripped screws.

Some older cabinets were built in place rather than being built and then installed. The best way to deal with these is to determine the building sequence the original builder followed. Then reverse the process, prying off one piece at a time.

At some point, you may have to drive a pry bar between a disposable piece of cabinet or trim and a piece you want to save. In that case, use your hammer to tap the 3-inch scraper into the joint. Drive the pry bar between the scraper and the disposable piece. The scraper should distribute the prying force well enough to prevent serious damage to the piece you want to save. See photo at right.

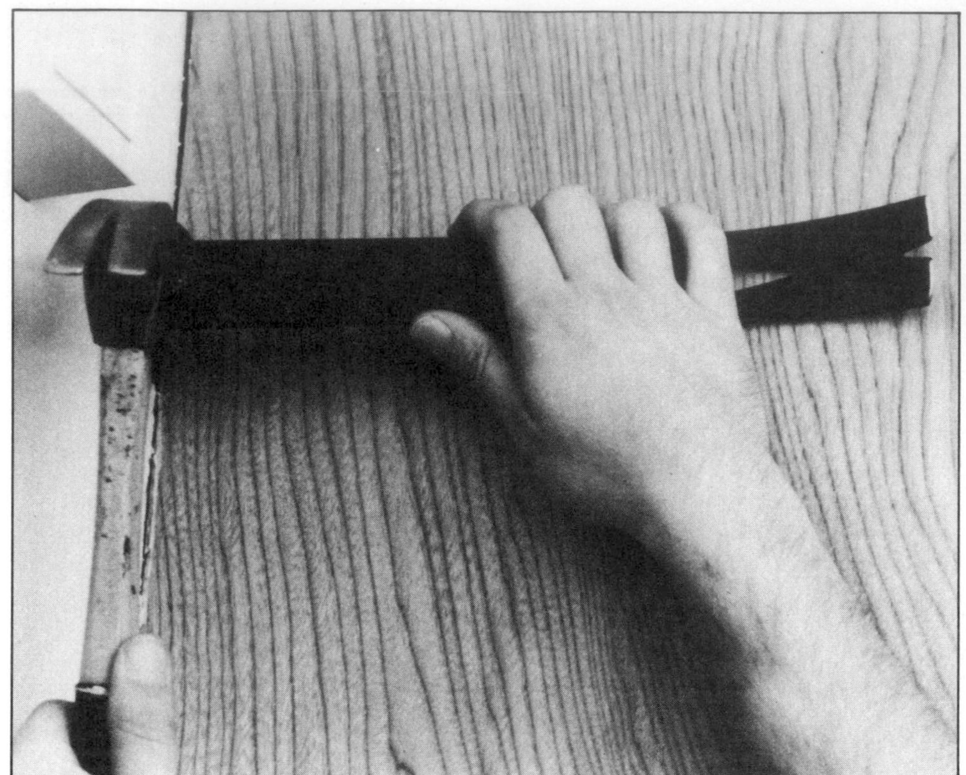

Wall cabinets that are nailed on, can be pried off wall. When replacing cabinets or installing new ones, use screws, not nails.

FLOOR COVERING REMOVAL

Most kitchen floors are covered with a resilient floor material, either sheet flooring or resilient tiles. A few homes have kitchens with wood floors, and occasionally, ceramic tile floors. Removal methods for all these floor coverings are discussed here.

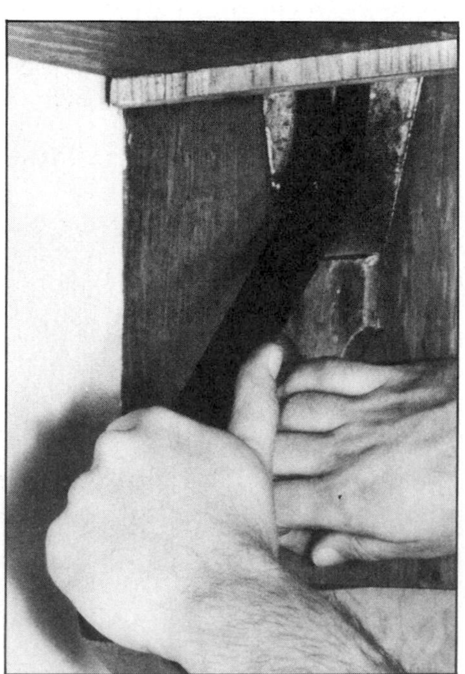

A scraper can be helpful in protecting adjacent surfaces while tearing out old fixtures.

Wood Floors—If your kitchen has a wood floor, consider refinishing it. At first glance, the old wood may not look like it's worth refinishing, but some judicious patching can greatly improve the prospects. In some kitchens, flooring under cabinets can be removed and used to patch the exposed areas. Normally, you can't find new flooring that exactly matches the old.

To take up a small section of wood strip flooring, either for patching material or to remove damaged strips, make two *pocket cuts* across the strips to be removed. Use a circular saw set to the thickness of the strip flooring. Make two cuts 1/2 or 3/4 inch apart. Remove the wood between the cuts with a hammer and wood chisel. Repeat at the other end of the strips. Strips can then be carefully pried up and reused in another location, if desired. To remove a single, damaged strip, split it down the middle with a chisel, then pry out the pieces.

To put down a small section in the middle of the floor, proceed the same as for new flooring, page 151. When you install the last strip in the patch, cut or plane the tongue off the strip and face-nail the strip in position. Sand and finish the floor as described on page 152.

Ceramic Tile Floors—Ceramic tile makes a great floor, but can present problems when you need to replace it. Once a ceramic tile floor is worn out, there's no effective way to refinish it, as you often can with a wood floor. The only two approaches are to rip it out or cover it up. If the ceramic tile was originally laid with a mastic adhesive, chip off the tiles with a hammer and *brick set.* A brick set is a chisel used to cut bricks, and can be bought wherever masonry tools are sold. Long sleeves, gloves and safety glasses or a face shield are required for this job.

If the ceramic tile was *mudset*—laid in a bed of wet mortar 1/2 to 2 inches thick—use the cover-up method described below, if at all possible. If both the tile and the mortar bed are in bad condition or breaking up, remove the entire floor down to the joists or concrete subfloor. Frame floors are usually constructed as shown at right. Joists under mudset tile often have tapered tops to minimize cracking. After removing tile and mortar bed, nail *scabs*, either 2x4s or 2x6s, alongside each joist to restore the bearing surface. Then lay a new subfloor as a base for the new flooring.

If the old ceramic tile floor is sound, and the extra floor height presents no problems, you can cover it with new flooring. Sand the tile surface thoroughly with coarse sandpaper. Then put down a layer of plywood underlayment with construction adhesive. Construction adhesive comes in cartridges to fit a caulking gun. Follow the instructions on the cartridge for flooring and underlayment work.

Resilient Floors—Decide whether you have to remove the existing resilient flooring. Not all old floor covering has to be removed. If the adhesive is holding and the surface is fairly smooth, old covering can serve as a base for the new. Just repair it and leave it in place. Reglue loose areas, cover with a layer of plastic wrap and add weights to force the surface flat. If the floor covering will not lie flat, soften it using a warm clothes iron over several layers of newspaper.

If your house has a wood subfloor and you're leaving the old floor covering in place, examine the subfloor from underneath. Use a screwdriver or icepick to probe around the sink area for signs of wood decay. If the subfloor is damaged, you'll probably

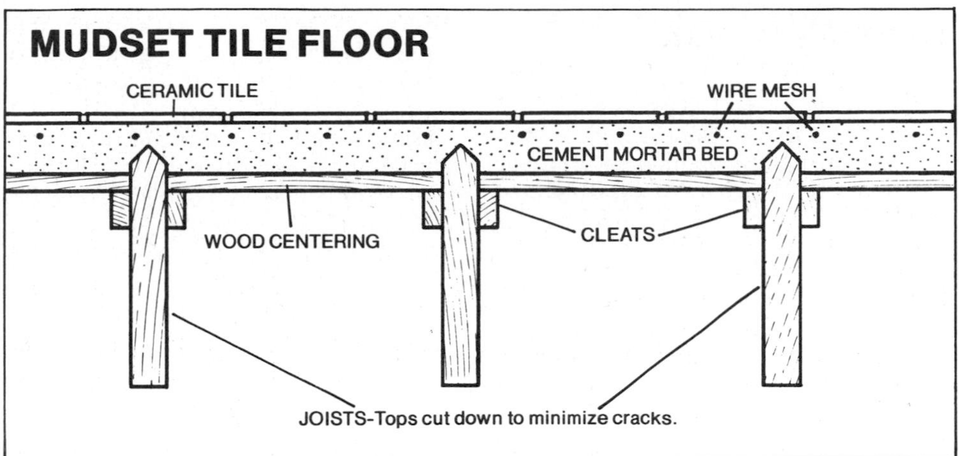

Mudset tile floors often have tapered joists. Scabs or cleats should be nailed alongside joists to provide bearing surface for new floor.

have to remove the finish flooring to make repairs. For more complete instructions on inspecting and repairing floors, see pages 132-135.

Broken areas, missing tiles, and miscellaneous dings and dents can be repaired with floor-repair compound. Do not repair these imperfections with materials with high shrinkage or low strength, such as plaster of Paris or drywall-joint compound. They'll pound out or disintegrate over the years.

Once the existing floor covering is repaired, you can remove meeting strips where the covering meets floor coverings in adjoining rooms. But it's better to leave meeting strips in place until just before you lay down the new flooring. This protects the edges of adjoining floor coverings.

Old floor coverings that are spot-glued or badly loosened can be eased up with the scraper and flat pry bar. Some of the backing will usually stay

If nothing else works, use hammer and chisel to remove old floor covering.

on the floor. This can be leveled off with the brick set and a hammer. Avoid digging up the subfloor while doing this.

Loose-laid sheet flooring can be rolled up and hauled off. It is sometimes helpful to slit sheet flooring into smaller pieces with a utility knife before removal.

WALL REMOVAL

If you've followed applicable procedures in this chapter so far, your kitchen is now stripped to the point where the original builder was just before the finish installation started. In many kitchen remodels, this is all the tear-out that needs to be done. But your project may require you to clear the way for major structural changes or repairs.

You can make small structural changes just before new work is done. Big changes, such as removing whole walls, should be done now. This section covers wall removal, step-by-step. Follow as many steps as necessary to accommodate the changes you'll make. For instance, if you're running new electrical or plumbing lines through a wall, you need only remove enough wall covering to provide access for the work to be done.

Drywall Removal—Use a utility knife to score deeply along all corners where drywall to be removed meets adjoining walls and ceiling. This prevents joint-reinforcing tape at corners from peeling off adjoining surfaces when drywall is removed.

To remove an entire wall surface, start at one side, near the bottom. Carefully use a hammer to knock a small hole in the drywall. Use the hammer claws or the hooked end of your flat pry bar to pull off chunks of drywall. Proceed carefully so you don't damage wiring or plumbing that might be in the wall. Remove nails as you get to them. When you've removed several square feet of drywall, you may find it easier to pull off some pieces by hand. Never hit or push the drywall inward—you might damage the opposite wall surface. Work carefully when removing drywall at corners. Use your utility knife to cut loose any tape holding drywall at the corner.

To remove only a section of drywall, mark pencil lines to indicate both sides of the proposed tearout area. Use a level or plumb bob to make lines exactly vertical. Keep in mind that the actual sides of the cutout should be centered over the nearest studs outside the proposed tearout area.

Starting at one side of the tearout area, hit the drywall sharply with a hammer several inches to the inside of the line. This should make a hole in the drywall the size of the hammer face. Slide the end of a tape measure sideways through the hole until it hits the nearest stud outside the tearout area. Transfer this measurement to the outside of the wall. Mark a second vertical line to indicate the side of the stud facing the tearout area. Repeat this process at the other side of the tearout area.

Unless you're removing a floor-to-ceiling section of drywall, use a framing square, pencil and straightedge to mark lines indicating the top and bottom of the cutout. Top and bottom lines should be exactly perpendicular to sides of cutout.

Make rough cuts along the outside vertical lines. At each cut, gently pry out the drywall attached to the stud to pop the nail heads. Remove nails and make final cuts centered over the studs. This provides a nailing surface for the edges of replacement drywall. Then make top and bottom cuts.

To cut drywall, score repeatedly with a utility knife until you've gone all the way through. Also cut a hand opening at the bottom side of the tearout area. Pull off the drywall in chunks, starting at the bottom. Be alert for places where the drywall you're removing is still attached to adjoining surfaces you wish to keep intact. Use a utility knife to cut these attachments free.

Plaster Removal—Removing an entire plaster wall is messy but straightforward. Use a hammer and brick set to separate the plaster to be removed from adjoining walls and ceiling. Keep the brick set at an extreme angle to avoid disturbing lath underneath and damaging plaster on adjoining walls. Drive the short end of your pry bar into the plaster at the center of the wall. Do not disturb the lath while doing this. Pry plaster off the lath in chunks, working your way out to the wall edges. Most plaster walls are edged with wood strips for leveling purposes. These are called *plaster grounds.* Remove these as you find them.

When all the plaster is off, remove the lath. Pry it off a piece at a time. Be careful not to hurt yourself on the many small nails in the lath. At adjoining walls, you may find that the ends of the lath extend behind the adjoining lath. If so, start at the bottom and ease out the free ends of a dozen or so pieces. Slide the brick set in behind these pieces and chop off nails holding them. Then work your way up the wall, levering each successive lath piece downward to pull its nail out. Do not pull lath directly toward you. This may damage plaster on the adjoining wall. See drawing below.

Removing part of a plaster wall is more difficult. The plaster to remain must not be dislodged from the lath behind it. The quickest but messiest method of removal is to use a circular saw with a *carbide-tip blade.* Do not use any other blade—the plaster and nails in the lath will destroy it.

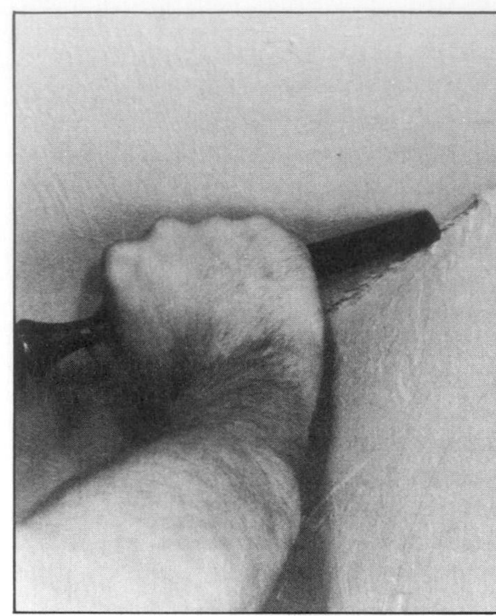

Before removing plaster, cut along corners with a hammer and chisel. Don't knock lath loose from back of plaster.

The safest way to cut plaster is to make a *plunge cut* near the bottom and push the saw up the wall. A plunge cut is made by holding the saw in one position with the blade centered over the cut line and raised slightly off the

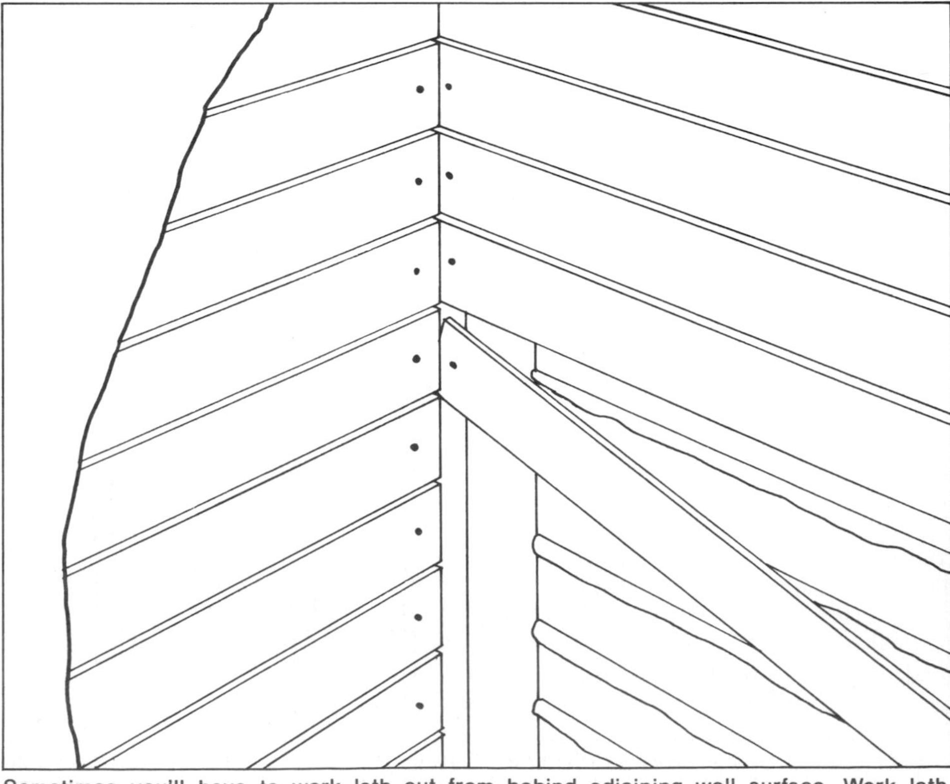

Sometimes you'll have to work lath out from behind adjoining wall surface. Work lath downward—don't pull lath outward from wall.

wall surface. The moving blade is then eased into the plaster until it bottoms out, then pushed forward along the cut line. This makes a fountain of plaster dust, so wear protective clothing, a mask and goggles. Set the saw blade only as deep as the bottom of the lath. Hold the saw firmly; it may kick back as you're cutting.

Cut slowly so the blade speed stays up and vibration stays down. If you have a hose-type vacuum, have a helper move the hose nozzle ahead of the saw as you cut. This catches most of the dust.

FRAMING REMOVAL

Before you remove wall framing, determine if you are working on a *bearing wall* or a *non-bearing wall.* See pages 106-108 to help make your determination. You can remove non-bearing walls at this time. You can also remove wall coverings from bearing walls. But bearing-wall framing should not be removed until you've provided adequate shoring to support the load the wall carries. Do not remove the wall until you're ready to build a permanent replacement for it. Temporary shoring should not substitute for a bearing wall any longer than absolutely necessary.

If you remove the wall covering from a bearing wall and leave the framing for more than a few days, brace it to prevent lateral movement. Nail on a 1x4 diagonal brace, extending from the top plate to the bottom plate. Nail the brace at each stud. Drive the nails all the way in. See drawing below. The nails used for this job are called *duplex nails.* A duplex nail has two heads, about 1/4 inch apart. Drive a duplex nail in to the first head. The second head protrudes so you can pull the nail easily.

Other than the required shoring techniques for bearing walls shown on page 108, removal is the same for both bearing and non-bearing walls. Use a circular saw to cut diagonally through the middle of each stud to be removed. Then pull the cut pieces off the nails at the top and bottom plates. Use a handsaw to cut the ends of the top and bottom plates flush with adjoining walls, then pry the plates loose.

TRASH DISPOSAL

Tearout work can make an unbelievable pile of trash. Remove trash from the work area on a daily basis—more frequently if it gets in the way of your work. You can put some of it in your garbage cans. But in most areas, ordinary garbage cans filled with 150 pounds of broken plaster will be left sitting at the curb forever.

You can sell old appliances and cabinets to offset some of the cost of your new kitchen. The easiest way to get rid of the bulkiest of the trash, the old cabinets, is to offer them to friends or neighbors. Or use the cabinets as storage units in another part of the house.

If you use a fireplace or wood stove in the winter, cut and stack the wood debris for kindling. Use a portable circular saw with a carbide-tip blade, because nails and other fasteners in the wood can ruin an ordinary saw blade.

Trash that can't be sold, given away or recycled will have to be thrown out. If you have access to a truck, you can make a few trips to the local dump. If you can't get a truck, check the newspaper classified section under "light hauling."

Individuals or companies that remove trash usually charge by amount of trash to be hauled and its location. The price is usually less if you put all the trash in one pile easily accessible to a truck.

If you have a lot of trash, call a dumpster service. Dumpsters are large trash containers that commercial businesses use. You've probably seen them behind the local supermarket. Dumpsters come in sizes that hold from 2 to 54 cubic yards of trash. Most dumpster companies have temporary drop and pickup services that are fairly economical. Provide enough space for the dumpster and access for its delivery truck.

TEMPORARY FACILITIES

If the kitchen can't be used during the remodel, you'll need to set up temporary cooking facilities. These don't have to be elaborate, but enough to get by with comfortably.

The best temporary facilities are informal and removed from the work area. One option is a travel trailer, motor home or other RV with cooking facilities. Even trailered boats with a galley can be used. If you're a camper or backpacker, use your camping gear. The family should be familiar with the equipment and the informal camping menus.

A bathroom, laundry room or garage with a sink can be used for washing dishes, and food preparation if large enough. Because of possible health hazards, don't use a bathroom for both kitchen and bathroom service. In other words, don't set up a kitchen in your only bathroom.

In a family room or dining room, set up a card table or folding table for portable cooking appliances, such as

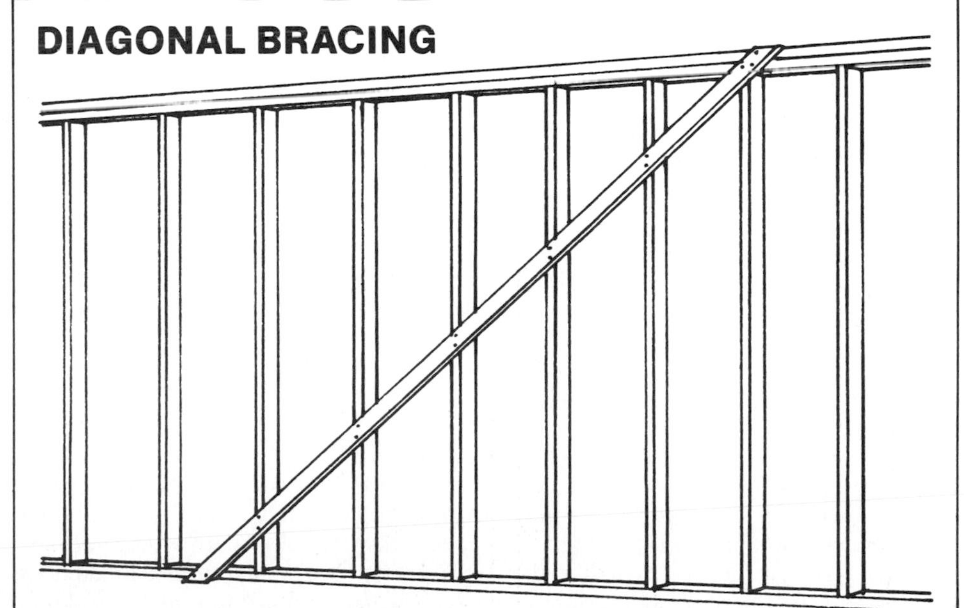

Use temporary diagonal bracing when you have to remove wall-finish material from both sides of bearing wall. Brace is best put on after you strip one side of wall, but before you strip other side.

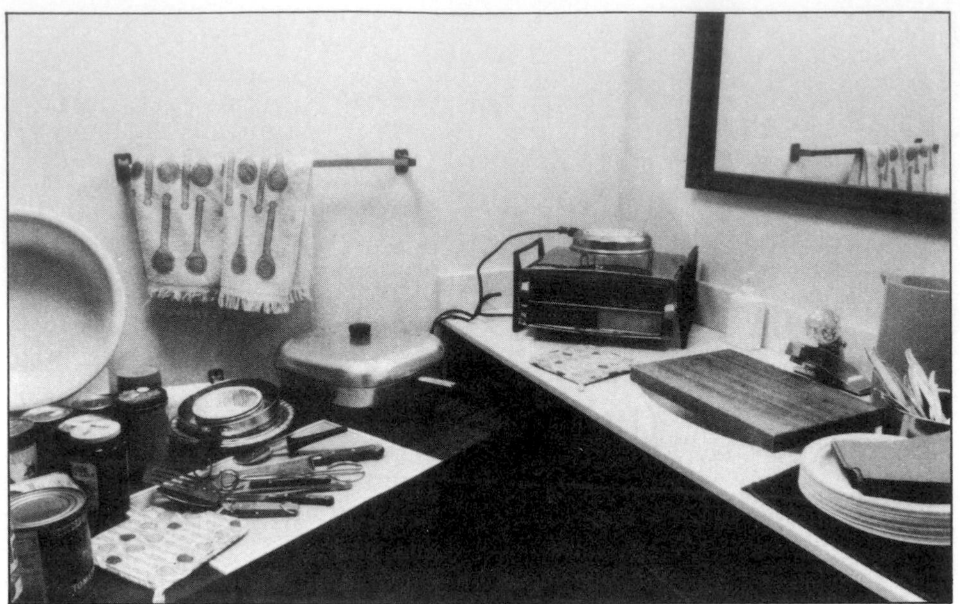

Temporary cooking facilities don't have to be elaborate. Equipment shown here is adequate for needs of most families.

camp stoves, electric frypans, broiler ovens and electric hotplates. If you use electric appliances, make sure you don't overload a circuit. If the appliance has a three-prong plug, don't try to adapt it to a two-prong, ungrounded outlet. See Electricity section at right.

If your temporary kitchen is located away from plumbing, keep a teakettle handy for storing cooking water. Keep a plastic dishpan handy for dirty dishes and utensils.

SAFETY PRECAUTIONS

Construction is a hazardous process. Those in the trades protect themselves as well as they can, and accept the occasional injury. But even a minor injury can take the satisfaction out of your kitchen project. Take every possible step to avoid injuries.

KNOW YOUR PHYSICAL LIMITATIONS

Honestly evaluate your physical abilities and limitations. Kitchen remodeling requires lifting many heavy objects, so pay attention to your back and its limits. Rest when your muscles tell you to. Get help moving heavy objects, or use a dolly, hand truck or other lifting device.

Knees and wrists are also prone to strains and sprains. Take protective steps if you need to. Use an Ace bandage to help support a weak wrist or knee when doing heavy work.

Do not work when you're tired, mentally or physically. Not only will you overexert yourself, but you're likely to make mistakes that can ruin the work or result in serious injury.

INFECTION

Tearout work, especially in kitchens, is incredibly dirty. You must protect yourself from exposure to infectious organisms.

The most dangerous disease you might encounter is *tetanus*, also known as *lockjaw*. Tetanus organisms can live indefinitely under the right conditions. If you haven't had a tetanus inoculation in the last few years, get one before you start working. Any of your tools or the old materials you're ripping out can carry tetanus. You can be infected through any minor scratch or puncture. Once contracted, tetanus is difficult to treat and is often fatal.

The second major health hazard is sewage. The buildup of organic materials inside drain lines and traps is an ideal growing medium for microorganisms, some of them dangerous. A few hours before you work on drain lines, flush them out with a cup of chlorine laundry bleach. This should kill much of the microbe population.

Maintain basic sanitation when working on drain and sewer lines. Don't eat, smoke, or otherwise touch your eyes, mouth or face while your hands might be contaminated. Don't contaminate any scratches or other damaged skin areas. Scrub down thoroughly when through working. Clean any tools that might have been contaminated.

A less serious but common source of disease is the buildup of food debris. These deposits occur in sink drains, range hoods, under the old stove—anywhere you can't clean without taking the kitchen apart. Food debris can harbor practically every major and minor food-poisoning organism, including *Salmonella*. When dealing with food debris, the basic sanitation measures outlined above should protect you. After you remove the debris, wipe down the area with a chlorine bleach solution to kill any organisms that remain.

HAND TOOLS

Use the right tool for the job. A screwdriver used to open paint cans will jump out of screw slots. Keep tools in good condition. A hammer with a loose or cracked handle can cause serious injury or damage if the head flies off.

Take time to sharpen cutting tools before they're completely dull. A well-maintained tool is easier to sharpen because the basic shape of the cutting edge is still intact so you don't have to reconstruct it. A sharp tool is safer and easier to use and does better work. A dull saw or chisel is much more likely to break or to slip and damage the work or injure you.

Never use a file without the correct file handle. If the file jams or your grip slips, the sharp tang of the file can injure you.

Always clean, oil, and sharpen tools before you put them away. Then store them so that both the tools and your family are safe. Most small children are fascinated with tools. They can seriously injure themselves on a wood chisel, plane or other cutting tool.

ELECTRICITY

Do not work on any electrical circuit unless the circuit is *turned off*. Cover the circuit breaker with a piece of tape to make sure that someone doesn't turn it back on while you're working. Loose wires should be capped and safely covered before the circuit is turned back on.

If you're relocating any of the old appliances for temporary use, don't try to jury-rig 240-volt or gas hookups. A Coleman stove or hotplates may be less convenient than the old stove, but they're safer to use than a jury-rigged stove.

Power tools and kitchen appliances draw large amperages. Share their electrical loads among several circuits. Check fuses or circuit breakers to determine the maximum amperage of the circuits you're using. If necessary, string heavy-duty extensions from other parts of the house to spread the load.

Power Tools—Power tools are the source of many injuries on home construction or remodeling jobs. All the standard safety precautions apply. Wear safety goggles, clamp down the piece you're cutting or drilling, and don't wear loose clothing that can get caught in the tool. All these precautions are detailed in the operating instructions that came with the tool.

One safety hazard not often mentioned in safety instructions is *distraction.* When using any power tool, don't let your mind wander. Force yourself to concentrate only on what you're doing. Don't let anyone or anything distract you until the power tool is shut off and secured.

Especially in enclosed areas, a big problem with power tools is noise. Tools such as the circular saw can do permanent hearing damage if used on a continuous basis. If you can't find suitable hearing protection where you buy your tools, check with a gunsmith or shooter's supply store.

The amperage draw of power tools and appliances can be found on the specification plate. Bear in mind that some motors draw a starting surge current that exceeds their rated amperage draw. If you can't find a stated amperage draw on a tool or appliance, determine motor horsepower or wattage. One motor horsepower is roughly equivalent to 6 amps at 120 volts. Or divide the voltage into the wattage to get the amperage.

Extension Cords—All tools should be either the newer double-insulated type or should be grounded. Tools that need to be grounded require three-wire, heavy-duty extension cords. Don't try to pull large amperages through household lamp-cord extensions. They work, but every second the current is flowing the wire is heating. This heat will quickly destroy the cord's insulation. As the cord heats, the voltage it delivers drops, causing the power tool to heat up. This can damage the tool's motor. Heavy-duty extension cords are a better solution. Look for an amperage rating on the cord label, and buy one rated above the current draw of your biggest power tool.

Electricity and Water—Be on the alert for wet conditions when you're using electricity. Water provides a good ground for any leaking current, through you. If you must work in wet conditions with electrical equipment, install a *ground fault circuit interrupter* (GFCI) in the circuit you're using.

Unlike a conventional circuit breaker, a GFCI detects the presence of potential current leakage, and shuts off the current before you get shocked. A GFCI does this by comparing the current going out and coming in on the two sides of the circuit. When it detects any current missing, it shuts off. GFCI's can be sensitive and under certain circumstances can shut off repeatedly. But the annoyance is nothing compared to the possible serious consequences of a major shock. If your house is wired with circuit breakers rather than fuses, you can unplug the breaker in the panel box and plug in a special GFCI breaker. Or you can wire a junction box into your extension cord and install the GFCI there.

DUST

Airborne dust from sanding or paint spraying can be a nuisance or it can be a direct health threat. Use a molded-paper respirator mask, available at paint stores. Avoid generating toxic dusts, such as those caused by sanding old lead-base paint or asbestos-bearing floor-tile backing.

SOLVENTS

A mask won't protect you from *volatile solvents* present in some materials you'll be using. A volatile solvent is one which evaporates quickly into the air. The fumes released from many solvents are highly toxic. Many adhesives, paints and varnishes, degreasers and cleaners contain toxic volatile solvents. Adequate ventilation is the key to safely using these products. Open doors and windows. Set up an electric fan if there isn't enough circulation. Or move the work outdoors if you can. Some of these solvents may make you sick only temporarily. Others can cause permanent injury.

Don't feel foolish about using safety gear—it's worth the trouble.

Aside from the exposure problem, some volatile solvents are flammable, or even explosive. Check labels carefully for indications in this regard and follow label instructions. *Extinguish all open flames,* including pilot lights, before using any flammable solvents. Some solvents are so sensitive that even a tiny spark from a light switch or a power tool can set them off. Also, solvent fumes can travel great distances to an ignition source. Provide adequate ventilation.

For More Information—If you're in doubt whether you need to be overly careful with a particular product or substance, contact your fire department. They can provide you with additional safety information.

Plumbing

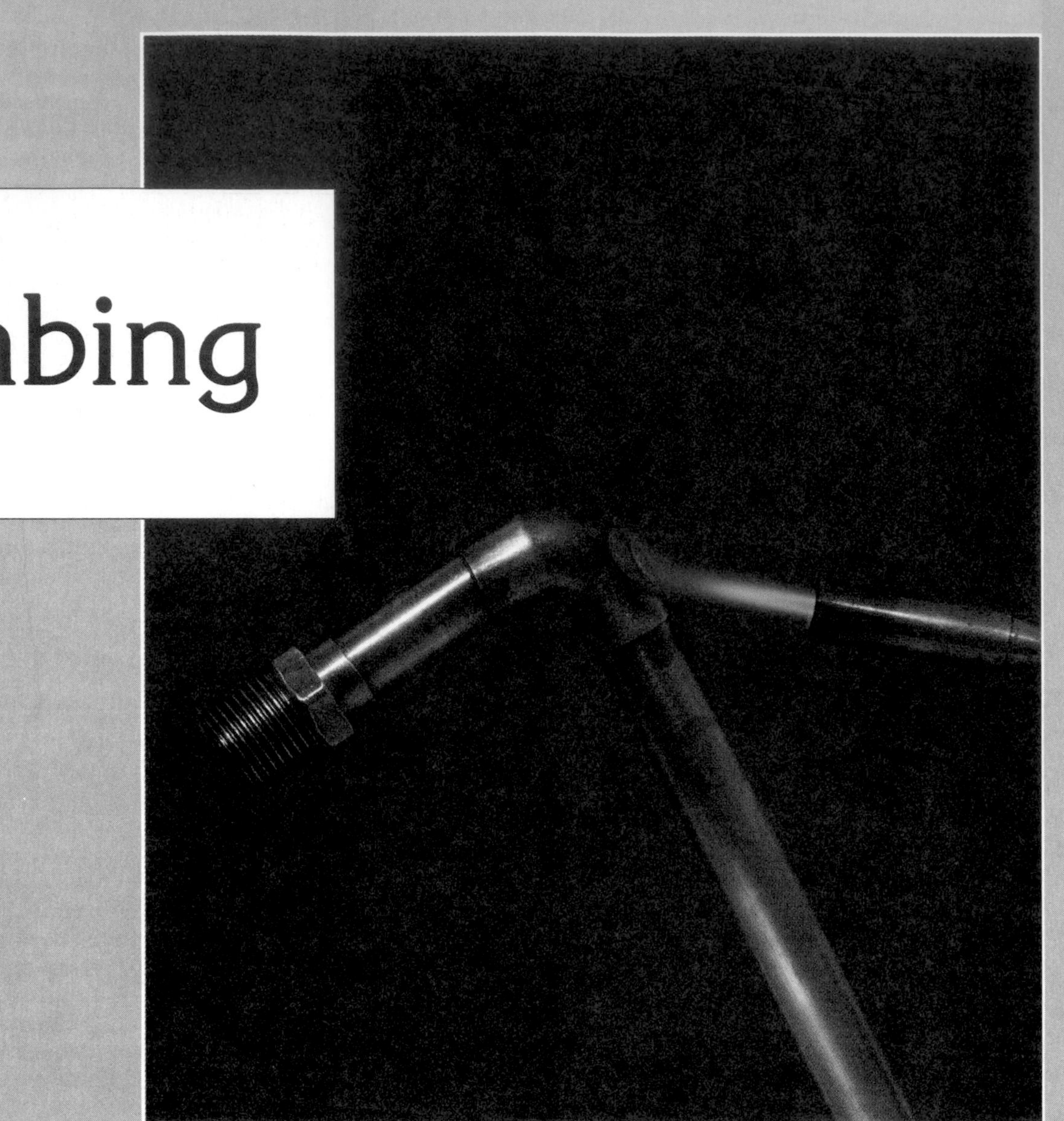

Soldering copper pipe is easier than you might think. See page 78.

The first part of this chapter describes how to modify existing plumbing systems to accommodate sinks, dishwashers and other plumbing fixtures. This work is referred to as *rough plumbing.* It includes all work done to water-supply and drain pipes to the point where they pass through the finished wall into the room. At this point, the pipes are *stubbed out,* or capped off, until you are ready to install and hook up the plumbing fixtures. Fixture installation and hookup, called *finish plumbing,* are covered in the second part of the chapter, starting on page 85.

Most building departments allow homeowners to do all of the plumbing work, provided correct permits are obtained. In a few localities, certain plumbing work must be done by a licensed individual to pass inspection. If this is the case where you live, don't try to do this work yourself. You might have to rip it out and have it redone.

ROUGH PLUMBING CHANGES

The first step in any plumbing system change is to locate existing pipe runs, lay out the change and make a materials list. Working from your cabinet layout, page 61, measure and mark on the wall the centerlines of all proposed plumbing fixtures and equipment—sinks, dishwasher, and so forth. If your refrigerator has an icemaker, you'll need to run a water line to the refrigerator location.

If changes are extensive or complicated, use a pencil and straightedge to mark on the walls and floor the locations of existing water supply lines and drain lines. Then mark proposed changes you'll make to them. Indicate where pipes will come through walls or floor. From this layout, determine the types of pipe and fittings needed for the job and amounts of each.

DRAINING THE SYSTEM

One rule applies to any modification you make to a water-supply system: Shut off and drain the system before you do *anything.* Especially on older systems, things can go wrong—such as a cracked pipe or a failed fitting—on even small repairs. If the water is turned on when this happens, the room may get flooded before you find a shutoff valve.

To turn off the water supply to your house, locate the main shutoff valve. If you don't already know where the shutoff valve is, start by finding your water meter. The meter is usually in a concrete or metal box recessed in the ground near one of the property lines. If you look inside the box, you may find a hand-operated shutoff valve. If there isn't one in the box, check along the house foundation on the side toward the meter. In warmer climates, the main water pipe often exits the ground near the foundation and enters the house above ground. Often, the shutoff valve is there, and usually a hose bib that's perfect for draining down the system after the valve is shut off.

If the main water pipe doesn't come above ground outside, look for another box like the one for the water meter, near the house foundation. The main valve may be there. This setup is sometimes used on crawl-space and slab-floor houses in colder climates.

If the shutoff valve is in none of these places, look inside the house. Check in the basement or crawl space, especially along the wall toward the water meter. Also check the utility room or garage, if they're on the side of the house toward the meter.

Still no sign of a hand-operated shutoff valve? Maybe there isn't one. Call the water company and ask them if they might know where your shutoff valve is. As a last resort, make arrangements with the water company to come by and shut off the water at the meter for a few hours, so you can install a shutoff valve, or repair or replace a frozen one.

In warmer areas, incoming water service will probably look like this. Shutoff valve is below faucet.

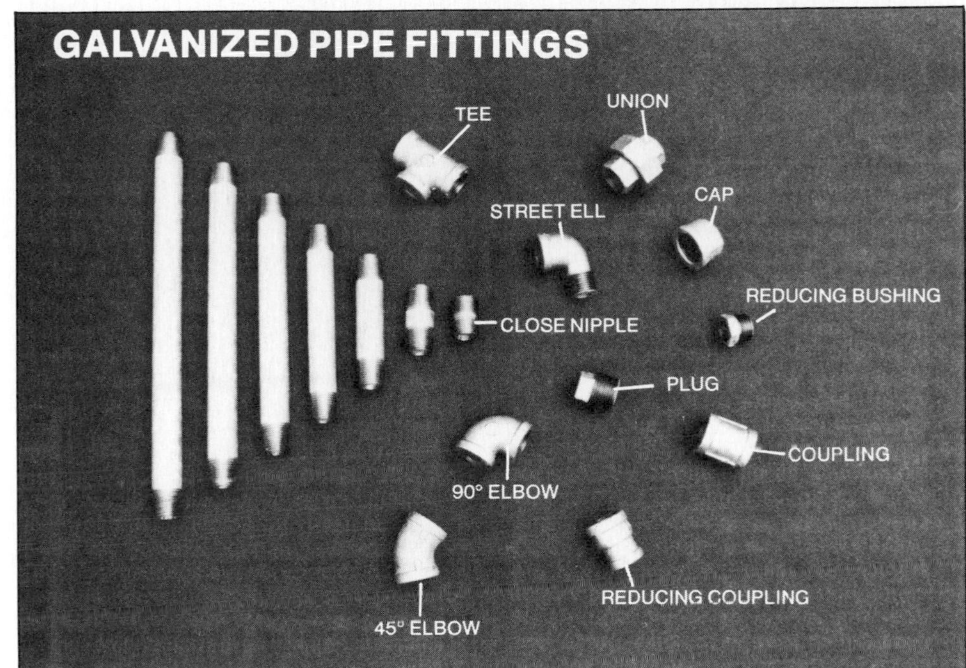

After you've successfully shut off the incoming water, drain the system below the level of the sections you'll be working on. Just open a low connection, such as a hose bib, to let out water and a high one such as a sink faucet, to admit air.

Water heaters—Your water heater can be damaged if it's allowed to operate without water. If there are valves on both inlet and outlet sides of the water heater, close them both before draining the rest of the system. Otherwise, turn off the water heater and let it drain along with the rest of the system.

Your existing water-supply system is probably either *galvanized pipe* or *copper pipe.* A few systems installed within the last decade use plastic pipes and fittings, either chlorinated polyvinyl chloride (CPVC) or polybutylene, though these systems are not yet common. Plastic pipe has only recently gained acceptance in most code jurisdictions. A few still prohibit its use.

When connecting new plumbing to an existing system, it's usually best to use pipes and fittings of the same material. Adding plastic pipe to a metallic-pipe system usually presents no problems. Mixing two kinds of metal pipe can lead to *electrolytic corrosion.* This can result in one or many holes in one or both pipes.

Dissimilar metal pipes, usually copper and galvanized, should be connected with a *dielectric union.* This connector looks like an ordinary union, in photo above, but it electrically insulates the two metals from each other. Without current flow there's no electrolytic corrosion.

Adapters—There are adapters to connect practically anything to anything in a plumbing system. Some situations may require you to use two adapters together. For example, if a former owner has used *flare connections* in a copper system, you can use adapters to convert to pipe threads and then to copper *sweat connections.* These connections are described on pages 78 and 80.

Describe adapters accurately when you go to buy them. First, look at the existing pipe end and write down what connects to it. That describes one end of the adapter. Then decide what you want to connect to the adapter and write down what fits that. That describes the other end of the adapter. Always write down the description of the adapter itself, as in "1/2-inch male IPS x 1/2-inch female CPVC." *IPS* stands for *Iron Pipe Size.*

Galvanized Pipe—This is iron or steel pipe coated with zinc to increase resistance to corrosion. Standard sizes are listed in the pipe sizing chart on page 82.

Galvanized pipe and fittings have threaded connections. The pipe threads are tapered, and fittings have a reverse taper. These threads are different from machine threads, which are straight. Never try to combine machine and pipe threads, even though some sizes seem to be identical.

The tapered threads and the malleable fittings are the reason why galvanized pipe systems stay leakfree in the face of vibration and changes in water temperature. As the pipe and fitting are threaded together, the taper forces the fitting to stretch to accommodate it. The heavy band at the end of the fitting remains in constant tension, squeezing the threads and preventing leaks.

Though galvanized pipe is not as corrosion resistant as copper or plastic pipe, it's still the most common pipe you'll find in an older home. Until recently, it was the least expensive pipe available. It is still cheaper than copper pipe but costs somewhat more than plastic pipe.

Have galvanized pipe cut to desired length and threaded when you buy it. Threaded-pipe nipples come in standard lengths from 1 to 12 inches, sometimes longer. You can buy pipe in lengths up to 21 feet, but you usually must thread them yourself or have the plumbing supplier do this. Most plumbing suppliers will cut pipes to your measurements and thread them for a modest fee.

To do your own cutting and threading, use a hacksaw, a sturdy vise and a *pipe threader.* This tool has a threaded cutting head, called a *die,* attached to a long handle. The die is positioned over the pipe end and twisted to cut the threads. Most pipe threaders come with interchangable dies for different-size pipes. Pipe threaders can be rented at tool rentals and plumbing suppliers.

Several tools are used for assembling and taking apart galvanized pipe. *Vise-grip pliers* and *Channel-lock pliers* can be useful in tight spaces.

If you're taking out or putting in much galvanized pipe, use the appropriate size *pipe wrenches.* Also called *Stillson wrenches* after their inventor, pipe wrenches are self-tightening as long as they're facing in the right direction. The movable jaw of a pipe wrench swivels to lock the teeth of both jaws solidly into the pipe or fitting. Be careful when using pipe wrenches. The jaw's swivel action develops enough force to distort a fitting or pipe end so severely that it won't mate with other threaded pieces.

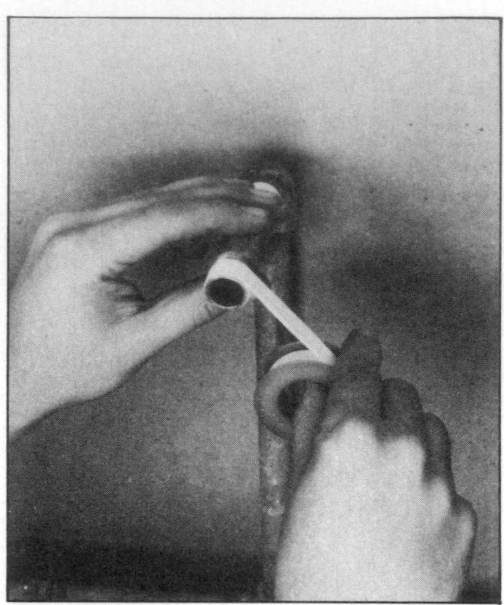
Teflon pipe-thread tape is clean and easy to use. Always wrap tape clockwise, as shown.

Always work with pipe wrenches in pairs. Use one to hold back against the other, one wrench on either side of the joint. This concentrates the force on just the one joint you're working on. See photo on facing page.

If additional force is needed to loosen a threaded connection, position the handles of both wrenches vertically and slightly apart from each other. Use both hands to squeeze handles together as you would a pair of pliers. Be careful not to pinch your fingers between the handles. If even more force is needed to break a joint loose, slip a length of pipe over each wrench handle to increase leverage.

When tightening threaded connections, don't overdo it. Tightening a connection too far risks splitting the fitting or stripping threads. When you have to apply heavy pressure with the pipe wrench to get another quarter turn, the connection is tight.

Pipe-joint compound should be used on all threaded connections for galvanized pipe, copper pipe and plastic pipe, unless pipe manufacturer's assembly instructions say otherwise. Pipe-joint compound does not act as a sealant, except where pipe threads are poorly cut or damaged. It's used to lubricate pipe threads, allowing a connection to be tightened beyond where it would if the threads were dry.

Many years ago, white lead ground in oil was used in place of pipe-joint compound. White lead is highly toxic. If you find an old can of white lead compound among your supplies, don't use it—dispose of it safely. This also applies to any unmarked bags of dark red powder, which is probably litharge, or red lead. This toxic substance was also used as a pipe-joint compound, mostly on boilers and steam piping. If you find white or red lead has been used on the pipe joints you're working on, clean it off with a wire brush and solvent. Use modern pipe-joint compound for reassembly.

Today, anything a plumbing supplier has on the shelf labeled "pipe-joint compound" is safe and will do the job. But the easiest and cleanest for the owner-builder is *pipe-thread tape.* This is a clean, dry roll of thin Teflon tape. One popular brand is called *Tape Dope.* Like pipe-joint compound, the tape acts as a lubricant. It has no adhesive.

Wrap the tape tightly onto the male threads of the pipe connection, so it takes on the form of the threads. With the threaded end of the pipe pointing toward you, wrap the tape clockwise around the threads. This way, when the connection is tightened, the tape wraps tighter around threads instead of bunching up. Two or three layers of tape are all that is needed. Don't be alarmed if you unscrew one of these connections and find the tape has smeared. This is the way it's supposed to work. Just apply another turn or two of tape and reassemble the connection.

A special lubricant can be used in conjunction with the tape, but you don't really need it, except on large pipe sizes. On small sizes, a drop of light oil or squirt of WD-40 will do. Pipe-thread tape makes the threads slick, so don't overtighten. One advantage of the tape is that it won't harden or dry out. This makes future dismantling easier.

Galvanized pipe is usually dismantled starting at the *downstream* end of the pipe run you're working on. The point where the water enters the house is called the upstream end. The last fixture in the pipe run is called the downstream end.

Unless there is a *union* nearby, it's hard to dismantle sections in the middle of a pipe run. A union is a fitting that allows you to unscrew the pipe run on either side of it. If there's no union nearby, find a short piece of pipe in the run or a fitting in a convenient location. Cut the pipe or fitting with a hacksaw. Then unscrew the cut ends. You can dismantle the pipe run in either direction from there. If you cut a short pipe length—called a *nipple*—it can be replaced with two shorter nipples and a union.

To make a new connection to the system, remove a length of pipe and substitute two shorter lengths with a *tee* in the middle. A tee is shown in the photo on page 75. An easier way is to find a convenient elbow or coupling. Remove it and substitute a tee.

You can't always make additional connections to existing pipe runs. Fixtures already connected to that run may have used up all of its legal or actual *flow capacity*. Flow capacity is the amount of water a pipe can carry. If too many fixtures are being used at the same time, and the pipe is not large enough to handle them, the water at each outlet will be reduced to a trickle. To make an additional connection, you may have to increase the size of the pipe upstream of the new connection. Refer to the pipe-sizing chart on page 82 for flow requirements for various fixtures.

Copper Pipe—There are two kinds of copper pipe—hard and soft. The only real difference between hard- and soft-copper pipe is that soft copper is bendable. This gives soft-copper pipe several advantages over hard-copper pipe. You can carry it home in a coil, rather than in straight 20-foot lengths. You don't need as many fittings, because you can bend it around corners. This makes soft copper pipe easy to thread into existing walls and floors. Also, the pipe can be bent to align to fittings and fixtures.

There are several difficulties in bending soft-copper pipe. Bends must be gradual and free of kinks. This requires a tool called a *bending spring*. This is a length of steel spring that slips over the pipe so it stays round and doesn't kink.

Also, it's difficult to straighten out curves at pipe ends. Because soft copper is malleable, you must be careful not to deform pipe ends when cutting, bending, and handling. Out-of-round pipe ends make it difficult to get leakproof connections. See *Soldering Joints* on page 78.

If the work area is easily accessible, hard-copper pipe is easier to work with. Because this pipe is less likely to deform, it's easier for the novice to cut, and to make good solder connections. Hard-copper pipe is slightly less expensive than soft-copper pipe.

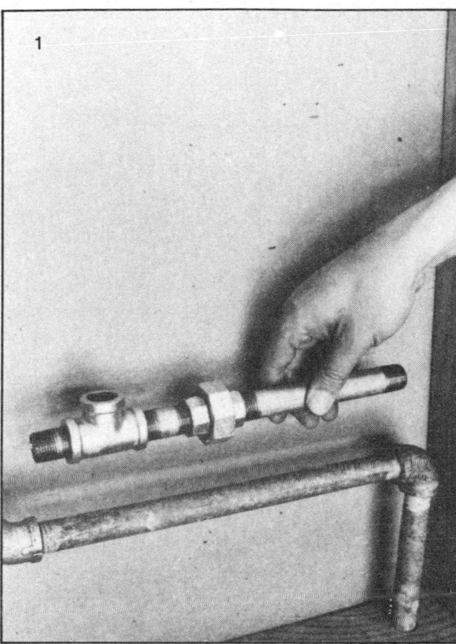

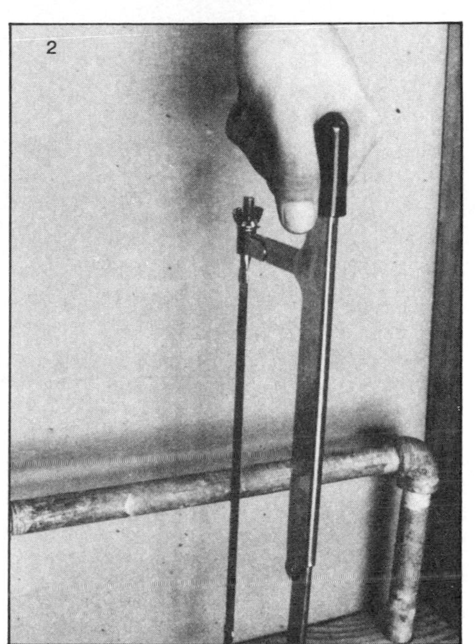

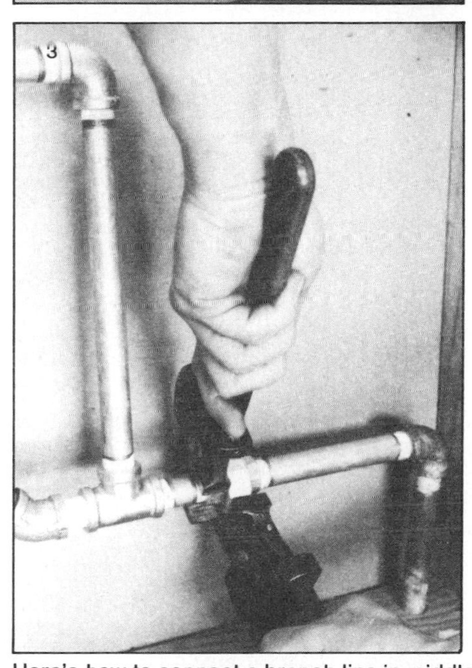

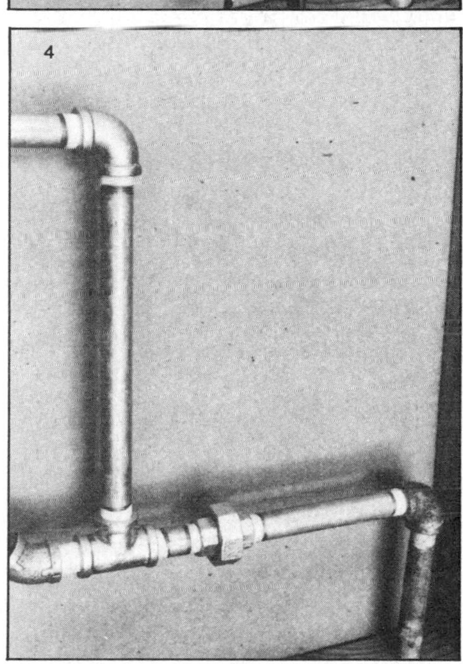

Here's how to connect a branch line in middle of a galvanized pipe run without having to take everything apart. 1. Get a *tee* fitting, a *union* fitting and correct size *nipples*. 2. Cut pipe section with hacksaw and unscrew ends. 3. Replace section with new fittings, working from both ends to union. Install union using two pipe wrenches. 4. Test completed assembly for leaks. The one pictured doesn't.

In general, hard-copper pipe is used for long, straight runs of pipe. If you don't have a way to transport 20-foot lengths of this pipe, take your measurements and a pipe cutter with you. Cut the pipe into convenient lengths before hauling it home.

Copper pipe is available in three wall thicknesses. The heaviest is *Type K*, which is available in hard and soft pipe. Type K is identified by a green stripe or green lettering. *Type L* is medium weight, available both hard and soft, and identified by a blue stripe or lettering. The lightest is *Type M*, available in hard pipe only. It has a red stripe or lettering. The difference between the types is primarily in their bursting strength. But even the lightest is safe for residential use. Still, local building codes may dictate which type you can use.

All copper pipe for rough plumbing is connected by *sweat-soldering* the joints. This technique is described on page 78. Copper pipe can also be connected with *flare fittings*, or *brass compression fittings*, as described on page 80. These fittings should not be used

continued on page 80

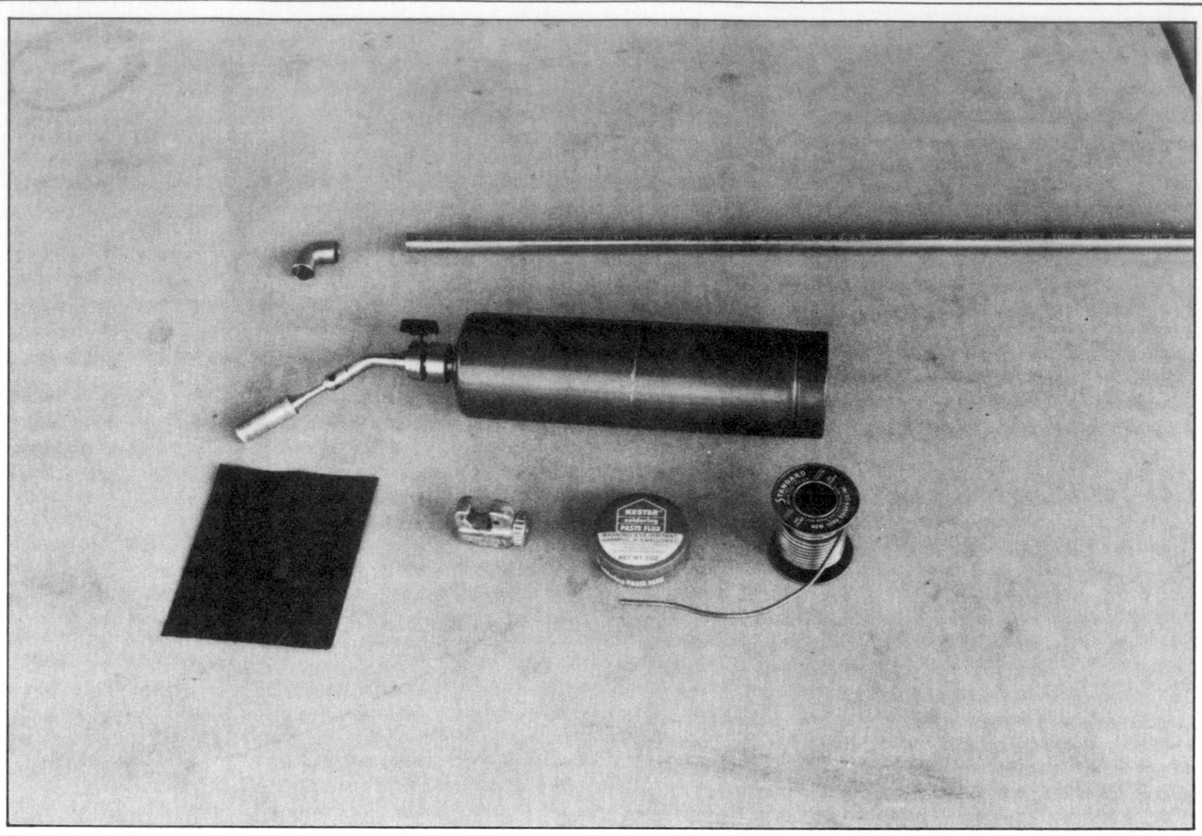

Basic tools for sweat-soldering copper pipe. Shown are torch, solder, flux, emery cloth and pipe cutter.

SOLDERING COPPER PIPE

Both hard- and soft-copper pipe are connected by a technique called *sweat-soldering.* The process of sweat-soldering is made simple by the high quality-control standards of today's pipe manufacturers. The outside diameter of copper pipe and the inside diameter of the fittings are carefully controlled. Thus, melted solder can be drawn into the thin space between pipe and fitting by capillary action.

Tools required are a propane torch, a pipe cutter, emery cloth, soldering flux and solid-core solder. See photo above.

Clean, Flux, and Assemble—Clean pipe end and inside of fitting with emery cloth. All traces of oxidation and foreign substances must be removed. A few twists of the emery cloth are all that's needed. Coat both surfaces with flux, either paste or liquid, to prevent new oxidation. Plug pipe all the way into the fitting socket. On most jobs, several joints can be prepared, and then soldered one after the other.

Heat—After pipe assembly is lined up correctly, light propane torch and adjust it. For small pipe sizes, the blue inner flame should be about 3/4-inch long; for large pipe sizes, 1-1/2 inches long.

If there is any white or orange in the flame, the torch-tip air openings are partially plugged. Shut off torch and *let it cool.* Remove torch tip and clean it.

Position tip of blue inner flame against side of joint. Move torch back and forth to distribute heat evenly. The flux will melt and then start to bubble and smoke a little. Test heat by touching pipe with the end of the solder. The joint is hot enough when solder melts after a second or so from heat in the joint, outside the torch flame.

Solder should spread freely, and have a shiny surface. If melted solder bubbles and becomes dry and porous-looking, the joint is too hot. Remove torch and pull joint apart carefully—it's hot. Reclean, reflux, and start heating again.

Feed Solder—Once the connection is heated to the correct temperature, start feeding solder. Use the somewhat cooler flame beyond the blue flame to compensate for heat the solder absorbs. Feed melting solder into joint from the top. When melted solder starts to run off bottom of joint, move flame away from joint, *but keep feeding solder.* As the joint cools, some of the melted solder will seem to disappear. It's being drawn into the joint. Keep feeding solder until enough heat has dissipated that the melting rate has slowed to almost nothing. As you feed solder, slide melting end around the joint, to form a *fillet.* This kind of fillet is pronounced "fill-it" and is a small radiused surface of solder covering the joint opening. Wipe off surplus solder with a damp cloth before it completely sets up. After the joint cools, clean off remaining flux.

Did It Work?—That fillet of solder indicates the joint is completely sealed. If you cleaned the joint correctly, saw the solder draw in, and have a complete fillet, you've got a good solder joint.

Safety—Whenever possible, do your soldering in the open. When you're forced to solder pipes in a wall or near framing members, protect them with a piece of sheet metal or 1/4-inch asbestos board, if you have it. If these aren't available, use a piece of 1/2-inch drywall. Wet the paper on the side toward the flame so it won't catch fire, and keep rewetting it periodically. Keep a fire extinguisher or a bucket of water handy.

The melting point of plumbing solder is fairly low, but melted solder can produce a burn on bare skin. Dripping solder won't ordinarily burn or set fire to clothing or shoes, but it does fuse and damage nylon, polyester and a few other synthetic fabrics. Solder spatters can be peeled off most fabrics after they cool. Remove solder spatters before putting clothes in the washing machine. The solder can damage the washer's pump.

When soldering, wear gloves to protect hands and safety glasses to protect eyes.

SOLDERING COPPER PIPE

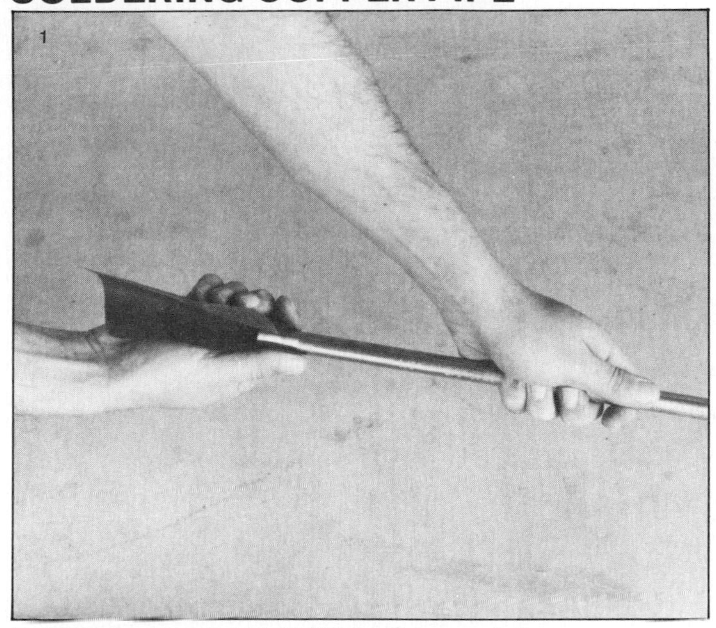
1

Polish pipe end and inside of fitting with emery cloth.

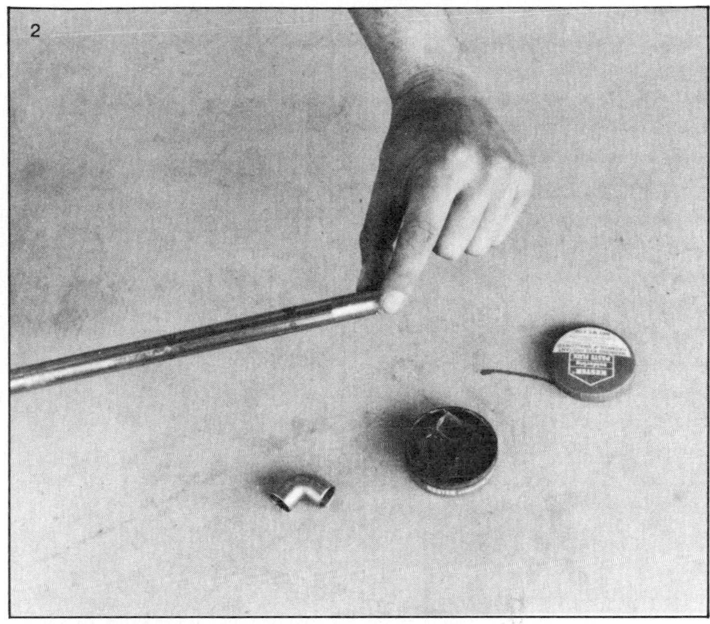
2

Coat both cleaned surfaces with flux immediately, even if you're not ready to solder yet. It helps keep cleaned surfaces from reoxidizing.

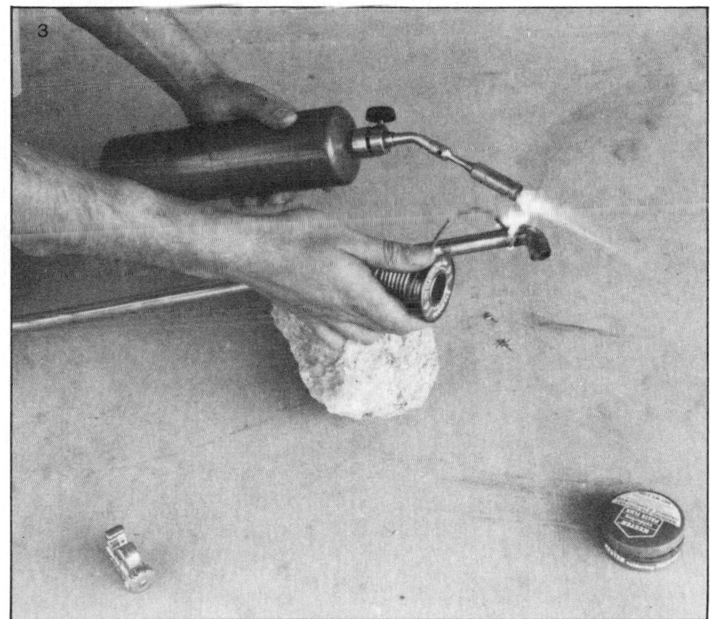
3

Use light blue-green inner cone of flame to bring a joint up to soldering temperature. Then use fainter outer cone of flame to maintain temperature. As you heat joint, keep testing heat level with solder, as shown. When solder melts from heat in joint, outside flame, back torch off and use outer part of flame to maintain heat level.

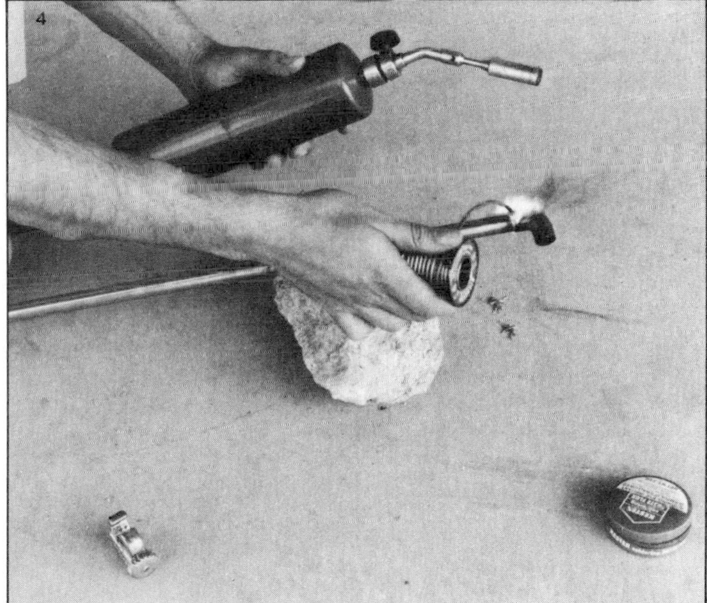
4

Feed solder into joint steadily as it cools to make sure joint stays full of solder.

on plumbing inside a wall or under a floor. These fittings can loosen and leak—to tighten them would require tearing into the wall or floor.

Plastic Pipe—Many jurisdictions now permit PVC (polyvinyl chloride) and CPVC (chlorinated polyvinyl chloride) plastic pipe for residential plumbing systems. Of the two, CPVC is much more resistant to heat, so use PVC on cold-water lines only. Both PVC and CPVC pipe are rigid. Fittings for plastic pipe are socketed much like copper-pipe fittings, but plastic pipe is solvent-welded into a single unit.

Cleaners, primers and solvent-weld cements are entirely different for PVC and for CPVC. If you have both kinds of pipe on the job, don't mix up either the pipe and fittings, or the cleaners, primers and cements.

Assembly procedures for plastic pipe are simple. Cut pipe to length with a fine-tooth handsaw and remove all burrs with sandpaper or a knife. See photos below. Clean pipe end and inside of fitting with the appropriate cleaner, available from the pipe supplier. Apply a thin coat of primer to pipe and fitting and let dry.

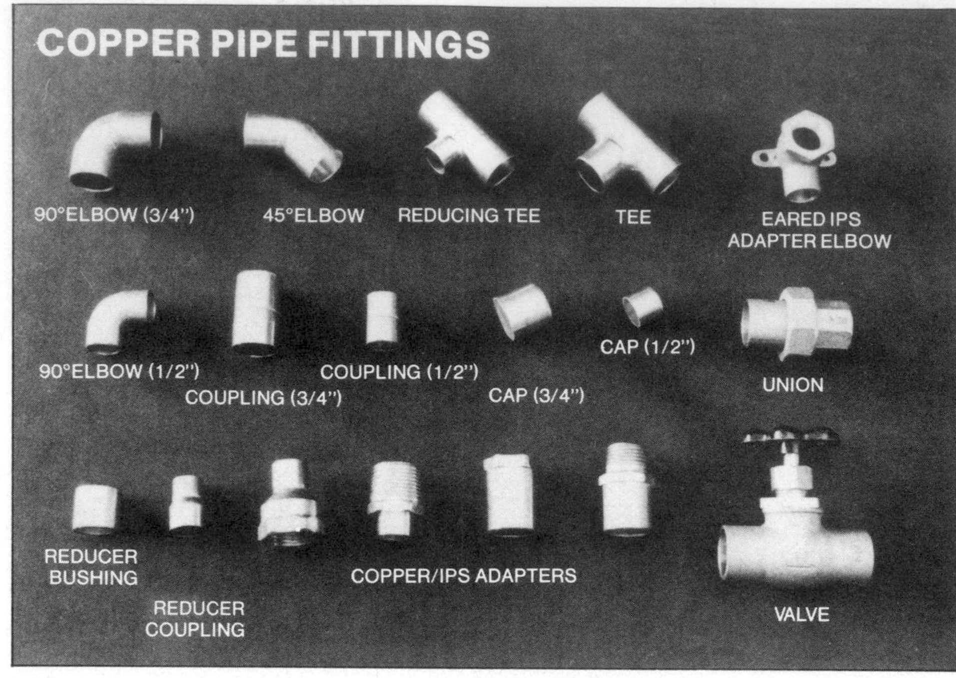

Solvent-weld cement sets up fast, so work quickly. You have to position pipe and fitting correctly on the first try. Use index marks across the joint if you need them. Coat the pipe end and inside of fitting with cement. Insert pipe end into the fitting with a continuous, smooth twisting motion. After the pipe bottoms out in the fitting socket, give it another 1/4 to 1/3 twist, stopping with the fitting in its correct position. In a few seconds the fitting will freeze there. Leave the joint undisturbed for a few minutes to set up.

If you make a mistake, don't try to readjust pipe and fitting. You'll create a leak. Let solvent cement set up a few minutes so you don't disturb nearby joints. Saw off the pipe a few inches back from the fitting, and discard the fitting. Install a coupling and a short length of pipe, and a new fitting.

Work carefully with plastic pipe. An error on one joint creates at least one extra cut and three extra joints.

Testing the System—After all changes have been made to your water-supply system, cap all the open pipe ends. Then *slowly* turn on the water. Examine the entire system carefully for leaks. Incidentally, the reason you turn on the water slowly is because there may be a joint you forgot to cement, solder or tighten up. These result in *big* leaks, and possible water damage.

Let the system stand under pressure

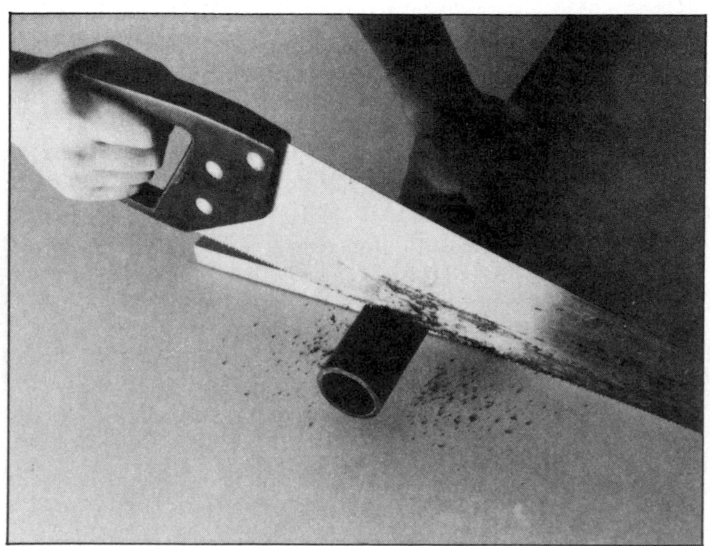

If you have a large copper-pipe cutter, it will work on most plastic pipe too. Otherwise a fine-tooth handsaw works just fine. Use a miter box if you can't make a square cut by eye.

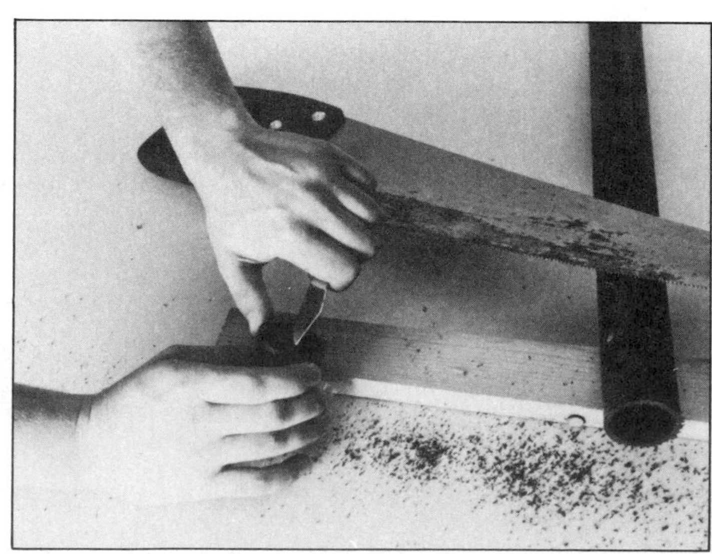

Clean up burrs and rough spots with pocket knife or sandpaper. Check and clean inside of fitting. Trial-fit pieces.

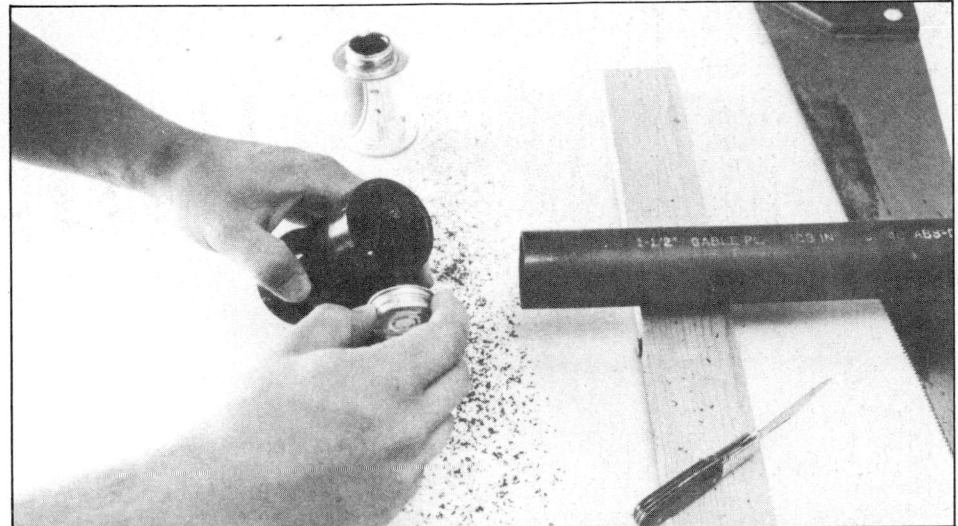

Once cement is applied, work fast. With ABS plastic as shown here, you can go directly to cement application. PVC and CPVC require a coat of special primer first. Make sure you extend colored primer an inch or so beyond cementing area so plumbing inspector can verify that you used it.

Fitting gets a thin coat of cement, pipe gets a thick coat.

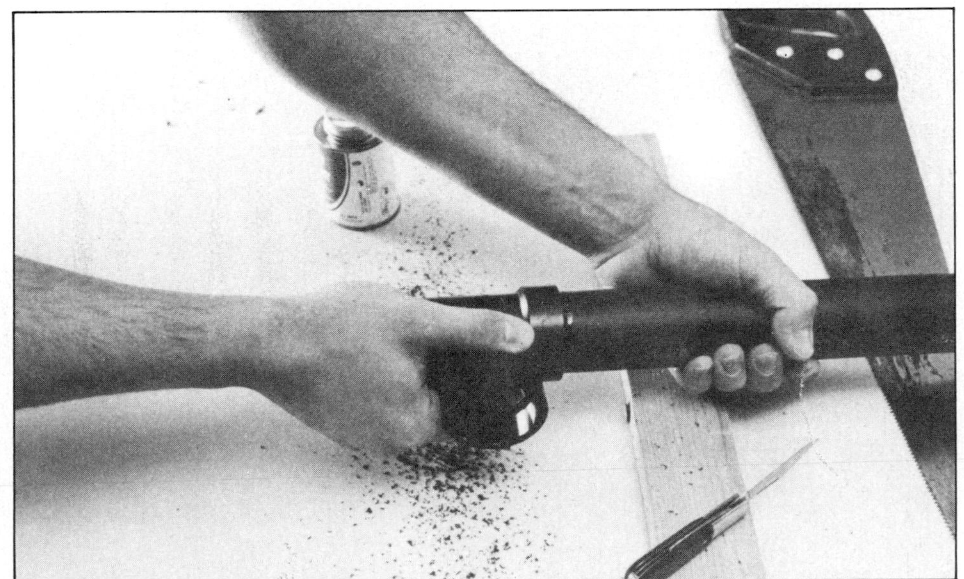

Once you start connecting joint, don't pause. Bottom out pipe end and twist parts into alignment before you let go. When you stop twisting, joint will set up fast. In difficult circumstances, trial fit (dry) and make index marks on both parts with a crayon.

for an hour or so and then check it again. This allows air in the system to escape and water to drip from any small leaks. If you find any leaks, drain the system, then fix the leaks.

DRAINAGE SYSTEM CHANGES

Changes to drain lines can be laid out in pencil on walls and floor the same as for water lines. Two main rules for drain lines must be observed at all times: *1. Sewage always runs downhill.* This means all lines must be sloped away from the fixture or inlet, at least 1/4 inch per foot. *2. All drainage systems must be vented to the atmosphere.* All vertical runs, called *stacks,* should extend up through the roof for venting. There are limits on how far you can run a horizontal drain line without providing a stack. Use the table on page 82 as a general guide. Check with your local plumbing inspector for any local code variations. Drain lines for island sinks require a loop to serve as an air break. Local codes vary on installation requirements. Check local codes.

If you're relocating a drain line closer to the present stack, slope is usually no problem. If you use the original stack opening, the slope for the new run will be even steeper than that of the original run, provided the new drain inlet is at the same level as the old drain inlet.

If you're moving the inlet farther away, it's not so simple. First check to see if there was enough extra slope in the original installation to permit you to get an acceptable amount of slope in the new run. Check slope by measuring from the floor the heights of stack opening and new drain inlet.

Adjust for any slope in the floor when you take your measurements. Divide the height difference between openings, in inches, by the horizontal pipe run in feet to get the number of inches drop per foot of run. As mentioned, you'll need a minimum of 1/4 inch slope per 1 foot of run.

Do not put in a drain line level or upsloped. If there isn't enough slope, raise the inlet at the fixture, if you can. Otherwise, open up the wall and rework the stack to lower the opening.

Cast-Iron Pipe—Depending on the age of your plumbing system, you may find several different types of cast-iron drain pipe.

Belled Cast Iron: In older systems, iron pipe was made in sections 3 or 4

MAXIMUM HORIZONTAL RUN FROM TRAP TO VENT

Pipe Size	Maximum Run
1-1/4"	2'-6"
1-1/2"	3'-6"
2"	5'-0"
3"	6'-0"
4" and over	10'-0"

DETERMINING MINIMUM PIPE SIZES

1. Make a list of fixtures on water line in question. Refer to chart and add up fixture units for each fixture. Left column is for sizing main pipe between hot-water heater and street service. This pipe carries combined hot- and cold-water demand for each fixture connected to it. Right column is for sizing individual hot- and cold-water branch pipes. In most cases you'll be working with branch pipes. See below.

	FIXTURE UNITS	
	Main pipe	Branch pipes
BAR SINK	1	.75
BATHTUB	2	1.5
DISHWASHER	2	1.5
HOSE BIBB	3	3.0
KITCHEN SINK	2	1.5
LAUNDRY SINK	2	1.5
LAVATORY	1	.75
SHOWER	2	1.5
WASHER	2	1.5
TOILET	3	3.0

2. Find the approximate total length of the water line you're sizing from the chart below. Then find the next-largest number that exceeds your total fixture-unit count, in the appropriate column below. The pipe size at the top of the column is the one to use.

MAXIMUM PIPE LENGTH	PIPE SIZE 1/2"	3/4"	1"	1-1/4"	1-1/2"
	TOTAL FIXTURE UNITS				
40'	9	27	60	168	270
60'	8	23	47	130	225
80'	7	19	41	106	193
100'	6	17	36	89	167
150'	5	14	30	66	128

Note: These figures are based on pipe of average interior roughness, and normal water pressure (46 to 60 PSI delivered to the house). It is also assumed that water meter and street-service line are at least as large as the pipe you're sizing. There may be local code variations.

feet long, with a bell-shape hub on one end. The straight end of one length was inserted into the belled end of the other. Then the bell was stuffed with a tarred ropy material called *oakum* and tamped. Finally melted lead was poured into the joint, allowed to cool, and then tamped tightly into place with a blunt chisel, called a *caulking iron.*

Belled cast-iron is difficult to modify. Replacement lengths and fittings are not readily available today. Also, because of the belled ends, you often have to take the system apart from the top end of the stack. When reworking the stack, it's best to dismantle it down to the stack opening, then replace the stack with ABS-plastic drain line to suit the new layout. See facing page. There's an adapter that fits into a cast-iron hub and accepts standard ABS pipe.

Gasketed-Belled Iron: Later cast-iron systems used the same belled-end pipe, but with neoprene gaskets instead of lead and oakum. These gaskets usually disintegrate if disturbed. Replacements are hard to find.

Also, you need a special tool to make connections. The tool is attached on either side of the joint with chains. A compound linkage then draws the two parts of the joint together. Again, it is easier to dismantle the stack and replace it with ABS drain line.

If you want to use the same kind of pipe for replacement, try to find an older plumber who has worked with this kind of pipe. Many younger plumbers won't know how to do this work.

No-Hub Cast Iron: More recent cast-iron systems use *no-hub pipe.* Straight lengths of cast-iron pipe are joined with couplings made of neoprene with a stainless-steel jacket. Because pipe sections butt together instead of interlocking, a section can be removed at any point in the run and modified.

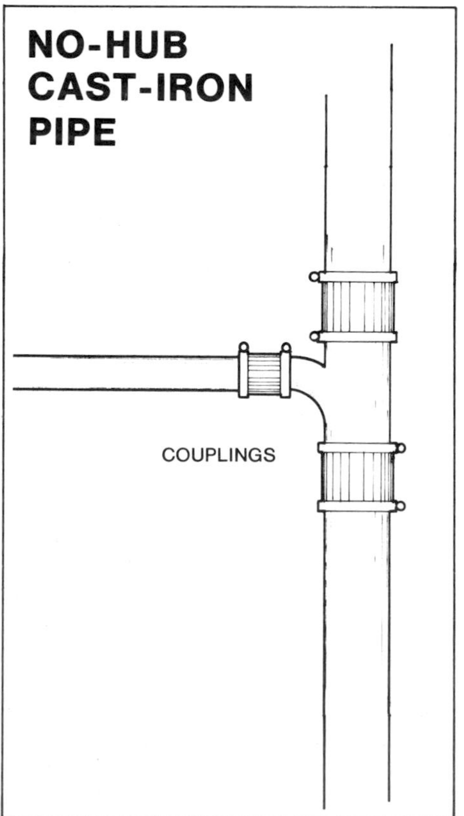

No-hub cast-iron pipe goes together easily, but it's heavy and needs bracing during assembly.

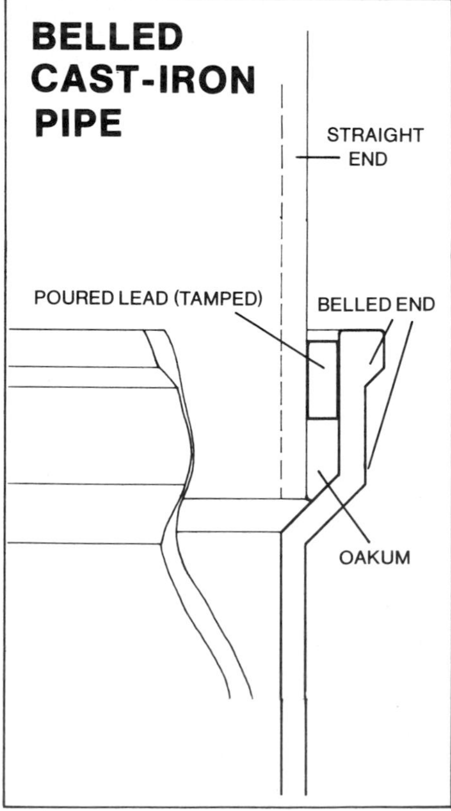

Belled cast-iron pipe must be installed by an experienced plumber.

Modifying ABS drain pipe systems is much easier than modifying cast iron. Usually, biggest problem is making necessary cuts inside a wall.

In tight quarters, you may need to slit drywall on other side to make room for saw. Make sure there are no obstructions on other side of wall.

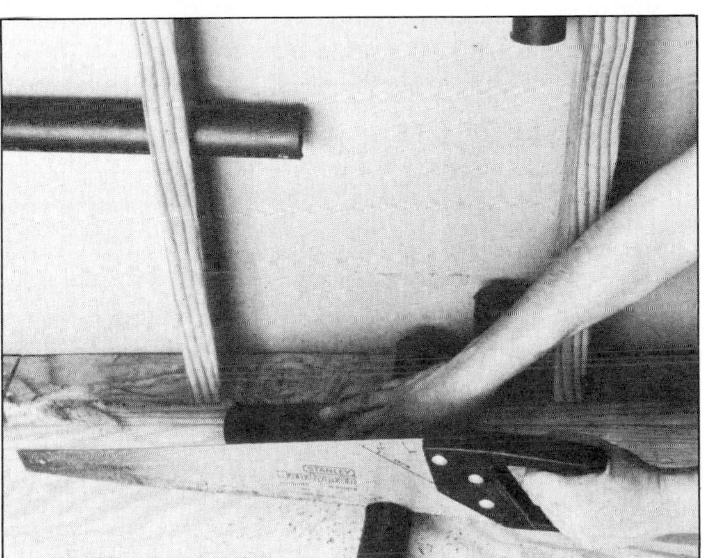

Once you have section loose, you can rework or replace it. Here a short length of pipe is being removed from below inlet to be reinstalled above it with repair couplings.

In this example, horizontal run had to be lowered so sink could be located farther away from stack. Only new parts used on stack were three repair couplings. New horizontal run can now be installed with adequate slope. Pipe at left will come in at lower level.

Support upper sections of a vertical stack before you remove a section from it. The means of support varies with stack location. One method is to tack a length of 2x4 across the studs in front of the stack. Then fasten the stack to the crosspiece with a C-clamp or perforated-metal strapping tape.

The neoprene-lined couplings should not be reused—buy new ones. Band tension is critical to permanent sealing of couplings. You'll need a special T-shape torque wrench. Torque wrenches should be available where you buy the couplings.

Cutting Cast-Iron: One or two cuts on cast-iron drain line can be made with a hacksaw or a hammer and cold chisel. You can also use a metal-cutoff blade in a portable circular saw. To cut with a hammer and cold chisel, mark a line all the way around the pipe. Make a light cut with the chisel along the cut line. Keep chiseling around the pipe, gradually deepening the cut, until you've cut all the way through. Do not use heavy blows. If you hit the pipe too hard, it will shatter.

If you have to make many cuts in cast-iron drain line, rent a device called a *squeeze cutter.* It looks like a large chain wrench, but the chain is lined with cutting wheels. The chain is wrapped around the pipe and gradually tightened until the pipe fractures.

ABS-Plastic Drain Line—Drainage systems for most new residential construction are built with *ABS* (acrylonitrile butadiene styrene) plastic drain line. ABS is easily modified and installed. The joints are solvent-welded, similar to other kinds of plastic pipe. See page 80. Once assembled, the separate parts form a single unit. ABS systems do not depend on mechanical joints.

Cut ABS-plastic drain line with a fine-tooth handsaw. See photos above. Don't use a hacksaw—the teeth clog up with plastic particles. Also, don't cut ABS with a power saw. Heat generated by the fast-moving blade causes the plastic to melt and stick to the blade.

You can easily modify ABS drain lines using a fitting called a *repair coupling*. This looks like a standard coupling, but does not have an internal ridge to serve as a pipe stop. This allows you to slide the coupling all the way onto one piece of pipe and slide it back down over the joint. If your plumbing supplier doesn't stock repair couplings, file the internal ridge off a regular coupling and use that.

A fitting in a vertical stack can be raised or lowered by making cuts in the pipe several inches above and below the fitting. Then cut off part of the loose piece and reattach the shorter piece with a repair coupling. Cut a piece of pipe to fill the gap at other end, or use the piece cut from the opposite end of the section. Use two repair couplings to complete the repair. See photos on page 83.

To make a new connection in an ABS-plastic drain line, mark on the pipe the locations of the bottoms of the hubs at each end of the new fitting. Measure 6 to 8 inches beyond the marks and make a second set of marks. Cut out the pipe section at these marks. Then cut the loose section at the first set of marks. Solvent-weld the cut ends of the loose section to the fitting. Attach this assembly to the drain line with two repair couplings.

Copper Drain Line—These are excellent systems, but not used much in residential work because of cost. They're much more common in commercial applications, so pipe and fittings should be available.

Copper drain lines are cut and connected exactly the same as copper water-supply lines, described on pages 77-80. You may need a large torch if you have to solder these larger pipe sizes.

Testing Drain Lines—Like water lines, drain lines are subject to inspection and testing. Required testing for a complete new drain system is the same in most jurisdictions. All openings in the system are capped or plugged. An air compressor is then used to increase air pressure in the system. If the pressure doesn't drop in a specified period of time, the system is tight. Then the plugs or caps are removed and the system can be connected.

Testing requirements vary when you've only changed part of the

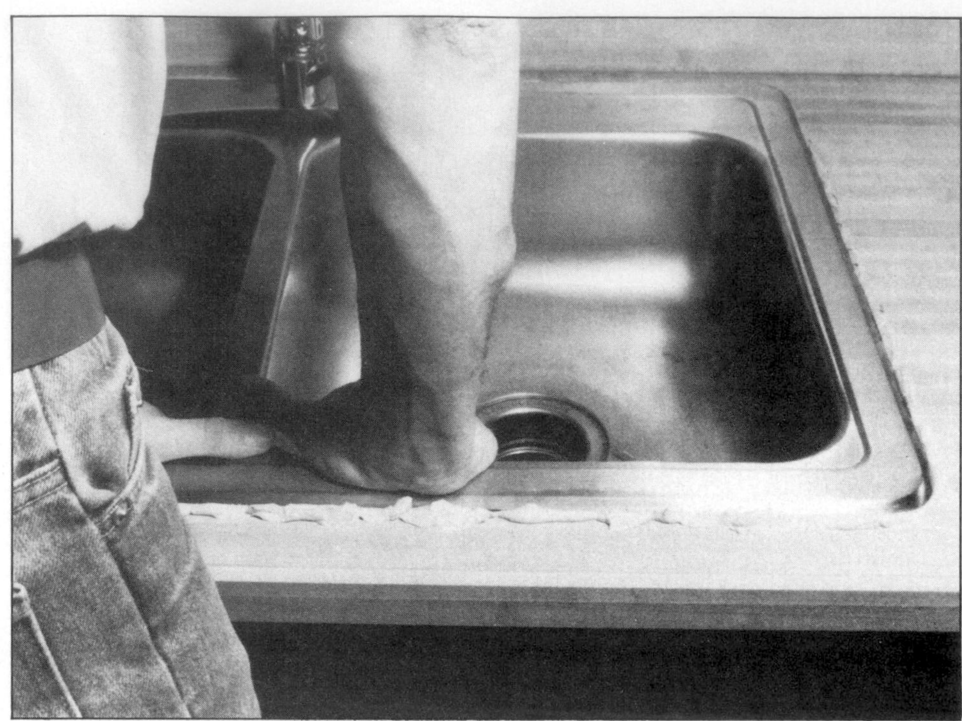

Make sure new sink is well sealed to countertop. Excess sealant—plumber's putty was used here—can be wiped away after sink is fastened down.

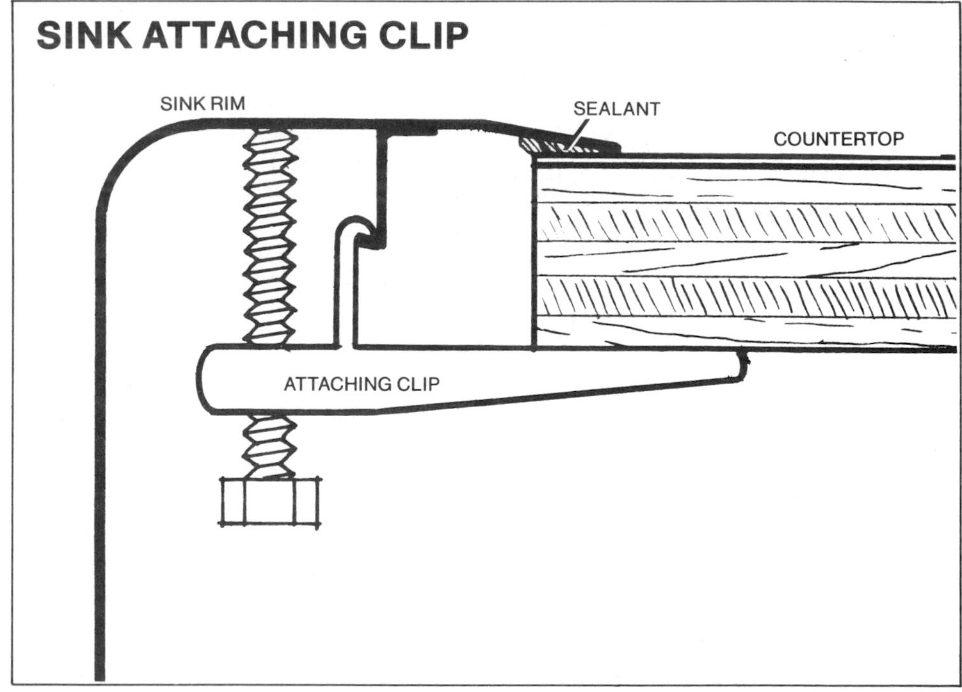

Sink attaching clips are used to fasten sink to countertop. You have to work from underneath sink to attach them. A socket wrench helps.

system. The only way to find out what's required is to discuss the work to be done with the building inspector. Small changes can often be approved on the basis of a simple visual inspection. If so, keep the work neat and tidy—it helps.

If you have to pressure-test a drain system, plastic systems are the easiest to cap off. Manufacturers make simple plugs that cement into any open ends. After testing the system, plugs are broken out with a screwdriver so you can make finish connections. Inflatable plugs and screw-on caps are used to close off the openings on copper and cast-iron systems. Inflatable plugs, pressure gages and air compressors can usually be rented from a local tool-rental company.

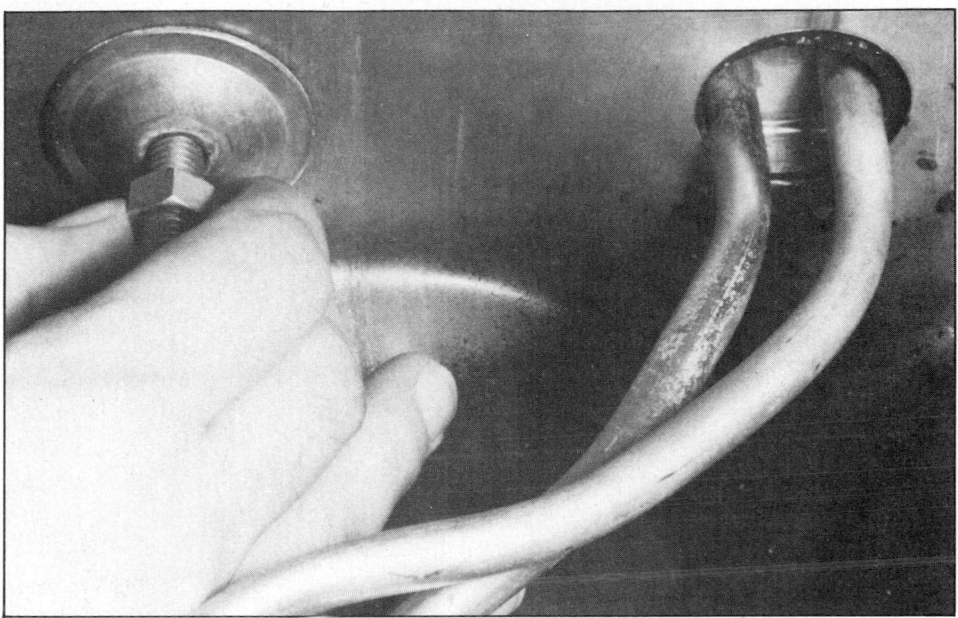

Most current single-control sink faucets attach as shown here, so they fit conventional 3-hole drillings on older sinks.

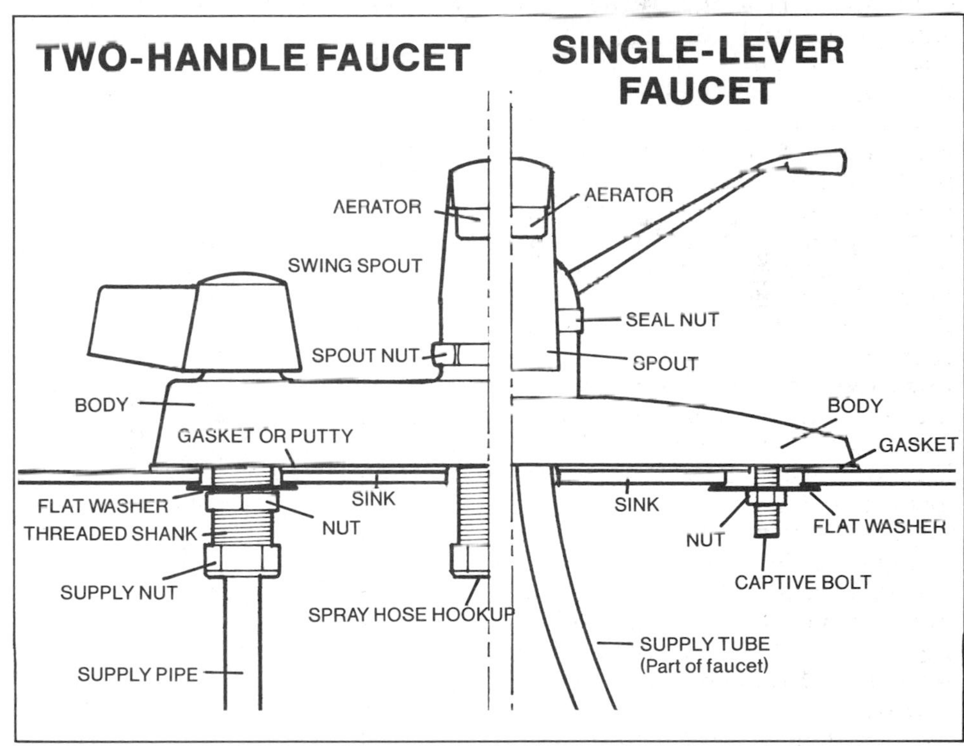

FINISH PLUMBING

Finish plumbing—installing and hooking up fixtures—can be one of the final phases of your remodeling project. After the rough plumbing is done, you can install the finish floor and walls, pages 118 and 135, cabinets and countertops, pages 154-169. Then do the remaining finish work, including installation of plumbing fixtures. Before you start any finish work, make sure required inspections have been made and approved.

SINK INSTALLATION

If you're installing a *self-rimming sink,* page 45, unpack and inspect it. Put the attaching clips where you can reach them from underneath the countertop. Put a narrow bead of tub-and-tile caulk or non-staining plumber's putty around the edge of the cutout in the countertop. Then lower the sink into place. Measure the spaces between the front corners of the sink and the edge of the countertop to make sure the sink is square.

Working from underneath, hook the attaching clips on the channel under the edge of the sink. Space clips evenly around the sink perimeter two or three on a side. Tighten every other clip a little at at time, until they're all snug. Wipe up excess tub-and-tile caulk or putty with a wet paper towel. Check the joint between the sink and the countertop for unevenness. Move or readjust the clips to correct uneven spots.

Faucet Installation—Most modern faucets come with a *base gasket,* so no sealant is needed between the faucet base and sink. If yours doesn't have a base gasket, put down a bead of tub-and-tile caulk or non-staining plumber's putty.

Drop the faucet into place on its base gasket or sealant and center it on the sink. If you can't center the faucet by eye, measure from reference points such as the edges of the sink.

From underneath, install and tighten the faucet *anchor nuts.* On some faucets these anchor nuts and washers thread onto the shanks of the water inlets. On others, nuts and large washers attach to *captive bolts* on the bottom of the faucet. The drawing above shows typical faucet installations with labeled parts.

Connecting faucets from behind a sink bowl can be difficult. The job is done much more easily with a tool called a *basin wrench.* A basin wrench has a shank with a T-handle at one end and a hook-shape swivel jaw on the other end. The jaw is reversible, to permit tightening or loosening connections in narrow spaces. If possible, mount faucet before installing sink.

Even if you use a a basin wrench, you may have to crawl underneath the sink to do the work. Use a small pillow to support the back of your head while you're working.

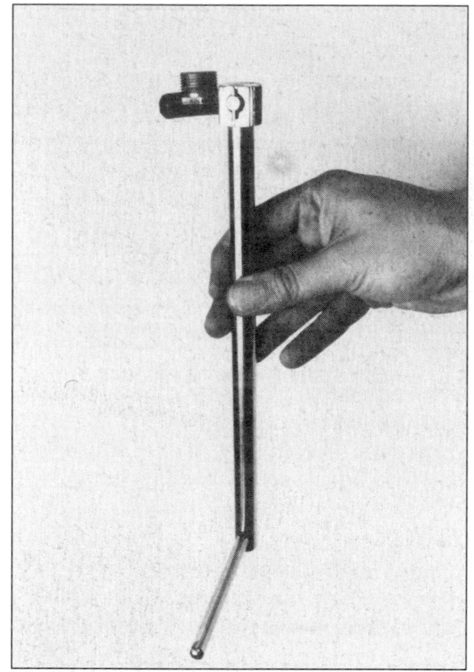

A *basin wrench* is best tool for attaching parts in tight spaces up behind a sink. Flip hook to opposite side of wrench head to operate in reverse direction.

Supply-Pipe Installation—Shut off and drain the water system. Remove the caps from water supply-pipe stubs under the sink. On a galvanized-pipe system, just unscrew the caps. On capped copper or plastic, cut the pipes just behind the soldered or solvent-welded caps.

Supply-pipe connections come in two parts: the *stop valve* and the *riser.* See photo above right. These parts are sold separately, so you can custom-make an unconventional supply pipe if you have an unusual situation. First install the *escutcheon* and then the *stop valve,* as shown in the photo.

On galvanized systems, unscrew the cap, apply pipe-joint compound and thread on the stop valve. Use a smooth-jaw wrench to avoid marring plating on the stop valve. For a completely exposed installation, use a plated supply nipple. Unscrew galvanized nipple from wall and install the plated one. Then install escutcheon and stop valve.

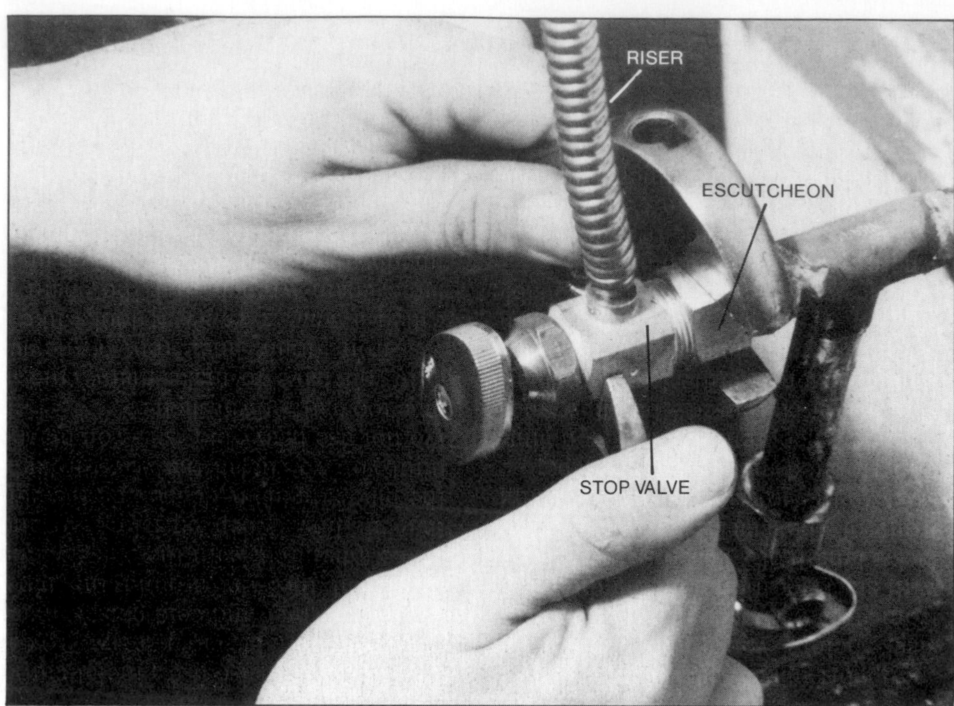

Use two wrenches, one to hold escutcheon and one to loosen or tighten stop valve. Align stop valve with riser as shown, then connect riser.

On copper and plastic systems, stop-valve installation depends on how you stubbed out the rough plumbing. If you finished the stubs with a *threaded adapter,* such as a 1/2-inch female sweat x 1/2-inch male IPS, unscrew the threaded cap on the adapter. Apply pipe-joint compound, and screw on the stop valve. This is also the best way to connect a plastic pipe system.

If you soldered caps on the copper pipe stubs, cut them off with about 1/2 inch of pipe. Solder the stop valve on, or use a stop valve with a *compression connection,* as shown in the photo at right.

To install a compression-type stop valve, put the *escutcheon* and the *compression nut* on the stub. Then put the *compression ring*—also called a *ferrule*—on the stub. Slide the back of the stop valve onto the stub until it bottoms out. Then thread and tighten the compression nut. Don't worry about the outlet position on the stop valve while tightening. Just make sure the stub stays bottomed. Then back off the compression nut until you can swivel the stop valve, position it, and retighten.

Shut off the stop valves, turn the water on and check for leaks. If the compression connection leaks, shut off the water, unscrew the compression nut and remove the stop. Wrap two thicknesses of pipe-thread tape onto the compression ring, and reassemble. Don't overtighten, and don't try to move the compression ring once you've made the connection.

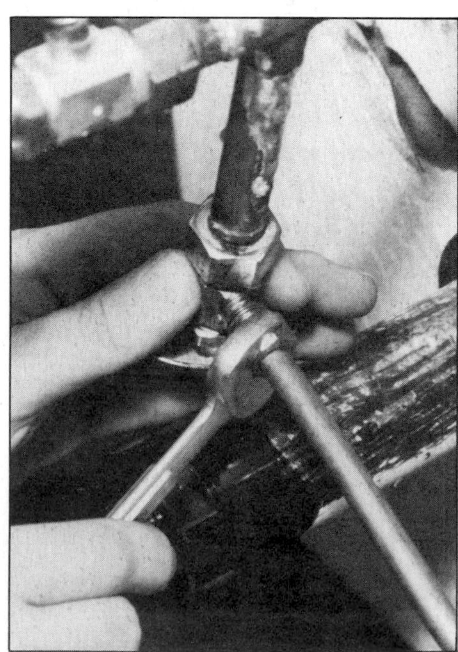

Water-supply line for dishwasher is usually 3/8" soft-copper pipe. Compression fitting shown here is used for hookup. Make sure line has a shutoff valve.

The risers usually are connected to the stop valve with compression connections. These connections have rubber-cone washers instead of compression rings. Before assembling the end connections on the riser, trial-fit each one. Trim and bend the riser to align with the stop valve and with the faucet connection. Make sure each end of the riser enters the socket straight, not at an angle. It's better to have a slight curve in the riser, rather than a straight run. The curve provides some flex to absorb small stresses without disturbing the end connections.

Swivel the stop valve slightly to one side to get a curve or to use up surplus riser length. Assemble end connections on the riser, thread and tighten. When bending risers, work slowly and carefully. They're easy to kink, and not easy to unkink. If the riser is badly kinked, it's better to replace it than try to unkink it.

Before turning on the water to check your work, remove the *aerator* from the faucet. The aerator is usually a small screw-on assembly in the end of the faucet spout. Then you can flush out any debris in the lines without clogging the aerator. If you do this before you install the drain or trap, put a bucket under the sink.

Sink Strainer Installation—Sinks are equipped with either basket-type or flat strainers, depending on the sink's use. Flat strainers are generally used on laundry sinks. All others use a basket strainer, so that debris can easily be removed by lifting out the basket and dumping it.

To install the strainer, apply a ring of non-staining plumber's putty around the hole in the bottom of the sink. Do not use glazing putty or tub-and-tile caulk in this location. Anything other than non-staining plumber's putty will deteriorate rapidly.

Remove the attaching parts from the drain body. Drop the drain body into the hole and center it. Push down firmly to bed the drain body in the putty.

From the underside of the sink, install the strainer's attaching parts and tighten. The attaching parts vary from one make to another, but are usually a neoprene ring, a large metal washer, and a large nut. Tighten the nut enough to compress the neoprene washer slightly. Much of the putty should extrude around the strainer. Clean off the surplus putty.

Now thread the *tailpiece* into the bottom of the drain body and tighten. If the tailpiece is already in, make sure it's tight.

Put a thick layer of plumbers' putty under lip of strainer body before installing it.

Shown are parts of basket-strainer assembly.

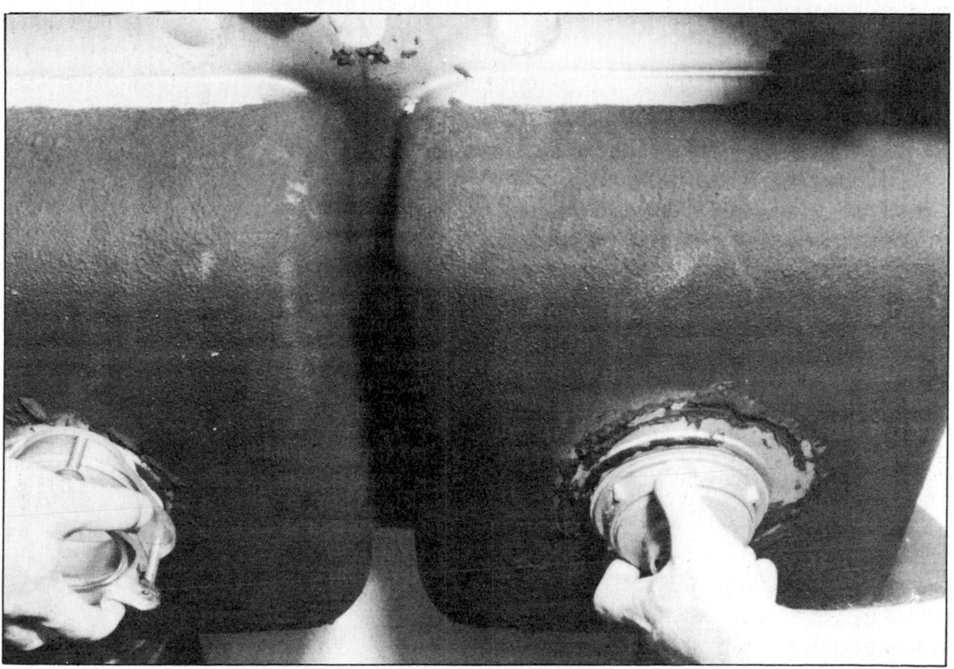

Tighten down large nut and sealing washers from underneath.

Sink Trap Installation—Traps are available in both metal and plastic pipe. Either type can be used on any drain system. If plastic traps are code-approved in your jurisdiction, they are preferable to the metal ones. They're non-corroding and the smooth interior does not collect debris or scale.

Both types install similarly. A male-thread trap adapter is required on the wall stub. Remove the cap from the drain-line stub and install the appropriate adapter.

Assemble the trap loosely with its nuts and rubber washers in place and trial-fit it. Cut off surplus pipe at the outlet end of the trap. If the outlet arm of the trap does not slope downward, reposition the parts. Or remove the strainer tailpiece and cut some off. Leave plenty of overlap at the various slip joints in the trap assembly. Hand-tighten all the nuts and recheck alignment of the parts. Then wrench-tighten the nuts.

Some plastic traps don't require a wrench. They have ribbed nuts that can be hand-tightened. This can be a handy feature if the trap gets blocked with debris at a crucial moment, such as while you're entertaining. The whole trap assembly can be

First section of trap is installed to drain outlet in wall. ABS assembly shown here need only be hand-tightened. Don't forget to install plastic seal washer.

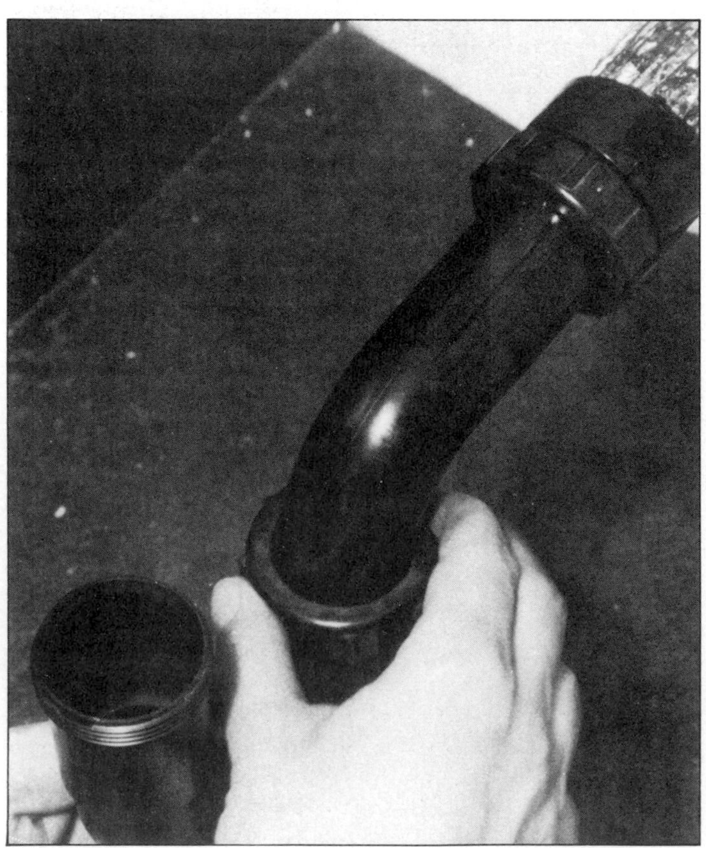

Next section of trap is installed. Make sure assembly aligns with sink outlet at this point.

Here, trap is being attached to sink-strainer tailpiece. Trim tailpiece to fit, if necessary. Horizontal pipe at right leads to other bowl in sink.

dismantled, cleared and reassembled in a few minutes, without tools.

Avoid plastic traps that are solvent-welded together. They're quick and easy to put in, but alignments of strainer and drain-line stub are critical. Also, you can't service the trap without cutting it apart with a saw.

Sink Wastes—Double- and triple-bowl sinks require a device called a *sink waste*. A sink waste attaches to the strainer tailpieces with slip connections, the same as a sink trap. The waste channels water into a single-outlet tailpiece, which is then connected to the trap.

Sink wastes are available with an end outlet or a center outlet. Install the sink waste first, then install the trap. If you don't have enough vertical space for tailpieces, sink waste, sink waste tailpiece and trap, there are sink wastes that thread directly to the bottoms of the strainers. This eliminates strainer tailpieces, and reduces the total assembly height.

Garbage Disposers—Garbage disposers are installed in place of a sink strainer. Because mounting systems on disposers vary so widely, no specific instructions for mounting can be given here. The installation instructions supplied with the disposer are usually sufficient. The disposer discharge outlet is usually connected into the drain system by a slip connection.

ICEMAKER INSTALLATION

The easiest way to hook up a refrigerator icemaker is to install a *1/2"x1/4" compression angle-stop valve* on the stub coming out of the wall. This valve is installed similarly to the one shown on page 86. Install valve for easy access—inside a nearby cabinet or under the sink—not behind the refrigerator.

When the valve is installed, run a length of 1/4-inch soft-copper pipe up the wall to the back of the icemaker. Connect it to the refrigerator according to the manufacturer's instructions. This usually involves making another compression connection from parts supplied with the icemaker. Leave enough excess coiled-up pipe behind the refrigerator so you can move it out.

DISHWASHER INSTALLATION

Dishwashers require three hookups. Water-supply connection and drain connection are covered here.

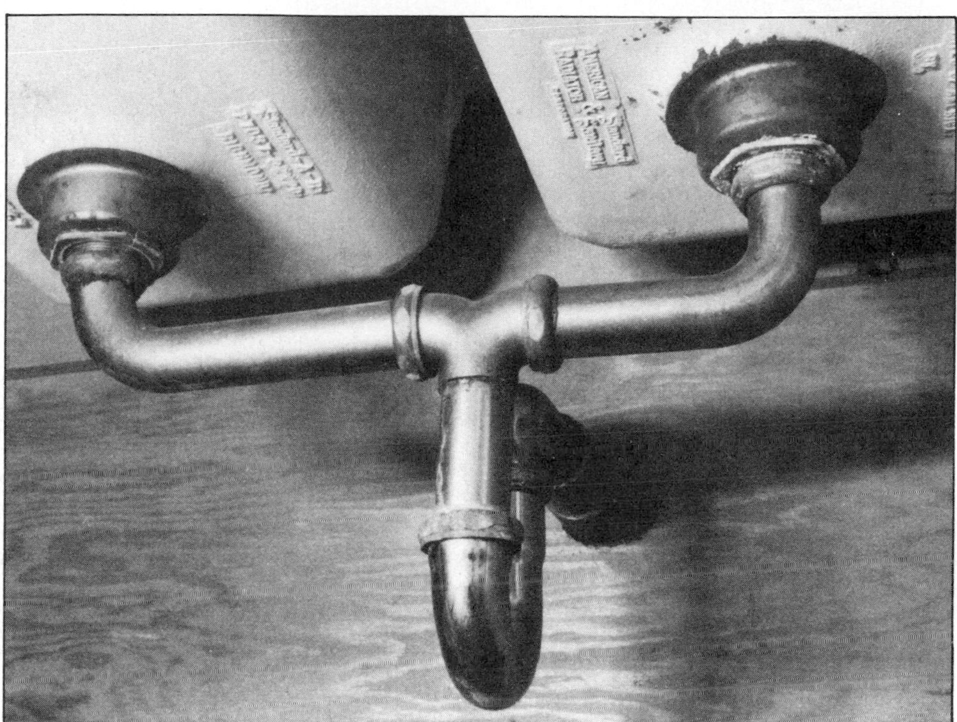

If vertical space is scarce, you can use sink waste shown here. It hooks directly to strainer bodies on sink and eliminates tailpieces.

Electrical connection is covered on page 95.

Water-Supply Connection—The easiest way to hook up water to a dishwasher is to use a *three-way angle-stop valve* on the sink faucet hot-water supply instead of a regular angle-stop valve.

Use a stop valve with an appropriate inlet for your installation, and two 3/8-inch compression outlets. Connect the riser leading from the sink faucet to one outlet of the stop valve. Cut enough 3/8-inch soft-copper pipe to reach from the stop valve to the dishwasher inlet. Connect one end to the other stop-valve outlet. Route the pipe to the dishwasher through the side of the cabinet, if the dishwasher is right alongside it.

If the dishwasher is some distance from the outlet, run the pipe through a hole in the bottom of the cabinet and through precut notches in the cabinet sides. The notches should be cut when the cabinets are installed. If you overlooked this step, run the line along the bottom rear of the cabinets until it reaches the dishwasher. Drill holes in any intervening cabinet sides.

Firmly anchor the pipe to the cabinets with pipe clamps. The valve in the dishwasher opens and closes quite abruptly, and a loose pipe can produce an annoying thump.

Hook up the other end of the supply line according to the instructions that come with the dishwasher. Hookup usually involves a compression connection.

Dishwasher Drain Connection—Drain connections for dishwashers require a special sink-strainer tailpiece with a small branch inlet. Or you can connect the dishwasher drain to a garbage disposer, if it has a connection for a dishwasher.

High-pressure neoprene hose is attached to the dishwasher outlet and the drain connection with hose clamps. Route the neoprene hose alongside the water line to the disposer or branch outlet in the sink-strainer tailpiece. If you're using the dishwasher connection on a disposer, you'll have to locate and remove a plug in the disposer before hooking up. Check the disposer installation sheet for details.

Some codes require an *airbreak* to be installed in the dishwasher drain line. An airbreak is a fitting that installs in a countertop or outside wall. It vents the dishwasher drain line so sewage or sewer gas can't be drawn back into the dishwasher. Many current-production dishwashers have a built-in airbreak.

Electrical Work

Here are some of the tools and materials used in electrical work.

Home electrical systems are complex and carefully regulated by codes. Some jurisdictions require all electrical work to be done by a licensed electrician, but most permit you to do some or all work yourself. Also, the electric utility company will insist that any work on the meter, the meter base, or wiring from the meter to the street must be performed by a licensed electrician or one of the company's own employees.

This section does not cover everything you need to know to rework your electrical system. It does cover basic circuit design and circuit installation. It also covers basic light-fixture installation.

Note: Information in this chapter is based on the U.S. National Electrical Code and applies to the United States only. In Canada and other countries, electrical codes and practices may differ from those described here. Consult local authorities before attempting any work described in this chapter.

ELECTRICAL REQUIREMENTS

The *service entrance* is the place where the utility company's wiring meets your house wiring. It usually includes a weather-protected main cable and one or more meters and meter bases. Generally the meters belong to the utility and the bases to you. It also includes a main-panel box, and sometimes a secondary panel box that contains fuses or circuit breakers for the individual *branch circuits.* The main-panel box contains the main switch and fuses, or main-circuit breakers that serve the same function. It may also contain fuses or circuit breakers for branch circuits.

Unless someone has made some dangerous modifications in the past, all the circuitry in your house has some sort of *overload protection.* Modern wiring systems usually have *circuit breakers.* These look like large switches and are marked with an amperage. Older systems may have replaceable fuses that have a screw base like a light bulb, or cartridge fuses that look something like a shotgun shell.

If your present service entrance is old and small, the installation of a new kitchen might dictate replacing the entrance with a larger one. Many service entrances installed years ago had a maximum capacity of only 25 or 40 amps. Modern installations generally won't be less than 100 amps, and may be 200 or even 400 amps.

Inside the service entrance main-panel box will be a pair of large-capacity circuit breakers or a pair of cartridge fuses. Cartridge fuses may be installed in an insulated, removable holder inside the cabinet, so they may not be readily visible. The capacity of the main-overload protectors will be the same as the total capacity of the service entrance. When examining your service entrance, *do not touch any metal inside the box.* On the meter side of the main-overload protectors, the only limits on current delivery are the capacity of the utility's wiring and the size of the transformer that supplies your street.

Repairing or upgrading your service entrance is a job for an electrician or, in some places, the utility company.

Many older homes have electrical service that doesn't fit requirements of modern kitchens. This one is 40 amps, 2-wire (120 volts only). When working on or near an old electrical service, stay clear of incoming wires from power pole, left. If insulation is deteriorated and you bump a wire with a tool, ladder, or an arm, you can get a serious shock.

Work only on wiring that can be *completely disconnected* while the work is being done. If you make a mistake on a branch circuit, the fuse will blow or the breaker will trip when you turn the circuit back on. If you make a mistake inside the main-panel box or meter base, you can disrupt service to the block or the whole neighborhood.

Connections inside the main-panel box provide two kinds of grounding for your electrical system. One is the *neutral ground* that enables the whole system to function. The other is the *safety ground* that protects you and your family when you use electrical devices. If either of these grounds is disturbed, your whole electrical system could go dead or become potentially hazardous to use.

To determine if your present electrical service will be adequate, calculate the total electrical demand of the whole house, including the new kitchen, in *watts*. The wattage of a demand source is the voltage multiplied by the amperage. The current National Electrical Code uses a base of 3 watts per square foot of house area to provide for general lighting and convenience-outlet demand. This base demand should include areas such as a garage or attic that might be enclosed or finished in the future.

To calculate total electrical demand, add the following items that apply to your home:

- Area of house in square feet times 3 watts per square foot.
- Two small-appliance circuits at 2,400 watts each
- One laundry circuit at 2,400 watts
- Range wattage
- Oven wattage
- Electric water heater wattage
- Electric furnace wattage
- Electric dryer wattage
- Air conditioner wattage
- Wattage of any other permanent appliances

If the total of the above list is less than the wattage of your service entrance, it has sufficient capacity. For instance, if your total above is 19,600 watts and your service entrance is 100-amp three-wire, you're OK. At 120/240 volts, 100 amps equals 24,000 watts. On the other hand, if you have a 40-amp two-wire service entrance, only 4,400 watts are available. Your house needs a new service entrance. In addition, 240-volt three-wire service may be needed for some new appliances. Three-wire circuits are discussed on pages 95-96.

If your house is older and has fuses instead of circuit breakers, consider updating to circuit breakers. This requires replacement of the branch-distribution panel box, if one is included in your system.

Interior of modern service entrance. Vertical strip on right edge is ground strip, where all neutral (white) wires and all safety grounds (green or bare) wires terminate. Grounding is completed through large white-striped cable at top of strip, supplemented by a bare-copper ground wire attached to nearby metal water pipe. To determine service entrance size, look at main breaker. It's the big one at top of box. Amperage will be stamped on breaker handle.

If you have a basic knowledge of home wiring, you can upgrade to circuit breakers, even if the branch-circuit fuses are in the main box. Turn the main switch off and install a new panel box near the old one. Disconnect each of the branch circuits from the old panel box. Reroute the wires and hook them up to the new panel box. Then install a feeder cable from the old box to the new. The new feeder cable should be the same size or larger than the old feeder cable. If you're unsure of your wiring capabilities, have an electrician do this work.

Replacing a branch-distribution panel box is relatively safe and straightforward if there's a main switch elsewhere that allows you to turn off the current to the box you're replacing. Substitute a new panel box and internal parts for old, following the wiring diagram for the new box. You can also provide circuit breakers for new branch circuits at the same time, as long as you don't exceed the service-entrance capacity.

BASIC KITCHEN REQUIREMENTS

Electrical codes generally require kitchens to have at least one permanently installed light fixture controlled by a wall switch. All electrical equipment and outlets for plug-in appliances in a kitchen are required to be grounded. All electrical circuits are required to be provided with overload protectors. This can be done at the branch-circuit panel box, or at a separate kitchen distribution box.

Two separate 20-amp circuits must be provided for the kitchen. The codes usually refer to them as *small-appliance circuits.* One circuit should supply the refrigerator. The other should supply all other outlets that might be used for small appliances, such as toasters or food processers. Generally, any section of countertop over 12 inches wide must be supplied with an outlet on the wall behind. A standard, grounded convenience outlet is all that's required. A separate circuit is required for each 240-volt appliance, and for each 120-volt appliance drawing over 12 amps.

CIRCUIT DESIGN

The first step in designing electrical circuits for your new kitchen is to make a sketch of the kitchen. Indicate the location of each electrical demand. Determine the amperage draw of each piece of equipment to be installed and note it on the sketch.

If the specifications for a piece of equipment indicate wattage, divide the wattage by the voltage to get the amperage. For example, 1,000 watts divided by 120 volts equals approximately 9 amps.

Figure convenience outlets at 1-1/2 amps each. No allowance is needed for switches. Figure light fixtures at the actual maximum wattage, but never less than 1 amp. If you haven't selected all equipment yet, or don't have information on what you've selected, ask your electrical supplier to get the figures for you.

MAKE A MAP

If you're remodeling, map existing electrical connections, not only in the kitchen but in adjoining areas. Some circuits may serve more than one room.

Draw in outlets, fixtures and switches you can see in the kitchen and adjoining rooms. Remove a fuse or shut off a circuit breaker that serves some part of the kitchen. Mark the circuit number next to each electrical connection that's inoperative. Use a switched-on lamp to find outlets that are on that circuit. If existing circuits aren't numbered at the panel box, number them with a felt-tip marker before you start.

After you've tracked down every outlet, light and permanently wired device on that circuit, turn on the circuit and turn off another one. Keep repeating the process until you've determined the location and the total load on each circuit you're concerned with. If you want, keep going until you have the entire house mapped. Such a map can make future repairs and changes easier.

WIRING SWITCHES AND LIGHT FIXTURES

Check existing switches. Mark a small "3" next to any switches you know to be the *three-way* type. A three-way switch allows a light to be controlled from two different points. On switches that are not three-way, remove the cover plate and see how the switch is wired. Ignore wires that are not connected to the switch. If a pair of wires from a single cable are connected to the switch, power for the light is fed in at the light. Note this on your map.

If one wire each from two different cables is attached to the switch, the power feeds to the switch, and from there to the light.

If three different wires are connected to the switch, you've found a three-way switch. In an older house, someone may have deactivated the other switch and covered it up. If so, find the other switch box and install the correct removable cover on it. Otherwise you risk having the whole job turned down by an alert electrical inspector. You may even consider reactivating the switch.

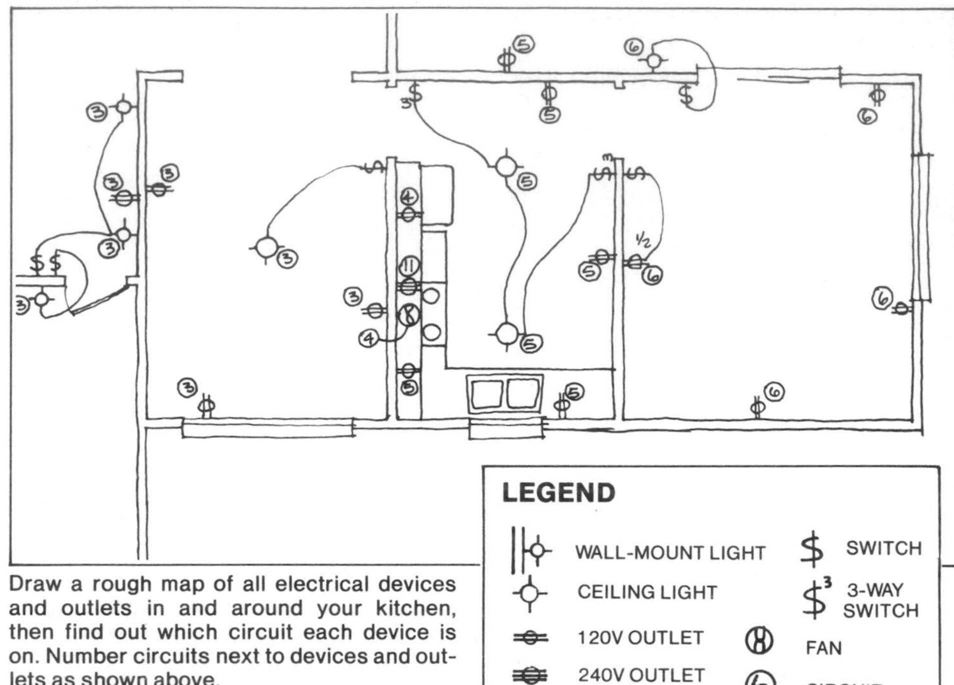

Draw a rough map of all electrical devices and outlets in and around your kitchen, then find out which circuit each device is on. Number circuits next to devices and outlets as shown above.

INSPECT EXISTING SYSTEMS

While you're determining how switches are wired, inspect the wiring. Conductor wires should be free of corrosion and should be at least 14-gage *solid* wire, not multistrand wire. The insulation should be intact and flexible, not brittle and deteriorated. Cables containing the wires should be firmly attached where they enter junction boxes. Junction boxes themselves should be free of corrosion and firmly attached to a stud or other framing member.

Switches and outlets should be serviceable and free of cracks, brittle insulation, paint and accumulated grime. Very little bare-copper wire should be visible at screw terminals and none at splices. This excludes safety ground wires, which are often bare copper for their entire length.

Taped splices in junction boxes were, and in some instances still are, permitted by code. But the tape should still be flexible, firmly in place, and covering all of the splice. Any splices *outside* junction or fixture boxes are not allowed by any code and should be enclosed in a junction box. All splices should be protected from mechanical strain and damage. Most junction boxes have clamps that firmly secure incoming and outgoing cables.

If you spot any of the problems described above, correct them as you remodel. A worn-out or improperly wired electrical system is dangerous.

LAY OUT NEW CIRCUITS

When you've mapped your existing electrical system, add the amperage on each circuit and compare it to the amperage of the fuse or circuit breaker to that circuit. If any circuits are overloaded, you'll need to reduce the load.

Mapping new or revised circuits is a process of trial and error. Put a piece of tracing paper over your layout. If you don't already have a layout, see pages 59-61. Start by noting the location of the main-panel box or fuse box. Then determine the shortest and least destructive path for any required new wiring. This will tell you where the new circuit wiring should arrive at the kitchen.

Bear in mind that your layout is two-dimensional, while your kitchen is three-dimensional. Use the appropriate notes for any locations where you'll have to run cable up or down a wall. This helps you estimate the amount of cable you'll need.

The object of the circuit-design process is to divide the electrical load equally among the circuits available. Keep trying different patterns until you find one where the load on various circuits is almost equal. The layout you want is one that uses the least amount of cable and requires the least amount of reworking and chopping out for access.

Certain elements of the electrical system can be determined quickly. All 240-volt appliances and 120-volt appliances over 12 amps must be on circuits of their own.

If you have many new circuits to install, or a long run from the main-panel box to the kitchen, consider installing a single, larger feeder cable from the main box to a sub-panel at the kitchen.

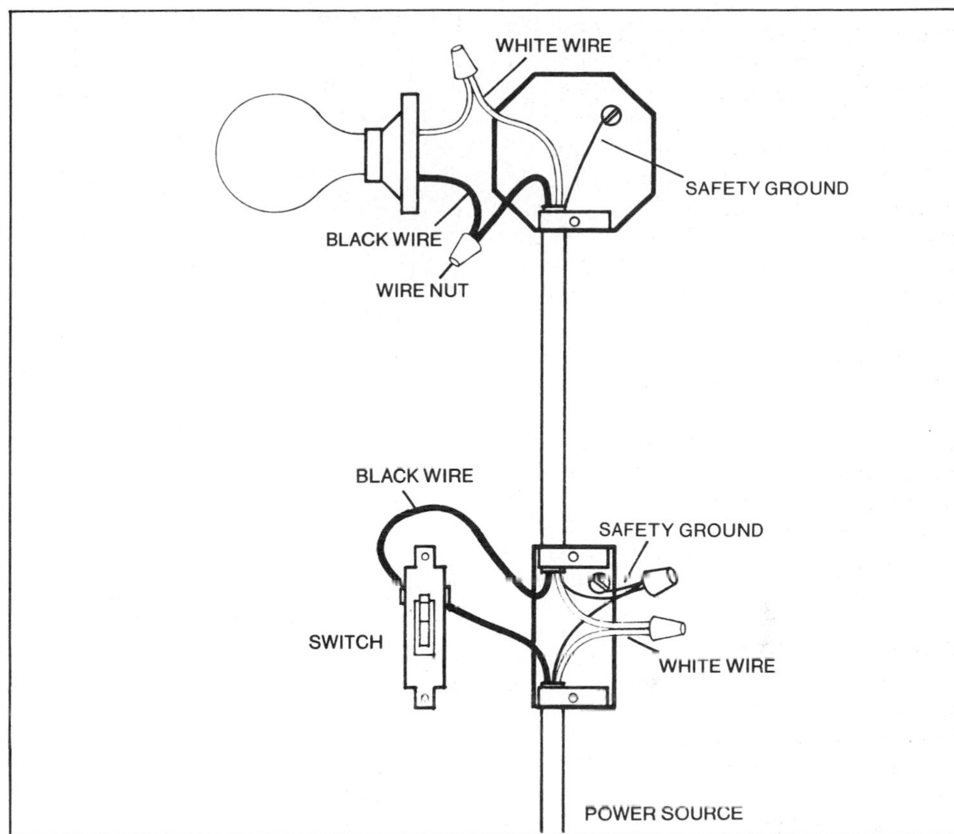

In this light circuit, power is fed in at switch.

WIRE SIZING AND SELECTION

Most jurisdictions now permit *non-metallic cable* for residential applications. A cable is a group of insulated wires wrapped together in a casing. Non-metallic cable is encased in a jacket of insulating material, usually plastic. Metallic cable uses a flexible, metallic jacket to encase the wires. The most common non-metallic cable types are type NM, type NMC, and type UF. Type NM is approved for clean, dry locations only. Type NMC is also approved for wet or corrosive locations. Type UF can be used in wet or dry locations, and is also approved for direct burial. There are many other cable types for different applications, and also a separate coding system for single wires. Your electric supplier or local building official can tell you which types your local jurisdiction permits.

Printing on the cable jacket will tell you wire type and gage, and the number and kind of wires. For instance, a cable marked "14-2" contains two 14-gage wires, one with black insulation and one with white.

If the cable is marked "-3" after the gage number, it contains a black wire,

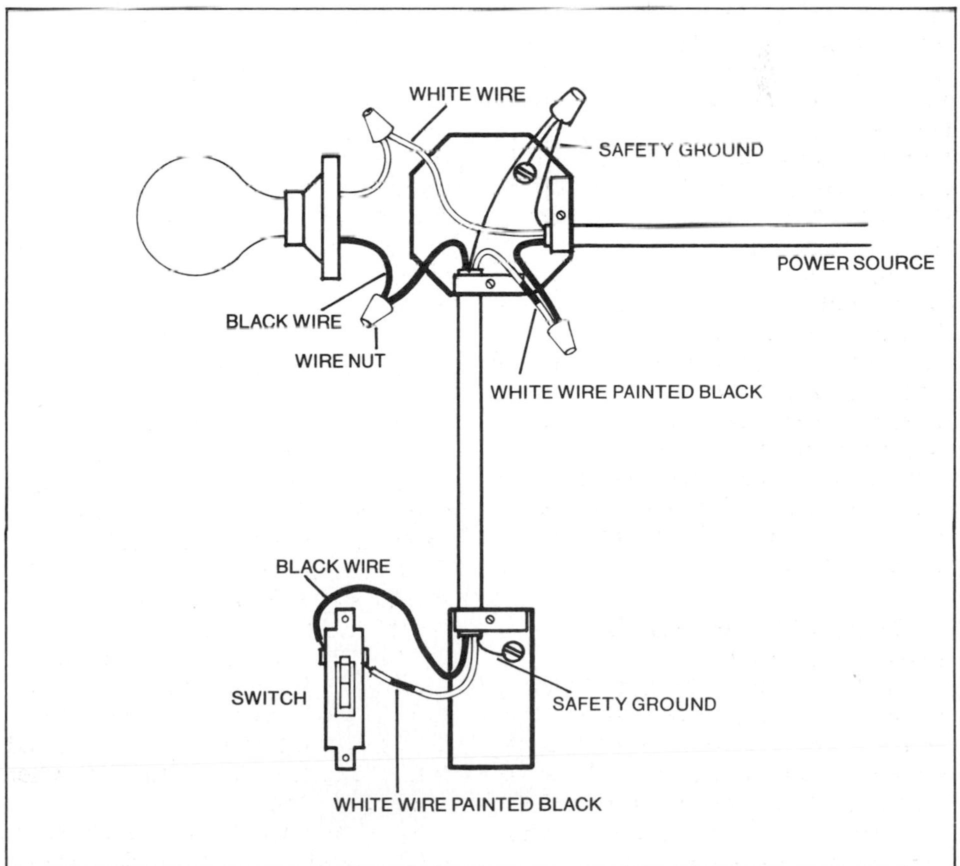

In this circuit, power is fed in at light.

a red wire and a white wire. If the cable is marked "with ground" after the gage and the number of wires, as in "12-2 with ground," the cable also contains a bare copper wire or a wire with green insulation. It is used for safety grounding.

Minimum wire size in most jurisdictions is 14 *AWG*—American Wire Gauge. Only solid wires can be used, except for connection leads in a light fixture. Correct wire size for a particular circuit depends on two factors. The first is the current-carrying capacity of the wire. Because current is measured in amps, this is the amperage capacity of the wire, called *ampacity*. The table at right shows the ampacities of the smaller wire sizes.

The other factor in correct wire size is the resistance of the wire to electrical flow. The larger the wire, the less resistance. Resistance causes voltage at the end of the wire to drop. Some electrical energy is dissipated along the way, as heat, to overcome the resistance. If a wire is long enough or small enough, no voltage will be available at the other end. Codes generally limit this *voltage drop* to a maximum of 5%, but for economical operation, it should be kept below 3%. The table at right shows maximum length for each wire size for an acceptable voltage drop.

Select wire sizes to meet minimum requirements for both ampacity and voltage drop. Overload current protectors, either fuses or circuit breakers, should be sized *no larger* than the total ampacity of the circuit they protect.

WIRING AMPACITY AND LENGTH

Wire Size (AWG)	Ampacity[1] (amperes)	Wire Length[2,3] (one way @ maximum amps @ 120v.)				
		VOLTAGE DROP				
		1%	2%	3%	4%	5%
14	15 amps	15'	30'	45'	60'	75'
12	20 amps	18'	36'	54'	72'	90'
10	30 amps	18'	36'	54'	72'	90'
8	40 amps	22'	44'	66'	88'	110'
6	55 amps	25'	50'	75'	100'	125'
4	70 amps	32'	64'	96'	128'	160'
3	80 amps	35'	70'	105'	140'	175'
2	95 amps	38'	76'	114'	152'	190'

[1]Information is for copper conductors only, with not more than 3 conductors per cable. Also assumes maximum 140F conductor temperature, maximum 86F ambient temperature. Some insulation types may have higher ratings, but none lower.

[2]Double lengths given for 240-volt applications.

[3]Amperage and voltage drop are proportional—lower amperage through same size wire means less voltage drop. Example: 8-gage wire at 40 amps-120 volts loses 2% voltage in 44 feet; 8-gage wire at 20 amps-120 volts loses only 1% in 44 feet.

WIRE COLORS

Wire colors are part of a coding system to help you keep track of wires in the electrical system. Black wires are always used for the electrically charged, or *hot* side of the system, and are always connected to brass-color terminal screws. White wires are always on the neutral side of the system, and are always connected to silver terminal screws. Red wires can be thought of as extra black wires.

The two primary uses of a red wire are in three-way switch circuits and in three-wire circuits, shown in drawings on the facing page. Green wires and bare copper wires are always used for safety grounding, discussed at right.

You may not be able to get a piece of cable with the particular combination of wire colors you need, and you don't have to. Use a cable with the right number of wires, and as close as you can get to the right colors. Then paint or tape the wrong-color wires with the right color, *at both ends*. For example, you may need two black wires in a cable, from the light to the switch as in example on page 93. Use a cable with a black and a white wire and wrap a strip of black electrical tape around the insulation on both ends of the white wire. You then have a black wire and a "black" wire.

SAFETY GROUNDING

Green wires or bare copper wires are used exclusively for safety grounding. The white wire that's part of the circuits, called a *neutral* wire, grounds the circuits. Also, every metal part in an electrical system must be independently grounded.

This safety ground does not form a part of the circuit. Every metal junction box, every appliance and all metal parts that might become charged, are grounded. The safety ground also connects to the third hole in convenience outlets, effectively grounding metal parts of any tools and appliances with a three-prong plug.

This kind of safety grounding has saved many lives. Before this practice was used, a loose wire or a frayed spot in insulation could make any nearby metal object part of the circuit, causing serious shock. The safety ground helps prevent such accidents.

It isn't necessary or required that you tear into walls and add safety grounding to an older electrical system. But the electrical inspector will require it on all new circuits. Always use non-metallic cable with a ground wire. Connect every piece of metal in the system to the safety ground, and connect the safety ground to a good main ground. A metal water pipe will usually do, if it's metal all the way to the underground street piping.

The best ground, if you can get to it, is the grounding strip in the service-entrance panel box. The grounding strip won't be hard to find—all the white wires are connected to it. If you're in doubt about the adequacy of a ground connection, check it with the electrical inspector on one of his inspections. Many electrical inspectors carry instruments that directly measure how well a ground connection is working.

ALUMINUM WIRING

Conductor wires in most electrical systems are made of copper. Cable with aluminum conductors has been used in the past and is common in very large wire sizes. Aluminum wiring can be perfectly safe, but specific installation techniques must be used.

When first introduced, aluminum wire and copper-coated aluminum wire was substituted for copper wire. Aluminum wire was on the market several years before the need for special installation techniques was discovered. If your house has aluminum wiring in the branch circuits, have a competent electrician check the entire system. He can quickly tell you if the system has been installed safely, or if it's a fire hazard.

If the system isn't safe, it can be made safe by replacing existing connection devices with the right ones, installed correctly. The wiring itself does not have to be replaced. Do not try to do this work yourself. Also, all new wiring should be copper.

CONNECTION DEVICES

Three basic connection devices in an electrical system are the *switch*, the *outlet* and the *wire nut*. Switches and outlets should be marked with the Underwriters Laboratories stamp or label. They should not be operated at a voltage exceeding that marked on the device. Switches and outlets shown in this chapter should not be installed on circuits over 20 amps. Other types of outlets are available for higher amperages and for 240-volt circuits. Consult your electrical supplier for the correct type of outlet for large appliances.

Appliances such as stoves and dishwashers can be wired directly into the circuit. But wiring and servicing is much easier if you provide an outlet for each. Order the correct cord and plug for each appliance when you buy it.

Switches are always installed in the black-wire side of a circuit (black-black) or the red-wire side (red-red). Never install a switch in the white (neutral) side. Crossing colors will create a short circuit when the switch is turned on. Three-way switches are a special case, shown on page 95. Outlets are always connected from black to white or from red to white, never from red to black. See photos on page 99.

Use wire nuts to connect a wire to one or more other wires. These conical plastic devices are lined with molded threads or with a small, conical metal spring. The insulation on the wires should be stripped and the wire cut to length so that no wire is left exposed after assembly. Screw the wire nut onto the ends of the wires until they're solidly joined together.

THREE-WIRE CIRCUITS

You can economize on the two required small-appliance circuits by running them in a single cable This is called a *three-wire circuit*. In a standard two-wire circuit, the cable contains a

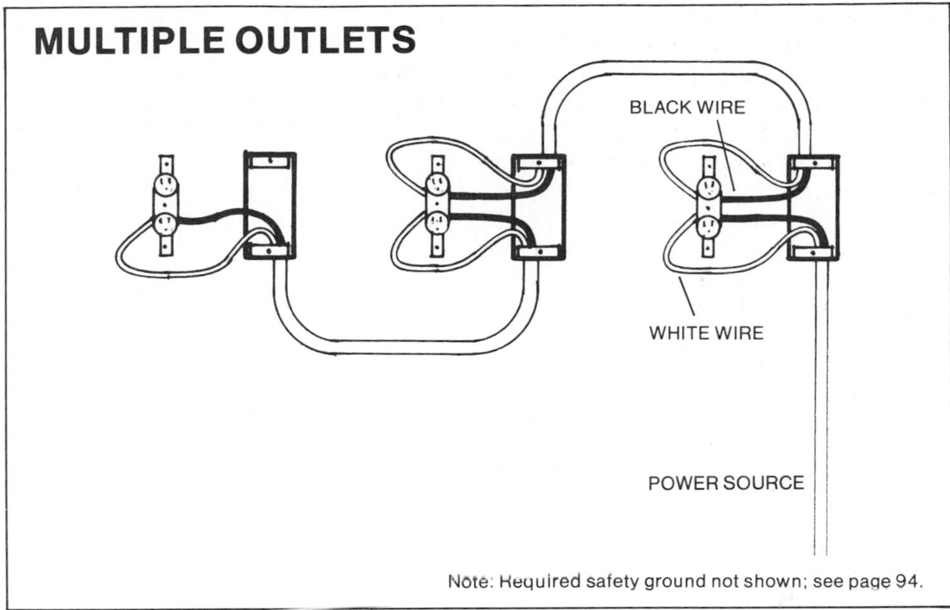

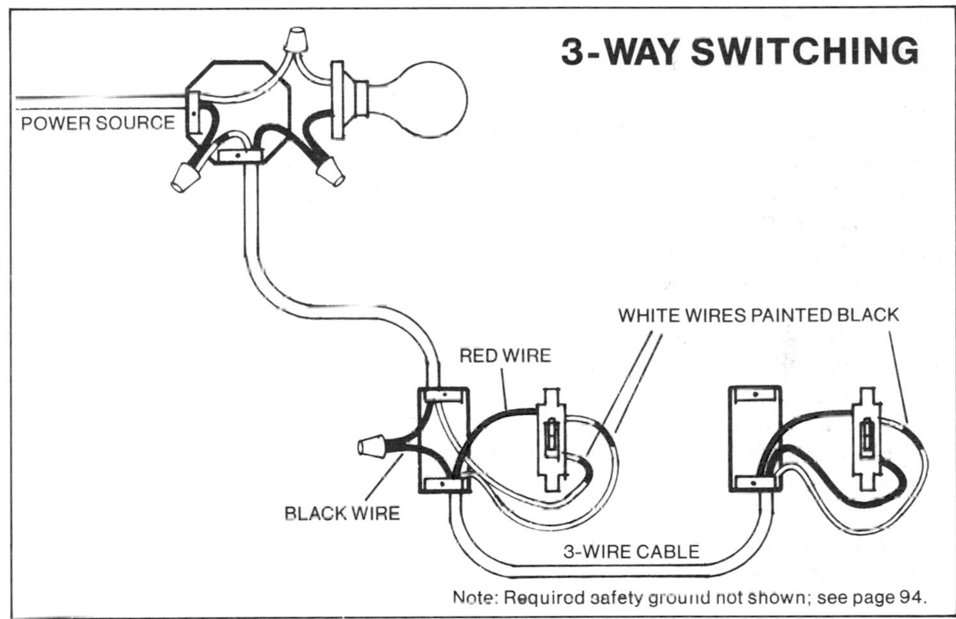

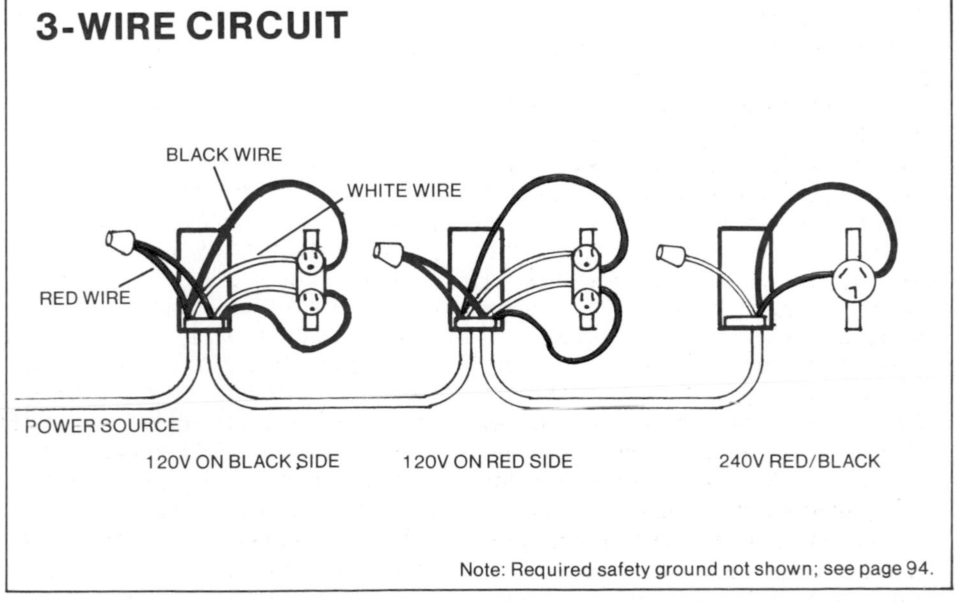

Nonconducting plastic electrical boxes are a relatively new development. Nails come premounted on box. Make sure box extends out as far as surface of finish wall material.

To suspend box for ceiling fixture when no joist or rafter is nearby, use a metal hanger strap. They're available for 16- and 24-inch centers. One shown is adjustable for odd spacings. Nail strap to adjoining joists or rafters from above. If you can't get to location from above, cut access hole from below and patch after installation.

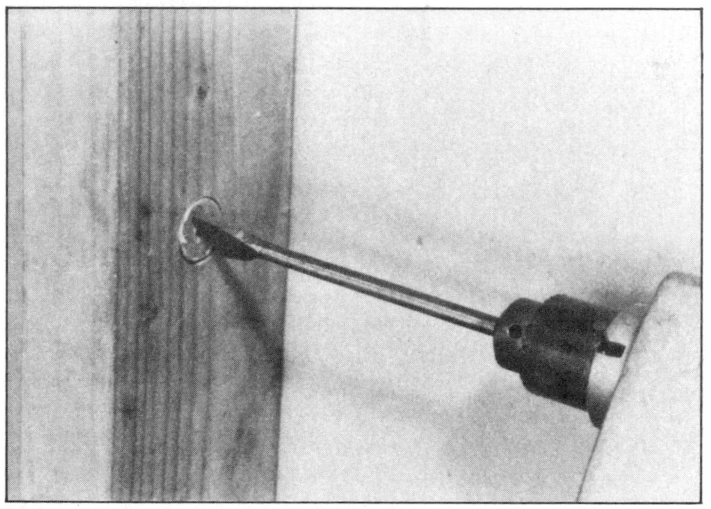

Make path for a new cable by boring holes through any intervening studs. Use a spade bit to drill holes.

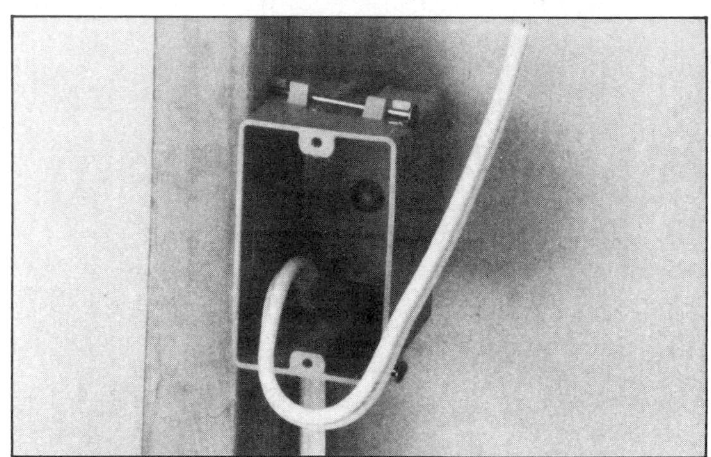

At end of a run or on a switch leg, leave 8-10 inches of cable.

black wire at 120 volts, a white wire which is neutral, and a green or bare wire which is used for grounding. Cable for a three-wire circuit contains a black wire at 120 volts, a red wire at 120 volts *attached to the other leg of the incoming 240-volt service*, a white wire which is neutral, and a green or bare grounding wire. See drawing on page 95. This means you can use black and neutral as one circuit and red and neutral as another circuit. *Note: If you use black and red as a circuit you get 240 volts. This will destroy 120-volt appliances.*

ROUGH-WIRING ELECTRICAL CIRCUITS

The installation sequence of rough wiring varies, depending on whether the wall framing is exposed or covered. Of course, it's much easier to install wiring in exposed framing.

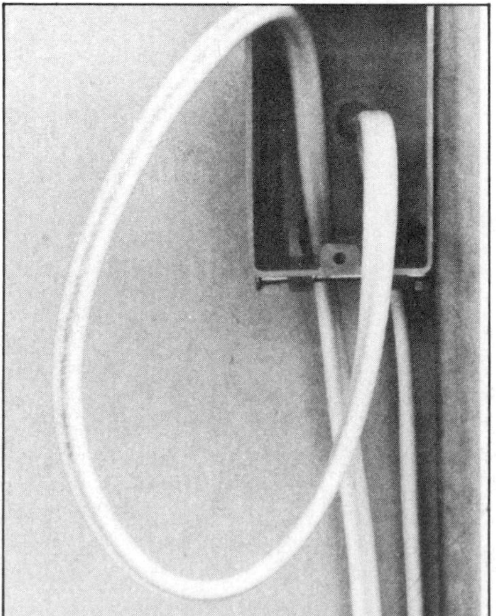

Don't cut cable when you come to a box in middle of a run. Feed cable into box and back out again, leaving a loop to be cut later. This allows you to adjust cable length as you anchor cable to framing. If you make cuts in middle of a run, you're stuck with length you cut.

ROUGH-IN WITH EXPOSED FRAMING

If wall framing is exposed, first install the switch and outlet boxes at the appropriate locations. The easiest boxes to use are ones that come with the attaching nails premounted on the side of the box. Just place the box alongside a stud and drive in the nails to anchor the box in place. Allow the box to project by an amount equal to the thickness of the planned wall-finish material. Switches are normally 44 to 48 inches from the floor, outlets 12 to 15 inches above the floor. Exception are switches and outlets above counters.

Light fixtures on walls can usually be mounted on an outlet box, but ceiling fixtures are installed differently. Remember, the ceiling box must also physically support the fixture, and some fixtures are quite heavy. Stamped-metal hanger straps are available to fit between ceiling joists on both 16- and 24-inch centers.

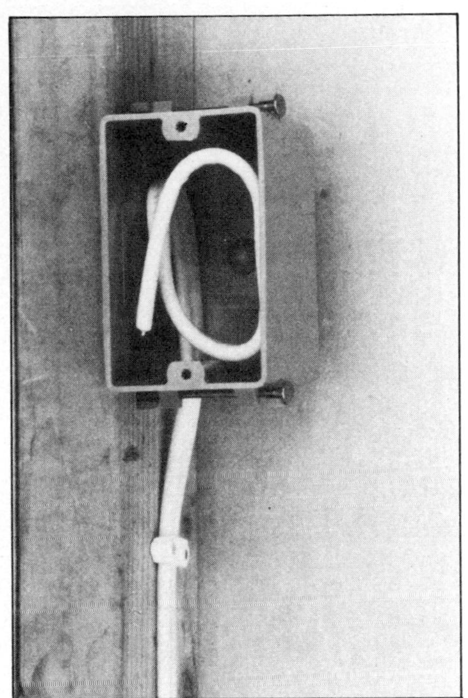

The code requires that cable be solidly attached to metallic boxes. Cable to nonmetallic boxes must be attached to framing within 8 inches of box. Plastic cable straps are preferable to metal staples, to minimize cable damage. Straps come with premounted nails.

The hanger strap is nailed into place between the joists first. An octagonal fixture box is then attached to the hanger strap's threaded stud using the nut provided. Again, the box should protrude beyond the framing enough to line up with the finish-ceiling surface. Hanger straps can also be used on walls when you're forced to locate a switch or outlet between studs.

Determine where cables will run inside the wall, floor and ceiling framing. Bore a series of holes in framing members to run the cable. Hole diameter in studs should not exceed 40% of the width of the stud. Holes in floor or ceiling joists must be at least 2 inches away from the top or bottom edge of the framing member. The diameter of any hole cannot exceed 1/3 the depth of the member. If any hole is less than 1-1/4 inch from the edge of a stud, the wiring must be protected from penetration by nails. Special 1/16-inch-thick steel protective plates are available for this purpose. Try to avoid notching for wiring. Notches provide a starting point for splitting of the framing member. Double-check with the building department before drilling holes in floor or ceiling joists—codes vary in different localities.

Pulling Cable—Run cable through the holes and into the boxes. Leave about 12 inches of cable hanging out of the boxes. If the box is in the middle of a cable run, loop the cable into and back out of the box—about an 18-inch loop. This may seem like a waste of expensive wire, but the code requires a minimum of 6 inches of each wire inside the box. The rest of the cable in the box will be used as you anchor the wires in place.

Don't stretch, crush or kink cable while you're installing it. You may damage the wires and insulation inside. Cables should not hang loose inside the framing. Use *cable straps* to anchor the cable to the side of the framing members at 4-1/2-foot maximum intervals. Cable straps are available at electrical-supply stores. Turn any corners with a gentle radius and make sure there is no stress on the cables. Tighten the clamps on the cables at box entrances.

ROUGH-IN WITH FINISHED WALLS

If you have to work with finish-wall material in place, start with the wiring instead of the boxes. Try to run wires so any cutting and patching done to walls will be hidden by cabinets or other fixtures.

First, determine the location of all switch, outlet and fixture boxes. Using the boxes as templates, mark and cut the box openings in the walls and ceilings. Before you cut, check the appropriate cover plates to make sure they will conceal the cutouts when you're done.

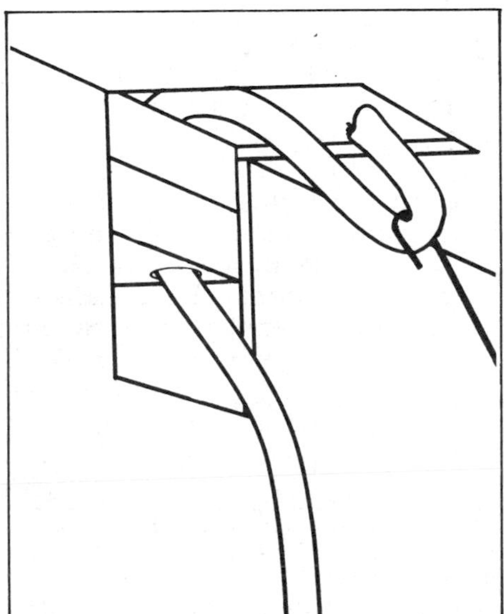

Turning a corner where wall meets ceiling requires two access holes and a coat hanger.

It helps to draw the circuit layout on the walls and ceiling as you figure it out. Try to run wiring parallel to the framing members to a location where access holes in the finish-wall material will be concealed. After you've decided where cables have to run, cut access holes. When you have to route a cable through a framing member, drill a hole crossways through the framing member. Extend the access hole in the finish-wall material 2 or 3 inches either side of the framing member. Then insert a drill in the access hole and bore a hole through the framing member on an angle.

Turning Corners—If the cable must turn a corner, such as at the junction of a wall and ceiling, cut two access holes. Position one in the ceiling, 2-3 inches from the corner. Locate the other in the wall just below the bottom edge of the double top plate.

Drill a slanted hole up through the top plates. Be careful not to drill through nails attaching framing members. The cable can then be doubled over and pushed up through the hole. Snag the doubled-over end and pull it into the ceiling. The hooked end of a wire coat hanger works well for this. The same technique works at corners where two walls meet.

Fishing Cable—Work the cable into walls and ceiling through the access holes, leaving 12-inch tails or 18-inch loops at each box location. Because cable is not very rigid, there will be times when you can't push it from one access hole to the next. In that case, use a *fish tape*. A fish tape is a roll of spring-tempered flat steel that is much more rigid than cable, but also quite bendable. It has a pulling loop on the end, so you can force it past obstacles and around corners, and then pull cable back through with it.

The fish tape can also be used to run cable across sections of exposed wall without having to cut into finish material. Cut an access hole in an adjacent concealed location and look for existing cable or pipe runs across the section of exposed wall. If you find such a run, work the fish tape through the holes alongside the existing run. Then connect the end of the new cable to the fish tape and pull it back through the holes.

Another effective but somewhat riskier technique is to detach the existing cable that runs across the exposed section of wall. The existing cable can be used to pull the fish tape through the holes in the studs to the other side. The fish tape can then be used to pull two cables back, the old one and the new one. This method avoids having to cut an access hole, but you do risk losing the existing cable in the wall if anything goes wrong.

Box Installation—The switch, outlet and fixture boxes are installed next. There are a variety of special boxes for use in existing finish walls. Most are anchored to the finish material by U-clamps or expanding clips. These special boxes are convenient, because they reduce the risk of losing the box and the cable ends inside the wall. But it's preferable to position the boxes adjacent to framing members, the same as in new work. They can then be solidly anchored after installation by drilling two holes in the side of the box and anchoring it to the framing member with screws. Mount boxes so the front edges will be level with the finish material, or slightly below it.

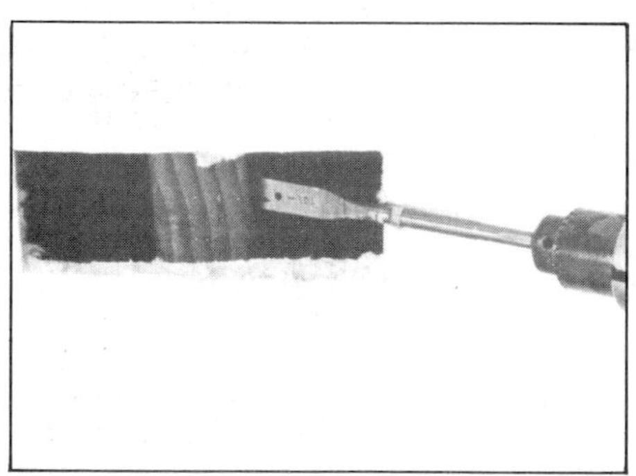

To get a new circuit past intervening framing members, cut access holes at each member. Drill through access hole, on as flat an angle as possible. Size of drill depends on number and size of cable to be pulled through: 3/8" is fine for one 14/3.

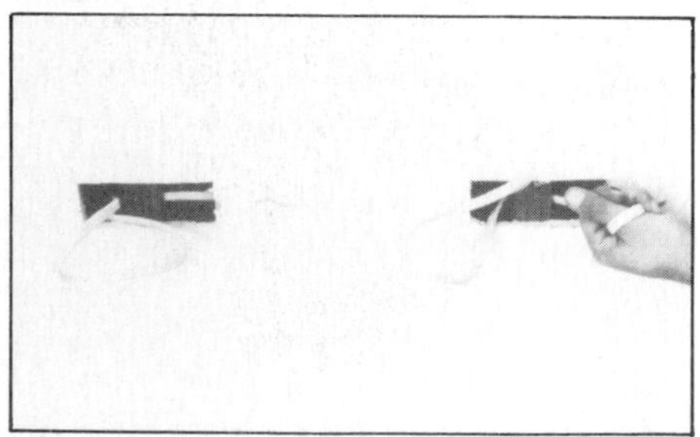

Feed cable through holes, keeping a loop of cable at each access hole to work with. Most cable is rigid enough to support itself over stud and joist spans of 16 to 24 inches.

FINISH INSTALLATION

The finish parts of an electrical circuit are not installed until after the finish wall is in place. In most cases, cabinets and countertops are also installed before finish electrical work is done. What's involved in finish electrical work is the installation of outlets, switches and light fixtures. Then you can hook up the circuit and test it.

OUTLETS AND SWITCHES

Connection methods for outlets and switches are essentially the same. Strip the cable jacket back to within an inch or two of where cable enters the box. Trim wires to approximately 6 to 8 inches in length. You now have a choice of methods. All modern switches and outlets still have traditional terminal screws on the sides. Most also have simple push-in connections on the back.

Screw Terminals—To connect to a screw terminal, strip enough insulation from the wire to make a loop 3/4 of the way around the screw shank, but not more than once around. The wire must not overlap itself under the head of the terminal screw. Form the loop with needle-nose pliers.

Hook the loop over the shank of the terminal screw and pinch it into place under the screw head with needle-nose pliers. The end of the loop should go clockwise rather than counterclockwise, so that tightening the screw will tighten the loop rather than expand it. Then snug down the terminal screw. The screw should be tight enough so you can't unscrew it using the wire as a lever. Don't tighten the terminal screw enough to deform the wire.

Do not connect two wires to the same terminal screw. A loop formed in a continuous wire will achieve the same result.

Push-in Connections—Far simpler and faster is to use the push-in connections in the back of the box. Strip the insulation off the end of the wire. There's a handy strip-length gage molded on the end or backside of switches and outlets. Then push the wire into the appropriate hole in the back of the switch or outlet. If you get it wrong, push a small screwdriver into the slot next to the hole and the wire will come free.

Mounting Procedures—Don't try to force the switch or outlet into the box on top of all the surplus wire. Fold the extra wire length a few times so it accordions neatly into the box without strain on the switch or outlet.

Start the top and bottom screws on the switch or outlet into the threaded holes in the box. Tighten the screws to pull the device down until the *plaster ears* on the device are resting firmly on the finish-wall surface. See photos on facing page. As you do this, you'll find you can adjust the switch or outlet position by means of the slotted screw holes. Adjust the device so it is vertical, whether the box is vertical or not. Now position the cover plate and snug down the screw or screws. Don't overtighten cover plate screws. The thin plastic plate is easy to break.

Wire Nuts—Connection of one wire to another is most easily done with a *wire nut.* Strip approximately 1/2 inch of insulation from the wire ends. Twist the ends together with pliers and screw on a wire nut of appropriate size. If any bare wire still shows, unscrew the wire nut and clip a little off the end of the wires. Then reapply the wire nut.

It's easy to tell if you're using the right-size wire nut for the number and size of wires to be joined. If the wire nut is too large, the wires will bottom out at the end of the nut but will not be firmly anchored. If the wire nut is too small, the wires won't thread very far into the wire nut, or may not start to thread in at all. If you're in doubt of the connection, try the next size nut and see if it works better.

FIXTURES

Fixture wires are generally connected to the circuit with wire nuts. Unpack the fixture and make sure all the pieces are there and intact. There will usually be an assembly sheet and a package of attaching hardware, including wire nuts. Fixtures are usually attached to the junction boxes by screws or a threaded center stud. Recessed fixtures are somewhat different. See facing page.

Screw-mounted Fixtures—The parts bag that comes with a screw-mounted fixture will contain a flat mounting strip with two threaded holes and two slotted holes. Slip the mounting strip over the machine screws on the face of the junction box, and tighten it down. Then assemble and wire the fixture, according to the instruction sheet. Insert finish screws from the parts bag through the canopy of the fixture and thread them into the threaded holes in the mounting strip.

Adjust the fixture canopy so it is centered over the junction box and completely covers the wall or ceiling opening. Then tighten the finish screws until the canopy of the fixture contacts the wall or ceiling surface. Don't overtighten, or you'll crush the canopy or pull the screws through it.

Stud-mounted Fixtures—The flat mounting strip for a threaded center-stud fixture will have two slotted holes for the junction-box screws, and a large threaded hole in the center. In some cases, the threaded center stud will be tubular and will serve as a conduit for the fixture wiring. In other designs, a decorative cap or hook goes on the end of the threaded center stud. Consult the assembly sheet for specifics. In any case, start the threaded center stud into the flat mounting strip, connect the wiring, then attach the fixture to the center stud. Add any additional parts to the threaded center stud that holds the fixture in place.

Heavy Fixtures—Large, heavy fixtures can sometimes exceed the strength of the box screws. Use the hanger straps, described on page 96, for such fixtures, even if the junction box is attached to a framing member. Then the hanger strap's threaded mounting stud can be used to support the fixture independent of the box itself.

Recessed Fixtures—Recessed fixtures can't be ignored until finish installation, as can other fixtures. In most cases, some part of the recessed fixture, usually a sheet-metal housing, must be installed at the rough-wiring stage. The rest of the fixture is installed after the finish-ceiling material is in place. Make sure the finish parts of the recess fixtures are kept in the original containers, stored safely, and are marked as to location. Recessed fixtures are so varied in their construction that no assembly specifics can be given here. Be sure to keep the assembly sheet with the rest of the finish parts.

Ceiling insulation placed directly on top of a recessed fixture can cause a potentially dangerous heat buildup. Either clear away such insulation, or make sure the fixture is marked *I. C.*, for *Insulated Ceiling*, on the UL label.

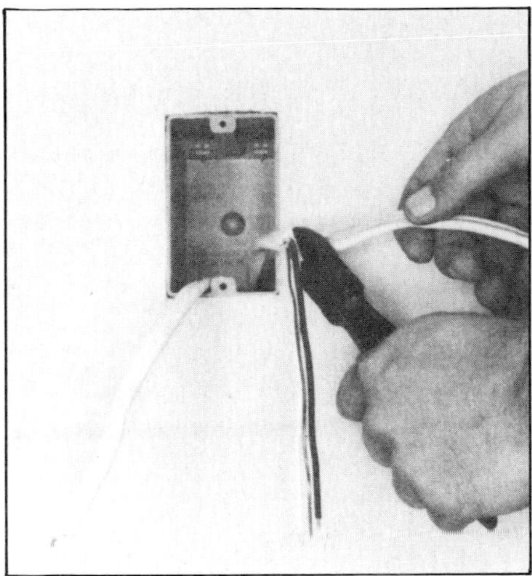

To strip outer jacket off cable, slit lengthwise with a utility knife. Don't nick insulation on wires inside. Clip off surplus jacket and any internal wrappers with wire cutters as shown.

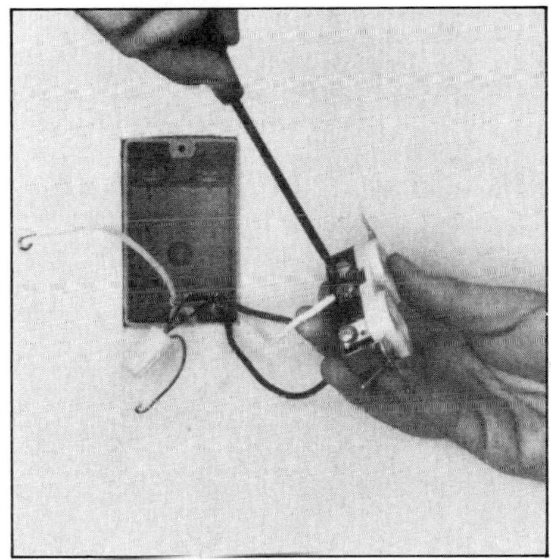

Hook up wiring, black wires to brass screws, white wires to silver screws.

Heavier fixtures are usually hung on tubular center stud. Other attachment variations are available. Check instructions packed with fixture.

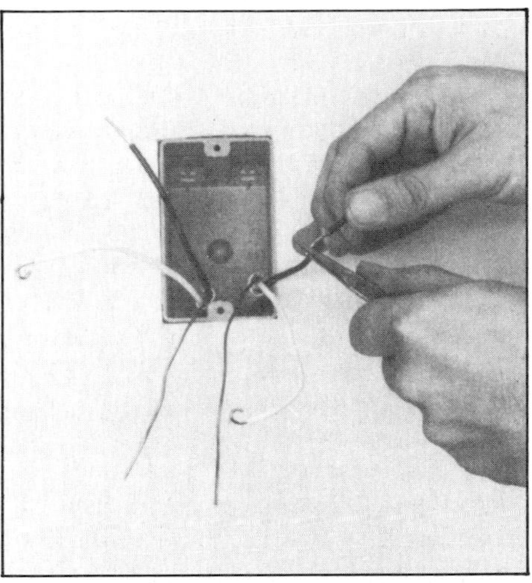

Cut wires to length—with some extra in case you misjudge when stripping. Strip off an inch or so of insulation. Form loops in each conductor wire with needle-nose pliers. Make loops relative to end of insulation, not end of conductor. Snip off excess conductor beyond loop.

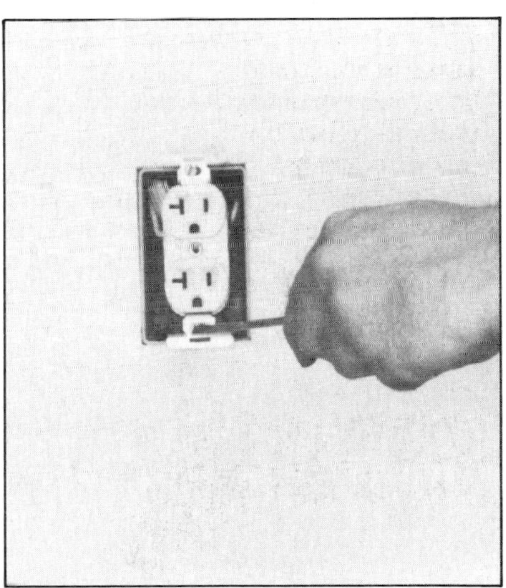

Install device in box, folding wires in behind it. Make sure device is vertical, even if box isn't.

This is most common way to mount fixtures that don't weigh more than 1 or 2 pounds. If holes in fixture line up with screw holes on box, cross-strap can be omitted.

Heating, Cooling & Venting

All kitchens require an exhaust system to vent heat, smoke and cooking odors. In most kitchens, a range hood does this job. This range hood features fold-down warming racks.

Behind every heating or heating-cooling system lies complex engineering and design work. Substantial modifications can disrupt the system balance, and even its function. Any resulting problems usually will not show up under normal circumstances, but under the most extreme ones. The coldest week in winter is not the time to try to straighten out your heating system.

Kitchen remodeling often requires changes to the present system. Certain changes are safe and often easy. Lengthening or shortening a duct by a foot or two, or moving a length of baseboard convector a few feet, usually won't affect the system enough to matter. For major changes, call a heating-and-cooling contractor.

HOT-WATER SYSTEMS

Hot-water heating systems generate hot water in a central boiler and circulate it through baseboard convectors or radiators to deliver heat to the rooms. Hot-water heating systems can be modified using the plumbing techniques described on pages 74-80.

If you're not familiar with the way your hot-water heating system works and the basic principles involved, consult a plumber or heating contractor on the modifications you want to make and have him do the work. If you have a working knowledge of your heating system, follow the guidelines given here.

Make sure the *flow rate* and *pressure drop* through the modified section closely approximates that of the original. In other words, make sure pipe length and size remains about the same, including pipe inside the baseboard unit. Also make sure the same number, size and type of fittings are in the system.

Some hot-water systems circulate water directly from one baseboard unit to the next. Others use a large-diameter circulating pipe, called a *main*, and move hot water into the baseboard units through a *diverting tee*. This is a tee with a small vane inside that redirects part of the water flow. The diverter tee is located on the upstream side of the pipe loop on the baseboard unit. If you have to rework the main, make sure you use a diverter tee where there was one before.

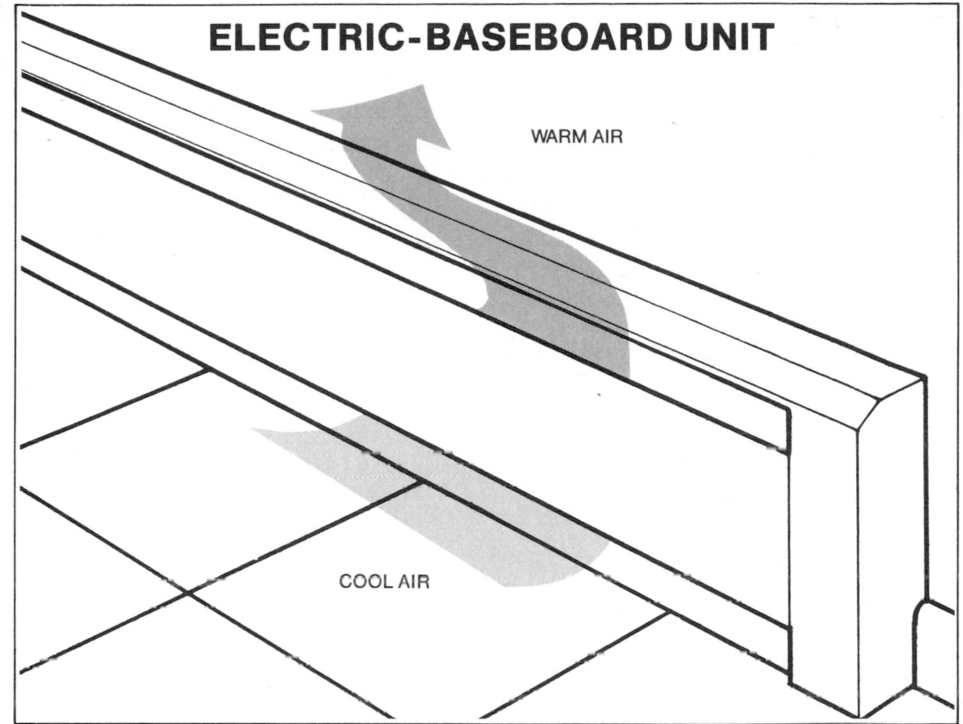

Electric-baseboard heaters are separate units installed in each room. They're wired like other electrical fixtures. They have separate thermostats.

If you've enlarged the kitchen or added any extra windows or doors, you may have increased the heat loss. To compensate, see if you can increase the amount of *finned element* in the kitchen baseboard convector or radiator. This may upset the balance of the system, requiring adjustment of the balancing dampers on all the baseboard units.

If the units don't have balancing dampers, balance them by using heavy-duty aluminum foil to block some of the air flow around finned elements of units that are emitting too much heat in other parts of the house. Just pull the cover off and wrap foil around part of the finned element.

If you've added finned elements to the system and the overall output doesn't seem adequate, inspect the limit-control settings on the boiler. It's possible that the operating-limit control is set fairly low and can be moved up 5 to 10 degrees. If the boiler operating temperature is in the 160F to 180F range, there's a possibility of increasing operating temperature. If operating temperature is in the 205F to 210F range, you can't get any more heat out of the boiler.

Note: If you're not completely *knowledgeable about boiler controls, call a serviceman to make any changes.*

Another way to get a small amount of extra capacity out of a hot water system calls for a substitution. If your boiler has a *tankless heater* to supply domestic hot water, you might consider installing a separate water heater. This can liberate some of the boiler capacity for room heating purposes. This is probably a job for a serviceman because the control system will have to be reworked.

If you've reduced heat loss, it's easy to compensate. Just turn the boiler operating temperature down a few degrees. If your boiler is oil-fired, a serviceman will often be able to install a smaller-size nozzle to reduce the fuel flow through the oil burner.

If your present hot-water heating system won't handle the additional heating requirements, consider adding an electric baseboard unit with its own thermostat.

ELECTRIC-BASEBOARD HEATING SYSTEMS

Electric-baseboard systems are easy to modify. Usually, there's a separate electrical resistance heating unit with its own thermostat in each room. The heating unit and the thermostat can be relocated just like any other electrical fixture. For more information on electrical wiring see pages 90-99.

In general, the heating unit should be located under or near the window, or at least on an outside wall. The thermostat should be located on an inside wall, away from drafts and away from heat sources such as an oven or range.

If you have a problem finding an open stretch of wall for an electric-baseboard unit, try using a fan unit instead. These are designed to fit under a base cabinet. They're supplied with electricity just like an electric-baseboard unit and warm air is blown out by a squirrel-cage fan.

WARM-AIR HEATING SYSTEMS

Warm-air heating systems typically generate warm air in a central furnace and circulate air to the house through a network of ducts. The duct network for central cooling systems is much the same. In many cases, heating and cooling systems share the same ductwork. Most ducts are sheet metal, though a few may be fiberglass board, or a round, flexible heat resistant plastic. Find a knowledgable heating contractor to modify a fiberglass-board duct, because special fabricating equipment is required. The flexible plastic ducts can be easily moved to a new location.

Changing a sheet-metal duct system requires more work. First, remove any registers in the area you're working on. Then, if the ducts aren't already exposed, remove as much wall- or ceiling-finish material as needed to provide working clearance. Shortening a duct can often be done by trimming off excess sheet metal with sheet-metal shears. More extensive changes usually require opening the wall or ceiling back to the first joint in the system to gain access. Measure and sketch the changes to be made before removing any sections of duct that are to be modified.

Duct sections are held together with sheet-metal screws or with *interlocking joints.* Interlocking joints are made by folding the edges of the metal duct back on themselves to form a "U". Then a C-shaped metal slide is driven into folded ends to lock them together.

To disconnect duct sections with interlocking joints, remove duct tape sealing the joint and fold up the end tabs on the metal slide. Then drive

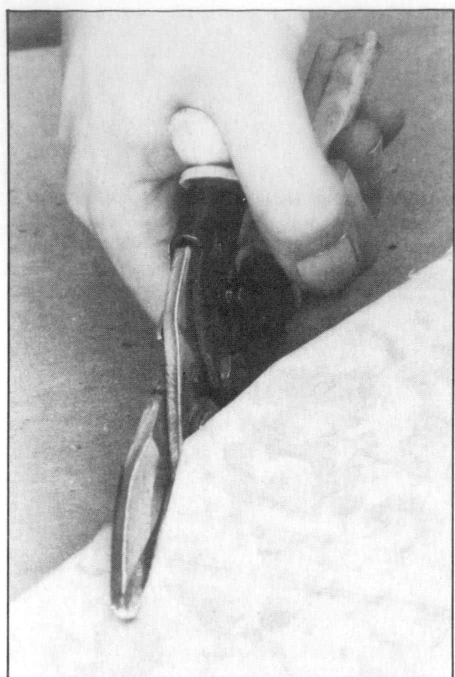

Most ductwork is made of galvanized sheet steel. It's easily cut and formed with hand tools. Best shears to use are *compound-linkage* or *aviation* type.

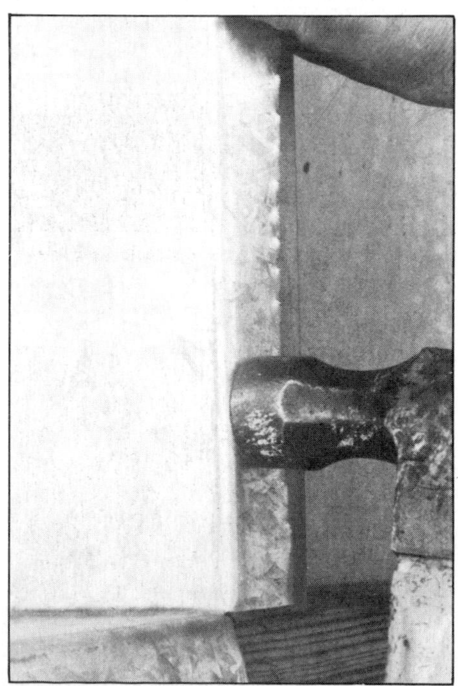

Bending and flanging galvanized steel is accomplished with repeated light hammer blows. Where ductwork terminates at a register, flange duct over framing before installing wall finish.

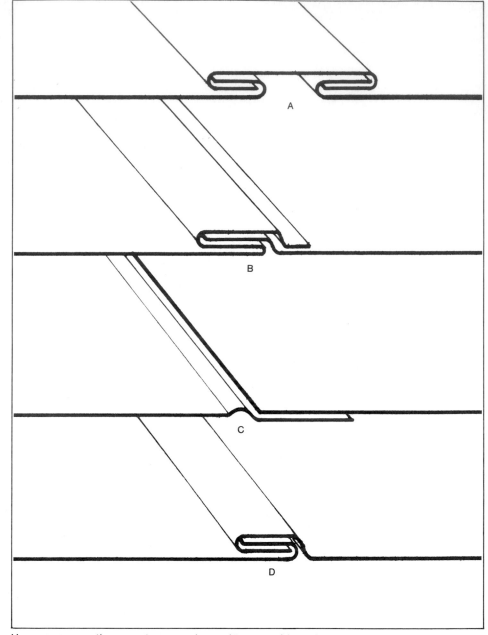

Here are connections most commonly used to assemble and connect ductwork: A. *Drive clip* is used to lock sections of rectangular duct together. B. *Snap lock* is used on long, side seam of round duct. C. *Crimp* allows one length of round duct to plug into the next. Secure with self-tapping screws. D. *Hammer lock* is earlier, simpler version of snap lock. It must be hammered closed to hold securely. For best sealing, all joints should be covered with duct tape.

the metal slide off the duct ends with a screwdriver and a hammer. If the duct was assembled with sheet-metal screws, remove duct tape, then remove the screws.

Take the piece of ductwork you removed and detailed measurements of the proposed modifications to a sheet-metal fabricator. They're listed in the Yellow Pages. They'll either rework the existing piece to suit the new dimensions or fabricate a new piece that replaces or attaches to the old. They should also be able to supply you with new attaching parts and a new register if you need one.

Before replacing duct sections reshape any joints that may have been deformed when taking sections apart. Replace insulation after sections are installed.

When installing a sheet-metal duct, box in the duct end on all four sides with framing members. Then clip the duct corners with sheet-metal shears and beat the four sides down flat against the framing members to form flanges. After the wall-surface mate-

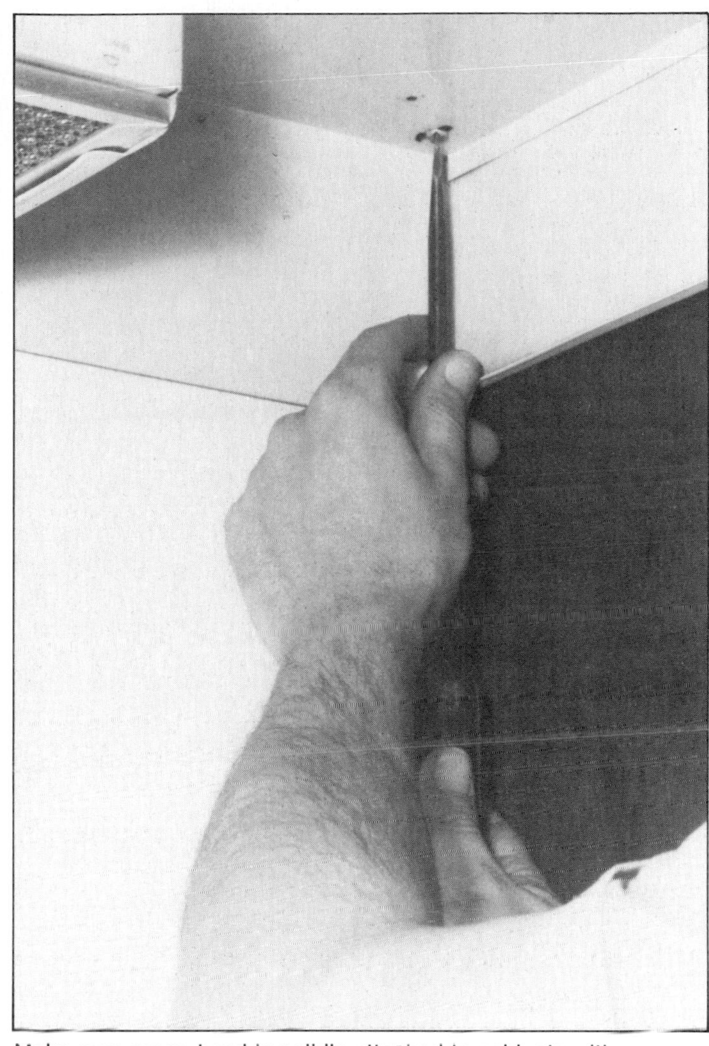

Make sure range hood is solidly attached to cabinets with screws. Check installation sheet for specifics.

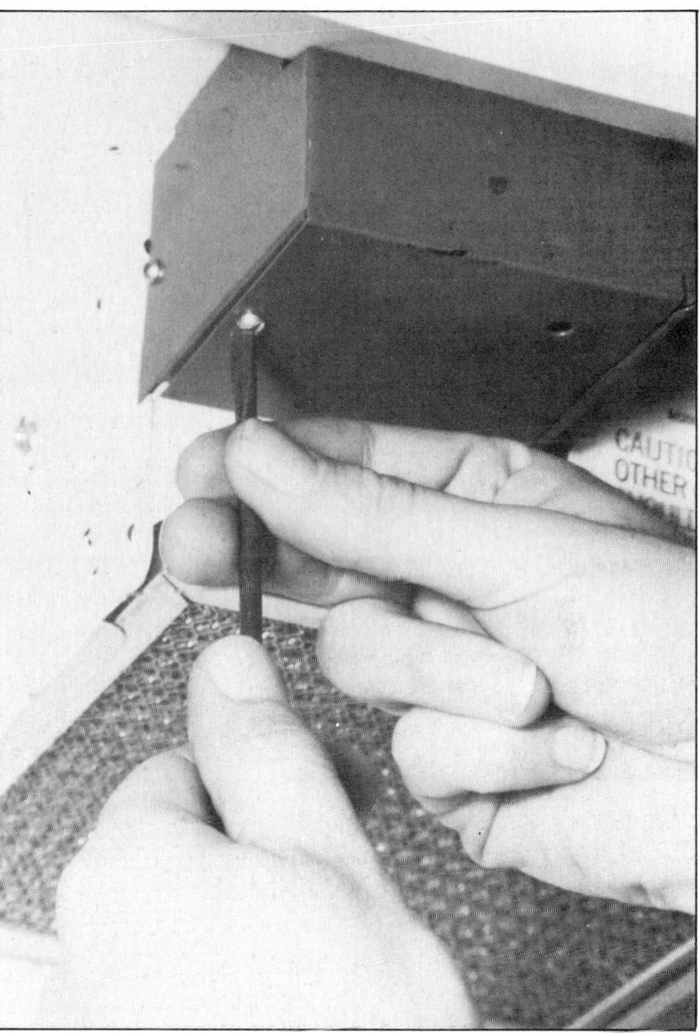

Cover for junction box is usually attached with screws. Remove cover for access to wiring. Replace when finished.

rial is installed and painted or papered, install the register. Make sure the sheet-metal screws that attach the register extend through the wall-surface material into the flanges in the end of the duct.

VENTILATION

Every kitchen needs some means of exhausting heat, moisture, smoke, airborne grease and cooking odors. In most kitchens this takes the form of a *range hood.* Range hoods come in so many shapes and sizes that you'll have to depend on the installation instructions packed with the hood for details on mounting it. Wiring hookup is much like a light fixture. All connections are made inside a junction box that's part of the range hood. Once again, check the installation instructions for connection details.

Note: While the term range hood is used here, the following instructions also

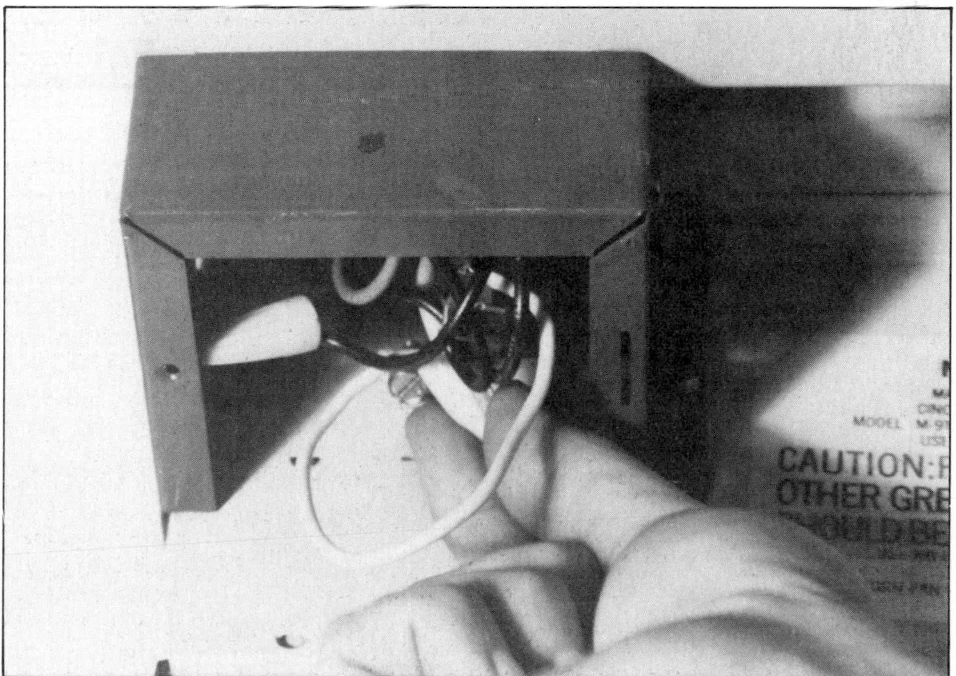

Use wire nuts to connect range hood wiring. Black wire is connected to black wire, white to white. Connect green or bare-copper ground wire to grounding screw inside box.

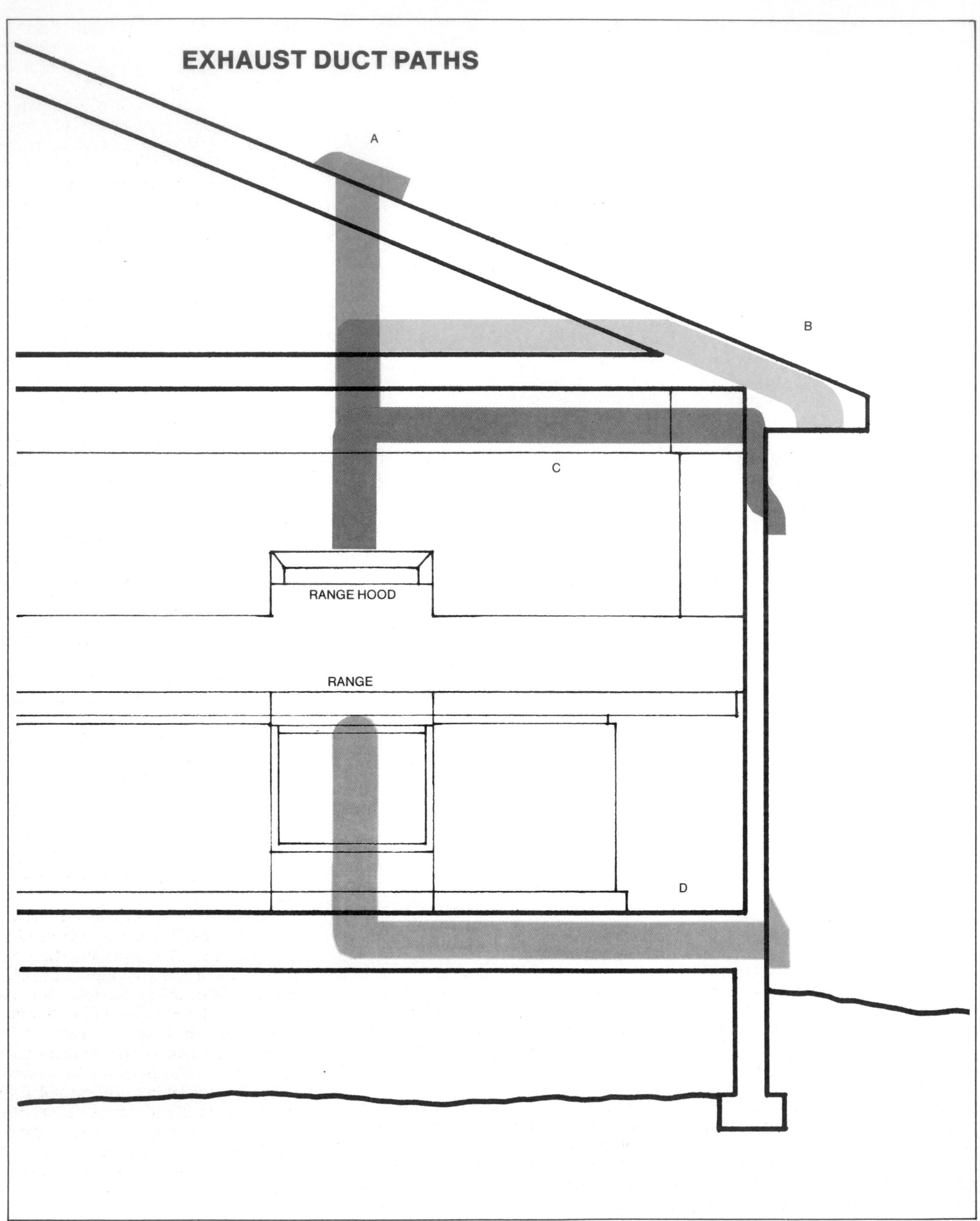

Shown here are common paths for ductwork: A. If appliance is on inside wall, shortest path is straight up through roof. B. In unfinished attic, vent is run over or between ceiling joists, exits at roof-soffit location. C. For house with second story or finished attic, duct is run between joists of first-floor ceiling. D. For down-venting appliances, duct can be run under house.

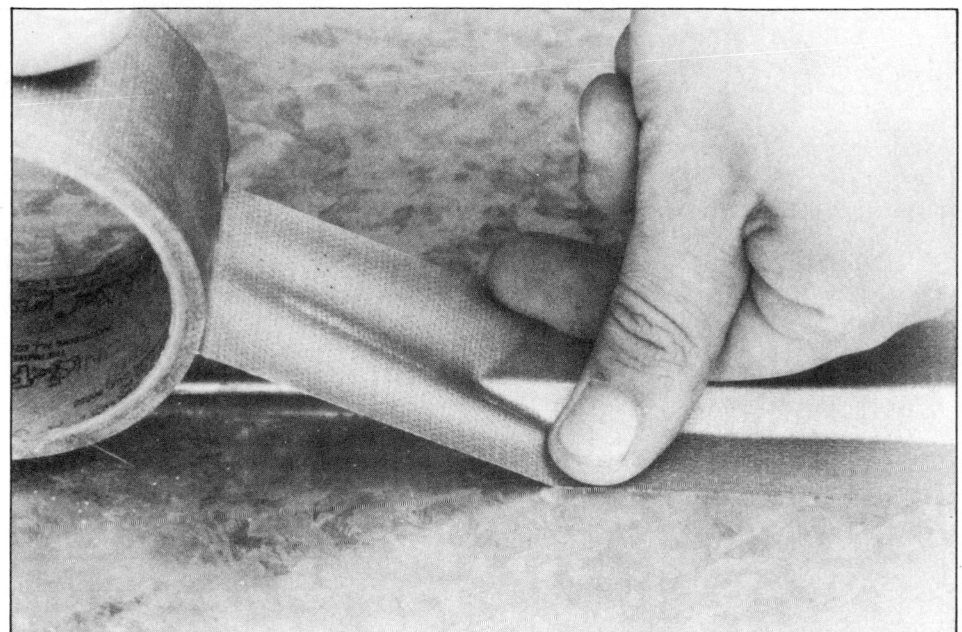

Tape all joints in any duct except flue pipes. When retaping joints in old duct, clean off dust and grease.

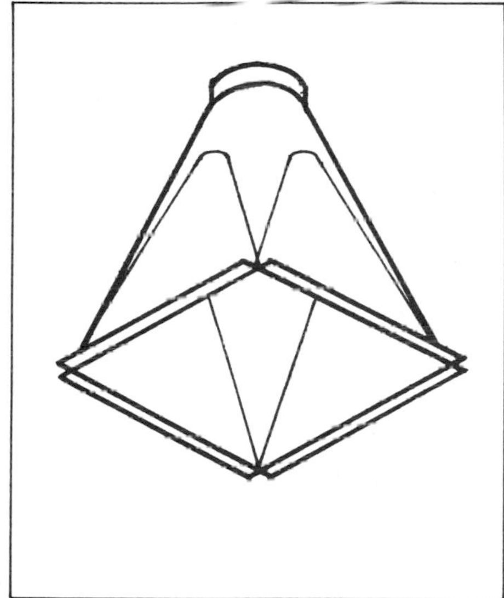

A transition fitting is often needed to connect range hood to duct.

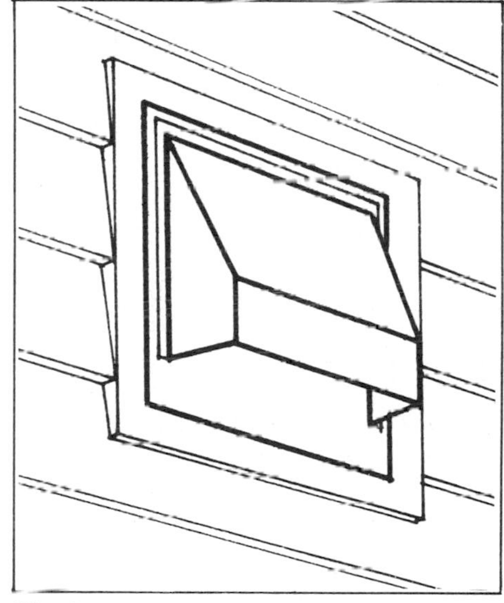

Weather cap covers duct at outside wall. If duct exits house through roof, a roof-type weather cap is needed.

apply to appliances with built-in vent systems, such as the self-venting cooktops and wall-oven units. Hookup is much the same.

Planning a Duct Layout—Unless you're installing the recirculating ductless type of range hood, you'll have to provide a duct to carry exhaust air outside the house.

First, plan a path for the duct. Basically, the shortest path is the best, but avoid framing members if you can. If your house has an attic, basement, or crawl space, plan on running the duct there.

Otherwise, you can use space between floor joists or ceiling joists to get to an outside wall. If the appliance is on an inside wall, the easiest path for the duct may be through the roof. You need to install flashing. Find or create a path where grease and condensation will run toward the outside of the house, and slope the duct in that direction as you install it. Insulate any duct that's in unheated areas, to minimize condensation of moisture within the duct.

Vent duct is available in round and flat shapes. Duct comes in a variety of cross-sectional areas. Flat duct is 3-1/2-inches wide, so it will fit inside a standard stud wall. It's useful in other places also.

Depending on the shape of the duct you're planning to install, you may need a *transition fitting* to connect the range hood to the duct. Check with the range-hood dealer or sheet-metal fabricator. You'll also need an outlet fitting such as a roof cap or wall cap. These fittings usually include some sort of automatic gravity-operated damper so wind doesn't blow back through the duct when the fan's not on. A transition fitting may also be needed to match the cap to the duct.

Plastic duct may be legal for range hoods in some areas, but it's not recommended due to the possibility of grease fires. Accumulated grease inside the duct can ignite and the resulting fire will melt plastic duct. For this reason, sheet-metal duct with well-anchored, airtight joints is preferred.

There's a limit to how long a duct you can use with any particular fan. Such limits are usually specified in the fan manufacturer's literature. Elbows and other restrictions count as the equivalent of extra duct length. As a rule of thumb, add 4-5 feet to the total duct length for each 90° elbow in the system. For a long duct run, you may have to use a more powerful fan assembly or include a booster fan. Or you may have to use a larger duct.

Installing the Duct—Vent ducts are best installed while doing rough electrical or plumbing work. Then all patching and finishing can be done at once. Much of what's covered under Warm-Air Heating Systems applies to vent ducts.

Remove any finish material necessary for access. Then cut holes needed for passage of the duct. Loosely assemble the duct in place. Use sheet-metal screws to fasten duct sections together solidly. Wrap all joints carefully with duct tape. Heavy, foil-backed duct tape will better resist heat and moisture the joints will be subjected to. When the duct is assembled in its final location, make sure it's securely supported. Use cross-blocking under horizontal runs, and loops of perforated-metal strapping tape on vertical runs.

Walls

Walls and ceilings provide background for kitchen cabinets and appliances. Choose materials carefully.

Most kitchen remodeling involves work on some or all walls. At the very least, walls may need repairs because of wear and tear, or to eliminate marks and irregularities left from tearing out the old kitchen installation.

Openings will have to be cut and then patched if you run new plumbing or electrical lines or modify old ones. Or you may have to remove sections of wall to create window, door or pass-through openings. You may need to close old openings. Your plans may require that you remove, relocate or add a wall. Any wall can be changed if you support the structure above it.

WALL CHANGES

Before making substantial changes to an existing wall, find out whether or not it's a *bearing wall.* Bearing walls are those that support the roof structure or the second floor of a two-story house. You must work on bearing walls much more carefully than non-bearing walls. Bearing walls require bracing while you're working, as described on page 108. Working on bearing walls without providing sufficient bracing can lead to structural collapse and possible major injury to anyone caught in the collapse.

FINDING BEARING WALLS

All exterior walls are bearing or should be considered so. Interior bearing walls are more difficult to identify. If the house is one-story or the work area is on the top floor, a look in the attic will reveal bearing-wall locations. If the roof is supported by *trusses,* none of the interior walls below are bearing, unless they support the end of a truss. A roof truss is a preassembled unit made up of many small members held together by metal fastening plates or plywood gussets. If the roof is constructed with rafters and ceiling joists, all walls supporting splices or overlaps in ceiling joists are bearing walls. Even if the ceiling joists are continuous over a wall, treat it as a bearing wall if you can't find a definite bearing wall within 12 feet or so. In general, you can suspect that any wall perpendicular to ceiling joists is a bearing wall.

If the beams or girders are visible below the plane of the ceiling, they're probably structural. Check to make sure they're not just hollow, decorative beams. Beams and girders are sometimes included in the roof structure above the ceiling so the ceiling is flush. If there's an attic above, you'll

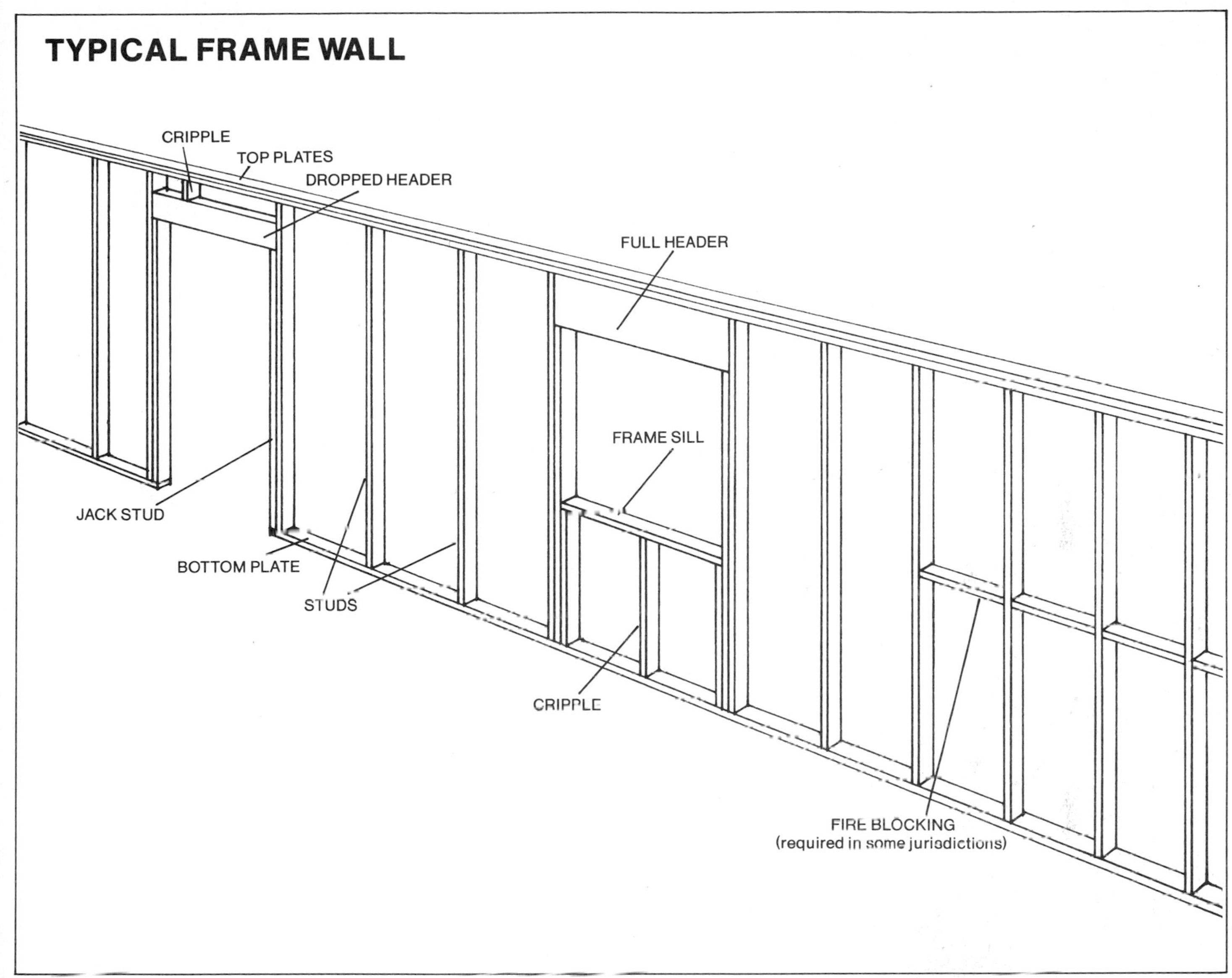

Become familiar with names of wall-framing members before you work on walls.

be able to see these beams or girders from there. Support must be maintained for both ends of such beams and girders.

If you remove the finish material from a wall and find two or three studs grouped together, don't take them out, even if the wall itself is non-bearing. That group of studs is probably holding up the end of a beam or girder you weren't aware of. Stop and investigate, cutting access holes if you have to, to make sure you don't disturb essential structural supports.

Another source of bearing-wall information is the basement or crawl space, if your house has one. All bearing walls will be supported from below by either a beam or by two or three floor joists spiked together.

When you're in the attic, basement or crawl space, measure where bearing walls are in relation to a convenient reference point. This could be the crawl-hole, one corner of the house, a nearby vent or drainpipe, or recessed fixture protruding through the ceiling or floor. Don't try to judge by eye which wall is involved. Unfinished spaces can be misleading, and you can easily misidentify a wall.

If you're working on a house with no attic or the first floor of a two-story house, finding bearing walls may be more difficult. All framing members will be concealed. If you can't find bearing walls from underneath the house, look closely at the ceiling for clues.

Hairline cracks where walls meet the ceiling indicate stress, which in turn may indicate the wall is bearing. See if you can detect a continuous drywall seam on the first-story ceiling, or pull up some carpet on the second floor and study the nailing pattern of the subfloor. These will indicate the direction the floor/ceiling joists run.

Sometimes the only way to find out how the second floor is framed is to cut some small holes in the ceiling near the wall and look. As mentioned, if the upper-floor joists are lapped over the wall, it's a bearing wall.

If there is blocking between joists over the wall, it may be bearing. Check another wall or two that you can be fairly sure are not bearing. Most framers block between second-story floor joists over beams and bearing walls, but not over non-bearing walls. Some framers will block above all walls and at midspan. If you've looked for all these clues and still don't know whether the wall is bearing, treat it as a bearing wall.

SHORING FOR BEARING-WALL WORK

Bearing walls are built like other walls, but they hold up some part of the structure above. When you remove or modify a bearing wall, you must first shore up the structure it supports. The purpose of shoring is to prevent movement and possible collapse of the structure. Movement of structural parts of a house loosens fasteners and pries off or cracks finish materials. Shoring can be rough and temporary, but it must be rigid, not flexible.

The most common shoring situation involves holding up the ends of members such as floor joists, ceiling joists, rafters or trusses that rest on a bearing wall. Leaving room to work between shoring and wall, tack a 2x6 or 2x8 to the floor and another to the ceiling directly above. Extend ends of these plates one or two joists beyond the bearing wall area you're going to work on.

Then install studs or posts between plates to carry the load. Size, spacing and type of studs or posts is a matter of good judgment. If load is heavy, or distance between floor and ceiling is large, use 4x4 posts or 2x6 studs spaced 16 to 24 inches apart. If load is light, 2x4 studs spaced 2 to 4 feet apart will probably suffice.

If you're not sure of shoring requirements, consult the building inspector.

To make stiff and cheap shoring posts, nail two 2x4 studs together in a T cross-section. The post will be almost as stiff as a 4x4. Similarly, if you need to add stiffness to top and bottom plates, spike a 2x4 on edge to one or both edges of the plate. Toenail studs or posts in place with a nail or two—at the top only. Slip a pair of shim shingles under the bottom of each stud or post.

Wedge shoring into place to remove load from bearing wall. Tap shim shingles under each stud or post in turn until load is transferred. Watch corner where wall and ceiling meet. If it starts to separate, you've shimmed too much.

You can sometimes tell the amount of load on a stud or post by tapping it with a hammer and listening. Tap a loose piece of 2x4 to get a representative sound, then tap shoring as you drive in shims. The sound will "tighten up" as stud or post takes the load. If stud makes a metallic ring, the load is excessive; ease off or add support on either side.

If members overlap wall from both sides, such as a bearing wall in the middle of a house, shore both sides. Take additional load into consideration. In general, it's better to overbuild shoring than underbuild it. You can reuse materials after you've removed temporary shoring.

Before erecting shoring, check carefully to make sure floor under shoring will carry the additional load. You may have to brace the floor to support shoring.

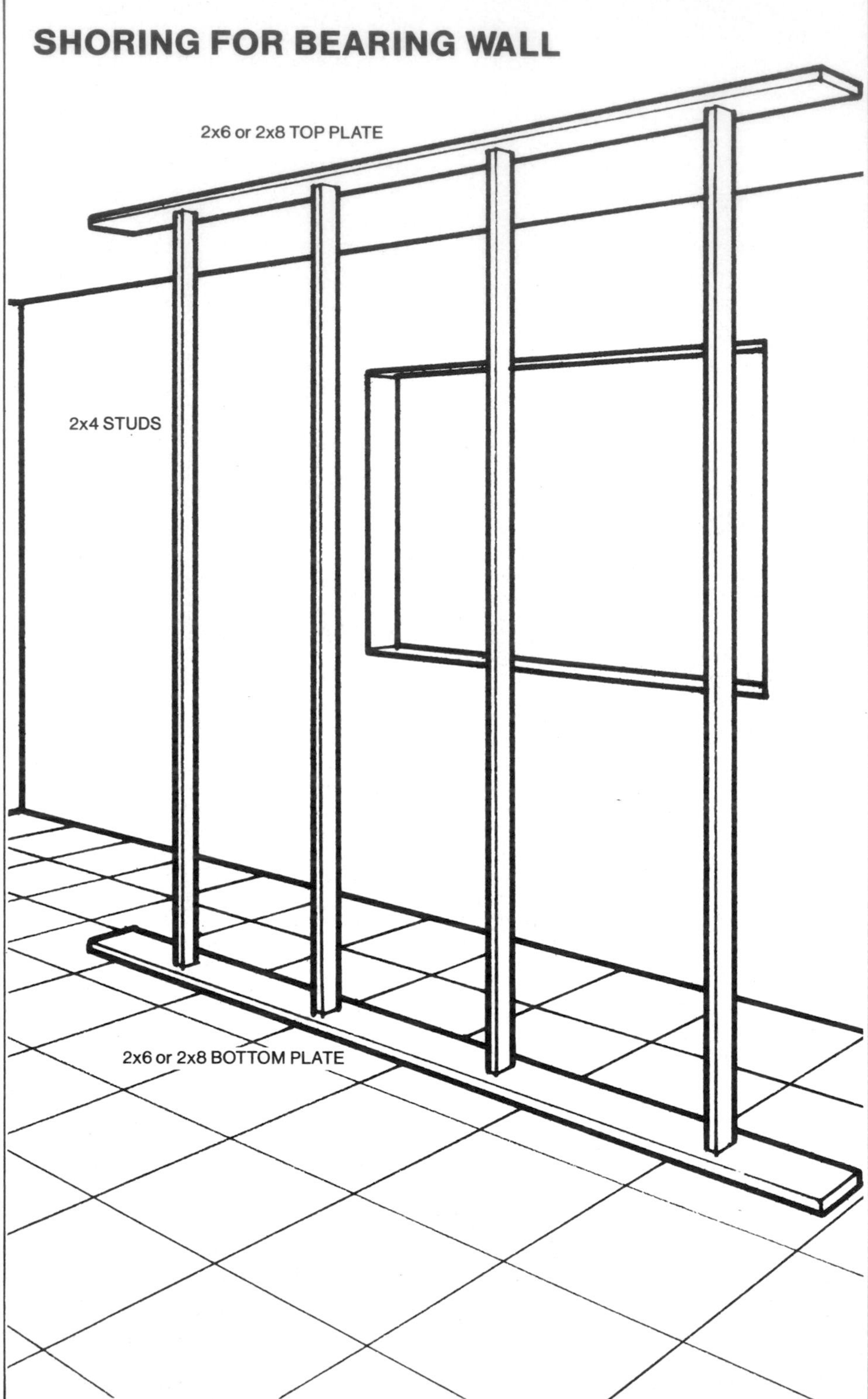

If bearing wall supports light load, the shoring above will be adequate. For heavier loads, such as a wall supporting part of a second-story structure, use 4x4 posts set close together instead of 2x4 studs.

WALL FRAMING

Frame walls look solid but are mostly empty space. The basic elements of a frame wall are a *bottom plate*, the vertical members called *studs*, and one or two *top plates*. Exterior walls and some interior bearing walls may include bracing that runs diagonally across the studs. Aside from diagonal bracing and a few nailing blocks, all other members used in standard wall construction are usually 2x4s. In some cases, 2x6s are used, such as for walls over 10 feet in height. Some code jurisdictions allow 2x3s to be used for interior, non-bearing walls. In post-and-beam construction, framing members may be 4x4s or larger, depending on the architectural style of the house.

Framing Materials—Two-inch lumber is *nominally* 2 inches thick, but actually measures 1-1/2 inches. You're not being cheated out of that other 1/2 inch. A 2x4 is rough cut from the log at an actual 2 inches by 4 inches. Once it's dried to a usable moisture level, and milled to a smooth surface and uniform size, it measures 1-1/2 by 3-1/2 inches. *Green* lumber has been milled, but not dried. A green 2x4 measures 1-9/16 x 3-9/6 inches.

The chart at right shows nominal and actual sizes of dimension lumber. Keep these sizes in mind when you're drawing your plans, pages 59-61, and taking measurements for framed walls and other structures.

STANDARD LUMBER SIZES

Nominal (inches)	Dry (inches)	Green (inches)
1	3/4	25/32
2	1-1/2	1-9/16
4	3-1/2	3-9/16
6	5-1/2	5-5/8
8	7-1/4	7-1/2
10	9-1/4	9-1/2
12	11-1/4	11-1/2

NAIL SIZES AND AMOUNTS

Penny Size	Length	Number Per Pound
2d	1"	
Common		876
Box		1010
Finish		1351
3d	1-1/4"	
Common		568
Box		635
Finish		807
4d	1-1/2"	
Common		316
Box		473
Finish		548
5d	1-3/4"	
Common		271
Box		406
Finish		500
6d	2"	
Common		181
Box		236
Finish		309
7d	2-1/4"	
Common		161
Box		210
Finish		238
8d	2-1/2"	
Common		106
Box		145
Finish		189
9d	2-3/4"	
Common		96
Box		132
Finish		172
10d	3"	
Common		69
Box		121
Finish		132
12d	3-1/4"	
Common		64
Box		94
Finish		113
16d	3-1/2"	
Common		49
Box		71
Finish		90

Note: Nail lengths are designated by *penny size (d).* Use a nail three times as long as the thickness of the top board you're nailing.

NAILING TIPS

Nails have great strength if used correctly. When using nails to attach framing members, there are a few simple rules to follow.

- **Use Nails Correctly**—When nailing a joint together, try to determine the stresses involved. The nail should be located crossways, or at least diagonally, to the direction of stress on the joint. If stresses on the joint are parallel to the nail direction, the nail will tend to pull out. Reposition the nail or rework the joint so the nail is crossways to the direction of stress. If these methods are impractical, use a wood screw to attach the members. Nails have great shear strength, crossways to stress, but little resistance to withdrawal.
- **Box Nails**—Box nails have slightly thinner shanks than common nails. They are less likely to split the wood and are easier to drive. Also, you get more nails of a given size per pound. On the other hand, box nails bend more easily. Use the smallest, thinnest nail codes and conditions will permit.
- **Splitting**—Don't work with short pieces of wood if you can help it. There's no way to avoid splitting the piece. If you must nail near the end of a piece of wood and splitting is likely, look at the point of the nail. A nail point is made with four flat surfaces, but the surfaces don't form a square. They form a diamond. When the wide part of the diamond is parallel to the wood grain, the nail tends to wedge the wood fibers apart, causing a split. If you position the wide part of the diamond across the grain, the nail point tends to crush its way into the fibers instead of wedging them apart. In extreme cases, rest the head of the nail on a wood block with the point up. Then tap the point with your hammer several times to blunt it. This will inhibit splitting still more, again by permitting crushing rather than wedging.
- **Hammers**—If you're constantly bending nails, don't be too quick to blame yourself or the nails. Look closely at your hammer. Replace any hammer with a chipped and worn face and a crack in the handle. This is necessary, if only to avoid throwing the head off the handle and injuring somebody. But beyond that, some hammers just aren't properly made or properly assembled. Buy the best hammer you can find. Choose one that feels balanced and comfortable in your hand.
- **Pulling Nails**—Don't pull a nail the way most people try to do it. The standard method of hooking the claws under the nailhead and using the hammer head as a rocker to pull the nail works fine for small nails. On framing-size nails, drive hammer claws into the shank of the nail at the wood surface. Then use the handle of the hammer as a lever to bend the nail over sideways. You'll find that you've easily withdrawn about an inch of nail. Hitch the hammer loose, drive the claws onto the shank of the nail again, and bend it over again. Continue this process until the nail is withdrawn.
- **Knots and Old Wood**—Sometimes a piece of wood won't take a nail. This often happens when working with existing framing in older houses. The wood has become rock-hard over the years. Or, you may occasionally have to drive a nail near or through a knot. In either of these cases, substitute a fluted, hardened concrete nail for an ordinary one. These nails are unbendable and will go through almost anything.

Wear safety glasses, a long-sleeve shirt and gloves when you use concrete nails. Hardened concrete nails will sometimes chip, or chip the hammerhead, and the fragment will have considerable velocity. This doesn't happen often, but when it does, you can be injured. Also, don't use your favorite hammer for this work.

Another option for hard-to-nail pieces is to drill a pilot hole and insert the correct-size flat-head wood screw.

Green lumber is used for outdoor building, but should *not* be used for house framing. It has a tendency to warp and shrink as it dries. The only way to be sure lumber is dry is to check the grade stamp for the letters *KD*, the words *Kiln-Dried* or the letters, *S-DRY.* Kiln-dried lumber has been dried in an oven or kiln to an acceptable moisture content, usually 19% or less. S-DRY lumber has been kiln- or air-dried to an acceptable moisture content.

In standard wood-frame construction, different circumstances call for walls of different thicknesses and different stud spacings. The smallest lumber size that can be used for free-standing walls is 2x3. This is used for interior non-bearing walls only, and only on 16-inch centers. The maximum permitted height of a 2x3 frame wall is 10 feet. Though 2x3s are less expensive and easier to work with, don't use them where plumbing must be run. Holes through studs are limited to 1 inch in diameter, because you can't make a hole exceeding 40% of the width of the stud. Also, doorways or pass-throughs in a wall framed with 2x3s can look skimpy.

The most common wall framing member is the 2x4. The maximum allowable height for a wall with 2x4 studs is 14 feet. In non-bearing walls, 2x4 studs can be spaced no wider than 24 inches on center. In bearing walls that support a ceiling and roof only, 2x4 studs can be spaced 24 inches on center, provided the wall is 10 feet tall or less. If the bearing wall supports a floor above, the studs must be 16 inches on center.

Codes do not permit 2x2s for free-standing walls. But if you want to increase the depth of an existing wall to make room for plumbing, nail 2x2s to existing 2x4 studs and plates. This will give you an extra 1-1/2" depth to run a 2-inch diameter drain pipe through the framing.

The maximum height for 2x6 wall framing is 20 feet. Any 2x6 wall can be spaced 24 inches on center, unless it is supporting a floor above. In that case, spacing must be 16 inches on center.

Any wall thicker than 2x6 should generally be constructed as two separate 2x4 walls.

In all cases, you're required to *fire-block* wall framing so that no vertical space exceeds 10 feet in height. Fire-blocking consists of a continuous row of horizontal blocks nailed between the studs. Blocks must be the same width as the studs. You must also fire-block where soffits meet wall framing.

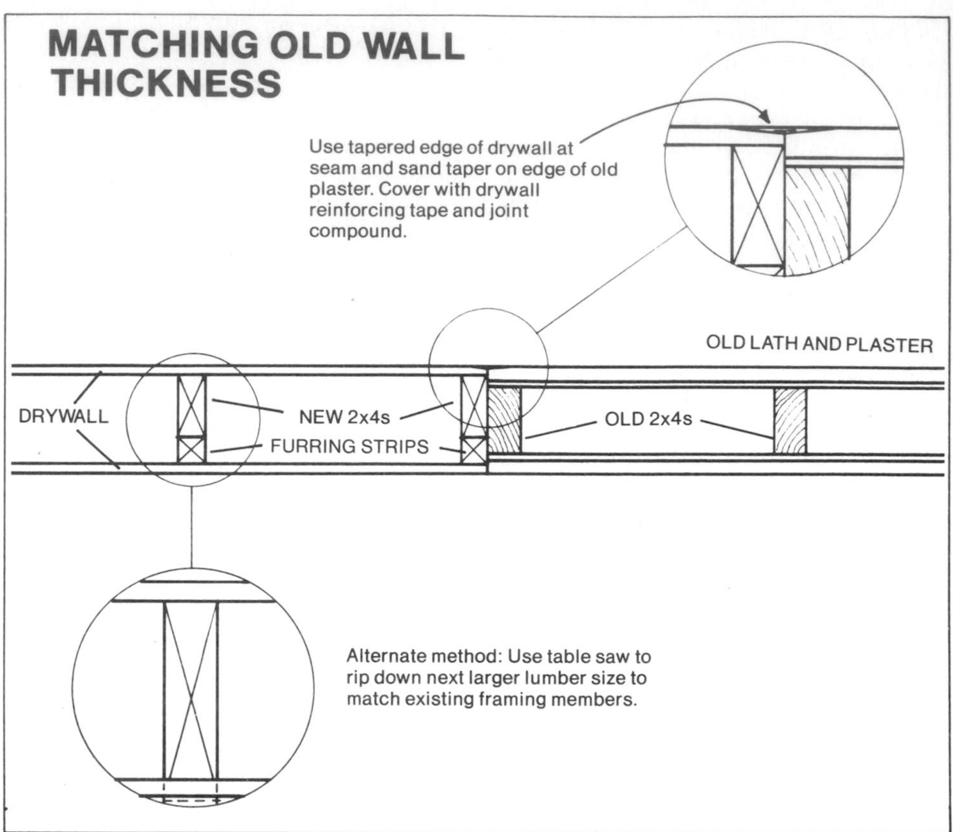
MATCHING OLD WALL THICKNESS
Use tapered edge of drywall at seam and sand taper on edge of old plaster. Cover with drywall reinforcing tape and joint compound.
OLD LATH AND PLASTER
DRYWALL
NEW 2x4s
FURRING STRIPS
OLD 2x4s
Alternate method: Use table saw to rip down next larger lumber size to match existing framing members.
If house is framed with older lumber, sizes may be larger. Use firring strips to shim out new framing members to match old. Alternate method is to cut down next-larger size of new lumber to match old.

In some code jurisdictions the requirements may be stricter than those given here. This is especially true if your area is subject to earthquakes or severe climatic conditions, such as high winds or heavy snows. Also, the above recommendations only apply to framing lumber graded "Standard & better," or "Stud." You may be able to substitute the less expensive "Utility" grade in your area and under certain circumstances. Check with your building department.

Don't use ungraded lumber. Most codes don't allow it. High-quality graded lumber is well worth the few extra dollars it costs. It's much easier and more satisfying to work with. The finished job will turn out better.

Old Lumber Sizes—If you're remodeling a kitchen in an older home, you may find the older framing members in walls and floor don't measure the same as new ones. Standard lumber sizes were introduced about 40 years ago. Since then, the standards have changed several times. The current standard sizes were introduced in 1970. Any houses built before this time are likely to have slightly larger framing members. Current standard sizes are listed on page 109.

Because it would be impractical to search for old lumber to match the house framing, you'll have to either build up the thickness of the next-smaller current size, or rip down the next-larger current size to match.

Building up, or *furring out*, studs and plates to the desired thickness is only practical if the size of the old lumber is the same as some combination of today's sizes. For instance, a standard 2x4 and furring strips cut from 1/2-inch plywood will match the full 4-inch studs used in many pre-1940 houses. Plywood comes in a number of thicknesses, from 1/8-inch to 1-1/4 inches, so you'll have little difficulty matching thicknesses of old studs. Also, lath or molding strips, either rough or finish grade, work well as furring strips. They may be cheaper than buying a whole sheet of plywood if only a few studs need to be furred out.

The same techniques can be used for aligning the surface of a section of new drywall with the surface of an existing plaster wall. Measure the thickness of the old wall in several places—plaster thickness can vary greatly. Subtract the thickness of one or two layers of 1/2-inch drywall, depending on plaster thickness. Then frame the new section of wall to the resulting dimension, centered on the old section. It's best to leave existing lath in place, if possible. For large areas, you can save materials by using only a single thickness of drywall.

HOW TO FRAME A WALL

In new construction, the wall framing is assembled on the floor then tilted up into position. This is often impossible to do in an existing structure because the ceiling prevents the wall from being tilted into an upright position. In most cases, you'll have to build the wall in place, first attaching the plates to the floor and ceiling, then attaching studs to the plates.

Measure and mark the new wall location on the floor, then snap a pair of chalk lines to indicate the width of the bottom plate. Keep in mind the width of the finished wall will equal the width of the framing plus the combined thicknesses of the wall surfacing materials on either side. For instance, if you're using 2x4 framing and 1/2-inch drywall, the total wall thickness will be 4-1/2 inches.

If the new wall will butt against existing walls, use a 4-foot level to continue the chalk lines up to the ceiling. If the end of the new wall is away from other walls, use a plumb line to transfer the marks to the ceiling. Then mark both sides of the new wall on the ceiling. Do not mark wall locations with center lines or the marks will be invisible under the plates. If you only mark one side of the new wall location, it's easy to get the wall on the wrong side of the line.

If the new wall runs parallel to floor joists below but is not positioned over one, install cross-blocking between floor joists under the new wall to help support its weight. Space blocking every 2 feet. The cross-blocking should be 2x6 or larger. If the trusses or ceiling joists are also parallel to the new wall, install cross-blocking every 2 feet so you will have solid backing to nail the plate into. In cases where there is no access to joists from above, you'll have to remove some of the

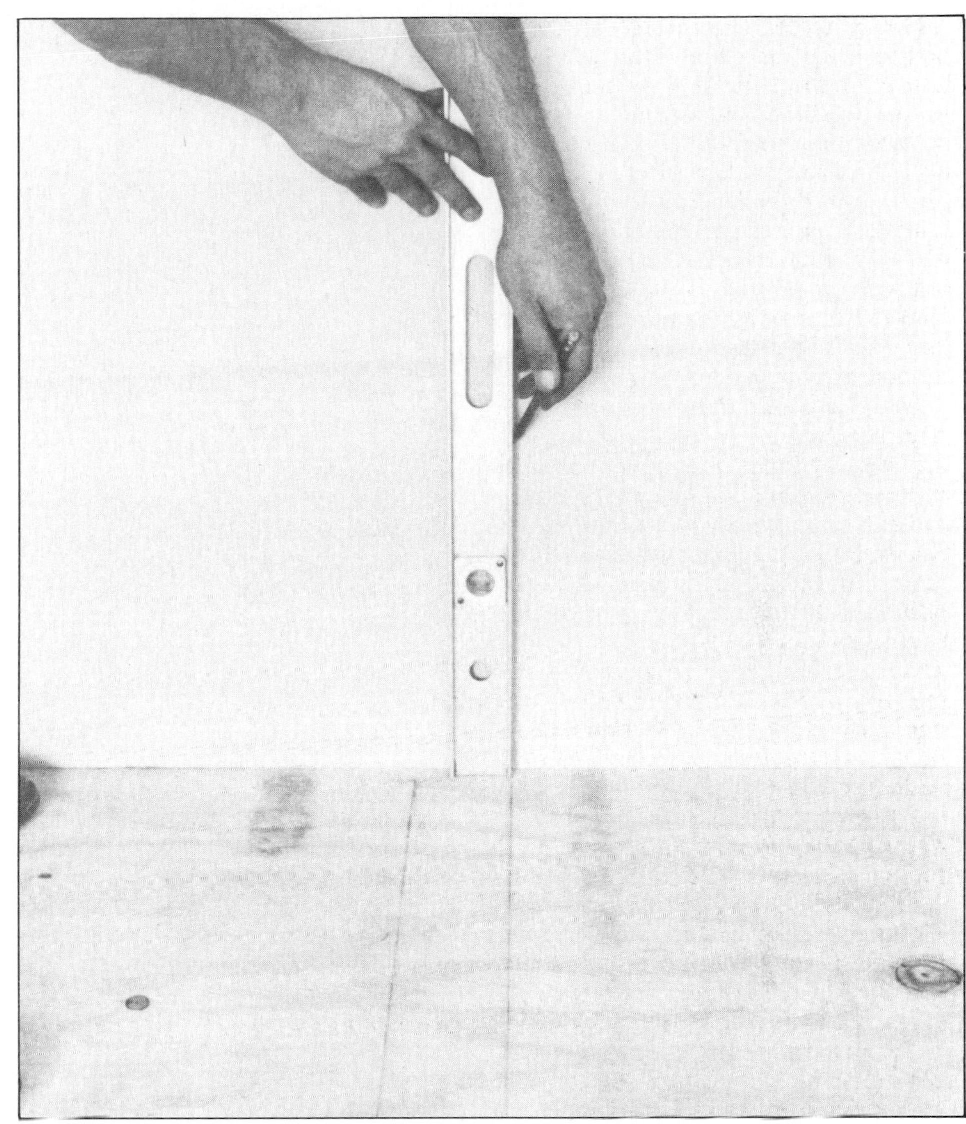

Snap chalk lines on floor at new wall location. Extend lines up any adjacent walls with a level. Use chalkline again to mark ceiling.

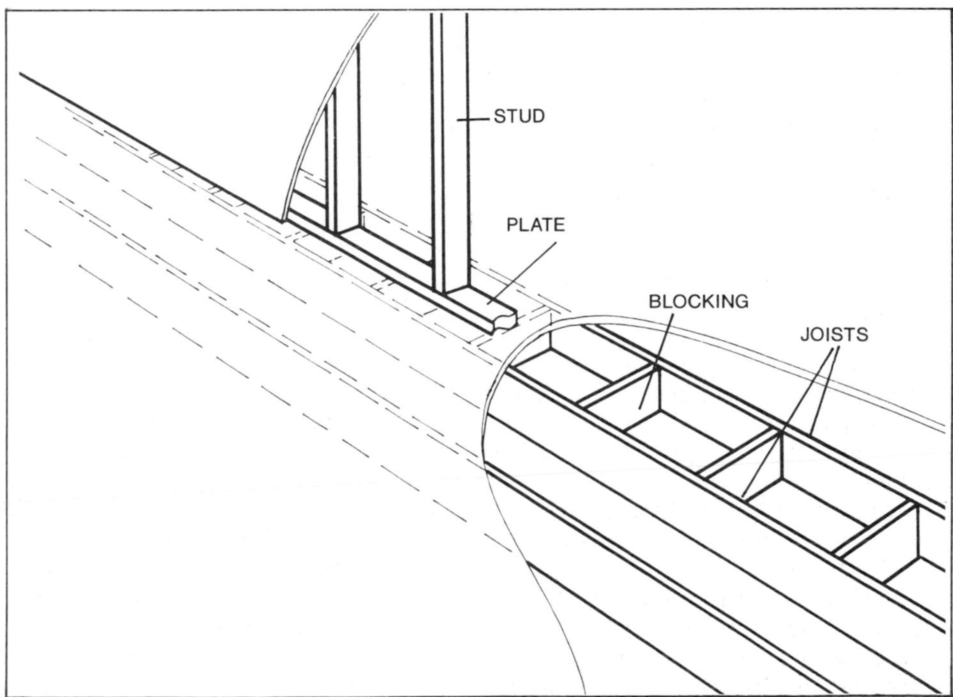

ceiling material to install the blocking.

If working from above, drive small nails through the ceiling on either side of the blocking so you can locate it from underneath when you nail the top plate to it.

Cut bottom plate and two top plates to length. Set them on edge across two sawhorses or on the floor. Position plates against each other with their ends in alignment, then use a pencil and try square to mark stud locations across the top edges of both plates. Make sure the plates remain in alignment while you're marking so the studs will be plumb. From one end, mark every 16 or 24 inches, depending on spacing requirements of the wall. These marks indicate the center lines of the studs. Also mark locations for window and door framing. See page 136 for details on window and door framing. Once the plates are marked, align them to marks on the floor and ceiling and nail them in. Use concrete nails to attach plates to slab floors.

Measure between top and bottom plates for each stud. Mark each measurement next to the stud's marked location on the bottom plate. Don't just measure in one spot and then cut all the studs the same length. No structure is ever perfectly straight, so stud lengths will vary slightly. After taking all the stud measurements, mark and cut the studs, then nail them in place, one at a time. Start with the longest studs first, and work your way down to the smallest. That way a miscut stud can be trimmed for a shorter location.

When cutting studs, cut to the outside of the marked line so the stud will fit tightly between the plates. The ideal fit for a stud requires a light tap or two to move it into position.

To attach studs, drive 16d nails part way into the top and bottom plates, 3/4-inch to one side of the stud center-line marks. These nails serve as stops to keep the stud from moving while you're nailing it. Use two 12d nails to toenail the stud into the top plate from the side opposite the stop nail. It's easier to drive these nails partway into the stud before lifting it into position. Toenail the stud to the bottom plate in the same manner. Remove the 16d stop nails. Then toenail each end from the other side—a total of four nails at each end of the stud.

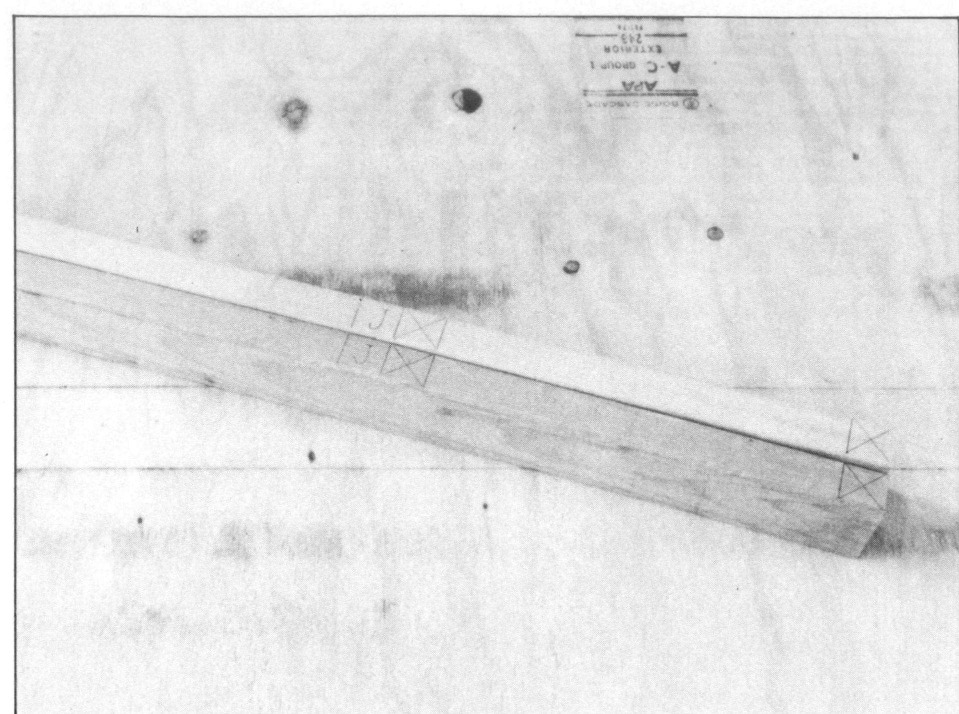

Mark top and bottom plates in pairs. An X indicates a full stud, a J indicates jackstud beside window or door opening, supporting end of the header.

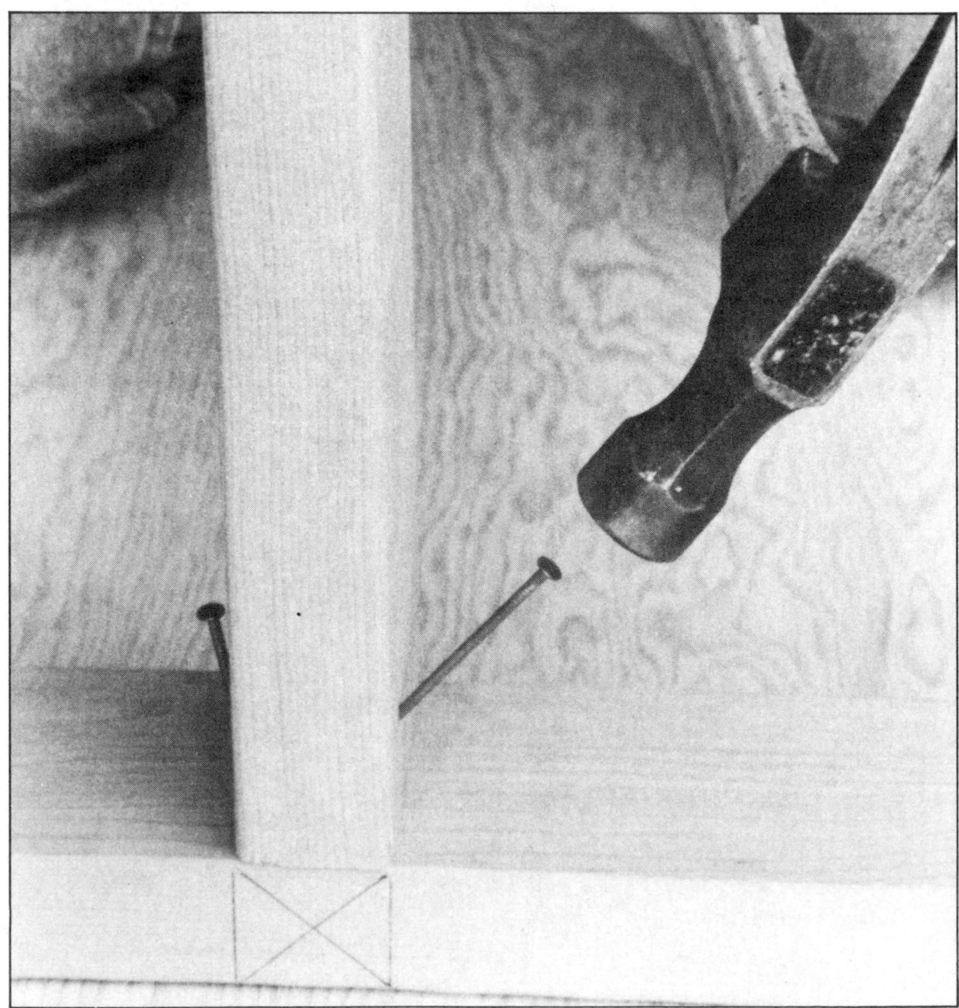

Toenailing studs isn't difficult if you use 16d nail for a backstop until you've got first two nails in. If you have much toenailing to do, cut a scrap piece of 2x4 that fits between studs for use as a backstop.

Wall Problems—Out-of-plumb adjoining walls must be detected early. If you have to work to an out-of-plumb wall, cut top and bottom plates to fit their locations. Tack the top plate temporarily into place. Use a plumb bob to get a reference mark on the top plate that's exactly above a similar mark on the bottom plate. When you position the plates side by side to mark the stud center lines, make sure these reference marks are lined up. That way the studs will be plumb.

When marking the stud center lines, measure from the wall-end of the longest plate. This ensures the first stud is 16 inches or less, or 24 inches or less, from the wall, but never more. This avoids having to fit small pieces of finish material later on.

If an adjoining wall is curved, the end stud that lies flat against the wall should be warped into place roughly to follow the curve, and nailed there. If the wall is concave by more than 1/8 inch, reduce the distance to the first stud center line by the amount of the curve.

If the floor or the ceiling slopes, do not set the studs at right angles to the sloping surface. It's far easier to trim the top or the bottom of the finish material instead.

If the tops of toenailed studs do not bear fully on the top plate, don't shim them. Instead, drive shim shingles flat between the upper top plate and the lower top plate over the problem stud, or between single top plate and ceiling joists near the stud.

WINDOW AND DOOR FRAMING

Standard framing for windows and doors consists of vertical studs and horizontal framing members. The horizontal member at the top of the window or door opening is called a *header.* The horizontal member at the bottom of a window is called a *sill.* There are usually no horizontal framing members at the bottom of a door opening. In most cases, even the bottom plate of the wall does not extend across the door opening.

Vertical members for window and door openings consist of *full studs* that run from bottom plate to top plate on each side of the opening, and partial studs, called *jackstuds,* that support the ends of the window or door header. See drawing on page 107. For extremely large beams or headers, building codes may require three or

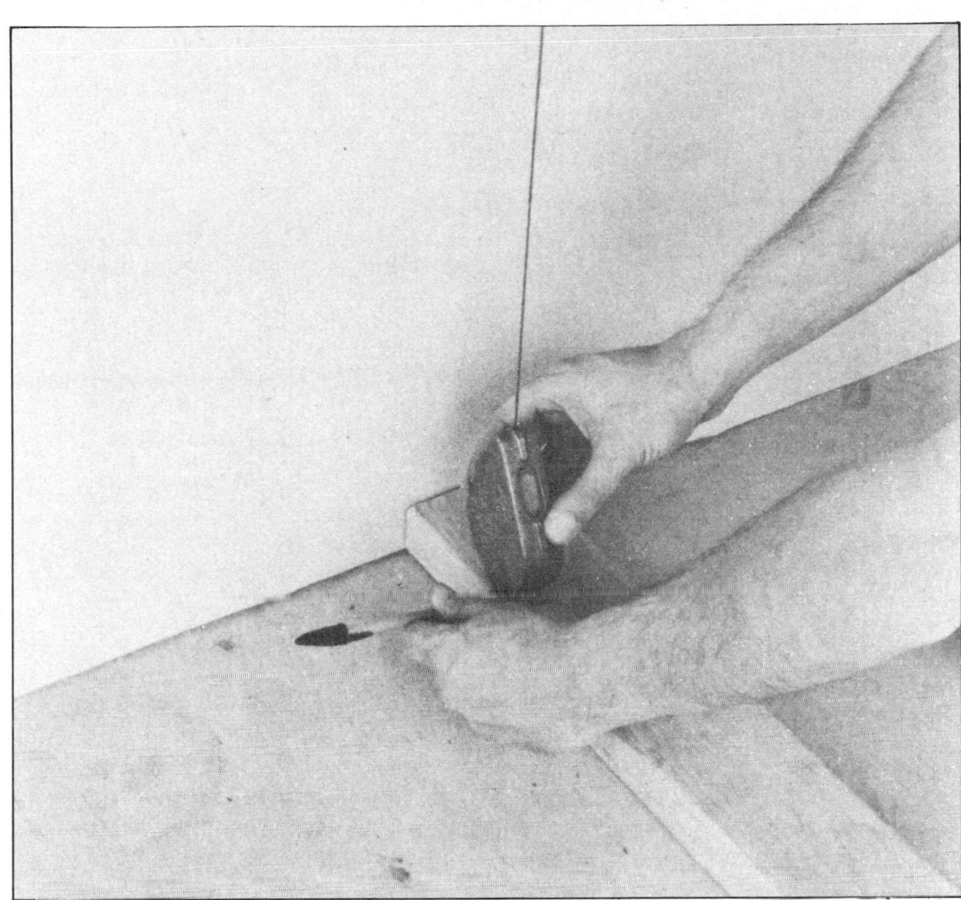

To lay out plates that run to an adjacent out-of-plumb wall, use plumb-bob to make reference marks that *are* plumb. Then line up plates to reference marks instead of wall.

ROUGH-OPENING SIZES

If possible, measure actual door or window unit or get exact rough-in dimensions from supplier or manufacturer's literature. Pre-hung doors and aluminum-frame doors and windows come in standard sizes, so dimensions given here can be used for them. Wood-frame windows and sliding doors can vary by several inches in both dimensions, so consult supplier or manufacturer in every case.

INTERIOR SWING DOORS (NO THRESHOLD)

DOOR OPENING	ROUGH OPENING[1]
2'-4"x6'-8"	2'-7"x6'-10"
2'-6"x6'-8"	2'-9"x6'-10"
2'-8"x6'-8"	2'-11"x6'-10"
2'-10"x6'-8"	3'-1"x6'-10"
3'-0"x6'-8"	3'-3"x6'-10"

EXTERIOR SWING DOORS (1" THRESHOLD)

DOOR OPENING	ROUGH OPENING[1]
2'-8" single	2'-10-1/2"x6'-10"
3'-0" single	3'-2-1/2"x6'-10"
3'-6" single	3'-8-1/2"x6'-10"
5'-4" double	5'-7-1/2"x6'-10"
6'-0" double	6'-3-1/2"x6'-10"

[1]Based on standard 2-1/8" case molding or wider.

ALUMINUM-FRAME SLIDING-GLASS DOORS

DOOR OPENING	ROUGH OPENING
5'-0"x6'-8"	5'-1"x6'-9"
6'-0"x6'-8"	6'-1"x6'-9"
8'-0"x6'-8"	8'-1"x6'-9"

ALUMINUM-FRAME WINDOWS

WINDOW	ROUGH OPENING
2'-0"x2'-0"	2'-1"x2'-1"
x3'-0"	x3'-1"
x4'-0"	x4'-1"
x5'-0"	x5'-1"
x6'-0"	x6'-1"
3'-0"x2'-0"	3'-1"x2'-1"
x3'-0"	x3'-1"
x4'-0"	x4'-1"
x5'-0"	x5'-1"
x6'-0"	x6'-1"
4'-0"x2'-0"	4'-1"x2'-1"
x3'-0"	x3'-1"
x4'-0"	x4'-1"
x5'-0"	x5'-1"
x6'-0"	x6'-1"
5'-0"x2'-0"	5'-1"x2'-1-1/4"
x3'-0"	x3'-1-1/4"
x4'-0"	x4'-1-1/4"
x5'-0"	x5'-1-1/4"
x6'-0"	x6'-1-1/4"
6'-0"x2'-0"	6'-1"x2'-1-1/2"
x3'-0"	x3'-1-1/2"
x4'-0"	x4'-1-1/2"
x5'-0"	x5'-1-1/2"
x6'-0"	x6'-1-1/2"

even four jackstuds supporting each side of the opening. The chart on page 113 shows rough-opening sizes for most standard doors and windows. For sizes not shown, call a window or door supplier for the information.

Once wall-stud center lines are marked on the top and bottom plates, mark the exact locations of window and door rough openings. Adjust the locations—but not the rough-opening sizes—if you can, to coincide with previously marked stud spacings.

To the outside of the rough-opening marks, mark positions of outside full studs and jackstuds. Label outside-stud positions with an X, for *full studs*, and inside-stud positions with a J, for *jackstuds*.

When you've marked locations for all full studs, including those for door and window openings, nail the studs to the plates. When all full studs are in place, cut and install jackstuds and headers as described below.

Installing Jackstuds—There are some pitfalls in determining the correct lengths of jackstuds. Because of the load on a header, the jackstuds holding it must bear fully on the header and on the bottom plate or floor. Don't just measure one side of of the opening and cut both jackstuds to the same length. If the floor slopes, the header will slope. Use a level to determine if the floor slopes, and mark the rough opening height at the high side of the opening. Then use a level—and a short length of 2x4 if necessary—to transfer the header height to the opposite side of the opening, as shown in the top photo. Once you've determined header heights for doors and windows, use one of the methods below to install the jackstuds. When the jackstuds are cut, mark them for location so you don't mix them up.

There are two methods of installing jackstuds. In both methods, the wall is framed with the bottom plate left in place below the window and door openings. In the first method, jackstuds rest on top of the bottom plate. After the jackstuds are in, the sections of plate within the openings are cut out. See photo at right. The bottom plate below window openings is left in place. See Method 1, on facing page.

An alternate method is often used for door openings. The wall is framed and the bottom plate is cut out at the door opening before the jackstuds and headers are installed. The jackstuds

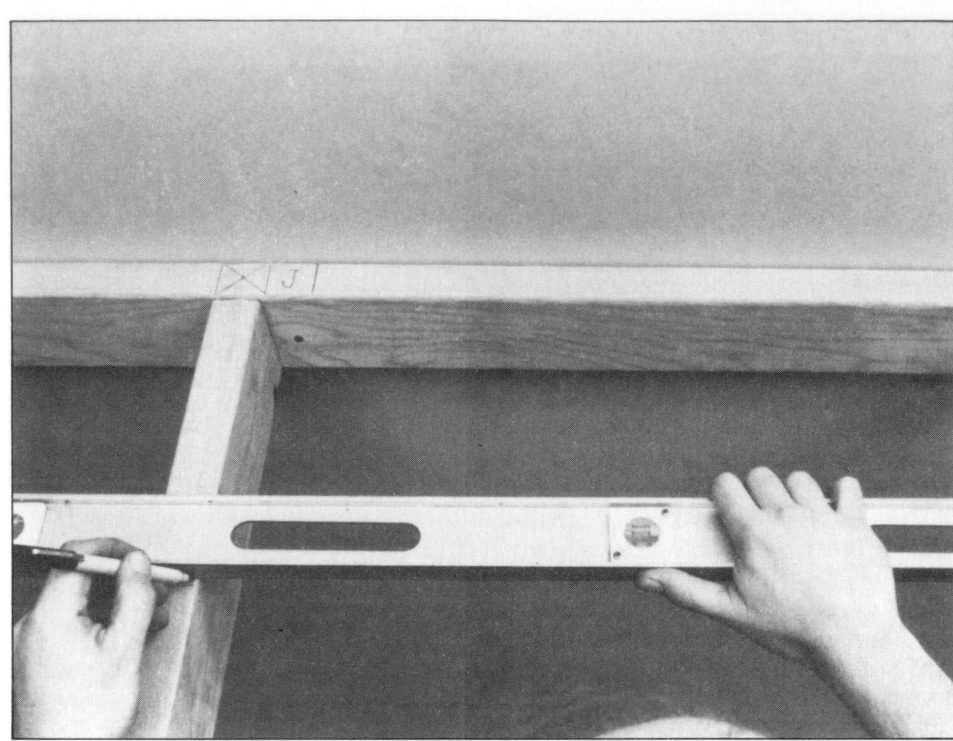

To mark header height when floor isn't level, find and mark high side of opening, then use level to transfer mark to other side of opening.

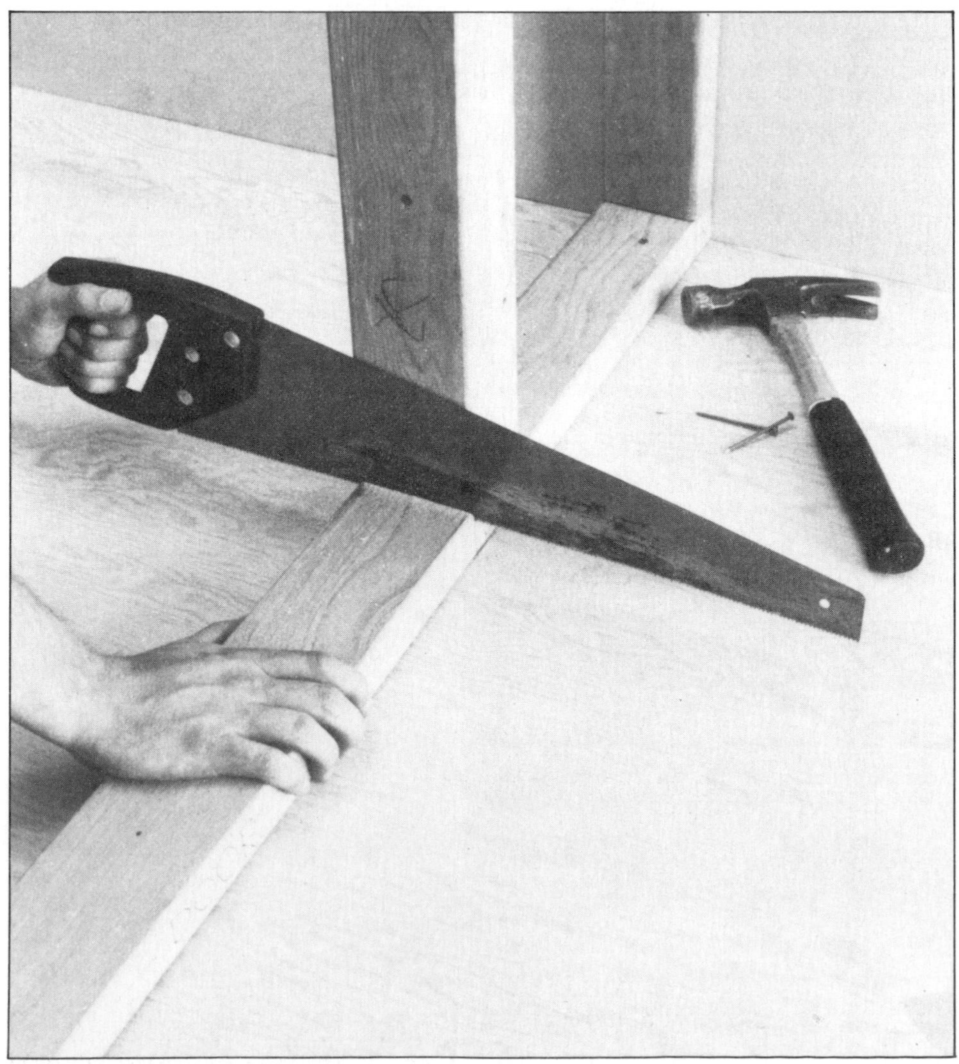
To preserve alignment across doorway, cut bottom plate out at doorways after wall is framed.

are then cut and installed so they rest directly on the subfloor. This method provides an uninterrupted surface for mounting the door jamb and makes a slightly stronger assembly. See Method 2, lower right. Do not drive nails into the plate within the door openings—the plate sections will be harder to remove.

Always run a continuous plate across door openings, then cut out the section after the wall is framed and the bottom plates are attached to the subfloor. If you leave out sections of plate while framing the wall you may save some material and time cutting the plates. But this method can result in problems with wall alignment on opposite sides of the opening. A warped door opening is even harder to fix than a warped door.

Installing a Sill—There are three ways to install a sill at a window opening, as shown in the drawings on pages 116 and 117. As mentioned earlier, the sill is the horizontal framing member at the bottom of the rough-window opening. The piece of finish wood at the bottom of a window that everybody calls a sill is correctly called a *stool.*

Method 1 in the drawing on page 116 is widely used, but is the weakest assembly. Cut the sill to fit between the jackstuds and toenail it in place. Method 2 requires cutting two *cripples* that are nailed alongside the jackstuds, as shown. The sill rests on the ends of the cripples. Just as sturdy and more economical is Method 3 on page 117. Before nailing in each jackstud, measure down from the top of the jackstud to the bottom of the rough opening and mark. Make a cut at the mark and another cut 1-1/2 inches below it. Nail lower segments of jackstuds to adjacent full studs, attach the sill, then nail in upper segments of the jackstuds. Then nail in the header.

Installing Cripples—Vertical members, called *cripples,* usually must be installed between the header and the top plate on window and door openings, and between the sill and bottom plate at window openings. Cripples take the place of studs to distribute the load on a bearing wall onto headers across the openings. Cripples under windows provide nailing for finish materials.

If the distance between header and top plates or sill and bottom plate is less than 5 inches, cripples are usually not needed in non-bearing walls.

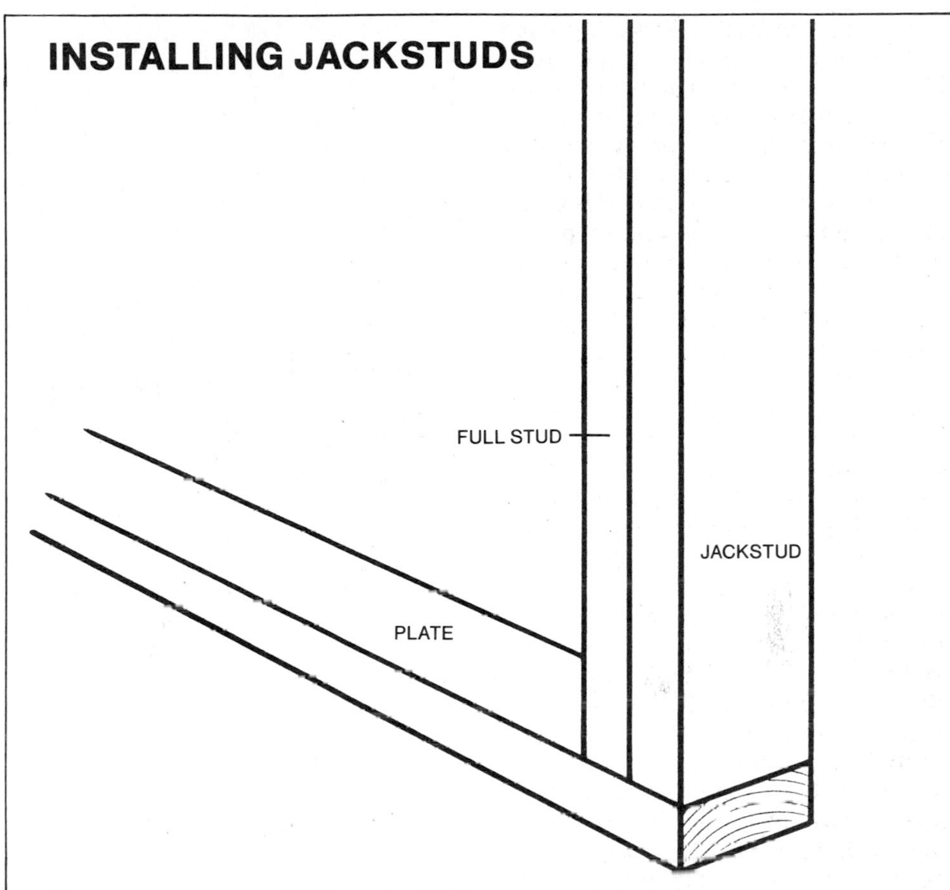

Method 1. Jackstuds are installed before plate is cut out at opening.

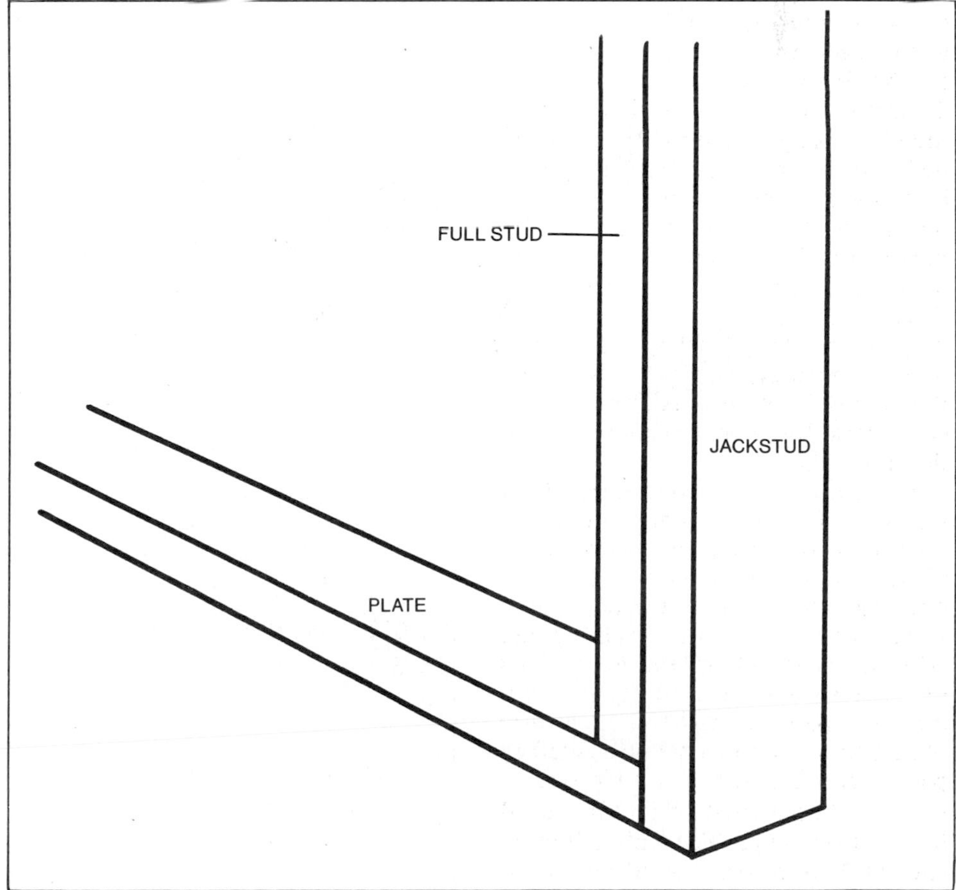

Method 2: Jackstuds are installed after plate is cut out at opening.

Check local building codes. For larger spaces and in bearing walls, cut cripples to fit and nail them to correspond with the stud spacing on either side of the opening. This keeps the spacing consistent for the installation of finish-wall material. Typical installation of cripples is shown in the drawing on page 107.

Installing Headers—Headers for openings in 2x4 bearing walls are normally constructed of two pieces of 2-inch-thick lumber on edge with a 1/2-inch plywood spacer, or of 4-inch-thick lumber on edge. Headers for openings in 2x6 frame walls are usually three pieces of 2-inch-thick lumber with two 1/2-inch plywood spacers, or of solid 6-inch-thick lumber on edge. Codes require that a header meet the same load requirements as a structural beam. This means the header must be large enough to bear the weight of all structural members above it.

As long as the header does not support any unusual loads, such as those described below, the following rule of thumb usually applies. The header height in inches—nominal—should be equal to the width of the opening in feet, plus 2 inches. In other words, a 4-foot opening usually requires a 4x6 header, or two 2x6s plus spacers. An opening up to 6 feet would require a 4x8 or two 2x8s plus spacers. Local codes may vary from this rule, so check with the building department during the planning stages.

An example of an unusual load on a header would be a beam terminating over an opening. The effect would be to add the total load the beam is carrying to the total load that the header carries. But the effect of the beam's load would be approximately doubled, because it's applied at a point instead of evenly distributed. Try to avoid complicated situations like this. If one can't be avoided, talk it over with a building official or a structural engineer. Mark proposed header sizes on the plans you submit for your permit. Ask the plan checker to double-check the sizing.

Blocking—After you've framed the wall, inspect the framing for any places where the edges of drywall sheets or other finish material will be unsupported. Install blocks between studs to support edges and provide backing for nailing. Make sure you have full backing for nailing where you plan to install molding.

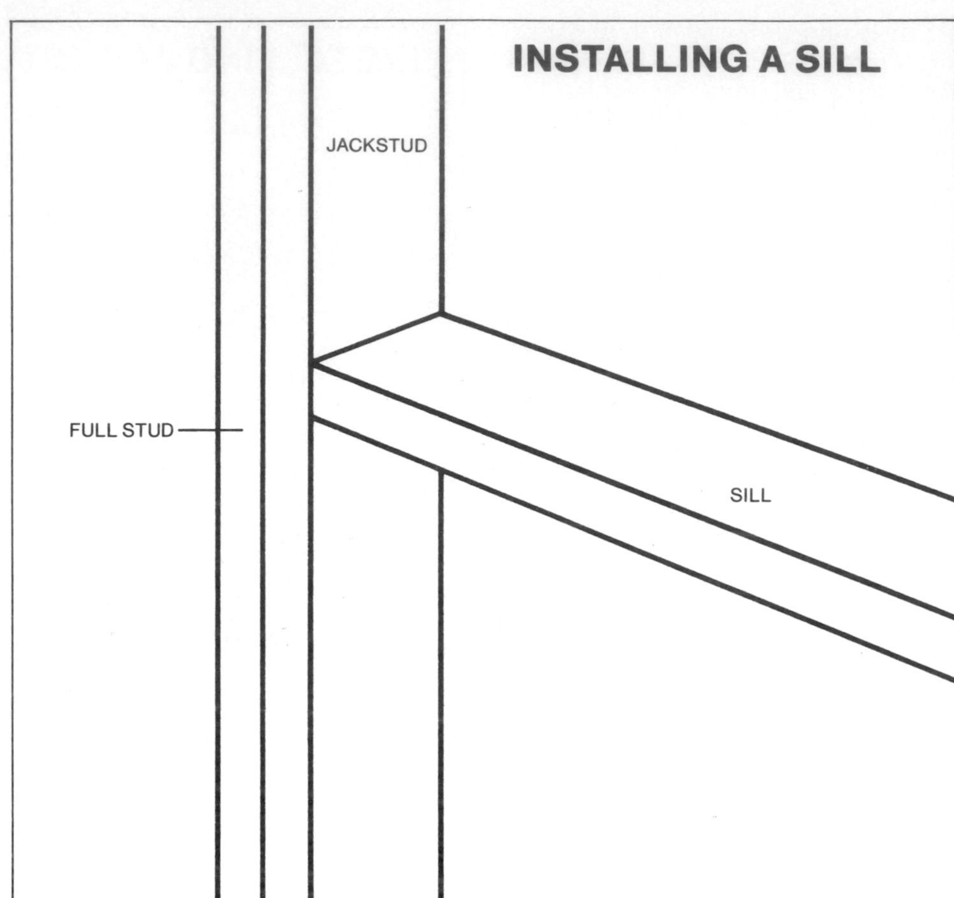

Method 1: Toenail sill between jackstuds in opening. This is weakest assembly.

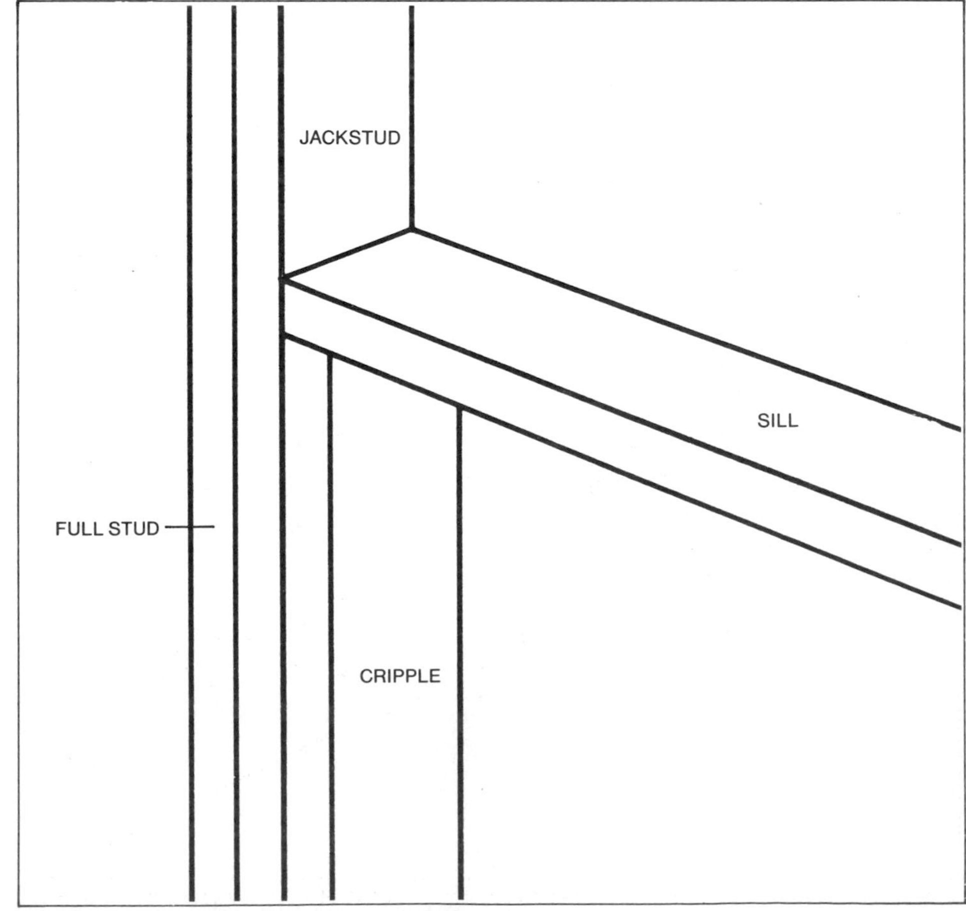

Method 2: Cut cripples and nail to jackstuds to support sill.

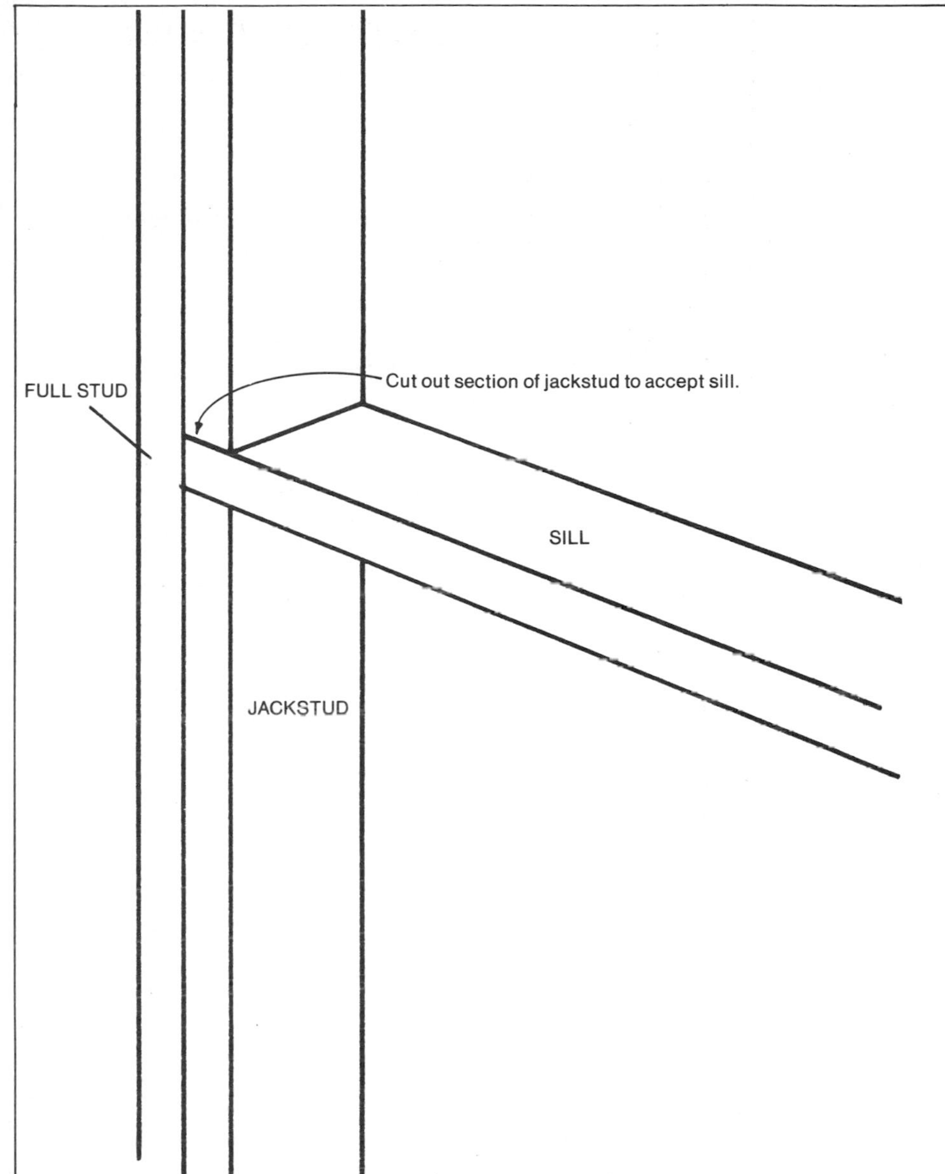

Method 3: Cut slot in jackstud to accept sill; toenail sill into full stud behind.

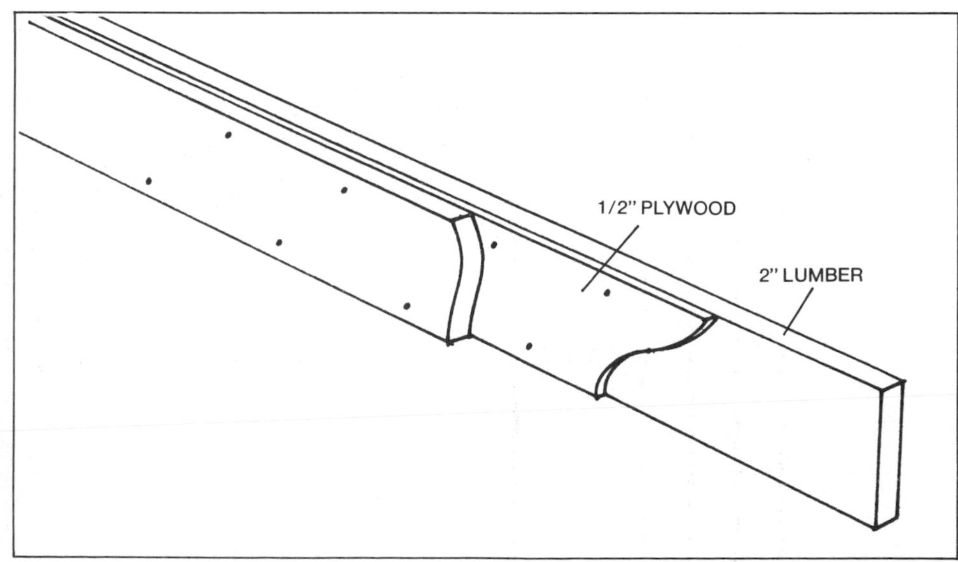

Instead of using 4-inch lumber for a header, nail two pieces of 2-inch lumber together, with 1/2-inch plywood spacer.

DRYWALL INSTALLATION

Drywall, otherwise called *gypsum board* or *Sheetrock,* has just about eliminated lath and plaster as a residential wall-surfacing material. Drywall consists of a layer of gypsum plaster between two layers of heavy paper. It's a great boon for the do-it-yourselfer because it's much easier to work with than lath and plaster.

Drywall is available in several types and sizes, depending on use. Most useful to the do-it-yourselfer is standard 1/2-inch-thick drywall in 4x8' sheets. Drywall also comes in 5/8-inch-thick sheets. Sheets also come in 12 and 16-foot lengths for special applications, but they are more difficult to work with and should be avoided if 8-foot sheets will suffice. The edges of the 8-foot sides are tapered inward slightly so the drywall joints can be taped and finished without the seam showing. See page 118.

Moisture-resistant drywall is used in areas exposed to water, such as behind kitchen sinks. Commonly known as MR board, these drywall sheets have a color-coded paper backing, usually green, to distinguish them from standard drywall.

INSTALLING DRYWALL

Drywall sheets come in pairs with the finish sides facing in. Sheets are held together with heavy paper tapes on the 4-foot ends. Because these pairs are heavy, you may want to pull the tape off the edges so you can move individual sheets to the work area. If you're buying much drywall, choose a supplier who will deliver and stack it near the work area, as long as his price is reasonably competitive.

Stack drywall lengthwise against one wall. Keep sheets close to vertical to prevent warping. Do not put more than 8 or 10 sheets in one stack. Any more than this can weaken or collapse a floor or push a wall out of plumb—drywall is heavy. On wood floors, make sure the bases of stacks run across the floor joists, not parallel to them. Locate stacks convenient to the work area, but not where they will be in the way.

Cutting and Trimming—In most instances, drywall is cut with a utility knife rather than a saw. For small jobs and repair work, any convenient straightedge or a 4-foot level can be

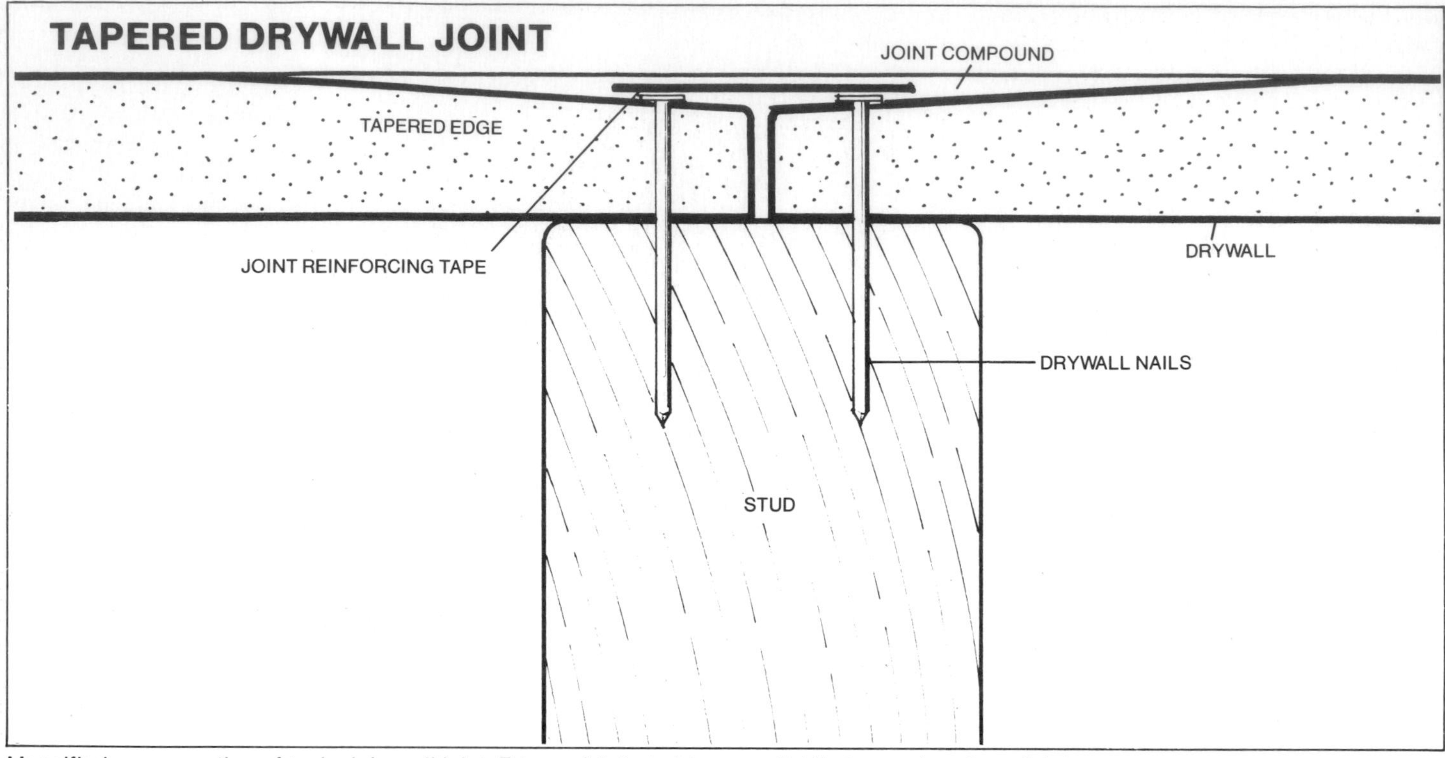

Magnified cross-section of typical drywall joint. Edges of 8-foot sides are slightly tapered so drywall-joint compound can be applied flush to surface.

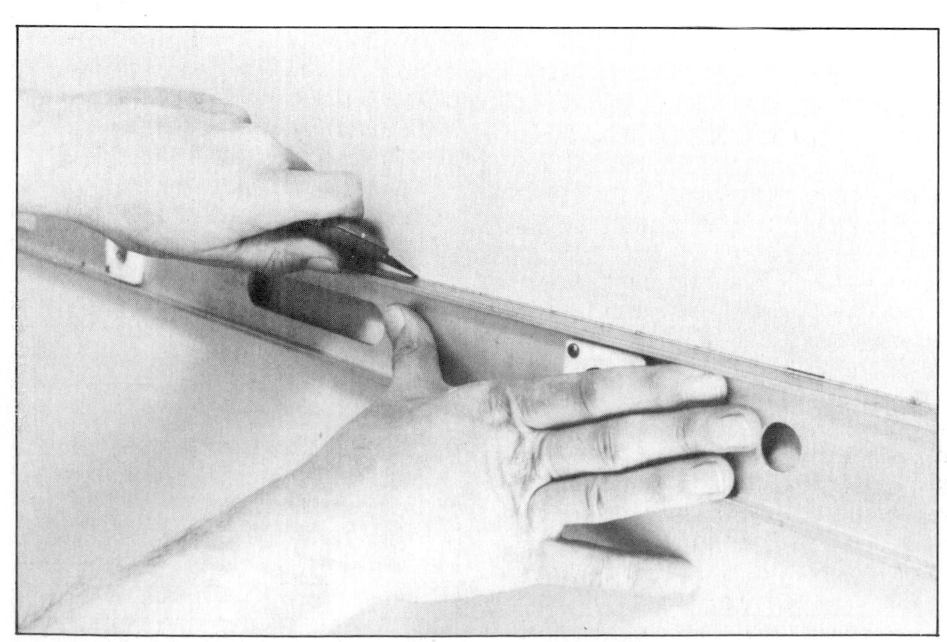

To cut drywall, slice through paper on one side with utility knife.

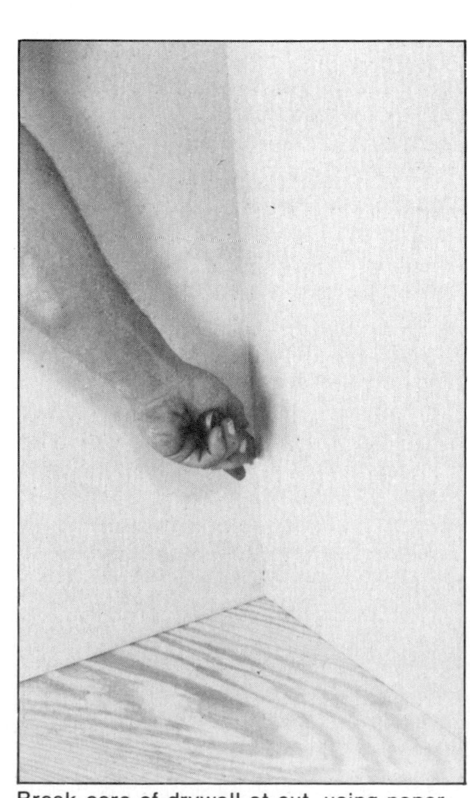

Break core of drywall at cut, using paper on other side as a hinge. Then cut paper on other side, as shown.

used as a guide, or cuts can be made freehand to a pencil line. But for larger jobs, you should consider investing in a drywall installer's *T-square.* This is a 4-foot-long straightedge, marked in inches and fractions, attached to a crosspiece that allows the device to slide on the top edge of the outer sheet of drywall on the stack.

To make a crosswise cut on a sheet of drywall, measure and mark the sheet right on the stack. Then lock the straightedge on the marks with your foot at the bottom and your hand on the top, to guide the knife blade for the cut. To make longwise cuts, position the straightedge on the marks and have a helper hold one end while you cut.

After you make the cut on the front side of the sheet, pull the sheet away from the stack. Then hit the back side of the sheet with the base of your fist, or with a hammer handle, directly behind the cut. The core material will fracture, and the sheet will hinge neatly on the back paper. Be ready for it—the core breaks easily and the sections can get away from you and fold up on the floor. Cut the backing paper along the fold, and the two pieces will come apart.

Don't try to use this technique on narrow strips. For narrow strips, cut the paper on both sides of the sheet and then break the core. If you want to use the narrow strip, lay the sheet down on the floor with a length of rope or extension cord under the cut line. Push down on the strip with the T-square or a length of wood to break the narrow strip cleanly. If you want the bigger piece and don't care what happens to the narrow strip, cut both sides and break off the narrow strip a foot or two at a time with your fingers.

Slight trimming to fit a piece of drywall can be done with the utility knife, or with a *Surform tool.* This is a rasplike tool that works similar in principle to a cheese grater. Most useful for drywall and trim work is the small, handsize model, shaped like a small block plane. It will easily smooth ragged edges with a few strokes. The perforated cutting plates on Surform tools are replaceable.

To cut a hole in drywall for a projecting obstacle, such as a pipe stub or electrical box, measure from two edges of the piece of drywall and mark the outline of the obstacle. Or rub some colored chalk from your chalk line on the obstacle and place the drywall in position against the obstacle. Tap the drywall lightly to transfer the outline of the obstacle on the back side of the drywall.

Cut the marked side with a utility knife. Drive a nail at each corner of the cutout and cut from nailhole to nailhole on the other side. Make sure the cuts are deep. Then tap the piece out from the front with a hammer. For circular cuts you can use a *keyhole saw.* This is a saw with a narrow, pointed blade. Don't use the saw any more than you have to, because drywall will dull the blade.

Ceiling Installation—Ceiling drywall should always be hung first, so the edges are supported by the drywall on the walls. Ceilings are the biggest challenge you'll face in working with drywall. You'll need at least two helpers to make the job reasonably easy.

If you have more than a sheet or two to hang, construct two *T-bars* from 2x4s for the helpers to use in positioning the drywall. The vertical leg should be slightly longer than the distance from floor to ceiling, minus 1-1/2 inches to allow for the thickness of the crossbar. The 2-foot crossbar should be centered on top of the vertical leg, as shown in the drawing at right. Use 8d or larger nails to attach the crossbar to the vertical leg. Scrap carpet can be used to pad the crossbar to avoid damage to the drywall.

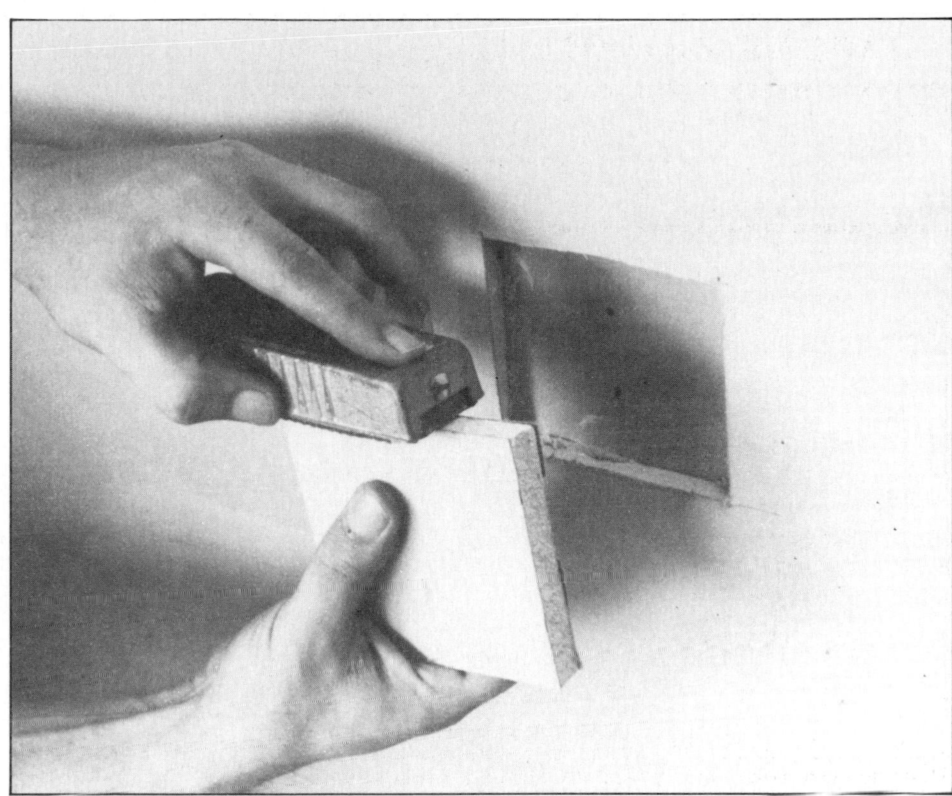
Small changes in size and shape of drywall piece are easily made with Surform tool. It works much like a cheese grater.

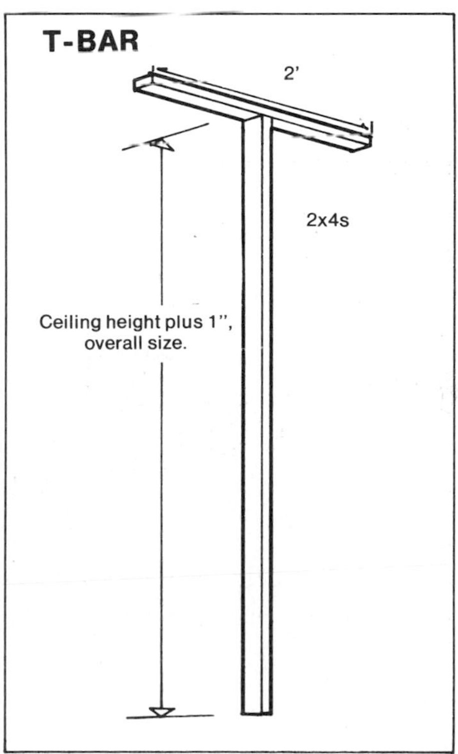

T-bar supports ceiling drywall while nailing.

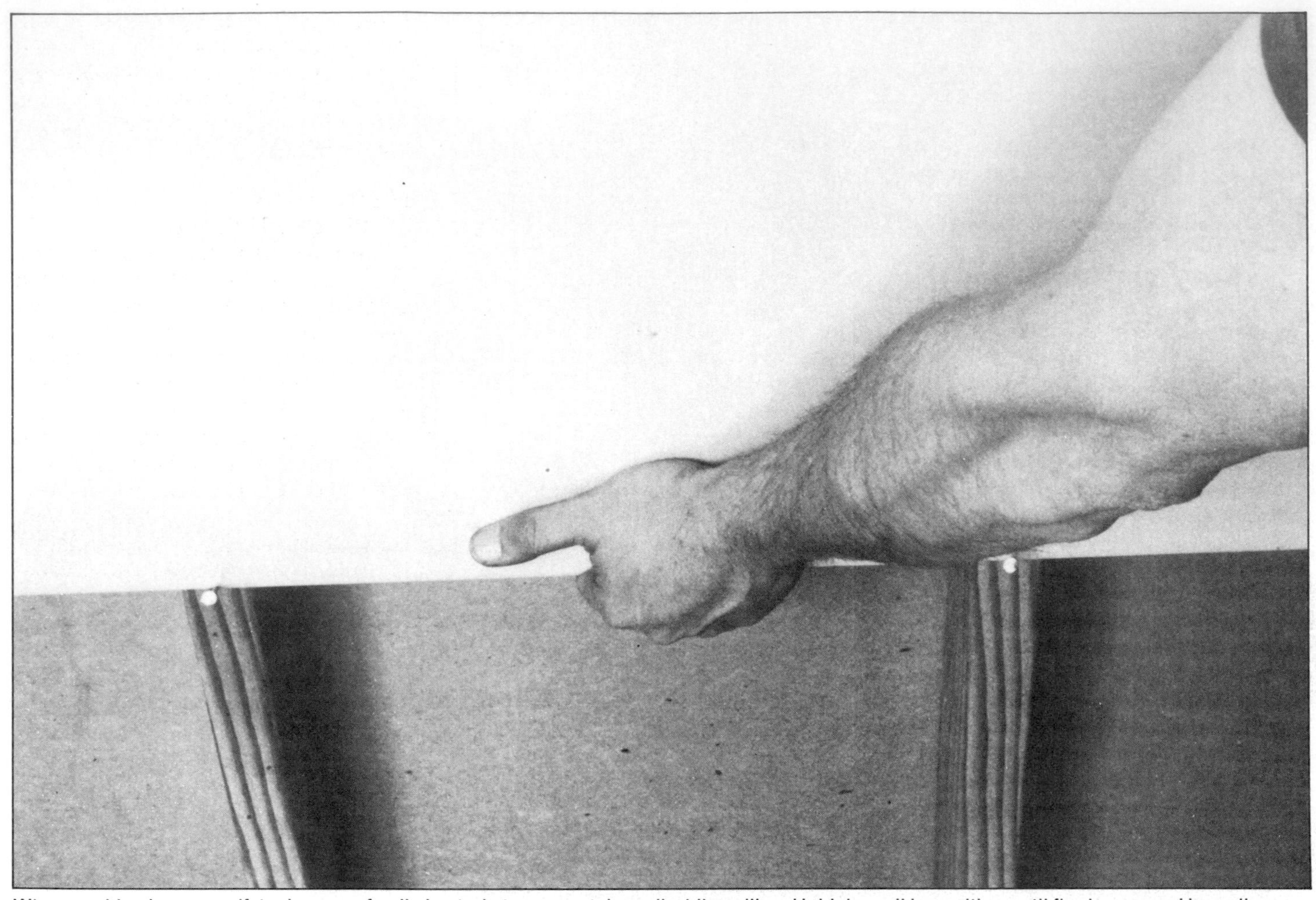

When working by yourself, tack a row of nails in studs to support drywall while nailing. Hold drywall in position until firmly secured by nails.

To hang ceiling drywall, the helpers carry the sheet to its approximate location. They then lift the sheet and balance it on their heads while the nailer hands a T-bar to first one helper and then the other. The helpers set the T-bars with the vertical legs angled away from the room corner, wall, or adjoining drywall sheet.The helpers lift the drywall with the T-bars and set it loosely against the ceiling framing, bracing the T-bars to hold it there. The nailer uses a pry bar or hammer to make any final adjustments in the position of the sheet. Then the helpers pin the sheet solidly into position by kicking in the bottom of the vertical leg of each T-bar.

The helpers then hold the T-bars to make sure they stay in position while the nailer fastens the sheet to the ceiling. The nailer stands on a plank on two sawhorses. The plank should be positioned so the top of the nailer's head is only two or three inches below the ceiling. This makes nailing easier, though nailing over your head is never really easy. Once the sheet is nailed you can leave the T-bars, plank and sawhorses where they are until needed for the next sheet of drywall.

Wall Installation—Drywall on a wall can be hung by one person. But two helpers make the work go more quickly. Two people cut and carry the drywall to the location and tack it in place while the third person does the finish nailing. If you can only get one helper, the work proceeds as if you were working single-handed. But one of you can finish the nailing on a sheet while the other is cutting or carrying the next piece.

Drywall on walls is hung with the long dimension—and the tapered edges—horizontal. Always start at the top of the wall with a full sheet. Then fill the rest of the wall, staggering the vertical joints.

If you're working by yourself, measure down 4 feet from the ceiling and drive three or four 8d nails into the studs. Angle the nails upward slightly to form a perch for the drywall. Then carry the sheet to the wall and rest it on the nails. Make sure you have your hammer and nails within reaching distance, because you'll have to hold the drywall in position once it's on the nails. Making sure that both ends of the sheet are at the center of a stud, and the top is butted tightly against the ceiling, drive a few nails in the top of the sheet to hold it in place. Then do the rest of the nailing. Pull the 8d nails out of the studs and hang the next sheet. Hang all of the top sheets on the wall or walls before starting the bottom ones.

When the top row of drywall sheets is in place, position the first of the lower sheets. To raise the lower sheet into position below the upper sheet, slip the straight end of a flat pry bar under the edge of the sheet. Then

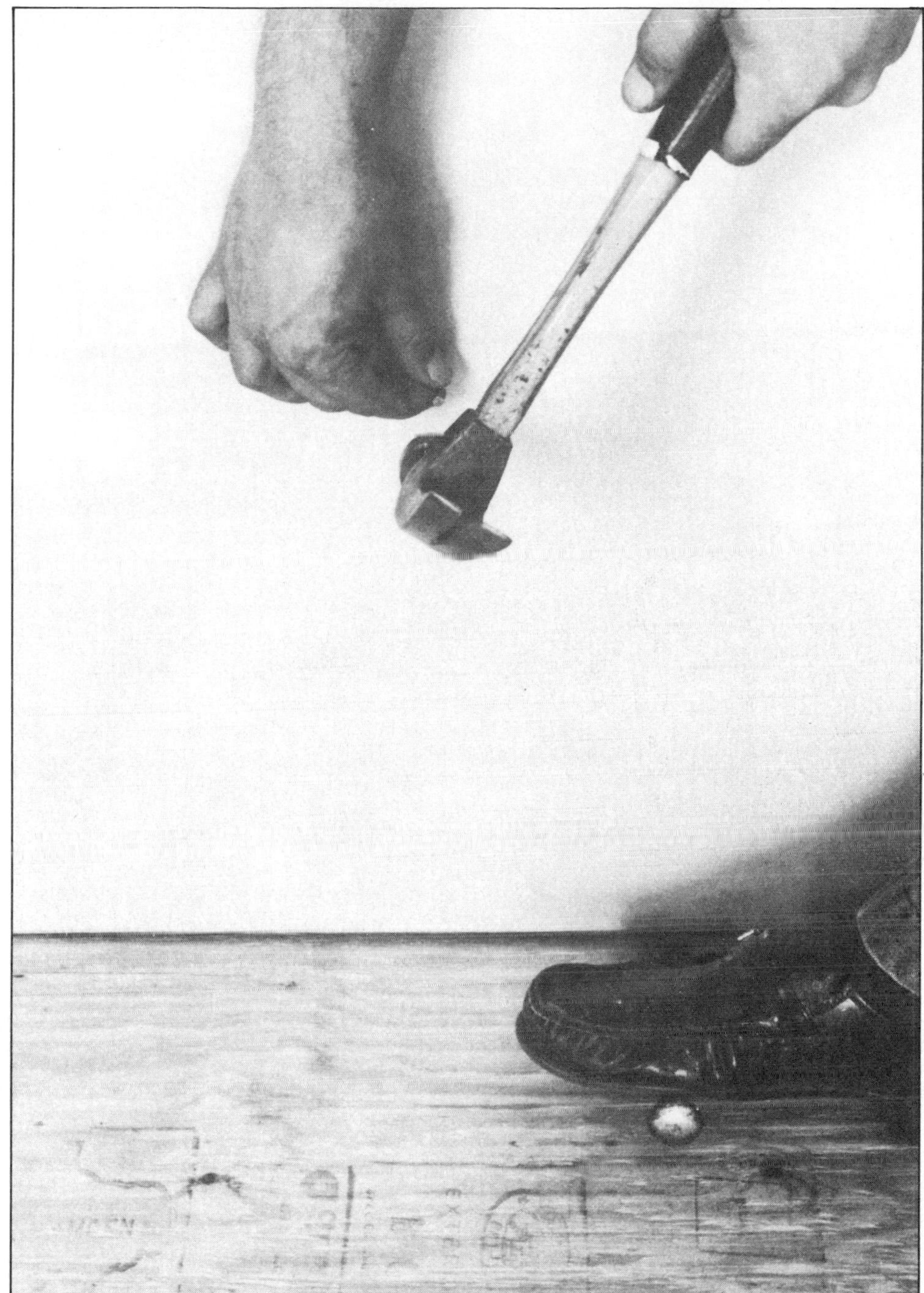

To lift sheet of drywall into final position, use pry bar and wood block. Step on prybar to lift sheet.

place a wood block under the pry bar for a fulcrum. Gently step on the outer end of the pry bar with one foot until the lower sheet butts tightly against the upper one. Hold the sheet in place with the prybar and drive several nails into the top of the sheet to hold it in place. Do not exert too much pressure on the prybar with your foot or you'll damage the drywall sheet.

Drywall Nailing—Space nails 7 inches apart along all framing members. The best nails to use are 1-1/4 inch annular-ring ones, especially on ceilings. Nails should have special large, cupped heads for drywall. If you have difficulty getting the drywall to pull down tight to the framing, drive nails in pairs, an inch or so apart.

Drive each nail into drywall until the hammer head makes a slight indentation into the drywall surface, but not enough to break the paper coating or the gypsum core. The indentation, or dimple, provides a recess for the joint compound that will cover the nailhead.

When nailing along drywall joints, place nails in pairs on each side of the joint. If you stagger nails on adjoining sheets, you can introduce a waviness that will make joint finishing much more difficult.

TAPING AND FINISHING DRYWALL

Finishing drywall involves two operations, taping joints and covering nailheads. Tools required are a 6-inch taping knife, a 14-inch taping knife, and something to hold a working supply of compound, such as a *hawk*. A hawk is a flat-blade tool with a handle on the bottom, in the center. A large concrete trowel can serve as a hawk. Or, you can use a long, rectangular pan for the joint compound. These pans are available at a building-supply store, or you can use a deep, rectangular bread pan. The pan makes joint compound easier to work with, and helps keep compound in the bucket from getting contaminated with bits of dried compound on the knife.

Putty knives and stiff, nicked up old scrapers should not be used in place of taping knives. Drywall finishing requires a flexible blade with a straight edge and sides.

Materials include *joint compound* and *drywall reinforcing tape*, available at home-improvement centers and paint stores. Premixed joint compound is much easier to work with than the dry powdered kind and costs about the same. Reinforcing tape is a roll of heavy, non-adhesive paper, usually perforated with tiny holes so joint compound will key into it.

Filling Nail Dimples—First, fill the nail head dimples that won't be covered by tape. This work can be done with the 6-inch knife and hawk. Put a small amount of joint compound on the edge of the knife, toward the center of the blade. Cover the nail dimple with a thick coat of compound. Make a second pass with the knife at right angles to the first to skim off excess compound. Use just enough pressure to level the joint compound. As you cover successive nail dimples, you'll develop a rhythm that will make work move along rapidly.

If your knife touches a nailhead while you're filling nail dimples, you'll feel it. Drive the nail a bit deeper with a hammer and reapply the compound. Don't bother to clean the joint compound out of the nail dimple to do this—just let it splatter. Drywall finishing is not a neat process.

As you're working, joint compound may squeeze out to the ends of the blade and drop off. To minimize this, periodically clean compound from the ends of the knife blade. If any compound falls on the floor, wipe it up immediately and dispose of it. If you don't, someone may slip on it or track it through the rest of the house. Don't use your taping knives to pick up compound from the floor, and don't reuse the dropped joint compound. The knives will get nicked, and you'll pick up debris that will mess up the work.

Taping Joints—When you've finished the nailheads, start taping the joints. During the taping and finishing process, keep taping knives clean and joint compound uncontaminated. If bits of compound dry on the knife, it will be difficult to get a smooth finish surface. The same is true if debris or bits of dry compound get into the compound you're working with. If you have excess compound on the knife or hawk after finishing a section of drywall, don't put it back in the container with the fresh compound. Dispose of it.

Use the following method for joints where the drywall edges are tapered. Working crossways to the joint, butter it liberally with joint compound. The object is to get a layer of compound in which to bed the tape, so be generous.

Unroll a length of reinforcing tape, and tear it from the roll. Starting at one end of the joint, lightly embed the tape in the compound. Cover the end with a small amount of joint compound. Then run the tape knife down the joint, lightly sticking the tape in the compound. Don't apply too much pressure, or the tape may slide or stretch.

If you didn't align the tape correctly and it drifted off the joint or got wrinkled, pull it loose and start over. In dry climates, the tape may be too dry to stick properly. If the tape is too dry, it will begin to shrink and pucker a few minutes after it's applied to the joint. If this happens, remove the tape. Dip it into a bucket of water and remove excess just before reapplying. Moisten successive lengths of tape before using them.

After the reinforcing tape is in place, use the 6-inch knife to apply a thin, even coat of joint compound over the tape. Start in the middle of the joint and work toward each end. If

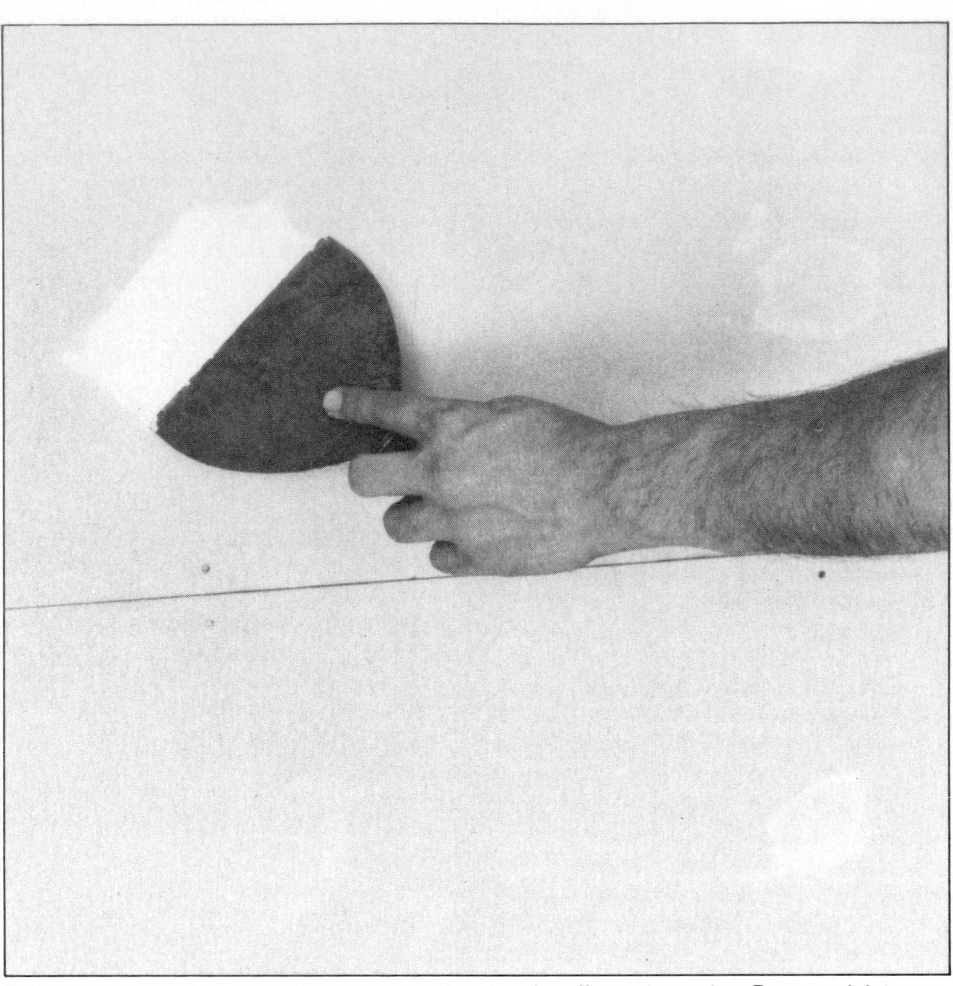

To finish nail dimples, apply joint compound and strike off at right angles. Because joint compound shrinks slightly, you may have to apply second coat.

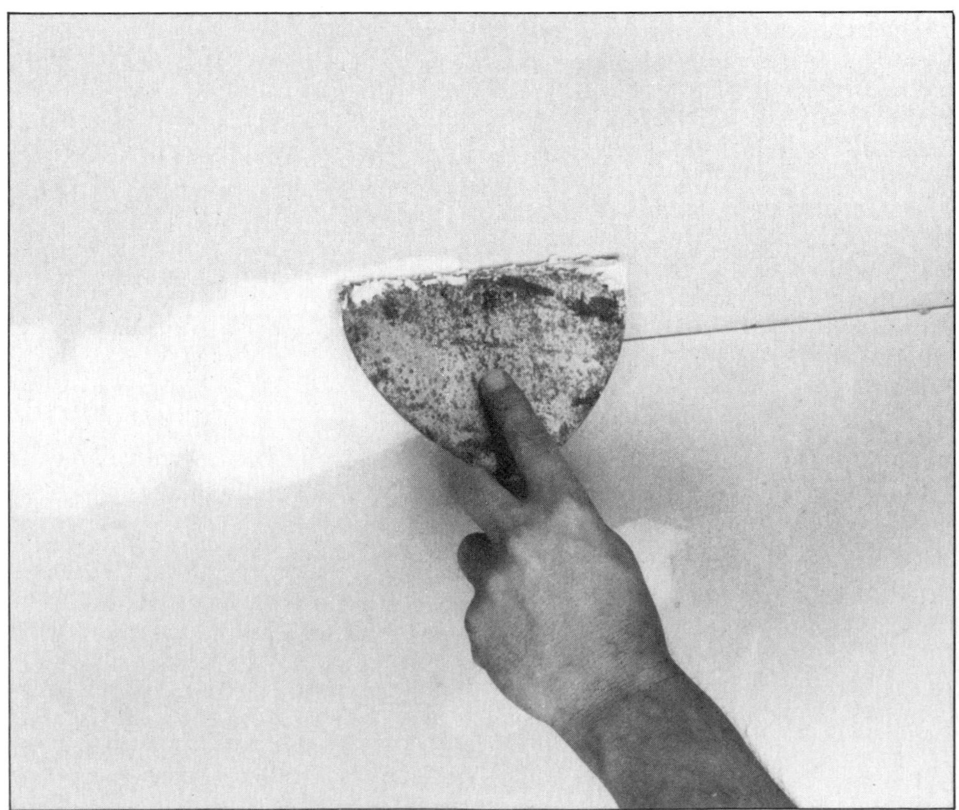

Butter joint liberally before bedding tape.

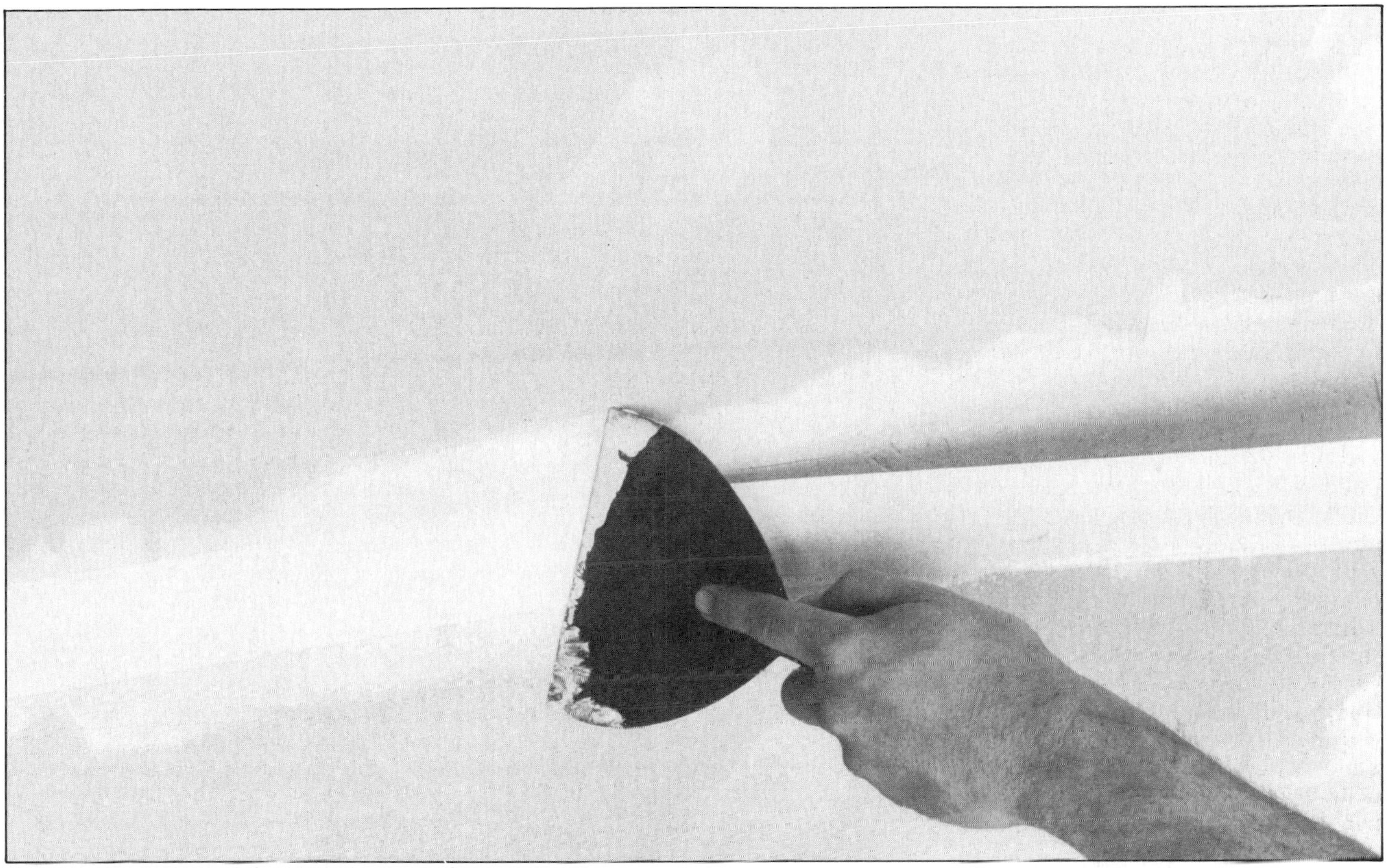

Bed tape into compound. Avoid wrinkles or air bubbles.

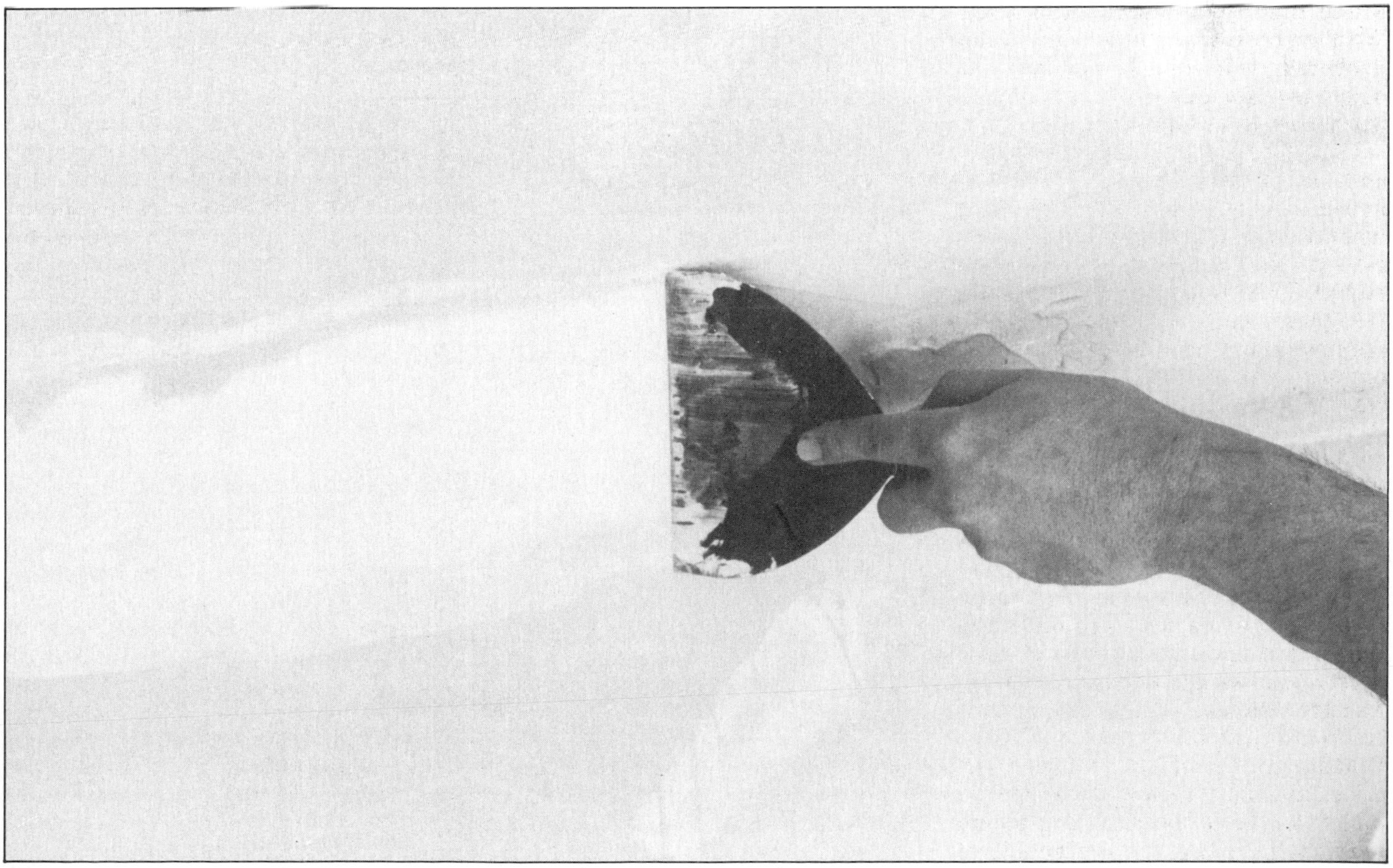

After tape is on, put another light coat on top, pressing tape firmly into compound.

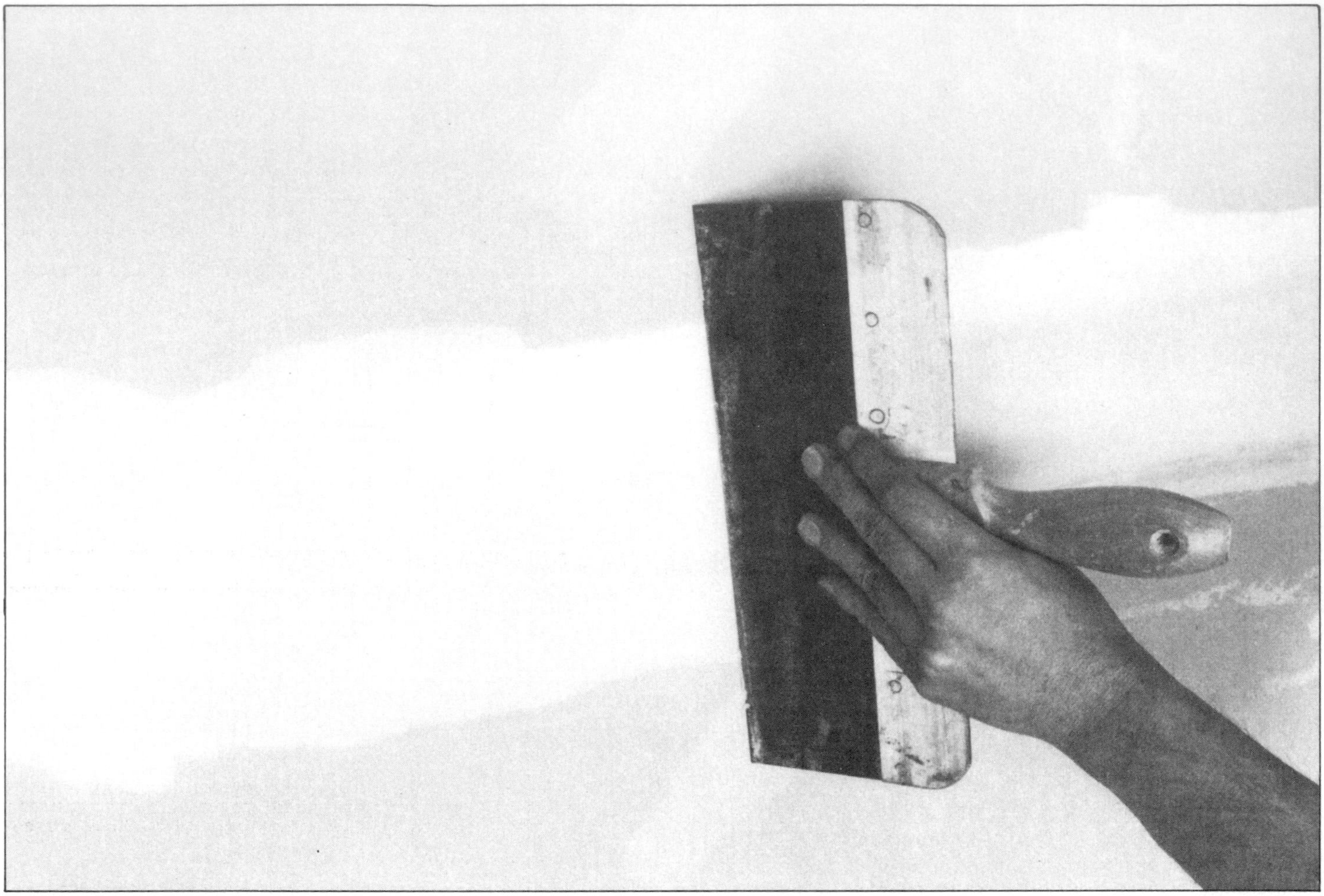

Apply last coat with a steady hand to avoid heavy finish sanding. Repeat pass if you're not satisfied.

the tape tends to slide out of position, hold it in place with your thumbnail while applying compound.

When the first coat of joint compound is dry, lightly sand the joint with 120- to 180-grit sandpaper attached to a sanding block, or wrapped around a short piece of 1x2. If you have very much sanding to do, you'll save time if you use a *pole sander.* This tool looks somewhat like a sponge mop, except it has a pivoting head to which the sandpaper is attached. A pole sander is especially useful for sanding ceiling joints. Special sandpaper is available for the sander.

Sand joints until you have taken down high spots and the surface is fairly smooth. Any voids or low spots in the joint compound can be filled with the second coat. Do not let the sandpaper cut into the reinforcing tape.

When all joints are sanded, apply a second coat of joint compound. Use the 6-inch knife to skim on a thin film of compound down the middle of the

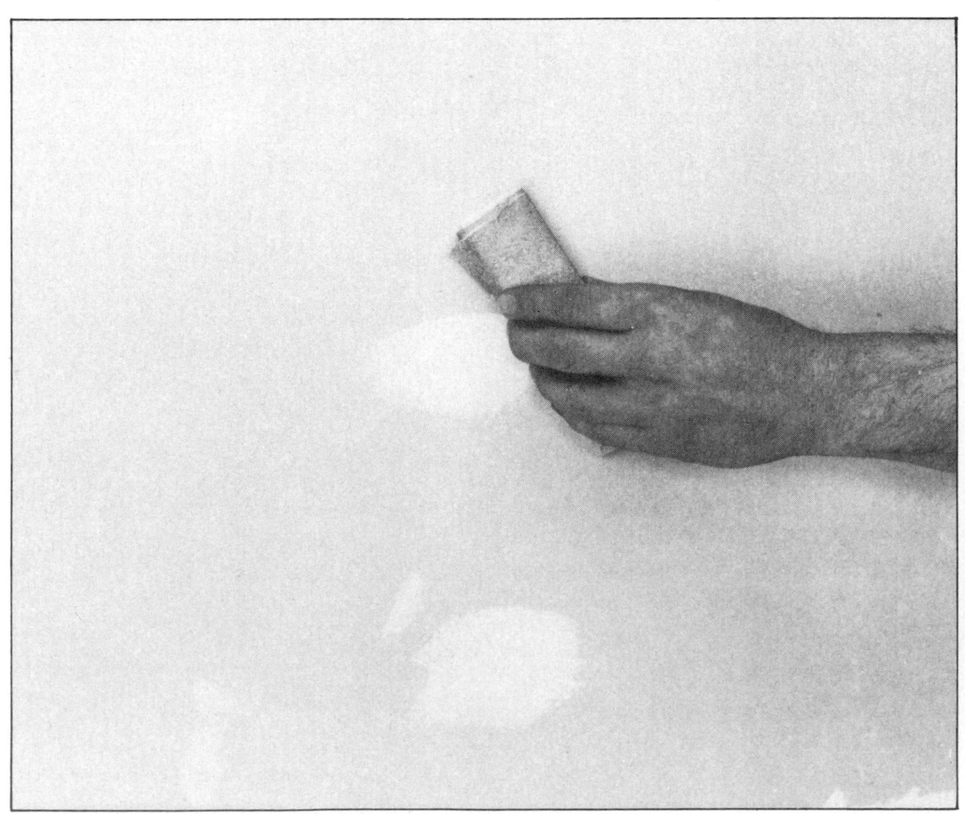

Sand down to a smooth surface. Every blemish will show under paint.

joint. Clean off the knife, then skim off any compound deposited outside the tapered area. Be careful not to remove compound inside the tapered area. See photo on page 123. Don't try to smooth out small ridges of compound on the tape when you're doing this. They can be sanded later.

When the second coat is dry, sand again. When sanding, carefully remove any ridges or high spots where the taper meets the flat drywall surface. Then use the 14-inch knife to skim a thin, even coat of compound over the joint. See photo on the facing page. Run the knife along the full length of the joint, in one even, smooth pass. This should be the final coat, so take your time. The compound should go on smooth and level—any irregularities will have to be sanded out completely. After the third coat is sanded, check with a straightedge and see if the joint is completely level with the rest of the wall. If it isn't, add a fourth coat, using the 14-inch knife. Sand out any irregularities.

Joints with Square Edges—You'll find that not all drywall joints have tapered edges adjacent to them. Joints at the 4-foot ends of sheets and joints between cut pieces will have square edges instead of tapered ones. Because the adjoining drywall edges aren't tapered, the reinforcing tape and drywall compound will be higher than the surrounding surface. You'll need to taper joint compound away gradually from the taped joint to hide this change in level.

To do this, apply reinforcing tape and cover it as described for tapered-edge joints, page 122. Before applying the third coat, hold a straightedge along the edge of your 14-inch knife. You'll find that the edge will probably have a slight bow to it. Use the side that most closely resembles the curve shown in the drawing above right. Warp the blade until it approximates the curve. Don't use a hammer to bend the blade. Put fingers on one side of the blade and thumb on the other and warp it gently. Check frequently while you're working to make sure the curve is still there. The curve allows you to apply the third coat, or fourth coat if needed, over the tape and joint compound that beds it. Pay particular attention to these square-edge joints when finish sanding. Sanding across the joint helps.

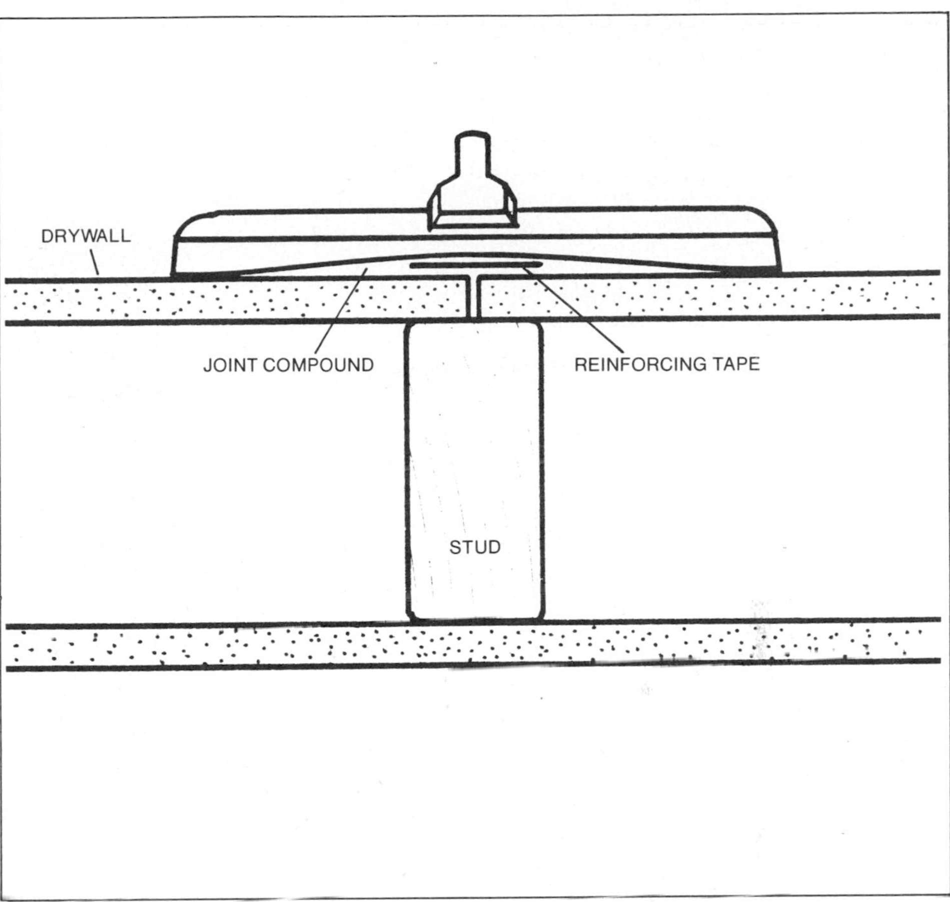

Warp a slight curve into tape knife when you have to finish square-edge joints. Curve is exaggerated here.

Finishing Corners—One of the most difficult and time-consuming parts of drywall finishing is taping the corners. There are special tools available for doing corners, but these are probably not worth the investment if you're doing one room or less. These tools also take getting used to. There is an easy, though slow, way to finish corners so they come out looking as good as those done with specialized tools.

First, look at your 6-inch taping knife. The working edge, of course, is straight. On most taping knives, at least one of the sides will have a straight section at least 1 inch long. If your's doesn't, file one side of the blade to provide a straight edge slightly less than 90° to the working edge.

If you file straight edges on both sides of the blade, it's helpful to have one that's just slightly under 90°, and the other with an angle between 60° and 75°. The second angle is useful for three-way corners, such as where two walls meet the ceiling.

Apply joint compound to adjoining drywall sheets along the corner. Tear off a length of reinforcing tape to fit. You'll find an indented line down the middle of the reinforcing tape. Crease tape along the line so it forms a right angle. Be careful not to cut your fingers on tape edges while creasing it. Pat the tape lightly into the bed of joint compound. Use the 6-inch knife to apply a skim coat of compound to one side of the tape along the corner. After a minute or two, go over that same side with the tape knife. Apply enough pressure to remove the skim coat down to the reinforcing tape. This beds the tape solidly on that side. Don't disturb the reinforcing tape, or rough it up while doing this.

Before compound on the first side dries, apply a skim coat to the other side of the tape. Position the tape knife so the straight section on the side of the blade is riding on side one. This prevents the joint compound from building up a bead on side one.

Let this coat dry thoroughly and sand off any irregularities. Then skim-coat side one, the same way as side two. Let dry, sand and skim coat side two. Repeat process, adding skim coats to alternate sides of corner, letting coats dry and sanding them until corner is done.

This technique produces perfect corners if you observe these precautions: Don't try to work on both sides of the corner at the same time. Sand off any ridges on both sides before you apply another coat of compound to either side. Where two walls and a ceiling meet, handle it as if you had a corner with three sides instead of two. The drawing at right shows the correct taping sequence.

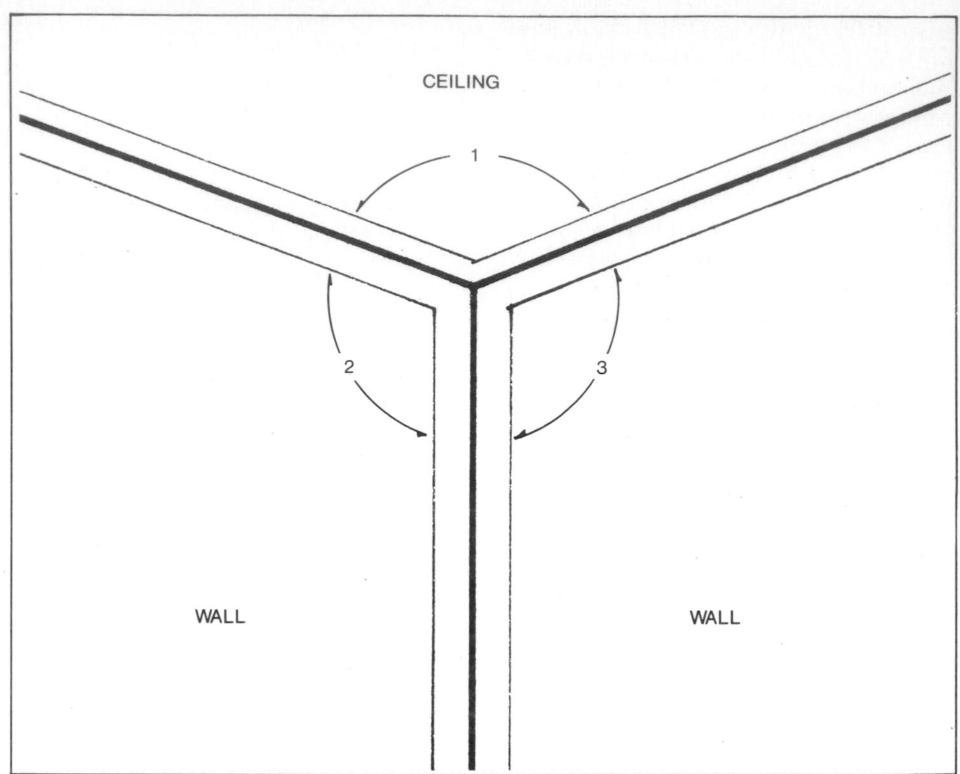

When working in a corner, apply joint compound to tape in sequence shown. After first coat dries, repeat sequence until joints are smooth.

REPAIRING WALL SURFACES

Remodeling often requires cutting access holes in a sound wall to run plumbing, wiring or ductwork. Many times, cabinet removal reveals a water-damaged wall surface, while wall framing itself is sound. Wall surfaces sometimes get damaged while remodeling. Or the wall may just be showing its age.

Often, only small portions of wall surface need to be repaired or replaced. The rest can be left intact. Because most kitchen wall surfaces are either drywall or lath and plaster, repair techniques for these surfaces are covered here.

REPAIRING DRYWALL

Inspect existing drywall for damage and deterioration. If the paper surface is scraped or otherwise damaged, clean off any loose material. Then restore the surface with a skim coat of joint compound.

If the gypsum core is broken or disintegrating from water damage, remove damaged drywall and put in a new section. If you have to remove drywall to gain access to plumbing or wiring, the repair method is the same.

Find the studs adjoining the area to be removed. To do this, remove a small section toward each side of the damaged area. Slide the end of a tape measure through the holes to locate the studs. If you'll be using the piece you take out, use a hammer and small nail to probe for the studs. Drive the nail through the drywall where you suspect a stud might be. If you don't find the stud, move about an inch left or right and try again. Don't move the nail more than 1-1/2 inches at a time, or you might skip over the stud.

After you've found adjoining studs, mark drywall along the stud center lines on either side of the damaged area. Use a framing square to mark

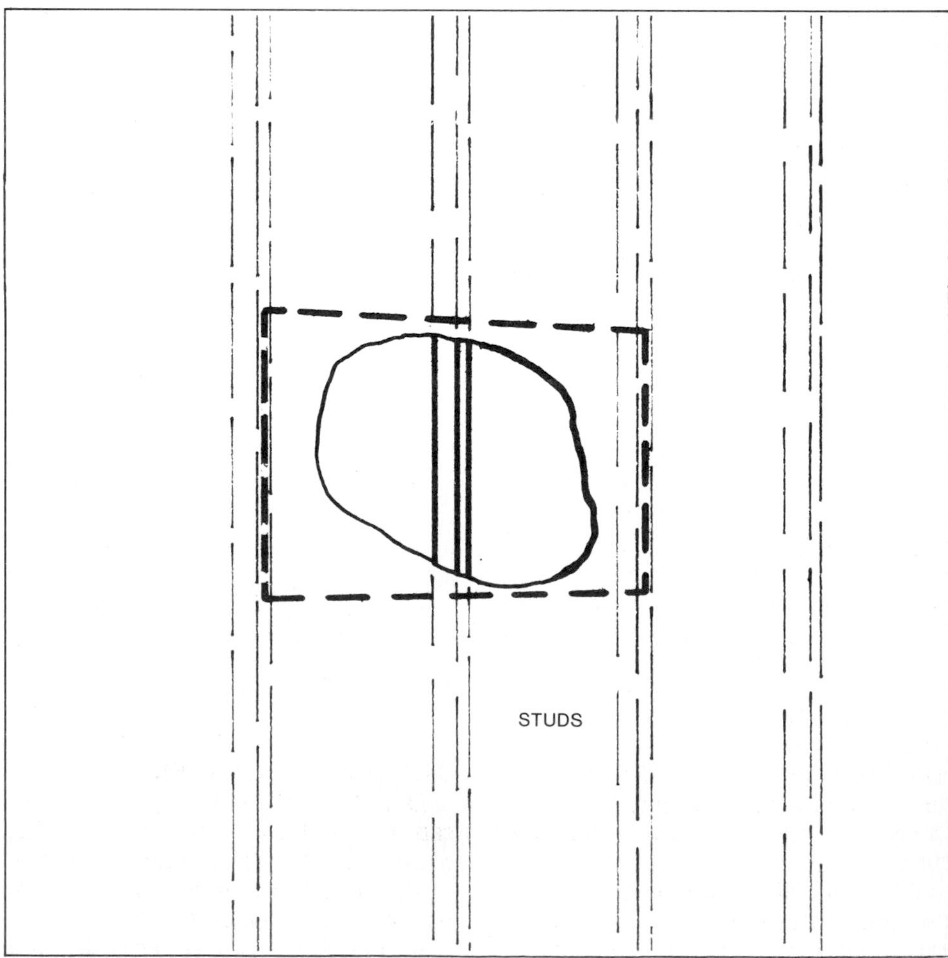

To repair large damaged area in drywall, cut back to framing members on at least two sides so you can nail in a patch.

perpendicular lines across the top and bottom of the area to be removed. The corners of the marked area should be exactly 90° so the cutout will be perfectly square. This will make it easier to cut and fit replacement drywall. To remove drywall, score along vertical lines with a utility knife and a straightedge until you've cut completely through the drywall.

You may hit one or more nails with the knife as you work. As you find nails, chip the old joint compound off the nailheads and drive nails into the stud with a nailset or pull them out. If you can't make the cuts along the middle of a stud, cut the drywall flush to the side of the stud that faces the work area. Then nail a length of 2x4 to the side of the stud to provide a nailing surface when you replace the drywall.

To save the cutout piece of drywall, gently pry it out with a chisel. Make sure you've cut completely through the paper backing or it will tear off when you remove the piece. If you're using new drywall for a patch, use the utility knife and straightedge to smooth any rough edges around the cutout area.

To close the hole you've made, replace the piece you removed. Or cut a piece of new drywall to fit, and nail it in place. Then tape and finish the joints as described for square-edge joints on page 125.

To repair small holes in drywall, you can enlarge the hole to the nearest adjacent studs and nail in a patch, as described above, or you can use the following method. Enlarge the hole to make it approximately square. Then cut a square backer of drywall with sides that measure a little less than the diagonal measurement of the hole.

Punch two small holes close together in the middle of the backer, and loop a length of wire through the holes. Apply a coat of joint compound around the edges of the backer where it will contact the backside of the surrounding drywall. Insert the backer through the hole, and pull it into place with the wires. Then place a small wood block across the hole and twist the wires around it to hold the backer in place while the joint compound dries.

After the joint compound has dried and glued the backer in place, cut off the wires. Cut a patch a little smaller than the hole. Glue this patch to the backer with joint compound. When this has dried, you can finish the patch.

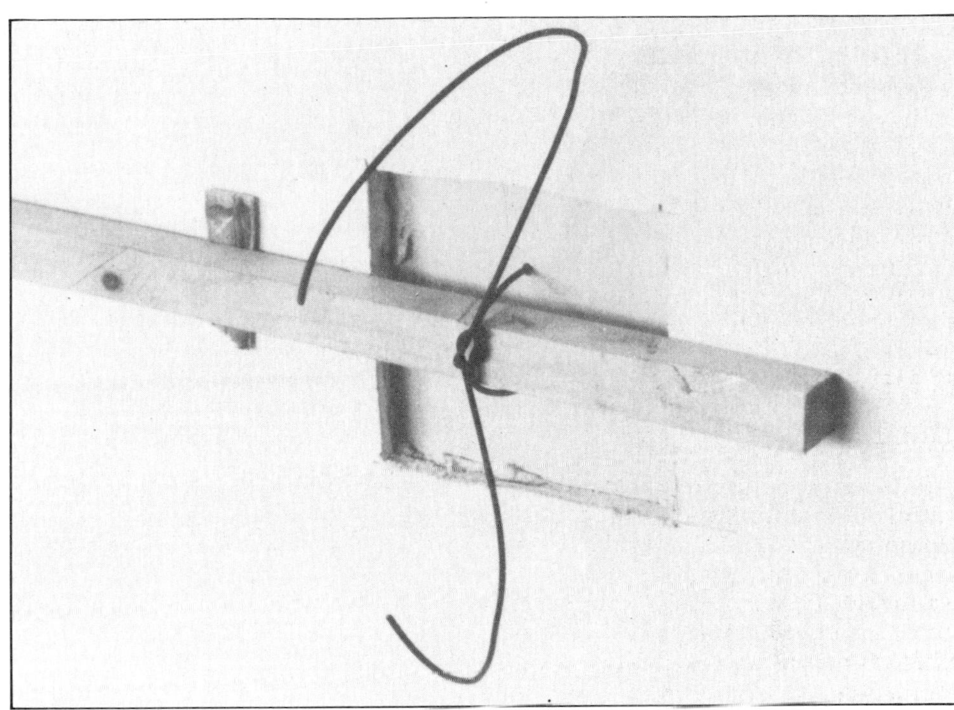

Small damaged area can be repaired by gluing in a backer and then gluing a patch on top.

Use several heavy coats of joint compound to fill patch. On small patches, drywall reinforcing tape isn't necessary.

REPAIRING PLASTER

Drywall materials and techniques can be used to repair plaster walls. Make sure all loose plaster is removed first, no matter how much of it there is. Don't try to patch together a disintegrating plaster wall—tear it all out if you have to.

If only the finish coat of plaster has loosened or been damaged, and the plaster undercoats and lath are still sound, a skim coat of drywall-joint compound will restore it. Add sand or fine sawdust to the compound to match the plaster texture.

If plaster has loosened from the lath or deteriorated all the way through, remove it, leaving the lath and surrounding sound plaster in place. See *Plaster Removal,* page 70. Then cut a piece of drywall to the size and shape of the opening and nail it right over the lath.

Nail the drywall along the studs, not to the lath. Edges of the drywall patch don't need to be supported by studs because the lath will hold them in place. The patch does not have to be exactly the same thickness as the existing plaster, because it only forms a base for a skim coat of joint compound. Because plaster is often wavy, a flush patch can sometimes present problems at the edges. The patch should be about 1/16 inch lower than the surrounding plaster.

If the plaster is thick, you may have to shim out the drywall patch, or even use two layers of drywall to get fairly close to the plaster surface.

After the drywall patch is in place, force joint compound into joints so that it *keys* the plaster and the drywall patch together, locking both to the lath. Keying happens when the joint compound squeezes out behind the joint and hardens. After this keying application is dry, finish the patch with one or more skim coats, feathering out onto the plaster at the edges.

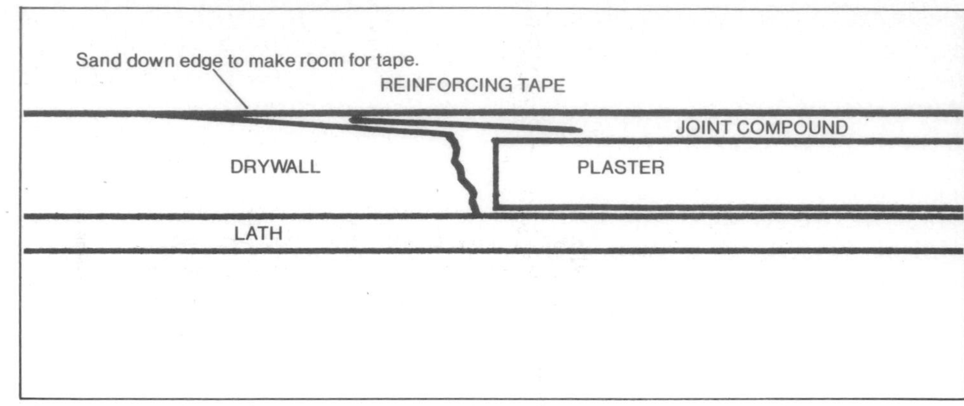

Use drywall as a base for a skim coat to repair damaged areas in plaster walls.

MATCHING TEXTURES

Patching and repair work may require you to match an existing textured-wall finish. Or you may decide to change the texture in the entire room. You can either buy a ready-mixed interior texturing product, or you can mix your own. Textured paints also work, but the surface you're coating must be even and level. Textured paint hides only small imperfections and won't hide dissimilar materials very well.

Mix Your Own—To mix your own wall texturing, thin drywall joint compound to a consistency like mayonnaise or pancake batter. Instead of water, use liquid synthetic latex, available at ceramic-tile suppliers. Or use half water and half cheap latex paint. Prepare a thick mix for heavy textures, and a thinner mix for finer textures.

You can add a variety of materials to modify the texture of the basic smooth mix. For a medium-coarse texture, use #30 silica sand, available at masonry suppliers, or sawdust. For a coarse texture, you can use kitty litter. Do not use the kind with disinfectant additives. Many of these materials will take up moisture from the texturing mix, so you may have to add water.

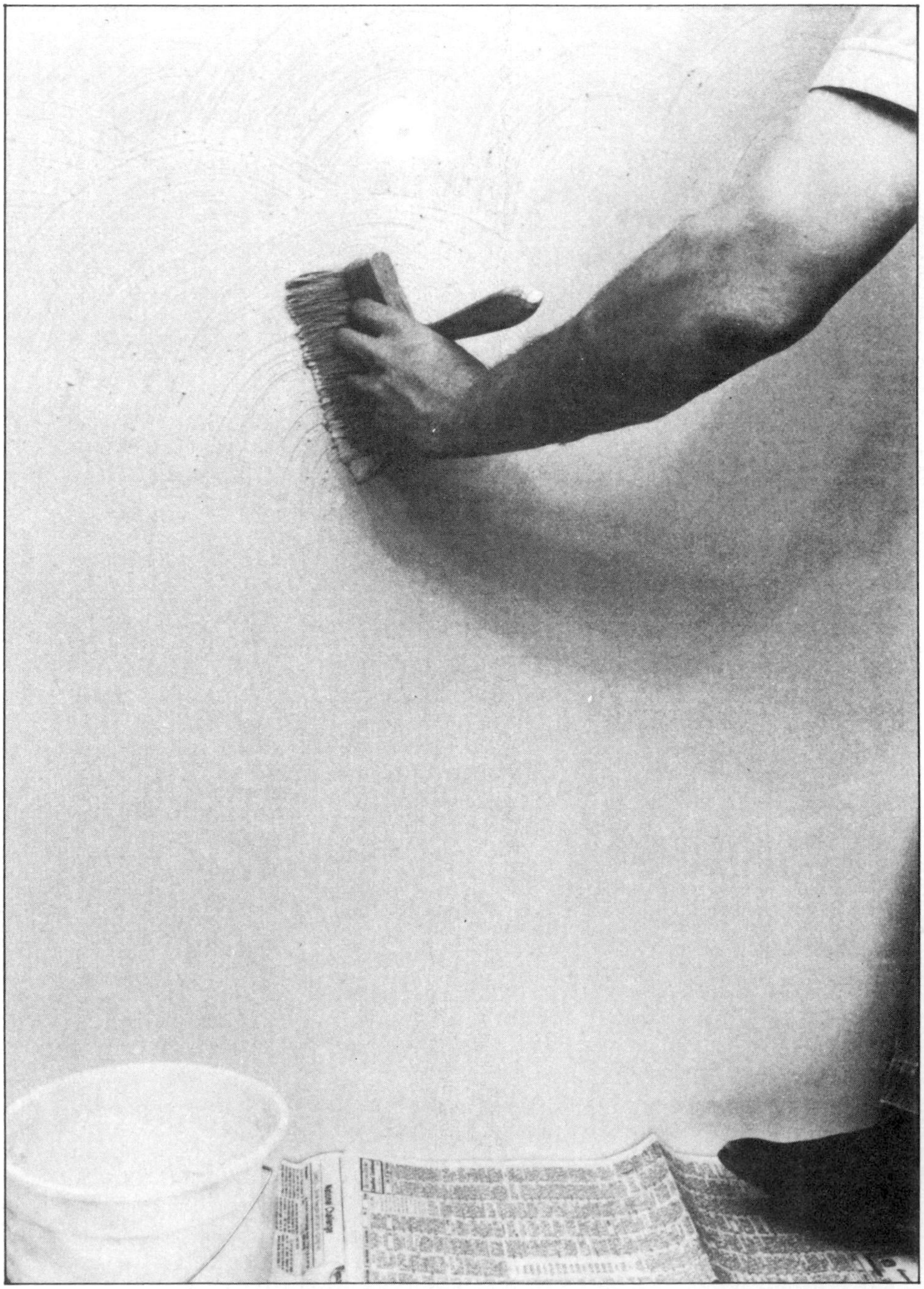

You can make your own texture coatings and apply them with sponge, brush, broom, trowel or taping knife. Here, wallpaper brush is used to give patterned texture. Texturing is messy, so protect floor.

The method of application also influences texture. A trowel, sponge or paint brush is often used. Large areas can be covered quickly with a large, soft-bristle brush used for applying wallpaper paste, or an ordinary broom. But anything at all can be used, from bare hands to a push broom. Experiment on a scrap piece of drywall or plywood until you find a mix and an application technique that matches surrounding walls, or one you like for doing a new texture. Start and finish texturing strokes in the unfinished area, and then cover with succeeding strokes.

A common texture that has to be matched in drywall repair is called a *skip texture.* Skip texturing is achieved by mixing several hands full of #30 silica sand into the basic smooth mix and applying the mixture with a 14-inch taping knife. The compound is applied in a quick skimming motion, with the knife blade almost parallel to the wall surface. This deposits compound in small, flat blotches across the surface of the wall.

WINDOW INSTALLATION

If you've done work on outside walls, may have windows to install. No matter what type of window it is, installation is similar.

Check the window assembly with a rafter square to make sure it's square. If the window assembly is wood, attach a 6- to 8-inch-wide strip of 6-mil polyethylene around the outside edges of the window frame. Staple it onto the sides so you can lap it over wall framing for an air seal. Then trial-fit the window in the opening. For information on making window openings, see pages 113-115.

Aluminum windows have a flange that seats against the outside edges of the framed window opening. The windows can be installed before the finish siding, with siding covering the flange, or after the finish siding. If your house has lapped siding, it's best to install the window first, then fit the siding to it. If the window is installed over the siding, the flange can be covered with 1x3 or 1x4 trim.

Wood and vinyl-clad wood windows have molding attached to the outside of the frame. They can be installed before or after the finish siding, depending on the type of siding involved. Lap siding is usually fitted to the sides of the window after installation.

To install the window, place it in the opening and level it. The window should be level, even if the framed opening isn't. Leave a gap of at least 1/4 inch at both top and bottom between the window frame and the header and sill. This prevents the window from jamming if the header or floor ever sags in the future. On horizontal-sliding windows, the gap at the top should be slightly larger than the one at the bottom. But the opening should not be so large that you can't nail the flange or outer molding on all four sides. The wider the opening, the more gap you need.

After the window is positioned and leveled, drive a few nails through flange or outer molding on each side. Don't drive nails through top or bottom flange or molding.

If you're installing a wood-frame window, go inside and fit temporary shims or wood blocks every foot or so between the bottom of the window and the sill. Also fit shims or wood blocks between the top of the window and the header. Drive *casing nails* next to each of the temporary shims. Casing nails look much like finish nails. Remove the temporary shims. This locks the window into the opening, but allows it to function independent of the header and sill.

On aluminum windows, punch vertical slots every foot or so in the top and bottom flanges with a screwdriver. Install nails at the centers of the slots. Leave a tiny gap between the nailhead and the slot, so nails can move in the slots if the header sags.

In severe-climate areas, consider installing a metal drip cap at the top of the window to protect the top joint from water penetration. In all cases, caulk joints where window assembly meets siding or trim.

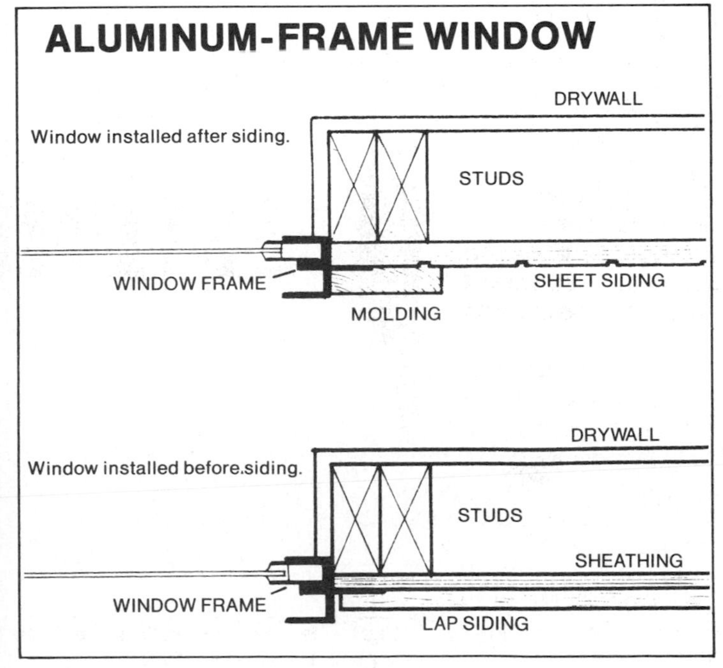

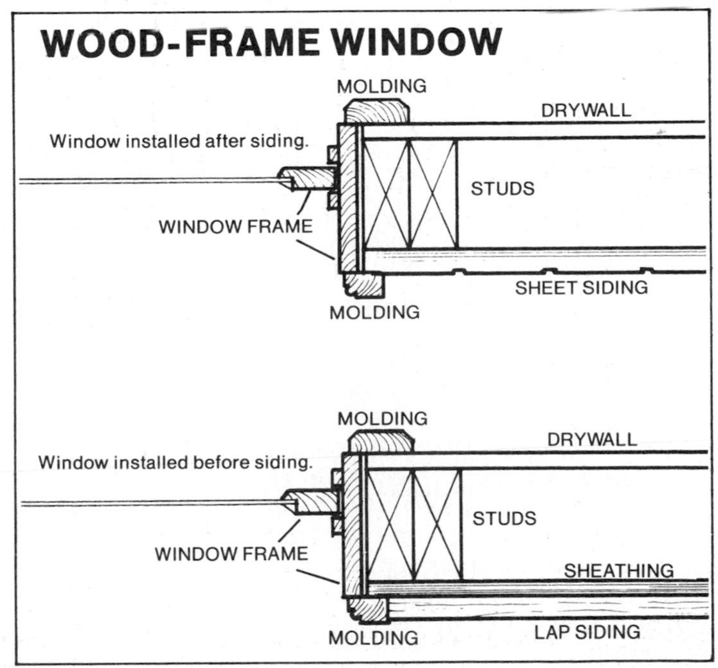

DOOR INSTALLATION

Doors provide a different set of installation problems from windows. Doors are susceptible to misalignment because of constant stresses placed on the jamb from opening and closing the door, and from the weight of the door itself. You must install doors in proper alignment and install them solidly enough to keep them in alignment.

PREHUNG DOORS

Prehung doors are factory-made assemblies that consist of the door, the *jamb*—or door frame—the door stop and hinges. The door usually has predrilled holes for locksets and the jamb is mortised to accept the striker plate. The case moldings are precut by the factory, and often installed on one side of the door. Doors come in left- and right-hand swing. Make sure you order and receive the correct one.

Prehung doors cost little more than if you had to buy the pieces separately. They save hours of work in installation. They're installed much like wood-frame windows.

To install a prehung door, use your level to determine if the floor at the door opening is level. If the opening isn't level, measure and note the amount of offset. Then measure down the side jambs and mark and trim the jamb bottoms to fit. Also use the level to make sure the wall is *plumb*—not leaning in or out. The opening doesn't have to be perfectly plumb. It can lean slightly left or right. See drawing above right.

On prehung exterior doors, either side jambs or doors may be pretrimmed to suit the height of the *threshold*. The threshold is a wood or metal strip that runs across the bottom of the door opening. Check the threshold height and trim jamb or door for it, if necessary. On interior doors, check the offset between the door bottom and the bottoms of the jamb. Adjust the jamb length to suit the finish floor you'll be installing.

Let the door supplier know your floor requirements so he can provide the right-size clearance at the bottom of the door assembly for the flooring.

Pull any nails, staples or cleats that hold the door and jamb together. Holding the door itself so the jamb hangs on it—don't pick up the prehung assembly by the jamb—stand the prehung assembly in the opening. Drive shims under the door on the lock side until the door just contacts the jamb at the top. Most prehung doors are shipped with a series of cardboard shims tacked on the edge of the door. This keeps spacing even between door and jamb. Don't remove shims until the installation process is complete—they allow for correct operating clearance.

It doesn't matter if sides of opening are slightly out of plumb in line of wall. You can compensate in shimming process. But if wall leans in or out more than 1/8" or so, it's hard to correct.

Wedge two or three shim shingles between the top of the jamb and the side of the opening on the lockset side. See drawing on facing page. Fit a similar group of shim shingles behind each hinge. Shimming should be done without disturbing the position of the door and jamb assembly. Both sides of the jamb assembly should be sitting squarely on the floor. Use your level to make sure the hinge side of the jamb is plumb.

Check shimming by pushing the lower end of the jamb on the lockset side away from the door, then open the door. It should neither fall open nor closed, from any position. If it does, the hinge side of the jamb is out of plumb. Use your level to find the problem. Realign the hinge side of the jamb by adding and removing shims at the correct locations.

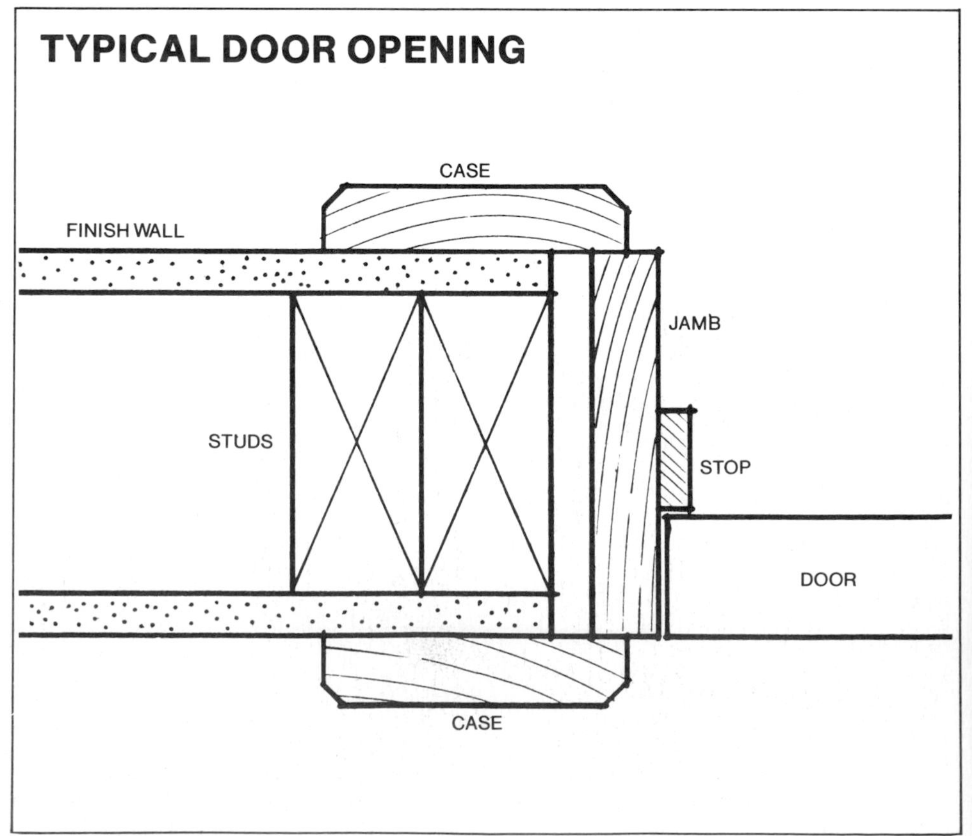

Sometimes the door will remain in position even though the hinge side of the jamb is out of plumb. This is because the new hinges are tight or are binding. If you're not sure whether or not the jamb is plumb, check it.

When the hinge side of the jamb is plumbed, drive pairs of casing nails on either side of each hinge, one just below the shims. That way, if the jamb loosens and the shims slip, they will be stopped by the nails. Try the door again to make sure you haven't misaligned the jamb while you were nailing.

Close the door and move the lockset side of the jamb into alignment with it. Add shims behind the striker-plate location and near the bottom of the jamb. When shims are lined up correctly, drive pairs of casing nails just below each shim. Line up the jamb to the door, not to the wall.

If the jamb doesn't line up to the wall, either the door or wall is warped. Find out which has the problem and fix it. Small warpage of the door can be corrected by removing the stop strips on the jamb and relocating them. Minor warpage of the wall opening can often be hidden with trim.

Remove spacers on the edges of the door itself. Check the door for smooth operation and make any needed adjustments.

To strengthen the door installation, remove the middle screws from all three hinges on the jamb side. Drill pilot holes and install longer flat-head screws that extend back into the stud behind the jamb. This stabilizes the hinge positions and keeps the casing nails from withdrawing.

To avoid distorting the assembly, attach the top and bottom hinges first. Pull the hinge pin on the middle hinge and put in the long screw for the middle hinge. Adjust the middle hinge long screw in and out until the hinge halves are lined up for the hinge pin. Recheck the door to make sure it operates freely.

Break off shim shingles level with the wall surface. If shingles are not easily broken, cut them with a hammer and a wood chisel. Then attach wood casing strips.

The final step in door assembly is to install the *lockset*—door-handle assembly—and *striker plate*. Because locksets differ slightly in assembly and installation, the best advice here is to follow instructions that come with the unit.

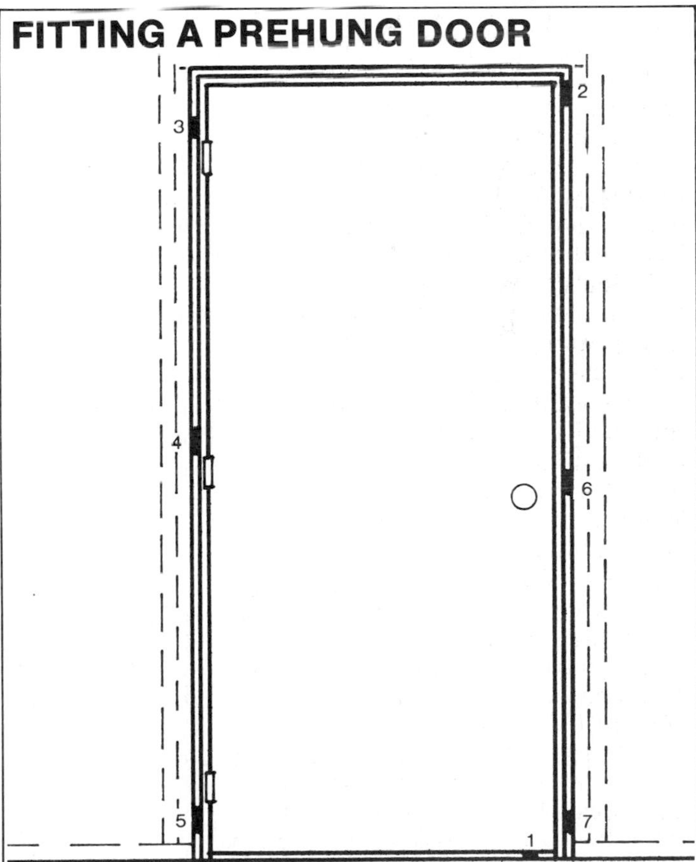

To fit prehung door into rough opening, follow this sequence: Loosely fit door and jamb into rough opening. Shim frame at position 1 to raise door to correct position in jamb. Shim at position 2 to hold jamb in position. Shim at positions 3 and 4; check upper half of hinge side of jamb for plumb. Shim at position 5 without loosening position 4. Shim at positions 6 and 7. Recheck plumb on hinge side of jamb. Check fit and alignment of door in jamb, and jamb in wall. Adjust if needed. Drive two casing nails through jamb just below each shim location. Open door to make sure it doesn't fall open or closed. Remove cardboard shims on door and check for free operation. Install one long screw in center hole of each hinge. Screw should extend into jackstud of rough opening. Break off projecting shims, install case trim, lockset and threshold.

Case covers up adjustments you made earlier. It's last step in installing a door.

Floors

Modern wood-strip flooring is easy to install. See page 151.

The first half of this chapter deals with required floor preparation for installing finish-floor materials. The second half deals with installation of more-popular finish-floor materials.

Preparation necessary for installing a finish floor will depend on type and condition of existing subfloor and type of finish-floor material you're installing. If you've not yet chosen a finish-floor material, see pages 34-37 in the chapter, *Surfaces & Equipment.*

Resilient flooring is the most popular type for kitchens. Installation procedures start on page 136. Ceramic tile installation starts on page 144, brick, page 148, and wood flooring, page 150. Before you start reworking the subfloor, read the section on the finish-floor material you've chosen. Then determine required preparation.

FLOOR REPAIR AND PREPARATION

An existing finish floor in good condition can be used as a base for the new finish floor. But some old floors are so badly chewed up or rotted that major repairs are needed. Don't be tempted to patch things over quickly and finish up. Floors take more of a beating in a kitchen than anywhere else in the house. A sound floor is crucial to a successful remodeling job. Even on new work, good floor preparation is essential.

Wood-frame floors rarely have to be reworked structurally. Joists and beams that support the floor won't need repair or replacement unless the floor is seriously sagging or the members themselves are decayed. More often, you'll need to make repairs to the *floor underlayment* and sometimes the *subfloor* beneath.

Subfloor repairs may range from renailing a few loose boards or plywood joints to replacing whole sections of decayed or damaged subflooring. Wood decay caused by water leakage is the most common cause of kitchen floor damage. See page 134.

If floor damage is relatively minor, you can fix it yourself, as described on the following pages. Dry rot or decay that has weakened the floor substructure—joists and beams—will require expert attention. Also, wood-frame floors may need additional bracing if they are to support a new wall or a heavy floor covering such as bricks, flagstones, or heavy tiles. If you want to use one of these materials as a floor covering, check with your local building department for subfloor requirements.

Concrete-slab floors don't require much work unless they're badly cracked. Small cracks or low spots can be easily patched as described on page 135.

REPAIRING WOOD-FRAME FLOORS

If the existing finish floor is undamaged, you may be able to install the new finish floor directly over it. First, make sure the new finish-floor material and its attachment method are compatible with the existing finish floor. Refer to installation instructions for various floor coverings, starting on page 135.

If new and existing floor coverings are not compatible, remove the finish floor down to the underlayment. See page 34 in the chapter, *Preparing to Build,* for details on removing floor coverings.

Depending on the condition of the underlayment and on the type of floor covering you're installing, some patching may be required to get a smooth, level surface. Different floor coverings may require different floor preparations.

If the existing finish floor is in bad shape, remove it. Examine the underlayment, if any, and the subfloor beneath. Probe with an ice pick or or small screwdriver for soft, spongy areas. Closely examine areas around sinks, dishwashers, and other water-prone locations. Slow leaks in old traps and supply pipes concealed by walls or cabinets can go undetected for years, causing much damage.

Use a pry bar to rip out soggy or disintegrated sections of flooring. Use a tape measure to locate floor joists and mark their locations on the surrounding floor. You can often tell where joists are by the subflooring nailing pattern.

Remove all damaged flooring and subflooring back to the nearest sound joists, as described in the following text. Now is also a good time to make structural changes to the area to meet your remodeling requirements.

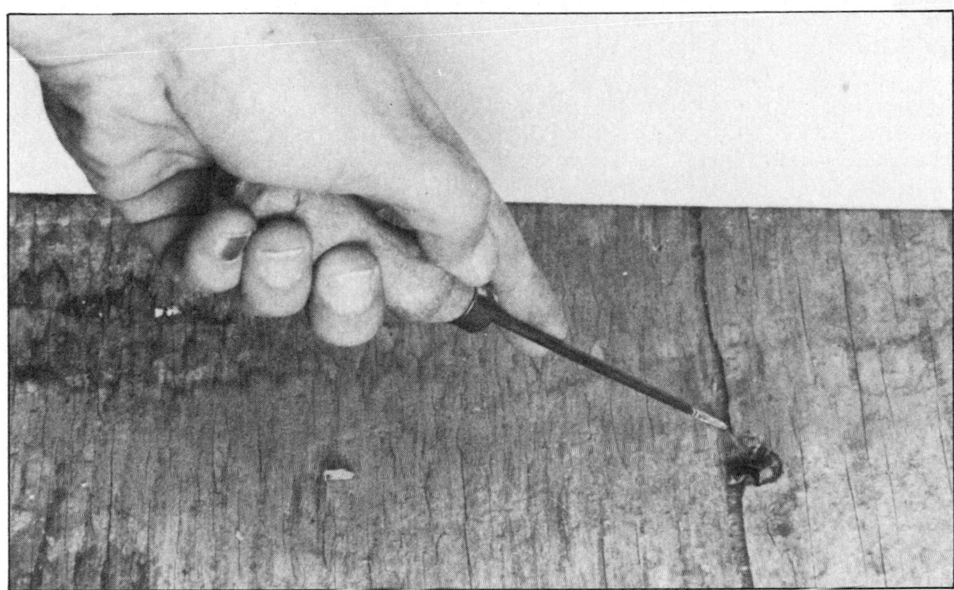

Probe thoroughly with ice pick or small screwdriver for deteriorated floor and wall materials, especially around old plumbing.

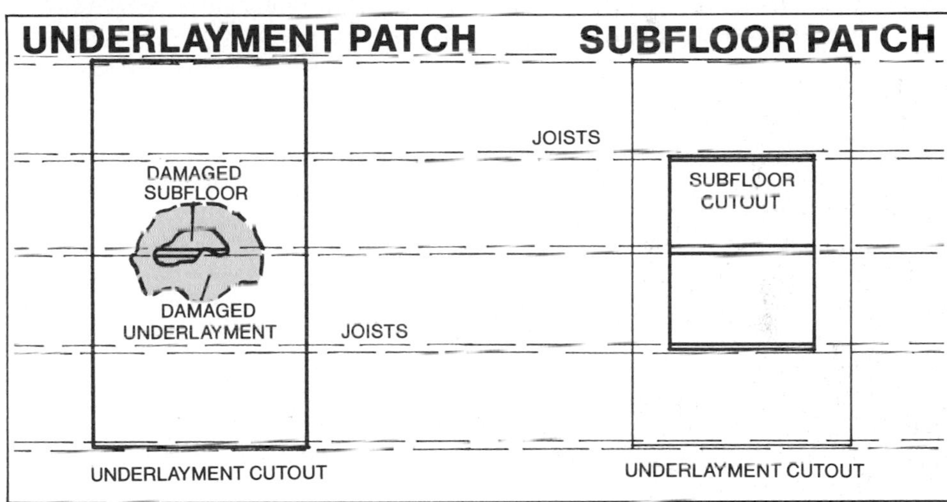

Remove damaged underlayment by making square cutout with two sides centered over joists. If subfloor is damaged, make cutout one joist larger each way than subfloor repair patch.

Lay out rectangular cutout for subfloor inside underlayment cutout. Center two sides over joists as shown.

Fixing Damaged Underlayment—If there is underlayment, lay out a rectangular cutout. Center two of the cutout edges over the nearest sound floor joists adjacent to the deteriorated area. Use a rafter square to square up the cutout. This simplifies cutting and fitting a replacement patch later.

If you have to repair the subfloor, remove a section of underlayment that's one joist span larger each way than the repair section in the subfloor. In other words, the underlayment replacement patch should overlap the subfloor replacement patch so patch seams won't coincide. Or, you can pry up the entire sheet or partial sheet of underlayment affected.

Use a circular saw with a carbide-tip blade to make cutouts in underlayment. Hidden nails can easily ruin an ordinary blade. Wear safety glasses and gloves to protect yourself against flying nail chips. Set the blade only as deep as the thickness of the underlayment, so you won't weaken sound areas of subfloor beneath.

Fixing Damaged Subflooring—After the underlayment is removed, mark joist locations on the subfloor. Lay out another rectangular cut inside the first one. Center the side lines of the cut over the joists. Again, use a circular saw with a carbide-tip blade and wear gloves and safety glasses.

Find and Repair the Cause of Damage—When the damaged area is removed, find the cause of the damage. The damage may have been caused by plumbing or fixtures you've already ripped out. If not, track down the source and repair it.

If necessary, leave the cutout area open to dry for a day or longer. Areas that don't dry out during this time indicate that there is a continuing leak. You may have to remove some sound flooring or part of an adjacent wall to find it. In most cases, you can trace leaks to the plumbing in the immediate vicinity of the kitchen sink, behind or beneath it. Prime suspects are a leaky trap, weeping packing nuts or washers on supply valves, or a deteriorated seal washer on the sink-strainer assembly.

Less frequently, floor damage can be a result of inadequate ventilation under a house, or a leaky window, door, or wall that lets in water from the outside, as described below.

Repairing Damaged Floor Joists—If underlayment and subflooring are damaged by water, the floor joists may also be damaged. Use an ice pick or awl to check the joists. Look for deterioration both on the top and bottom surfaces of the joists. Sometimes, water runs down a joist and accumulates on the bottom side, causing rot.

Slightly rotted joists can be repaired by attaching a length of 2x6 or 2x8 alongside the rotted portion of the joist. This provides a new bearing surface for the subfloor. If rot has structurally weakened the joist, replace it or install a new one alongside the old. It's best to have a building official inspect the damage and recommend a repair procedure. If you follow the recommended procedure, the work is more likely to pass inspection.

If you've provided adequate floor support as described above, you need not remove the rotted joist. Once the source of the water is removed, the rot won't spread. So-called *dry rot* is caused by decay-producing organisms that can only survive under wet conditions. Wood kept at a low moisture content will not rot. What appears to be dry rot has taken place under wet conditions, and the source of water was later removed. Soggy, punky or rotted wood can be scraped out if it smells bad or otherwise offends you.

Allow wet areas to dry completely before making repairs and patching the hole. To speed the drying process, direct a portable electric heater or fan into the area.

After a day or two, if the area *still* smells swampy, check under the house for adequate ventilation, ground-water seepage or leaky plumbing elsewhere under the house. Other leaks can be caused by windows, doors, poorly placed downspouts or inadequate flashing around the house foundation, to mention a few sources. If you can't identify and repair the source of damage, seek help from a qualified building contractor.

Replacing Subflooring—After joists are repaired and underfloor work has been done, measure the thickness of the subfloor. It needn't be replaced with the same material, but the patch should be the same thickness.

Due to its strength and durability, plywood is the best patching material. The face grain should run perpendicular to joists. Cut a patch to size. Allow 1/16- to 1/8-inch clearance around the edges of the patch to allow for expansion and contraction of materials.

Trim patch to avoid wedging it into place. Then nail patch in, using *annular-ring nails.* These nails have grooved shanks to reduce withdrawal.

Replacing Underlayment—Match the thickness of the underlayment and cut the patch. Nail it down with annular-ring nails. Before you install the underlayment patch, inspect the underlayment around it, especially the nails. If some of the nails are backing out, don't just drive them in. Pull a few out and examine them. If they're smooth-shank and uncoated, they'll keep backing out. This isn't a problem under certain types of finish floors, such as tile or brick. Loose nails can damage resilient-flooring materials.

Plywood underlayment in good condition can be pulled up and reused. Remove the nails, and renail with annular-ring nails. Particle-board underlayment probably won't survive that much handling.

If the particle board is in good condition, pull any loose or protruding nails you can with your pry bar or hammer. Use your nail set or punch to set remaining loose nails completely through the particle board into the subfloor beneath. Patch nail holes with floor-repair compound. Renail with annular-ring nails.

If the old underlayment is lumpy and torn, rip it up. Otherwise, install new underlayment directly over the old. Use 1/4-inch PTS (plugged, touched and sanded) plywood and annular-ring nails. Nail plywood into the joists.

If you're installing resilient flooring, even underlayment in fairly good condition requires some preparation.

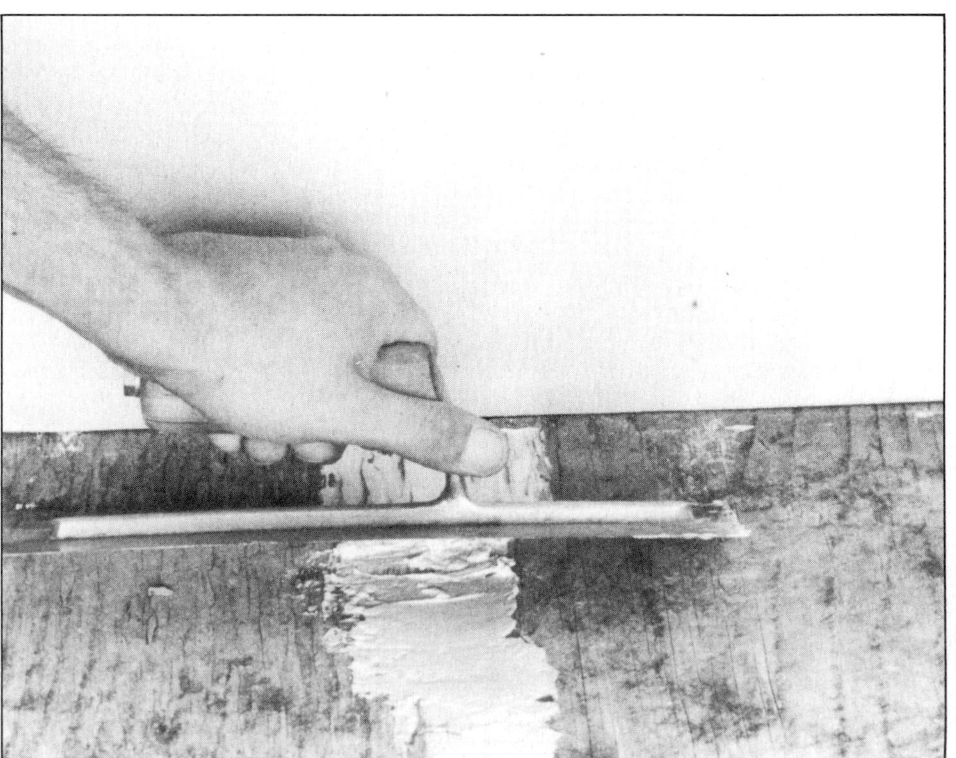

Fill all imperfections with floor-repair compound, even if you've installed new underlayment. The thinner and more flexible the floor covering, the smoother the underlayment must be.

Small imperfections in the underlayment surface can telegraph through and show up in the finish-floor surface.

Redrive protruding nails and remove loose ones. Renail with annular-ring nails where necessary. Use floor-repair compound to fill cracks, dimples, hammer dents or splintered wood.

Occasionally you'll find that a *void* in the plywood underlayment has collapsed. A void refers to an area inside the plywood where a piece of one of the inside plys is missing. This forms a hollow, or indentation in the floor surface. Cut out the top ply over the void and fill with floor-repair compound.

REPAIRING CONCRETE FLOORS

Poured-concrete floors don't usually require much preparation. Remove floor covering, if necessary, as described on page 68. Examine the floor for defects. Chip off high spots and fill low ones with floor-repair compound.

Closely examine any cracks to determine their cause. If a crack is a simple shrinkage or stress crack, it will not be offset, either horizontally or vertically. These cracks can be filled with floor-repair compound.

If the crack is offset more than 1/4 inch, chop out the broken section of concrete. Determine the cause of the crack. If the cause is a leaky pipe that has caused dirt to settle under the floor, fix the pipe and patch the concrete as described below. If major cracking has occurred over a large portion of the slab, consult a masonry contractor. Also have any exposed soil treated for termites before replacing concrete or patching a hole.

To patch a hole in concrete, wet the dirt in the hole and tamp it down firmly. Use a length of timber such as a 4x4, 6x6 or railroad tie for tamping. Wet concrete edges around the hole. Make sure edges are free of dirt, dust or mud. For small holes, use a concrete-patching compound, available at masonry suppliers or home-improvement centers. Follow instructions on package.

For large holes use mortar or concrete mix. Mix it to a stiff consistency in a bucket or wheelbarrow. Dump the mix in the hole, adding wet chunks of the broken concrete to raise the mortar level even with the surface of surrounding concrete.

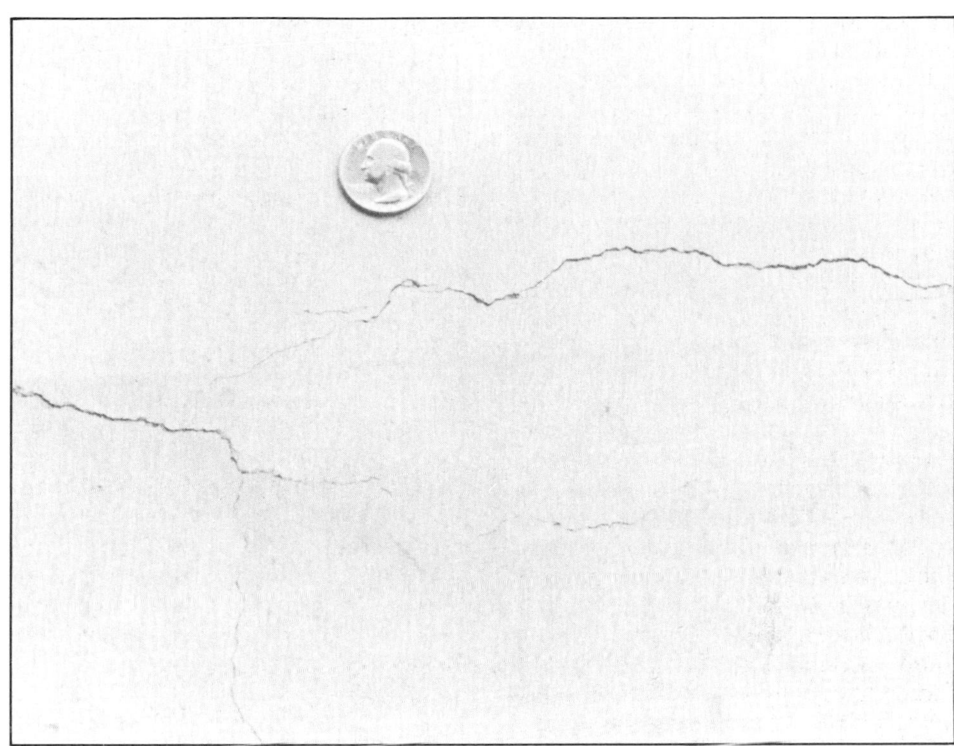

This kind of concrete crack is caused by shrinkage during setting period and isn't significant. Chip off any high spots and fill with floor-repair compound. Thin compound so you can force it into crack.

Use a board to strike off the patch surface. Allow patch to set up about an hour. Then use a mason's trowel to put a smooth finish on the patch. Don't walk on the patch for at least 2 days. Keep the patch damp so the mortar or concrete cures properly.

If you're using floor-covering adhesives, do not apply them over the patch for several weeks. Keep this in mind when sequencing your remodeling work. Make concrete repairs early so you can work on other phases of the project while the patch is curing. Check instructions on adhesive label for specific times.

If a concrete floor shows any signs of moisture, find the cause and fix it before installing the finish floor. Plumbing leaks and other causes of moisture are discussed on the facing page. To check for moisture, tape a piece of plastic wrap, on all four sides, over a small section of floor and leave it for two days. If moisture condenses on the underside of the plastic, the floor is too damp to install the finish floor without some type of waterproofing. If you can't correct the moisture problem, find out from the flooring dealer what type of waterproofing is required for the floor material you're installing.

FLOOR COVERING INSTALLATION

All floor coverings are not necessarily installed at the same time during the construction sequence. Materials such as quarry tile and brick should be installed before the cabinets, though any floor covering can be. This approach saves a lot of cutting and fitting around the cabinet bases. You don't have to cover the entire floor area under the cabinets, so you needn't use much more material. Just extend the floor covering a few inches beyond the proposed edges of cabinet bases. Plan on protecting the finish floor from accidental damage during subsequent operations.

When to install floor covering depends on the construction sequence for your particular kitchen remodel. All wall and ceiling work should be done, including painting.

If practical, install floor coverings before applying any trim that contacts the floor, such as baseboard and door trim. The trim, prepainted or otherwise prefinished, will then cover most of the floor-covering edges. This way, cuts at edges don't have to be as precise. See top photo on page 136.

Install permanent appliances, such as dishwashers or trash compactors, before installing floor covering. For more information on determining the construction sequence for your kitchen remodel, see page 64.

RESILIENT FLOOR COVERINGS

Linoleum, asphalt, vinyl asbestos, solid vinyl and cushioned vinyl are all classified as *resilient* floor-covering materials. They are available in either *sheet goods* or blocks, called *tiles*. General installation procedures for both sheet goods and tiles are covered in this section. Each flooring material has its own specific installation procedures, recommended adhesives and seam sealers. The dealer can provide specific instructions for the resilient-flooring material you've chosen. He'll also supply you with the right tools and materials for the job. For more information on types of resilient-floor coverings, see pages 34-37.

Sheet-Floor Coverings—The stiffer sheet-floor coverings such as heavy inlaid vinyl cannot be unrolled in a room and fitted. Stiff floor coverings are fitted by making a pattern and transferring the shape from the pattern to the floor covering. This technique also works for more flexible materials, especially on complicated floor shapes. Some cushion vinyls can be unrolled and trimmed to fit freehand—a few are as flexible as a throw-rug.

Make A Pattern: You can make a pattern of almost any material, but heavy flooring felt is best. It looks like 15-pound building felt, but contains no asphalt. The pattern paper you use should lie flat on the floor. It should not wrinkle when you crawl around on it, or stretch out of shape.

Position pattern paper where the flooring will go, overlapping about 6 inches where pieces meet. Trim the paper an inch or so from all edges of the room. If the floor is wood, use pushpins, thumbtacks or staples to tack the pattern paper down flat. Remember to pull these fasteners out before you install the floor covering.

On concrete floors, use a utility knife to cut out a 3- or 4-inch square every 3 or 4 feet along each piece of the paper. Then put an "X" of strapping tape or duct tape over each hole to stick the pattern paper to the floor.

On either a wood or concrete subfloor, cut another row of squares

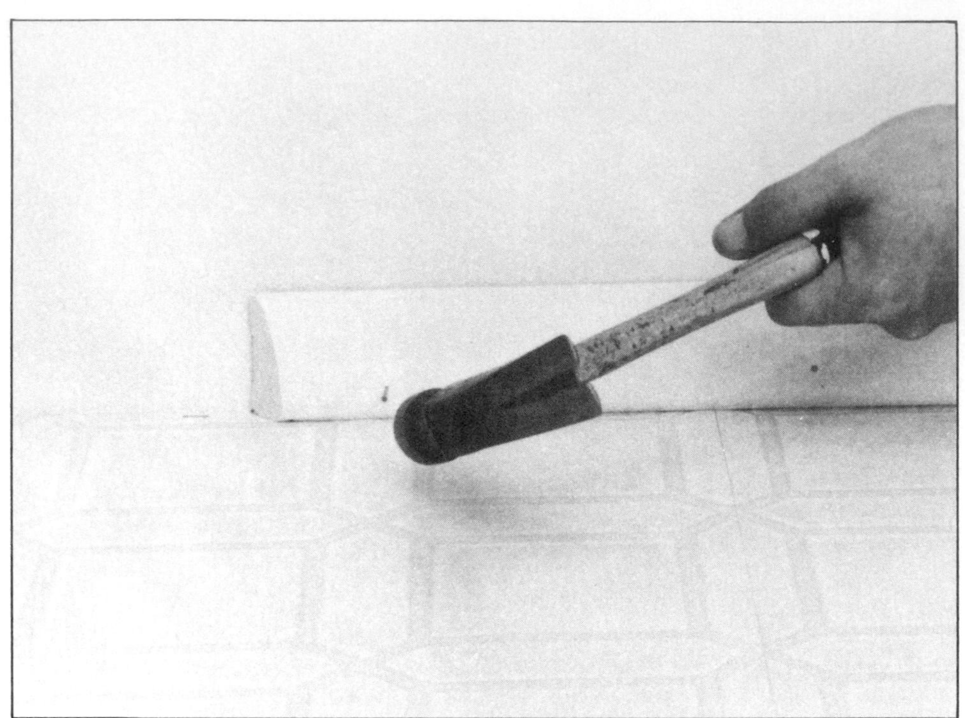

If you wait to put down baseboard after flooring, need for precise edge-trimming is reduced. Paint or stain baseboard *before* you put it down. Fill and touch up nail holes after.

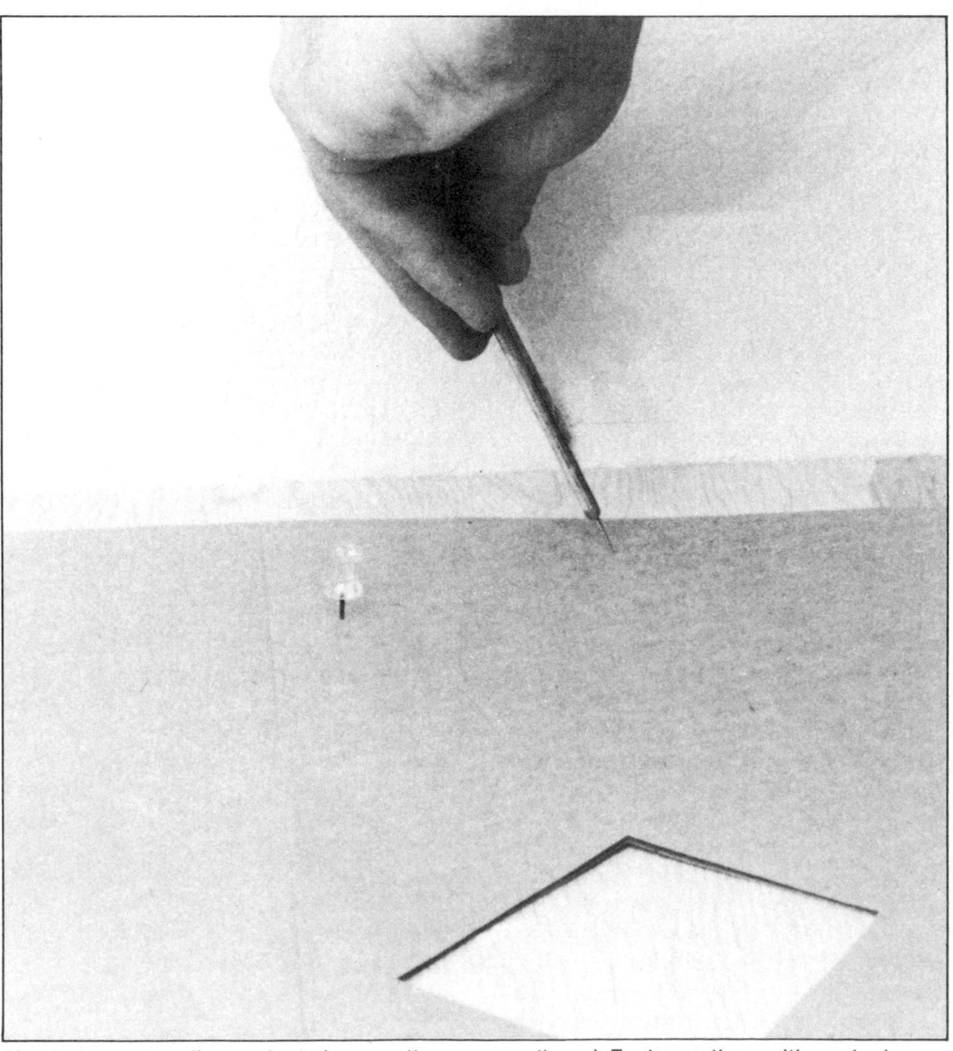

Use holes and scribe marks to keep pattern paper aligned. Fasten pattern with push pins, or with tape over holes. Don't let paper drift as you scribe.

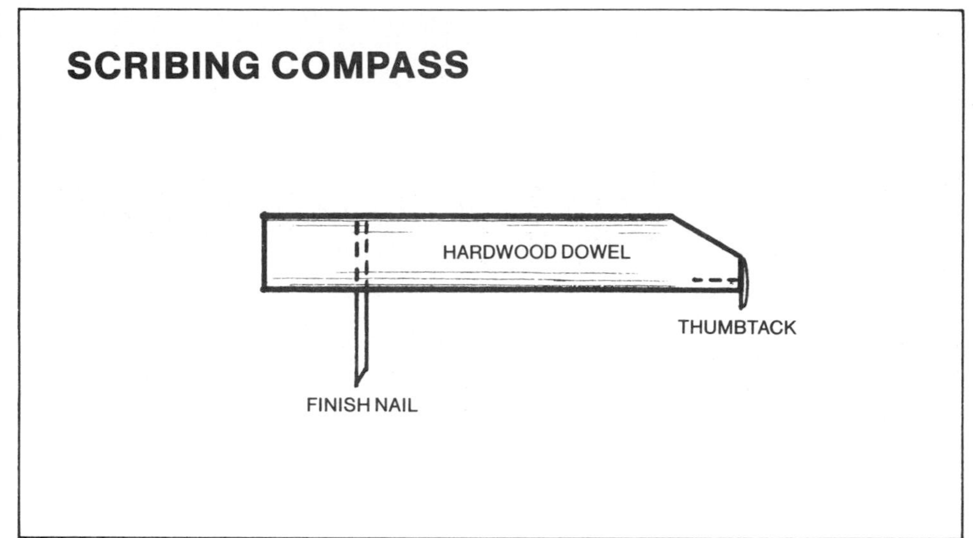

A simple scribing compass can be made from readily available materials.

every 3 or 4 feet along each overlap in the paper. These squares should be cut with the utility knife blade held at 90°. The cut edges enable you to realign the pieces of pattern paper. Number pieces if there are more than a few, and put an "up" arrow on each one.

Mark the pattern with a *scribing compass*. Most floor covering dealers and hardware stores carry this tool. It is an adjustable compass with a sharp point on each end. Try to find one with a locking adjustment. If you can't find a scribing compass that locks, set the points at some convenient and easily remembered spacing, such as 2 inches. Check frequently to be sure the adjustment hasn't been disturbed. You can make a scribing compass from a dowel, thumbtack and finish nail as shown in the drawing above.

Hold the compass at exactly 90° from the wall. Pull it along the wall in that position to make a scratch on the pattern paper. The vertical position of the scribing compass doesn't matter. You can tip it in any convenient direction but keep the points perpendicular to the wall.

Use the same technique where the floor covering meets pipes, cabinets doorways or other obstructions. You can check any marking you're unsure of. Hold the point at the wall stationary and swing a radius on the pattern paper with the scratching point. The radius should just touch the scribed line. Anyplace you drift off 90°, you'll have to trim excess material to get a fit. But you can't cut the floor covering too small unless you let the scriber point move away from the wall.

To follow a complicated curve or shape, move the point at the wall along 1/8 inch at a time and make a series of radii to be connected later. See drawing below.

Cut Floor Covering: Unroll the floor covering on a large, flat surface near the work area, such as the floor in an adjacent room. The surface must be flat and clean.

Let the floor covering relax until it's completely flat and at the same temperature as the kitchen. The dealer can tell you if there are steps you need to take to acclimate the material to its new location.

Take up the strips of pattern paper and reassemble them on top of the floor covering. To install floor covering in multiple pieces, rough cut the pieces and lay them out side by side and match up the pattern, if there is one. Position the pattern paper on the floor covering so the floor-covering design is straight and symmetrical. Tape the pattern in place at the holes.

Use the scribing compass to transfer the scratch line from the pattern to the floor covering. *Keep the scribing compass exactly perpendicular to the line you're transferring.* If you let the compass get off 90°, your final cut will be short of the wall.

After you mark the floor covering, cut along the line with a utility knife. Where possible, use a steel straightedge as a guide. Take your time and make short, straight cuts. If you drift off the line, be sure you drift to the outside, into the scrap area. To fit the floor covering around isolated objects such as pipes, use the steel straightedge and make a cut to the nearest edge. Try to place the cut in an unobtrusive location.

Remove and discard the pattern. Loosely roll up the floor covering and carry it into the kitchen. Fit the floor covering in place. Trim or sand the edges to fit tight spots.

Cut Seams: Some sheet floor coverings are patterned all the way to a precision-cut edge. All you need do is butt the edges together and align the pattern. Others have either one or two unpatterned *selvage edges* that have to be cut off to make a seam. Or you may need to make a seam between two previously cut edges.

To make a seam, overlap the two pieces until the pattern matches. Use a straightedge and a utility knife to cut through both pieces at the same time.

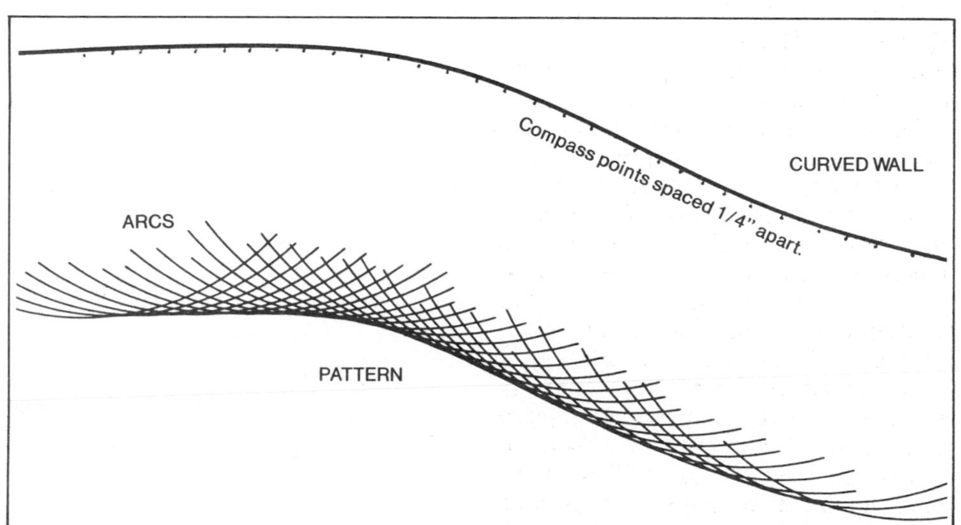

At curved walls or obstructions, hold compass point steady at wall, scribe a radius onto pattern paper. Move point at 1/8- to 1/4-inch intervals along wall or obstruction, scribing a radius at each location. Contour of outline is scribed on paper, as shown.

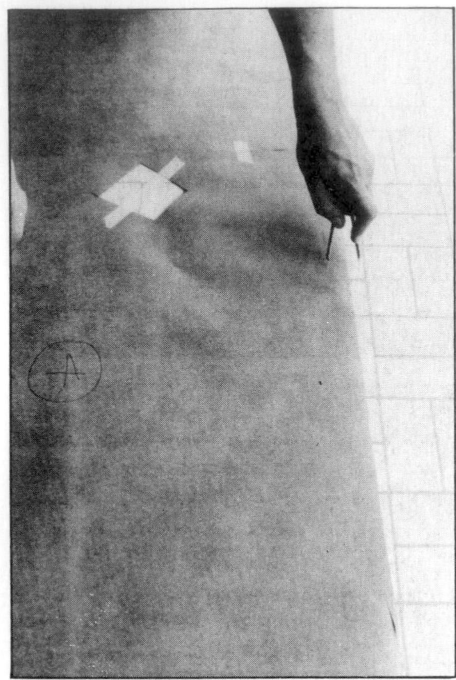

Be careful transferring from pattern to sheet flooring. Errors in scribing will show up later as gaps in flooring.

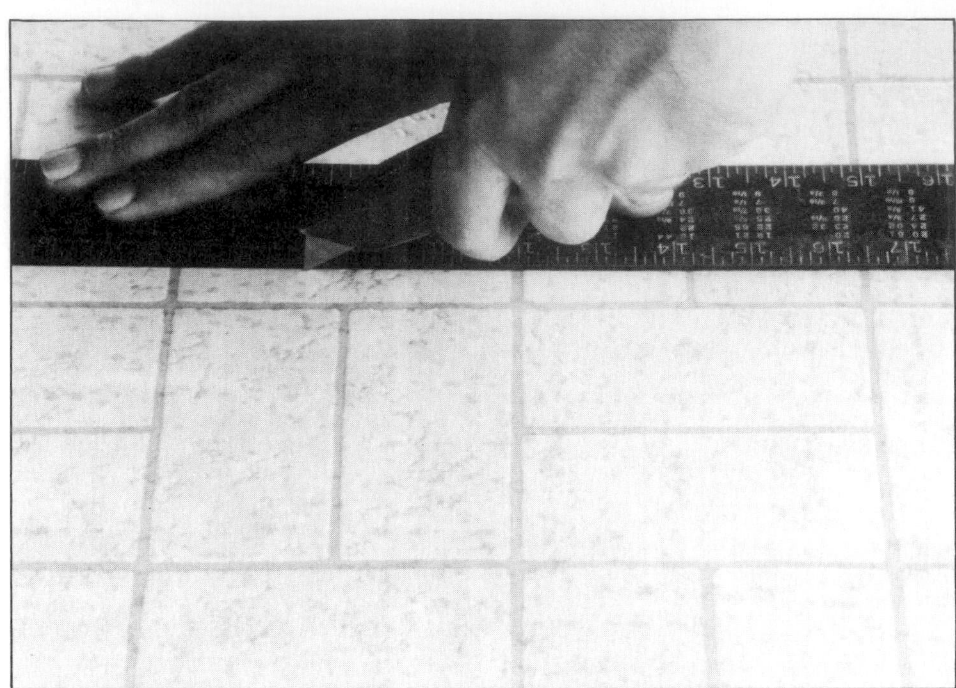

Use steel straightedge to shield floor covering. This way, slips or mistakes will be made on scrap side of line.

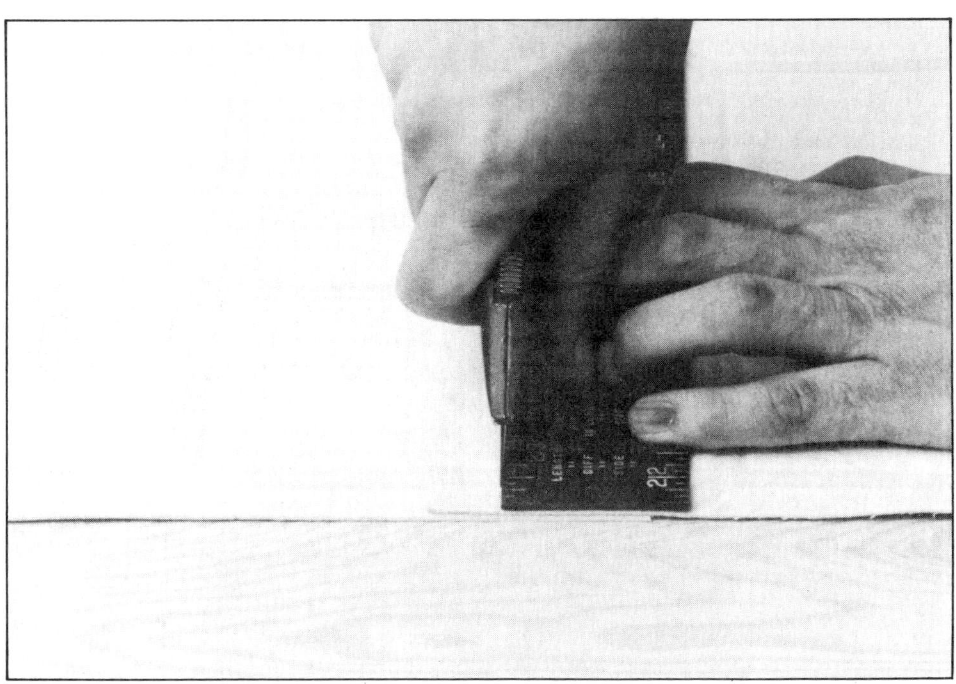

Keep utility knife exactly vertical when cutting seam. Thickness of knife-blade compensates for slight offset.

Hold the knife exactly vertical when cutting. It's OK if the knife wanders from the cut line, as long as it's held exactly vertical. Use weights or have several helpers stand on the material to anchor the two pieces so they don't shift while you're cutting. Remove scrap from underneath and the seam will drop into place.

If the floor covering is too thick or heavy to cut two thicknesses at once, cut one thickness with a utility knife and a straightedge. Put this piece underneath and use it as a guide for a marking tool called an *underscriber.* When the underscriber is correctly adjusted, it makes a mark on the upper layer that exactly corresponds with the edge of the lower layer. Then cut the upper layer to the scribed line.

If you don't have an underscriber, cut one thickness with a utility knife and straightedge as before. Put the cut piece *on top* of the uncut piece. Then cut the second piece, using the edge of the cut piece as a guide. Hold the utility knife at 90°, with the blade flat against the edge of the cut piece.

Attach Floor Covering: After the seam is cut, align the floor covering and adhere it to the floor with adhesive. Follow manufacturer's recommendations for attaching the floor covering to the floor. Some coverings require an adhesive, called *mastic,* over the entire floor surface, others just around the perimeter. Some can be attached with double-face tape or staples. Some materials can be loose-laid, though for safety reasons you should secure any exposed edges such as at doorways. The floor-covering dealer can recommend fastening methods for the floor covering you've selected.

Trial-fit the floor covering before applying adhesive. If you don't, you'll have no time to make corrective cuts before the mastic sets up. Also, once the floor covering is down, you can't take it up to rework it.

Remove all debris from the floor before laying the floor covering. This includes removing crumbs, chips, and other lump-makers. Then apply adhesive, if you're using it, and attach the floor covering.

If you're fastening the floor covering with double-face tape, start at the seams. Lift one edge of the seam and draw a pencil mark along the floor, using the other side of the seam as a guide. Then lift the other side of the seam and put a strip of double-face tape on the floor centered on the pencil line. 2-inch tape works well for seams. Peel the release paper from the top of the double-face tape and lower the two sides of the seam into contact. Smooth out bubbles or waves in both pieces of floor covering. Press or roll seam to get a good bond.

Fasten edges with 1-inch or 1-1/2-inch double-face tape. Roll back the edge, apply the tape to the floor, remove the release paper and press down the edge.

Some floor coverings must be stapled at the edges. Drive staples where they will will be hidden by moldings, if possible. Space staples 2 or 3 inches apart. Stapling is usually combined with a special adhesive for seams and exposed edges.

The perimeter-adhesive method is similar to the double-face tape method. Start with the seams. Fold back the edges and apply a strip of adhesive about a foot wide, stopping 6 or 8 inches from the walls. Adhesive should be put down with a notched spreader or trowel. The notches should be the size specified by the manufacturer. See recommendations on the adhesive can or in the floor-covering manufacturer's installation instructions.

After seams are done, do the edges. Lift one edge at a time and put down a 6- to 8-inch-wide strip of adhesive along the wall. Make sure the floor covering lies completely flat. If adhesive instructions call for it, use a floor roller to bond the floor covering to the adhesive. The floor-covering dealer should be able to supply a floor roller, if you need one.

For the full-adhesive method, lay back half of a piece of floor-covering and apply an even coat of adhesive to the floor surface. Once again, use a notched trowel or spreader of the recommended notch size. Do not apply adhesive to the back of the floor covering unless recommended in manufacturer's instructions.

Lay down the covering and bed it in the adhesive. Then do the other half of the same piece. Use a floor roller, if required, before laying the next piece of floor covering.

If you're not using a floor roller, use a heavy push broom to work out any bubbles. Just push bubbles toward an edge and out. If you have several pieces of floor covering, it's generally best to work out bubbles from a wall to a seam, then from seam to seam, then to the other wall.

You can slightly adjust the position of a floor-covering piece during the *open time* of the adhesive, unless you roll or walk on the piece. Open time is the amount of time it takes the adhesive to set, or harden. After it's walked on or rolled, the floor covering is down to stay, so make sure seams are aligned first.

After adhesive work is done, promptly clean up any drips with solvent specified on the adhesive can. Then seal the seams.

For most floor coverings, clear-liquid seam sealers in special applicator bottles are available. Fit the little guide on the applicator tip into the seam. Lay down a bead of seam sealer to bond the two pieces together.

Attach Trim Strips: The last step in installing sheet-floor covering is finishing doorways and other exposed edges. If the floor covering meets another hard-surface material, you can put down a metal trim strip with screws or tacks. Many types of strips are available from your floor-covering dealer, in an array of colors, widths and offsets.

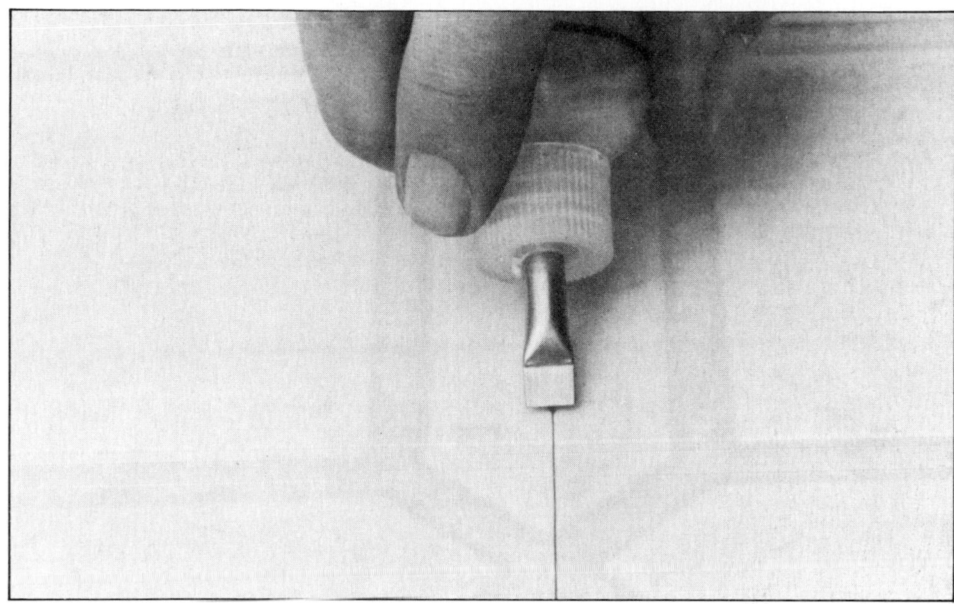

Use seam sealer to close seams permanently.

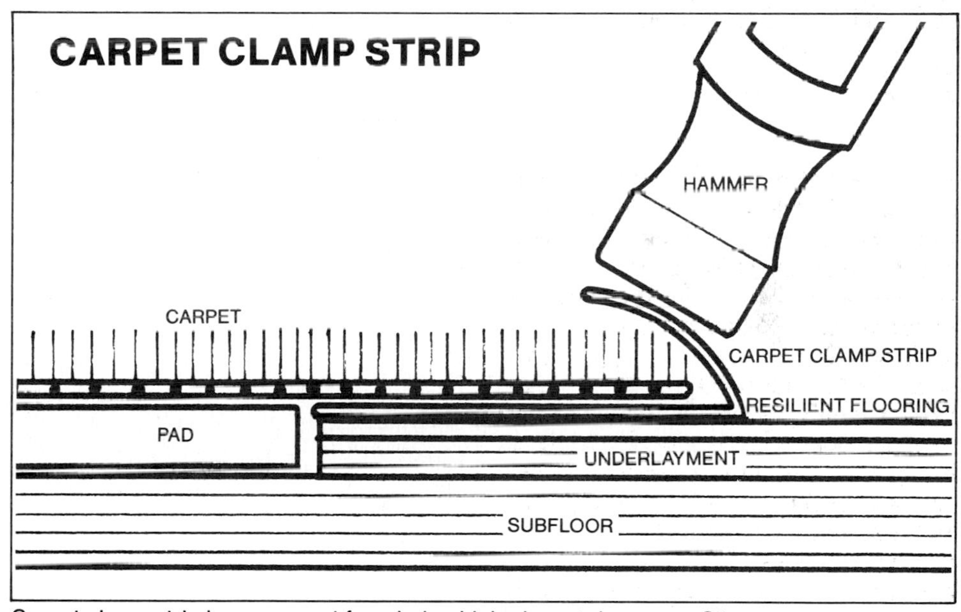

Carpet clamp strip keeps carpet from being kicked up at doorways. Slip carpet into strip and knock down flange with hammer.

If the new floor covering meets carpet, lift up the carpet edge and run the floor covering 1-2 inches under it. After the floor covering is in, slide a piece of clamp-down metal carpet trim under the carpet edge and nail it to the subfloor. Then use a hammer and a wood block to bend the free edge of the clamp-down strip to anchor the carpet. See drawing on page 139. On deep-pile carpets, trim pile along carpet edge so the clamp-down won't trap too much of it.

Freehand Fitting: Not all sheet-floor coverings require pattern making. Some are flexible enough to install directly over the floor. This involves a process similar to carpet installation. The floor covering is trimmed to fit by creasing it at the walls and cutting along the crease.

Measure the floor and roughly cut the floor covering to size. Allow 1 to 2 inches extra around the room perimeter. Roll out the floor covering in the room, so the edges run up the walls on all sides.

If one of the room walls is fairly straight, and in the right place, you may be able to butt one factory edge of the floor covering against it and start from there. Otherwise, start at a long wall and trim both ways from the center, a little at a time.

Push several feet of the floor-covering edge into the angle between floor and wall. It probably won't bend to a right angle, but make as small a radius as you can. Then cut along the top of the radius with your utility knife. Don't cut in the middle of the radius or remove too much surplus material at a time. See photo above.

After you've cut along the perimeter of the first side, go back and make a second, tighter cut. You'll be able to make a smaller radius at the wall this time. The radius size and the position of the cut on the radius varies for different floor coverings, depending on thickness, composition, and even the temperature and humidity.

Work down the curve of the radius until you find the right cutting location. Note that the bending characteristics of your floor covering may be different in one direction than in the other.

To fit the floor covering to a corner, first cut out a square at the corner. Don't cut the bottom of the square below the level of the next trim cut, or you risk cutting it short.

When trimming the floor covering, make many small passes with the knife, each coming a little closer to a tight fit. After all pieces are fitted, cut in the seams, if any, as described on page 137. Then fasten down the floor covering.

Some Armstrong floor coverings are so flexible that the manufacturer recommends going directly to a finished trim cut, using the following method: Lay out the floor covering in the room and align any seams. Use a rafter square to push the floor covering squarely into the angle between floor and wall. Using the rafter square as a guide, cut the floor covering with a utility knife held at a 45° angle. The floor covering should drop into place with only one guided cut. Use this method only if it's specifically recommended for the floor covering you've selected. It will crack less-flexible material.

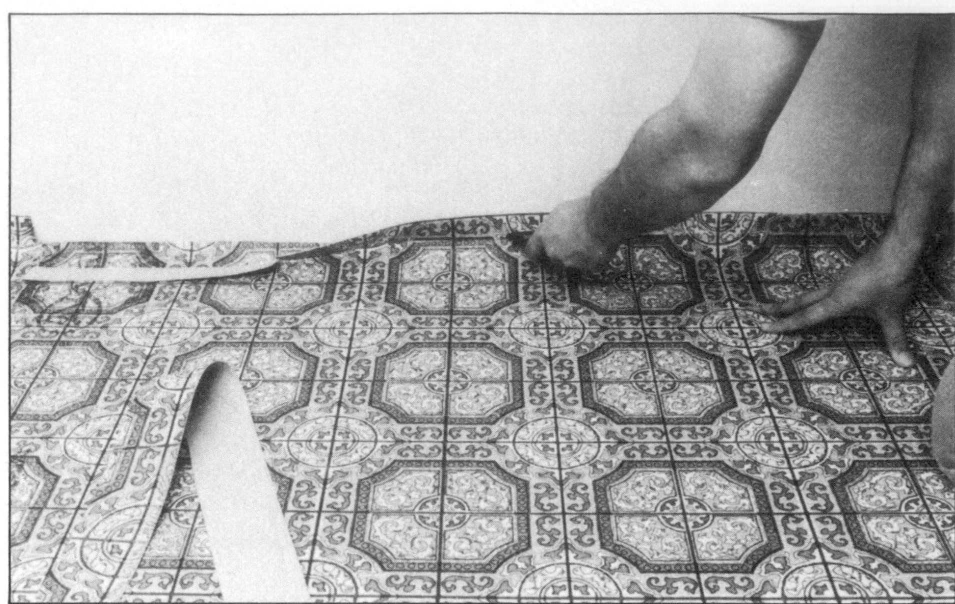

Several cuts may be needed to get floor covering to drop into place at walls. Keep a slight upward angle on knife handle so top surface of floor covering comes out with tightest fit.

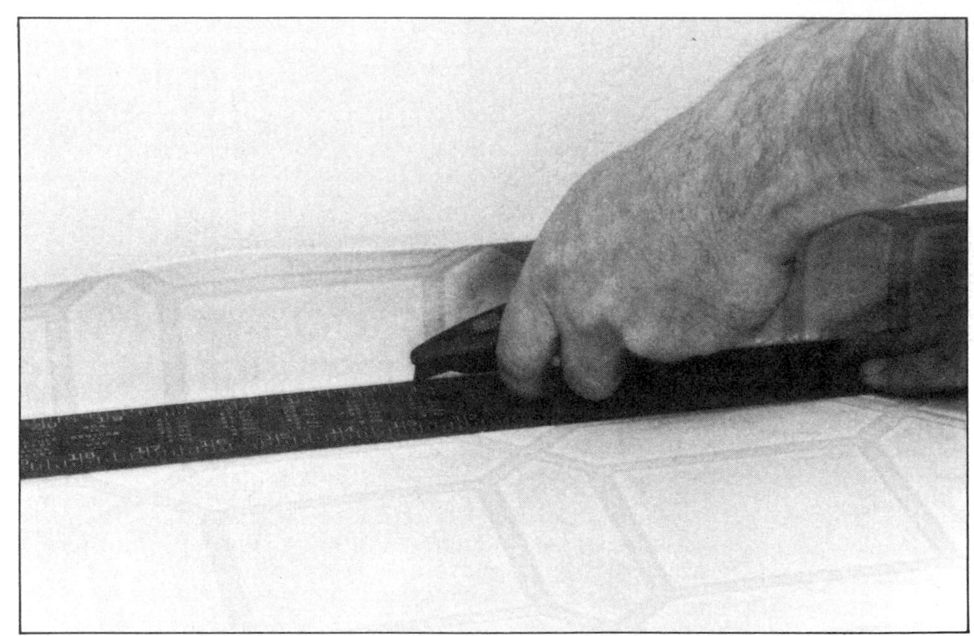

Thin, flexible floor coverings can be cut directly into place. Only one cut is necessary.

Resilient Tile—First work out the layout lines for the tile. This procedure is the same as for ceramic tile. See page 143. Unless you're using self-stick tiles, apply the recommended adhesive, following label instructions. Lay the whole tiles first, then the cut ones.

Resilient tiles should be at room temperature when they're laid. Don't slide tiles into position or adhesive

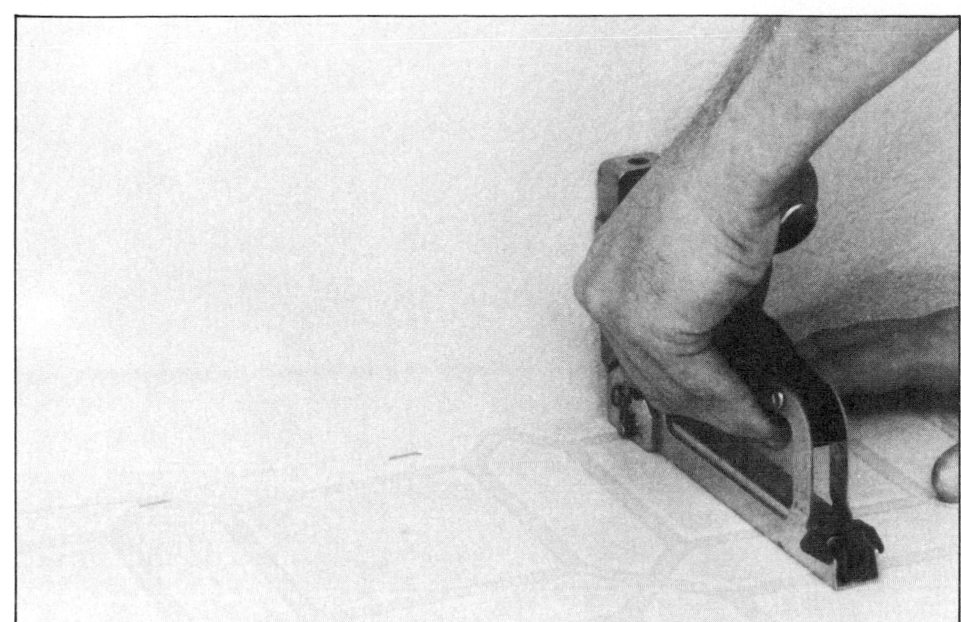

Some thin floor coverings can be attached by stapling perimeter.

will pile up at the seams. Butt one side of the tile against a tile already in place, line up the corners, and lower the tile onto the floor. As you lower the tile, warp down the corner toward the adjoining tile just enough so the edges don't catch. Work along, then outward from, your layout lines.

If you're laying more than one box of resilient tile, don't use up one box and then start the next. This applies even if the boxes have the same lot number. It can result in a slight change of color or reflectivity where tiles from one box meet those from another. Mix up tiles from two boxes as you work so slight changes are disguised. The best way is to use the first half of the first box. Then alternate the second half of the first box with the first half of the second box. Then alternate the second half of the second box with the first half of the third box, and so on.

Determine Pattern: Some tiles have a directional pattern, even if they're a solid color. The pattern may be subtle when comparing individual tiles, but will show up in the finished floor. Check information on or in the box, or any markings or arrows on the back of the tile itself.

You don't have to lay tiles all in one direction. You can vary the pattern by laying one row of tiles straight, the next row 90° to the first, alternating the rows. Or you can alternate the directions of successive individual tiles. Another choice is to alternate tiles or rows straight, 90° right, reversed, then 90° left. If you do any of these rotations, lay them out before adhering them to the floor. Then look at the layout under a strong light.

As you lay tiles, be alert for mixed pattern directions within the same box. If you're rotating pattern directions, stagger the rotation when you start a new row. If the change in pattern direction is hard to see, indicate direction with a grease pencil along edges of whole tiles where they meet partial tiles. This will help you orient partial tiles when you cut them.

As a rule, marble-pattern tiles are never laid in one direction. But that doesn't mean you have to lay them in the traditional checkerboard pattern. Tile can be laid in alternating rows, in a herringbone pattern, or even in a chevron pattern. Experiment with loose tiles to find pleasing patterns. See drawings below.

Cut And Fit Tiles: The method you use for cutting resilient tile depends on its composition. The thinnest and softest tiles can be cut with scissors. Most self-stick tiles are of this kind. Thicker and more rigid tiles can be cut with a utility knife. The thickest and most rigid tiles are scored repeatedly with a utility knife and straightedge, then snapped apart.

To fit partial pieces of tile along walls and other obstacles, use the following technique: Place a loose tile on the full tile adjacent to the space you want to fit. Position the loose tile to

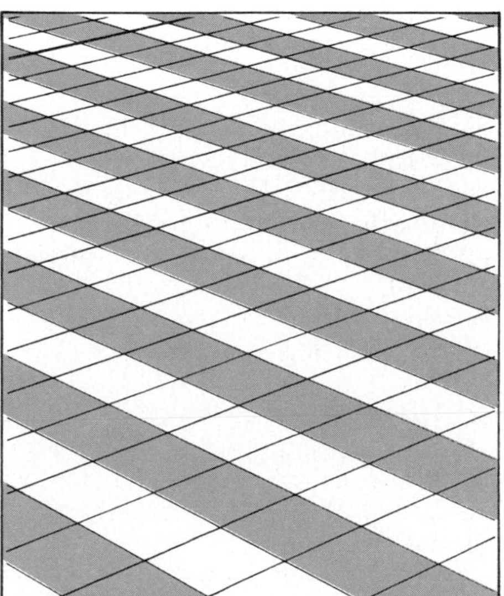

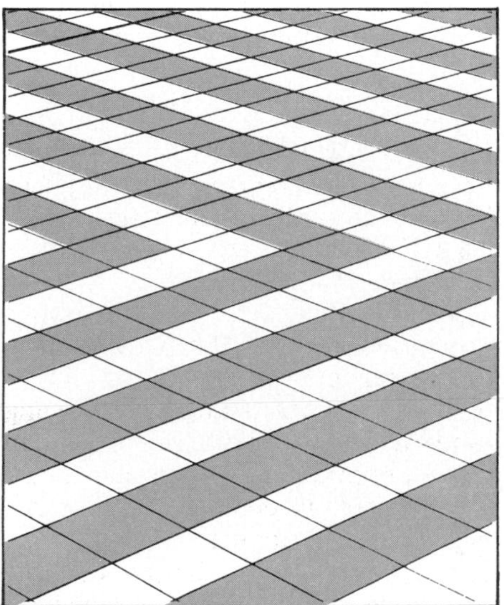

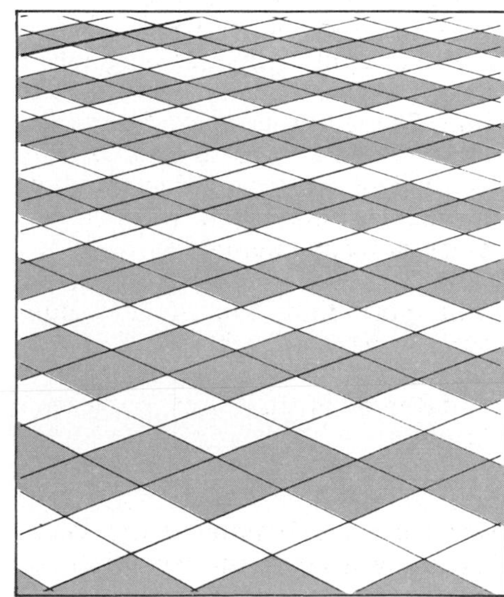

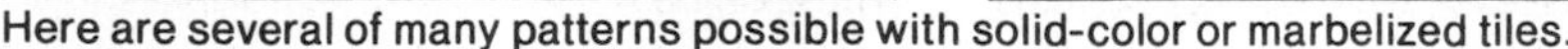

Here are several of many patterns possible with solid-color or marbelized tiles.

match the pattern you're creating. Don't align the loose tile to the one it's on—position it for the space you're filling. See drawing at right.

Place another full tile on top, pushed sideways to the wall or obstacle. Use the edge of this second loose tile to mark the first loose tile. When you cut on this line, the piece farthest from the wall should fit the space perfectly. If you've laid out the floor correctly, the cutoff piece will be less than half a tile, and you can throw it away. If you have a few cut locations that are less than a half tile in size, you may be able to use the cutoff pieces in those locations. This can be done by placing the cut piece on the far edge of the adjoining full tile. Mark and cut as shown at right.

Odd-shape cuts such as inside and outside corners and offsets are made by a variation of the same technique. Place the tile you're fitting on one adjacent whole tile and then on the other adjacent tile until you've transferred all of the necessary measurements. Then cut the tile to fit. See drawing at right.

Fitting Around Irregular Objects: To fit irregular objects such as pipes, make a paper pattern. Grocery-bag paper works well. When the fit of the paper pattern is satisfactory, transfer the pattern to the tile. Cut out the shape with a utility knife using short, firm strokes.

Before cutting stiff or thick tiles, warm them in the oven at a low temperature for a few minutes. This makes them easier to cut. When making complicated cuts in inlaid-vinyl tiles, small segments of the pattern may fracture. Segments can be cemented in separately, if necessary.

If an irregular object, such as a pipe, is away from the wall, cut a straight slit from the object to one edge of the tile. Place the slit in the most unobtrusive place you can, such as to the adjoining wall.

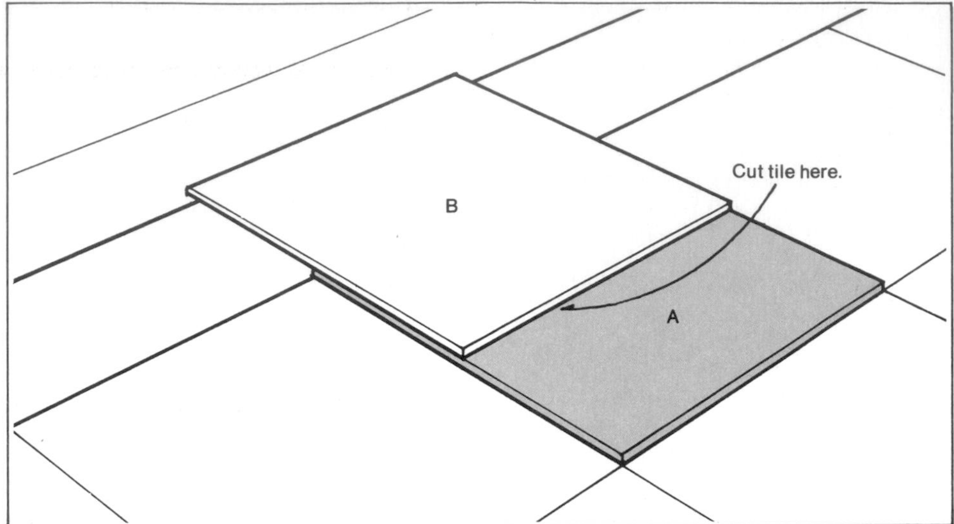

Position full tile (A) over tile adjacent to space being fitted. Adjust tile right or left to align with space, if necessary. Place another full tile (B) over tile A in position shown. Mark and cut tile A as indicated.

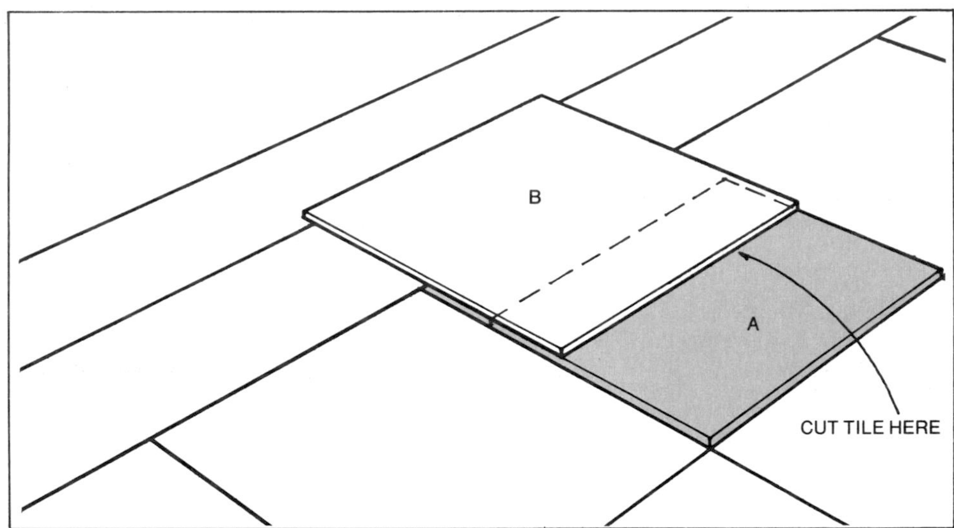

To cut partial tile to fit space, first position partial tile (A) over tile adjacent to space being fitted. Place second full tile (B) over tile A. Mark and cut tile A. Exposed piece of tile A will fit cut location.

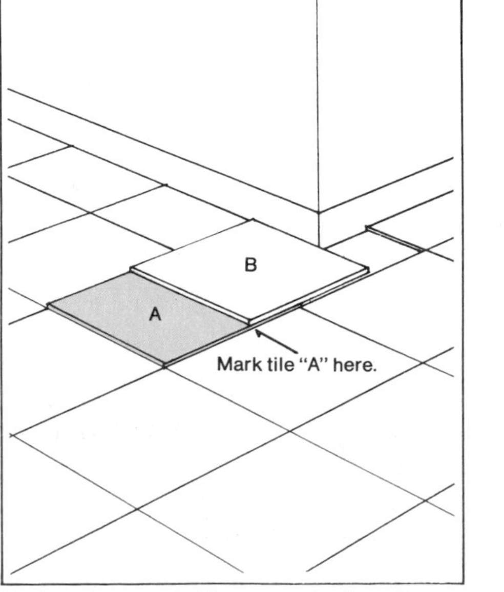

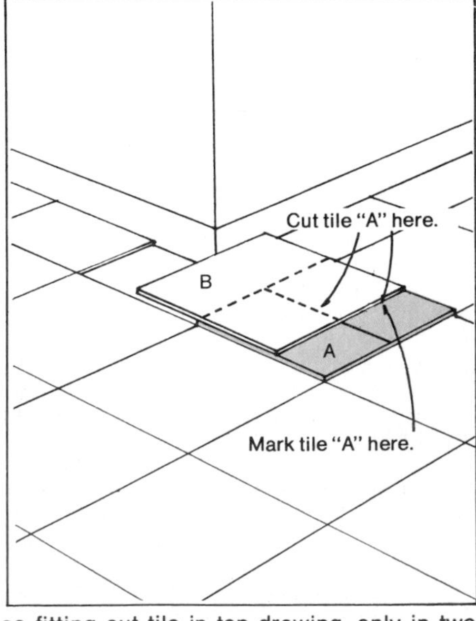

Fitting tile to outside corner is done the same as fitting cut tile in top drawing, only in two directions.

LAYOUT LINES

When you set tiles on a floor, start from *layout lines.* You can't start from a wall—they're rarely parallel.

Check room dimensions. Divide length and width of room by width of tiles. If result is an odd number of tiles and a partial tile, center layout line and run tiles in each direction from it. See top drawing. If result is an even number and a partial tile, working from a centered layout line will cause cut pieces at walls to be less than half a tile. Move layout line half a tile to either side of center to end up with tiles over half size at walls.

Layout lines should average out the variance in direction of each pair of walls, and should cross in the middle at an exact right angle.

Measure and mark centerpoints of long walls. In top drawing, distances A and B should be equal, as should distances C and D. Snap a chalk line between centerpoints of opposite walls. Mark centerpoints of short walls, E equal to G and G equal to H.

Use two nails to string a chalkline between centerpoints of short walls. Before you snap the line, use a rafter square to see if intersection in middle is an exact 90° angle. If it is, distances A to H are all equal—all walls are square and the same length. Snap chalkline and get on with the job. If intersection of layout lines is not 90°, adjust them.

To adjust, mark center intersection on floor. Then move end points of chalkline until intersection in middle is 90°, and mark two new end points. Don't move intersection as you do this. Find midpoint between old and new marks at each end of chalkline. Connect chalkline to midpoints at each end and snap.

Rub out first center line that runs perpendicular to the one you just marked. Set chalkline over rubbed-out line, across short dimension of room. Adjust chalkline until it's exactly at 90° to long chalk mark, *through original center intersection.* Snap chalkline. Both center lines should now intersect at 90°.

To make layout lines for a diagonal floor, first set up layout lines as described above. Measure out from center intersection several feet, in any three directions along lines—points A, B and C in bottom drawing. All measurements from center should be equal.

Tack a nail into floor at points A, B and C. Hook end of a tape measure on each nail in turn. Hold pencil against tape measure at distance equal to that between nails and centerpoint. Draw four arcs on floor, as shown in drawing. Arcs should intersect at points E and F. Snap chalklines between D and center intersection, and E and center intersection. Continue lines to wall.

On a diagonal floor, you'll have small, partial tiles at walls, unless you hit all four walls so you can split blocks corner to corner. Lay out a row of diagonal tiles to see what size partial tiles are required at walls. Adjust layout lines for best pattern of cut pieces at walls.

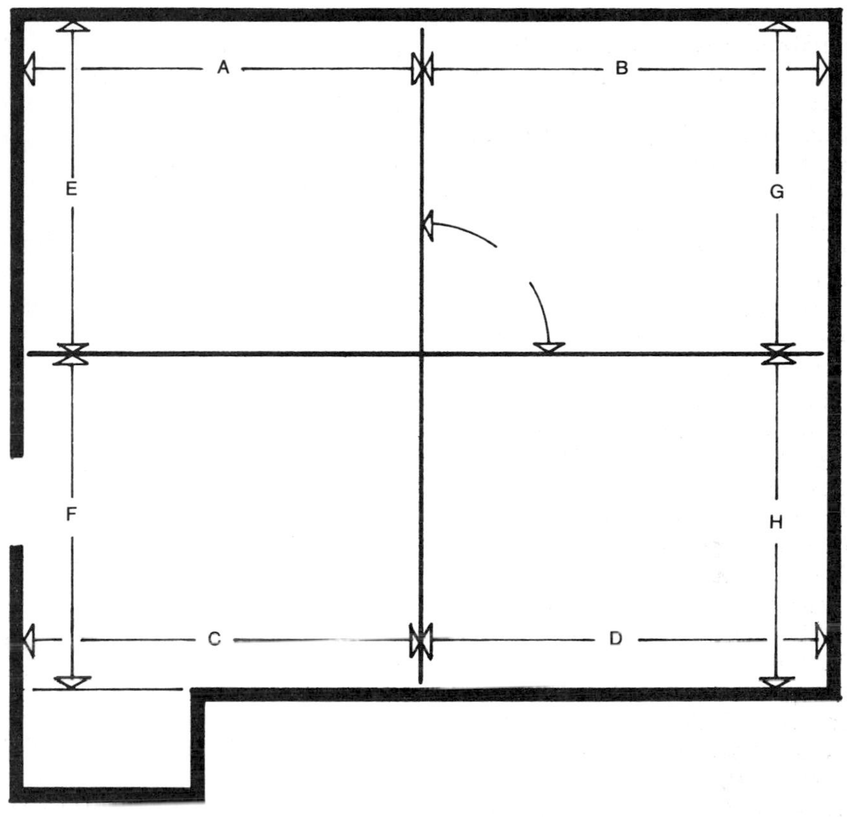

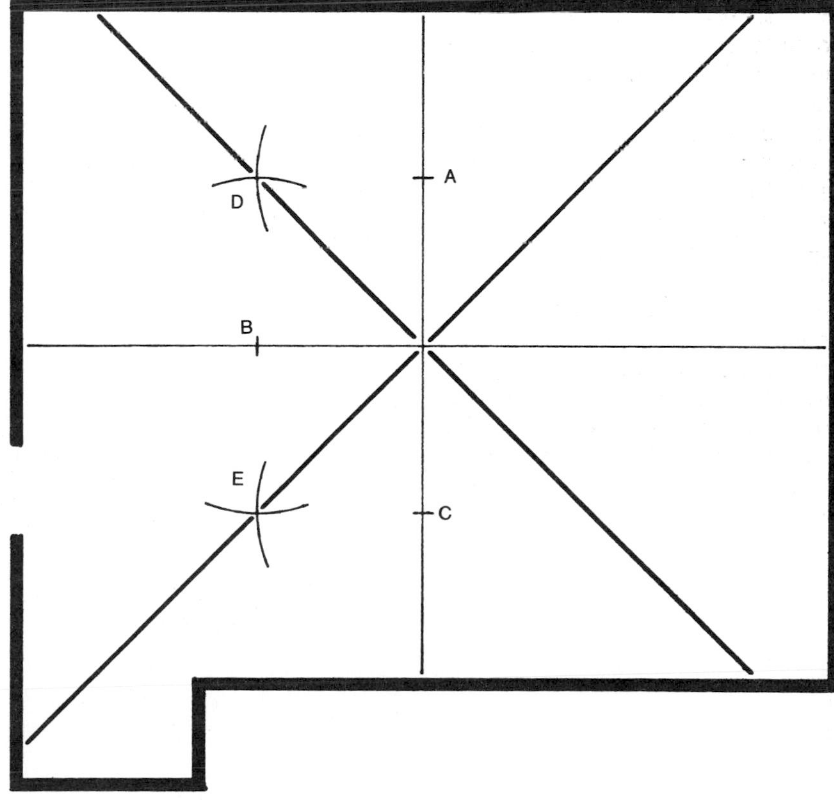

CERAMIC TILE

Traditionally, ceramic tile was laid in a thick mortar bed. The work was difficult and was done by a specialized group of craftsmen. Today, ceramic tile floors can be installed with modern adhesives, as discussed on page 164. Thinner and more regular ceramic tiles are usually laid in mastic adhesives. Thicker tiles such as Mexican tile and quarry tile are set with thinset-type cement adhesive. Application techniques for tile are much the same for both adhesive types. Of course, the traditional mortar bed can still be used.

Generally, the larger the individual tile, the faster the floor goes down. But surprisingly, the smallest tiles available—mosaic tiles—often go down as fast as the biggest. This is because these intricate tiles come premounted on either a backing mesh (that stays on) or on a facing paper (that is soaked off after installation). Among the slowest tiles to lay are the standard 4-1/4 x 4-1/4" tiles, without *spacer lugs*. Spacer lugs are protrusions molded into the tile edges to keep them evenly spaced.

Application—After you've set up your layout lines and applied the mastic, start setting whole tiles diagonally out from the intersection of the layout lines. Don't bed tiles solidly into the mastic until you have a number of them down and you're satisfied with the alignment and spacing. Then use a short length of 2x4 wrapped in an old towel to beat the tiles into solid contact with the adhesive. Don't push any of the tiles too far into the mastic at the edges of the field.

If the tiles you're laying don't have spacer lugs at the edges, use tile spacers, available at your tile dealer. For larger grout joints, space tiles with small strips of wood or hardboard.

Large, heavy Mexican tiles and other quarry tiles require additional layout lines to keep the grout joints spaced evenly.

Overall size, shape, and thickness of individual tiles can vary greatly, so you can't use a spacer system to make uniform grout joints. As you work, add extra chalk lines to form a *grid block* that's two tiles on a side, two by three tiles, or three by three tiles, depending on tile size. Run the chalk lines down the centers of the grout joints. Apply adhesive to one grid block at a time.

Drop tiles into contact with adhesive using a slight twisting motion. Don't let adhesive pile up between tiles.

Irregular Mexican handmade tile requires extra layout lines to make grout joints even. Avoid using obviously cupped tiles.

Place and level the tiles in that grid block. Then ease the tiles around until all grout joints are spaced evenly. Remember that the edges of most quarry tiles are curved. The shoulder of the tile controls the width of the grout joint, not the actual gap between the tiles.

Recheck level and give each tile a firm push with the flat of your hand to ensure solid bedding. Then start with the next grid block.

Lay all whole tiles in a room before you start fitting and laying cut tiles. To do this, you may have to work while standing or kneeling on newly laid tiles. This is tricky, because you can easily sink tiles into the adhesive or slide them out of position. Place large pieces of plywood or hardboard on newly laid tiles to distribute your weight. Move carefully so you don't slide the plywood. Or, you can set the cut tiles the following day.

Cutting and Fitting—How you cut ceramic tile depends on the kind of tile and the nature of the cut. To make a quantity of straight cuts on medium- to large-size, glazed or semiglazed tile, use a device called a *tile cutter.* The tile dealer may loan or rent you one. A tile cutter has a scoring wheel on the central handle. Score the tile on the cut line, and then push down on the handle to snap the tile at the score.

If you have only a few medium- or large-size glazed or semiglazed tiles to cut, use a glass cutter and a straightedge.

Score the tile at the cut line. Then position a length of insulated wire directly under the score line and push down evenly on both sides.

Unglazed quarry tiles and Mexican tiles can't be cut by scoring and snapping. Some tile dealers have water-cooled *tile saws* and make cuts to your marks for a small fee. If you have a large quantity of cuts to make, it might be worthwhile to rent a tile saw to make the cuts.

Unless you have to make enough cuts to justify using a tile saw, cut quarry and Mexican tiles by hand. Most hardware stores carry hacksaw blades that have carbide grit bonded to the edge. Installed in a standard hacksaw frame, one of these blades will make hundreds of cuts in quarry and Mexican tile. There is also a wire version of this blade for making tight, curved cuts in glazed and unglazed tiles.

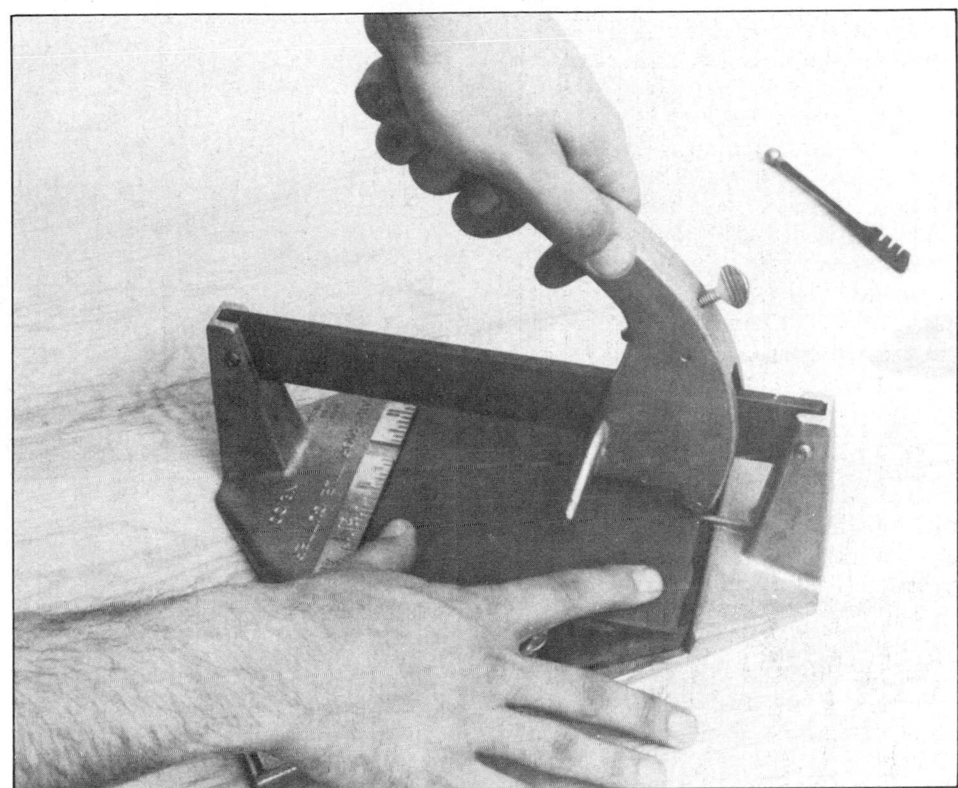

A tile cutter easily makes straight cuts in glazed tile.

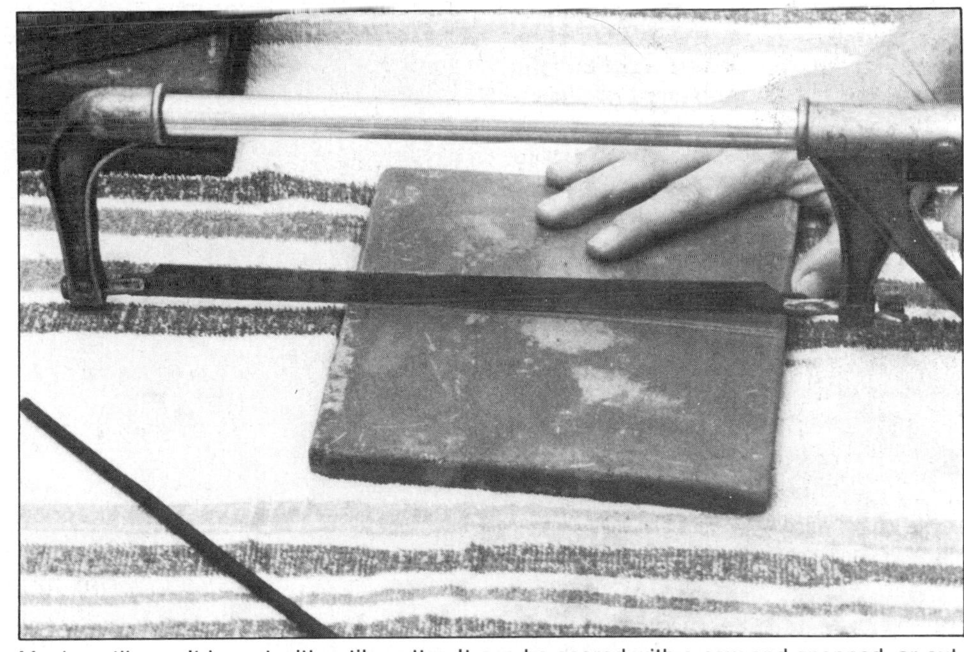

Mexican tile can't be cut with a tile cutter. It can be scored with a saw and snapped, or cut with a water-cooled tile saw. Shown is hacksaw with carbide-tip blade.

To make straight cuts with a carbide-grit hacksaw blade, cut with the blade flat to the surface of the tile to make a groove about 1/16-inch deep. Extend the groove down the radii on curved-tile edges. Place the tile on a towel, over a length of insulated wire. Push down sharply on both sides to snap it. For thick tile, you may have to groove both sides in order to get a clean snap. Don't use a straightedge to guide a carbide-grit blade. It will ruin the straightedge in two or three strokes.

The best way to make curved or irregular cuts in tile is to use *nibbling pliers.* These are available at the tile dealer. Use the pliers to nibble away at the surplus part of the tile until you've gnawed it down to the desired shape. Remember, the tile needs only have an even contour at the finished surface. If the cut edge is uneven down in the grout joint, it won't show.

Mosaic tile in sheets presents some problems of its own. Whole tiles are easy to separate from the sheet with a utility knife. Cutting individual tiles is more difficult. They can be cut with nibbling pliers, but the pliers may leave surface fractures on highly glazed mosaics. It's difficult to get a really straight clean cut.

A technique borrowed from the diamond cutters works well with some mosaics. Turn the tile face down on a piece of plywood and support each edge with lengths of wire. Then place the cutting edge of a chisel over the cut line. Make sure the cutting edge is squarely in contact with the back of the tile, and the front of the tile is squarely in contact with the wires. Then strike the chisel handle with a hammer. You may have to try several cuts to determine exactly how the tiles respond to this technique. Don't use your best wood chisel for this. Tile will chip or dull the cutting edge.

Grout—Small floor tiles with small grout joints are usually grouted with *prepared-cement grout. Epoxy grouts* are used in extreme-wear areas. Epoxy grouts are difficult for the inexperienced tile-setter to work with.

For a tile floor with small grout joints and fully glazed tiles, mix prepared-cement grout to about the consistency of pancake batter. Protect adjoining surfaces and wear rubber gloves. Pigment particles in powdered grout should be broken up and evenly distributed throughout the mixture.

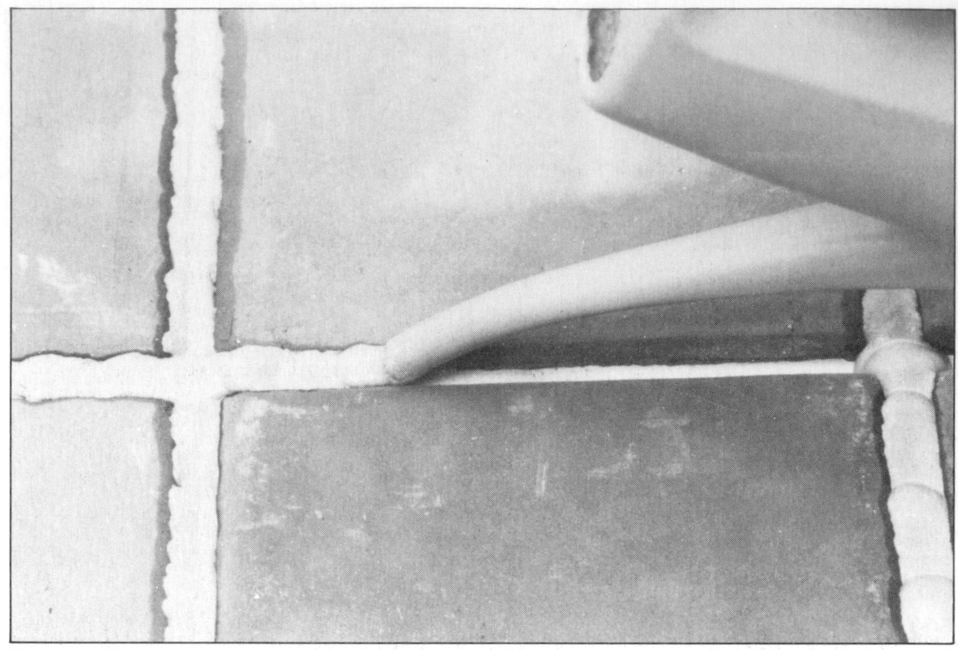

Use container with pour spout to apply grout to Mexican or quarry tiles. Job is tedious, but grout will stain tile if you spread it over whole surface. Then you would have to wash whole floor with muriatic acid, a messy and hazardous process.

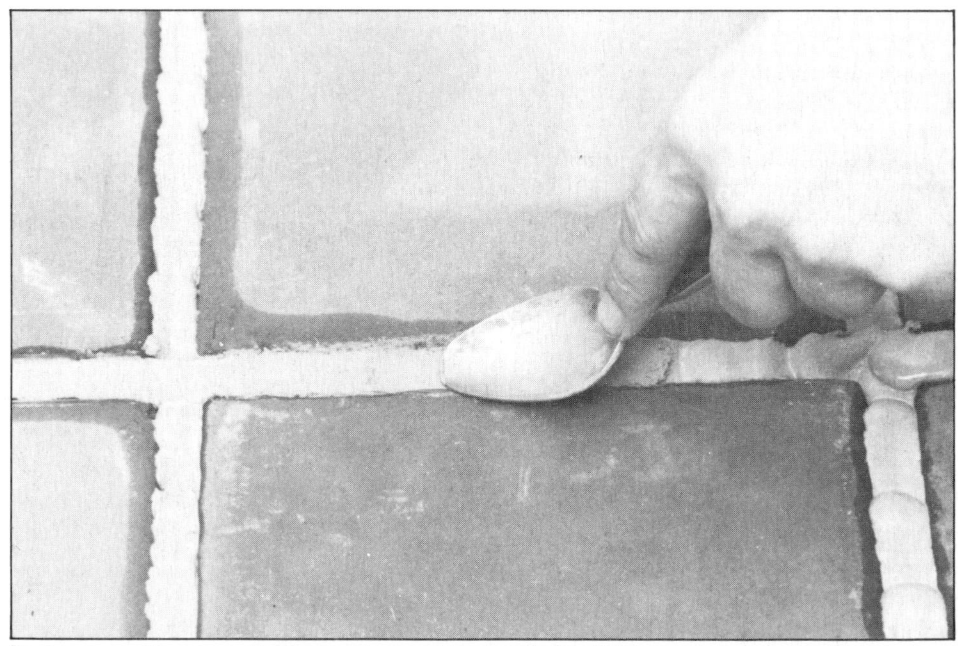

Tool grout with any suitable wood or metal object. Don't let grout set up too hard before tooling.

Even some white grouts contain pigment for a uniform color.

Apply grout with a squeegee or with a sponge float and work the grout into the joints. If necessary, work a putty knife up and down in the joint to remove air bubbles in the grout. Use a piece of plywood to protect your knees while you work.

After the whole floor has been grouted, use a nearly dry sponge to wipe up as much surplus grout as you can. Run the sponge diagonally across the joints. Too much pressure on the sponge will scrape the grout out of the joints, so work carefully.

After the grout has started to set up, tool or *strike* the joints with a suitable implement. You can buy joint strikers to work with, but improvising is OK too. Depending on the size of the grout joint, you can use the handle of an old toothbrush, an old spoon or any piece of scrap metal that's the right size and shape. The tool should compress the grout to the desired shape, rather than scraping it off. Don't use soft metals like aluminum. They can leave a metallic streak on the tiles next to the grout joint.

The grout will start to dry within a few hours of application. At this stage remove more surplus grout to save work later. Wrap a piece of coarse cloth around a short piece of 2x4 and buff the floor diagonally. Don't use cloth with a heavy nap, such as terrycloth, because it can disturb the grout joints. If tiles are large, you can carefully clean the face of each tile at this time.

When the grout is completely dry, buff off haze or surplus grout with a coarse cloth. High spots in grout joints can be leveled by wrapping the coarse cloth around your joint-striking tool and buffing vigorously.

Mortar Grout—Large floor tiles with large grout joints are generally grouted with mortar—a mixture of Portland cement and sand. Don't use ordinary sand for mortar grout because the color and grain size is variable. You can buy uniformly graded white silica sand in sacks at the masonry-supply yard where you get the cement.

The basic mix is 1 part Portland cement to 3 parts #30 white silica sand. To improve plasticity, add a small amount of *hydrated lime*. The lime content is not critical, but should not exceed 10% or the grout will be too stringy. Use the basic 1 to 3 mix for grout joints 1/2 inch or wider. For narrower grout joints, the mix should be richer in proportion, up to 1 part cement to 1 part sand for the narrowest grout joints. Joints narrower than 1/4 inch or so should be grouted with prepared grout.

If the tile is glazed, mortar grout won't stick to the glazed surface. With glazed tiles, you can shovel grout into place with a trowel and strike it off with a flat piece of wood or squeegee.

Mortar grout will cause permanent stains on the faces of unglazed tiles. For these tiles, mix mortar grout thinner—almost a slurry—and pour into place. Use a plastic watering can with a long, thin spout or a sturdy canvas bag with a hole in it, similar in use to a cake decorator's pastry bag.

The mortar will start to set up a few minutes after application. This stage is easy to determine because the mortar loses its *water sheen*, or becomes dull in appearance. Tool the mortar to final shape and surface compactness before it sets completely. Masons' joint tools work well on glazed tile, but they're difficult to use on unglazed tile.

Buff off remaining grout haze after grout is completely dry.

For unglazed tile, put in only as much mortar as is needed, and tool it with something that can be handled more carefully, such as an old stainless-steel tablespoon. After tooling grout joints on unglazed tiles, clean tile surfaces with a damp sponge or cloth wrapped around your index finger. This removes minor mortar stains on the tiles. It also evens and compacts the edges of the mortar grout.

Mortar grout must be kept damp for it to cure properly. Grout that has dried too quickly will shed sand grains for years. Use water in a spray bottle to keep grout damp for the first 24 hours or so. If you can't be around to spray periodically, spray the grout heavily and cover the floor with plastic dropcloths to keep in the moisture.

If you find the mortar grout is drying out too quickly during application, the tile itself is probably too dry. If so, use the spray bottle to moisten the grout joints before you apply the mortar grout.

Sealing—While glazed tile is impervious to most dirt and stains, grout is not. Especially in a kitchen, grout joints should be sealed. Unglazed tiles are also susceptible to dirt and stains. They should be sealed with the same sealer used for grout.

Several materials are available to seal tile and grout. If you don't want the sealer to show, use *silicone sealer*. Silicone sealer is swabbed on with a brush or cloth, and the surplus wiped up a few minutes later. After drying, it's invisible. Test by pouring on some water and wiping it up after a while. If the surface remains damp after wiping, apply another coat of sealer.

If you want a semigloss surface, use an *acrylic emulsion*. For a small area, use one of the self-polishing floor waxes, such as Johnson's Futura. For big areas, use commercial concrete sealer, available from a janitorial supplier.

The easiest way to apply these products is with a 4- or 5-inch paintbrush or a thick lamb's-wool paint roller. Don't brush on the sealer too vigorously. You'll create bubbles that will show after the sealer dries. On porous tiles and grout joints, several coats may be necessary. To get a uniform satin gloss, use an electric floor buffer after the acrylic emulsion is dry.

Floors sealed with acrylic emulsion should be damp-mopped periodically, and need a light reapplication of sealer every 6 to 12 months. Some commercial-maintenance services add a small amount of acrylic emulsion to the water when damp-mopping and follow up with a light buffing. Unglazed-tile floors treated this way never need full reapplication, yet don't build up an excess of acrylic.

BRICK FLOORS

Brick for floors can be thought of as thick tile. The installation techniques are practically identical. Don't construct brick floors of any brick other than *pavers.* Pavers are specifically made for the heavy wear of flooring use. They're available either full thickness or half thickness, called *split pavers.*

Brick floors are heavy and thick. The weight doesn't create problems on a concrete slab, but wood-frame floors must be strong and rigid enough to support the brick.

If the subfloor is at all springy, a brick floor can cause a permanent sag. A subfloor can be springy and more than strong enough, or rigid but weak.

If there is a crawl space or basement below, additional girders or joists can be installed to add rigidity or strength. An additional layer of 5/8 or 3/4-inch plywood can be installed to compensate for flex in the subfloor itself.

Flexibility can be detected by jumping up and down on the floor while another person stands nearby to feel how the floor reacts. Strength can be determined by noting the size, spacing and span of all subfloor members. From that information, your local building department should be able to tell you if you can safely install brick on the existing floor structure, or if additional bracing is needed. Most building departments have charts that prescribe the type of subflooring required for various-size loads.

The additional thickness of a brick floor can cause problems where the bricks meet other floors. If you're building a new floor structure, you can lower the brick areas to compensate. Or, if the ceilings are high enough, you can build a platform to raise the brick—and the kitchen—a full step up from surrounding floors.

The platform solution mentioned can be useful if you have to cope with problems of floor strength or excessive flexibility. Properly designed, the platform can add enough strength or stiffness to make brick feasible. Like any thick flooring material, it's best to put brick down before cabinets are installed.

Acrylic emulsion makes semigloss finish. It gives grout joints a slightly damp appearance.

Dry-laid Brick—The simplest brick floor is laid dry. No mortar is used, so the subfloor must be smooth and level before you start.

Put a layer of 30-pound building felt over the entire floor. Do not overlap the seams and do not wrinkle the felt. Use a few staples or small dabs of construction adhesive to keep the felt from moving around underfoot. Set up your layout lines on the building felt as you would for any kind of block flooring. See page 143.

Put down all whole bricks, pushed tightly together, working outward from the layout lines.

There will probably be a slight variation in the dimensions of the bricks. Undersize or oversize bricks can be segregated and used together to avoid gaps. One advantage to dry-laying brick is if a section doesn't look right or you make a mistake in the pattern, you can take the bricks up and start over.

After the whole bricks are in place, mark and cut the partial bricks. Brick is an unglazed-clay product and is cut much the same as quarry tile or Mexican tile, page 145. In non-critical areas such as under cabinets, cut bricks by scoring and splitting with a hammer and brick set.

When all brick is in place, sprinkle the floor with fine sand and sweep the sand into cracks. After the floor has been in place for a few days, it can be sealed or finished as shown above for unglazed tile.

If the subfloor is uneven, lay brick in a mortar bed. Over wood subfloors, the mortar bed should be put down on 15- or 30-pound building felt, and should be a full 1-1/2 inches thick. On a clean concrete subfloor, the mortar bed need only be 1/2-inch thick. The mortar mix used is 3 parts sand to 1 part Portland cement, with up to 10% hydrated lime added to improve plasticity.

Starting from the layout lines, put down about 2 square feet of mortar. The area covered does not have to be precise. Then seat a row of bricks along one layout line. Use a level to get the top surfaces even and level. To level a brick, just push or tap it into the mortar bed.

Clean excess mortar from edges you won't immediately be adding bricks to. If you're allowing for mortar joints between the bricks, space them apart with small strips of wood.

Continue the above process until all whole bricks are laid. As you work, remove mortar from locations where cut bricks will go. Make all cuts in bricks at one time, so you can use up extra pieces. Then use a narrow trowel to lay down a mortar bed in the cut-brick locations.

Remember, if you lay brick without mortar joints, there's no place for the mortar to squish out as you level the cut pieces. Make sure you put down the right amount of mortar under the cut pieces.

Avoid walking on mortared bricks until the mortar has set. If you have time, lay all whole bricks in mortar and allow the mortar to set for a day or two. Then set the cut pieces. If you have to work over freshly laid bricks, wait several hours for the mortar to set up partially. Use large pieces of plywood or hardboard to distribute your weight as you work.

After laying the brick, keep it wet for a day or two, to allow mortar to cure properly. If the floor has no mortar joints, sweep fine sand into the cracks. If the floor will have mortar joints, grout and seal them the same as for unglazed tile. See page 147.

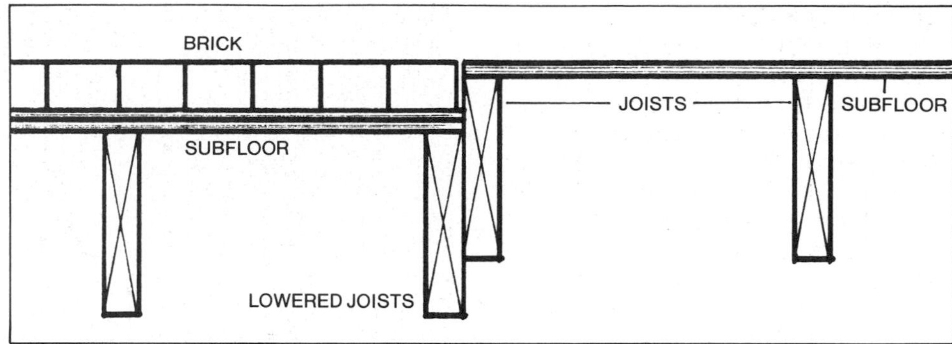

Rework subfloor so brick surface is even with finish flooring in adjacent rooms.

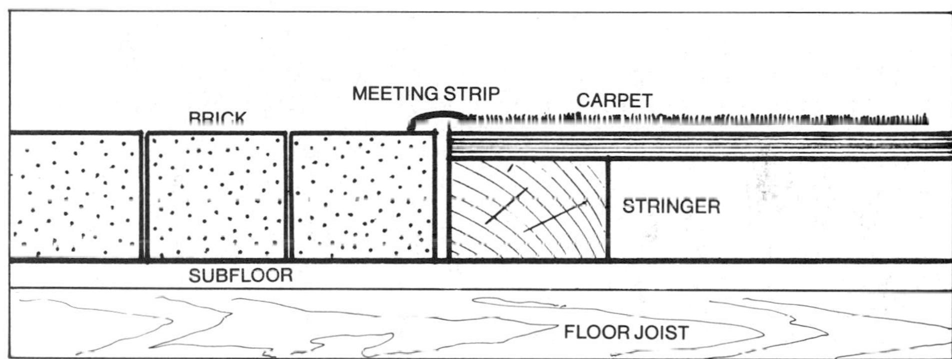

If brick is laid on existing subfloor, raise floors in adjacent rooms so finish flooring is flush to brick. Use appropriate meeting strip to cover gap between floors.

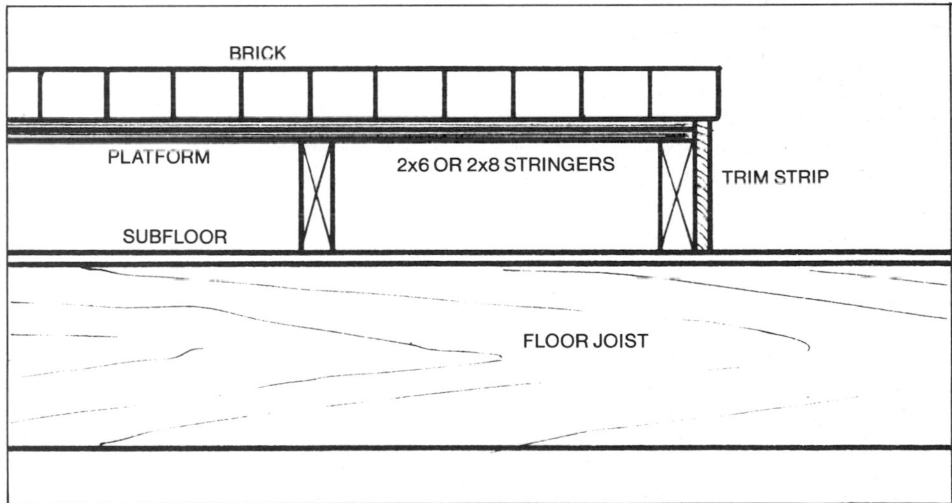

Another alternative is to build platform to raise brick floor a full step above adjacent floors. Edge bricks at openings must be securely mortared in place.

WOOD FLOORING

The two major types of wood flooring are *strip flooring* and *wood-block flooring,* also called *parquet.* Wood flooring materials come prefinished, sanded and unfinished, and unfinished requiring sanding. A more complete description of the flooring types appears on page 36.

Parquet Installation—Parquet flooring requires a subfloor that is sound, tight, smooth and dry. Repairs to subfloor and floor underlayment are described on pages 132-134. If you're laying parquet over a concrete-slab floor, check with the flooring dealer for subfloor requirements.

Set up layout lines as for other block flooring and trowel on adhesive. Apply only as much adhesive as you can cover during the adhesive's *open time.* The open time, or *setting time,* is shown on the adhesive can.

Start at the intersection of your layout lines and put down a row of six or eight blocks. Some parquet blocks will have tongues on one edge and grooves on the opposite edge. This allows them to interlock. Carefully align the face of the block, not the tongue, with the layout lines. Fit the blocks together hand-tight. The corners of the tiles should line up exactly with each other.

Then start the next few rows on one side, step fashion. Keep setting blocks in the steps until 1/4 of the room is done. The stepped blocks enable you to back your way out of the corner, fitting cut blocks as you go along. There's a knack to seating the blocks without sliding them on the adhesive, despite the tongue-and-groove edges. With practice you'll be able to slide the tongues and grooves together while you drop the block flat into position.

When several blocks are in position, use a hammer and a padded wood block to bed them solidly into the adhesive. Doublecheck intersections of block corners before you bed the blocks. This is where any misalignment will show up. Realign blocks by twisting them slightly.

Cutting and Fitting: Parquet floors should always have clearance around the floor perimeter and at any obstructions. This allows for expansion and contraction. Cutting and fitting perimeter blocks is simpler than with other materials. Use a spacer strip of 1/2-inch plywood along any

Align parquet blocks so all four corners meet perfectly. Check every time you lay a block and adjust if necessary.

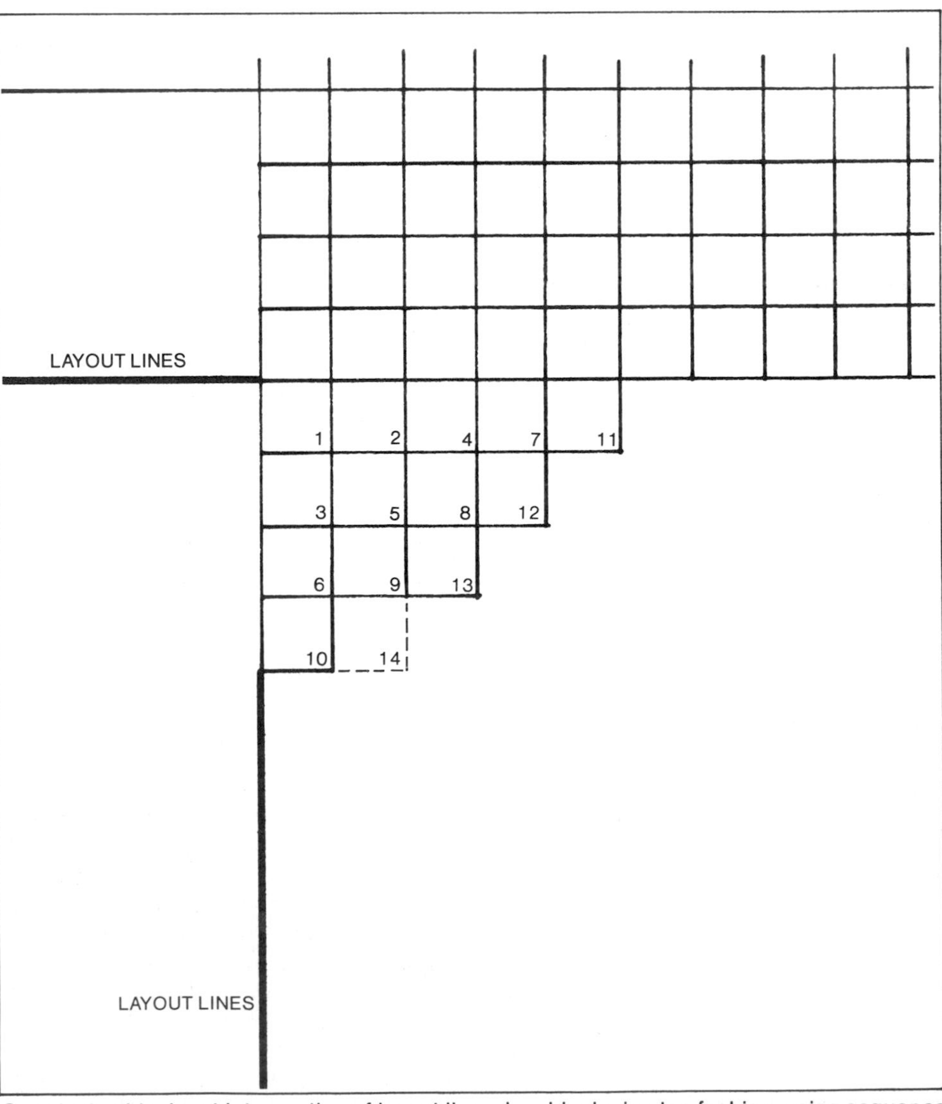

Start laying blocks at intersection of layout lines. Lay blocks in step fashion, using sequence shown here. When one quarter of floor is finished, lay blocks in next quarter, and so forth.

walls and around obstacles. The expansion gaps are then covered by moldings.

With the spacer strip in place along a wall, place the block to be cut exactly on top of the adjacent whole block. Use another block with the tongue trimmed off as a gage to mark the loose block for cutting. The exposed piece beyond the gage block will fit the space. Use a fine-tooth handsaw or saber saw to cut the block. If you use a table saw or radial-arm saw, use a finish blade.

Difficult areas should be fitted by making a paper template first. Pencil the shape of the template onto the block for cutting. Because most parquet is rigid, you may have to cut a block in two pieces to make a cutout for a free-standing obstacle. Detach the obstacle, if you can. Then drill a hole in the parquet block, install it, and replace the obstacle.

Finishing: Many parquet-flooring products are prefinished. All that's needed is a coat of any good paste wax. Some types come prewaxed. If you're working with unfinished parquet, use finishing techniques discussed for strip flooring on pages 152-153. Parquet should be sanded on alternate diagonals.

Cut parquet flooring as gently as possible to avoid loosening laminates. A block nailed to a 2x4 makes a good guide.

Sand parquet floors diagonally.

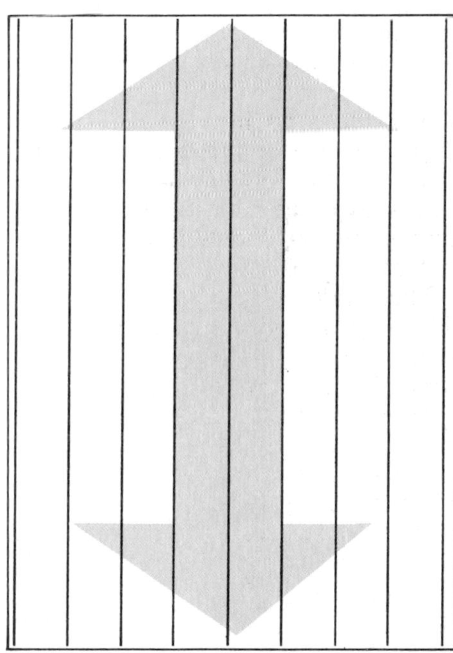

Sand wood-strip floors parallel to grain.

Wood Strip Installation—It's easiest to install wood-strip flooring longways in the room. This requires the least cutting and fitting. If the strip pattern is visible from doorways and other rooms, make sure the strip direction gives you the desired space illusion.

If you're laying wood-strip flooring over a concrete-slab floor, check with the flooring dealer for subfloor requirements. Do not put wood flooring over concrete floors that show signs of moisture unless floor can be waterproofed. See page 135.

On wood-frame floors, you can run wood-strip flooring in any direction you want to without reference to joists beneath. It depends on the strength and stiffness of the subfloor material. Thin strip flooring will require a sturdy subfloor of 1-inch plywood or 2x6 tongue-and-groove subflooring. If you're using 2-inch (nominal) planks for the finish floor, a subfloor may not be required, but flooring must run perpendicular to the joists. If you're in doubt, consult the building department.

Referring to your layout lines, pencil in the base-cabinet layout on the floor. Layout lines should average out any walls that aren't parallel to each other. But the cabinet fronts will be parallel to the wall the cabinets are attached to. Use a tape measure and chalkline to determine if the last flooring strip will be parallel to the cabinet front. If not, try to adjust your layout lines to minimize the problem in the most visible areas.

Application: If possible, start laying wood strips from a wall that's close to parallel to your central layout line. Sort out the short pieces in the flooring bundles and save them for use under cabinets and for cut pieces. Put down a strip of *resin paper* (available at the flooring dealer) or 15-pound floor felt. Snap a chalk line 1/2 inch from the wall and align the first strip to it. This will allow room for expansion and contraction of the flooring.

Snap a line 1/2 inch from the adjacent wall. Align flooring-strip ends to this line as you lay them. Face the tongue on the first strip away from the wall. Drive nails through the top surface of the strip, along the back edge, so the nails will be covered by molding. This procedure is called *face nailing.* See drawing at right.

Nail size and spacing will vary with the type of wood-strip flooring you use. If nailing instructions aren't provided with the flooring bundles, ask the flooring dealer for this information.

Maintain the 1/2-inch spacing at the end wall. Keep adding pieces until you reach the wall opposite the starting point. Mark and cut a piece to close out the run. Ends of flooring pieces will often have tongues and grooves the same as the edges. This is called *end-matched* flooring. With end-matched flooring, use the cutoff piece from the end of the last run to start the new run.

After the first strip in each run is face nailed, *blind-nail* remaining strips in the run. Strips are blind-nailed through their tongues, so nails won't show. This can be done by hand if the floor area is small. For large areas, use a *hammer-actuated nailer.* This device hooks onto the tongue-edge of the strips and is loaded with strips of nails or special staples. When you hit the plunger with a special hammer, the strip of flooring is driven up tight and nailed through the tongue. You can rent a hammer-actuated nailer from the flooring dealer or a tool-rental company. Get a supply of the special nail or staple strips and the special hammer that goes with the nailer.

Starting with the second run of wood-strip flooring, no face-nailing is necessary. All strips can be blind-nailed until you get to the opposite wall. If the flooring is running across the joists, try to catch the joists as you nail. An occasional miss doesn't matter, but a large area of flooring that isn't solidly nailed to underlying joists is prone to squeak.

If you find any warped strips in the bundle, put them aside. You can use them later for cutting shorter, straight sections. If you have to use a warped strip, cut off badly warped ends, if any. Then nail a short 2x4 block to the subfloor as shown at right. Use a pry bar to force the warped strip into position. Nail down another 2x4 block to pin the pry bar into position. Then blind-nail the warped piece, nailing every 4 or 5 inches.

As you complete the floor, the last few strips will be so close to the wall that a hammer-actuated nailer won't fit between the flooring and the wall. If strips are fairly wide, you may be able to blind-nail the next-to-last strip with an ordinary hammer. Otherwise, face-nail the last few strips as unobtrusively as possible.

If nails show, set them below the floor surface. Fill nail holes with a wood filler that matches the wood color. Maintain the 1/2-inch expansion clearance on the last wall. Use a pry bar and a wood block to wedge the last few strips in place.

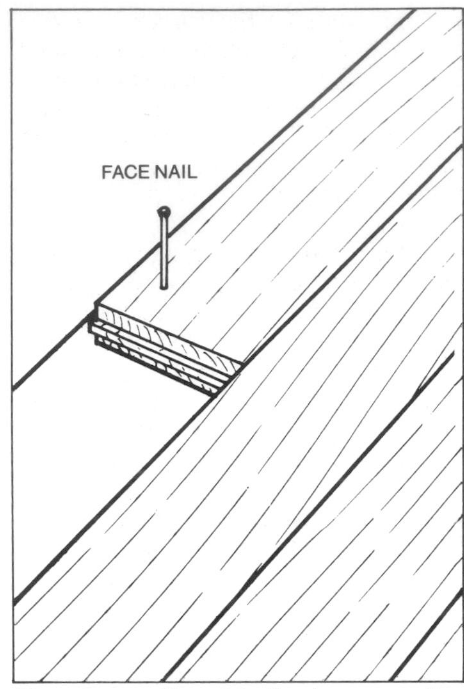

When face-nailing strip flooring, use nailset to avoid hammer-dents.

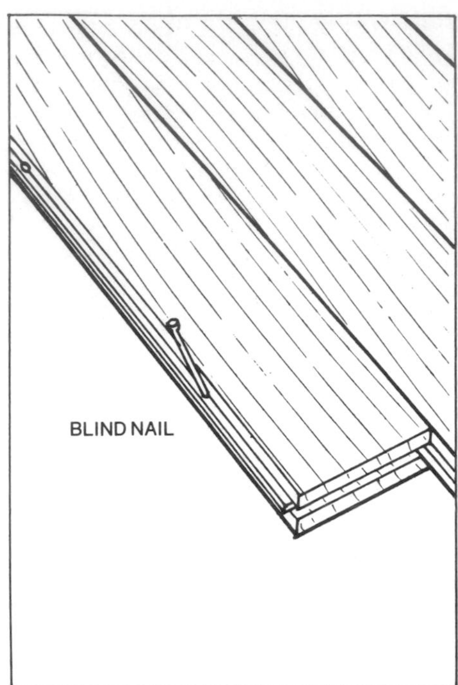

If you don't have a hammer-actuated nailer, you'll have to blind-nail flooring with hammer and nailset. After you've driven nail almost flush with end of nailset, turn nailset on its side for last stroke.

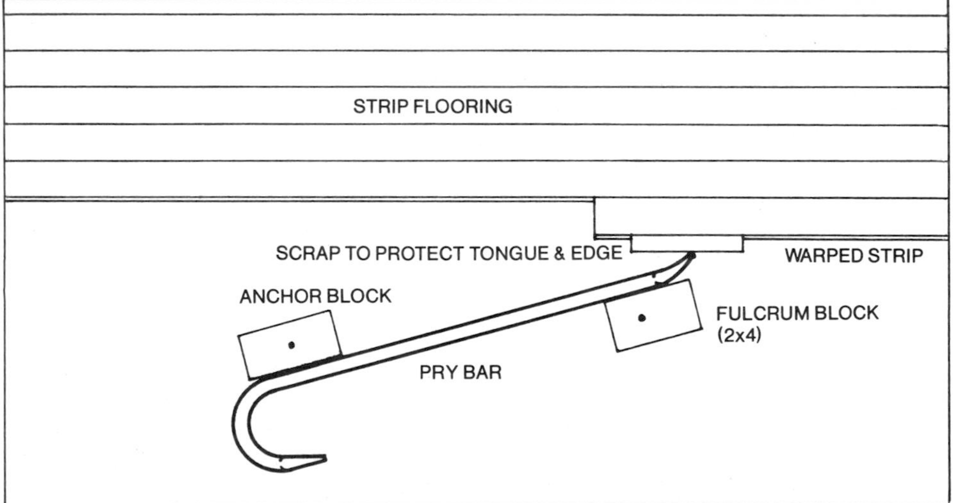

Use prybar to force warped strip into position. Use short block to pin prybar into position.

Finishing: If you've installed prefinished wood-strip flooring, apply a coat of any good paste wax. If you've installed unfinished flooring or are reconditioning an old wood floor, use the following procedure. The only difference is that a new unfinished floor won't require as much sanding as an old one.

You'll need two rented tools to sand a wood floor—a large *drum sander* and an *edger.* The drum sander looks like a large lawnmower with a handle on the back. The edger is either rotary or a variation of a belt sander. Of the two types of edgers, the belt type is preferable. The tool-rental company or flooring dealer should also carry sandpaper belts for the machine you rent. You'll need belts with coarse, medium and fine grits for the drum sander, and medium and fine grits for the edger. If the machines don't have decals showing how to load the sandpaper, ask the people at the rental company or flooring dealer how to do it. The machines vary.

Before sanding, use a nailset or punch to set all nails below the floor surface. Remove large splinters and renail loose spots in the floor.

Start with coarse paper in the drum sander. Position the sander close to one wall and turn it on. Hold the drum clear of the floor until it reaches full speed. Gently and smoothly lower the drum into contact with the floor.

Let the moving drum guide you and the machine across the floor, parallel to the grain. At the other wall, gently and smoothly lift the drum off the floor and pull the machine back to the far wall. Try to keep the drum from notching the floor or producing ridges in it. Keep the sander moving in a straight line along the grain of the wood. Move the drum sander slowly enough to remove irregularities in the surface and offsets between boards. Don't move too slowly, or you'll remove more wood than you need to.

The second pass with the drum sander is more difficult than the first. Lap the drum a few inches over the previous pass and move across the floor *at the same speed as the first pass.* If you go faster or slower, the second pass will remove too much or too little wood, making a ridge. Keep a measured pace as you work. Speed becomes less critical with fine-grit sandpapers, because ridges are smaller and more easily sanded out.

After you've sanded the whole floor with the drum sander, reverse the machine direction and carefully sand the strip along your starting wall. Stay with the grain.

Park the drum sander in the middle of the room with the drum elevated. A hot drum resting on the floor can cause a scorch mark. Then repeat the entire sanding process, using medium-grit sandpaper. Load the edger with medium sandpaper. Sand the border where the drum sander could not reach.

Sand along the grain, where possible. You'll probably have to sand across the grain where strip ends meet the wall and in some tight spaces. Sand all edges level with the main surface. In tight locations such as corners, you may have to sand by hand.

When you've sanded the entire floor with medium-grit sandpaper, fill any imperfections with wood putty. If you're going to stain the floor, the wood putty should match the stain color. To make your own wood putty, mix some of the sanding dust with a 1-to-1 mixture of white glue and water. To match the putty color to the wood, add a small amount of water-base or alcohol-base wood stain to the mixture. Let the wood putty dry before final sanding.

Load the drum sander with fine-grit sandpaper and make a final pass over the floor. Then touch up edges and remaining rough spots with the edger or by hand.

During final sanding try to keep dirt and stains off the wood. Wear socks over your shoes, clean your knees, and make sure tools don't leave metal marks. Vacuum up any sawdust that escaped the bags on the sanders. If your vacuum cleaner has a metal nozzle, wrap it in masking tape to protect the floor. Use a brush attachment if your vacuum has one. Empty the vacuum-cleaner bag frequently. Marks, dirt or imperfections left on the floor will show under the finish.

Apply Finish: The actual finishing procedure you use for your new or reconditioned floor is largely up to you. If you want the finished floor to be darker than it is now, you can stain it. To see the true color of the wood, moisten a cloth with paint thinner—water will raise the grain—and wipe a spot on the floor. Until the paint thinner dries, the spot will be the color of the floor with a clear finish. If you like the color, you don't need to stain. If you want a lighter floor color, you'll have to bleach the wood before you apply the clear finish. Wood bleaches are available at paint stores.

To stain a wood floor, take a piece of leftover flooring to a paint store or flooring dealer to try stains on. Stain can be applied separately, or as part of the finish. If you've sanded an old wood floor the old finish may still show in cracks between boards. To hide color difference, stain the whole floor the same shade or darker than it was. Open-grain wood species such as oak require filling before applying stains and finishes. Other species require sealing before staining to prevent uneven stain absorption.

Use brush to apply finish to wood floor after sanding. Make sure you brush finish into cracks between strips.

A number of penetrating sealers, sealer-waxes and surface finishes can be used on wood floors. If you want a high-gloss finish, use a surface finish like polyurethane. Satin or matte finishes are available in all types. The best way to make the final decision on finish is with the help of the flooring dealer or a paint store. If you use more than one finish material, buy them from the same supplier or finish manufacturer.

Because there are so many combinations of wood species, colors, and finish-material systems, no specifics can be given here on finish application. The finish supplier and manufacturer can give you detailed instructions for your particular set of circumstances.

Cabinets & Countertops

Cabinets and countertops form framework that defines a kitchen.

The heart of a kitchen is its cabinets. In many ways they're the easiest part of a kitchen installation. But they must be installed carefully and with attention to detail, especially the finished surfaces. With adequate preparation, most cabinets can be installed in an average kitchen in a single day.

PREPARATION WORK

You must install cabinets level and square, whether the surface to which they're attached is level and square or not. Use a level and a straight, 6- to 8-foot-length of lumber to locate and mark the high spots on the floor, walls, and ceiling or soffit. A soffit is shown on page 181. If high spots can't be sanded or chipped down, shim out the cabinets to clear them as described here.

When the high spots on wall and ceiling surfaces have been found and marked, draw a layout of the cabinets full size on the walls and floor. The layout should be drawn from reference marks made to match the high spots. For instance, the highest spot on the floor that will contact a cabinet bottom may be 1/2 inch above the floor at the wall line. Use the stick and the level to transfer this height to the walls. Draw a level line on the wall at that height. Then lay out the base cabinets up from the level line rather than from the floor.

Similarly, use the level to transfer the height of the lowest spot on the ceiling or soffit to the wall. Draw a level line on the wall at that height and lay out the wall cabinets down from that line. If your cabinets don't butt up under a soffit or ceiling, measure up from your bottom reference line 54 inches and draw a level line around the walls. This line marks the bottom of a standard 30-inch-tall wall cabinet. Other sizes can be measured up or down from the line. For more information on planning cabinet heights, see pages 38-39.

If you have any full-height cabinets in your plan, measure from the soffit or ceiling down to the floor level line at the cabinet location. Check this measurement against the dimensions of the full-height cabinets. Cabinets should have 1/4-inch minimum clearance from the ceiling. If they don't, check the cabinet manufacturer's literature to see if the cabinets can be trimmed.

On many full-height cabinets, the top can be trimmed, if necessary. On others, you'll have to trim the base or toe-board area. In the latter case, you'll also have to trim the toe boards of all the base cabinets to match. If you run into this problem, consider reworking the high spot on the floor or the low area of the soffit, especially in a kitchen with a lot of cabinets.

If the full-height cabinets fit under the soffit or ceiling, don't be concerned if they extend above the level guideline you've marked at the soffit or ceiling location. Start the next wall cabinet slightly dropped down on the side of the full-height cabinet.

Look over the cabinet layout on the wall to make sure available moldings and fillers will cover any gaps that will occur. Don't be tempted to slope a cabinet run to close a gap. If gaps at tops of upper cabinets are going to be large, rework the soffit or ceiling to alleviate the problem.

Gaps in base cabinets usually occur where the toe board meets the floor. That's easily fixed by installing a dummy toe board over the existing one when you trim out the rest of the kitchen.

Tap with a hammer to find the approximate locations of studs in walls where cabinets will be hung. Then use a nail to verify exact locations of stud centers and mark them. Make sure you locate the exact center of the studs, because the cabinet-mounting screws will be carrying a lot of weight. The most convenient location for the stud marks is above the back of the base cabinets. The marks will later be covered by the countertop backsplash.

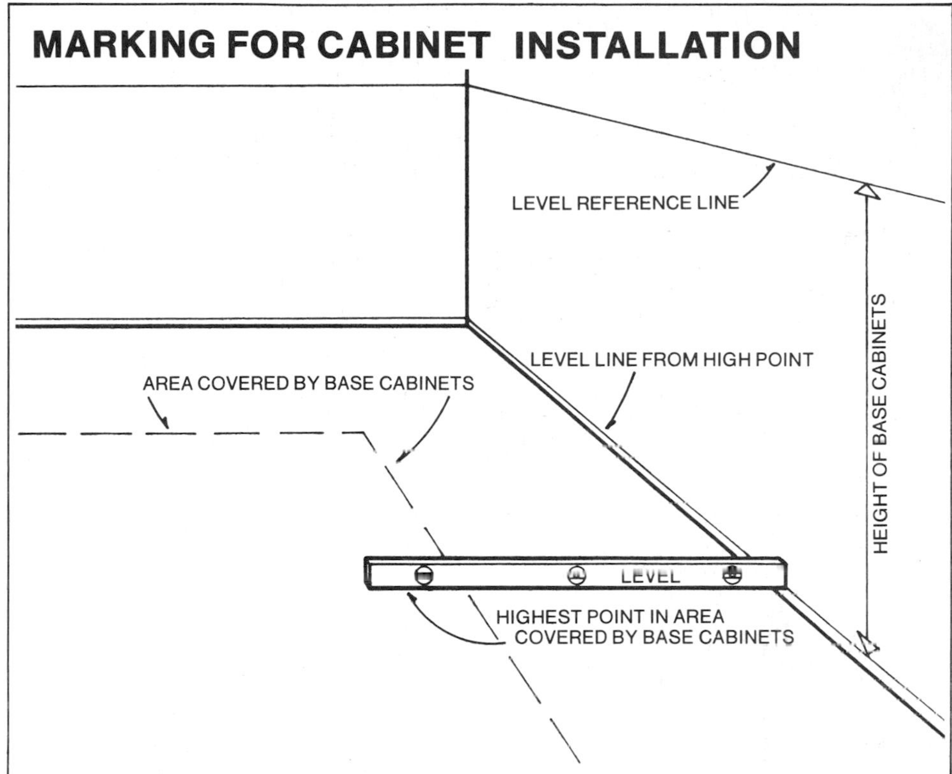

Locate and mark high spots on wall, floor and ceiling. You can either rework wall to eliminate high spots, or shim cabinets to clear them.

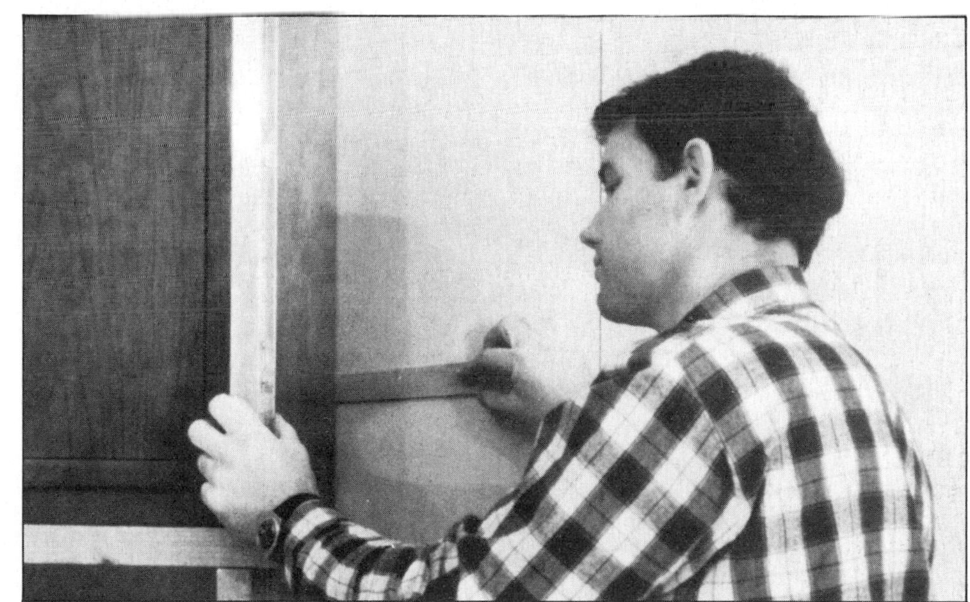

Level first wall cabinet and shim in correct position.

WHICH COMES FIRST?

If you don't have any full-height cabinets, install wall cabinets first, without base cabinets in your way. If you have a full-height cabinet located at a logical starting point for the cabinets, install it first. Then install wall cabinets and finally, base cabinets. If you have full-height cabinets in difficult locations such as the middle of a cabinet run, start with the base cabinets. If you're applying plastic laminate to the wall between countertop and wall cabinets, do this before mounting wall cabinets.

INSTALLING WALL CABINETS

Before installing factory-made cabinets, open each carton and inspect the cabinet. Make sure the cabinet is the right size and type, and there hasn't been any shipping damage. Then slip it back into the carton to protect it. Custom-made cabinets may not come as individual units like factory cabinets. They may be in larger subassemblies. Carefully check custom-made cabinets when they're delivered, not only for transit damage, but for flaws and dimensional errors.

Installing the First Cabinet—The first cabinet must be installed carefully because it will determine level, plumb and exact height for all the rest. Start with a corner cabinet, if possible. Line it up to the marks on the wall, particularly the soffit- or ceiling-level line.

Using your level as a guide, insert shims as needed to get the cabinet absolutely plumb and level in all directions. *Shim-shingles* are low-grade cedar shingles made up in small bundles for this use.

Select shims only a little thicker at the thick end than the space you're shimming. Otherwise the thick end of the shingle sticking out beyond the side of the cabinet will interfere with the fit of the next cabinet. If you can't find a shim shingle the right thickness, select a thicker one, mark it and cut off some of the thick end. The quickest way to cut shim shingles is with a large pair of *diagonal wire cutters.* See photo at right. Crunch the shingle on the cut line from one side, and then from the other. Then snap it off with the cutters.

By now you may be wondering how you're supposed to hold a bulky wall cabinet in precise position while you cut and fit shims, hold the level and do the rest of the fitting work. Even a couple of strong helpers may tire before you can get all the fitting work done. There are three basic methods of holding a cabinet in position while you work on it. Which you use depends on the circumstances of the job.

If you've already installed the base cabinets and either the finish countertop or a temporary one, make a four-sided frame of 1x2s or 1x3s. Nail four scrap pieces together so two sides of the frame are slightly longer than the distance between countertop and wall-cabinet bottom.

If cabinet bottoms are at two different heights, construct the adjacent sides of the frame to fit the second height. That way you can use the frame in one place on its side and the other on its end. Tack a scrap of carpet or old towel on two sides to pad it.

The frame is used by warping it into a parallelogram and wedging it under the cabinet you're working on. Angle the frame away from the corner or previously installed cabinet, so the cabinet you're working on is stable. Position the frame forward of the cabinet centerline so the cabinet leans against the wall. A little experimentation will enable you to perch a cabinet on the frame and make position adjustments without disturbing cabinet stability.

One innovative cabinet installer padded the seat of an old-fashion piano stool and used this on the countertop to position and support wall cabinets. It was the kind that has a large screw and a round top, so that he could adjust the height by spinning the top of the stool.

If you haven't installed base cabinets, make up a *T-brace* by nailing a short length of 1x3 or 1x4 to the top of a length of 2x4. The vertical 2x4 should be a little longer than the most common floor-to-wall-cabinet distance. Pad the crossbar with a scrap of carpet or an old towel. The T-brace is used as a prop to position the wall cabinet you're working on.

Angle the bottom of the T-brace slightly outward, and position the top of the T-brace forward of the center of the cabinet. You'll soon find the right position for the cabinet to rest securely so you can work on it.

If the wall between the countertop and the wall cabinets has not been finished yet, nail a 1x3 or 1x4 cleat to the wall with the upper edge on the lower cabinet line. Then lower the back edge of the wall cabinet on the cleat. If there is a soffit or ceiling immediately above, the cabinet can be pinned in place by tapping a shim shingle into the space between the top rail of the cabinet and the surface above, as shown on the facing page. Or the T-brace or frame mentioned above can be used to support the front edge.

Anchoring—When the first wall cabinet is resting securely in place and is

Use diagonal wire cutters to cut shim shingles. Mark shingle, crunch one side with cutters, then opposite side. Use cutters to snap shingle.

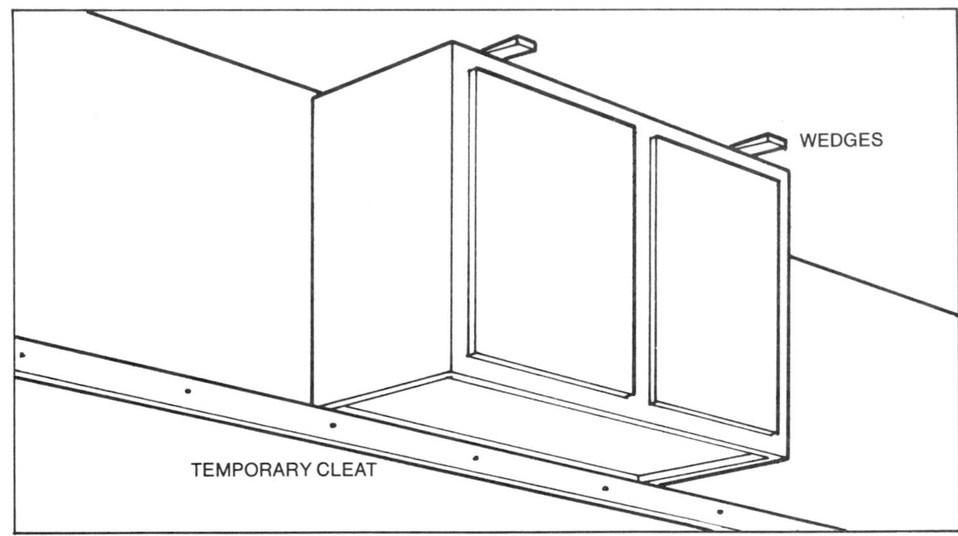

Use cleat at bottom and wedge at top to temporarily pin wall cabinet in place.

correctly shimmed and leveled, drill 3/32-inch holes in the mounting rails for screws. Attach the cabinet with two screws to every stud it crosses. Locate one screw 1/2 to 3/4 inch above the floor of the cabinet, and one 1/2 to 3/4 inch down from the top. If mounting screws come with the cabinets, use them. Otherwise, use #7x1-3/4-inch pan-head screws as a minimum size. Drive screws almost tight. Make sure all shims are equally clamped by the cabinet. Recheck level and plumb frequently as you work. Then fully tighten the screws and remove the support.

If shims do not adequately support the mounting rails in the cabinet back, the cabinet may warp or pull apart when the mounting screws are tightened down. Slight warping will be apparent on inspection. The cabinet door will no longer be completely square with the cabinet frame. Or the door may appear to be warped. If this happens, loosen the cabinet-mounting screws one at a time until you find the source of the problem. Then reshim to correct the condition.

Installing the Next Cabinet—Once you have the first cabinet in place, the installation technique changes slightly. Prop the second cabinet in place next to the first one and roughly shim it into position. Carefully align the front frames with each other and clamp them together with two padded C-clamps. The better you match up the front frames, the better the finished job will look.

Drill two 3/32-inch holes edgeways through one front frame and a short distance into the other. Countersink the holes and drive in two #7 flat-head wood screws of appropriate length. This permanently ties the two frames together and gives a smooth line to the exposed cabinet fronts.

Make final shim adjustments and put in the mounting screws, as you did with the first cabinet. Repeat this process for successive cabinets.

INSTALLING BASE CABINETS

Base cabinets are much easier to install than wall cabinets. No props or helpers are needed to install them, although a helper makes the work go faster.

Installing the First Cabinet—As with wall cabinets, install the first cabinet at a corner. Shim up the cabinet and level it to the wall reference line. Then drill a 3/32-inch hole through the upper mounting rail of the cabinet at each stud mark. The hole should be about an inch down from the top of the cabinet. Insert a #7x2-1/2-inch pan-head screw each hole and drive into stud. As with wall cabinets, draw the screws down lightly and check for warpage.

On a base cabinet, it's easy to see warping or twisting taking place as you tighten the screws. Check door and drawer fronts. Drawers sometimes need final adjustment, but the doors should remain in alignment with the face frame and each other. They should not look warped.

If the corner cabinet is a Lazy Susan or a reach-in cabinet that doesn't extend all the way to the wall, install a 1x3 or 1x4 cleat to support the countertop. Attach the cleat at the corners and to the closest studs out from the corners, using the same techniques as for a cabinet.

Installing the Next Cabinet—Place the second cabinet next to the first, and shim it into position. Then clamp the front faces of the two cabinets tightly together with two padded C-clamps. Drill two 3/32-inch holes edgeways through one of the front frames and partway into the other. Countersink the holes and drive in two #7 flat-head screws. Shim the back edge of the cabinet as required. Screw the cabinet to the studs as you

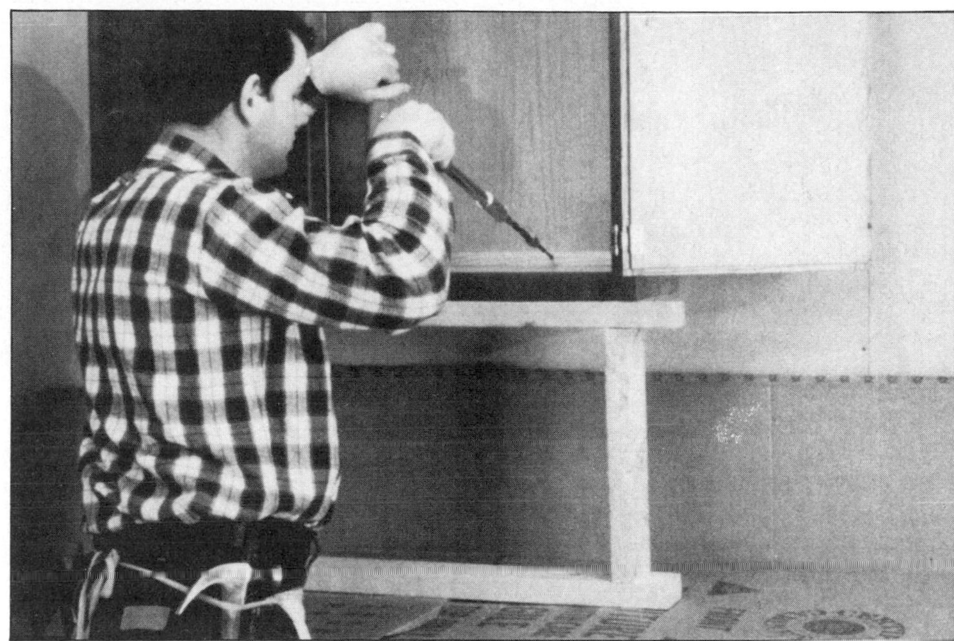

Attach cabinet to wall by driving screws through top and bottom mounting rails of cabinet into wall studs. Frame used to provide temporary support for cabinet is described on facing page.

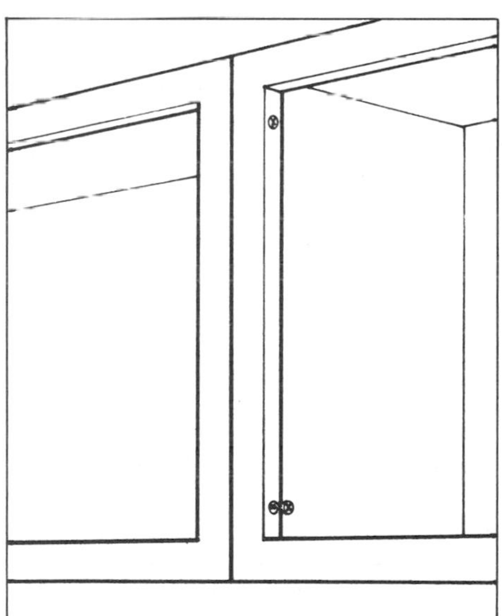

Use screws to connect face frames of first and second wall cabinets cabinets before shimming second cabinet.

When tightening mounting screws, be careful not to warp cabinet. One indication of warp is misaligned doors, as shown here. Loosening screws and reshimming will correct problem.

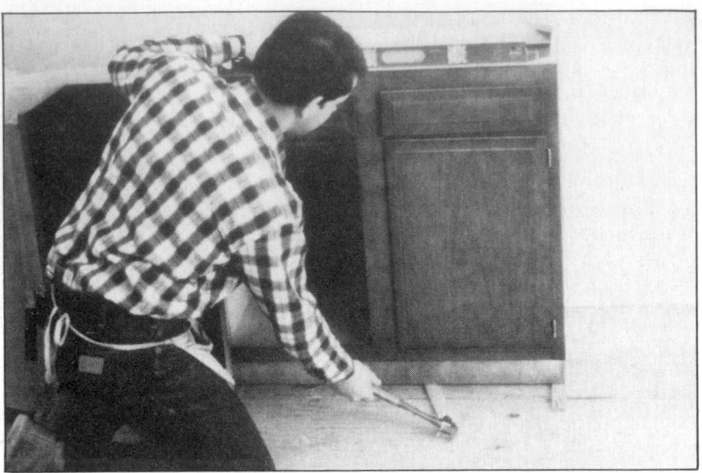

Drive shims under base cabinet to level.

Attach base cabinet to wall by driving screws through mounting rails into studs. If there's a gap between cabinet back and wall, use spacer blocks behind screws to prevent cabinet from warping.

If floor is uneven and you must shim base cabinets up from floor, use additional piece of toe board or base-shoe molding to cover gap.

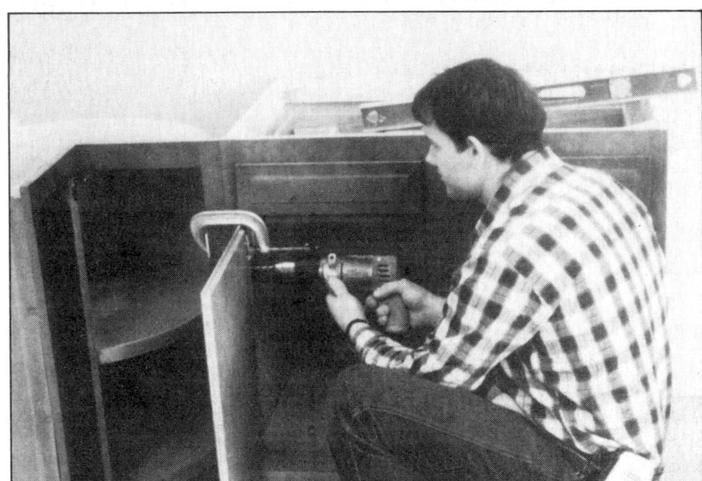

Connect face frames of base cabinets together the same as with wall cabinets.

did with the first one. Repeat this process for successive cabinets.

Spaces for Appliances—To bridge the gap where an appliance will be installed, use two straight 6 or 8 foot lengths of 1x3 or 1x4. Clamp these to the top front and top rear of the cabinets you've already installed, so they extend across the appliance location. Measure and mark on the wood strips the rough-in width of the appliance. Use the wood strips as guides for the setting of the next base cabinet. Double-check for the correct rough-in dimension at the bottom of the gap, both front and rear, before you anchor the cabinet.

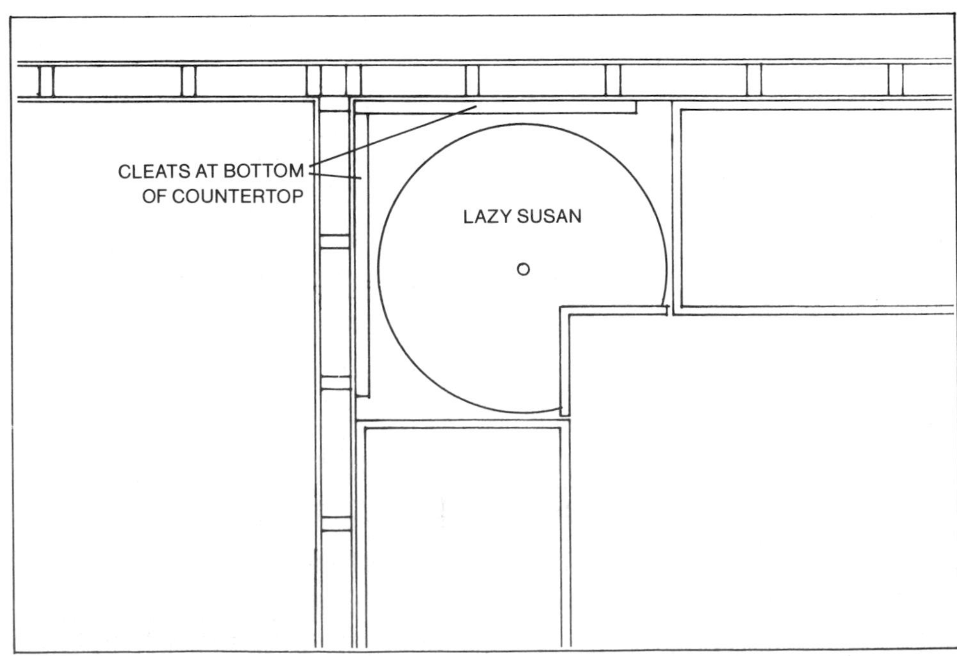

When installing a Lazy Susan, attach cleats to wall, level adjacent cabinet tops. Cleats support countertop at back edge.

FILLERS

Custom-made cabinets are generally made to exact measurements. But factory-made cabinets come in fixed sizes, usually in 3-inch increments. If you have a space that's 10 feet 2-1/4 inches long, you can only fit in 10 feet of factory cabinets. The last 2-1/4 inches is closed off with a *filler.* Fillers commonly come in 3- and 6-inch widths. They can be cut to narrower widths. Every cabinet manufacturer can supply prefinished fillers to match their cabinets.

Fillers can be installed at the end of a cabinet run or in the middle between two cabinets. But fillers have another use besides simply taking up space. They separate cabinets and appliances so both can function correctly. This is most important at corners. Most cabinets and many appliances have doors or handles that project beyond their faces. When placed at right angles to another cabinet or appliance, projecting doors or handles can interfere with operation of adjacent doors or drawers.

If possible, avoid placing an appliance directly in a corner. Water splashed from a dishwasher or heat from an open oven door can damage adjacent cabinets. If you have to locate an appliance near a corner, use at least a 3-inch filler on each side of corner to provide clearance for doors and drawers.

Fillers can be trimmed to desired width or lapped behind adjacent cabinets to fit. If used at a corner, a filler can provide clearance *and* lengthen a cabinet run, solving two problems.

Installing Fillers—Attach fillers to adjoining cabinets with screws through the front frame of the cabinet. If two fillers meet at a corner, screw them together into an L before attaching. Some cabinet manufacturers supply preassembled L-shape corner fillers.

Wide Stiles—Some cabinet manufacturers eliminate need for fillers by providing cabinets with extra-wide stiles on one or both sides. Sometimes these can be made to exact measurements, but wider stiles are usually a standard oversize such as 3 inches. Trim or lap oversize stile to exact width the same as a separate filler.

COUNTERTOPS AND BACKSPLASHES

When the cabinets are installed, install the countertops. The easiest type to install is the post-form countertop, though its use has limits. Butcher block, synthetic marble and DuPont Corian complete the list of materials that can be applied directly over the base cabinets. Plastic laminate and ceramic tile require the construction of a platform or substructure on the base cabinets.

POST-FORM TOPS

When you buy post-form top material, get pieces larger than your measurements. Buy an extra 3 inches for each overhanging end and an extra inch for each flush end. The mitered ends come precut. Make sure which miters are supposed to be left-hand and which right-hand. You can't turn the piece over to reverse the miter. To replace an existing top, refer to page 67 for instructions on removal of the old top.

Problem Miters—If your walls and corners aren't square, avoid using a post-form countertop. To check a miter cut, turn the piece over on a padded surface. Use a framing square to draw a line from the front end of the miter cut, square to the back edge of the countertop. Then measure from the line to the back corner of the miter. This measurement should be exactly the same as the overall width of the countertop. If it isn't, the miter isn't cut correctly. Take the top back to the dealer.

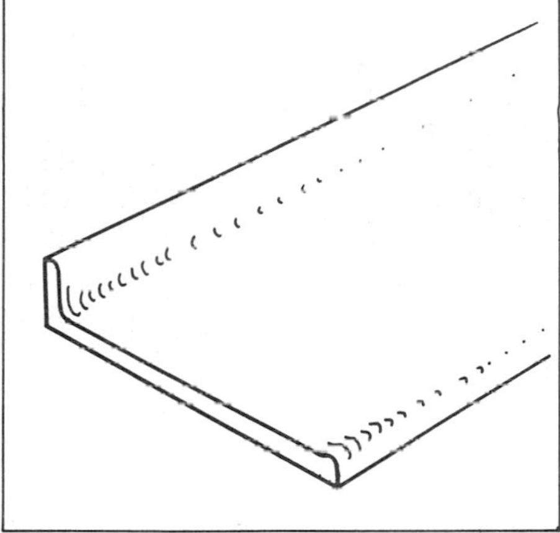

Post-form countertop material is sold by the running foot, usually in 2-foot increments. Check cut ends for square when you buy top. Cut ends must be covered with end cap.

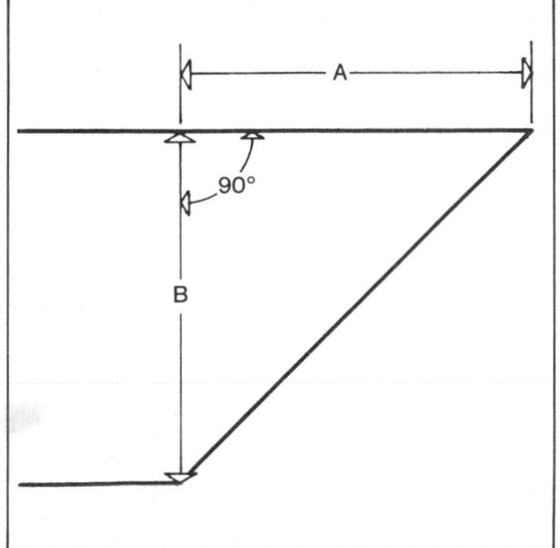

Check precut miters on post-form tops to make sure they're cut exact. Distances A and B, shown above, should be equal.

Rough Cutting—If your new top isn't yet in the correct number of pieces, refer to your sketch and recheck the measurements. To allow for trimming, add 3 inches to each overhang and at least 1 inch to each flush end. Transfer the measurements to the top material, using a rafter square. Double check all factory cuts for square before doing any cutting of your own. Factory cuts aren't often off. When they are, you'll have to return the top to the dealer.

Where you mark cut lines depends on what tool you're using to cut the tops. If you're using a circular saw or saber saw, mark and cut the top from the underside. That way the saw teeth cut into the finish surface instead of out of it. If you get confused while marking the underside, mark the top side first. Then mark the underside and make sure your marks match.

Handsaws and tablesaws cut away from you, so for them you can mark and cut from the top side. Fine-tooth plywood blades and finish blades work best. Make cuts to the outside of your marks, especially on the finish cuts. Don't cut down the middle of the line.

Fitting—Drop each rough piece into place and check for problems. Mark each end on the underside where it clears the cabinet below. If some of the pieces are similar, number them on the bottom. Write the number on the wall behind the piece location.

The countertop ends at the stove location should be adjusted to the stove rough-in dimension. All other open ends should be given an overhang equal to the front overhang and marked for final cutting. Cross out any earlier marks so you don't cut off the overhang by mistake.

Cutouts—With the top pieces in their locations, mark off any cutouts that have to be made. Fixtures such as sinks can be turned upside-down on the countertop for marking. Position the sink or other fixture upside-down on the countertop. Use a tape measure to make sure the sink is square to the top. Run a pencil around the edge, then measure in from your marks the width of the rim. Lay out the cut lines. If you have any trouble working out exact locations for cutouts, measure inside the cabinet on the underside of the top to find a centerpoint. Then drive a nail through from underneath and measure from the nail. Make sure at this point that the items you're installing will clear the cabinet structure below.

Make cutouts after you've made the final end cuts. Match the corner radius of the fixture that goes in the cutout. Bore a hole at each corner from the top side. Flip the top over and connect the holes from underneath with a saber saw or a router. If you're cutting with a handsaw, work from the finish side instead.

End Caps—When all pieces are cut, sand the open ends to prepare them for the precut end caps. Use a hard wood block behind the sandpaper to keep the cut surface perfectly flat. Angle sanding strokes away from the finish surface so you don't chip it. Take your time sanding. It makes a big difference in the appearance of the finished job. Trial-fit end caps frequently as you sand. When you're satisfied with the fit, glue on the end caps. Use the same gluing procedures as for plastic laminate, page 163.

Mounting—With the top off the cabinets, drill a vertical 3/16-inch hole in the front and back corner blocks of the cabinets. Holes should clear the threads of the screws you're using to anchor the top—#10 drive screws are recommended. Screws should be long enough to extend about two-thirds the way into the countertop.

If you have help to lift a large assembly, assemble miters and bolt them solidly together. Use special *miter bolts,* available from the countertop supplier. Drop the assembled top into position. If you don't have help for a large assembly, position pieces on the cabinets before you assemble miters.

Insert drive screws up through the predrilled holes. Drive them into the top. A magnetic bit in a variable-speed drill is the best tool for driving these screws. If you use a screwdriver, drill pilot holes for screws.

Caulking—When the top is fastened in place, run a bead of tub-and-tile caulk along the joint between the wall and the backsplash. If the colors of the top or the wall are strong, use colored latex exterior caulk. Pump some of the caulk down behind the backsplash as you go. Apply the bead about a yard at a time, then quickly go back and squeegee the excess off with a wet finger. The amount of caulk that builds up on your finger as you do this will indicate whether you're putting on too much caulk.

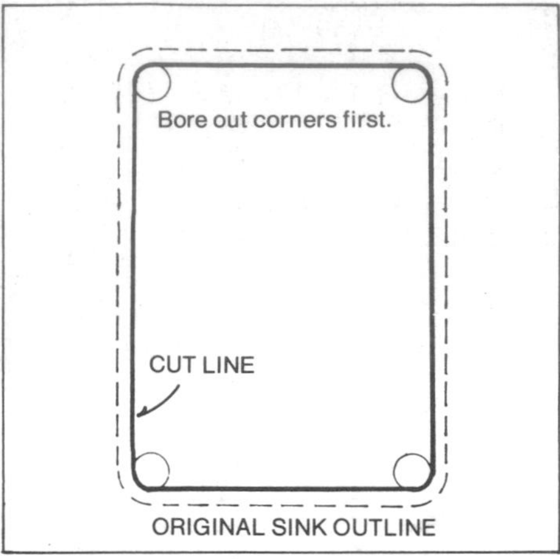

Flip new sink over and align carefully before marking outline on countertop. Inset cutting line from tracing so sink doesn't fall through cutout. Same process works for other fixtures to be mounted in cutout.

Drill out corners of sink outline before cutting. Square corners tend to start cracks.

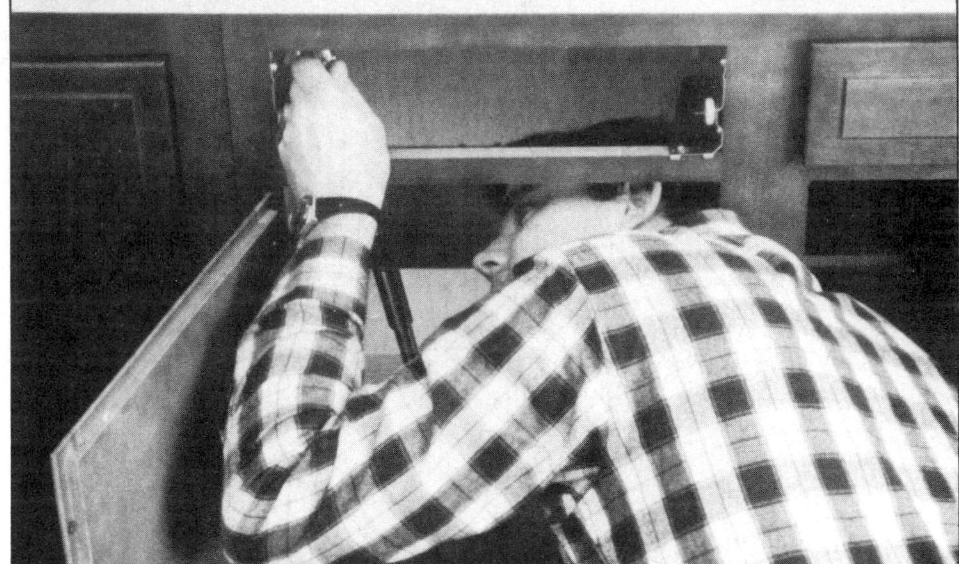

Tie new top down solidly from below. Choose screws that extend about 2/3 the way into top.

ROUGH TOP FOR LAMINATE OR TILE

Plastic laminate and ceramic tile are the two most common materials for countertops. If you're planning to use either one, you'll need a platform or substructure to put them on.

Materials—When you select material for the rough top, consider the finish materials, and the location of the top. Particle board works well under plastic laminates and is commonly used. It's inexpensive and provides a smooth surface for gluing laminates. But particle board is hard on saw blades, tends to be brittle and can disintegrate when repeatedly exposed to water. On installations with long overhangs or other structural problems, or those with potential for water exposure, use plywood. This especially applies to ceramic-tile surfaces. The grout joints are susceptible to water leaks.

Whichever material you use, the thickness should be 3/4 inch. Plywood should be grade-marked PTS (plugged, touched, sanded) on at least one side. Plywood stamped "interior with exterior glue" is preferable. Use exterior grade if water exposure will be severe.

Layout and Cutting—Make a sketch of the countertop area. If you'll be applying plastic laminate, plan how you'll lay it out. Butt joints in the rough top should not coincide with butt joints in the laminate. It's easier to adjust rough-top layout than laminate layout.

Measure, cut, and fit according to the layout. Add a 1-1/2-inch overhang on all open edges as you do. If the top will have a wood edging, add 3/4 inch instead of 1-1/2 inch. Start with a piece that extends into a corner and work out from there. On tricky areas, rough out a piece, put it in place, and mark it for finish cutting.

If the kitchen has wavy walls, the rough top should be fitted to them. Cut to the finish-top width plus a little more than the maximum depth of the wall irregularities. Then tape a pencil to a small piece of scrap wood. Hold the block flat against the wall at the biggest gap with the pencil point down. Move the top piece away from the wall to where the pencil can just mark the piece. Then run the block and the pencil along the wall to mark a line. Cut on the line and the piece should fit perfectly. Refer to pages 163-164 for instructions on backsplash installation for wavy walls.

Assembly—When the rough top parts are cut and set in their final location, take them off the cabinets. Reassemble the parts of the rough top in their correct positions, upside down, on a reasonably flat and level floor.

Before you assemble the countertop, make sure you can turn it right side up after assembly. An L-shaped countertop with two 16-foot arms will not turn over in a room with an 8-foot ceiling. It doesn't matter how big the room is, just how high the ceiling is. If you run into this problem, assemble the countertop in manageable sections and do the final assembly rightside up.

Tie all splices together with corrugated fasteners and glue. Cut trim strips of the same 3/4-inch material about 3 inches wide. Glue and nail them to the perimeter of the top. Use 1-1/4-inch annular-ring nails. No clamping is required. Match the edges as carefully as possible while you're doing this—it saves a lot of work later. Stagger splices in strips so they stiffen the splices in the rough top itself.

Final Fitting and Cutouts—If the rough top is big, get someone to help move it. Pick the top up, turn it over, and try it on top of the cabinets. If you've moved any of the pieces when reconstructing the top upside down, small corrections may be required. Trim, fill or otherwise rework to get a good fit. The fit doesn't have to be perfect—within 1/16 inch or so is OK.

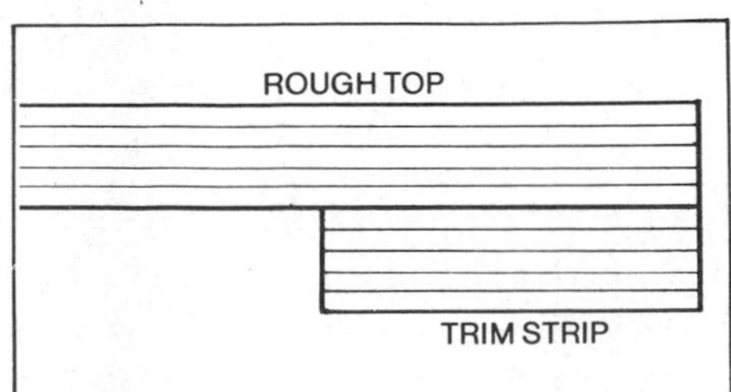

Cut and attach trim strip to bottom edges of rough countertop. Strips are cut from countertop material and are about 3 inches wide.

Mark exact locations of cutouts. Items like sinks can be turned over, positioned on the rough top, and traced in. Offset the cut lines inside the mark by the width of the sink rim. Otherwise the sink will fall through the hole. Other top-mounted appliances will have either a trim ring or a template packed in the box with them. Make sure there is clearance underneath the counter for the equipment. If you have difficulty centering a cutout, find its center underneath the countertop by measuring. Drive a nail up through the top and take measurements from the nail.

Once the cutouts are marked—and checked—drill a hole that matches the radius at each corner of each cutout. Make straight cuts with a circular saw or saber saw. Make cuts carefully, because you'll be trimming the finish material to the cutouts. Excess cutout could be visible in the finished job.

Backsplashes—While the finished rough top is sitting in place, measure and cut backsplashes, if your countertop will have them. The standard height for backsplashes is 4 inches, but you can make them higher, lower, or omit them altogether.

Remove countertop from cabinets to mount backsplashes. Drill a row of 3/16-inch holes in the countertop about 1 foot apart. Center holes on a straight line, 3/8 inch in from the back edge of the top. Countersink holes on the underside of the countertop to accept flat-head wood screws.

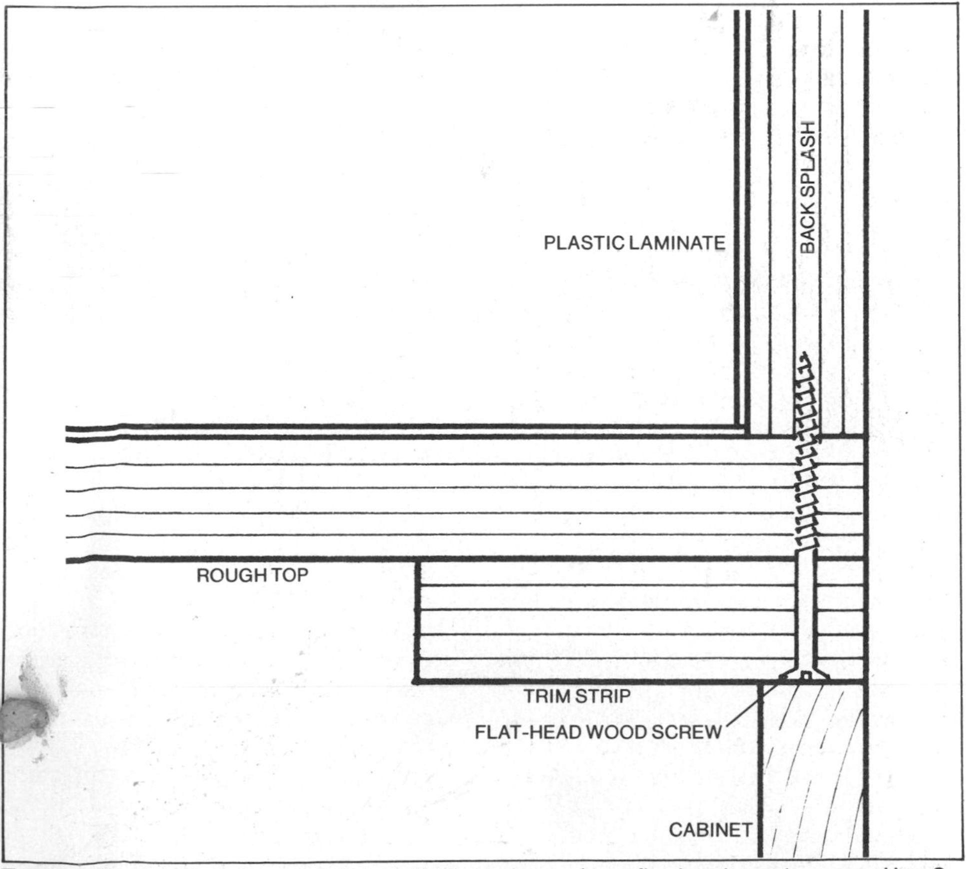

To attach backsplash to countertop, drill pilot holes and use flat-head wood screws. Use C-clamps to hold backsplash in position while drilling holes and attaching screws.

Line up the backsplash sections and clamp them in place with C-clamps. Drive in flat-head screws from the bottom. Also use wood screws to tie the backsplash pieces together at corners.

Mounting—Before anchoring the rough top to the cabinets, do any sanding and squaring that might be difficult to do later. Watch edges and surfaces that will be adjacent to the wall. If you're going to use plastic laminate for the top, everything needs to be flat and square. Use a hard sanding block and a small plane to smooth any rough edges. Do final sanding and cleaning up after mounting.

To fasten the top in place, lift it off the cabinets if you haven't already done so. Drill vertical 3/16-inch holes in the corner blocks of the cabinets. Then move the top back into final position and drive in screws from underneath. Use #10x1-1/4-inch hex-head drive screws. A magnetic screw bit in a variable speed drill is the quickest way to drive the screws. Do not use glue to attach the top—you might need to remove it sometime in the future.

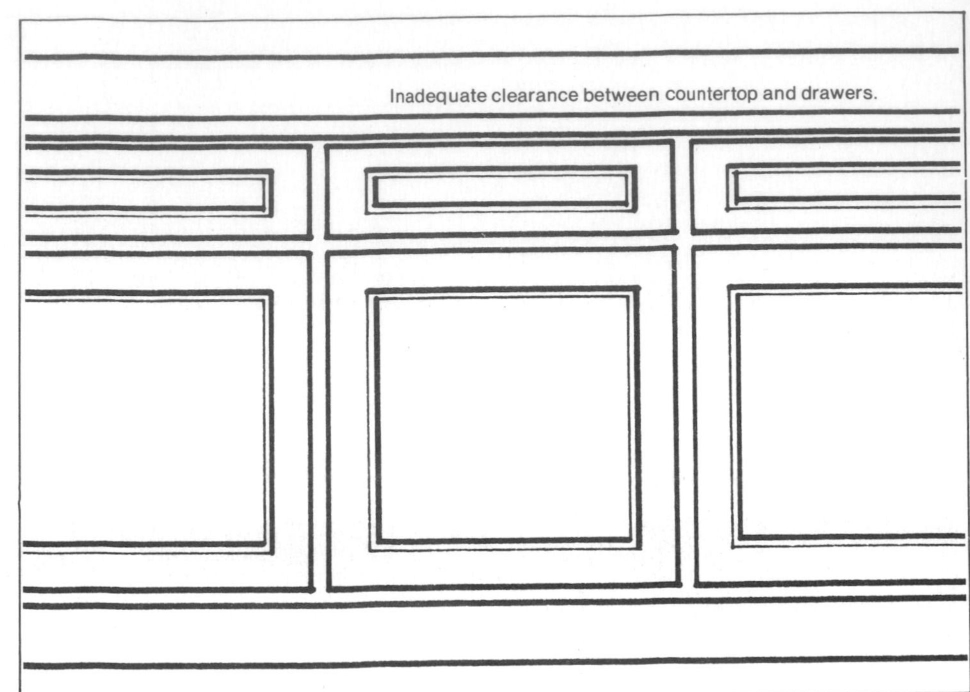

When mounting rough top, make sure there's at least 1-1/2 inches clearance between base-cabinet drawers and top. Countertop above is too close to drawers, resulting in a finger-pinching situation. Install thicker trim strips if necessary.

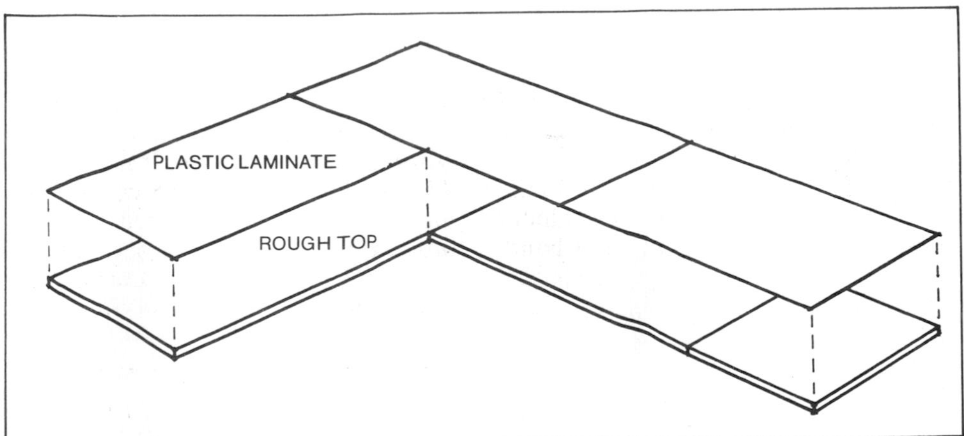

Cut laminate pieces so joints don't align with those of rough top.

PLASTIC LAMINATE

Before starting any project with plastic laminate, reread the earlier section on safety, pages 72-73. If you're using solvent-base contact cement, read label directions carefully, and follow them. The principal dangers are explosions and overexposure to fumes. Solvent fumes can dull your thinking, which can lead to a progressive carelessness. This carelessness can lead to injuries, or to severe overexposure.

Solvent fumes can be explosive. Even a stray spark from a switch, electric motor or power tool can set them off, causing an explosion. Extinguish all open flames, including pilot lights. Provide good ventilation to the work area or do the work outside. If you can't do either, use the slower but safer water-base contact cement.

Preparation—Thoroughly clean the plastic laminate and the surface you're applying it to. Remove all grease, oil, wax and sawdust.

New laminate can be applied over existing laminate. The existing surface must be roughened thoroughly with coarse sandpaper and cleaned with mineral spirits or alcohol.

If the surface is the least bit loose, all loose material must be removed. In this case, check the compatibility of the new adhesive with the old. If the old surface is in poor condition, you may prefer to rip it out and build a new rough top. Fill small surface imperfections with floor-patching compound.

Layout and Cutting—Lay out all cuts on the plastic laminate with a grease pencil or washable felt-tip marker. Leave 1 inch excess material on all sides to allow for trimming. Lay out pieces so the straight, factory edges can be used for butt joints where pieces will meet. If the job is complicated, or if you haven't ordered enough extra material, you may have to make paper patterns. This allows you to make more exact cuts and to save layout time.

You can make all rough cuts with a power circular saw. Tape heavy paper to the bottom of the saw to protect the laminate. Sheet-metal shears also work. Most straight cuts in plastic laminate can also be made with a special carbide-tipped scriber and a steel straightedge. Score the face of the plastic laminate deeply with the scriber. Then insert a strip of wood under the score line and push down to snap off the piece.

Cementing—If you are making a self-edge top, coat the countertop edges with contact cement. Also coat the backs of appropriate laminate pieces.

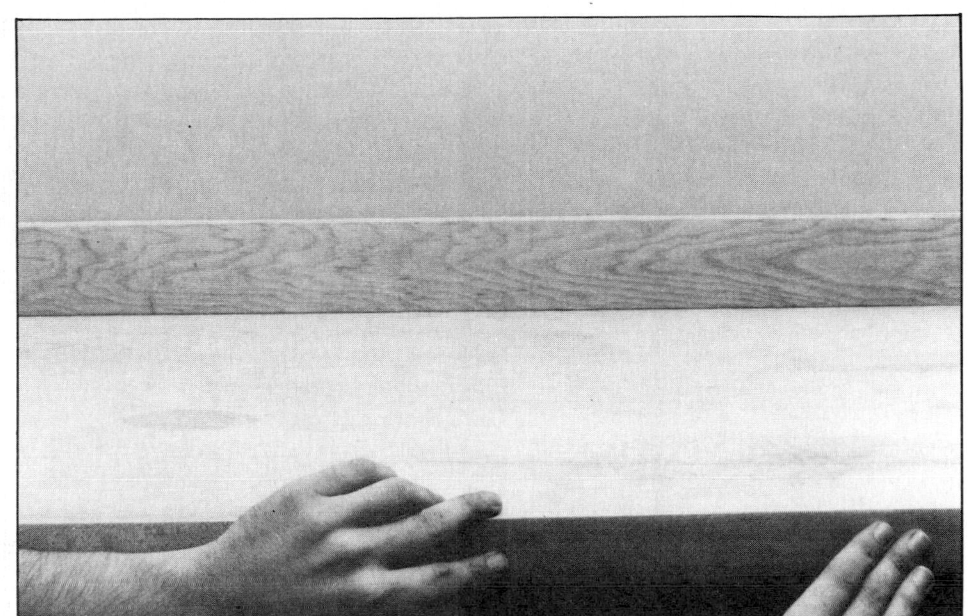
Apply laminate on ends, then long edges, then on the main surfaces. Plan on making the exposed edges as unobtrusive as possible.

Apply side pieces first, then front edges, then top pieces. Contact cements have open times from 20 minutes to 2 hours, so there's no need to rush. After application, the contact cement is ready when it's tacky, but no longer tends to lift when you touch it with your finger.

If dull spots appear anywhere in the cement coatings, it means the cement has been absorbed and will not bond. If this happens, let the surface dry, then recoat. The first coat will serve as a sealer.

Laminate edge pieces over 3 feet in length require help with alignment when you attach them to the top. On long pieces, a small misalignment at one end can turn into several inches misalignment at the other. Once the two coated surfaces come into contact, they're stuck permanently in that position. You can't adjust them. Clean any contact cement off your hands before touching coated surfaces.

After you've applied the laminate to the edges, tap it into contact with a padded wood block and a hammer. Use a hand towel wrapped around a length of 2x4.

Trimming—Trimming the overhanging edges of plastic laminate is the most intimidating part of the whole job. While it can be done with a saw, plane, file and sandpaper, it's difficult and tedious that way. The best way to trim laminate is with a router. If you have a router, or are borrowing or renting one, be sure to get the required bits.

Special router bits are made for plastic laminates. These bits have small ball bearings to guide the cut. In a pinch, or for a small job, you can use similar bits made to be chucked in your electric drill. Don't try to do a big job with a drill-mounted bit. Your drill is designed for thrusting forces, not lateral forces. Drill bearings will survive small jobs, but not large ones.

Horizontal Surfaces—After the plastic-laminate edge strips are trimmed flush with the surface of the rough top, apply contact cement to the top and to the laminate. On large, horizontal surfaces, use spacers between the top and the laminate to keep the two separated until you adjust the laminate to its final position. Use wood strips, metal rods or thin strips of cardboard for spacers.

Lay spacer strips so they prevent contact until you're ready to attach the laminate. Position strips so you can withdraw them as you lower the laminate to the top. Make sure spacers won't leave any debris, such as splinters or sawdust, in the cement.

When the laminate is positioned over the rough top, start sticking down the laminate at the tightest location, such as a corner. Ease out the spacers and let the laminate down until all the spacers are out.

Beat the laminate firmly into place with a padded block and a hammer, especially along the edges. Trim it with a router. The final edge can be trimmed square, or with a bevel. Use fine sandpaper and a block to remove any sharp edges. Make any cutouts and trim off the surplus material with a router.

Laminate on Walls—Plastic laminate is sometimes applied to the exposed wall between the upper and lower cabinets. Do this before the upper cabinets are mounted. Refer back to your cabinet layout and mark the

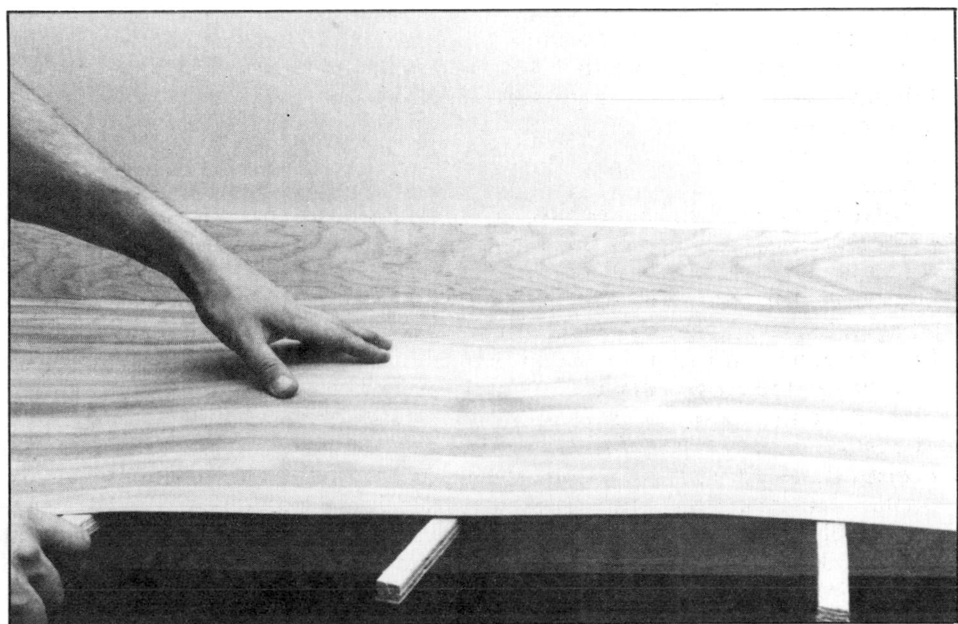
For large horizontal areas, use spacers. A small misalignment can grow to inches in 8 or 10 feet. Here, wood strips are used to hold up glued laminate. Brown wrapping paper keeps laminate between strips from contacting rough top. Strips and paper are carefully removed as laminate is pressed into place.

upper-cabinet locations on the walls. Then lay out and cut laminate pieces that extend up behind the cabinets. You may have trouble getting a completely tight joint between the wall and the countertop. If so, use a metal-cove molding to hide the gap.

Most wall surfaces require at least one extra coat of contact cement, due to absorption. Usually, the wall laminate can be easily tilted into place.

Wavy-Wall Problems—If you have wavy walls to work to, use a standard 4-inch backsplash. But you have to approach the job somewhat differently than the standard method described on page 161. Instead of attaching the rough backsplash to the rough top, leave it loose. Also leave the rough top loose from the cabinets. Scribe the rough top to fit the wall, as described on page 161.

Apply laminate to both the rough top and the backsplash. Then drill a row of 3/16-inch holes every 8 inches along the back edge of the top, about 3/8 inch in from the edge. Run a thin bead of tub-and-tile caulk along the line of holes. Position one end of a backsplash section so the back of the backsplash is flush with the scribed back edge of the counter. Position a padded C-clamp next to each of two or three screw holes and tighten. Then drive in the first two or three wood screws to pin the backsplash into place. Do not remove the C-clamps.

Warp the backsplash in or out until it lines up at the next screw hole, and apply another clamp. When you have another two or three holes lined up, put the screws in. After several feet have been fastened, remove the first of the clamps and reuse them. Continue until the backsplash is securely fastened in place.

The backsplash should now fit the wall at least as well as your original scribing of the rough top. A careful caulking job at the top of the backsplash should take care of any remaining gap.

Use a wet paper towel to clean up excess caulk as you work. The caulk may get smeared around by the backsplash, so you may have to reapply caulk when necessary.

CERAMIC TILE

Tile looks like it's expensive and difficult to install. It used to be, when it was set in a thick mortar bed. But new adhesives have made tile work easy.

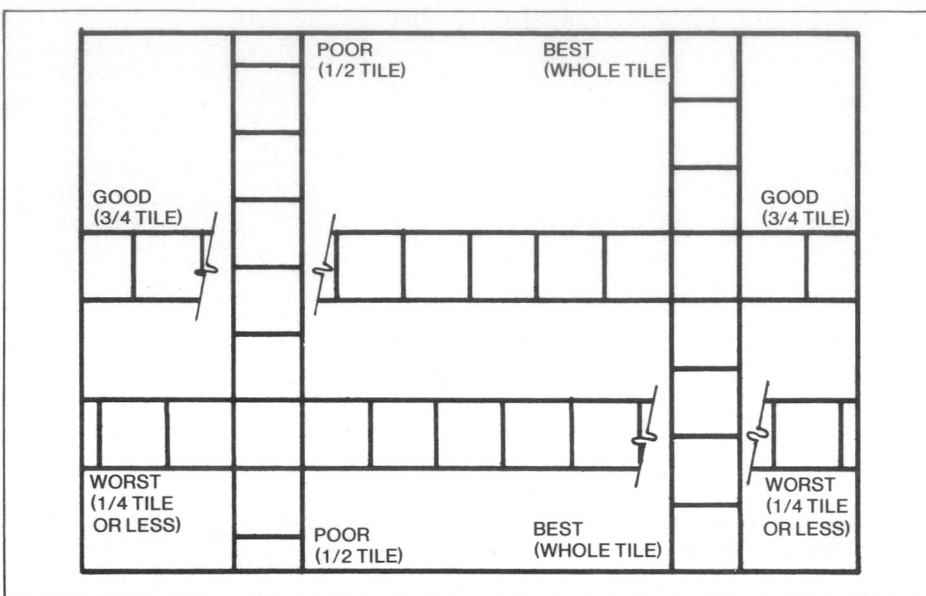

Do a trial layout of tile so you'll have as few cut tiles as possible. Try to position any cut tiles at back of countertop.

Adhesive types suitable for countertops are organic water-base, organic solvent-base, and epoxy adhesives. The organic water-base will tolerate some water exposure, but not a lot. Organic solvent-base will withstand a lot of water exposure. Epoxy will stand up to anything the tile will, with the exception of a few industrial solvents. Pick the adhesive best suited to your circumstances.

Most tile adhesives come in *floor* and *wall* grades. Either grade can be used in either area. Wall grades set up more slowly and take more time to set completely. Floor grades are completely set in 24 hours, but you have to work quickly. Pick the grade best suited to your working speed.

A tile dealer can loan or rent you two of the three specialized tools you'll need. One is a *tile cutter* used for straight cuts. The other special tool is a pair of *nibbling pliers,* used for making curved or irregular cuts.

The third specialized tool is a notched trowel. After you've chosen an adhesive, look on the can for the recommended trowel-notch size. Trowel notches control the adhesive-film thickness, which is critical. If you'll be setting tile for more than 1 day, buy a second trowel for the second day. It's much easier and less expensive to discard the used trowel than it is to clean one properly.

Trial Layout—The most important part of any ceramic-tile job is a trial layout. Starting with any outside corner, lay out a single row of tiles in both directions. If you're planning to use an outside-corner tile on the edge, lay out the first row of whole tiles. See drawing above.

Many tiles have protrusions, called *spacer lugs,* along their edges to pro-

Most tiles come with *edge lugs* to space grout joints. See large tile at left of photo. For tiles without lugs, use appropriate-size tile spacers. Spacers are removed before grout is applied.

vide for grout joints. If your tiles don't have these, buy a bag or two of *spacers*. These small plastic crosses fit into the corners between tiles. They're available in several sizes at the tile dealer.

Use a carpenter's square to run single rows of tiles at right angles to the long rows. This will reveal any awkward-looking areas or small cuts. Cuts less than a half tile in width are less obtrusive at the back edge of the counter, rather than the front edge. Small cuts at the ends of straight runs can usually be eliminated by shifting the whole layout half a tile left or right. Rework the trial layout until it suits you. Then make a sketch, or draw reference marks on the countertop. Remove the single rows of tile.

Tile Application—Some adhesives require a sealer or a preliminary skim coat of that adhesive when they're used over raw wood. If yours does, brush or trowel on the sealer or skim coat and let it dry. If you've removed

Tools for working with ceramic tile include framing square, tile cutter, nibbling pliers, glass cutter, notched trowel for applying adhesive and squeegee for applying grout. Hammer and wood block are used to bed tiles into adhesive. Sponge is used to clean grout joints.

Lay all whole tiles on surface first.

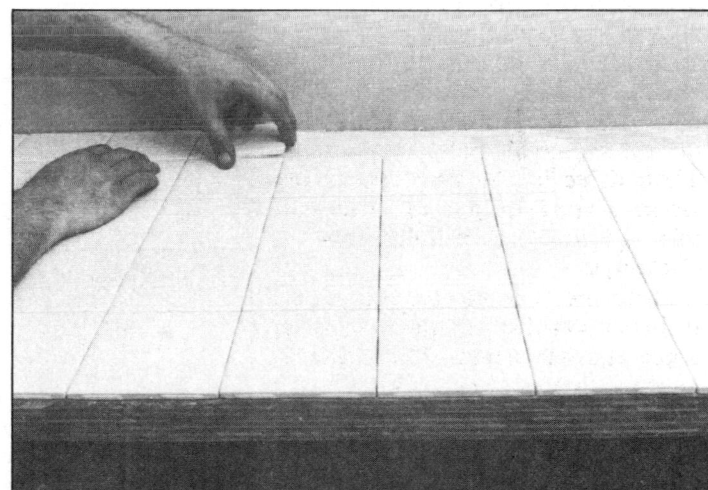

After whole tiles are laid, lay cut tiles.

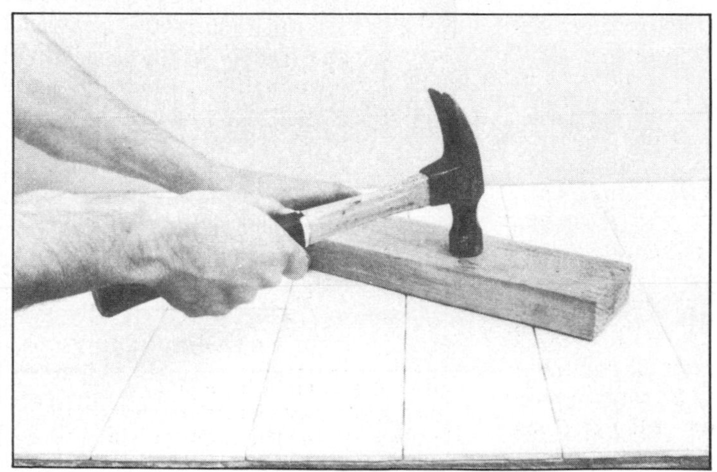

Tap tiles in place with hammer and padded wood block.

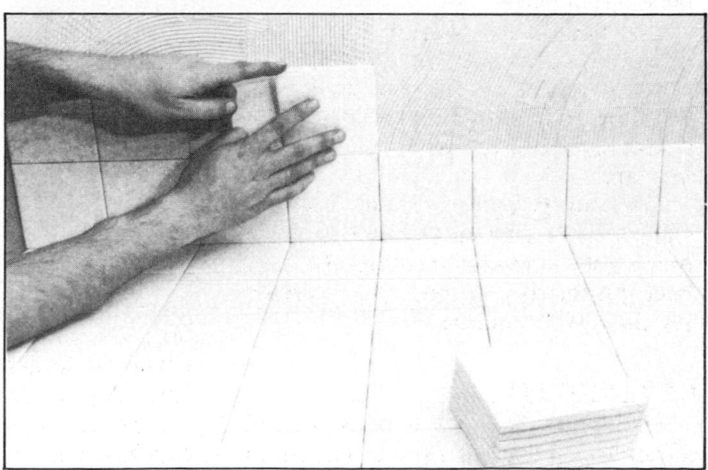

Lay tiles on backsplash.

existing finish materials, make sure the new adhesive will stick to the surface.

If you're using outside-corner tiles on the edge, apply them first. Butter the back of the outside-corner tiles with adhesive and apply them according to your layout marks.

Use the notched trowel to spread adhesive over a portion of the rough top. Spread only as much adhesive as you're sure you can cover with tile before the adhesive sets up. If you're using a wood edge strip, the first row of tiles should be a grout joint's width back from the edge of the top. Install all whole tiles first. Do not apply adhesive to the cut-tile locations at this time. It is easier to cut and fit all partial tiles at the same time, after you've done the whole tiles.

Lay whole tiles by setting them down slightly out of position. Then twist or slide them into final position. The movement should be slight, so you don't pile up adhesive in the grout spaces.

After all whole tiles are in place, lightly tap them into the mastic with a padded wood block and hammer. This levels the tiles and ensures good contact with the mastic. A towel wrapped around a piece of 2x4 or 2x6 will do.

Tile Cutting—Insert a marked tile into the tile cutter and score it. Push down on the lever handle to snap the tile at the score line. If only a few cuts are needed, you don't need a tile cutter. Score the cut line with a glass cutter. Position the score line over a pencil or piece of wire and press down sharply with both hands. Small or irregular cuts are best made with nibbling pliers, also available at the tile dealer.

All cuts for a surface should be made at one time. Put cut pieces near their final location so you don't mix them up. Then butter the back of each cut piece and ease it into position. The adhesive under the cut pieces should be the same thickness as the rest of the adhesives. When cut tiles are in place, tap them with a padded wood block and hammer until they are level with surrounding tiles.

Grouting—After all tiles are in place and the mastic has set, grout the joints. If you're using wood edging strips, install and finish them before grouting. Grouting is a messy job. Protect nearby surfaces. Wear rubber gloves—most grouts are slightly caustic. Mix powdered grout according to the package directions, usually to a consistency a little thicker than pancake batter.

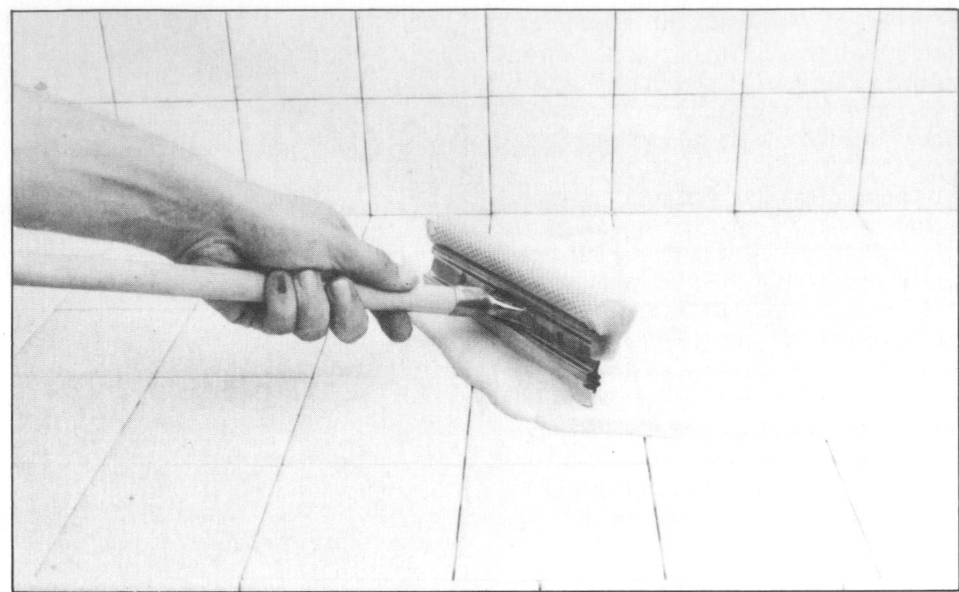

Use squeegee to work grout into joints. Run squeegee diagonally across joints.

A few hours after grouting, use rag, preferably burlap, to remove excess grout from tiles. Be careful not to remove grout from joints.

Spread grout over the entire surface with a squeegee. Working on the diagonal, force grout into all joints. Use the squeegee to remove as much surplus grout as you can. Then remove some more with an almost-dry sponge. Do this until the grout is level with the tile surface or slightly below it.

In an hour or so, the grout will be ready for another cleanup. Package instructions will often tell you to let the grout set overnight. If you do, the tile won't clean up as easily. Wait until grout is starting to show dry patches. Use a cloth wrapped around a wood block to remove surplus grout from tiles and polish off the grout haze. Don't use terrycloth or other fabric with a nap. It will dig the soft grout out of the joints. Burlap is the best material for this job. Work the grout in the joints down to its final level and contour. Don't try to remove every last trace of haze. Touch up any low spots or air bubbles with more grout. You can use any smooth object to shape the grout as needed. The handle of an old toothbrush works well. Use an old spoon for wider grout joints. The next day, after the grout is completely dry, buff off remaining haze.

Sealing—After the grout has completely cured, apply silicone sealer to the grout joints. Several applications may be necessary to protect grout from moisture and staining. Swab on sealer with a brush, wait a few minutes, then polish it off the tile surface with a cloth.

After the sealer has dried, it will be invisible on the grout. To see if more sealer is needed, put a drop or two of water on a joint. Wipe the water off in a few minutes. Any sign of dampness in the grout means it needs more sealer. Clean grout and reapply sealer once a year.

EDGING

One of the handsomest edge treatments for counters is wood edge strips. Wood edge strips can either match or contrast with the cabinets. Strips are available from some cabinet manufacturers, or you can make them. If you're working with a custom cabinetmaker, he can make matching edge strips. Have them milled to a shape that matches or harmonizes with the cabinets.

Wood edge strips are usually 1-1/2 to 2 inches wide and 1/2 to 3/4 inch thick. They can be used with almost any countertop-finish material. A close-grain non-splintery hardwood with good wear characteristics should be selected for edging. Provide adequate clearance between the bottom of the wood edge strip and the drawer tops or appliance doors below. If a finger-pinching situation develops, or if the spacing doesn't look good, remove the countertop, add plywood-spacer strips, and remount the countertop.

On laminate counters, wood edge strips are mounted after the laminate is applied. On ceramic-tile counters, strips are best applied after the tile but before the grout. On synthetic marble or Corian tops, wood edge strips are best installed last. If you've ordered countertops from a fabricator, see if edge strips can be mounted for you. Or, tell the fabricator where you'll apply wood edge strips so he can keep edges square and straight for you.

Installation—In general, wood edge strips should be sanded and finished before they're installed. Sanding and finishing without disturbing adjoining finished surfaces can be difficult.

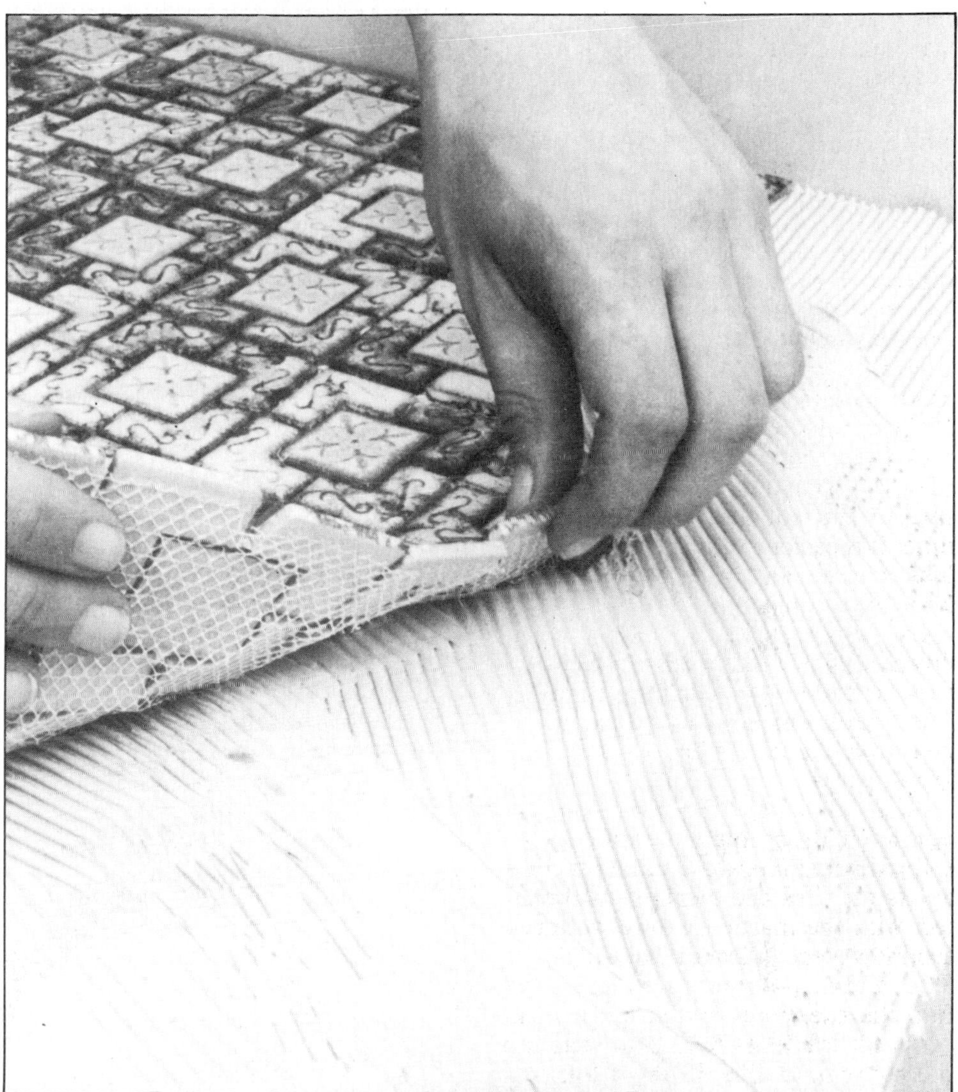

Mosaic tile is easier to lay than individual tiles. Cut mosaic sheet to size. Starting at one end of countertop, gently lay sheet over adhesive. Keep edges aligned and do not pull or stretch sheet as you lay it.

To cut individual mosaic tiles, use glass cutter to score along cut line. Center cut line over piece of metal wire and press down to snap tile.

Keep oil and wax-base finishes off areas where adhesives will be applied.

On ceramic-tile counters, the alignment of the top edge of the wood strip is not critical. Grout will hide small irregularities. On plastic-laminate tops, all irregularities must be taken care of during edging installation. It's difficult to remove high spots and refinish without damaging the laminate.

If you're patient and skillful, you can fit wood edges for laminate tops, finish them, and mount them with contact cement without visible attachments. Otherwise, plan on using countersunk screws with matching or contrasting plugs made from wood dowels. Plugs made from brass or aluminum rod can also be used.

Lay out the fastener locations on the roughly fitted wood edge strips in a neat and evenly spaced pattern. Use small nails to tack the strips in place. Place one nail at each fastener location, but drive it partway in. Nail holes will serve to relocate the pieces as you work.

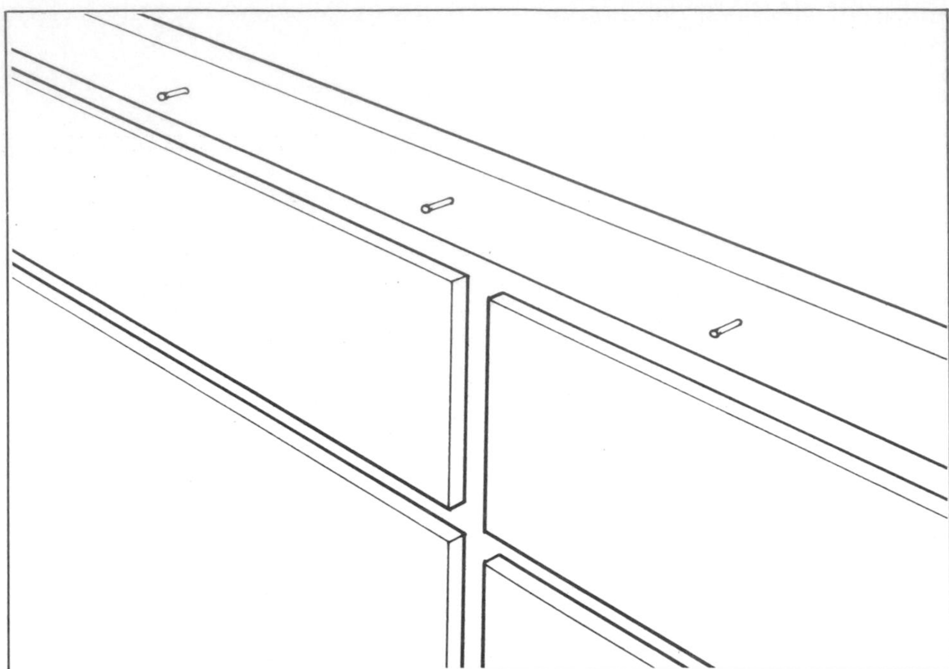

Tack wood edge strip to countertop with finish nails. Leave enough of nail protruding so it can be pulled with pliers later. Mark high spots on strip. Remove strip, leaving nails in it, and sand down high spots. Realign nails in strip to nail holes in countertop and attach strip. Replace nails one at a time with screws.

Working with one strip at a time, mark any high spots by scribing a line on the back of the strip with the point of a utility knife. Remove the strip with the nails still in it, sand it down, and replace it. When that strip fits perfectly, move to the next and fit it.

After all strips are fitted and replaced, remove one nail. Using the nail hole as a guide, drill a screw-pilot hole and a countersunk pocket for a wood plug. Drive the screw in the hole. Then do the same with the next hole. Do not disturb the position of the strips as you work.

When all screws are in place and strips fit perfectly, remove screws and strips. Stain and seal strips. Apply woodworking glue to the back of each strip and to end joints. Reinstall the strips with the screws. Remove excess glue with a damp cloth.

To plug the holes, start with a dowel or metal rod of appropriate diameter. Sand dowel end smooth and square. Gently press dowel in hole to check fit. Sand as needed to get a good fit. Insert dowel and pull the end slightly clear of the hole bottom. Mark the dowel. Cut the plug off the dowel at the mark. Taper the cut end slightly with sandpaper.

Put a drop of glue into the hole and line up the plug grain with the wood strip grain. The smooth-sanded end of the plug should face out, and the tapered end in. Start the plug in the hole. Push the plug into position with a smooth metal object, such as the end of your level. Do this carefully. If you've put too much glue in the hole, there won't be room in the hole for both the glue and the plug. The plug won't go all the way into the hole. You'll then have to sand the plug flush with the surface after the glue dries. Also, if you push the plug too far into the hole, you'll have to sand the whole strip to the level of the plug.

Another problem occasionally occurs with plugs and dowels. Air pressure built up when the plug is pushed in can sometimes push the plug back out again before the glue dries. This can happen if the fit of the plug is too loose. Check plugs every few minutes while the glue is drying and push in any that move out. The air pressure will dissipate eventually, and plugs usually stay put the second time.

BUTCHER BLOCK

Butcher block is quite easily fitted and installed, because it can be treated as a single piece of wood. Take care to keep the butcher block clean as you work, to minimize sanding. Joints and miters should be tied together with angled wood screws on the underside.

After final fitting and sanding, coat the butcher-block top *on all sides* with two heavy coats of pure mineral oil. This is the recommended finish if the butcher block is to be used for cutting and food preparation. Don't use salad or cooking oil on butcher block, because it will eventually turn rancid or oxidize.

Let oil soak in overnight, then wipe off any that remains on the surfaces. Coating all surfaces helps prevent warping due to differences in the moisture absorption of the surfaces.

Before positioning the butcher-block top, drill 3/16-inch vertical holes in the corner blocks of the cabinets every foot at front and rear of the base cabinets. Position the top and drill small pilot holes up through the 3/16-inch holes.

The size of the pilot holes should fit the size of the screws you're using. #10x1-3/4" hex-head sheet-metal screws work well. When you drive the screws, don't put them in too tightly. Butcher block is rigid. You can distort the cabinet if there's a misalignment between cabinets and the top when you tighten the screws.

Butcher block is not often used for backsplashes, although it can be. If you do use it, fasten the backsplash to the top from underneath with wood screws. Seal the top to the backsplash with tub-and-tile caulk. Finish with a heavy coat of mineral oil on the working surfaces.

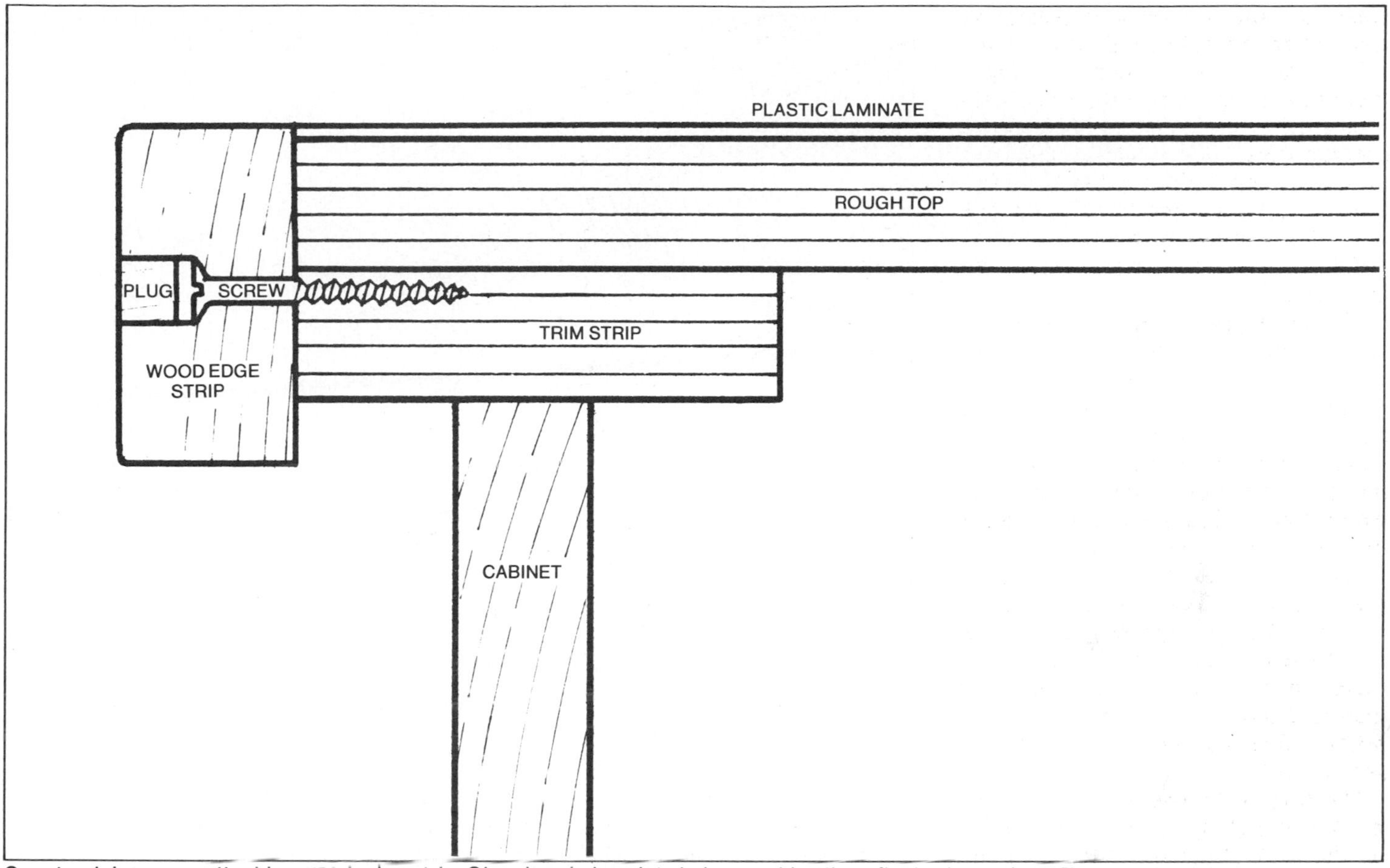

Countersink screws attaching wood edge strip. Glue dowel plugs into holes, pushing them flush with surface. Top of edge strip should be flush with finish-countertop surface.

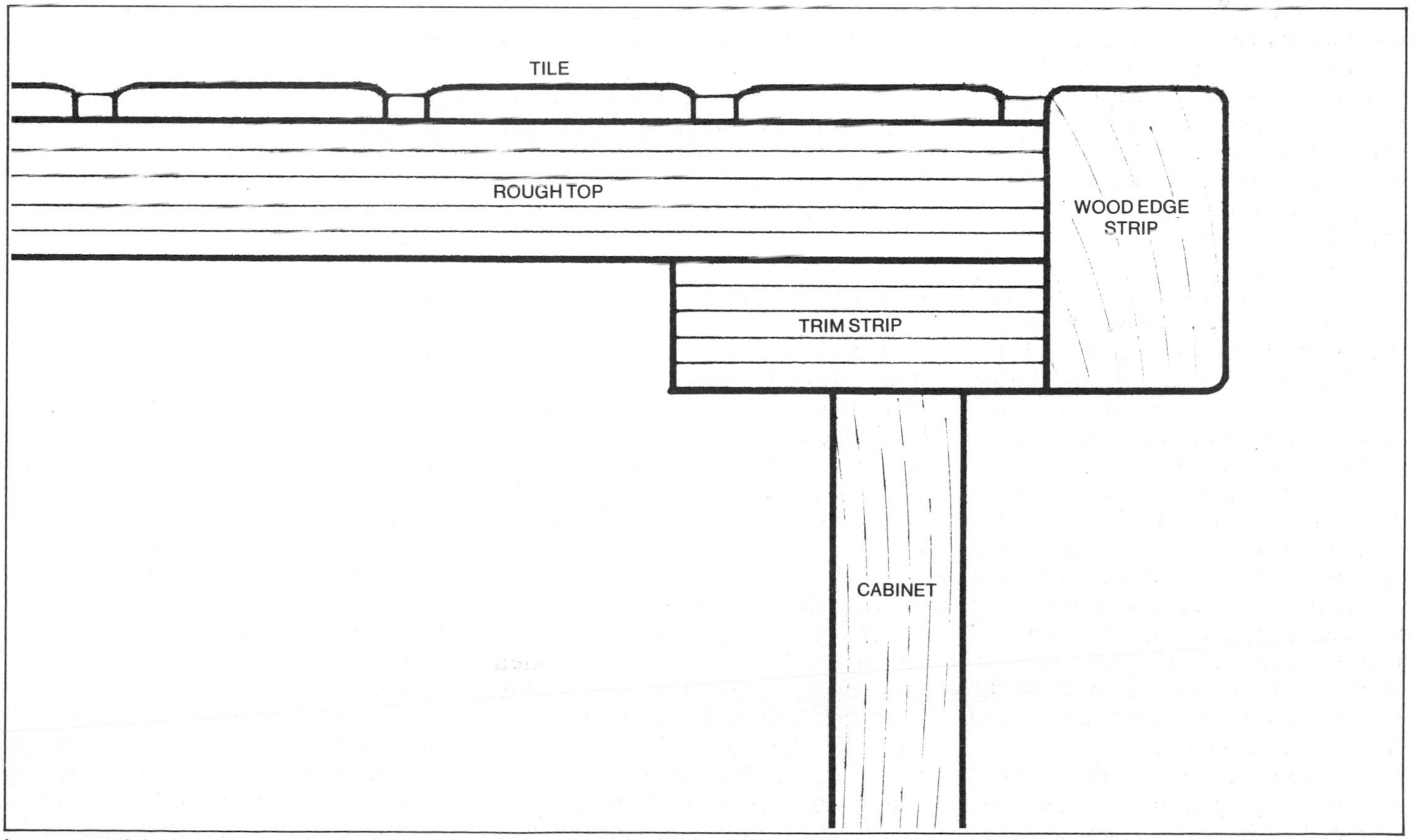

Leave grout joint between wood edge strip and ceramic tile. Use masking tape to protect wood strip while grouting.

Trim Work

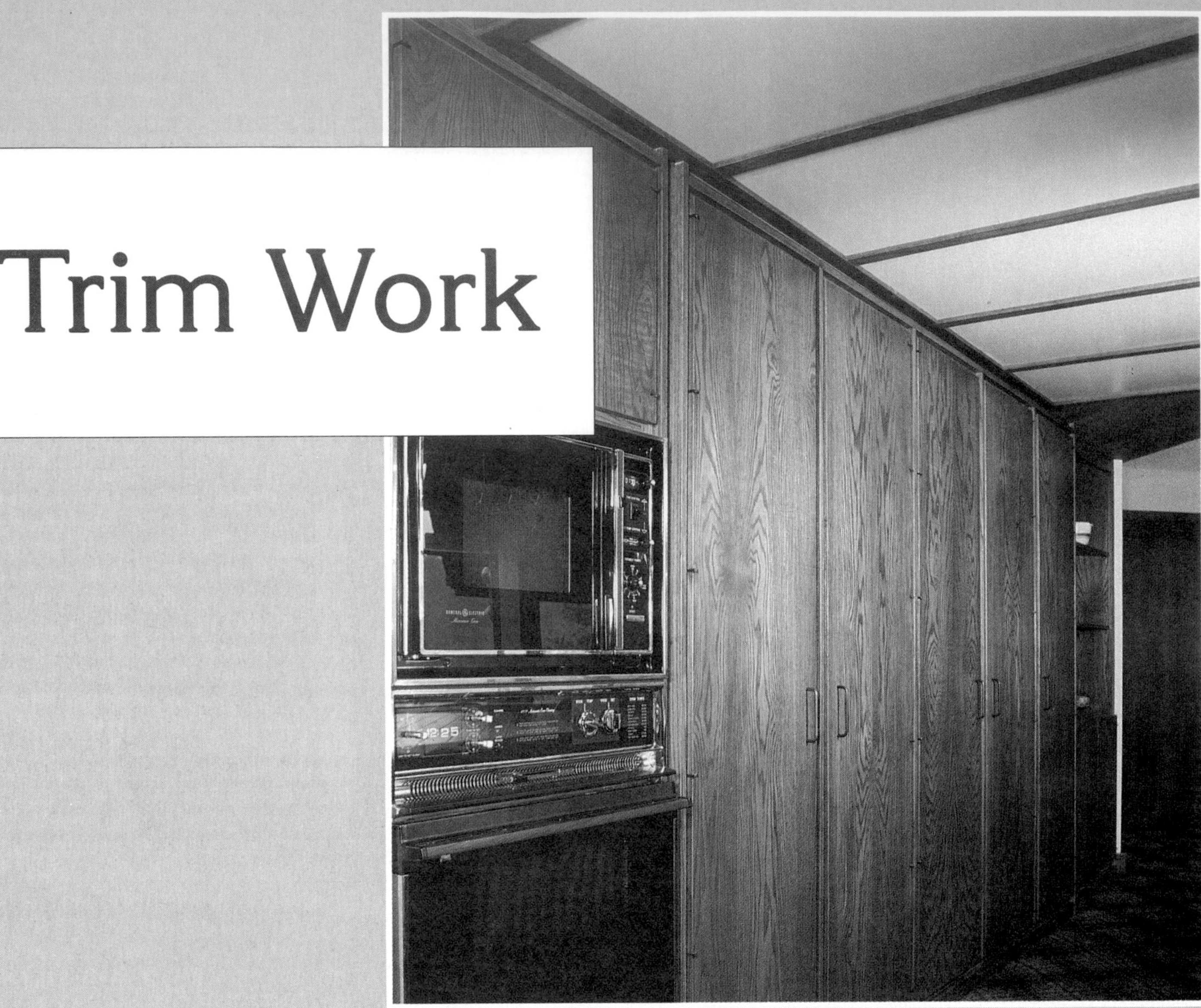

Moldings and trim cover all cracks and gaps in a kitchen. They're also a unifying design element. Here moldings are used to add dimension to ceiling and break flat expanse of pantry doors.

Kitchens have more cracks, gaps and expansion-contraction spaces than any other room in the house. They're the result of fitting all the parts and pieces together, with their various tolerances and clearances. If you've installed the cabinets, gaps should have already been closed off by the moldings and fillers of the cabinet system. Others around doors and along the bottoms of walls will be covered by moldings, to be discussed here.

This chapter also covers procedures for installing finish trim for luminous ceilings and skylights.

WOOD MOLDINGS

You can use a number of materials for door, window and base moldings. Strictly speaking, the term *molding* applies to wood that has been milled to a decorative surface. But many unmilled materials such as rough-sawn cedar or redwood can be used as moldings, so the strict definition won't apply in this chapter. You can use anything that works and looks good. Molding can match the walls, the floors, the cabinets, the doors, or you can choose a contrasting molding. Installation techniques are similar for all types.

All moldings should be painted or otherwise finished before installation. This saves work cutting in paint or finish next to other surfaces. The trim can then be touched up after mounting.

Joints—Basic joints in moldings are the *square end,* the *splice,* the *coped joint,* and the *miter joint.* Except for the coped joint, all should be made with a good-quality miter box. Simple wooden miter boxes work for a few cuts, but the guide slots soon become frayed and inaccurate. If you have many miter cuts to make, buy a good metal miter box, either the U-channel type or the blade-guide type.

If you have a lot of miter cuts, rent or buy a power tool called a *chop saw.* This is basically a power miter box. The saw portion is similar to a circular saw, mounted on an adjustable pivot. If you have a good table saw or radial-arm saw, you don't need a miter box or a chop saw. Check the accuracy of the angle settings of your mitering tools before you start. Also remember when working with moldings that you have to consider not only the angle of a cut in one plane, but in two.

The square-end joint is the simplest cut to make—the name is self-explanatory. To make this cut, position the angle setting on your miter box or saw at exactly 90°.

A splice is used to connect two short pieces of molding to make a long piece. Cutting is straightforward, but the installation of a splice joint can be tricky. Splices tend to gap after the pieces are firmly attached. Crowd the joint slightly as you're attaching the pieces, but not enough to cause an overlap.

The miter joint comes in inside and outside forms, and consists of two 45° cuts. Miters can be made from the narrow face or the wide face of the molding. See drawing at right.

The coped joint makes a much smoother inside corner than an inside miter does. Make a miter cut on the end of the piece at one side of the inside corner. Let the piece on the other side of the corner run straight through. Then use a coping saw to cut out the section of wood on the second piece beyond the miter line of the first. If you saw carefully, the cutout section will fit neatly over the molding on the other side of the corner. See photo at right.

Especially on remodeling work, true cuts on moldings are as rare as straight walls. To make a good fit, some variation from the expected cut will often be required. Unfortunately there's no good way to measure these small variations in advance. The expert trimmer sees the needed adjustment and makes it. For the novice, it's usually a process of trial and error.

Moldings that are small in width and thickness can usually be cut true and installed without making adjustments. But moldings that are over 1 inch or so in either width or thickness must be adjusted as you cut.

For the novice, the best substitute for experience is to use precut guides to test the accuracy of cuts. Cut two short lengths of the molding you're using to serve as guides. Cut one end of each piece exactly square and the other end at a 45° angle. These pieces can be pushed into the position of most joints, and will make the needed adjustments obvious. Then adjust cuts on the molding you're installing to fit the space.

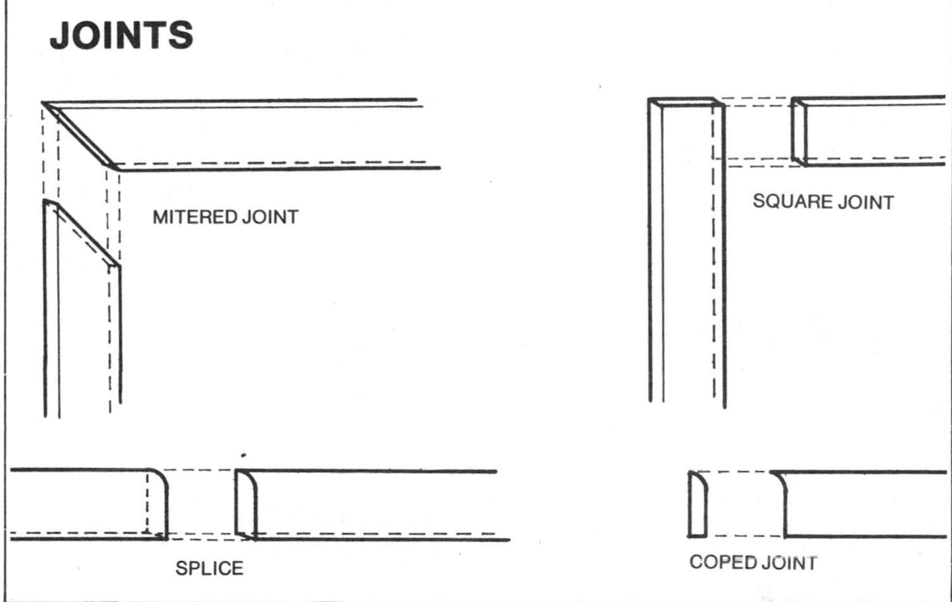

Coping a joint takes little if any more time than mitering. Technique enables you to deal with curved or complex molding shapes.

Always cut molding an inch or two longer than the final, installed length. This allows you to make adjustments to the cut without ending up with a too-short piece. Surplus molding at the opposite end can then be trimmed off or cut to fit.

The only time guide pieces won't work is when you're fitting moldings around doorways. Door jambs are rarely flush with the surrounding wall surface. If you put your guide piece in place, you'll find the jamb is either in or out from the wall. If it's out, the miters at the top corners will tend to gap at the inside. If the jamb is in from the wall, the miters at the top corners will tend to gap at the outside. The angle of the cut must be adjusted to fit, in both planes, and the adjustment should be the same for both halves of each cut.

Scribing—Not all surfaces you want to fit a molding against are straight. You may have to recut the edge or end of a molding to fit an irregular contour. Start by placing the length of molding as close as possible to its final position. Use a compass to measure the width of the widest space between the molding and the irregular surface. An inexpensive pencil compass will work.

Draw the compass along the length

of the molding. The point should follow the line on the surface where you want the molding to fit, while the pencil makes a parallel mark on the molding.

To cut to the line you've marked, use any tools that seem suitable. On small moldings, scribe along the pencil line with the point of a utility knife. Then shave off surplus material, using the utility knife or a wood rasp. Smooth the shaved surface with sandpaper. On larger moldings and hardwoods, a coping saw or saber saw may be needed to remove surplus material.

When you've cut the molding back to the marked line, remove some extra material behind the visible surface. This enables the molding to clear any projections on the irregular surface it will be fitted to.

Trial-fit the molding as you work to detect any problems. If you must have a perfect fit, apply chalk to the irregular surface. Trial fit the molding and tap it a few times. Shave or sand off the places where the chalk transfers, until the chalk transfers along the whole length of the molding.

Wood flooring must be free to expand and contract. Use paper shims to provide clearance between floor and molding.

Moldings—Finish nails are most often used to attach moldings. The nail size should be suited to the molding thickness, not width. Use the smallest nail that will reach through the molding and 1/2 inch or so into solid wood behind any intervening softer material, such as drywall. If wood tends to split near the molding ends, chuck a finish nail of the same size in an electric drill and use it to drill pilot holes. Construction adhesive can also be used where necessary, to minimize nail holes or to cope with difficult situations.

Finish materials such as wood flooring are subject to expansion and contraction. Make sure adjoining moldings don't bind against these materials. Don't nail the moldings to them, but to the adjacent surface. For instance, if the floor is subject to expansion and contraction, nail the molding to the wall. Insert a piece of thick paper or thin cardboard between the molding and the finish-flooring material to maintain clearance while you're nailing.

Dark wood molding defines skylight. Molding is installed using simple miter joints.

LUMINOUS CEILINGS AND SKYLIGHTS

Luminous ceilings that emit artificial light, and skylights that let in natural light, start out as a hole in the kitchen ceiling. The interior of luminous-ceiling recesses and skylight openings should be lined with drywall or plaster. They should be painted white for maximum reflectivity.

Diffuser panels of glass or plastic are used to cover a luminous ceiling, and sometimes a skylight. A metal or wood molding is used to hold the diffuser panels in place. See drawings on facing page.

The simplest means of holding diffuser panels in place is a metal L-channel and T-channel made for suspended ceilings. The opening should be framed to fit standard 2x2' or 2x4' diffuser panels. If it isn't, measure and mark the opening so that cut diffuser panels on the sides or ends are equal in size.

Install channel all the way around the opening. If the diffuser panels are to be flush with the ceiling, use T-channel, as shown in the drawing at right. If the diffuser panels are to be recessed into the opening, use L-channel.

Recessed diffusers should not be leveled when installed. They should

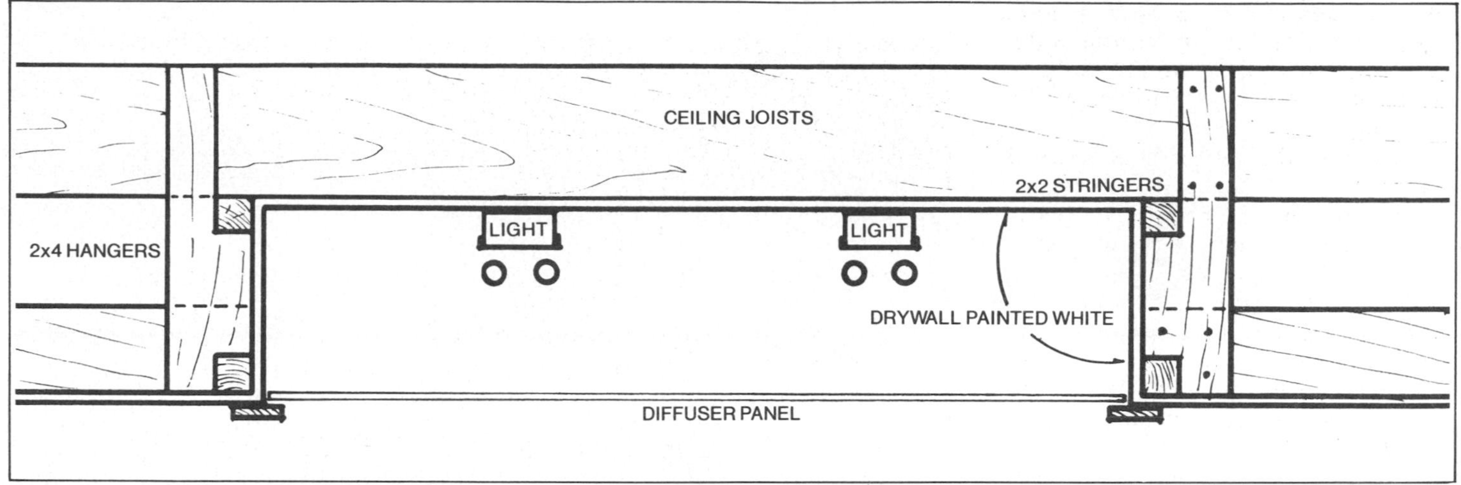

Cross-section shows framing details of luminous ceiling. Ceiling is usually dropped for this type of installation.

follow the slope of the ceiling, if any. If the ceiling isn't level, make the recess measurement equal all the way around the opening. Twist diffuser panels slightly to fit. Install T-channel across the shortest dimension of the opening, spaced to accept the diffuser panels. You may need to add screw-eyes and suspension wires if the channel spans are long. Consult manufacturer's instructions. Then snap in *cross-Ts* in the opposite direction. Then drop in the diffuser panels.

Luminous ceilings and skylight openings can also be trimmed with wood, either to match other openings in the ceiling, or to match cabinets. Installation techniques are the same as detailed under moldings on facing page, but you should use annular-ring nails or screws to attach moldings. Smooth-shank finish nails will have a tendency to pull out, due to gravity.

A problem you'll encounter in installing wood-trimmed luminous ceilings is sag. If the moldings don't have a generous vertical dimension, install vertical 1x2 or 1x3 stringers and attach the crossbars to the stringers. On long spans, use screw-eyes and suspension wires if you have to.

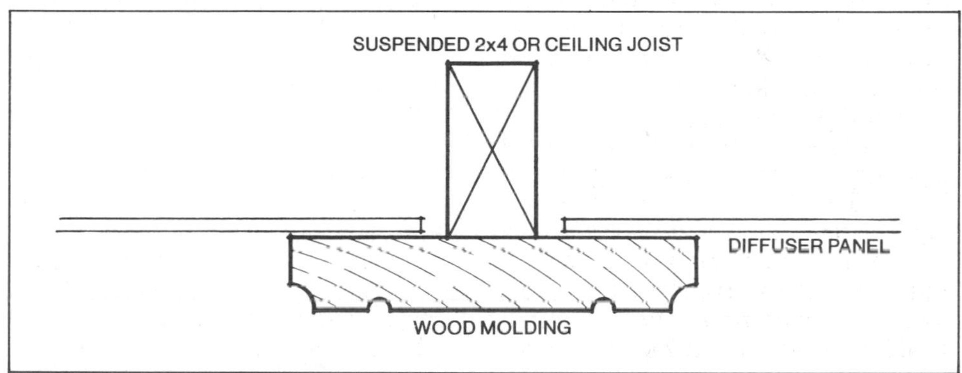

Decorative wood molding is used to hold diffuser panels for luminous ceiling. Use screws or annular-ring nails to attach moldings.

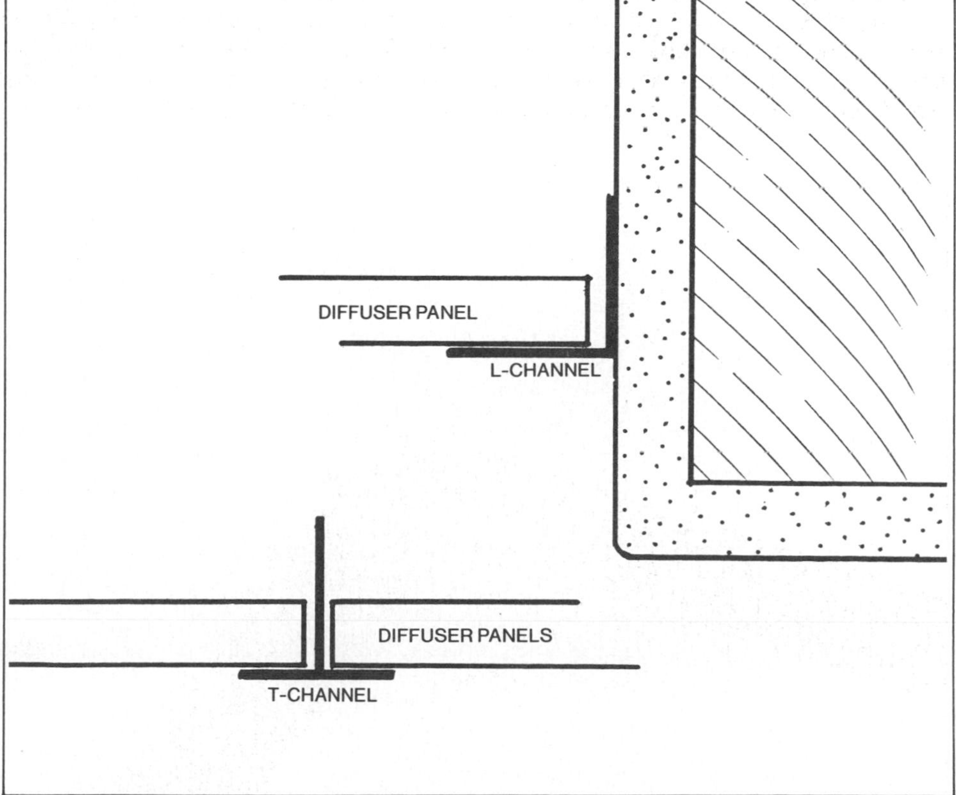

Metal L-channels,top, and T-channels,bottom, are most often used for luminous ceilings. Use T-channels to make panels flush with ceiling, L-channels for recessed panels.

Special Areas

Small serving clean-up area between dining room and kitchen includes dishwasher, sink and dish-storage cabinet. Food warmer is under top cabinet at right. Wood panel on dishwasher is grooved so mounting trim strips don't show. Sink includes instant hot-water dispenser and a disposer.

Special areas in or near the kitchen help link it to the rest of the house. Some of these special areas work along with the kitchen. Others remove functions from the kitchen when these can be located elsewhere.

A pantry is a good example of a special area that's directly related to the kitchen. So is a dining area. Both directly relate to the kitchen, and should be planned along with it. Other special areas relate to the kitchen but are additional to it. Planning centers and outdoor serving and eating counters are in this group.

Mixing and serving drinks is often done in the kitchen, but doesn't have to be. It's an unrelated function that can be moved elsewhere. Laundry facilities are often located near or even in the kitchen. But modern laundry equipment is so automatic that it can be located near bedrooms where clothes are kept.

SERVING AREAS

Small kitchens can include space for serving meals in the kitchen itself. Large kitchens should have a serving area, and perhaps some support equipment, close to the dining room. This is particularly useful if you do much entertaining. The purpose of a serving area is to reduce the steps required to get a meal and utensils to and from the table. Look for a place that's just out of the main traffic path, preferably within arm's reach of the path.

The staging area can be large, or small like the one shown on facing page. Only 4 feet in length, this serving center has enough room for bar sink, dishwasher, food warmer and storage space for serving china. The rest of this kitchen is shown the cover and on pages 14-16 and 179. You can see how well the serving counter fits the traffic path to and from the dining room.

The serving counter at right is reminiscent of an old-style butler's pantry. It's in a passageway between kitchen and dining room of a renovated house. The house was originally designed by Southwestern architect, Josias T. Joesler.

The use of this serving counter is somewhat different than the others. Counter and wall cabinets are designed to store all serving dishes so that none have to be kept in the kitchen. Prepared food can be brought from the kitchen and put into serving dishes on the counter. Or empty serving dishes can be set on the counter and taken to the kitchen, one by one, to be filled.

Often, there's a problem serving an outdoor-eating area from an inside kitchen. In the kitchen at right, the cook ordinarily takes extra steps around the end of the kitchen, and wrestles with serving dishes and doors at the same time. The problem is neatly solved by providing a counter outside the kitchen window. Food and utensils pass through easily.

For an outdoor-serving area of this sort, arrange for the window bottom to be as close as possible to outside-counter height. If you live in a mild climate, this sort of serving counter also functions as an outdoor snack bar.

Counter behind sink extends to form outdoor serving area. Sliding-glass window can be closed during bad weather.

BARS

One way to make your kitchen function better for its main purpose, cooking, is to move secondary functions to a separate area. For example, mixing and serving drinks is best done at a well-equipped bar. Bottles, glasses, ice, measuring utensils, corkscrews, decanters and other mixing and serving items form an easy-to-move group. A small sink at the bar facilitates mixing, especially if the bar is any distance from the kitchen. Optional items include a small refrigerator and icemaker.

Space for a bar can be taken from the kitchen, as shown at right. A corner cut off the kitchen can make a more useful area on the other side in a dining room or family room. In this example, the traffic flow was greatly improved by the relocation.

After you've decided to move the bar from the kitchen, locate it anywhere that works well. A well-designed bar in a family room or recreation room remote from the main kitchen can also function as a minikitchen.

When a kitchen and a bar are within sight of each other, a unifying element is needed. For the bar on facing page, top left, the tie-in is stonework. Stone around the bar extends to form the massive fireplace. It also echoes stone wrapped around the kitchen at the other end of the family room.

In a family room near the kitchen, the connection between bar and fireplace is a natural one. Shown at right on facing page is the opposite end of the room from the kitchen on page 24. Cabinets are the same, but the top material has been changed to a dark-plastic laminate. The stemware racks and mirror behind them lend sparkle.

A bar can be elegant as well as functional. The bar shown on facing page, bottom left, has louver doors that can be closed when the bar is not in use. Additional storage cabinetry is located at right, in the corner.

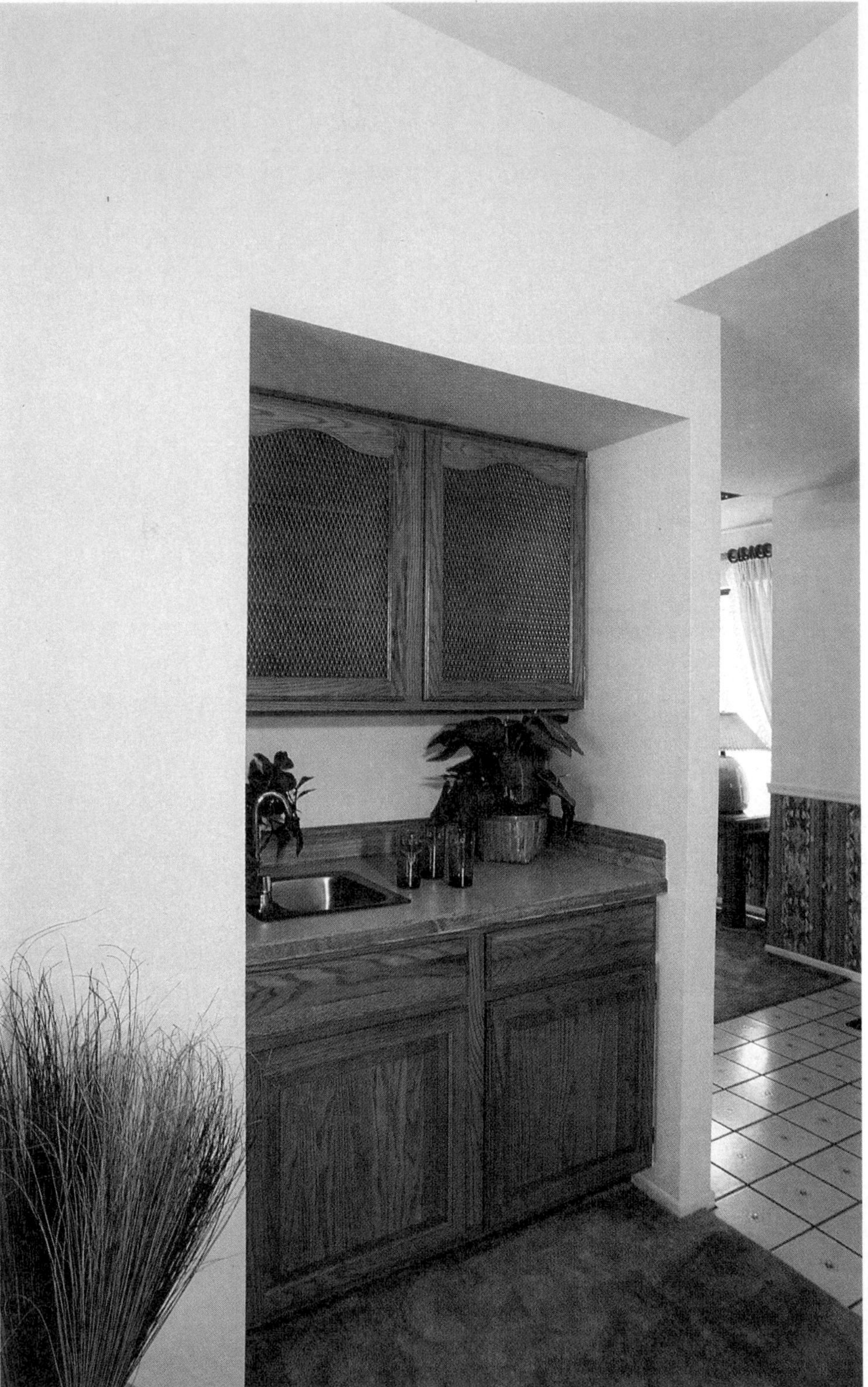

Space was taken from kitchen to accommodate alcove bar in family room.

Stonework across bar is extension of massive fireplace in family room.

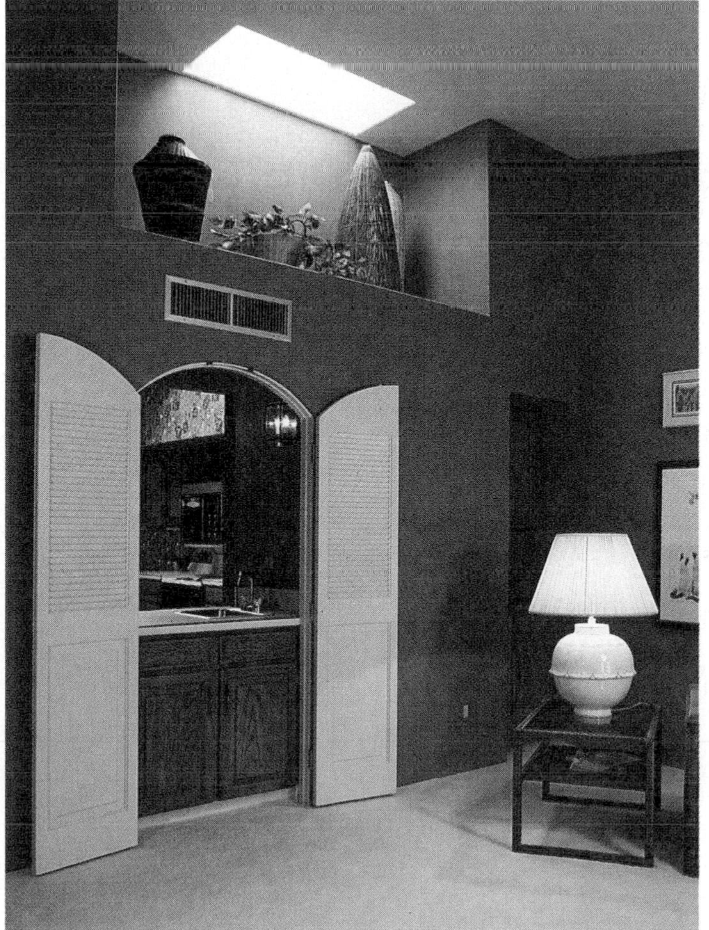

Pass-through bar can be used from kitchen and living room.

Cabinetry for this bar matches that in kitchen. Stemware racks and mirror make bar focal point in room.

PLANNING CENTERS

The kitchen is the nerve center of a household. All too often, there's no planned space for bookkeeping, note-taking and phone calls. Little room exists where you can sit and write a menu plan or shopping list, read recipes or jot a letter while food cooks. A more-complete planning center might include a personal computer for computing household finances, making shopping lists and storing recipes. A snack bar or breakfast table can handle some of these tasks, but a special planning center is better.

The essentials of a kitchen planning center include an area of countertop dropped to about 30 inches high, knee space, drawers and bright lighting. The planning center shown below is a good example. A fluorescent fixture under the wall cabinets provides ample lighting. Chair pushes into a knee space so it's out of the way when not being used. Chair matches those at the breakfast table for extra seating there.

The planning center/office below right overlooks the front entry and the family entrance through an adjoining laundry room. The window looks out on the front drive. This allows observation of the comings and goings of a large and busy family.

The custom-built rolltop desk at right matches kitchen cabinets and bar on pages 24, 25, and 177. The cover rolls down to conceal the work surface, large key rack and cubbyholes for filing.

Rolltop desk is custom made to match kitchen cabinets and bar shown on pages 24, 25 and 177.

Dropped section of countertop provides comfortable desk height. Fluorescent fixture under wall cabinet provides light.

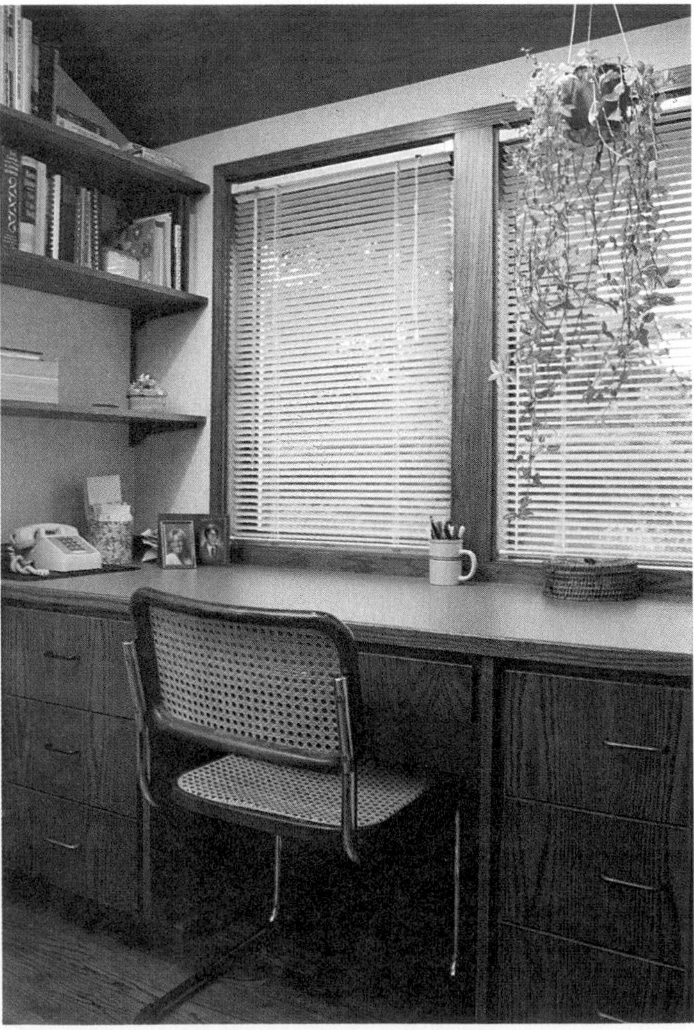

Large window provides light and view of front drive.

LAUNDRY ROOMS

Laundry areas have much in common with kitchens. Both have cabinets, appliances, countertops and floors that should be water-tolerant. Laundry areas can be part of the kitchen or planned along with them.

The laundry room shown below is around the corner from the kitchen on the cover and pages 14-16. It shares the same cabinets and sense of organization. The drip-dry enclosure at left has pull-out rods at different heights for hanging clothes. It is built much like a small ceramic shower. There's plenty of counter space for sorting clothes without stooping over. The washer-dryer is a combination model—no need to transfer wet clothes from the washer to the dryer.

Three separate cabinet groupings form the triangular laundry room shown at right. The deep sink next to the washer and dryer is useful for pre-soaking or washing clothes by hand. It's also a good spot for watering and potting plants. Ample storage room is allowed for supplies. The extra counter to the left can serve as a special-project area or for folding laundry. The closet on the diagonal wall includes a fold-out ironing board and space to hang finished clothing.

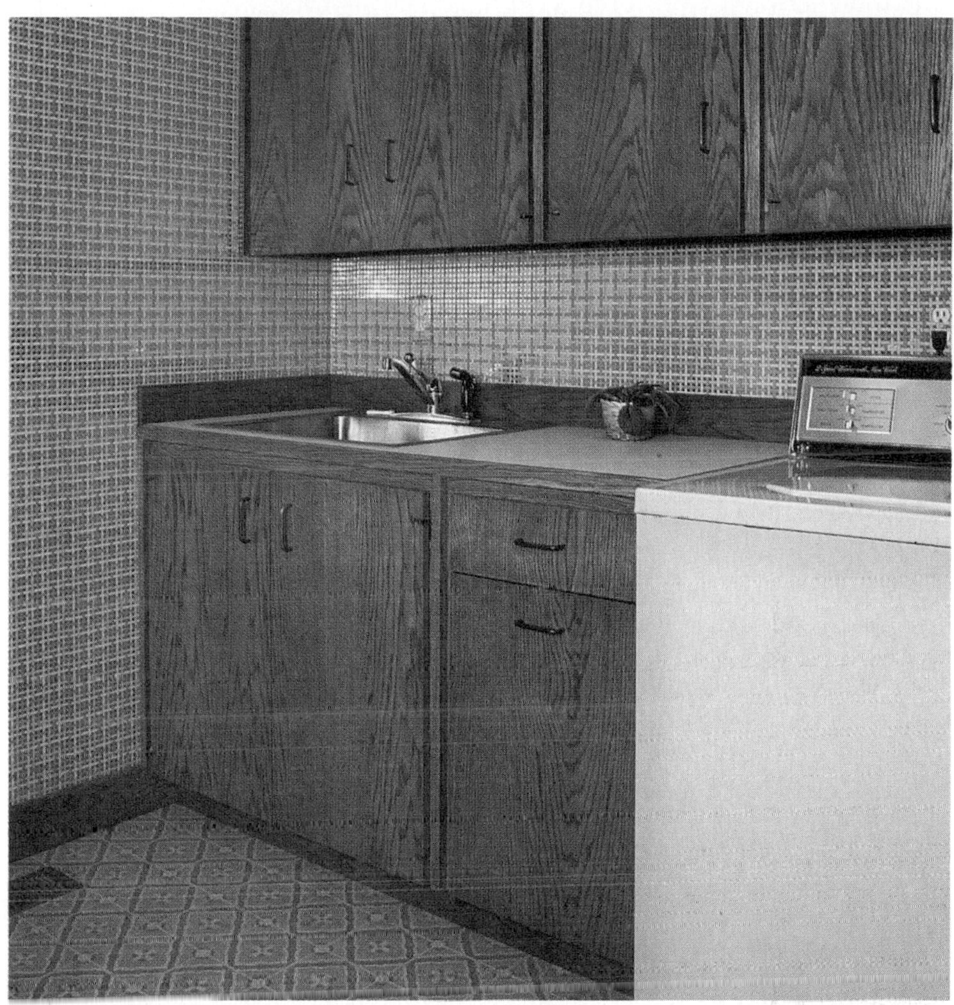

Laundry room includes deep sink for hand-washing clothes, plenty of cabinet space.

Drip-dry enclosure at left of laundry room is built like small ceramic-tile shower. It includes a swing-spout faucet 17 inches above the floor for filling buckets for flower arranging.

Quick Projects

One or more lights to sink can be run off wiring for existing ceiling lights. Here, lights are recessed into soffit.

LIGHT UP THE SINK

Does your kitchen have a light in the center of the ceiling, no light over the sink and no cabinet above it to mount a light on? You can wire one or more additional lights into the box for the existing ceiling light, as described here.

Check wiring above ceiling. If there's an attic, it's easy to add a light over the sink from above. First, be sure there's enough capacity on the circuit that carries the ceiling light, and tie-in the new one there. Details on how to wire are given in the chapter, Electrical Work.

If there's no access from above, you'll have to run wiring between the joists from below. Choose a lightweight fixture with a cupped base to conceal a thin electrical box mounted directly on the ceiling. Drill a hole at the new location in the same joist bay as the old ceiling light. Turn off power and dismantle the old light fixture.

Remove a knockout plug in the old electrical box. Push a length of nonmetallic cable into the ceiling in the direction of the new fixture. When the cable end is over hole for the new light, jiggle the cable. A helper can snag the end and pull it through the hole. Mount a shallow box on the ceiling with toggle bolts. Wire and mount the new fixture. Wire cable into the existing fixture box and reassemble. Both new and old fixture will work on the same switch. In photo above, recessed fixtures light sink area.

UPGRADE YOUR WORK LIGHTING

Are there places in your kitchen where you work in your own shadow? Many older kitchens have a light fixture or two in the middle of the ceiling. No light is directed at the countertops where the work is done. Small fluorescent-light fixtures can be added beneath cabinets to provide countertop light. They are available at most hardware stores and home-improvement centers. A home-lighting center will carry the widest selection of incandescent and fluorescent fixtures.

Installing the light fixture or fixtures usually involves mounting them to the underside of the wall cabinets or soffit. Bottoms of cabinets may be too thin to hold mounting screws. Mark and drill at screw-hole locations, and use small, countersunk flat-head machine screws and nuts. Drill a hole in cabinet. Run cord up through hole where you can inconspicuously drop it to a nearby electrical outlet.

If the cord on a light fixture isn't long enough to reach the closest outlet, don't splice it to another cord. Remove short cord and replace it with a longer one.

If you wish to conceal the fixtures, install a 3- or 4-inch-wide skirt on the underside of the wall cabinets. Use any material that harmonizes or matches the cabinetwork. Attach the skirt from inside the wall cabinets with wood screws.

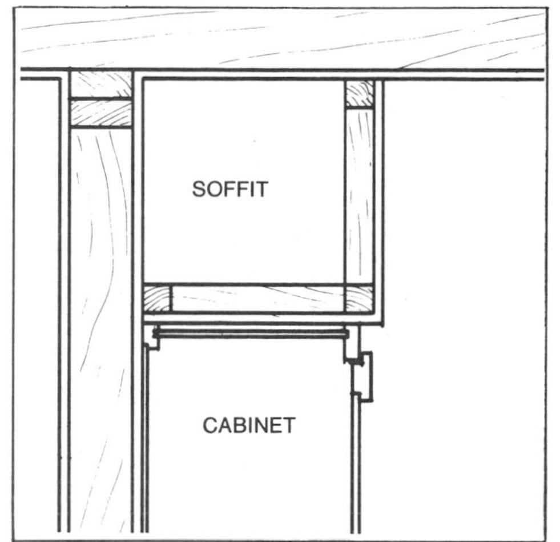

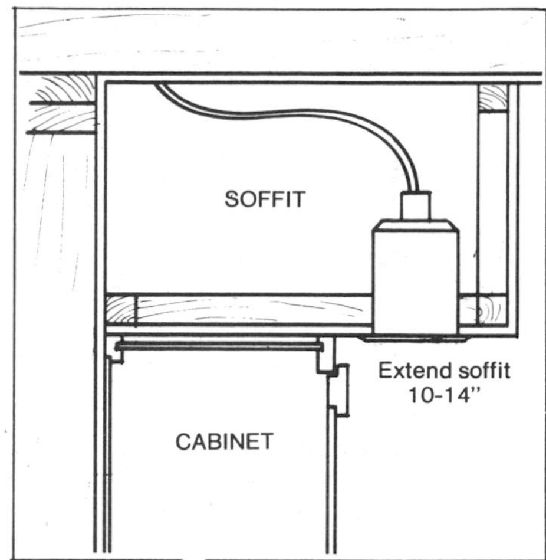

To provide lighting over wall cabinets, extend soffit and install recessed lights.

Under-cabinet lighting brightens work area over sink. Wood skirt hides fluorescent fixture.

Practical application of drawing above includes soffit lights over each wall cabinet.

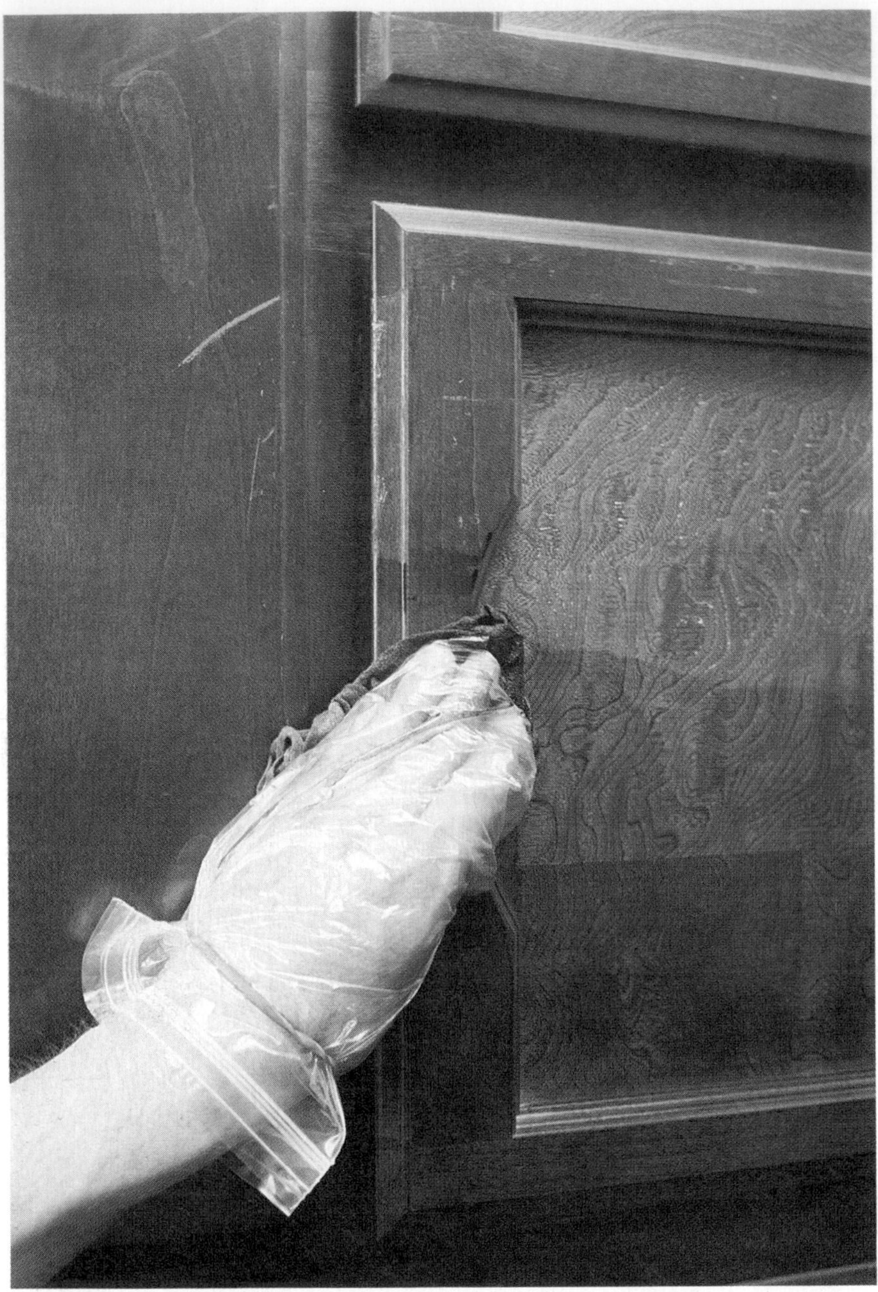

Stain-wax is a quick way to give new life to old cabinets.

SPRUCE UP YOUR CABINETS

In a kitchen, the finish on wood cabinets can look dingy after a few years. Grease and smoke film builds up, fingerprints accumulate and nicks and scratches appear. You can restore wood cabinets to near-new appearance in less than a day at minimal cost.

Several manufacturers make a wood-finishing product called *stain-wax.* Stain-wax contains solvents, waxes and pigment in liquid form. The most widely distributed brand is Minwax. The label on the can says not to put the product on over old finish, but don't be concerned. It works anyway, though not as well. You are sprucing up, not refinishing. If you go to the trouble to strip the cabinet finish, you might as well restain and seal cabinets.

Use the color chart available at the store to match the stain-wax to your cabinets. A pint goes a long way for this kind of use. See label for amount of stain coverage.

Wipe cabinets with a damp sponge. Put newspapers down to protect floors and countertops. Shake the can vigorously before opening. When applying the stain-wax, it is best to replace the lid every few minutes to shake the can. If not mixed frequently, the pigment tends to settle. Put a plastic bag over your hand and secure with a rubber band to avoid staining your hand.

Dampen a pad of cheesecloth or an old washcloth in the stain-wax and wipe it on cabinets. Wipe back over the area with more stain-wax before the first coat dries, then buff. The cloth doesn't have to be saturated, just damp. Solvents remove film and fingerprints. Pigment helps hide scratches and dings. Wax buffs up to a shine.

ORGANIZE!

Your kitchen may not seem to have enough storage space. When was the last time you had space to spare? Probably not since you moved in. A complete reorganization often frees up space you didn't know you had.

Kitchens tend to become cluttered with unused or rarely used items. Such items should be removed and stored in a garage or attic, disposed of or given to someone who can use them.

Set two cardboard boxes in the middle of the kitchen. Empty a cabinet on the counter and look at the contents. If you use an item regularly, put it aside on the counter. If you haven't used an item in the last year, put it in one box. If you haven't used an item in 2 years, put it in the second box.

Continue this process until you've gone through everything in the kitchen. When you're done, consider disposing of the contents in the second box. Or you can donate it to a charitable organization or sell it at your next yard sale. Things you want to save can be stored in the attic, basement or garage.

Put the first box in a nearby closet for a year, in case you want to retrieve something from it. After the year is up, store or dispose of what's left.

Organize what remains into functional groups. A few more cardboard boxes can be helpful here. The utensils you use every day should be within arm's reach of where they're used.

When the everyday tools are where they belong, look at the other categories. Study the remaining storage space. Find places for those other groups of kitchen items as close as possible to where they are used. When everything is reorganized, you may find a surprising amount of space left over.

A kitchen accumulates a lot of clutter. Poor organization eats up space, makes things hard to find and difficult to get out for use.

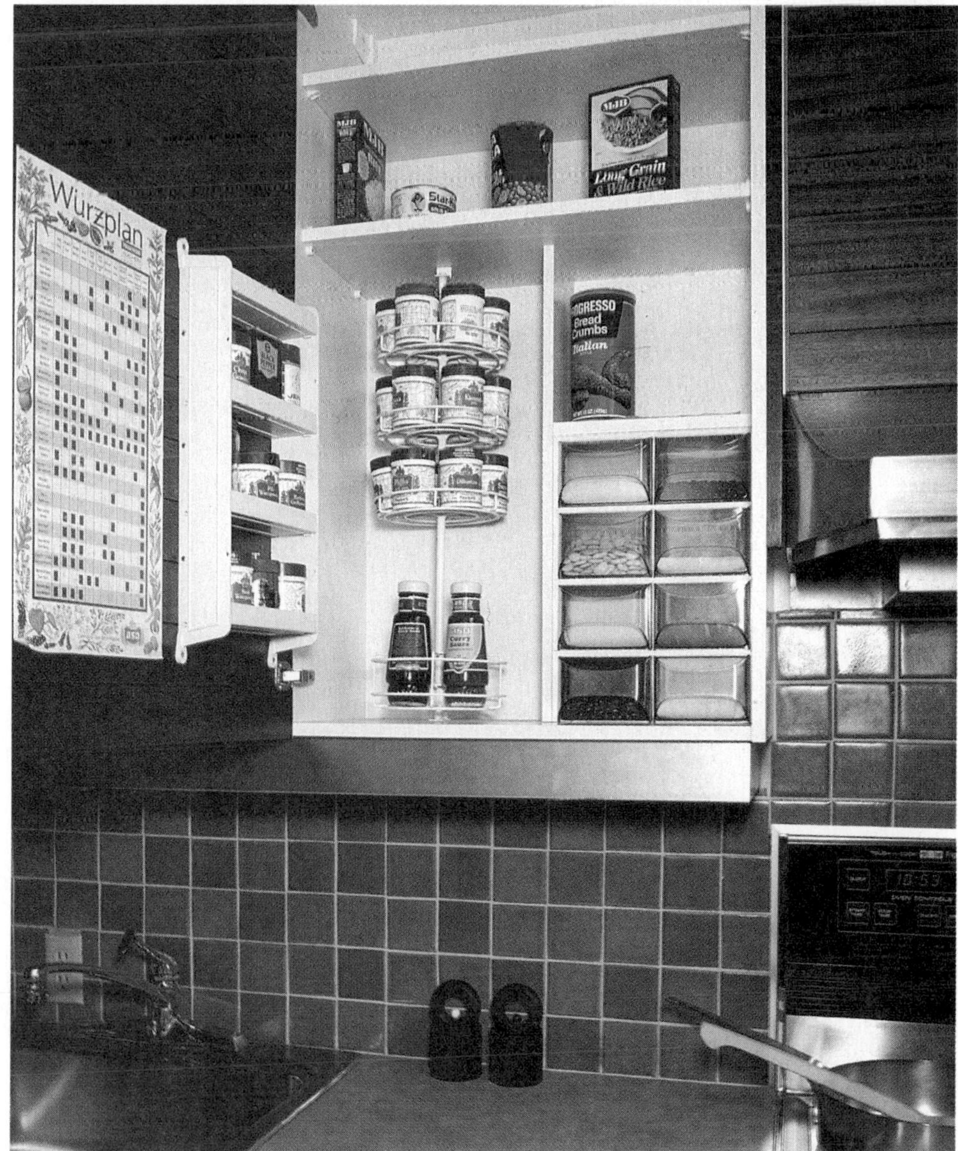

Racks and bins help organize supplies. Store things close to where they're used.

A QUICK NEW FLOOR

If your resilient-tile floor is in good condition and firmly attached, but you're tired of the design, you can put a new floor over it. The easiest way is to use self-adhesive resilient tile.

First, clean the floor thoroughly and strip off old wax. Unless the floor was poorly laid out, it isn't necessary to measure and calculate new layout lines. Mark two chalk lines in a cross to divide the room in quarters. Lines should be slightly offset from existing tile joints. Peel release paper off backs of tiles and press each into place. Follow instructions that come with the new tiles.

When all the whole tiles are down, use scissors to cut partial tiles. Instructions on page 142 show an easy way to fit partial tiles at walls and around obstructions. After tiles are installed, apply a coat of acrylic floor wax.

Clean floor *thoroughly* to remove all old dirt and wax. Use sandpaper if you have to. Then repair old floor, pages 133-135. Or you can remove old floor covering and repair the underlayment, page 69. Set up layout lines as shown on page 143. Open carton and peel protective paper off back of a tile. Set first tile at intersection of layout lines, aligning it carefully. Work out from first tile until you've put down all tiles in one quarter. Then do next quarter and so on.

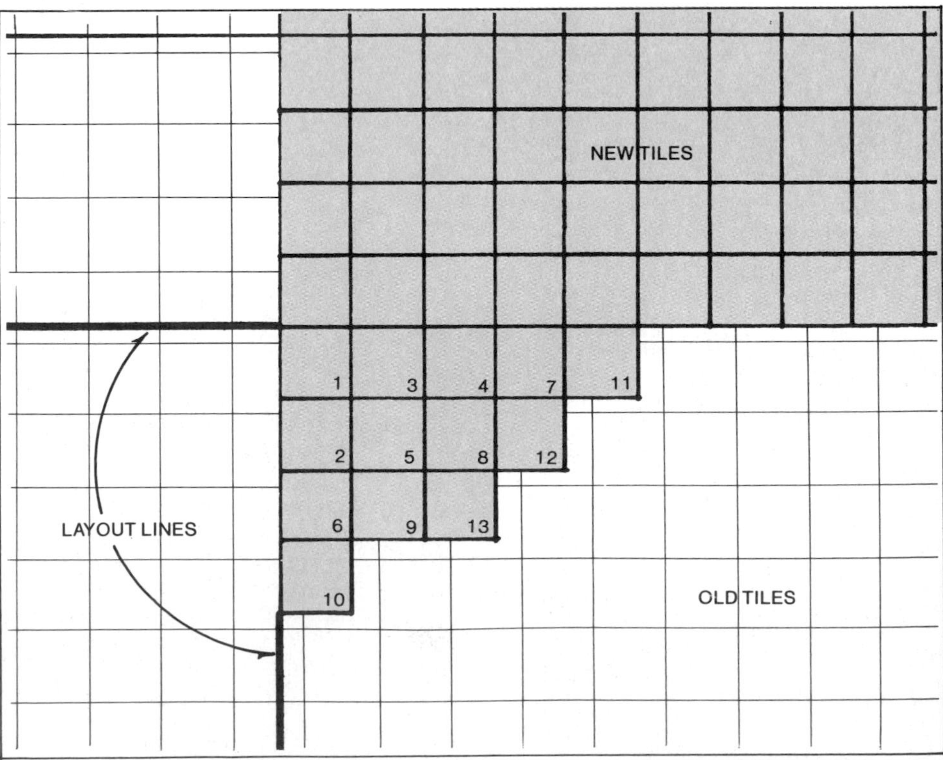

If you're setting new tiles over old, layout lines should be slightly offset from existing tile joints. If existing tiles are well laid out, joints can be used as guides for new layout lines. Lay tiles in sequence shown.

As you work, use grocery bag to dispose of protective papers. They're slippery and pile up in a hurry. As you lay tiles, make sure floor and backs of tiles are clean. The adhesive acts like a magnet for small particles that can make a bump under new floor. This can be a problem when you're cutting partial tiles. Make sure corners of tiles meet as you put them down.

Fitting partial tiles requires nothing more than a pencil and heavy pair of scissors. Use marking techniques shown on page 142 and cut tiles to fit. You may have to trim back protective paper on a tile or two so you can mark to cut. Finishing steps for tile you're using will be marked on box, or on instruction sheet inside box.

A NEW FAUCET

The one piece of kitchen equipment that takes the most punishment is the sink faucet. If your faucet is over 5 years old, it's probably time for replacement, perhaps with one of the single-handle models. There's even a replacement faucet on the market that doesn't require any tools for installation. You will need some hand tools to get the old faucet out. Before you buy a new faucet, note the size and location of the water-supply pipe hookup on the old one. This way you will buy the right-size faucet.

To remove an installed faucet, you'll need large and small crescent wrenches, and a basin wrench for under-counter work. If the old faucet is the captive-bolt type described on page 85, you'll also need the correct-size open-end wrench to remove nuts on the captive bolts.

Begin by turning off water. Place a pan directly under the faucet to catch drips. Disconnect supply pipes from old faucet and remove any fasteners that hold old faucet to sink. Fasteners are usually nuts and washers. They are located on captive bolts holding faucet to sink, or on shanks where hot- and cold-water lines connect to underside of faucet. Use a mirror and flashlight to see up behind sink bowls while working. After removing old faucet, clean top of sink with a putty knife and pot scrubber or steel wool.

Insert new faucet and anchor it to sink. Many new faucets come with a base gasket that fits between faucet and sink top. If faucet doesn't have a base gasket, set new faucet on a thin layer of tub-and-tile caulk or non-staining plumber's putty. Then reconnect supply pipes. You may have to recut or rebend water-supply pipes to fit. Use new rubber *cone washers* at supply-pipe connections. They should be same size as those removed when you disconnected pipes.

Remove aerator from new faucet spout. Turn water on and open both hot and cold water to flush-out pipes. Check for leaks, then reinstall aerator.

When you replace faucet, consider amenities such as hot-water dispenser or spray unit.

DRAWERS BEHIND DOORS

Drawers can store about three times as much as standard-cabinet shelves. The easiest way to add drawers is to install them inside an existing base cabinet. Stock-size drawers are available at better kitchen dealers. Most drawers have a groove on each side panel and a matching wood runner. Get accurate measurements of base cabinet, inside and out, before you go shopping.

To install drawers, remove existing shelves and attach wood runners to insides of cabinet. You may have to trim the runners or shim them out to get a good fit. Then slide drawers into place.

You can also use roller-type drawer glides which make drawers easier to use. This hardware allows drawers to extend all the way out for better access to items at backs of drawers.

Drawers provide easy access to cooking utensils and supplies.

OVERLOOKED DECORATING SPACE

Almost every kitchen has space between the tops of the wall cabinets and the ceiling. If it's open space, the cabinet tops can serve as display shelves for plants or decorative items.

A soffit presents other possibilities. If side walls are close enough, install a shelf. Nail lengths of molding on the ends and back of the space and drop the shelf into place. Paint or stain to match.

Another treatment for soffits is to build in niches. Cut some access holes to locate the soffit structure. Then cut rectangular holes in the material covering the face of the soffit, working around the structure. Construct boxes of thin plywood with one open end, the same size as the holes. Attach trim molding around the open end, flush with the inside of the box. Extend out to form a frame. Stain or paint the boxes and slide them in. They can later be pulled out if you want to paint or paper the wall.

Open shelves over cabinets make good display nooks.

ADD AN ICEMAKER

You can make your kitchen more efficient and convenient by installing an automatic icemaker. Installation kits are available for many refrigerators. Get the model number from the identification plate on your refrigerator. Contact your dealer to see if an icemaker is made for that model.

Details of installation will vary from one refrigerator to another. Check instructions that come with the kit. In general, you install a clamp-on stop valve on the nearest cold-water pipe, then run a length of 1/4-inch soft-copper pipe through base cabinets to the refrigerator. Allow an extra coil of pipe behind the refrigerator so you can pull it out without having to disconnect the pipe.

Some icemakers may require electrical connections to the refrigerator. Wire to existing terminals in the refrigerator by using spade clips.

Icemakers are available for many older refrigerators. This refrigerator was over 12 years old when icemaker was installed.

Where to Find Out More

The following list includes many manufacturers of equipment and supplies used in kitchens. You can write to manufacturers for product information and brochures, or for the names and addresses of local suppliers of their products.

APPLIANCES

Note: Key identifies appliances made by manufacturers, indicated by letters under each name.

APPLIANCE KEY

CT	Cooktops
D	Disposers
DW	Dishwashers
FP	Food Processors (built-in)
MO	Microwave Ovens
O	Built-in Ovens
R	Ranges
RF	Refrigerators and Freezers
TC	Trash Compactors
V	Ventilating Equipment and Range Hoods

Admiral Division of Magic Chef Inc.
1701 E. Woodfield Road, Schaumburg, IL 60196
CT, D, DW, MO, O, R, RF, V

Amana Refrigeration Inc.
Amana, IA 52204
CT, MO, O, R, RF, V

Anaheim Mfg. Co. Division of Tappan Co.
4240 E. La Palma Ave., Anaheim, CA 92803
D

Aubrey Mfg. Co.
S. Main St., Union, IL 60180
V

Broan Mfg. Co. Inc.
926 W. State St., Hartford, WI 53027
V

Caloric Corp.
Topton, PA 19562
CT, D, DW, MO, O, R, TC, V

Dayton Electric Mfg. Co.
5959 W. Howard St., Chicago, IL 60648
D

Elkay Mfg. Co.
2222 Camden Court, Oak Brook, IL 60521
D

Filtex Division of Natter Mfg.
9440 Gidley St., Temple City, CA 91780
FP

Frigidaire Co., Division of White Consolidated Industries Inc.
PO Box WC4900, 3555 S. Kettering Blvd., Dayton, OH 45449
CT, D, DW, MO, O, R, RF, TC

General Electric Co.
Appliance Park, Bldg. 6, Rm. 218, Louisville, KY 40225
CT, D, DW, MO, O, R, TC, V

Gibson Appliance Co.
Gibson Appliance Center, Greenville, MI 48838
CT, DW, MO, O, R, RF

Glenwood Range Co., a Raytheon Co.,
Route 140, Industrial Park, Taunton, MA 02780
DW, R, V

Hotpoint
2100 Gardiner Lane, Suite 301, Louisville, KY 40205
CT, D, DW, MO, O, R, RF, TC, V

In-sink-erator Division of Emerson Electric Co.
4700 21st St., Racine, WI 53406
D, DW, TC

Jenn-air Corp.
3035 Shadeland Drive, Indianapolis, IN 46226
CT, MO, O, R

Kelvinator Appliance Co.
930 Ft. Duquesne Blvd., Pittsburgh, PA 15222
CT, D, DW, MO, R, RF, V

Kitchenaid Division of Hobart Corp.
World Headquarters, Troy, OH 45374
D, DW, TC

Litton Microwave Cooking Products
PO Box 9461, 1405 Xenium Ln. N., Minneapolis, MN 55440
CT, MO, O, R, V

Magic Chef Inc.,
740 King Edward Ave., Cleveland, TN 37311
CT, D, DW, MO, O, R, RF, V

The Maytag Co.
403 W. Fourth St. N., Newton, IA 50208
D, DW

Miami-Carey
203 Garver Road, Monroe, OH 45050
V

Modern Maid, a Raytheon Co.,
PO Box 1111, Chattanooga, TN 37401
CT, D, DW, MO, O, R, TC, V

Monarch Ranges and Heaters
Division of The Malleable Iron Range Co.
715 N. Spring St., Beaver Dam, WI 53916
R

Nutone Division of Scovill Inc.
Madison and Red Bank Roads, Cincinnati, OH 45227
FP, V

O'Keefe & Merritt Co.
PO Box 606, Mansfield, OH 44901
CT, D, DW, MO, O, R, RF, TC, V

Oster Corp.
5055 N. Lydell Ave., Milwaukee, WI 53217
FP

Panasonic Co.
1 Panasonic Way, Secaucus, NJ 07094
CT, MO, RF

Rittenhouse Division of Emerson Electric Co.
475 Quaker Meeting House Road, Honeoye Falls, NY 14472
V

Ronson Corp.
1 Ronson Road, Bridgewater, NJ 08807
FP

Roper Sales Corp.
PO Box 867, 1905 W. Court, Kankakee, IL 60901
CT, D, DW, MO, O, R, RF, TC, V

Sears Roebuck & Co.
Sears Tower, Chicago, IL 60684
CT, D, DW, MO, O, R, RF, TC, V

Sub-Zero Freezer Co. Inc.
4717 Hammersley Road, Box 4130, Madison, WI 53711
RF

Tappan Appliance Division
Tappan Park, Mansfield, OH 44901
CT, D, DW, MO, O, R, RF, TC, V

Thermador/Waste King
5119 District Blvd., Los Angeles, CA 90040
CT, D, DW, MO, O, R, TC, V

Waste King—See Thermador Waste-King

Westinghouse—See White/Westinghouse

Whirlpool
Benton Harbor, MI 49022
CT, DW, MO, O, R, RF, TC, V

White/Westinghouse Corporate Headquarters
930 Ft. Duquesne Blvd., Pittsburgh, PA 15222
CT, D, DW, O, R, RF, TC, V

CABINETS

Acorn Mfg. Co. Inc.
PO Box 31, Mansfield, MA 02048

Aristokraft Cabinets
PO Box 420, Jasper, IN 47546

Belwood Division of U. S. Industries Inc.
PO Drawer A, Ackerman, MS 39735

Birchcraft Kitchens Inc.
1612 Thorn St., Reading, PA 19601

Bruce Cabinets, a Triangle Pacific Co.
4255 LBJ Freeway, Dallas, TX 75234

Coppes Inc.
401 E. Market St., Napannee, IN 46550

Del Mar Division of Triangle Pacific Corp.
16803 Dallas Parkway, Dallas, TX 75248

Diamond Cabinets, Division of Medford Corp.
PO Box 547, Hillsboro, OR 97123

H. J. Scheirich Co.
PO Box 37120, Louisville, KY 40233

Haas Cabinet Co.
625 W. Utica St., Sellersburg, IN 47172

IXL, a Triangle Pacific Co.
PO Box 110, Route 4, Elizabeth City, NC 27909

Kemper Division of Tappan Co.
701 South N St., Richmond, IN 47374

Kitchen Kompact Inc.
KK Plaza, Jeffersonville, IN 47130

Long-Bell Cabinets Inc.
PO Box 579, Longview, WA 98632

Mastercraft Industries Corp.
6175 E. 39th Ave., Denver, CO 80207

Merillat Industries Inc.
2075 W. Beecher Road, Adrian, MI 49221

Mutschler Division of Triangle Pacific Corp.
302 S. Madison St., Nappanee, IN 46550

Micarta—See Westinghouse Corp. Micarta Division

Poggenpohl U.S.A. Corp.
222 Cedar Lane, Teaneck, NJ 07666

Quaker Maid Division of Tappan Corp.
Route 61, Leesport, PA 19533

St. Charles Mfg. Co.
1611 E. Main St., St. Charles, IL 60174

Triangle Pacific Corp.
PO Box 220100, Dallas, TX 75222

Westinghouse Corp. Micarta Division
PO Box 248, Hampton, SC 29924

CERAMIC TILE

American Olean Tile Co.
PO Box 271, 1000 Cannon Ave., Lansdale, PA 19446

Cambridge Tile Mfg. Co.
PO Box 15307, Cincinnati, OH 45215

Florida Tile Division of Sikes Corp.
PO Box 447, Lakeland, FL 33802

Franciscan Tile
2901 Los Feliz Blvd., Los Angeles, CA 90039

Marazzi U.S.A. Inc.
PO Box 58163, Suite 9063 World Trade Center, Dallas, TX 75258

Monarch Tile Mfg. Inc.
PO Box 2041, San Angelo, TX 76901

Sherle Wagner International
60 E. 57th St., New York, NY 10022

U. S. Ceramic Tile Co., Division of Soartek Inc.
1375 Raff Road SW, Canton, OH 44710

Wenczel Tile Co.
PO Box 5308, Klagg Ave., Trenton, NJ 08638

COUNTERTOPS

See also Ceramic Tile

DuPont Co.
1007 Market St., Wilmington, DE 19898

Formica Corp., Subsidiary of American Cyanamid
859 Berdan Ave., Wayne, NJ 07470

Nevamar Corp.
8339 Telegraph Road, Odenton, MD 21113

Westinghouse Corp. Micarta Division
PO Box 248, Hampton, SC 29924

Wilsonart Division of Ralph Wilson Plastics Co.
600 General Bruce Drive, Temple, TX 76501

LIGHTING

Armstrong World Industries Inc.
PO Box 3001, Lancaster, PA 17604

Celotex Corp.
1500 N. Dale Mabry, Tampa, FL 33607

Day-Brite Lighting Division of Emerson Electric Co.
1015 S. Green St., Tupelo, MS 38801

Dayton Electric Mfg. Co.
5959 W. Howard St., Chicago, IL 60648

Duray Fluorescent Mfg. Co.
2050 W. Balmoral Ave., Chicago, IL 60625

Eagle Electric Mfg. Co.
45-31 Court Square, Long Island City, NY 11101

General Electric Co., Lighting Systems Dept.
Hendersonville, NC 28739

GTE Products Corp., Lighting Products Group
100 Endicott St., Danvers, MA 01923

KEENE Corp. Lighting Division
2345 Vauxhall Road, Union, NJ 07083

Kent, subsidiary of Kidde Inc.
Grandview Ave., Bellevue, KY 41073

Laurel Lamp Mfg. Co.
111 Rome St., Newark, NJ 07105

Lightolier Inc.
346 Claremont Ave., Jersey City, NJ 97305

McGraw Edison Co., Lighting Products Division
PO Box 1205, Racine, WI 53405

Nutone Division of Scovill Inc.
Madison & Red Bank Roads, Cincinnati, OH 45227

Omega Lighting Co., Division of Emerson Electric
270 Long Island Expressway, Melville, NY 11747

Panasonic Co.
1 Panasonic Way, Secaucus, NJ 07094

Remcraft Lighting Products
4565NW 37th Ave., Miami, FL 33142

Scovill—see Nutone.

Thomas Industries Inc.
PO Box 35120, 207 E. Broadway, Louisville, KY 40232

Vistalite Division of Eco Electric Mfg. Co.
PO Box 67, 445 W. 26th St., Hialeah, FL 33010

Westinghouse Electric Corp., Lighting Division
PO Box 824, Vicksburg, MS 39180

RESILIENT FLOORING

Amtico Flooring Division of American Biltrite Inc.
3131 Princeton Pike, Lawrenceville, NJ 08648

Armstrong World Industries Inc.
PO Box 3001, Lancaster, PA 17604

Azrock Floor Products
PO Box 34030, San Antonio, TX 78233

Congoleum Corp.
195 Belgrove Drive, Kearny, NJ 07032

Kentile Floors Inc.
58 Second St., Brooklyn, NY 11215

Magee Carpet Division of Shaw Industries Inc.
PO Box 2128, Dalton, GA 30720

Mannington Mills Inc.
PO Box 30, Salem, NJ 08079

Masonite Corp.
29 N. Wacker Drive, Chicago, IL 60606

SINKS AND FAUCETS

American Brass Mfg. Co.
5000 Superior Ave., Cleveland, OH 44103

American-Standard
PO Box 2003, New Brunswick, NJ 08903

Brass-Craft Mfg. Co. Inc.
700 Fisher Building, Detroit, MI 48202

Briggs
PO Box 22622, Tampa, FL 33622

Central Brass Mfg. Co.
2950 E. 55th St., Cleveland, OH 44127

Chicago Faucet Co.
2100 S. Nuclear Drive, Des Plaines, IL 60018

Crane Co., Plumbing Division
300 Park Ave., New York, NY 10022

Delta Faucet Co.
PO Box 40980, 55 E. 111th St., Indianapolis, IN 46280

DuPont Co.
1007 Market St., Wilmington, DE 19898

Eljer Plumbingware—Wallace Murray Corp.
Three Gateway Center, Pittsburgh, PA 15222

Elkay Mfg. Co.
2222 Camden Court, Oak Brook, IL 60521

Gerber Plumbing Fixtures
4656 Touhy, Chicago, IL 60646

Indiana Brass Inc.
PO Box 369, Frankfort, IN 46041

In-sink-erator Division of Emerson Electric Co.
4700 21st St., Racine, WI 53406

J. A. Sexauer Inc.
10 Hamilton Ave., White Plains, NY 10601

Just Mfg. Co.
9233 King St., Franklin Park, IL 60131

Kitchenaid Division of Hobart Corp.
Troy, OH 45374

Kohler Co.
High St., Kohler, WI 53004

Manville Mfg. Co.
342 Rockwell Ave., Pontiac, MI 48053

Milwaukee Faucets Inc.
4250 N. 124th St., Milwaukee, WI 53222

Moen Division of Stanadyne
377 Woodland Ave., Elyria, OH 44036

Nibco Inc.
500 Simpson Ave., Elkhart, IN 46515

Piazza Faucet Inc.
11602 Knott Ave. Suite 13, Garden Grove, CA 92641

Price Pfister Division of Norris Industries
13500 Paxton St., Pacoima, CA 91331

Speakman Co.
301 E. 30th St., Wilmington, DE 19899

Sterling Faucet Co.
1375 Remmington Road, Schaumburg, IL 60195

Streamway Corp.
875 Bassett Road, Westlake, OH 44145

Symmons Industries Inc.
31 Brooks Drive, Braintree, MA 02184

U. S. Brass Division of Wallace Murray Corp.
901 Tenth St., Plano, TX 75074

Vance Industries Inc.
7401 W. Wilson Ave., Chicago, IL 60656

Wallace Murray Corp.—see Eljer.

WINDOWS AND SKYLIGHTS

Alcan Building Products
PO Box 511, Warren, OH 44482

Anderson Corp.
Bayport, MN 55003

Caradco
PO Box 920, Rantoul, IL 61866

Cathedralite
820 Bay Ave., Suite 302, Capitola, CA 95010

Crestline
910 Cleveland Ave., Wausau, WI 54401

Filon Division of Vistron Corp.
12333 S. Van Ness Ave., Hawthorne, CA 90250

Howmet Aluminum Corp., Building Products Division
PO Box 4515, Lancaster, PA 17604

Hurd Millwork Co.
520 S. Whelen
Medford, WI 54451

Kalwall Corp.
PO Box 237, 1111 Candia Road, Manchester, NH 03102

Kennedy Sky-lites Corp.
3647 All American Blvd., Orlando, FL 32810

Louisiana-Pacific Corp.
1300 SW Fifth Ave., Portland, OR 97201

Marvin Windows
Warroad, MN 56763

Peachtree Doors
PO Box 700, Norcross, GA 30091

Pella/Rolscreen Co.
100 Main St., Pella, IA 50219

Rolscreen—see Pella/Rolscreen

Remington Aluminum Division of Evans Products
100 Andrews Road, Hicksville, NY 11801

Velux America Inc.
PO Box 3208, Greenwood, SC 29646

Weathershield Mfg. Inc.
PO Box 309, Medford, WI 54451

WOOD FLOORING

Bangkok Industries
4562 Worth St., Philadelphia, PA 19124

Bruce Hardwood Floors, a Triangle Pacific Co.
16803 Dallas Parkway, Dallas, TX 75248

Comtex Industries Inc.
1666 Kennedy Causeway, Suite 503, Miami Beach, FL 33141

Connor Forest Industries
PO Box 847, Wausau, WI 54401

Crown Mosaic Parquet Flooring Inc.
PO Box 272, Sevierville, TN 37862

Harris Mfg. Co.
PO Box 300, Johnson City, TN 37601

Masonite Corp.
29 N. Wacker Drive, Chicago, IL 60606

Sykes Flooring Products Division of Masonite Corp.
PO Box 999, Warren, AR 71671

Weyerhaeuser Co.
Tacoma, WA 98401

Wood Mosaic, Olinkraft Division
PO Box 21159, Louisville, KY 40221

Index

8.426200718430